Economic Analysis and Policy before, during and after a Public Debt Crisis, a Pandemic and an Inflationary Outburst

Economic Analysis and Policy before, during and after a Public Debt Crisis, a Pandemic and an Inflationary Outburst

Guest Editor

Angeliki N. Menegaki

MDPI

Basel • Beijing • Wuhan • Barcelona • Belgrade • Novi Sad • Cluj • Manchester

Guest Editor
Angeliki N. Menegaki
Department of Business
Administration and Tourism
Hellenic Mediterranean
University
Heraklion
Greece

Editorial Office
MDPI AG
Grosspeteranlage 5
4052 Basel, Switzerland

This is a reprint of the Special Issue, published open access by the journal *Economies* (ISSN 2227-7099), freely accessible at: https://www.mdpi.com/journal/economies/special_issues/Z8018142N2.

For citation purposes, cite each article independently as indicated on the article page online and as indicated below:

Lastname, Firstname, Firstname Lastname, and Firstname Lastname. Article Title. *Journal Name* **Year**, *Volume Number*, Page Range.

ISBN 978-3-7258-7498-9 (Hbk)
ISBN 978-3-7258-7499-6 (PDF)
https://doi.org/10.3390/books978-3-7258-7499-6

Contents

About the Editor

Angeliki N. Menegaki

Angeliki N. Menegaki Angeliki Menegaki holds a Ph.D. from the University of Stirling (UK) and an MSc from the University of Leeds (UK). She also holds undergraduate degrees in Economics (University of Crete) and Language & Literature of Black Sea Countries (Democritus University of Thrace), with specialization in the Turkish language.

She has taught at universities in Greece and abroad and has held managerial positions in both the public and private sectors. Until June 2024, she served as a Full Professor at the Agricultural University of Athens (Department of Regional and Economic Development). She currently holds a professorial appointment at the Hellenic Mediterranean University, specializing in energy and environmental economics.

Dr. Menegaki has published over 100 articles in peer-reviewed international journals and has authored or edited 11 academic books in Greek and English. Her scholarly work has received more than 3,400 citations in Scopus (H-index: 32) and approximately 5,900 citations in Google Scholar (H-index: 37). Her primary research interests include renewable energy economics, energy policy, environmental valuation, energy transitions, and sustainable development. She has extensive editorial experience, including service as Associate Editor for several Elsevier journals and as editor of collective academic volumes.

Since 2020, Dr. Menegaki has been included in the Stanford University–Ioannidis database among the top 2% of the most influential scientists worldwide in the field of energy. Her research has been published in leading journals such as *Renewable Energy, Energy Economics, Applied Energy, Energy Policy, Energy, Energy for Sustainable Development, Ecological Economics, Ecological Indicators*, the *Journal of Economic Psychology*, and the *Journal of Choice Modelling*.

Preface

This Reprint brings together twelve peer-reviewed contributions originally published in the Special Issue focusing on economic analysis and policy responses before, during, and after major systemic shocks, including public debt crises, the COVID-19 pandemic, and recent inflationary pressures. The aim of the Special Issue was to provide a rigorous and pluralistic platform for examining how economies respond to uncertainty, disruption, and structural change, using a variety of theoretical frameworks and empirical methodologies. The contributions address topics such as macroeconomic policy, financial stability, inequality, institutional performance, and growth dynamics across different regional and development contexts. This Reprint is addressed to academics, researchers, graduate students, and policymakers interested in contemporary economic challenges and evidence-based policy design. The Special Issue was prepared in honor of Professor George Agiomirgianakis, whose academic work and public engagement have significantly shaped economic thought and policy debate. The Guest Editor gratefully acknowledges all contributing authors and reviewers for their valuable insights and commitment to scholarly excellence.

Angeliki N. Menegaki
Guest Editor

economies

Editorial

Economic Analysis and Policy Before, During, and After Public Debt Crises, the COVID-19 Pandemic, and Inflationary Outburst

Angeliki N. Menegaki

Department of Business Administration and Tourism, Hellenic Mediterranean University, PC71410 Heraklion, Crete, Greece; amenegaki@hmu.gr

Since the mid-2000s, the global economy has experienced a sequence of profound shocks that have reshaped economic structures, policy priorities, and analytical frameworks. Public debt crises, financial instability, the COVID-19 pandemic, energy and supply chain disruptions, and the subsequent inflationary resurgence have not occurred in isolation. Rather, these shocks have variably interacted, revealing structural vulnerabilities while testing the limits of established economic policy tools. This Special Issue was conceived to capture studies that critically examine these dynamics through rigorous economic analyses and empirically grounded policy discussion.

The motivation behind this Special Issue was to provide a forum for addressing how economies respond before, during, and after systemic crises, with particular attention to debt accumulation, inflationary pressures, financial market behavior, and institutional capacity. The twelve contributions in this Special Issue reflect this goal: researchers combined diverse methodological approaches, regional perspectives, and thematic emphases. Together, the included studies offer a multidimensional understanding of economic resilience, fragility and adjustment in an era characterized by heightened uncertainty.

A central theme through several contributions is the role of public and external debt in shaping macroeconomic performance. A paper focusing on South Africa (Mah, 2025) provides a timely analysis of the asymmetric effects of foreign and domestic debt on economic growth. By moving beyond linear assumptions, Mah highlights how different types of debt exert distinct and nonuniform impacts on growth dynamics, particularly in the aftermath of the COVID-19 pandemic. This insight is echoed and reinforced by those of a study examining the nonlinear relationship between foreign debt and inflation in Brazil (Sharaf et al., 2024). The researchers employed advanced econometric techniques to demonstrate that debt–inflation linkages vary among regimes and economic conditions. Together, these papers underline the importance of distinguishing debt composition from debt dynamics when designing fiscal and monetary policy.

Inflation, as a macroeconomic outcome and as a policy constraint, occupies a prominent position in this Special Issue. The resurgence of inflation following the pandemic challenged long-standing assumptions about price stability, particularly in economies that had previously experienced prolonged periods of low inflation. Contributions addressing inflation and investment behavior, such as a study on foreign direct investment in a subnational U.S. economy (Wright & Wu, 2025), reveal how sustained inflation can generate differences in the responses between new and existing investment flows. These findings suggest that inflation does not uniformly deter investment but instead reshapes its composition and timing, with important implications for regional development and policy coordination.

Financial markets and instability constitute other major analytical themes in this Special Issue. Several contributions explore how crises propagate across markets, institutions, and regions. A study on intermarket reactions among asset classes before and after COVID-19 provides qualitative insights into the changing relationships among gold, oil, and digital assets under varying volatility regimes (Bannerjee et al., 2025). This perspective complements a more quantitative analysis of contagion dynamics in international equity portfolios (Floros et al., 2024), which demonstrates how macroeconomic conditions and regime shifts influence portfolio allocation and risk transmission. Together, these papers deepen our understanding of financial interconnectedness and the mechanisms through which uncertainty is transmitted across markets.

Banking sector stability and financial distress are also examined in detail. Researchers focused on banks in the MENA region (Metwally et al., 2025) to investigate the interaction among financial performance indicators, macroeconomic conditions, and financial distress, drawing on contagion and financial instability theories. The results highlight the vulnerability of banking systems to macroeconomic shocks, particularly in environments characterized by weak growth and inflationary pressures. These insights are especially relevant in the context of post-pandemic recovery, where financial institutions are playing a critical role in supporting investment and economic activity.

Beyond macroeconomic and financial variables, the papers in this Special Issue focus on the structural and institutional factors shaping economic outcomes. Governance and fiscal decentralization in Latin America (Pinilla-Rodríguez & Hernández-Medina, 2024) are examined through an empirical lens, revealing how institutional quality conditions the effectiveness of decentralized fiscal systems. The findings show that decentralization alone does not guarantee improved economic performance; rather, decentralization must be accompanied by strong governance structures and accountability mechanisms. This institutional perspective aligns with broader debates on fiscal sustainability and public sector efficiency in times of crisis.

Firm-level performance and productivity dynamics are also explored, notably through an analysis of business efficiency in the Visegrad Four countries before, during, and after the COVID-19 pandemic (Durana et al., 2025). This contribution illustrates how efficiency and asset management practices influence firms' resilience to shocks and capacity to recover in turbulent economic environments. By situating firm behavior within a broader macroeconomic context, the authors bridge microeconomic analysis and macroeconomic outcomes, highlighting the importance of enterprise-level adjustment in aggregate recovery processes.

The role of technological change and structural transformation features prominently in this Special Issue. A study on technological innovation and agricultural productivity in Nigeria (Adeyemo et al., 2024) addresses the challenges faced by resource-dependent economies undergoing energy transitions. By examining the contribution of innovation to productivity outside the oil sector, the authors show the importance of diversification and technological adoption for sustainable growth. Complementing this perspective, an analysis of information and communication technology (ICT) advancements and economic growth in European Union countries provides robust empirical evidence on the growth-enhancing effects of digitalization (Magoutas et al., 2024). These contributions collectively highlight technology as a buffer against shocks and a driver of long-term structural change.

Sustainability and responsible finance are increasingly important dimensions of economic analysis in the context of systemic crises. Researchers examined the relationship between credit ratings and environmental, social, and governance (ESG) scores in banking, reflecting a growing recognition that financial stability cannot be fully understood without considering ESG factors (Vortelinos et al., 2024). By linking ESG performance to market

https://doi.org/10.3390/economies14040111

valuation and credit risk, this contribution demonstrates how sustainability considerations are becoming embedded in financial decision-making and risk assessment.

This Special Issue also includes a comprehensive review of Greece's economic trajectory, which situates recent developments within a longer-term historical and structural context (Makantasi & Valentis, 2024). The review highlights persistent challenges related to growth, public debt, and institutional reform, while identifying pathways forward in a post-crisis environment. As a synthesis of experience from successive crises, the case provides valuable lessons for other economies facing similar constraints.

Methodologically, the contributions in this Special Issue reflect a strong commitment to analytical rigor and innovation. The use of nonlinear models, regime-switching techniques, panel data analysis, and qualitative approaches demonstrates the value of methodological pluralism in addressing complicated economic phenomena. These different methods enhance the robustness of the findings and allow for a richer interpretation of economic dynamics under stress.

Although each paper addresses a specific research question, several overarching messages emerge from this Special Issue. First, economic crises tend to amplify existing structural weaknesses rather than create entirely new ones. Second, policy effectiveness is highly context-dependent and closely tied to institutional quality, credibility, and governance. Finally, the economic consequences of crises extend beyond short-term fluctuations in output or prices, affecting investment behavior, inequality, financial stability, and long-term development trajectories.

This Special Issue is dedicated to Professor George Agiomirgianakis on his retirement. His academic career has been marked by sustained engagement with macroeconomic policy, financial markets, and applied economic analysis, as well as by a commitment to bridging theory and practice. The thematic breadth and analytical depth of the contributions included here reflect the intellectual legacy of the field he served and the influence on generations of researchers and students.

The completion of this Special Issue would not have been possible without the dedication of the contributing authors, whose work forms the core of this scholarly endeavor. I would also like to express my sincere appreciation to the anonymous reviewers for their careful evaluations and constructive feedback, which significantly increased the quality of the published papers. Finally, I acknowledge the support of the editorial team for their professionalism and efficiency throughout the publication process.

This reprint is addressed to academics, researchers, graduate students, and policymakers seeking to understand the economic challenges posed by debt, inflation, financial instability, and structural change. My hope is that the insights provided here will inform future research and contribute to more resilient and inclusive economic policy design in an increasingly uncertain global environment.

Conflicts of Interest: The author declares no conflict of interest.

References

Adeyemo, J. T., Ahmed, A., Abaver, D. T., Riyadh, H. A., Tabash, M. I., & Lawal, A. I. (2024). Technological innovation and agricultural productivity in Nigeria amidst oil transition: ARDL analysis. *Economies*, *12*(9), 253. [CrossRef]

Bannerjee, S. S., Pillai, R., Tabash, M. I., & Al-Absy, M. S. M. (2025). Unveiling inter-market reactions to different asset classes/commodities pre- and post-COVID-19: An exploratory qualitative study. *Economies*, *13*(3), 66. [CrossRef]

Durana, P., Kovalova, E., Blazek, R., & Bicanovska, K. (2025). Business efficiency: Insights from visegrad four before, during, and after the COVID-19 pandemic. *Economies*, *13*(2), 26. [CrossRef]

Floros, C., Vortelinos, D., & Chatziantoniou, I. (2024). Crises and contagion in equity portfolios. *Economies*, *12*(7), 168. [CrossRef]

Magoutas, A. I., Chaideftou, M., Skandali, D., & Chountalas, P. T. (2024). Digital progression and economic growth: Analyzing the impact of ICT advancements on the GDP of European union countries. *Economies*, *12*(3), 63. [CrossRef]

https://doi.org/10.3390/economies14040111

Mah, G. (2025). An asymmetric analysis of the impact of foreign and domestic debt on South Africa's economic growth. *Economies*, *13*(6), 164. [CrossRef]

Makantasi, E., & Valentis, H. (2024). Greece's economic odyssey: Persistent challenges and pathways forward. *Economies*, *12*(6), 139. [CrossRef]

Metwally, A. B. M., Yasser, M. M., Ahmed, E. A., & Ali, M. A. S. (2025). Financial and economic determinants of banks financial distress in MENA region. *Economies*, *13*(2), 56. [CrossRef]

Pinilla-Rodríguez, D. E., & Hernández-Medina, P. (2024). Governance and fiscal decentralisation in Latin America: An empirical approach. *Economies*, *12*(8), 207. [CrossRef]

Sharaf, M. F., Shahen, A. M., & Binzaid, B. A. (2024). Asymmetric and nonlinear foreign debt–inflation nexus in Brazil: Evidence from NARDL and Markov regime switching approaches. *Economies*, *12*(1), 18. [CrossRef]

Vortelinos, D., Menegaki, A. N., & Alexiou, S. (2024). The relationship between credit rating and environmental, social, and governance score in banking. *Economies*, *12*(6), 152. [CrossRef]

Wright, R., & Wu, C. (2025). Divergence between new and existing FDI in times of sustained inflation post the COVID-19 pandemic: The case of a subnational economy in the U.S. *Economies*, *13*(2), 55. [CrossRef]

https://doi.org/10.3390/economies14040111

economies

Article

Asymmetric and Nonlinear Foreign Debt–Inflation Nexus in Brazil: Evidence from NARDL and Markov Regime Switching Approaches

Mesbah Fathy Sharaf [1,2,*], Abdelhalem Mahmoud Shahen [3,4] and Badr Abdulaziz Binzaid [4]

[1] Department of Economics, Faculty of Arts, University of Alberta, Edmonton, AB T6G2H4, Canada
[2] Department of Economics, Faculty of Commerce, Damanhour University, Damanhour 22514, Egypt
[3] Department of Economics, Faculty of Economics Studies and Political Science, Alexandria University, Alexandria P.O. Box 5424041, Egypt; halem@alexu.edu.eg
[4] Department of Economics, College of Economics and Administrative Sciences, Imam Mohammad Ibn Saud Islamic University (IMSIU), P.O. Box 5701, Riyadh 11432, Saudi Arabia; bazaid@imamu.edu.sa
* Correspondence: sharaf@ualberta.ca

Abstract: This paper augments the sparse literature on the inflationary impact of foreign debt in Brazil while addressing methodological caveats in previous studies. We depart from the linearity assumption and employ two nonlinear techniques: the nonlinear autoregressive distributed lag (NARDL) model and a Markov Switching Regression (MSR) to investigate the connection between foreign debt and inflation within a multivariate framework. The analyses consider the presence of structural breaks via assessing variable stationarity using the Zivot and Andrew unit root test and incorporating a residual-based cointegration test proposed by Gregory and Hansen. Additionally, we apply a multiple structural breakpoints test by Bai and Perron to determine the presence of structural breaks in the impact of foreign debt on inflation. Our findings robustly indicate that the domestic money supply has a statistically significant positive effect, while the nominal effective exchange rate has a negative effect on inflation in both the short and long run. The NARDL model reveals that only positive changes in foreign debt have a statistically significant negative effect on inflation in the short run, whereas both positive and negative foreign debt changes significantly affect inflation in the long run. The results from the MSR model are generally consistent with those of the NARDL model.

Keywords: asymmetry; Brazil; foreign debt; inflation; nonlinearity

1. Introduction

Developing economies usually need help accumulating capital and financing their increasing public expenditures. This leads them to rely on foreign borrowing to fund their development needs and address their budget deficits and trade imbalances (Aimola and Odhiambo 2020). On the opposite view, foreign debt could create an acute debt overhang issue, and if the foreign debt becomes unsustainable, it can cause economic uncertainty and instability. There is substantial empirical evidence that high levels of foreign debt can lead to inflation and solvency issues, which pose significant risks to a country's financial stability and vulnerability to foreign shocks. Moreover, borrowing to plug budget deficits can impact inflation by monetizing foreign debt (Reinhart and Rogoff 2013; Mweni et al. 2016).

Statistics reveal that Brazil has increasingly relied on foreign borrowing to finance its rising developmental needs. However, it is crucial to acknowledge that this reliance on foreign debt could adversely affect macroeconomic indicators, including inflation. The increasing levels of foreign debt and inflation in Latin America have prompted questions about the nature of their relationship.

There is considerable literature that examines the effect of foreign debt on inflation in several countries, using a variety of econometric methodologies and covering different periods, with inconclusive findings.[1] A common feature among most empirical studies is that they assume that inflation responds symmetrically to changes in foreign debt. The mixed findings regarding the inflationary effect of foreign debt might be due to the failure of previous studies to consider the potential asymmetry in the inflationary effect of foreign debt, which the current study aims to overcome.

Meanwhile, although the relationship between foreign debt and inflation has garnered growing attention, very few studies have examined this nexus in Brazil, and the existing ones were published quite a long time ago. Instead, the focus has been on the linkage between Brazil's foreign debt and economic growth rather than inflation (e.g., Koyuncu Çakmak and Demirhan 2020; Afonso et al. 2020).

The main objective of this study is to unmask the nature of the relationship between foreign debt and inflation in Brazil over the period 1980 to 2020 within a multivariate framework while addressing methodological caveats in previous related studies. In particular, this study contributes to the sparse literature on the inflationary effect of foreign debt in Brazil along several dimensions. Firstly, it departs from the conventional linearity and symmetry assumptions and utilizes nonlinear and asymmetric methodologies, such as the nonlinear autoregressive distributed lag (NARDL) model and the Markov Switching Regression (MSR). Methodologically, we also address concerns regarding the presence of structural breaks when checking stationarity and cointegration between the variables. Secondly, to date, we are not aware of any study that investigates the asymmetric and nonlinear nexus between foreign debt and inflation in Brazil, as well as the potential regime shifts in regard to this relationship, and the current study aims to fill this gap in the literature.

The current study's findings based on linear models suggest no significant foreign debt effect on inflation; nonetheless, nonlinear models counter this, revealing a substantial negative effect for both positive and negative foreign debt shocks on inflation. Our findings also robustly indicate that the domestic money supply has a positive effect, while the nominal effective exchange rate has a negative effect on inflation. The results also revealed the existence of structural breaks in the examined variables and their underlying relationships.

These findings underscore the necessity of considering asymmetries and structural breaks for a comprehensive understanding of how foreign debt influences inflation in Brazil. We expect these findings to offer valuable insights for policymakers in Brazil, potentially aiding in devising more effective strategies for managing inflation and foreign debt levels.

The remaining structure of the paper is set as follows: Section 2 provides an overview of Brazil's foreign debt and inflation rate trends over the past four decades. Section 3 reviews the related theoretical and empirical literature. Section 4 presents the econometric methodology. Section 5 summarizes the empirical results, which are then discussed in Section 6.

2. Evolution of the Foreign Debt and Inflation Rate in Brazil over the Period 1980 to 2020

Figure 1 displays the evolution of Brazil's foreign debt and inflation rates from 1980 to 2020. The figure suggests a dynamic and fluctuating relationship between foreign debt stocks (% of GNI) and the inflation rate in Brazil from 1980 to 2020.[2]

The figure also illustrates the correlation between these two variables and how their relationship has changed over the past four decades. Specifically, the data show a fluctuating trend in foreign debt stocks and inflation rates with an apparent structural break. This structural change in the trends can be easily visualized by dividing the study period into two sub-periods: the 1980s to mid-1990s sub-period (Figure 1a) and the mid-1990s to 2020 sub-period (Figure 1b).

The figure clearly illustrates a structural break in these three series around 1995. This notable structural break serves as the primary rationale for dividing the study into two distinct periods, with the year 1995 serving as the demarcation point that distinguishes the two segments depicted in Figure 1.

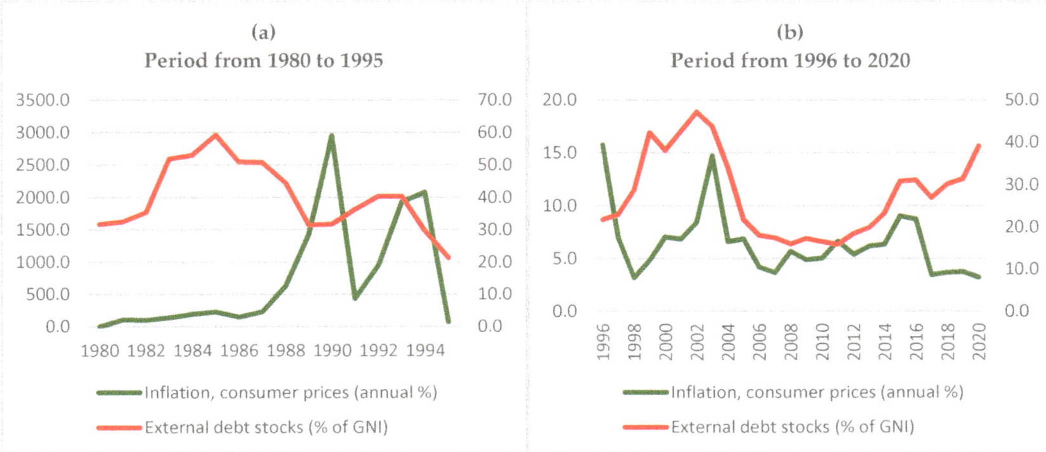

Figure 1. Brazil's external debt and inflation rate during the period (1980–2020). Source: Authors' compilation based on data from (WDI).

As demonstrated in Figure 1a, in the initial period spanning from the 1980s to the mid-1990s (the first period), Brazil's foreign debt as a percentage of GNI exhibited fluctuations within the range of 30% to 60%. During this same period, the country grappled with elevated inflation rates ranging from 100% to over 2900%. Notably, 1989 marked a significant turning point as Brazil experienced a dramatic surge in its annual inflation rate, reaching an unprecedented 1430.7%. This event signaled the onset of hyperinflation, leading to severe economic instability and a substantial devaluation of the Brazilian currency, the Cruzeiro.[3] By 1990, inflation had peaked at an alarming 2947.7%, the highest point recorded throughout the study period.

Concurrently, 1989 represented a pivotal year in Brazil's political evolution, as the nation held its first direct presidential elections in nearly three decades, ultimately electing a democratic government (Bethell 2000). Therefore, 1989 is a radical turning point, impacting Brazil's economic and political domains.

The 1980s is known as the "lost decade" due to the economic instability and debt crisis experienced by many Latin American countries, including Brazil. Brazil's version of the "lost decade" was characterized by economic stagnation, hyperinflation, and a significant burden of foreign debt (Grinberg 2008; Valença 1998).

The high foreign debt in Brazil posed a significant challenge in repaying loans, which, in turn, led to reduced investment and growth, resulting in elevated inflation rates. During this period, a clear positive correlation between foreign debt and inflation emerged, signifying that high levels of foreign debt were linked to soaring inflation. The economic crisis in Brazil during the 1980s and early 1990s was primarily driven by the simultaneous issues of high inflation and foreign debt, coupled with a lack of fiscal discipline. The government's implementation of multiple economic stabilization plans aimed to address these challenges, but these efforts were largely ineffective in quelling hyperinflation.

The second period commenced with Brazil adopting the Real Plan in 1994. This initiative was designed to stabilize the economy and control inflation, and it included the introduction of a new currency, the Brazilian real (BRL), in the same year (Barata 2019).

The program achieved partial success, leading to a substantial reduction in inflation, decreasing from 2076% in 1994 to 3.2% in 2020, as depicted in (Figure 1b). However, the percentage of foreign debt to GNI remained a crucial variable during this period, with fluctuations ranging from 16% to 47% of GNI. On the other hand, Brazil managed to lower its inflation rates from the mid-1990s until the end of the study period, resulting in a more stable economy and bringing some relief to the country. The relationship between foreign debt and inflation following the implementation of the Real Plan became less straightforward, with some years showing a positive correlation between the two variables while others showed no clear relationship. For instance, in 2015 and 2016, there was an increase in foreign debt as a percentage of GNI, but inflation remained stable. Similarly, in 2017 and 2018, foreign debt as a percentage of GNI rose again, but inflation remained low. In 2019 and 2020, foreign debt as a percentage of GNI continued to rise while inflation rates experienced a slight decline.

During the second period, the implementation of the Real Plan marked a relative success in curbing inflation and achieving economic stability in Brazil. It ushered in a period of stability and attracted higher levels of foreign investment. Concurrently, Brazil initiated a phase of economic openness to international trade, which significantly fueled its economic growth. Notably, the increased export of agricultural products and other commodities played a pivotal role in boosting the nation's economy.

Overall, the time series data indicate a positive correlation between foreign debt and inflation in Brazil. High foreign debt has previously been associated with high inflation rates and economic instability. However, this relationship has become less definitive in recent years. It is worth noting that other factors, such as government policies, economic growth, and international trade, also influence inflation rates. Therefore, the relationship between foreign debt and inflation in Brazil is complex.

3. Theoretical and Empirical Literature

Theoretically, there are several pathways through which debt can influence inflation. The first is through an increase in government deficits and debts, which can raise a country's overall wealth if bondholders of the new debt rule out the possibility of using future taxes to cover the deficit. In this non-Ricardian context, a rise in the nation's wealth increases the demand for goods and services, leading to higher prices. The second channel is the crowding-out effect, whereby an increase in government budget deficit and the associated increase in public debt raises interest rates, depressing private domestic investment, reducing the country's future productive capacity, decreasing aggregate supply, and driving up prices. Finally, the monetization of debt can be the third channel, where an increase in government debt may lead to an increase in seigniorage, allowing the government to balance its budget. This can increase the amount of printed money, propping up demand and increasing prices (Barth et al. 1987; Davig and Leeper 2007).

Earlier studies, such as those by Catão and Terrones (2005), Bajo-Rubio et al. (2006), and Lin and Chu (2013), provide evidence that inflation is not uniquely a monetary issue but also a fiscal concern due to large fiscal deficits and excessive public debt. Thus, coordinating monetary and fiscal policy is crucial in controlling inflation, and fiscal policy is increasingly recognized as an essential factor in determining inflation.

The Fiscal Theory of the Price Level, which asserts that debt plays a pivotal role in determining the price level, has been a subject of extensive debate and has spurred a substantial body of literature, such as studies by Cochrane (2005), Gordon and Leeper (2002), Cochrane (2001) and Sims (1994). Additionally, some studies suggest that an active monetary policy with a passive fiscal policy can stabilize prices. An independent central bank with a clear inflation target and the ability to adjust interest rates can effectively stabilize the economy and control inflation. These studies argue that the effects of debt management policy on the economy can be offset by changes in other policies, such as monetary policy (Assadi 2015; Davig and Leeper 2007, 2009; Leeper 1991).

Regarding empirical research, we observed that the bulk of the empirical literature predominantly focuses on examining the connection between inflation and public debt rather than foreign debt, such as the work of Aimola and Odhiambo (2022) in Gambia, Aimola and Odhiambo (2021a) in Ghana, Aimola and Odhiambo (2021b) in Nigeria, Van Bon (2015) across various developing countries, and the comprehensive study by Reinhart and Rogoff (2010) which covers 44 countries. Recently, a growing number of studies have probed the intricate relationship between foreign debt and inflation using a variety of econometric methodologies and covering different countries and periods, with inconclusive findings. Notably, research conducted by Enongene and Etape (2023) in Cameroon, Sharaf and Shahen (2023) in Sudan, Gathendu (2021) in Kenya, Uganda, and Tanzania, and the collective work of Arisa (2020) and Mweni et al. (2016) in Kenya, have explored this nuanced association. While a positive relationship between foreign debt and inflation is supported by some studies (e.g., Choong et al. 2010; Mweni et al. 2016; Arisa 2020), others indicate a negative relationship (e.g., Karakaplan 2009; Sharaf and Shahen 2023), and a third category of studies asserts no discernible relationship (e.g., Essien et al. 2016; Aimola and Odhiambo 2021b). These empirical studies share a common feature where they assume that inflation responds symmetrically to changes in foreign debt. However, recent evidence suggests that the effect of foreign debt on inflation could be asymmetric. The findings of some recent studies seem to support the asymmetric hypothesis, which indicates that positive foreign debt shocks could have a different effect on inflation than negative debt shocks (see, for example, Enongene and Etape 2023; Sharaf and Shahen 2023; Aimola and Odhiambo 2022).

Table 1 briefly reviews the empirical studies exploring the intricate connections between foreign debt and inflation, employing various research methodologies like ARDL bounds testing, NARDL, vector autoregression models, and regression analyses. The amalgamation of these methodologies has yielded a spectrum of results, showcasing varied conclusions, encompassing positive, negative, and inconclusive relationships. This diversity underscores the complexity of economic interactions. Additionally, these studies encompass multiple countries and timeframes, enriching our comprehension of how foreign debt and inflation interplay across different economic contexts. This breadth emphasizes the influence of contextual factors, emphasizing the need to consider diverse scenarios when formulating policies or theories related to foreign debt and its impact on inflation.

Table 1 shows that there is a significant research gap regarding the foreign debt–inflation nexus in Brazil. In particular, very few studies have investigated this relationship in Brazil, often within a comparative framework involving multiple countries, and these studies were published quite some time ago. Instead, the focus was on the linkage between Brazil's foreign debt and economic growth rather than inflation (e.g., Koyuncu Çakmak and Demirhan 2020; Afonso et al. 2020). Among the few studies that examined the connection between inflation and foreign debt in Brazil, Cardoso and Fishlow (1990) focused on the mid-1980s period. At that time, Brazil had a foreign debt of more than one-third of the country's GDP and was also facing high inflation rates. The authors argue that inflation and foreign debt are related problems with the same underlying issue. The study showed that shifting from foreign to domestic deficit finance has increased real interest rates and inflation. In another study, Koluri and Giannaros (1987) tested the monetarist view that deficits and money growth are the leading causes of inflation in Mexico and Brazil. The study findings indicate that the federal budget deficit has not significantly contributed to money growth in Brazil and Mexico. However, there is evidence of a direct impact of deficit spending on inflation in Mexico.

Moreover, the research supports the idea that changes in money supply directly affect the inflation rate in both countries. Foreign debt is a significant factor in money growth in both countries, with a possible indirect effect on inflation. The study suggests that expansionary fiscal policy can lead to inflation by impacting the central bank's monetary policy. However, the results should be interpreted cautiously due to sample size limitations. The study by Farhan and Younes (2021) is the most up-to-date research on the foreign debt–inflation nexus in Brazil. The study found that an increase in foreign debt leads to a rise in inflation rates, a persistent issue affecting the Brazilian economy and many other Latin American countries.

Table 1. A brief review of related Empirical studies.

Study	Study Period	Country/Region	Methodology	Public Debt/ Foreign Debt	Relationship in General
(Enongene and Etape 2023)	(1980–2020)	Cameroon	NARDL	Foreign debt	Positive (In the long run)
(Sharaf and Shahen 2023)	(1970–2020)	Sudan	ARDL bounds testing approach	Foreign debt	No relationship (In the long run)
			NARDL		Negative (In the long run)
(Aimola and Odhiambo 2022)	(1978–2019)	Gambia	NARDL	Public debt	Positive
(Aimola and Odhiambo 2021a)	(1983–2018)	Ghana	ARDL bounds testing approach	Public debt	Positive
(Aimola and Odhiambo 2021b)	(1983–2018)	Nigeria	ARDL	Public debt	No relationship (In the short and long run)
(Gathendu 2021)	(1988–2018)	Kenya, Uganda and Tanzania	VECM	Foreign debt	Positive
(Arisa 2020)	(1993–2018)	Kenya	Vector auto regression model Diagnostic tests	Foreign debt	Positive
(Mweni et al. 2016)	(1972–2012)	Kenya	Regression model	Foreign debt	Positive
(Essien et al. 2016)	(1970–2014)	Nigeria	Vector Autoregressive model Granger causality test Impulse response Variance decomposition of various innovations	Foreign debt	No relationship
(Van Bon 2015)	(1990–2014)	Developing Countries	GMM Arellano-Bond	Public debt	Positive
(Choong et al. 2010)	(1970–2006)	Malaysia	Cointegration test	Foreign debt	Positive
(Reinhart and Rogoff 2010)	200 years	44 countries	Examination of pertinent statistical data	Public debt	Positive (Emerging countries)
(Karakaplan 2009)	44 years	121 countries	GMM technique	Public debt	Negative (Advanced countries)
(Kwon et al. 2009)	(1963–2004)	Some developing and developed countries	Vector autoregression model	Public debt	Positive (Developing countries) - Specially indebted developing countries
(Janssen et al. 2002)	Past 300 years	U.K.		Public debt	No relationship
(Taghavi 2000)	(1970–1997)	Large European economies	Hybrid cointegration analysis Vector autoregressive model	Public debt	Positive (In most cases in the long run)

In summary, although the relationship between foreign debt and inflation has garnered growing attention, very few studies have examined this nexus in Brazil, and the existing ones were published quite a long time ago and suffer from several methodological caveats. In particular, these studies failed to consider the potential asymmetry in the inflationary effect of foreign debt, as well as the potential regime shifts in regard to this relationship that may result from the presence of structural breaks, and the current study aims to overcome these methodological limitations.

Consequently, a research gap exists concerning the specific relationship between foreign debt and inflation in Brazil. Further research is essential to establish a comprehensive and widely applicable understanding of how foreign debt influences inflation within the Brazilian context. Addressing this gap requires a detailed examination of the potential mechanisms through which foreign debt affects inflation, necessitating a more nuanced analysis of the dynamic nature of this relationship. Our ongoing research aims to bridge this gap by emphasizing the importance of considering structural changes and accounting for nonlinearities and asymmetry. This approach is crucial in unveiling the dynamic and multifaceted nature of the interplay between foreign debt and inflation in Brazil.

4. Data and Methods

We use annual time series data from 1980 to 2020 on the consumer price index (CPI), the foreign debt stock as a % of gross national income (Xdebt), the nominal effective exchange rate (NEER), and the broad domestic money supply (M). The period under investigation is dictated by data availability. The CPI, Xdebt, and M data are obtained from the World Development Indicators. Data on the NEER come from Bruegel's database Darvas (2021). All the variables are measured in natural logarithmic form.

To estimate the impact of foreign debt, within a multivariate framework, on the price level, we use the model in Equation (1).

$$CPI_t = \theta_0 + \theta_1 Xdebt_t + \theta_2 M_t + \theta_3 NEER_t + \varepsilon_t \tag{1}$$

We first check the stationarity of the variables under investigation. The ARDL bounds test of cointegration validity requires that none of the series be integrated of order more than one. The order of integration of the variables is checked using the Augmented Dickey–Fuller (ADF) unit root test and the Zivot and Andrews (2002) unit root test, allowing for an endogenously determined structural break in both the intercept and the trend. After checking the stationarity property of the data, we check the nonlinearity of the variables by employing the Broock, Dechert, and Scheinkman (BDS) test developed by Broock et al. (1996). The results of the BDS test will be used to validate the use of the NARDL approach. We also use a residual-based cointegration test proposed by Gregory and Hansen (1996) that allows for a structural break in the cointegration vector. We then will incorporate a time dummy variable to represent the structural break when estimating the VECM to estimate the short- and long-run elasticities of the price level to the examined factors. Lastly, we estimate foreign debt's symmetric and asymmetric short-run and long-run impact on inflation using linear and nonlinear ARDL models and then conduct a Markov Switching regression (MSR) as a robustness check.

Foreign debt's symmetric (linear) effect on the price level is examined using the ARDL model presented in Equation (2).

$$\begin{gathered}\Delta\, CPI_t = \alpha_0 + \sum_{i=1}^{p} \lambda_{1i} \Delta CPI_{t-i} + \sum_{i=1}^{q} \lambda_{2i} \Delta Xdebt_{t-i} + \sum_{i=1}^{r} \lambda_{3i} \Delta M_{t-i} + \\ \sum_{i=1}^{s} \lambda_{4i} \Delta NEER_{t-1} + \varphi_1\, CPI_{t-1} + \varphi_2\, Xdebt_{t-1} + \varphi_3\, M_{t-1} + \varphi_4 NEER_{t-1} + \varepsilon_t\end{gathered} \tag{2}$$

where Δ is a first difference operator, p, q, r, s are the optimal lag length based on the Schwarz Information Criterion (SIC).

The short-run coefficients are estimated by presenting the ARDL model in an error correction form, as shown in Equation (3).

$$\begin{gathered}\Delta\, CPI_t = \tau_0 + \sum_{i=1}^{p} \tau_{1i} \Delta CPI_{t-i} + \sum_{i=1}^{q} \tau_{2i} \Delta Xdebt_{t-i} + \sum_{i=1}^{r} \tau_{3i} \Delta M_{t-i} + \\ \sum_{i=1}^{s} \tau_{4i} \Delta NEER_{t-1} + \varnothing ECT_{t-1} + \varepsilon_t\end{gathered} \tag{3}$$

We use the NARDL model of Shin et al. (2014) to investigate the asymmetric impact of foreign debt on inflation. The intuition of this model is that it decomposes the foreign debt changes into negative changes $\left(Xdebt_t^- = \sum_{i=1}^{t} \Delta Xdebt_t^- = \sum_{i=1}^{t} \min(Xdebt_i, 0)\right)$ and positive changes $\left(Xdebt_t^+ = \sum_{i=1}^{t} \Delta Xdebt_t^+ = \sum_{i=1}^{t} \max(Xdebt_i, 0)\right)$. $Xdebt_t^-$ and $Xdebt_t^+$ are the partial sums of the negative and positive changes in the foreign debt, respectively.

Equation (4) presents the NARDL formulation of the model in Equation (1). It is used to uncover an asymmetric equilibrium relationship between foreign debt and inflation within a multivariate setting by incorporating the other covariates, NEER and M.

$$\Delta\,CPI_t = \varphi_0 + \sum_{i=1}^{p}\omega_{1i}\Delta CPI_{t-i} + \sum_{i=1}^{q}\omega_{2i}\Delta M_{t-i} + \sum_{i=1}^{r}\omega_{3i}\Delta NEER_{t-1} + \sum_{i=1}^{s}\omega_{4i}\Delta Xdebt^{+}_{t-i} + \sum_{i=1}^{v}\omega_{5i}\Delta Xdebt^{-}_{t-i} + \vartheta_1\,CPI_{t-1} + \vartheta_2 M_{t-i} + \vartheta_3 NEER_{t-i}\,\vartheta_4 Xdebt^{+}_{t-1} + \vartheta_5 Xdebt^{-}_{t-1} + \varepsilon_t \quad (4)$$

Equation (5) shows the error correction representation of the NARDL model in Equation (4) and is used to estimate the short-run asymmetric effect of foreign debt on inflation.

$$\Delta\,CPI_t = \varphi_1 + \sum_{i=1}^{p}\eta_{1i}\Delta CPI_{t-i} + \sum_{i=1}^{q}\eta_{2i}\Delta M_{t-i} + \sum_{i=1}^{r}\eta_{3i}\Delta NEER_{t-1} + \sum_{i=1}^{s}\eta_{4i}\Delta Xdebt^{+}_{t-i} + \sum_{i=1}^{v}\eta_{5i}\Delta Xdebt^{-}_{t-i} + \varnothing ECT_{t-1} + \varepsilon_t \quad (5)$$

In Equations (3) and (5), the error correction term coefficient measures the speed of recovery from short-run disequilibrium in the aftermath of a shock to the long-run equilibrium path. Dynamic stability requires $\varnothing$ to have a negative sign and is less than unity.

We also run a multiple structural breakpoints test of Bai and Perron (1998) to check the presence of structural breaks in the impact of NEER, M, and foreign debt on the CPI. Equation (6) presents a multiple structural breakpoints linear model with T periods and m structural breaks.

$$CPI_t = \gamma_i Xdebt_t + \varphi_i\,NEER_t + \psi_i\,M_t + u_t \quad (6)$$

In which γ_i, φ_i and ψ_i are the regime-dependant coefficients for $i = 1, \ldots, m+1$, and u_t is the error term. The number of statistically significant structural breaks, m, is determined endogenously by a sequential algorithm as proposed by Bai and Perron (1998).

Finally, we estimate a nonlinear Markov Switching Regression (MSR) as a robustness check to determine if there is a regime shift in the impact of foreign debt on inflation.

5. Empirical Results

Results of the ADF unit root test, presented in Table 2, show that CPI, M, and NEER are stationary at level in one of the versions of the test and non-stationary in the other versions.

Table 2. Results of the ADF unit root test.

		CPI	M	NEER	Xdebt
		At Level			
With Constant	T-Statistic	−2.5749	−3.2326 **	−2.5877	−2.3552
	Prob.	(0.1067)	(0.0259)	(0.1041)	(0.1607)
With Constant and Trend	T-Statistic	−1.8663	−2.5808	−1.9279	−2.6338
	Prob.	(0.6526)	(0.2906)	(0.6210)	(0.2684)
Without Constant and Trend	T-Statistic	−2.3888 **	−0.3375	−2.6546 ***	−0.0677
	Prob.	(0.0181)	(0.5567)	(0.0093)	(0.6539)
		At First Difference			
With Constant	T-Statistic	−1.7557	−1.2856	−1.8892	−3.9091 ***
	Prob.	(0.3962)	(0.6260)	(0.3338)	(0.0046)
With Constant and Trend	T-Statistic	−2.4705	−2.2844	−2.5496	−3.8752 **
	Prob.	(0.3401)	(0.4316)	(0.3042)	(0.0228)
Without Constant and Trend	T-Statistic	−1.5565	−1.1474	−1.6111	−3.9602 ***
	Prob.	(0.1111)	(0.2242)	(0.1001)	(0.0002)

, * indicate rejection of the null hypothesis (series is non-stationary) at the 5%, and 1% significance level, respectively. Lag length is based on SIC. *p*-values are in parenthesis.

Foreign debt is non-stationary at level across the three versions of the ADF test. The ADF also shows that foreign debt is the only stationary variable at first difference. One shortcoming of the conventional ADF unit root test is its failure to allow for existing structural breaks in the series, which causes a bias in conducting the unit root test. Results of the Andrew–Zivot unit root test of the variables at level and first difference are presented in Table 3.

Table 3. Results of Andrew–Zivot unit root test.

Unit Root Test of Variables in Level							
CPI		**M**		**Xdebt**		**NEER**	
T-Statistic	Time break	T-Statistic	Time break	T-Statistic	Time break	T-Statistic	Time break
−6.38 ***	1992	−7.89 ***	1992	−4.03	2005	−6.43 ***	1992
Unit root tests of variables in first difference							
−9.41 ***	1995	−8.02 ***	1995	−5.41 **	1995	−10.91 ***	1995

, * imply rejection of the null hypothesis of a unit root with a structural break at the 5%, and 1% significance level, respectively.

The test shows that, but for foreign debt, all of the variables (CPI, M, NEER) are stationary at level at the 1% significance level. More importantly, at their first difference, all the variables become stationary, with one structural break in 1995 for CPI, M, and NEER and in 2003 for foreign debt. The Andrew–Zivot unit root test results align with the time series plots in Figure 2, which also reveals the existence of a structural break in the consumer price index, money supply, and the nominal effective exchange rate series around 1995.

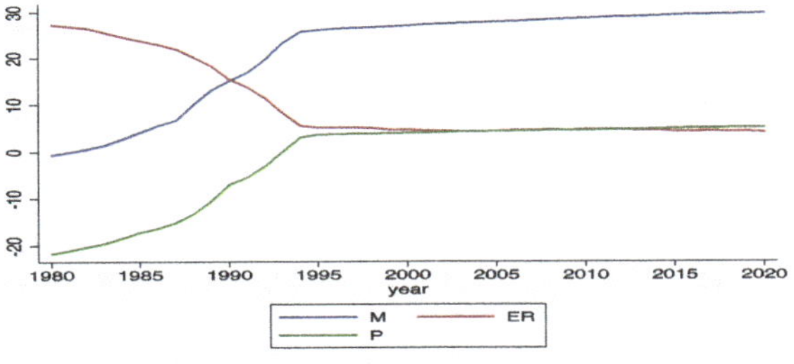

Figure 2. Evolution of the consumer price index, money supply and the nominal effective exchange rate over 1980–2020. Source: Authors' compilation based on data from (WDI).

Results of the BDS test, displayed in Table 4, confirm nonlinearity patterns in the data of the variables, which allow us to proceed with the nonlinear (asymmetric) NARDL approach. According to the BDS test, the null hypothesis that data in a time series are independently and identically distributed (iid) is rejected for all the variables.

Results of the Gregory–Hansen test for cointegration with regime shifts are shown in Table 5. According to this test, the ADF and Zt statistics both exceed their asymptotic critical values at the 5% significance level, confirming cointegration between the price level and the other variables with an identified structural break in 1999.

The Schwarz Information Criterion selected an ARDL (1, 2, 1, 0) and a NARDL (1, 2, 1, 1, 0) model. Results of the cointegration bounds test for both the symmetric and asymmetric ARDL models, presented in Table 6, show both a linear and a nonlinear cointegration between CPI, M, NEER, and Xdebt since the F- and t- statistics are greater than their upper critical bounds at the 5% significance level.

Table 4. Results of the BDS Test.

BDS Test for CPI				
Dimension	**BDS Statistic**	**Std. Error**	**z-Statistic**	**Prob.**
2	0.2075	0.0141	14.7009	0.0000
3	0.3512	0.0226	15.5192	0.0000
4	0.4487	0.0271	16.5064	0.0000
5	0.5122	0.0285	17.9120	0.0000
6	0.5531	0.0278	19.8635	0.0000
BDS Test for M				
Dimension	**BDS Statistic**	**Std. Error**	**z-Statistic**	**Prob.**
2	0.2073	0.0139	14.8805	0.0000
3	0.3508	0.0224	15.6316	0.0000
4	0.4489	0.0270	16.5707	0.0000
5	0.5149	0.0286	17.9803	0.0000
6	0.5570	0.0280	19.8791	0.0000
BDS Test for NEER				
Dimension	**BDS Statistic**	**Std. Error**	**z-Statistic**	**Prob.**
2	0.2075	0.0141	14.7009	0.0000
3	0.3512	0.0226	15.5192	0.0000
4	0.4487	0.0271	16.5064	0.0000
5	0.5122	0.0285	17.9120	0.0000
6	0.5531	0.0278	19.8635	0.0000
BDS Test for Foreign Debt				
Dimension	**BDS Statistic**	**Std. Error**	**z-Statistic**	**Prob.**
2	0.1135	0.0077	14.6836	0.0000
3	0.1800	0.0124	14.4366	0.0000
4	0.2023	0.0150	13.4327	0.0000
5	0.2031	0.0159	12.7570	0.0000
6	0.1868	0.0155	11.9930	0.0000

Table 5. Results of the Gregory–Hansen Test for cointegration with regime shifts.

Testing Procedure	Test Statistic	Breakpoint	Date	Asymptotic Critical Values		
				1%	5%	10%
ADF	−6.77	21	2000	−5.77	−5.28	−5.02
Zt	−5.60	20	1999	−5.77	−5.28	−5.02
Za	−33.20	20	1999	−63.64	−5.58	−48.65

Source: Authors' estimation. The optimal lag length is automatically chosen based on Bayesian criterion.

Table 7 shows the results of the estimated ARDL and NARDL models. The results of the ARDL model show that current and lagged values of the domestic money supply have a statistically significant positive impact on inflation in the short run.

The NARDL model results show that the current value of the domestic money supply has a positive effect, though not statistically significant, on the inflation rate, while the lagged value of the money supply positively affects inflation in the short run. Results of both the ARDL and NARDL models reveal that the nominal effective exchange rate has a statistically significant negative impact on inflation in the short run. This means a nominal appreciation of the Brazilian real lowers the inflation rate. The estimated time dummy variable coefficient is positive and statistically significant, which confirms the importance of controlling for the structural break in the time series.

Table 6. Results of the symmetric and asymmetric cointegration bounds test.

				95% Critical Bounds	
Dependent Variable	**Explanatory Variables**	**Specification**	**F-Statistic**	**I(0)**	**I(1)**
Δ(CPI)	M, NEER, Xdebt	**ARDL (1, 2, 1, 0)**	12.54 ***	2.45	3.63
			T-Statistic	I(0)	I(1)
			−5.46 ***	−1.95	−3.33
Δ(CPI)	M, NEER, $Xdebt_t^+$, $Xdebt_t^-$	**NARDL (1, 2, 1, 1, 0)**	F-statistic	I(0)	I(1)
			8.69 ***	2.26	3.48
			T-Statistic	I(0)	I(1)
			−3.65 **	−1.95	−3.60

, * indicate statistical significance at the 5%, 10% level, respectively. The lower and upper bound critical values are obtained from Pesaran et al. (2001).

Table 7. Estimated short and long-run coefficients of the symmetric and asymmetric ARDL models.

	ARDL (1, 2, 1, 0)		NARDL (1, 2, 1, 1, 0)	
	Coefficient	**Std. Error**	**Coefficient**	**Std. Error**
Short-run coefficients				
ΔM	0.0850 **	0.0366	0.0360	0.0356
ΔM_{t-1}	0.1139 ***	0.0331	0.0922 ***	0.0319
ΔNEER	−0.8884 ***	0.0570	−0.9943 ***	0.0592
D_{95}	0.0334 *	0.0203	0.2019 ***	0.0330
$\Delta Xdebt^+$			−0.7451 ***	0.1365
ECT_{t-1}	−0.4804 ***	0.0647		
Long-run coefficients				
M	0.3279 ***	0.0164	0.2505 ***	0.0329
NEER	−0.6946 ***	0.0182	−0.7500 ***	0.0104
Xdebt	−0.5223***	0.1213		
$Xdebt^+$			−0.5701 ***	0.1926
$Xdebt^-$			−0.6761 ***	0.2182
Diagnostic checks				
Breusch–Godfrey Serial Correlation LM Test	$\chi^2(2) = 0.15$ *p* value (0.92)		$\chi^2(2) = 2.40$ *p* value (0.30)	
Heteroskedasticity Test: Breusch–Pagan–Godfrey	$\chi^2(8) = 2.18$ *p* value (0.21)		$\chi^2(10) = 2.39$ *p* value (0.77)	
Ramsey RESET Test	F (1,30) = 1.02 *p* value (0.33)		F (1,28) = 0.66 *p* value (0.15)	
Normality	Jarque-Bera = 1.48 *p* value (0.47)		Jarque-Bera = 1.45 *p* value (0.48)	
	R^2 = 0.99 Adjusted R^2 = 0.99		R^2 = 0.99 Adjusted R^2 = 0.99	

*, **, *** indicate statistical significance at the 10%, 5% and 1% level, respectively. Lag length is based on SIC.

As for the impact of foreign debt in the short run, the symmetric ARDL model shows that foreign debt does not affect inflation in the short run. In contrast, the results of the NARDL model show that only positive changes in foreign debts have a negative and significant effect on inflation in the short run.

The estimated long-run coefficients of the symmetric ARDL model show that M, NEER, and Xdebt have a statistically significant long-term effect on inflation. According to the estimated long-run elasticity coefficients, a one percent increase in money supply raises the inflation rate by 0.32 percent. An increase in the nominal effective exchange rate (a nominal appreciation of the Brazilian real) by one percent lowers the inflation rate by 0.69 percent. Analogously, a one percent increase in foreign debt lowers the inflation rate by 0.52 percent.

The results of the NARDL model are generally similar in the long run. In particular, money supply has a statistically significant long-term positive effect on inflation. A rise in domestic money supply by 1% raises the inflation rate by 0.25 percent. Analogously, a 1% rise in the nominal effective exchange rate of the Brazilian real lowers inflation by 0.75% in the long run. Regarding the effect of foreign debt on inflation, the estimated long-run coefficients of the NARDL model reveal that positive and negative foreign debt changes have a significant impact on inflation at the 1% significance level. A 1% rise in foreign debt lowers inflation by 0.57% in the long run, while a 1% drop in foreign debt raises inflation by 0.68 percent. The dynamic asymmetric multiplier of the NARDL model presented in Figure 3 portrays this.[4] It is evident in Figure 3 that the dynamic asymmetric multiplier is statistically significant at the 5% significance level, where the asymmetry plot lies within the 95% confidence level as reflected by the upper and lower thin dashed red lines.

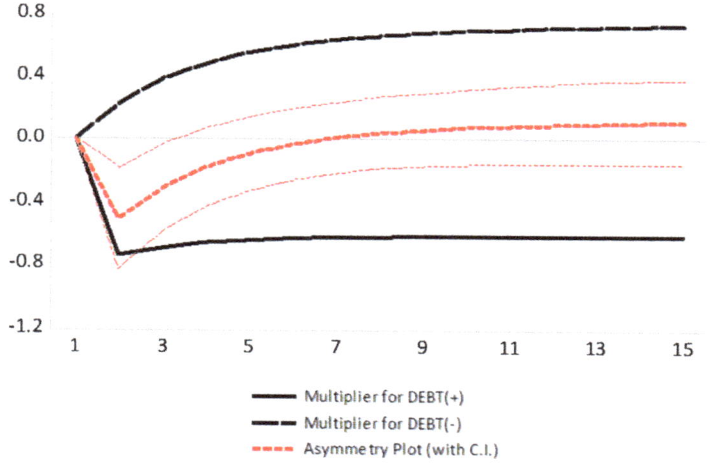

Figure 3. Dynamic asymmetric multiplier of the NARDL model.

The estimated coefficients of the error-correction term of both the symmetric and asymmetric ARDL models are both less than unity, are statistically significant, and have a negative sign. The ARDL error correction model shows a speedy restoration to long-run equilibrium, where 48% of the past period's disequilibrium is corrected in the current period. This implies that following a shock, restoring the long-run equilibrium between CPI, M, NEER, and foreign debt takes about two years. The NARDL error correction model shows a slower speed to restore equilibrium, where 33.5% of the past period's disequilibrium is corrected in the current period. This means that following a shock, it takes about three years for examined variables to restore their long-run equilibrium relationship.

We checked the soundness of the estimated symmetric and asymmetric ARDL models using a set of post-estimation diagnostic tests. The results of these tests indicate that the estimated ARDL and NARDL models are free from heteroskedasticity, serial correlation, specification errors, and non-normality of the residuals at the 5% significance level. Parameters stability diagnostics as reflected by the cumulative sum of recursive residuals (CUSUM) test and the cumulative sum of squares of recursive residuals (CUSUMSQ) test, displayed in Figures 4 and 5, reveal that the estimated coefficients of the ARDL and NARDL models are stable at the 5% significance level.

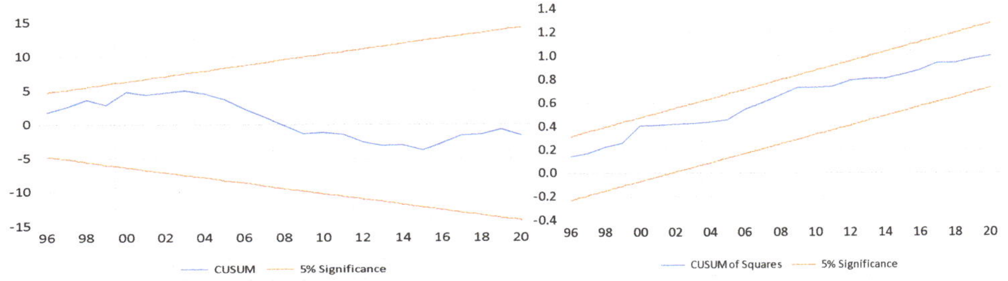

Figure 4. CUSUM and CUSUMSQ stability plots of the ARDL (1, 2, 1, 0) model.

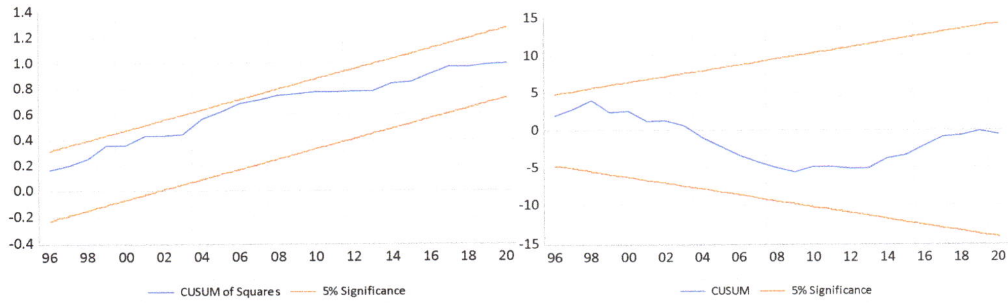

Figure 5. CUSUM and CUSUMSQ stability plots of the NARDL (1, 2, 1, 1, 0) model.[5]

The Bai–Perron multiple breakpoint test results, presented in Table 8, indicate the existence of two structural breaks in 1989 and 1997 in which the null hypothesis of a two-regime (one break) model is tested versus the alternative of a three-regime (two breaks) model and the null hypothesis is rejected at the 5% significance level.

Table 8. Bai–Perron multiple breakpoint test of L + 1 vs. L sequentially determined breaks.

Break Test	F-Statistic	Critical Value **
0 vs. 1 *	51.78	16.19
1 vs. 2 *	37.78	18.11
2 vs. 3	4.067	18.93
Break dates:		
	Sequential	Repartition
1	1991	1989
2	1997	1997

* Significant at the 0.05 level. ** Bai–Perron (Bai and Perron 2003) critical values.

The Bai and Perron multiple structural breakpoint test is implemented with a maximum of five breaks and a trimming parameter of 0.15 to test the null hypothesis of L + 1 versus L sequentially determined structural breaks.

Table 9 presents the results of the discrete threshold regression associated with the Bai–Perron multiple structural breaks estimation over 1980–2020.

Table 9. Discrete Threshold Regression.

Variable	Coefficient	Std. Error	T-Statistic	Prob.
		1980–1989		
M	0.4018 ***	0.0396	10.147	0.000
NEER	−0.6031 ***	0.0590	−10.211	0.000
XDEBT	0.3017 **	0.1261	2.3923	0.023
		1990–1997		
M	0.5560 ***	0.0580	9.5833	0.000
NEER	−0.3969 ***	0.0685	−5.7947	0.000
XDEBT	−0.9903 ***	0.1975	−5.0131	0.000
		1998–2020		
M	0.4009 ***	0.0320	12.507	0.000
NEER	−0.2014	0.1466	−1.3739	0.179
XDEBT	−0.0282	0.0846	−0.3333	0.741
		Non-Breaking Variables		
C	−5.8452 ***	1.6675	−3.5053	0.001

Break type: Bai–Perron tests of L + 1 vs. L sequentially determined breaks. **, *** indicate statistical significance at the 5% and 1% level, respectively.

The break model for the sub-period 1980–1989 shows that both the broad money supply and the foreign debt have a statistically significant positive effect on the CPI, while the NEER has a statistically significant negative effect. For the sub-period 1990–1997, the effect of money supply on CPI remains positive and significant, and the effect of the NEER is negative and statistically significant. However, foreign debt has a statistically significant negative impact on the CPI in that second sub-period. Notably, in the third sub-period, 1998–2020, the effect of foreign debt on CPI is negative, though not statistically significant. While money supply continues to have a statistically significant positive effect on CPI, the effect of the NEER is negative but not significant.

Table 10 presents the results of the Markov Switching Regression. The findings of Markov Switching Regression in the two regimes (regime 1 and regime 2) are generally similar. In particular, M and NEER negatively and statistically significantly impact the price level in both regimes.

Table 10. Markov Switching Regression (BFGS/Marquardt steps).

Variable	Coefficient	Std. Error	z-Statistic	Prob.
		Regime 1		
M	0.374 ***	0.064	5.836	0.000
NEER	−0.600 ***	0.078	−7.613	0.000
Xdebt	−0.202 *	0.122	−1.655	0.097
C	−2.762	2.439	−1.132	0.257
		Regime 2		
M	0.254 ***	0.035	7.220	0.000
NEER	−0.817 ***	0.047	−17.23	0.000
Xdebt	−0.066	0.153	−0.429	0.667
C	1.294	1.082	1.195	0.232
		Common		
LOG (SIGMA)	−2.286	0.155	−14.66	0.000
		Probabilities Parameters		
P1-C	−0.591	0.723	−0.817	0.413
Mean dependent var	−1.703	S.D. dependent var		9.521
S.E. of regression	0.286	Sum squared resid		2.627
Durbin–Watson stat	0.432	Log likelihood		22.41
Akaike info criterion	−0.605	Schwarz criterion		−0.187
Hannan–Quinn criter.	−0.453			

*, *** indicate statistical significance at the 10% and 1% level, respectively.

However, although foreign debt has a negative impact on the CPI in both regimes, the impact is statistically significant in the first regime at a 10% significance level and not significant in the second regime.

6. Discussion

This study augments the existing literature investigating the relationship between foreign debt and inflation. It does so by examining this nexus in the context of Brazil, within a multivariate framework, from 1980 to 2020. In addressing methodological concerns in previous studies, our research diverges from conventional linear assumptions and employs two nonlinear approaches: the nonlinear autoregressive distributed lag (NARDL) model and a Markov Switching Regression (MSR). Additionally, the study considers the presence of structural breaks via utilizing the Zivot and Andrews (Z–A) unit root test and incorporates a residual-based cointegration test developed by Gregory and Hansen (G–H). Moreover, the study employs a multiple structural breakpoints test by Bai and Perron (B–P).

The merit of this study lies in recognizing the importance of incorporating structural breaks in time series analysis, which highlights the dynamic nature of economic relationships and emphasizes the necessity of addressing regime shifts. This significance stems from the limitation of the conventional unit root tests, which do not account for structural breaks in time series data, resulting in bias that weakens the ability to detect a false unit root null hypothesis. We employed the Z–A unit root test to address this issue, revealing that most variables exhibited stationarity at their levels with one structural break around

1995. This corresponds to the period following the introduction of the Real Plan in Brazil in 1994, an initiative aimed at stabilizing the economy and controlling inflation. Another contribution of our study concerning structural breaks is the utilization of the Gregory–Hansen test, which examines the presence of cointegration in the context of structural breaks, verifying its existence between the price level and other variables, with a structural break identified in 1999.

The results obtained from the linear ARDL model suggest that the influence of foreign debt on inflation in Brazil has no statistical significance. These findings are consistent with Sharaf and Shahen's (2023) study, which found no statistically significant effect of foreign debt on inflation in Sudan over the period from 1970 to 2020. Similarly, these findings align with the research conducted by Aimola and Odhiambo (2021b), focusing on the relationship between public debt and inflation in Nigeria, spanning from 1983 to 2018. The findings of another study conducted by Essien et al. (2016) corroborate and fortify the conclusions that utilizing the linear ARDL model in the analysis may not detect a statistically significant inflationary effect for foreign debt.

To consider the possible asymmetry in how foreign debt could affect inflation, we employed a nonlinear ARDL model. The rationale for using this nonlinear model is the recognition that the link between foreign debt and inflation might not exhibit symmetry and could depend on whether the foreign debt shock is in a positive or negative direction. The results of the NARDL model reveal that positive foreign debt shocks have a statistically significant negative impact on inflation in the short run. This relationship remains negative and significant in the long run as well. This finding contradicts the conventional belief that excessive foreign debt can lead to inflation through currency devaluation and increased import demand.

Nevertheless, these results coincide with the research conducted by Sharaf and Shahen (2023), demonstrating that debt negatively affects inflation in Sudan when the NARDL model technique is utilized. Likewise, Karakaplan (2009) also indicated that debt has a negative effect on inflation in certain advanced countries. Furthermore, these results are consistent with the study conducted by Bleaney (1996), which suggested that debt has a negative influence on inflation during particular periods.

The negative effect of foreign debt on inflation can be explained by various economic mechanisms, notably the rise of debt service costs associated with the mounting foreign debt. In response, governments may employ monetary strategies, such as tightening the money supply, to mitigate the inflationary impact. Additionally, the accumulation of foreign debt can influence exchange rates and, if managed effectively, contribute to inflation control. Fiscal measures, such as austerity, are also deployed to ensure the proper management of the debt burden while averting inflationary pressures. These outcomes underscore the active role of governments in mitigating the potential inflationary consequences of increasing foreign debt through a fusion of monetary and fiscal approaches.

The findings derived from the ARDL and NARDL models present contrasting perspectives regarding the influence of debt on inflation. Findings of the linear ARDL model imply an absence of a statistically significant long-term impact of foreign debt on inflation, aligning with studies such as Aimola and Odhiambo (2021b) and Essien et al. (2016) on Nigeria and Janssen et al. (2002) on U.K., whose findings also suggest no significant association between debt and inflation. Conversely, the NARDL model results reveal a statistically significant long-term relationship between foreign debt shocks and inflation. These NARDL findings align with several empirical studies emphasizing asymmetric effects in adjusting economic variables, particularly regarding critical elements like debt and inflation. Noteworthy research endeavors, including studies by Enongene and Etape (2023) on Cameroon, Sharaf and Shahen (2023) on Sudan, and Aimola and Odhiambo (2022) on the Gambia, further substantiate and bolster these conclusions and support the asymmetric hypothesis which indicates that positive foreign debt shocks could have a different effect on inflation than negative debt shocks.

Using the nonlinear ARDL approach often leads to distinct results compared to the linear models in these studies. For example, previous investigations using a linear ARDL approach did not reveal significant long-term impacts of foreign debt on inflation in Sudan until the study conducted by Sharaf and Shahen (2023), where the ARDL approach suggested an absence of a statistically significant impact from foreign debt on long-term inflation. In contrast, the findings from the NARDL model imply that positive and negative shocks in foreign debt wield a statistically significant influence on long-term inflation. Consequently, applying the nonlinear ARDL method in their research revealed the asymmetric effects of alterations in Sudan's foreign debt on inflation from 1970 to 2020, presenting critical supplementary insights in our research.

To sum up, the use of asymmetry analysis in the current study reveals a significant impact of foreign debt shocks on inflation, underscoring the importance of accounting for nonlinear dynamics. The research suggests that changes in foreign debt levels can gradually reduce inflationary effects over time. Furthermore, the study demonstrates that the relationship between foreign debt and inflation is nonlinear, indicating that the magnitude and direction of the shock can influence how foreign debt affects inflation. These conflicting results underscore the complexity and nuances in comprehending the intricate relationship between debt and inflation, emphasizing the necessity for more detailed analyses and considerations of multifaceted factors in future research.

On the other hand, the findings of both linear (symmetric) and nonlinear (asymmetric) ARDL models, for both short-term and long-term periods, concerning domestic money supply and nominal effective exchange rate, reveal that domestic money supply (M) has a significant positive effect on inflation, while the nominal effective exchange rate (NEER) has a statistically significant negative effect on inflation.

The results related to the impact of M on inflation align with the Quantity Theory of Money, a fundamental concept in monetary economics that suggests that an expansion of the money supply causes inflation. This correlation is supported by multiple empirical investigations, including studies conducted by Gharehgozli and Lee (2022), Helmy (2021) in Egypt, Abate (2020) in Ethiopia, and Benati (2021) across 27 countries. For instance, Gharehgozli and Lee (2022) illustrated that the lockdowns in 2020, coupled with expansive fiscal and monetary policies, triggered an unprecedented surge in the money supply. This excess of money supply subsequently contributed to the rise in the core inflation rate during and after COVID-19.

Similarly, the results for the NEER correspond to economic theory, suggesting that a stronger currency can reduce inflation by lowering import costs and enhancing the competitive position of local producers. These findings are also supported by empirical evidence, such as the studies conducted by Sharaf and Shahen (2023) and Baharumshah et al. (2017) in Sudan. Both studies employed a NARDL model and concluded that a stronger currency has a negative and statistically significant impact on inflation, implying that it can reduce inflationary pressures in Sudan. However, our findings contrast with those of Sharaf et al. (2023) in Jordan, who found that a nominal depreciation of the Jordanian Dinar led to increased short- and long-term inflation rates spanning from 1970 to 2020.

A distinctive aspect of our study, focusing on structural breaks, involves the application of the Bai–Perron multiple breakpoint test to identify such breaks in different periods. The test detected structural breaks in 1989 and 1997, revealing varying effects of the variables on the price level within distinct sub-periods. These structural breaks indicate significant relationship changes between the variables and the inflation during those years. As a result, these findings provide insight into shifts in economic conditions in Brazil during those specific periods. Notably, the economic landscape in Brazil showed marked differences in the distinct years of 1989 and 1997, which represented pivotal moments in the nation's economic history. In 1989, Brazil grappled with hyperinflation and underwent a significant political transition. Conversely, in 1997, the introduction of the Real Plan marked a shift towards relative economic stability and the initiation of trade liberalization in the country.

The current study is not free from limitations. One limitation is that the data used cover the period 1980–2020 annually, which might pose a challenge due to the relatively small sample size. Nonetheless, a sample size of about 40 observations is acceptable in empirical research. Also, it is worth mentioning that our use of annual data, instead of quarterly data, for instance, and the choice of the study period are dictated by data availability for all the variables included in the analysis.

7. Conclusions

This study investigated the relationship between foreign debt and inflation in Brazil from 1980 to 2020 while addressing the methodological limitations of earlier studies. Analyzing structural breaks and implementing nonlinear models uncovers pivotal insights into the nature of the foreign debt–inflation nexus. While linear models suggest no foreign debt impact on inflation, nonlinear models counter this, revealing a substantial negative effect from positive foreign debt shocks, thus disrupting established beliefs. These revelations underscore economic links' intricate and dynamic nature, stressing the importance of acknowledging regime shifts and asymmetry in economic analyses. Additionally, the research pinpoints significant years like 1989 and 1997 as pivotal economic milestones, emphasizing the Brazilian government's proactive role in managing foreign debt levels to stave off potential inflationary consequences. Ultimately, this study enriches our comprehension of the intricate interplay between foreign debt, inflation, and other economic factors, offering indispensable guidance for policymakers navigating economic transformations. In conclusion, these findings corroborate earlier research, illustrating the multifaceted impact of foreign debt on inflation. We expect these findings to aid policymakers in Brazil in designing more effective strategies for managing inflation and foreign debt levels by providing a better understanding of how the two variables are interrelated.

Author Contributions: Conceptualization, M.F.S., B.A.B. and A.M.S.; methodology, M.F.S., B.A.B. and A.M.S.; software, M.F.S., B.A.B. and A.M.S.; validation, M.F.S., B.A.B. and A.M.S.; formal analysis, M.F.S., B.A.B. and A.M.S.; investigation, M.F.S., B.A.B. and A.M.S.; resources, M.F.S., B.A.B. and A.M.S.; data curation, M.F.S., B.A.B. and A.M.S.; writing—original draft preparation, M.F.S., B.A.B. and A.M.S.; writing—review and editing, M.F.S., B.A.B. and A.M.S.; visualization, M.F.S., B.A.B. and A.M.S.; supervision, M.F.S. and B.A.B.; project administration, M.F.S. and B.A.B.; funding acquisition, M.F.S. and B.A.B. All authors have read and agreed to the published version of the manuscript.

Funding: This work was supported and funded by the Deanship of Scientific Research at Imam Mohammad Ibn Saud Islamic University (IMSIU) (grant number IMSIU-RP23016).

Data Availability Statement: The CPI, Xdebt, and M data are obtained from the World Development Indicators. Data on the NEER come from Bruegel's database Darvas (2021).

Acknowledgments: The authors would like to thank the assigned editor and the anonymous reviewers for the constructive comments and suggestions that significantly improved the paper.

Conflicts of Interest: The authors declare no conflict of interest.

Notes

1. Aimola and Odhiambo (2020) offer a systematic review of the related literature.
2. M denotes the broad domestic money supply; E.R. is the nominal effective exchange rate; P is the consumer price index. All these variables are expressed in natural logarithmic form.
3. The "cruzeiro" was Brazil's former currency before it was replaced by the Brazilian real (BRL) in 1994.
4. DEBT $(+)$ and DEBT $(-)$ are the partial sums of the positive and negative changes in the foreign debt, respectively.
5. CUSUM refers to the cumulative sum of recursive residuals, and CUSUMSQ is the cumulative sum of squares of recursive residuals.

References

Abate, Tadesse. 2020. Macro-economic Determinants of Recent Inflation in Ethiopia. *Journal of World Economic Research* 9: 136. [CrossRef]

Afonso, António, Sergio Gadelha, and Agatha Silva. 2020. Public Debt and Economic Growth in Brazil. *SSRN Electronic Journal*, 1–39. [CrossRef]

Aimola, Akingbade U., and Nicholas M. Odhiambo. 2020. Public Debt and Inflation: A Review of International Literature. *Folia Oeconomica Stetinensia* 20: 9–24. [CrossRef]

Aimola, Akingbade U., and Nicholas M. Odhiambo. 2021a. Public debt and inflation: Empirical evidence from Ghana. *Development Studies Research* 8: 1872392. [CrossRef]

Aimola, Akingbade U., and Nicholas M. Odhiambo. 2021b. Public debt and inflation nexus in Nigeria: An ARDL bounds test approach. *Cogent Economics & Finance* 9: 1921905. [CrossRef]

Aimola, Akingbade U., and Nicholas M. Odhiambo. 2022. Is the effect of public debt on inflation symmetric or asymmetric? Evidence from the Gambia. *Croatian Review of Economic, Business and Social Statistics* 8: 41–57. [CrossRef]

Arisa, Gibson Marienga. 2020. Impact of External Debt on Inflation and Exchange Rate in Kenya. Master's thesis, Kenyatta University, Nairobi, Kenya. Available online: https://ir-library.ku.ac.ke/handle/123456789/21755 (accessed on 15 January 2023).

Assadi, Marzieh. 2015. *Monetary and Fiscal Policy Interactions: National and International Empirical Evidence*. Glasgow: University of Glasgow. Available online: https://theses.gla.ac.uk/6796/ (accessed on 15 January 2023).

Baharumshah, Ahmad Zubaidi, Abdalla Sirag, and Norashidah Nor. 2017. Asymmetric Exchange Rate Pass-through in Sudan: Does Inflation React Differently during Periods of Currency Depreciation? *African Development Review* 29: 446–57. [CrossRef]

Bai, Jushan, and Pierre Perron. 1998. Estimating and Testing Linear Models with Multiple Structural Changes. *Econometrica* 66: 47. [CrossRef]

Bai, Jushan, and Pierre Perron. 2003. Critical Values for Multiple Structural Change Tests. *The Econometrics Journal* 6: 72–78. [CrossRef]

Bajo-Rubio, Oscar, Carmen Diaz-Roldan, and Vicente Esteve. 2006. Is the budget deficit sustainable when fiscal policy is nonlinear? The case of Spain. *Journal of Macroeconomics* 28: 596–608. [CrossRef]

Barata, João. 2019. Chapter 7 Brazil: Taking Stock of the Past Couple of Decades. In *Foreign Exchange Intervention in Inflation Targeters in Latin America*. Washington, DC: International Monetary Fund. Available online: https://www.elibrary.imf.org/display/book/9781484375686/ch007.xml (accessed on 22 October 2023).

Barth, James R., Michael D. Bradley, and Paul C. Panayotacos. 1987. Understanding International Debt Crisis. *Case Western Reserve Journal of International Law* 19: 31.

Benati, Luca. 2021. *Long-Run Evidence on the Quantity Theory of Money*. Bern: Departement Volkswirtschaft, Universitaet Bern.

Bethell, Luca. 2000. Politics in Brazil: From Elections without Democracy to Democracy without Citizenship. *Daedalus* 129: 1–27.

Bleaney, Michael. 1996. Inflation and Public Debt. *Australian Economic Papers, Wiley Blackwell* 35: 141–55. [CrossRef]

Broock, William A., José Alexandre Scheinkman, W. Davis Dechert, and Blake LeBaron. 1996. A test for independence based on the correlation dimension. *Econometric Reviews* 15: 197–235. [CrossRef]

Cardoso, Eliana, and Albert Fishlow. 1990. *External Debt, Budget Deficits, and Inflation*. Cambridge: National Bureau of Economic Research, Inc. NBER Chapters, pp. 318–34. Available online: https://econpapers.repec.org/bookchap/nbrnberch/8948.htm (accessed on 2 April 2023).

Catão, Luis A. V., and Marco E. Terrones. 2005. Fiscal deficits and inflation. *Journal of Monetary Economics* 52: 529–54. [CrossRef]

Choong, Chee-Keong, Evan Lau, Venus Khim-Sen Liew, and Chin-Hong Puah. 2010. Does debts foster economic growth? The experience of Malaysia. *International Scholars Journals* 5: 1–12.

Cochrane, John H. 2001. Long-Term Debt and Optimal Policy in the Fiscal Theory of the Price Level. *Econometrica* 69: 69–116. [CrossRef]

Cochrane, John H. 2005. Money as stock. *Journal of Monetary Economics* 52: 501–28. [CrossRef]

Darvas, Zsolt. 2021. Timely Measurement of Real Effective Exchange Rates. Bruegel | The Brussels-Based Economic Think Tank. Available online: https://www.bruegel.org/working-paper/timely-measurement-real-effective-exchange-rates (accessed on 14 March 2023).

Davig, Troy, and Eric M. Leeper. 2007. Generalizing the Taylor Principle. *American Economic Review* 97: 607–35. [CrossRef]

Davig, Troy, and Eric M. Leeper. 2009. *Monetary-Fiscal Policy Interactions and Fiscal Stimulus*. NBER Working Papers 15133. Cambridge: National Bureau of Economic Research, Inc. Available online: https://ideas.repec.org//p/nbr/nberwo/15133.html (accessed on 23 February 2023).

Enongene, Betrand Ewane, and Felix Mejame Etape. 2023. Does External Debt Stocks Have an Asymmetric Effect on Inflation Dynamics in Cameroon? An Application of Nonlinear ARDLL. *American Journal of Economics and Business Innovation* 2: 17–23. [CrossRef]

Essien, Sunday N., Negozi T. I. Agboegbulem, and Ogochukwu G. Onumonu. 2016. An Empirical Analysis of the Macroeconomic Impact of Public Debt in Nigeria. *CBN Journal of Applied Statistics* 7: 125–45.

Farhan, Saadoun Hussein, and Samah A. Younes. 2021. Inflation in light of the external debt constraint in Latin American countries/Brazil as a model. *Tikrit Journal of Administration and Economics Sciences* 17: 218533. Available online: https://www.iasj.net/iasj/article/218533 (accessed on 2 April 2023).

Gathendu, Jane Joy Wairima. 2021. Effect of External Debt on Inflation: The case of Kenya, Tanzania and Uganda. Available online: http://hdl.handle.net/11071/12567 (accessed on 24 December 2023).

Gharehgozli, Orkideh, and Sunhyung Lee. 2022. Money Supply and Inflation after COVID-19. *Economies* 10: 101. [CrossRef]

Gordon, David, and Eric Leeper. 2002. *The Price Level, the Quantity Theory of Money, and the Fiscal Theory of the Price Level*. NBER Working Paper 9084. Cambridge: National Bureau of Economic Research, Inc. Available online: https://econpapers.repec.org/paper/nbrnberwo/9084.htm (accessed on 2 April 2023).

Gregory, Allan W., and Bruce E. Hansen. 1996. Residual-based tests for cointegration in models with regime shifts. *Journal of Econometrics* 70: 99–126. [CrossRef]

Grinberg, Nicolas. 2008. From the "Miracle" to the "Lost Decade": Intersectoral transfers and external credit in the Brazilian economy. *Brazilian Journal of Political Economy* 28: 291–311. [CrossRef]

Helmy, Heba. 2021. The external debt-inflation nexus in Egypt. *Journal of Public Affairs—Wiley Online Library* 22: e2802. [CrossRef]

Janssen, Norbert, Charles Nolan, and Ryland Thomas. 2002. Money, Debt and Prices in the United Kingdom, 1705–1996. *Economica* 69: 461–79. [CrossRef]

Karakaplan, Mustafa Uğur. 2009. The conditional effects of external debt on inflation. *Sosyal Ekonomik Araştırmalar Dergisi* 9: 17.

Koluri, Bharat R., and Demetrios S. Giannaros. 1987. Deficit and External Debt Effects on Money and Inflation in Brazil and Mexico: Some Evidence. *Eastern Economic Journal* 13: 243–48.

Koyuncu Çakmak, Tuğba, and Hüseyin Demirhan. 2020. Impact of External Debt on Economic Growth in Brazil: An ARDL Bound Testing Approach. *The Journal of International Scientific Researches* 5: 674985. [CrossRef]

Kwon, Goohoon, Lavern McFarlane, and Wayne Robinson. 2009. Public Debt, Money Supply, and Inflation: A Cross-Country Study. *IMF Staff Papers* 56: 476–515. [CrossRef]

Leeper, Eric M. 1991. Equilibria under 'active' and 'passive' monetary and fiscal policies. *Journal of Monetary Economics* 27: 129–47. [CrossRef]

Lin, Hsin-Yi, and Hao-Pang Chu. 2013. Are fiscal deficits inflationary? *Journal of International Money and Finance* 32: 214–33. [CrossRef]

Mweni, Fedrick Tsofa, Amos Njuguna, and Timothy Oketch. 2016. The Effect of External Debt on Inflation Rate in Kenya, 1972–2012. *International Journal of Financial Research* 7: 198. [CrossRef]

Pesaran, M. Hashem, Yongcheol Shin, and Richard J. Smith. 2001. Bounds Testing Approaches to the Analysis of Level Relationships. *Journal of Applied Econometrics* 16: 289–326. [CrossRef]

Reinhart, Carmen M., and Kenneth S. Rogoff. 2010. Growth in a Time of Debt. *American Economic Review* 100: 573–78. [CrossRef]

Reinhart, Carmen M., and Kenneth S. Rogoff. 2013. *Financial and Sovereign Debt Crises: Some Lessons Learned and Those Forgotten*. WP/13/266. Washington, DC: International Monetary Fund.

Sharaf, Mesbah, and Abdelhalem Shahen. 2023. Does external debt drive inflation in Sudan: Evidence from symmetric and asymmetric ARDL approaches. *Journal of Business and Socio-Economic Development* 3: 293–307. [CrossRef]

Sharaf, Mesbah, Abdelhalem Shahen, and Badr Binzaid. 2023. *Estimating the Causal Relationship between External Debt and Inflation in Jordan: Evidence from an ARDL and Toda-Yamamoto Approaches*. Working Paper 1641. Cairo: Economic Research Forum. Available online: https://econpapers.repec.org/paper/ergwpaper/1641.htm (accessed on 31 December 2023).

Shin, Yongcheol, Byungchul Yu, and Matthew Greenwood-Nimmo. 2014. Modelling Asymmetric Cointegration and Dynamic Multipliers in a Nonlinear ARDL Framework. In *Festschrift in Honor of Peter Schmidt: Econometric Methods and Applications*. Edited by Robin C. Sickles and William C. Horrace. Berlin: Springer, pp. 281–314. [CrossRef]

Sims, Christopher. 1994. A Simple Model for Study of the Determination of the Price Level and the Interaction of Monetary and Fiscal Policy. *Economic Theory* 4: 381–99. [CrossRef]

Taghavi, Majid. 2000. Debt, growth and inflation in large European economies: A vector auto-regression analysis. *Journal of Evolutionary Economics* 10: 159–73. [CrossRef]

Valença, Márcio Moraes. 1998. The Lost Decade and the Brazilian Government's Response in the 1990s. *The Journal of Developing Areas* 33: 1–52.

Van Bon, Nguyen. 2015. The Relationship Between Public Debt and Inflation in Developing Countries: Empirical Evidence Based on Difference Panel GMM. *Asian Journal of Empirical Research* 5: 9.

Zivot, Eric, and Donald W. K. Andrews. 2002. Further Evidence on the Great Crash, the Oil-Price Shock, and the Unit-Root Hypothesis. *Journal of Business & Economic Statistics* 20: 25–44. [CrossRef]

economies

MDPI

Article

Digital Progression and Economic Growth: Analyzing the Impact of ICT Advancements on the GDP of European Union Countries

Anastasios I. Magoutas [1,2], Maria Chaideftou [1], Dimitra Skandali [2] and Panos T. Chountalas [1,3,*]

1 School of Social Sciences, Hellenic Open University, 26335 Patras, Greece; amagoutas@ba.uoa.gr (A.I.M.); maria.chaideftou@gmail.com (M.C.)
2 Department of Business Administration, National and Kapodistrian University of Athens, 10559 Athens, Greece; dskandali@ba.uoa.gr
3 Department of Business Administration, University of Piraeus, 18534 Piraeus, Greece
* Correspondence: pchountalas@unipi.gr

Abstract: This research thoroughly examines the dynamic relationship between the European Union's economic growth and rapid advancements in Information and Communication Technology (ICT). Specifically, it assesses how certain ICT indicators are associated with significant economic growth. Utilizing an extensive dataset from the Digital Economy and Society Index 2022 (DESI), the Statistical Office of the European Union (EUROSTAT), and the Organisation for Economic Co-operation and Development (OECD), this study encompasses data from all 27 European Union member states. Employing structural equation modelling, our analysis illustrates the positive correlation between ICT development and the Gross Domestic Product (GDP) index. Our findings highlight the critical role of swiftly evolving technological landscapes, emphasizing the growing influence of new Artificial Intelligence (AI) technologies in business sectors. Furthermore, this study showcases the need to enhance human capital and expedite the growth of e-government technologies. These advancements are pivotal in strengthening the infrastructure supporting citizens and public enterprises across European countries, thereby contributing to their economic vitality.

Keywords: economic growth; gross domestic product; information and communication technology; digital technology integration; artificial intelligence; e-government technologies; European Union

1. Introduction

Over the past two decades, Information and Communication Technology (ICT) has experienced remarkable growth (Lucky 2004; Cave et al. 2006). Its expansion has significantly transformed Europe's digital infrastructure and has shaped the economic landscape through advancements such as enhanced mobile broadband coverage and the accelerated spread of high-speed internet. The pervasive impact of digitalization has revolutionized numerous facets of daily life, including government services, education, online commerce, and diverse business transactions (Kiss and Páger 2023). These changes are evident in the evolving modalities of business operations, workplace dynamics, educational methods, social interactions, and the exchanges between citizens, businesses, and governmental entities (de Clercq et al. 2023).

The consistent and rapid growth of the ICT sector justifies a thorough examination of its impact on the economic growth of European Union countries. This area has attracted considerable attention from researchers who have explored the influence of ICT expansion on economic development at a national level. Notably, Rai et al. (2019) and Makridakis (2017) have delved into the effects of ICT technologies on economic growth. Kumar et al. (2016) offered a detailed analysis of how ICT investment enhances overall productivity in macroeconomic variables. They employed an extended Solow (1956) model, the Autoregressive Distributed Lag (ARDL) bounds testing approach to cointegration, and Granger causality tests to confirm their findings. Understanding the relationship between

ICT growth and economic development within the European Union becomes increasingly important because new virtual environments, such as the metaverse, are currently in their infancy, according to Dwivedi et al. (2022). Therefore, identifying the necessary conditions for technology to exert a positive influence on economic dynamics is imperative. This will not only clarify the role of ICT in shaping economic trajectories but also inform strategic investments and policy decisions in the digital sector.

This study's innovative contribution lies in its integration of three distinct global databases: the Digital Economy and Society Index (DESI), the Statistical Office of the European Union (EUROSTAT), and the Organisation for Economic Co-operation and Development (OECD). Using Structural Equation Modelling (SEM) analysis, the research explores the potential links between ICT development and economic growth within the EU member states. Panel data serve as the foundation of analysis, and it enables a thorough examination of how various ICT dimensions affect important economic indicators at different levels. More specifically, this study examines the impact of ICT on the Gross Domestic Product (GDP) per capita (GDPM_CUER), in terms of millions of euros, and the GDP per capita (GDPM_CUSD), in millions of US dollars, compared against employment rates. This research also employs the Partial Least Squares (PLS) technique to synthesize data from multiple sources. This approach allows for a more comprehensive understanding of the relationship between ICT growth indicators and economic metrics, marking a significant contribution in the field of economic and technological research.

This study is structured as follows. It begins with an introduction, setting the stage for the subsequent in-depth review of relevant literature. The presentation of the conceptual model and a thorough analysis of the hypotheses follow. The research methodology is described in detail, followed by the empirical analysis of the available data. This study concludes with a presentation and discussion of the results, leading to the final section where conclusions are drawn.

2. Literature Review

The relationship between ICT and economic growth has been extensively explored through a multitude of economic theories and research studies (Vu 2011; Mattalia 2013; Kumar et al. 2023; Albiman and Sulong 2017). Tracing the evolution of this discourse, the Solow (1956) and Swan (1956) model, first suggests that ICT growth is a significant contributor to GDP growth through its contribution to increased productivity. Central to the Solow–Swan model is the assumption that consistent capital and labor units are employed within the economic framework, implying that identical capital and labor inputs should yield consistent outcomes over time. Consequently, any observed increases in productivity not justified by increases in capital and labor are attributed to the exogenous influence of ICT development and investment. The model highlights the transformative role of ICT in driving economic efficiency and growth and provides a robust and fundamental theoretical framework to help in the understanding of the intersection of technology and economics.

Vu (2011) presents a compelling theoretical and empirical analysis of the correlation between ICT growth and economic growth. He suggests that ICT penetration boosts economic growth by fostering knowledge exchange and innovation, enhancing resource efficiency for households and enterprises, reducing production costs, spurring demand, and stimulating investment. Particular emphasis is placed on internet penetration as a key driver of economic expansion. Vu suggests that prioritizing investments in infrastructure, as well as interventions in advancing education and training, which prepare individuals for the digital era and promote internet use in business and government sectors, will help countries realize economic growth benefits. Expanding on this perspective, Mattalia (2013) provides an in-depth examination of the role of technological change and revolution in economic growth. He introduces a model that segments the economy into four distinct sectors: final goods, equipment, intermediate goods, and research and development (R&D). Through this framework, Mattalia analyzes the impact and spillover effects of what he terms "ICT-driven growth episodes". His findings reveal that increased productivity across these sectors not only propels ICT growth but also leaves a lasting, long-term impact on the economy. This study underlines the profound influence of ICT growth on sectoral productivity and its cascading effect on overall economic development.

Albiman and Sulong (2017) provide an insightful analysis of the impact of ICT penetration on Sub-Saharan African (SSA) economies, concluding that middle-income countries experience a more pronounced effect compared to low- or high-income counterparts. Their model clearly demonstrates the positive and linear influence of internet penetration on the economic growth of lower-middle-income countries, underlining the importance of fixed telephone line infrastructure. Building on this, Njoh (2018) employs a Solow–Swan-based theoretical framework to investigate the relationship between ICT and economic development in Africa. His findings highlight a positive correlation between these variables, reinforcing the notion that ICT is a driver of economic progress in the region. Bahrini and Qaffas (2019) extend the analysis to the Middle East, North Africa (MENA), and SSA regions, using a panel Generalized Method of Moments (GMM) growth model. Their study confirms the superior performance of MENA countries in terms of internet usage and broadband adoption compared to SSA countries, illustrating the varying levels of ICT impact across different regions. Kurniawati (2022) delves into the relationship between ICT and economic growth in high- and middle-income Asian nations. Employing panel cointegration and estimation methodologies, she addresses concerns of endogeneity and cross-sectional dependence. Her findings indicate that high internet penetration significantly fosters economic development in high-income Asian countries.

Recent studies have made significant strides in unpacking the complexities of the modern Solow paradox. Capello et al. (2022) provide a methodical and empirical analysis of the seemingly incongruous relationship between the widespread adoption of ICT and labor productivity growth in various regions. Their research demonstrates that the adoption of new technologies generally enhances productivity in the industries where they are integrated. Complementing this, Kaygisiz (2022) adopts the input-oriented Charnes Cooper and Rhodes (CCR-O) Model to ascertain digital intensity levels. This approach enables the evaluation of countries' digital transformation performance, offering a comprehensive indicator of their progress in the digital domain. Further contributing to this field, Cornet et al. (2023) explore the interplay between the Digital Entrepreneurship Indicator (DEI) and the location quotient of small ICT firms. Employing geographically weighted regression, their study highlights a positive correlation between these factors.

Jemala (2022) supports the idea that there is a significant shift in Asian countries' focus towards technological innovation, moving away from traditional reliance on Europe and North America. His hypothesis is centered around the increased attention to three non-patent forms of technology protection: industrial designs, trademarks, and utility models. This suggests a strategic redirection in the protection and commercialization of technological innovations in Asia. Conversely, Ibrahimi and Fetai (2022) conduct a detailed investigation into the impact of ICT on GDP growth in Western Balkan countries over the period 2000–2019. Their methodology encompasses a variety of econometric techniques, including pooled Ordinary Least Squares (OLS), fixed effects, random effects, and the Hausman Taylor model augmented with instrumental variables. This comprehensive approach provides a robust analysis of the economic implications of ICT in this region. Meanwhile, Pan et al. (2022) employ the Competitive Advantage Theory to examine the effects of internet convergence on the competitive advantage of manufacturing businesses at different stages. Using a unique dataset of hand-collected patent data from Chinese manufacturing firms listed between 2005 and 2018, Pan, Bai, and Ren's findings reveal a nuanced impact: while technology and market convergence enhance the competitive edge of manufacturing enterprises, business convergence appears to have a diminishing effect. This study contributes valuable insights into the strategic importance of convergence in technology and markets for manufacturing competitiveness in the evolving digital landscape.

3. Conceptual Model and Hypothesis Analysis

This research builds upon prior studies to identify the key ICT factors influencing economic growth (EG), as measured by the GDPM_CUER and GDPM_CUSD. Consequently, our central hypothesis suggests a direct and positive correlation between the evolution of ICT and EG in EU member states. Thus, we state that: H1. ICT has a positive and significant impact on GDP.

According to Eurostat (2022), the Digital Economy and Society Index (DESI) has extensively documented the growth of ICT in EU member states. Eurostat's methodology encompasses a comprehensive array of indicators, systematically tracking the progress of the ICT sector across four primary dimensions: Connectivity, Integration of Digital Technology, Human Capital, and e-government. The detailed methodological approach DESI follows, including the full list of indicators and their definition and measurement, is included in the link provided in Appendix A. In this section, we present these subcategories of ICT development and some key findings about each, as detailed in Table 1. This approach ensures a thorough understanding of the various facets of ICT growth and their potential impact on the economic landscape of the European Union.

Table 1. ICT subcategories and indicators from DESI being examined: initial model *.

Construct	Subcategory I	Subcategory II	Indicators	Abbreviations
ICT	Connectivity	Broadband price	Broadband price index	BPI
		Fixed broadband coverage	Fixed very high capacity network coverage	VHCN
		Fixed broadband set up	At least 100 Mbps fixed BB take-up	AL
	Integration of Digital Technology	Digital technologies for business	Electronic information sharing	EIS
			Cloud	CL
			Artificial intelligence	AI
			e-invoices	EINV
		e-commerce	SMEs selling online	SMO
			e-commerce turnover	EC
			Selling online cross-border	SOC
	Human Capital	Internet user skills	At least basic digital content creation skills	DCS
		Advanced skills	Female ICT specialists	FS
			Enterprises providing ICT training	EPT
			ICT graduates	GR
	e-government	-	e-government users	EGU
		-	Digital public services for citizens	DP

* Note: The underlined variables were used at the subsequent stage. Source: Authors' edit using DESI's categories.

3.1. Connectivity

The connectivity dimension primarily assesses the availability of infrastructure, measuring both mobile and landline coverage and uptake. The EU-27 region is generally regarded as a mature market in terms of connectivity. However, disparities persist, particularly in coverage between urban and rural areas. In evaluating connectivity across nations, Denmark emerges as the top performer, closely followed by the Netherlands, Spain, Germany, France, and Ireland. On the other end of the spectrum, Belgium and Estonia occupy the lower ranks, with Poland and Croatia not far behind. This study focuses on three key indicators to measure connectivity: the Broadband Price Index (BPI), Fixed Very High Capacity Network (VHCN) coverage, and the uptake of fixed broadband services with speeds of at least 100 Mbps (AL). These metrics provide a comprehensive view of the connectivity of the EU-27 region and enable an in-depth analysis of the capabilities of its infrastructure and its digital readiness.

3.2. Integration of Digital Technology

The integration of digital technology is a crucial measure used to assess the performance of businesses, regardless of size. The adoption of digital technologies enhances business efficiency and productivity, improves services and products, and expands market reach. The European Union has set ambitious goals, aiming for 90% of small and medium enterprises (SMEs) to have achieved basic digital integration by 2030, reflecting the critical importance of digital technology in contemporary business practices. To thoroughly analyze this subcategory of ICT integration, our study uses seven distinct indicators. These include Electronic Information Sharing (EIS), Cloud Computing (CL), the application of Artificial Intelligence (AI) in business, the use of Electronic Invoices (EINV), the proportion of SMEs engaging in online sales (SMO), e-commerce turnover (EC), and cross-border online sales (SOC). Each of these indicators offers a unique perspective on the extent to which digital technologies are being incorporated into business operations and provides a multifaceted view of digital integration in the EU's business sector. This comprehensive approach allows for a detailed understanding of how digital technology integration is shaping the business landscape in the European Union.

3.3. Human Capital

The Human Capital dimension measures the existence and level (basic or advanced) of digital skills EU member states. Despite widespread internet access, with at least 85% of households connected and 87% of Europeans engaging with the internet regularly (ranging from weekly to daily usage), only 54% of the population possesses at least basic digital skills, as reported by Eurostat (2021). This disparity highlights the significance of not only ensuring access to the internet, but also equipping individuals with the necessary skills to effectively use digital technologies. This is a critical factor in monitoring and fostering the growth of the ICT sector. In assessing Human Capital, our study incorporates four specific indicators: the proportion of individuals with at least basic digital skills in internet usage (DCS), the percentage of female ICT specialists (FS), the prevalence of advanced skills in enterprises providing ICT training (EPT), and the number of ICT graduates (GR). These indicators collectively provide a comprehensive picture of the digital competencies within the EU, highlighting areas of strength and opportunities for improvement in digital literacy and specialization. This holistic approach is essential for understanding the role of human capital in the development of the ICT sector in the European Union.

3.4. e-Government

The provision and accessibility of e-government services have experienced a significant increase, a trend further accelerated by the COVID-19 pandemic. During this period, digital interactions became not only the norm but often the sole means of executing certain tasks, as outlined by Rodríguez-Núñez et al. (2023). The European Union has set an ambitious goal: ensuring that 100% of key public services for businesses and citizens are available online by 2030. According to Eurostat (2021), the current average for online public services availability in the EU stands at 67.3%. However, there are vast differences in the rate of availability of e-government services between member states. Estonia and Finland are at the forefront, very close to the 100% mark. On the other hand, Greece and Romania face substantial challenges, with only about 40% of their services currently available online. In assessing the impact of e-government, our study focuses on two key indicators: the use of e-government services (EGU) and the availability of Digital Public Services (DP). These indicators allow us to evaluate the effectiveness and reach of e-government initiatives across the EU and offer insights into the current state of digital governance and its effect on the public and private sectors within the European Union.

Having identified the indicators that represent ICT growth in EU member states, we proceed with selecting the most suitable measure to represent economic growth as compared against employment rates. In our model, we have used Gross Domestic Product GDP as a proxy for economic growth, and, more specifically, we use three sets of variables: Gross Domestic Product, GDP current per head vs. Employment in Millions of Euros, GDP current per head vs. Employment in Millions of US Dollars, and GDP constant per head vs. Employment in Millions of US Dollars.

Table 2 presents the list of indicators used to measure the impact of ICT on the economic growth of the 27 EU member states.

Table 2. Variables measuring EG: initial model *.

Construct	Subcategory I	Indicators	Abbreviations
Economic Growth (EG)	Gross Domestic Product	GDP current per head vs. Employment in Millions of Euros	GDPM_CUER
		GDP current per head vs. Employment in Millions of US Dollars	GDPM_CUSD
		GDP constant per head vs. Employment in Millions of US Dollars	GDPM_COUSD

* Note: The underlined variables were used at the subsequent stage. Source: Authors' edit using EUROSTAT's and OECD'S databases.

4. Methodology

This study aims to demonstrate the relationship between ICT and economic growth within the context of the European Union. Recognizing the pivotal role a country's economic level plays in this relationship, as per the research performed by Mayer et al. (2020), our research focuses on 16 distinct metrics across the EU's 27 member states, spanning from 2017 to 2022. These metrics are selected to reflect key areas of ICT development and their subsequent impact on GDP growth.

The Structural Equation Modelling (SEM) method, which is supported by Fernández-Portillo et al. (2020), is used to test our main hypothesis, which is that ICT has a positive and enhancing effect on economic progress. This approach facilitates a detailed analysis of the causal links between ICT and economic growth (Chin 1998).

Data for this analysis were sourced from official, licensed databases of the Digital Economy and Society Index (DESI), the Statistical Office of the European Union (EUROSTAT), and the Organisation for Economic Co-operation and Development (OECD). These sources provide robust data to assess the relationship between various ICT indicators and GDP metrics, specifically: GDP per capita versus employment in millions of euros (GDPM_CUER), GDP per capita versus employment in millions of US dollars (GDPM_CUSD), and GDP per capita at constant prices versus employment in millions of US dollars (GDPM_COUSD), for the period 2017–2022. The datasets used are available via the links provided in Appendix A.

To predict latent variables, the analysis was executed using SmartPLS software version 4.0.9.2, leveraging the estimation capabilities of the ordinary least squares method as per Henseler et al. (2015). This advanced statistical tool enables a precise and reliable examination of the interdependencies and influences within our dataset, ensuring the integrity and accuracy of our findings.

5. Results

5.1. Assessment of the Measurement Model

The initial step in our analysis involves a comprehensive evaluation of the measurement model, focusing on assessing its reliability and validity. Figure 1 illustrates the conceptual map of the model.

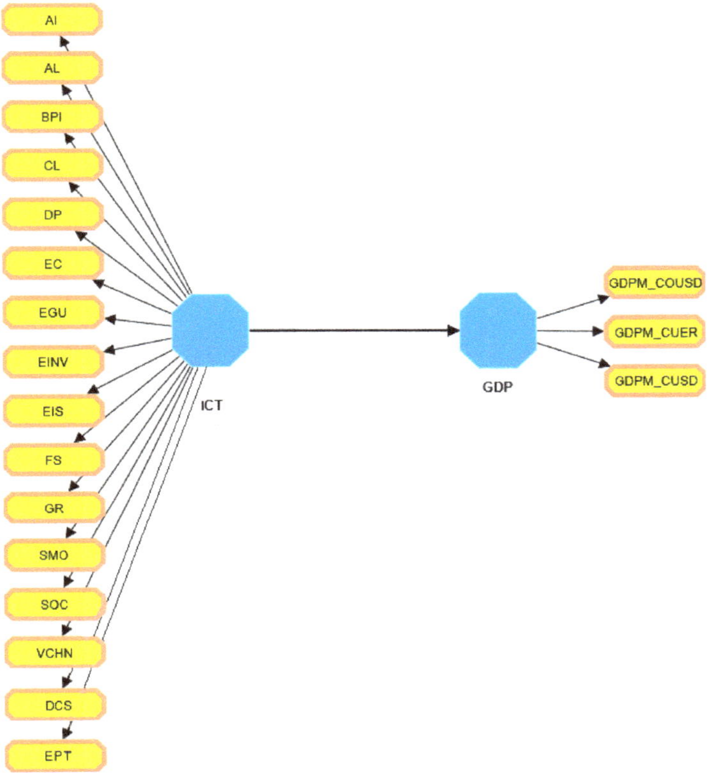

Figure 1. Initial model in the first stage. Source: Authors' edit.

For the reliability analysis, we examined both composite reliability and Cronbach's alpha values, as the data set includes results from surveys conducted by Eurostat. Please refer to Appendix A for a link to DESI's methodological note for more information. In our study, these values stand at 0.91 and 0.876, respectively, thereby satisfying the established theoretical criteria set by Gefen et al. (2000). This indicates a high level of internal consistency within our constructs, ensuring the reliability of our measurement model. Additionally, to establish convergent validity, we analyzed the outer loadings of each construct. The values obtained were as follows: AI = 0.758, DCS = 0.891, DP = 0.760, EGU = 0.844, and EPT = 0.834. These figures meet the standards for convergent validity as outlined by Bagozzi and Yi (1988), confirming that our model's constructs are adequately measured by their respective indicators. In the final part of this analysis, we addressed the Average Variance Extracted (AVE). Our calculation yielded an AVE of 0.671, which surpasses the threshold of 0.5. This result signifies that there are no issues related to convergent validity in our study, as detailed in Table 3. This comprehensive assessment of the measurement model ensures its robustness and appropriateness for further analysis.

Table 3. Reliability and validity analysis.

Construct	Items	Loading >0.704	Alpha >0.7	CR >0.7	AVE >0.5
ICT	AI	0.758	0.876	0.91	0.671
	DCS	0.891			
	DP	0.760			
	EGU	0.844			
	EPT	0.834			
GDP	GDPM_CUER	0.996	0.992	0.996	0.992
	GDPM_CUSD	0.996			

Note: The deleted items from the model due to low factor loadings are BPI, VCHN, AL, EIS, CL, EINV, SMO, EC, SOC, FS, GR, and GDPM_COUSD. Source: Authors' edit.

In our study, we also assessed the discriminant validity as per Fornell and Larcker's (1981) criteria. This involved confirming that the square root of the Average Variance Extracted (AVE) for each construct—GDP at 0.996 and ICT at 0.819—exceeds all corresponding inter-construct correlations. The details of this analysis are presented in Table 4.

Table 4. Discriminant validity analysis.

Constructs	1	2
1. Gross Domestic Product	**0.996**	
2. Information and Communication Technology	0.361	**0.819**

Note: Values on the diagonal (bold) represent the square root of the average variance extracted, while the off diagonals are correlations. Source: Authors' edit.

Following this validity assessment, we refined our measurement model by removing any indicators that did not adhere to the established quality standards outlined by Hair et al. (2021). This process of selection and elimination ensured that our measurement model only included indicators that met the highest criteria of analytical vigor. The revised measurement model presented in Figure 2, reflects these adjustments and the resulting streamlined structure. This step is critical in enhancing the model's precision and reliability, ensuring that the subsequent analysis is based on the most robust and valid constructs.

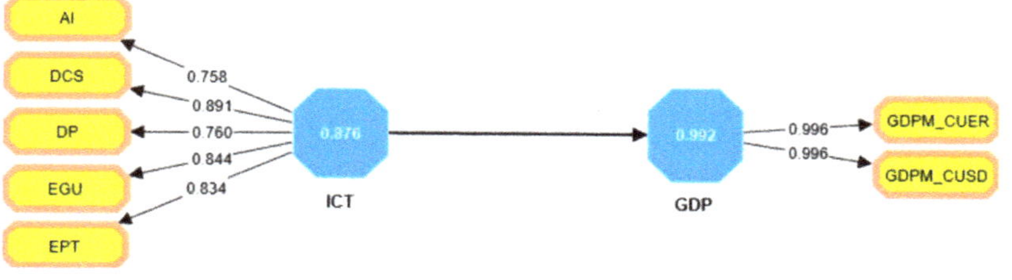

Figure 2. Graphical representation of assessment of measurement model. Source: Authors' edit.

In summary, we have taken all the necessary steps to ensure our measurement model is robust. We have eliminated indicators with low factor loadings ensuring we include the indicators that are present closest to the dataset's mean, therefore the most relevant. We have also ensured each construct is unrelated to the others, therefore reaffirming the model's validity. We present the result of these actions in Tables 3 and 4 and a graphical representation of our final model is in Figure 2 above.

5.2. Structural Model

5.2.1. Hypothesis Testing

For the hypothesis testing phase of our structural model, we employed the bootstrapping method, utilizing a sample size of 5000 as recommended by Ringle et al. (2015) to ensure robust hypothesis results. This approach provides a more accurate estimation of the standard errors and strengthens the reliability of our findings. Table 5 presents the detailed results concerning the direct effect of ICT on GDP and, hence, on EG. This table outlines the crucial importance of ICT's impact on the economy.

Table 5. Hypothesis testing direct effect.

Hypothesis	Direct Relationships	Std. Beta	Std. Error	T Values	P Values
H1	ICT → GDP	0.361	0.183	1.977	*

Note: Indicates significant paths: * $p < 0.05$, ** $p < 0.01$, *** $p < 0.001$, NS = not significant. Source: Authors' edit.

According to Hypothesis 1, a positive direct effect between ICT growth and GDP exists. The analysis revealed a path coefficient (β) of 0.361 and t-statistics of 1.977, indicating a statistically significant positive relationship between ICT growth and GDP growth. Therefore, based on this evidence, Hypothesis 1 is accepted, as illustrated in Figure 3. This acceptance highlights the crucial role of ICT in fostering economic growth, as reflected in GDP increases. Evidently, the large sample size, the strict bootstrapping method, and the clear presentation of the results presented in Table 5 and Figure 3 all support the validity and strength of our findings in relation to the proposed hypothesis.

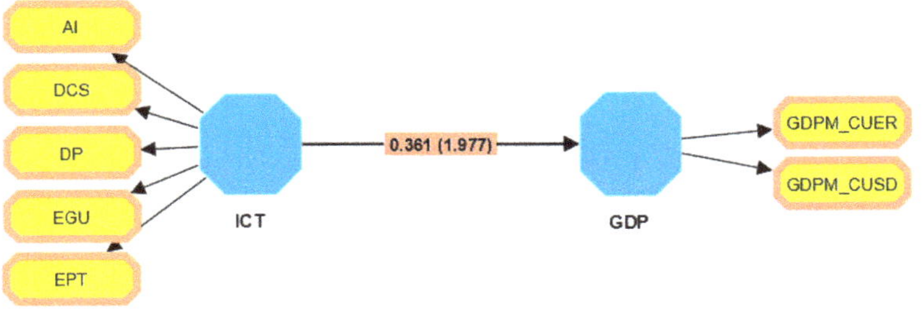

Figure 3. Graphical representation of the structural model. Source: Authors' edit.

We proceeded with hypothesis testing and have clearly demonstrated a direct positive effect between ICT and GDP growth, as confirmed by beta values and t statistics, therefore confirming our hypothesis. A graphical representation of our findings is presented in Figure 3, above.

5.2.2. Quality Criteria

We also used quality criteria to verify the suitability of our model and the validity of the results as presented above.

R-square, F-square, and Q-square values are shown in Table 6.

Table 6. R^2, F^2 and Q^2.

Latent Variables	R^2	R^{2Adj}	Q^2	F^2
GDP	0.131	0.096	0.078	
ICT → GDP				0.150

Source: Authors' edit.

Figure 4 provides a visual depiction of both R-square (R^2) and effect size (F^2) values, which are key metrics in evaluating the explanatory power and impact of our model. The R-square value of 0.131, while representing a small effect, is significant in the context of our study. It indicates the proportion of variance in an endogenous construct that is explained by its predictor constructs, as outlined by Hair et al. (2021). This value is crucial in assessing the strength and relevance of the model in explaining the relationship between the constructs. Furthermore, the effect size (F^2) in this study is calculated at 0.150, which, according to Cohen (2013), signifies medium effects exerted by the exogenous latent variable on the endogenous construct. This measure is instrumental in understanding the practical significance of the exogenous variables within our model.

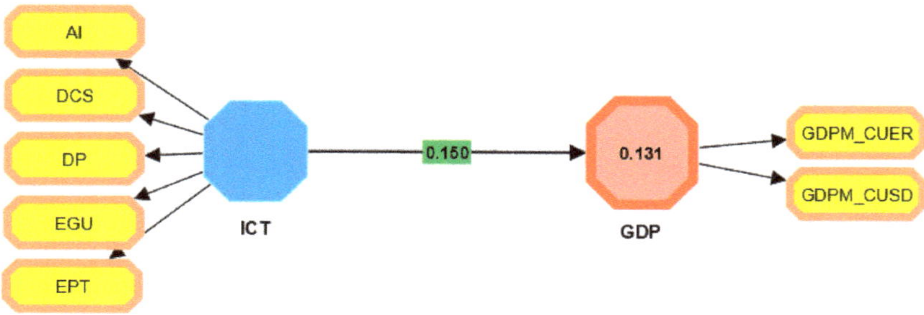

Figure 4. Graphical representation of R^2 and F^2. Source: Authors' edit.

Additionally, the Q-square (Q^2) value at 0.078, indicates a small but meaningful effect for the latent constructs within our model. This value also confirms the model's predictive relevance, as suggested by Chin (1998), given that Q^2 is above zero. The positive value of Q^2 underlines the model's ability to predict endogenous constructs with a degree of accuracy. The graphical illustration of the Q^2 values in Figure 5 provides a clear visual representation of the model's predictive power. This visualization aids in the interpretation and understanding of the model's predictive relevance, enhancing the overall understanding of this study's findings.

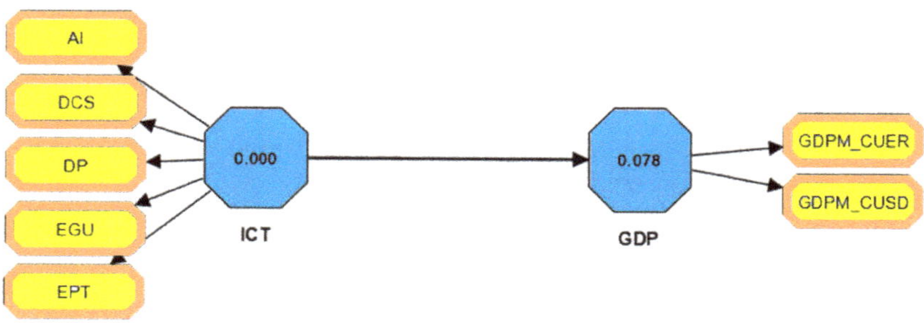

Figure 5. Graphical representation of Q^2. Source: Authors' edit.

The results of our analysis confirm Hypothesis 1 (H1) and demonstrate that ICT growth has a direct and positive influence on GDP growth. This hypothesis has been validated with a statistical significance exceeding the 95% confidence level, and it is further reinforced by the confidence interval test and the path coefficient analysis. Five of the ICT indicators we have examined in our model emerge as critical factors that GDP growth, and therefore economic development, in the 27 EU member states. Human Capital emerges as the most influential indicator in the model and, in particular, the indicator measuring at least basic Internet User Skills (DCS = 0.891) has the highest score. This is followed in second place by e-government usage, as measured by E-Government Users (EGU =

0.844). These indicators are followed by another Human Capital indicator in Advanced Skills of Enterprises in providing ICT training (EPT = 0.834), and the critical contribution of e-government in offering Digital Public Services (DP = 0.760). The fifth significant indicator which measures the Integration of Digital Technology, for the first time, highlights the role the adoption Artificial Intelligence (AI = 0.758) plays in enhancing the GDP index. These insights collectively confirm the multidimensional impact of ICT, and, in particular, Human Capital and e-government services, in fostering economic growth within the European Union, and they highlight the strategic importance of these factors in the region's economic development.

6. Discussion

The analysis of this study prominently positions the Human Capital factor as a key driver of ICT growth. This is echoed in the works of Pradhan et al. (2018), as well as Bahrini and Qaffas (2019), who emphasize the critical importance of ensuring that internet users possess at least basic Internet User Skills. This finding also reveals a broader implication: the indispensable role of education in fostering these necessary digital competencies. To effectively equip individuals with fundamental internet skills, there is an urgent need to develop a comprehensive educational framework. Such a framework should not only aim to promote digital literacy but also provide essential knowledge and skills for the use of technological tools and media. This will ensure that individuals can effectively navigate and benefit from the digital landscape. In the realm of advanced research, Herrera et al. (2023) employ machine learning algorithms to obtain insights into the intersection of ICT, education, and income distribution in Brazil. Their findings highlight the transformative potential of education in the digital era. Furthermore, Billon et al. (2009) observe that, in countries with high ICT adoption levels, education is a key factor shaping digitalization patterns, influencing GDP, and forging a multidirectional relationship between these variables. As we progress into an increasingly digitalized world, the importance of education and training becomes ever more paramount. Both education and training are not only beneficial but essential to the continued growth and integration of ICT in various sectors. The need for strategic focus on educational initiatives that can keep pace with and enhance the ongoing evolution of ICT emerges as more important than ever.

This study's findings also bring to the forefront the role of advanced skills in enterprises providing ICT training, significantly contributing to the European Union's economic prosperity. This observation extends the earlier findings about the crucial role of the Human Capital and the importance of at least basic internet user skills. Such skills are crucial for consumers, and, in certain contexts, notably in Sub-Saharan African (SSA) countries, the presence of basic ICT skills, including internet user skills, has been identified as a mitigating factor against poverty's severity and intensity, particularly when combined with targeted financial development actions (Ofori et al. 2021). In contrast, countries with mature ICT infrastructures, such as the top-performing OECD nations included in our study—Denmark, Iceland, and South Korea—have implemented strategies to promote and facilitate the use of ICT, which have resulted in increased levels of economic growth (Ali et al. 2020). This contrast highlights a divergence in ICT skill requirements based on the country's stage of ICT development.

In the European business context, however, basic ICT skills or internet user skills are not sufficient to foster economic growth. In the contrary, more advanced skills are needed. Ala-Mutka (2011) suggests that there is a need to obtain more sophisticated abilities and expertise, particularly in areas such as interaction and cooperation, information management, problem-solving, learning, and meaningful engagement. This advanced skill set is crucial in leveraging ICT for economic growth and innovation and underlines the need to invest in the continual evolution of skills along with the advancing technological landscape.

Inextricably linked to the preceding indicators, e-government users and digital public services for citizens are fundamentally intertwined with economic growth. These elements are mutually dependent, and the availability of digital services does not guarantee their effective use. Essential to the use of e-government services is the population's proficiency in basic internet skills. Van Deursen and van Dijk (2009) conducted a comprehensive analysis of digital skills among Dutch internet and e-government service users. Their findings reveal that the population's digital skill level significantly influences not only the usage of these services but also the accessibility, comprehension, and utilization of information available on the internet. They advocate for the implementation of policies aimed at enhancing government websites and digital services, as well as the digital competencies of e-government service users. Hyytinen et al. (2022) note an increase in e-government users, attributing this trend to the strategic involvement of policymakers and the application of what they term 'informational and social impact nudges'. This observation suggests that targeted governmental policies play a significant role in the increase ion e-government users and their impact on economic growth. Furthermore, Panagiotopoulos et al. (2023) emphasize the need for coordinated efforts to improve the provision of e-government services. They argue that enhancing these services' effectiveness and efficiency requires a transformation in their strategic management and operational models, which, in turn, would contribute to a better understanding of their positive impact on economies. Zoroja (2015) argues that governments that create an inclusive and transparent environment, particularly by offering e-government services, are likely to stimulate economic growth. This aligns with multiple studies that have explored the correlation between digitalization and the economic growth of businesses.

Artificial Intelligence (AI) has been, for the first time, identified in this study as a significant driver of economic growth in the 27 EU member states, particularly in the context of the Integration of Digital Technology in Business. Makridakis (2017) already predicted a substantial expansion of AI, along with its anticipated impacts on various industries and sectors. Brodny and Tutak (2022) highlight the varied levels of AI adoption across different EU-27 enterprises, correlating them with each country's position in the Digital Economy and Society Index's digitalization rankings. In their research, Pallathadka et al. (2023) explore the applications of AI in enhancing business performance and customer interactions, particularly in e-commerce, business management, and the finance sectors. Their findings suggest that AI contributes to sales growth, profit maximization, and sales forecasting, thereby influencing the economic performance of enterprises and, by extension, the GDP. Rai et al. (2019) explore the integration of AI with business operations, including hybrid models that combine AI and human intervention. Similarly, sector-specific research by Petrescu et al. (2022) investigates AI's role in Business to Business (B2B) marketing, incorporating perspectives from both academia and industry practitioners. Kulkov (2021) further examines AI's transformative impact in the pharmaceutical industry, noting that its application varies based on company size and specific needs. He observes that smaller firms benefit from AI in research and development, while larger entities leverage AI to enhance sales, marketing, and manufacturing processes, directly contributing to profit generation and operational efficiency. The use of AI also raises ethical considerations across various fields, including healthcare (Kumar et al. 2023), education (Chiu et al. 2023), and business education and skills development (Sollosy and McInerney 2022). These ethical dimensions highlight the need for further research to trace and assess the impact of AI adoption in business practices, its effectiveness, and its indirect influence on economic growth more accurately. Such comprehensive research will aid the understanding of and allow us to maximize AI's potential benefits while addressing its challenges and ethical implications.

This study's findings also yield an unexpected observation: the impact of connectivity, particularly the role of broadband, which is extensively explored and recognized in the works of Pradhan et al. (2018) for the Group of 20 (G20) countries, as well as by Bahrini and Qaffas (2019) for the MENA and SSA regions, is absent in our refined measurement model. This discrepancy can be attributed to the varying influences of mobile band and mobile network integration in different economic contexts. Research, including Kumar et al. (2016), indicates that these factors have a more pronounced impact on GDP in emerging and low-income countries. Conversely, as Edquist et al. (2018) suggest, their effect is more muted in developed economies. The absence of connectivity indicators in our model suggests that EU countries, generally, have already achieved a high degree of ICT infrastructure integration, despite some differences between rural and urban areas, as de Clercq et al. (2023) observed. Such a scenario indicates a more advanced stage of digital development in the EU, where the incremental impact of further connectivity improvements on GDP might be less pronounced compared to less-developed regions.

The outcomes of this research demonstrate a clear connection between the development of ICT and GDP growth, corroborating findings from prior studies, notably those conducted by Ishnazarov et al. (2021) and Chen et al. (2023). Ishnazarov et al. (2021) provide an in-depth analysis of the interplay between ICT and economic growth within the digital economy, highlighting innovation as a key driver of growth across diverse nations and regions. Their comprehensive study, which examined data spanning over 170 countries from 1990 to 2019, concluded that the ICT index has a considerable impact on GDP growth. This finding reinforces the transformative role of ICT in shaping economic trajectories on a global scale. Chen et al. (2023) delves into the concept of Digital Financial Inclusion (DFI-ICT), highlighting how ICT strategies can be leveraged to promote sustainable long-term growth and economic stability. This approach emphasizes the strategic use of digital technologies to enhance financial inclusion, thereby facilitating broader economic development.

7. Conclusions

This study explores the ICT sector's development and its relation to economic growth. This study follows a unique approach, as it integrates three comprehensive global datasets (DESI, EUROSTAT, and OECD) in its analytical model. This study uses Structural Equation Modelling analysis from year 2017 to year 2022, aiming to demonstrate the positive correlation between ICT and economic growth in 27 EU member states.

The ICT sector's growth has undeniably influenced key sectors in European economies, such as research, education, and business, fundamentally transforming social interactions and the dynamics between enterprises, governments, and the broader market for products and services. Our findings reveal that the primary factors connecting ICT development to GDP growth are Human Capital, e-government, and the Integration of Digital Technology.

These findings are in line with studies such as García-Muñiz et al. (2022), who demonstrate that the critical factors that influence economic growth include individuals with basic internet skills, users of e-government services, and professionals with advanced skills acquired through firm-sponsored training. The crucial role of education in acquiring digital skills emerges as a result. Furthermore, enhancing basic digital literacy, by integrating training initiatives to maximize the use of digital tools and media, should be the foundation of public policies that aim to stimulate economies. Indeed, advanced skills are needed and used by enterprises, and this is another deciding factor affecting economic development.

It is also not unexpected that, in regions where the corporate adoption of the internet and e-commerce is widespread and well-established, these factors also serve as key drivers of economic growth (Tsachtsiris et al. 2022). The business environment and the underlying framework in which companies operate have a considerable influence on economic growth, as demonstrated by a shift in online and remote services due to the COVID-19 pandemic and recorded in Eurostat's DESI year-on-year results. These services have become instrumental in the business sector's adaptation and evolution in the current digitally driven era. Moreover, the significant impact of e-government users on national economic trajectories suggests that policymakers and political leaders should prioritize and amplify investments in ICT and education.

Last, but not least, this study highlights the increasingly important role that AI technologies play in their application to business practices therefore indirectly driving economic growth. AI's rapid expansion fundamentally alters corporate dynamics and places the human–robot interaction at the forefront of current and future considerations (Savarese et al. 2016). Going forward, it is critical that we increase our understanding of the evolving relationship between humans and AI, both in current business contexts and in anticipation of future developments, as well as across sectors such as service provision and education.

This study therefore builds on the work of Fernández-Portillo et al. (2020) and brings to the surface ICT indicators which have been considered previously and continue to be very important (i.e., basic internet skills), along with others which are gaining prominence (i.e., advanced skills), while previously instrumental indicators, such as broadband connectivity and the use of the internet, are no longer detected as statistically important. It also highlights the emerging importance and role of indicators that have not been detected/or have not been measured before (i.e., AI technologies).

As demonstrated in both studies, it is evident that Human Capital is the differentiating factor when we explore the relationship between ICT and GDP growth. Basic internet skills are the pre-requisite for both consumers and employees in all areas of business as more and more aspects of the EU countries' economic lives and business transactions are digitalized.

However, we now also have clear indications that basic skills are not enough to navigate an increasingly digitalized landscape. On the supply side of services and goods, more digitalized services should be offered to citizens and businesses, while more advanced skills are also increasingly needed by employees for businesses, and therefore for European economies, to grow. On the demand side, consumers and citizens increasingly demand access to digital services due to their speed and efficiency benefits, but also face a more complex landscape that they need to be equipped and supported to navigate. The role of education and well-designed and thought-out economic policies that encourage and integrate advanced ICT skills training has become apparent, now more than ever.

In an era of rapid technological advancement, the transformative and increasingly more visible role of machine-generated outputs in aid of efficiency in the production process and in various sectors can also not be denied. More research is needed to further explore the numerous facets of ICT sector development on economic growth, particularly focusing on the complex interplay between technology, human capital, and economic outcomes. Such research is not only pertinent but necessary to fully grasp the intricate dynamics at play and to inform policy- and decision-making processes that will shape the future economic landscape of the EU and beyond.

Author Contributions: Conceptualization, A.I.M. and M.C.; methodology, A.I.M. and D.S.; software, A.I.M. and P.T.C.; validation, A.I.M., M.C. and P.T.C.; formal analysis, A.I.M. and P.T.C.; investigation, M.C. and D.S.; resources, A.I.M., M.C. and D.S.; data curation, A.I.M. and P.T.C.; writing—original draft preparation, A.I.M., M.C. and P.T.C.; writing—review and editing, M.C. and D.S.; visualization, A.I.M. and M.C.; supervision, A.I.M. and P.T.C.; project administration, A.I.M. and P.T.C. All authors have read and agreed to the published version of the manuscript.

Funding: This research received no external funding.

Informed Consent Statement: Not applicable.

Data Availability Statement: The data used for this study is publicly available. The data sets and the links to access them are provided in Appendix A.

Conflicts of Interest: The authors declare no conflict of interest.

Appendix A

Table A1. Indexes and data sources.

INDEXES	Links
DESI	
Entire dataset including all indicators for DESI 2022	https://digital-decade-desi.digital-strategy.ec.europa.eu/api/v1/chart-groups/desi-2022/facts/, accessed on 27 February 2023
List of DESI 2022 indicators	https://digital-decade-desi.digital-strategy.ec.europa.eu/datasets/desi-2022/indicators accessed on 27 February 2023
DESI 2022 Methodological note	https://ec.europa.eu/newsroom/dae/redirection/document/88557 accessed on 27 February 2023
OECD	
GDPM-COUSD	https://www.oecd-ilibrary.org/economics/data/aggregate-national-accounts/gross-domestic-product_data-00001-en accessed on 27 April 2023 Data set available on this link with results filtered based on requirements. Dataset available for download.
GDPM-CUER	https://www.oecd-ilibrary.org/economics/data/aggregate-national-accounts/gross-domestic-product_data-00001-en accessed on 27 April 2023 Data set available on this link with results filtered based on requirements. Dataset available for download.
GDPM-CUSD	https://www.oecd-ilibrary.org/economics/data/aggregate-national-accounts/gross-domestic-product_data-00001-en accessed on 27 April 2023 Data set available on this link with results filtered based on requirements. Dataset available for download.
Eurostat	
Real GDP per capita	https://ec.europa.eu/eurostat/databrowser/view/sdg_08_10/default/table?lang=en accessed on 27 April 2023
Labour Force Survey	https://ec.europa.eu/eurostat/databrowser/view/TIPSLM16/default/table Employment vs GDP accessed on 27 April 2023

References

Ala-Mutka, Kirsti. 2011. *Mapping Digital Competence: Towards a Conceptual Understanding*. Sevilla: Institute for Prospective Technological Studies, pp. 7–60.

Albiman, Masoud Mohammed, and Zunaidah Sulong. 2017. The Linear and Non-Linear Impacts of ICT on Economic Growth, of Disaggregate Income Groups within SSA Region. *Telecommunications Policy* 41: 555–72. [CrossRef]

Ali, Mohammad Afshar, Khorshed Alam, Brad Taylor, and Shuddhasattwa Rafiq. 2020. Does ICT Maturity Catalyse Economic Development? Evidence from a Panel Data Estimation Approach in OECD Countries. *Economic Analysis and Policy* 68: 163–74. [CrossRef] [PubMed]

Bagozzi, Richard P., and Youjae Yi. 1988. On the Evaluation of Structural Equation Models. *Journal of the Academy of Marketing Science* 16: 74–94. [CrossRef]

Bahrini, Raéf, and Alaa A. Qaffas. 2019. Impact of Information and Communication Technology on Economic Growth: Evidence from Developing Countries. *Economies* 7: 21. [CrossRef]

Billon, Margarita, Rocio Marco, and Fernando Lera-Lopez. 2009. Disparities in ICT Adoption: A Multidimensional Approach to Study the Cross-Country Digital Divide. *Telecommunications Policy* 33: 596–610. [CrossRef]

Brodny, Jarosław, and Magdalena Tutak. 2022. Analyzing the Level of Digitalization among the Enterprises of the European Union Member States and Their Impact on Economic Growth. *Journal of Open Innovation: Technology, Market, and Complexity* 8: 70. [CrossRef]

Capello, Roberta, Camilla Lenzi, and Giovanni Perucca. 2022. The Modern Solow Paradox. In Search for Explanations. *Structural Change and Economic Dynamics* 63: 166–80. [CrossRef]

Cave, Martin, Luigi Prosperetti, and Chris Doyle. 2006. Where Are We Going? Technologies, Markets and Long-Range Public Policy Issues in European Communications. *Information Economics and Policy* 18: 242–55. [CrossRef]

Chen, Yanyu, E. Kusuma Kumara, and V. Sivakumar. 2023. Investigation of Finance Industry on Risk Awareness Model and Digital Economic Growth. *Annals of Operations Research* 326: 15. [CrossRef]

Chin, Wynne W. 1998. The Partial Least Squares Approach to Structural Equation Modeling. *Modern Methods for Business Research* 295: 295–336.

Chiu, Thomas K.F., Qi Xia, Xinyan Zhou, Ching Sing Chai, and Miaoting Cheng. 2023. Systematic Literature Review on Opportunities, Challenges, and Future Research Recommendations of Artificial Intelligence in Education. *Computers and Education: Artificial Intelligence* 4: 100118. [CrossRef]

Cohen, Jacob. 2013. *Statistical Power Analysis for the Behavioral Sciences*. New York: Academic Press. Available online: https://books.google.com/books?hl=el&lr=&id=rEe0BQAAQBAJ&oi=fnd&pg=PP1&dq=%22Statistical+Power+Analysis+for+the+Behavioral+Sciences%22+Cohen&ots=sxTVJsMRo6&sig=f8ND8nEyvlDsjxofUhPhpVsGyyc (accessed on 5 March 2023).

Cornet, Dorine, Jean Bonnet, and Sébastien Bourdin. 2023. Digital Entrepreneurship Indicator (DEI): An Analysis of the Case of the Greater Paris Metropolitan Area. *Annals of Regional Science* 71: 697–724. [CrossRef]

de Clercq, Michaël, Marijke D'Haese, and Jeroen Buysse. 2023. Economic Growth and Broadband Access: The European Urban-Rural Digital Divide. *Telecommunications Policy* 47: 102579. [CrossRef]

Dwivedi, Yogesh K., Laurie Hughes, Abdullah M. Baabdullah, Samuel Ribeiro-Navarrete, Mihalis Giannakis, Mutaz M. Al-Debei, Denis Dennehy, Bhimaraya Metri, Dimitrios Buhalis, Christy M.K. Cheung, and et al. 2022. Metaverse beyond the Hype: Multidisciplinary Perspectives on Emerging Challenges, Opportunities, and Agenda for Research, Practice and Policy. *International Journal of Information Management* 66: 102542. [CrossRef]

Edquist, Harald, Peter Goodridge, Jonathan Haskel, Xuan Li, and Edward Lindquist. 2018. How Important Are Mobile Broadband Networks for the Global Economic Development? *Information Economics and Policy* 45: 16–29. [CrossRef]

Eurostat. 2021. *Digital Economy and Society Statistics—Households and Individuals*. Brussels: European Commission.

Eurostat. 2022. Digital Economy and Society Index (DESI) 2022. *Thematic Chapters*. Available online: https://Digital-Strategy.Ec.Europa.Eu/En/Library/Digital-Economy-and-Society-Indexdesi-2022 (accessed on 27 February 2023).

Fernández-Portillo, Antonio, Manuel Almodóvar-González, and Ricardo Hernández-Mogollón. 2020. Impact of ICT Development on Economic Growth. A Study of OECD European Union Countries. *Technology in Society* 63: 101420. [CrossRef]

Fornell, Claes, and David F. Larcker. 1981. Structural Equation Models with Unobservable Variables and Measurement Error: Algebra and Statistics. *Journal of Marketing Research* 18: 382–88. [CrossRef]

García-Muñiz, Ana Salomé, María Rosalía Vicente, and Margarita Billon. 2022. ICT Research Networks and Regional Competitiveness: An Analysis of the 7th Framework Program. *European Planning Studies* 30: 2063–83. [CrossRef]

Gefen, David, Detmar Straub, and Marie-Claude Boudreau. 2000. Structural Equation Modeling and Regression: Guidelines for Research Practice. *Communications of the Association for Information Systems* 4: 7. [CrossRef]

Hair, Joseph F., G. Tomas M. Hult, Christian M. Ringle, Marko Sarstedt, Nicholas P. Danks, and Soumya Ray. 2021. *Partial Least Squares Structural Equation Modeling (PLS-SEM) Using R: A Workbook*. Berlin: Springer Nature. Available online: https://library.oapen.org/handle/20.500.12657/51463 (accessed on 2 December 2022).

Henseler, Jörg, Christian M. Ringle, and Marko Sarstedt. 2015. A New Criterion for Assessing Discriminant Validity in Variance-Based Structural Equation Modeling. *Journal of the Academy of Marketing Science* 43: 115–35. [CrossRef]

Herrera, Gabriel Paes, Michel Constantino, Jen-Je Su, and Athula Naranpanawa. 2023. The Use of ICTs and Income Distribution in Brazil: A Machine Learning Explanation Using SHAP Values. *Telecommunications Policy* 47: 102598. [CrossRef]

Hyytinen, Ari, Jarno Tuimala, and Markus Hammar. 2022. Enhancing the Adoption of Digital Public Services: Evidence from a Large-Scale Field Experiment. *Government Information Quarterly* 39: 101687. [CrossRef]

Ibrahimi, Arta Ejupi, and Besnik Fetai. 2022. The Impact of ICT on the GDP Growth of Western Balkan Countries. *SEEU Review* 17: 105–19. [CrossRef]

Ishnazarov, Akram, Nargiza Kasimova, Shakhnoza Tosheva, and Arletta Isaeva. 2021. ICT and Economic Growth: Evidence from Cross-Country Growth Modeling. In *International Conference Proceedings Series*. New York: Association for Computing Machinery, pp. 668–71. [CrossRef]

Jemala, Marek. 2022. Systemic Technology Innovation Management and Analysis of Other Forms of IP Protection. *International Journal of Innovation Studies* 6: 238–58. [CrossRef]

Kaygisiz, Esra G. 2022. Determination of Digital Density Efficiency by Data Envelopment Analysis: EU Member States. *Selçuk Üniversitesi Sosyal Bilimler Enstitüsü Dergisi* 49: 175–90. [CrossRef]

Kiss, Eva, and Balázs Páger. 2023. Spatial Patterns of Manufacturing Sectors and Digitalisation in Hungary in the Age of Industry 4.0. *European Planning Studies* 32: 668–93. [CrossRef]

Kulkov, Ignat. 2021. The Role of Artificial Intelligence in Business Transformation: A Case of Pharmaceutical Companies. *Technology in Society* 66: 101629. [CrossRef]

Kumar, Pranjal, Siddhartha Chauhan, and Lalit Kumar Awasthi. 2023. Artificial Intelligence in Healthcare: Review, Ethics, Trust Challenges & Future Research Directions. *Engineering Applications of Artificial Intelligence* 120: 105894. [CrossRef]

Kumar, Ronald Ravinesh, Peter Josef Stauvermann, and Aristeidis Samitas. 2016. The Effects of ICT* on Output per Worker: A Study of the Chinese Economy. *Telecommunications Policy* 40: 102–15. [CrossRef]

Kurniawati, Meta Ayu. 2022. Analysis of the Impact of Information Communication Technology on Economic Growth: Empirical Evidence from Asian Countries. *Journal of Asian Business and Economic Studies* 29: 2–18. [CrossRef]

Lucky, Robert W. 2004. Yesterday's Dreams and Today's Reality in Telecommunications. *Technology in Society* 26: 223–33. [CrossRef]

Makridakis, Spyros. 2017. The Forthcoming Artificial Intelligence (AI) Revolution: Its Impact on Society and Firms. *Futures* 90: 46–60. [CrossRef]

Mattalia, Claudio. 2013. Embodied Technological Change and Technological Revolution: Which Sectors Matter? *Journal of Macroeconomics* 37: 249–64. [CrossRef]
Mayer, Walter, Gary Madden, and Chen Wu. 2020. Broadband and Economic Growth: A Reassessment. *Information Technology for Development* 26: 128–45. [CrossRef]
Njoh, Ambe J. 2018. The Relationship between Modern Information and Communications Technologies (ICTs) and Development in Africa. *Utilities Policy* 50: 83–90. [CrossRef]
Ofori, Isaac Kwesi, Mark Kojo Armah, Francis Taale, and Pamela Efua Ofori. 2021. Addressing The Severity and Intensity of Poverty in Sub-Saharan Africa: How Relevant Is the ICT And Financial Development Pathway? *Heliyon* 7: e08156. [CrossRef]
Pallathadka, Harikumar, Edwin Hernan Ramirez-Asis, Telmo Pablo Loli-Poma, Karthikeyan Kaliyaperumal, Randy Joy Magno Ventayen, and Mohd Naved. 2023. Applications of Artificial Intelligence in Business Management, e-Commerce and Finance. *Materials Today: Proceedings* 80: 2610–13. [CrossRef]
Pan, Maomao, Min Bai, and Xiaoxiao Ren. 2022. Does Internet Convergence Improve Manufacturing Enterprises' Competitive Advantage? Empirical Research Based on the Mediation Effect Model. *Technology in Society* 69: 101944. [CrossRef]
Panagiotopoulos, Panagiotis, Aimilia Protogerou, and Yannis Caloghirou. 2023. Dynamic Capabilities and ICT Utilization in Public Organizations: An Empirical Testing in Local Government. *Long Range Planning* 56: 102251. [CrossRef]
Petrescu, Maria, Anjala S. Krishen, Sheen Kachen, and John T. Gironda. 2022. AI-Based Innovation in B2B Marketing: An Interdisciplinary Framework Incorporating Academic and Practitioner Perspectives. *Industrial Marketing Management* 103: 61–72. [CrossRef]
Pradhan, Rudra P., Girijasankar Mallik, and Tapan P. Bagchi. 2018. Information Communication Technology (ICT) Infrastructure and Economic Growth: A Causality Evinced by Cross-Country Panel Data. *IIMB Management Review* 30: 91–103. [CrossRef]
Rai, Arun, Panos Constantinides, and Saonee Sarker. 2019. Next Generation Digital Platforms: Toward Human-AI Hybrids. *Mis Quarterly* 43: iii–ix.
Ringle, Christian M., Sven Wende, and Jan-Michael Becker. 2015. SmartPLS 3. SmartPLS GmbH, Boenningstedt. *Journal of Service Science and Management* 10: 32–49.
Rodríguez-Núñez, Estibaliz, Amparo Cervera-Taulet, and Iñaki Periáñez-Cañadillas. 2023. Assessing Social Value Derived from Social Innovation Capacity: A Review on the European Urban Context. *European Planning Studies*. [CrossRef]
Savarese, Maria Francesca, Luigi Orsi, and Fiorenza Belussi. 2016. New Venture High Growth in High-Tech Environments. *European Planning Studies* 24: 1937–58. [CrossRef]
Sollosy, Marc, and Marjorie McInerney. 2022. Artificial Intelligence and Business Education: What Should Be Taught. *International Journal of Management Education* 20: 100720. [CrossRef]
Solow, Robert M. 1956. A Contribution to the Theory of Economic Growth. *Quarterly Journal of Economics* 70: 65–94. [CrossRef]
Swan, Trevor W. 1956. Economic Growth and Capital Accumulation. *Economic Record* 32: 334–61. [CrossRef]
Tsachtsiris, George, Anastasios Magoutas, and Theodore Papadogonas. 2022. ICT and Economic Growth in EU: A Macro Level Comparison of Estimated ICT Output Elasticities. *Journal of Global Information Technology Management* 25: 202–16. [CrossRef]
Van Deursen, Alexander J.A.M., and Jan A.G.M. van Dijk. 2009. Improving Digital Skills for the Use of Online Public Information and Services. *Government Information Quarterly* 26: 333–40. [CrossRef]
Vu, Khuong M. 2011. ICT as a Source of Economic Growth in the Information Age: Empirical Evidence from the 1996–2005 Period. *Telecommunications Policy* 35: 357–72. [CrossRef]
Zoroja, Jovana. 2015. Fostering Competitiveness in European Countries with ICT: GCI Agenda. *International Journal of Engineering Business Management* 7. [CrossRef]

economies

MDPI

Review

Greece's Economic Odyssey: Persistent Challenges and Pathways Forward

Evmorfia (Fay) Makantasi * and Helias Valentis

diaNEOsis, 15125 Marousi, Greece
* Correspondence: fay.m@dianeosis.org; Tel.: +30-213-0023-000

Abstract: Two years after the COVID-19 pandemic, the Greek economy seems to have overcome the turmoil of the pandemic crisis as well as that of the following energy crisis. Nevertheless, it would be wrong to assume that the Greek economy has returned to a sound state, since this was not really the case even before the pandemic. Furthermore, the anemic growth rates of the pre-pandemic period were followed by an equally weak average growth rate (including the impact of the pandemic), as some of the significant fundamental weaknesses of the Greek economy, which had accumulated over time and constituted the real origin of the Greek crisis, have not been properly addressed yet. This paper attempts a complete mapping of the current state of the Greek economy, offering an insight into the external and internal determinants affecting it.

Keywords: Greece; Greek economy; Greek crisis; Greek debt; Greek competitiveness; development policy; investment strategy; eurozone

1. Introduction

In 2023, the Greek economy seems to have had a satisfactory registered growth (of 2.2%, according to the latest[1] European Commission (EC) estimates[2], European Commission and Directorate-General for Economic and Financial Affairs (2023b)), especially given the adverse timing on an international financial level. The rapid recovery following the pandemic crisis lost its momentum due to disruptions in the supply chain and the energy market, which, combined with the significant geopolitical instability, resulted in the considerable deceleration of most great developed economies, in combination with very high inflation rates. As the monetary authorities set monetary stability as their top priority, they were obligated to function restrictively by increasing the key interest rate level immediately and drastically, instead of functioning invigoratingly for their economies in a period of trends towards a recession.

This is the case to a considerable extent with the eurozone, with significantly adverse consequences for Greece. The Greek economy finds itself much farther from regularity in relation to the rest of the EU and eurozone economies as a result of an intense debt crisis that led to three successive bailout programmes[3] and the adoption of extreme fiscal austerity measures, resulting in a very deep and lasting economic recession. Since it is the only economy among the EU and the eurozone that has not yet recovered from the great economic crisis of the previous decade (by the end of 2023, it is estimated that it was at −18.4% of the 2008 GDP in real terms), it becomes clear that it is in the greatest need of faster economic growth. This presupposes a rapid investment rate, which is rendered considerably harder by the restrictive monetary policy. It is noted that, in the 2010–2021 period, Greece suffered a cumulative loss of standard capital amounting to EUR 94 bn. This loss must be replenished so that the country's production possibilities can at least be restored to those before the crisis.

Contrastively, the influx of very significant European resources by Next Generation EU (NGEU), to the extent that they are directed towards an investment activity and mobilize adequate, additional, private resources towards investments, can neutralize the negative impact of the restrictive monetary policy over the financing terms. The considerably increased incoming flow of foreign direct investments (FDIs) as well as the creditworthiness upgrade of the Greek state on an investment level are significantly helpful in the aforementioned process. This upgrade substantiates the depletion of the idiosyncratic risk of the Greek economy and also releases considerable investment resources from systemic investors. Many of the aforementioned factors, however, have served as a policy alibi for not prioritizing all the necessary structural changes and reforms required so that the Greek production and development model can be purged. In any case, this will involve a considerably demanding struggle that will last many years and necessitate constant effort as well as alertness to achieve a rapid readjustment to any unexpected development.

Therefore, this paper attempts to provide a thorough and cohesive mapping of the present state of the Greek economy as well as of the risks and opportunities involved in its course in the immediate future and aims to shed light on all the fields that have margins for improvement or are in need of it[4].

2. The Magnitude of the Greek Economic Crisis

The impact of the COVID-19 pandemic on various economies is clearly evident. Initially, there was a necessary shutdown in the production process of many goods and services—including many intermediate goods and services that constitute a crucial influx into other sectors—due to personnel infections, the border being shut down for long periods of time and the quarantine on means of transport (e.g., the cargo ships at their first port of call of every additional country during their voyage). Subsequently, there was a disruption in the supply chain and the added value chain, concerning the majority of end products, as well as a sudden and unprepared transition to teleworking for many employees and other factors that made the aggregate supply suffer from a significant global negative shock. At the same time, the restrictive measures for the pandemic to the extent that they also restricted the consumption behavior (confinement to the house, the shutdown of specific shops, the border shutdown, quarantine, etc.) alongside the atmosphere of uncertainty regarding the citizens' financial/work status or their health, made the aggregate demand suffer from an equally significant global negative shock as well. These bilateral negative shocks resulted in a deep and sudden recession in 2020 for all the world's economies and the ones more prone to external trade were more severely struck.

According to the quarterly data, it seems that the Greek as well as the global economy had already fully recovered from this recession since the beginning of the third quarter of 2021 (2021-Q3) despite the fact that there was still a considerable degree of uncertainty regarding the course of the pandemic crisis and due to several new focal points of risk, such as the energy crisis and the global inflation wave. However, it would be wrong to assume that, after the pandemic and all the aforementioned uncertainties, the Greek economy has returned in a good state, as this was not really the case before the pandemic, either.

We often refer to the Greek economic crisis that started in 2009 as a past state, which, depending on the narrator, lasted until 2016, 2018 or 2019. The truth is, though, that the Greek economy never exited this crisis. On the contrary, when the pandemic started, it was still approximately 25% below its level of economic activity in the distant 2008. As becomes apparent in Figure 1, although Greece escaped the considerably negative growth rates after 2013, its economy was in a virtual standstill until 2016 (with an average annual growth rate of −0.07%) and then it "paddled along" and grew slightly for 3 years (with an average annual growth rate of only 1.55%) until the advent of the pandemic crisis. As a result, when the pandemic struck at the beginning of 2020, the Greek economy registered at −23.1% of the 2008 GDP and lacked substantial, developmental "momentum". The 2020 pandemic recession was very deep (−9.3%)—as a matter of fact, it was the second deepest in the EU-27—but it proved to be temporary. The bouncing of the economy occurred instantly in 2021 (with a full recovery until 2021-Q3) and was followed by a considerable growth rate in

2022 as well, which can be partly explained in terms of base impact, for the first half of 2022 (until 2022-Q2) when compared with the first half of 2021. Thus, the post-pandemic growth rate of the Greek economy appears to be among the highest in the EU-27 (an average annual rate at 6.96%, which is the fifth greatest performance within the EU). Nevertheless, to a considerable degree, this is due to the previous 2020 recession, which was also one of the biggest in the EU-27. If one includes the pandemic period, it becomes clear that, by the end of 2022, the Greek economy had cumulatively grown by 3.74% since 2019 (with an average annual rate of 1.23%). This performance ranks 18th in the EU-27. At the same time, Greece stands much farther from its long-lasting balance, in comparison with the rest of the EU countries. According to the latest EC (European Commission and Directorate-General for Economic and Financial Affairs (2024)) estimates, the actual Greek GDP grew further by 2.2% in 2023, and as a result, it now registers at −18.4% of the 2008 GDP level, whereas by the end of 2025 it will have exceeded the −15% level.

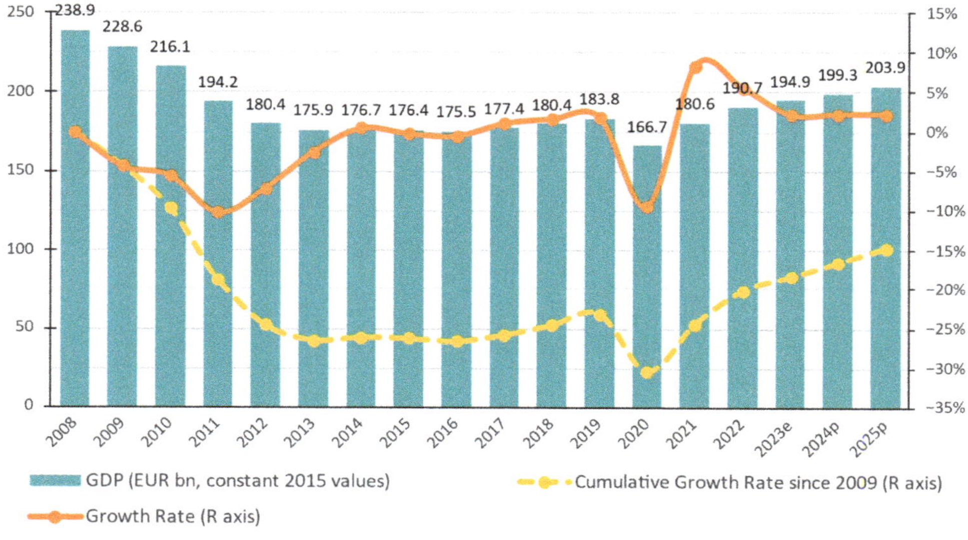

Figure 1. GDP and growth rate. e = estimation; p = forecast. Source: Eurostat and European Commission (AMECO), diaNEOsis editing.

It becomes clear from the aforementioned rates that the Greek economic crisis by no means belongs to the past. On the contrary, the Greek economy still has to come a very long way.

The true components of the GDP are none other than the added value contributed by every business in the country during a specific year. Consequently, a decrease in GDP is caused by a reduction in the added value of the country's businesses, leads to a reduction in the products available for every use and, thus, a consequent decrease in social welfare. Therefore, such a significant and sustained decrease in GDP can only register, in product value terms, accordingly dramatic alterations in the microeconomy (the finances of every business and every household), employment, real income, social prosperity and social coherence. Indicatively, Figure 2 presents the repercussions of the aforementioned GDP course, in terms of total and long-term unemployment.

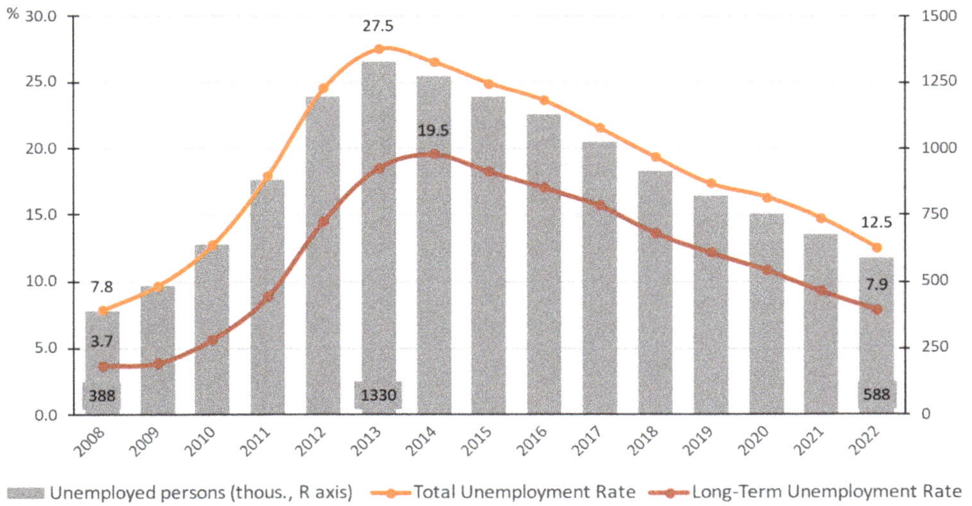

Figure 2. Total and long-term unemployment. All rates are expressed in terms of the total workforce. Long-term unemployed are those who remain unemployed for 12 months or more. Source: Eurostat (Labor Force Survey).

It is clear that unemployment skyrocketed by almost 20 percentage points (pp) from 2009 to 2013, as the GDP was shrinking dramatically. This added approximately 1 million unemployed people. Since then, unemployment has de-escalated, but at a very slow rate (an average annual decrease of 1.67 pp or ~82.500 people). This rate seems to have been affected by the pandemic only marginally and temporarily. In accordance with the latest available annual data, in 2022, unemployment remained at over 12.5% (the second highest rate in the EU, after Spain at 12.9%), the total number of unemployed people exceeding 588.000. Another phenomenon that gives rise to serious concern is the portion of the long-term unemployed (that is, those who have been continuously out of work for over 12 months) in the total number of unemployed. Whereas fewer than half of the people out of work were long-term unemployed in 2008, in 2014, they became almost three-quarters of the total number. Subsequently, their numbers decreased, but their portion remained at over 70% in 2019 and over 63% in 2022. The estimate and the recording of the consequences of long-term unemployment on individuals and societies do not lie within the scope of the present paper, but it is obvious that this specific social group, and especially its portion that remain unemployed for much longer than 12 months, deserve special solicitude from the state.

It is a particularly common misconception to view the Greek economic crisis as a subcase of the global financial crisis of 2007–2008 or as a simple case, albeit with certain peculiarities, of the frequent inherent circularity that is common in all the world's economies. On the contrary, the "Greek crisis" is a distinctive situation, prompted by the global financial crisis of 2007–2008, but caused by significant accumulated and fundamental weaknesses of the Greek economy, which deteriorated considerably, evidently, because of the very poor political and economic treatment that it received. As depicted in Figure 3, the Greek crisis is one of the deepest and longest economic crises of a developed economy in modern history, if not the deepest and longest. The "Great Depression" of 1929 in the USA caused more intense recession rates during the first 4 years, but the cumulative recession did not exceed 26.3% and the economic activity returned to pre-recession levels by 1936. The United Kingdom, in its deepest recession in modern history, suffered the greatest, cumulative loss of 14.9% in the period after the First World War (1920–1924) and returned to pre-recession levels within 5 years.[5] The widely known recession in Argentina started in 1999 and the cumulative loss of real GDP did not exceed 18.4%, whereas it surpassed pre-recession levels within 6 years. Subsequently, the Argentinian economy grew at the fastest pace. In contrast with the aforementioned cases, Greece suffered cumulative losses in terms of real GDP that exceeded 26% (26.38% in 2013), as opposed to the level before the crisis and it still registers cumulative losses at over 18.5% to the present day.[6] Regarding the European economies that entered recession at the same time as Greece, due to the financial crisis of 2007–2008, it is clear from the data that the depth of their recessions is not at all comparable with the case of Greece. Only the Italian economy manifests prolonged recession and—like the Greek economy—still registers anemic recovery rates. The case of Ireland is particularly interesting, as its course was similar to the course of Greece in the first 2 years of recession, with a maximum cumulative loss of 9.4%. However, it stabilized immediately afterwards, and by mainly exploiting foreign direct investment, it exceeded the pre-crisis levels of economic activity within 6 years and has achieved explosive growth since then.[7]

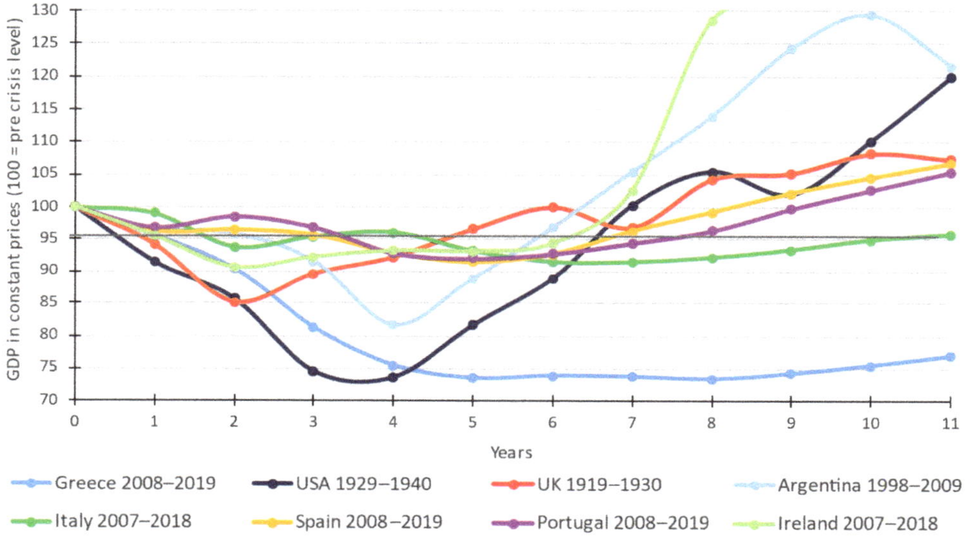

Figure 3. The Greek crisis vs other major economic crises. Sources: Eurostat, Bureau of Economic Analysis (USA), World Bank, Federal Reserve Bank of St Louis.

The important question raised at this point is why the Greek economy appears to have such a great difficulty in recovering from this economic crisis, which lasted over a decade, as opposed to its immediate recovery in 2021, after the severe recession of 2020, though in the midst of uncertainties due to the continuing pandemic, and contrary to all the other aforementioned cases of countries. To start with, the performance of the Greek economy, as it becomes apparent from the course of its real GDP and the rest of its qualitative and quantitative features, bears no resemblance to the usual recurrent recessions that appear during the economic cycles. On the contrary, it exhibits the features of a rather permanent, violent correction—downwards—because of fundamental, systemic and structural weaknesses,[8] which were possibly exposed to the financial markets due to the financial crisis of 2007–2008. These weaknesses include the distorted and state-funded production model, the deficit in competitiveness, the vast public debt, the unfair and ineffective tax system, the deficient and non-transparent capital market, the unsustainable public insurance system, the distorted savings and investments model, the extremely tardy administration of justice combined with the existence of an excessive number of—in many cases contradictory—laws and poor legislation, the cumbersome bureaucracy, the quality of the political system, etc., many of which have not yet been fully dealt with, despite the important efforts made.

To many people, the slowness of the Greek economy to contain the economic shrinkage and the anemic growth that it subsequently exhibited are due to the fiscal policy of strict austerity followed. If a significant fiscal extension had been permitted, even temporarily, during the first years of the economic crisis, the outcome would have been completely different. Although this is a valid claim, it excludes the need to correct the aforementioned weaknesses and does not include the fact that the public debt crisis is one of the main components of the Greek economic crisis. The degrees of freedom in fiscal policy had already been lost before the Greek economy reached its lowest point, while the external factors that now defined the fiscal policy ultimately aimed at making an example out of Greece for other European countries and not at the recovery of the Greek economy. The political timing, mainly at a European level, during which the Greek crisis occurred, clearly constitutes an important factor in its course. However, it remains an absolute fact that it is imperative for Greece to deal with the aforementioned fundamental, systemic and structural weaknesses.

Another aggravating circumstance, usually ignored in public discourse, is the fact that the very depth of a recession and, primarily, its duration become preventive factors for recovery possibilities. The reduction in the whole production of an economy is by definition equivalent to a corresponding—but not necessarily proportional—reduction in the use of its resources. These resources include the available raw materials, the soil, the physical capital as well as labor. Under the—plausible, in the case of Greece—hypothesis that the prior state of the economy was not a in state of overuse of its resources, a recession would clearly cause a corresponding underutilization of such resources. A severe and/or persistent underutilization of capital resources devalues them due to the increased actual depreciation of physical and human capital[9] and provides incentives for their transfer elsewhere, which results in the loss of these resources in the economy under recession[10]. To put it briefly, if, for some reason, the total product of an economy is much and/or for too long less than its potential product, then its potential product tends to decrease and, as a consequence, the development prospects of this economy are also reduced. There is no doubt that this mechanism has operated in the Greek crisis. The so-called "brain drain" is a well-known issue, but it is not equally perceived that it is only a part of a broader problem of devaluation and outflow of disposable resources, as well as that this has already negatively influenced the growth prospects of the Greek economy. It is worth noting that for the half a million young and educated people who left the country in 2008–2016, the Greek state is estimated to have invested EUR 8 billion in their education, while their host countries gained EUR 50 billion in GDP and EUR 12.9 billion in public revenues.[11]

3. The Effects of the Crisis on Disposable Income

During the Greek economic crisis, the average Greek citizen had to face the increase in average taxation, apart from their reduced average income, due to the strictly restrictive fiscal policy. It is indicative that, while from 2008 to 2016 the loss of the country's GDP was at 27%, the corresponding loss in the total tax revenue of the state was at only 7%, in accordance with a relevant study by diaNEOsis (diaNEOsis and IOBE (2018)). The obvious cause of this discrepancy is the dramatic increase in taxation. In an attempt to examine the overall impact of recession and over-taxation on the average Greek, we carried out the exercise of subtracting per capita taxes and compulsory social security contributions from per capita domestic income. The combined results appear in Figure 4, in constant 2015 values and in juxtaposition with the individual per capita consumption.

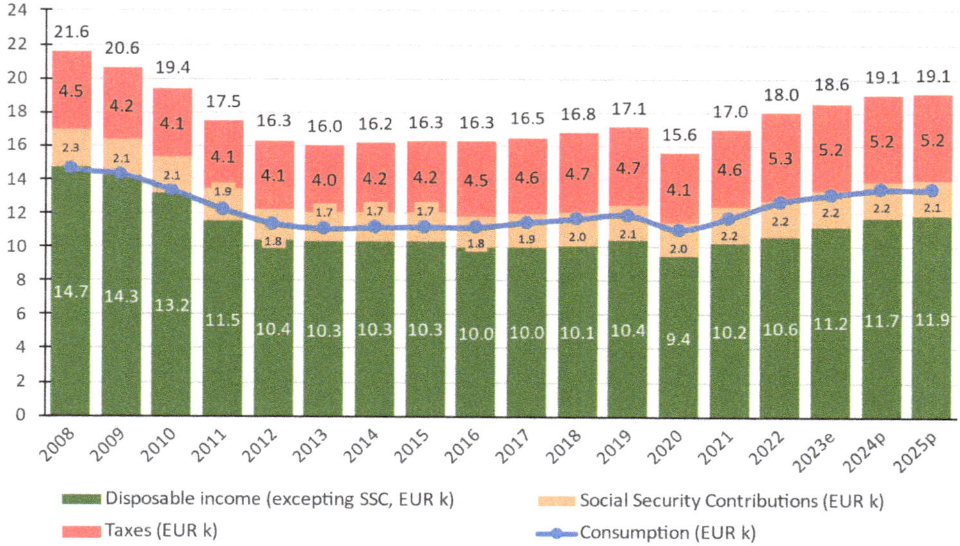

Figure 4. Per capita disposable income, taxes and SS contributions vs consumption. In constant 2015 values. e = estimation, p = forecast. Source: European Commission (AMECO), diaNEOsis editing.

It is absolutely clear from the results that the tax policy became an additional aggravating factor for the average Greek citizen, while their income was depressed by the severe recession. More precisely, from the end of 2008 to the end of 2013, when the average domestic income was reduced by 25.6%, the average disposable income was reduced by an additional 4.5 pp (30.1%). The total of per capita taxes and contributions amounted to 31.8% of the domestic per capita income in 2008, but, in 2013, this ratio had risen to 35.9%. After that, an increase in average income by 6.9% was rendered possible by the slow growth of the Greek economy until 2019, but the average disposable income remained almost stable (with an increase of approximately 0.8%), as the average share of taxes and contributions on the analogy of the income had already reached 39.5%. Therefore, in the complete course of the Greek economic crisis, the tax policy further aggravated the already sharply decreasing per capita incomes, during the shrinkage phase, and it absorbed every profit, during the slow growth phase. In the pandemic of 2020, the share of taxes and contributions remained stable (at 39.5%) and, thus, the significant reduction in per capita income was transferred proportionally to disposable income (with a reduction of −9.1% in both). During the recovery years after the pandemic recession (in 2021 and 2022), the considerable growth in average income was combined with the share of taxes and contributions, which was on the increase and reached 41.4% in 2022. As a result, the increase in disposable per capita income was mitigated. The estimated course of these figures in the following years is encouraging. By 2024, the disposable per capita income is expected to exceed its 2011 level for the first time in 13 years and the share of taxes and contributions on total income is estimated to continue decreasing.

It is of particular interest to juxtapose the aforementioned data with per capita final consumption. As the Greek pension system is primarily redistributory, the greater part of social security contributions is returned to the private economy as pensioners' income. For this reason, the individual consumption should be compared with the disposable income with contributions (the sum of the green category and the orange one, in every bar, in Figure 4).[12] This specific comparison is revealing not only regarding the course of the average Greek person's margin for saving, but also concerning the domestic market ability to hope for invigorated consumption. The average share of consumption expenditure on disposable income with contributions rose to 96.2% in 2018 from 85.6% in 2008. Respectively, the remaining average saving dropped from EUR 2449 in 2008 to only EUR 455 in 2018, which is less than one-fifth of its initial level. In 2019, the situation was marginally improved (at 95.2% in terms of average consumption share on disposable income with contributions and EUR 596 remaining income). This changed, however, in 2020 (96.1% and EUR 443, respectively) due to the severe shrinkage in average disposable income. Despite the additional significant disruption in consumer behavior in 2020, because of exogenous restrictions on the range of consumer choices, caused by the lockdowns and due to the significant increase in economic uncertainty on the consumers' part (reduced consumer confidence), the independent consumption and the phenomenon of consumption smoothing led to a fairly smaller alteration in the average consumption. This was probably also the result of the very important counterbalancing state subsidies given to households and businesses. Since then, the average individual consumption growth rate has been observed to marginally exceed the alteration rate in average disposable income with contributions. As a result, its share is estimated at 98% in 2023 and the average saving from the remaining income amounts to EUR 261.[13] In conclusion, it becomes clear that there is no space for stimulating domestic demand via increasing domestic consumption spending, as the latter is actively limited by disposable income, combined with the additional negative impact on savings, which are completely depressed. The reinforcement of disposable income constitutes an obviously deliberate goal, which, however, is a rather unrealistic measure for stimulating domestic demand.

4. The Production Structure of the Greek Economy

Before investigating which available options would be really effective for the reinforcement of the Greek economy, it is worth examining to what extent the Greek economic crisis exerted a uniform influence over its separate sectors or whether there was considerable asymmetry among the burdens involved. To this end, we grouped all Greek economy sectors for which there are gross value added (GVA) data in 14 initial categories[14]. Figure 5 depicts the contribution of each one of these groups to the Greek total GVA, during the years 2005–2020, and the total GVA value, in these years, in constant 2015 values.

To begin with, we can observe a period of sharp total GVA reduction, from 2008 to 2014 (with an average annual reduction rate of 4.4%), and a period of very slow growth, in the years 2015–2019 (with an average annual growth rate of only 0.7%). During the overall period of 2007–2019, the total GVA was reduced by 21.2% or EUR 43.5 billion, in constant 2015 values.[15] What is more, according to individual data, the economic crisis seems to have caused significant structural changes in the Greek economy. In 2007, the three primary sectors were the following: 1. wholesale and retail trade (with a 14% share), 2. manufacturing (at 11.9%) and 3. real estate activities (at 10.4%). In 2019, the three more important sectors remained the same, but with quite differentiated shares and in a different order: 1. real estate activities (at 17.5%), 2. wholesale and retail trade (at 11.7%) and 3. manufacturing (at 10%).

More specifically, from 2007 to 2019, the construction sector suffered a dramatic shrinkage in its GVA by almost 70%—a percentage change more than triple than the total GVA—and, as a result, its share was greatly reduced. The professional and administrative/support service activities sector also performed similarly, to a somehow smaller degree, as it was reduced by 43.2%—which was more than double the alteration of the total GVA. Other sectors that registered percentage reduction greater than the corresponding reduction in total GVA, and therefore exhibited reduced shares in Greek production, were classified in the following order: 1. human health and social work activities (at −37.7%), 2. wholesale and retail trade (at −37.2%), 3. manufacturing (at −36.3%), 4. transportation and storage (at −36%) and 5. the sector of public utility service provision (energy (excluding oil products), water and telecommunications, at −35.5%). At the very opposite end, three sectors not only registered increased relevant shares in the Greek economy, but also exhibited increased GVA. The top performing sector was real estate activities, which increased its GVA by 32.6%

(or EUR 7.1 billion). The agricultural sector (agriculture, forestry and fishing) followed with a 25.8% increase (or EUR 1.5 billion) and then the sector of accommodation and food service, with an increase of 6.6% (or EUR 650 million). It should be noted that the accommodation and food service sector constitutes a superset of the tourism sector, transportation excluded. Unfortunately, there are no open data available for its further division nor for the division of the transportation sector into passenger transfer and transportation of goods, so tourism cannot be analyzed in more depth. Under the plausible hypothesis that tourist transfer does not generate a particularly large GVA in Greece[16] and, surely, this does not exceed the GVA created in food service by customers who are not tourists, it is deduced that the direct effect of tourism on the Greek economy does not exceed 6.8%. To this share, which is in total harmony with relevant estimates by the Organization for Economic Cooperation and Development (OECD) (OECD (2020)), indirect effects should be added, insofar as domestic inputs are used in the tourism supply chain, in order to calculate the total impact of tourism on the country's total output. Finally, three more sectors increased their shares in the country's total GVA, although they suffered reductions in their GVA— these reductions were relatively smaller: the sector of "public administration, defense and compulsory social security" (at −8%), the sector of financial and insurance activities (excluding social security, at −9.7%) and the education sector (at −16.4%).

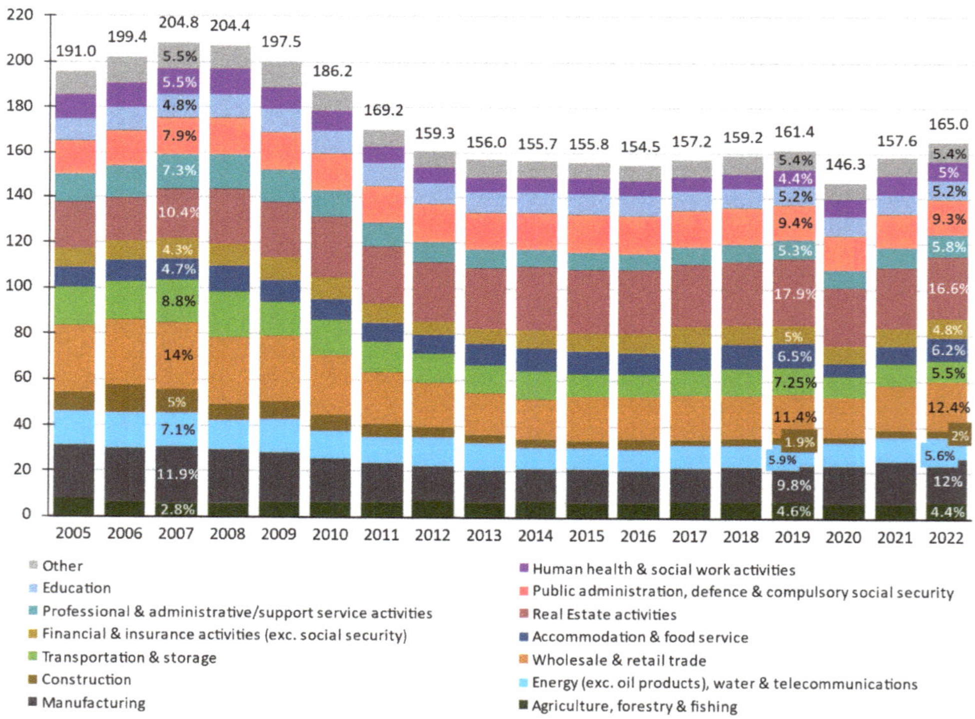

Figure 5. Gross value added by sector (EUR, billion, constant 2015 prices). Source: Eurostat, diaNEOsis editing.

4.1. The Asymmetric Effects of the Pandemic

Important conclusions can also be drawn regarding the consequences of the pandemic crisis on the individual sectors of the Greek economy. The country's total GVA dropped by 9.4% or EUR 15.1 billion in 2020 in comparison with 2019. With the only exceptions being utilities [energy (excluding oil products), water and telecommunications, at +3.8%], manufacturing (at +3.5%) and health (human health and social work activities, at +1.2%), all sectors were aggravated, but the allocation of this aggravation was not at all symmetrical. More specifically, almost one-third of the loss came from the accommodation and food service sector, which registered an almost 50% loss of GVA (at 48.2%), due to the dramatic decrease in tourist influx. The transportation and storage sector suffered a very high decrease in produced value added (by 24.3% or EUR 2.8 billion), the champion being air transport, (a decrease of 59.3%). Secondly, the real estate activities sector suffered a reduction of 11.9% or EUR 3.4 billion) and this sector contributed to almost one-fifth of the total loss, due to its large share. Thirdly, some of the sectors grouped above under the "other" category are such examples, the primary sector here being "arts, entertainment and recreation" (a reduction of 29.6%). All the other sectors, apart from manufacturing and utilities, suffered clearly smaller GVA losses, quantitively fluctuating between 0.8% and 11.9%. In conclusion, the pandemic crisis aggravated the Greek economy in a particularly unequal way, by exercising multiple pressures on the tourism-related sectors and, more generally, the final provision of services as well as transportation and arts.

4.2. The Current Production Structure

During the recovery years from the pandemic crisis (2021–2022), the total GVA was not only fully restored to pre-pandemic levels, but it also registered a small further growth (at +2.3%, compared with the 2019 levels). Apart from the return of the total GVA level, we can also observe a general restoration of the production structure of the Greek economy to the pre-pandemic structure (2019), which, however, included some differentiations. The main differentiation, pointed out by the data, has to do with the manufacturing sector, which grew much more than the overall economy (at +22.3% since 2019) and as a result, its share increased. Furthermore, the sectors of wholesale and retail trade (at +12.1%), professional and administrative/support service activities (at +12.1%) and construction (at +10.1%) also registered a great growth, which was considerably bigger than the overall economy. At the very opposite end, the transportation and storage sector failed to neutralize—until 2022—the majority of its losses caused by the pandemic (at −21.7% in 2019, whereas in 2020, at −24.3%). Real estate activities only partly recovered (at −4.9% in 2019, whereas at −11.9% in 2020). In spite of this difficulty, the real estate activities sector remains the principal activity sector for the contemporary Greek economy, with a share reaching 16.6%, a considerably upward overall trend and with very powerful prospects for the future (as substantiated also by the very big volume of foreign direct investment directed towards real estate)[17]. The sector of wholesale and retail trade also considerably contributes to the Greek produced product, with a share exceeding 12.4%, despite the compression of consumption abilities. Moreover, the course of the manufacturing sector has been particularly encouraging mainly over the recent years, having already established the third highest contribution before the pandemic, and it now registers a very powerful and uninterrupted upward trend.

5. Competitiveness and External Balance of the Greek Economy

5.1. The Current Account Deficit and the External Imbalance

Another issue worthy of analysis has to do with the competitiveness and external balance of the Greek economy. When a country imports more than it exports, without being able to cover the discrepancy, via incomes or transfers from abroad, then it faces a deficit in its current account balance (CAB). The funding of this deficit requires international, private, and public borrowing on the part of the country or a divestment of a part of its assets abroad, that is, a reduction in its net worth abroad. Consequently, the sustainability of a deficit in CAB depends on the current and expected level of the country's net worth abroad, that is, on past or expected future equivalent surpluses in CAB. The achievement of surpluses in CAB is a process that is anything but platitudinous, as it requires either a significant improvement in business competitiveness—so that exports can be increased and imports decreased, to a certain degree—or a considerable decrease in consumption expenditure—so that imports can be reduced—with whatever this entails regarding social prosperity.[18]

Unfortunately, all the aforementioned information does not seem to have ever been communicated in a simple and comprehensible manner in public discourse; so, the Greek economy has kept having deficits in CAB, throughout the period after the democracy's restoration.[19] The general state of the structure of CAB during this period includes an enduring, particularly negative balance of goods and a diachronically positive but of a smaller size services balance, which is determined to a high degree by the sectors of tourism and transportation. The rest of the minor balances (primary and secondary income balances) register quantitatively lower values, below and above zero.

Until Greece's accession into the eurozone, the CAB deficits were generally small (lower than 4% of GDP), with the exception of some isolated temporary spikes, mainly because of fluctuations in oil price—in conjunction with the dependence of the Greek economy on energy imports—and the election cycle[20]. Until 1990, the monetary/currency policy was used in the pursuit of the external balance—more specifically, the policy used was that of the constant decline of the drachma, with further emergency devaluations—but with decreasing effectiveness. The policy of drachma as "hard currency"—that is, the policy of decline restriction—was adopted from 1990 onwards and, consequently, the pursuit of the external balance came into the field of fiscal and employment policy.

Following the country's accession into the eurozone, the subsequent reduction in interest rates and the loss of the monetary/currency policy, the CAB deficit deteriorated significantly and, initially, it was stabilized at approximately EUR 15 billion or 7–9% of GDP. From 2006 onwards, as clearly indicated in Figure 6, the CAB deficit was even more enlarged, as a matter of fact to an excessively high degree, reaching EUR 36.6 billion or 15.1% of GDP by 2008. Given these levels, the CAB deficit exposed a fundamental external imbalance in the Greek economy to the markets, which could not be sustainable, a fact that contributed decisively to the course of the Greek economy later on, with the outbreak of the international financial crisis of 2007–2008. The so-called "twin deficits", that is the fiscal balance deficit and the CAB deficit, constituted the basic indications of non-sustainability of the Greek economy and led to the Greek crisis.

During the crisis, the CAB state significantly improved, primarily due to the considerable shrinkage in disposable income, which resulted in a compression in domestic consumption expenditure and a reduction in total imports rather than thanks to the improved competitiveness. More specifically, since 2009, the CAB deficit has started decreasing drastically and, as a matter of fact, in the years 2014–2015, it was almost reduced to zero, as it registered under EUR 1.5 billion and 1% of the GDP. It becomes clear from the data on the goods and services exports and imports that this adjustment was achieved almost completely by reducing imports by 32.1% (from EUR 84.8 billion to EUR 57.5 billion), whereas exports rose by only 0.7% (from EUR 56.1 billion to EUR 56.5 billion). After 2015 and until the advent of the pandemic, the overall imports seem to have been changing at the same pace as the total exports, thus keeping the CAB deficit low. More analytically, during the 2015–2016 period, both were reduced, because of the difficulties brought about by capital controls, among other factors, whereas later, both aspects of international trade grew rapidly. This growth in the exports of goods and services was a particularly encouraging factor, because it suggested improved competitiveness and extroversion on the part of Greek businesses. As a matter of fact, the total exports in 2019 reached the historically high percentage of 39.6% of GDP (EUR 72.6 billion). Nevertheless, it must be noted that, despite the significant improvement in CAB, during this period, no CAB surplus was achieved in any of the aforementioned years.

Figure 6. International trade and current account balance (EUR, billion, current values). e = extrapolation of available monthly data to the whole year. Source: Bank of Greece, diaNEOsis editing.

The advent of the pandemic in 2020 caused global disruption to international trade at both goods and services levels. The considerable share of tourism in Greek total exports and inflexible Greek imports were contributing factors to this disruption that derailed the CAB once again. More specifically, the diachronically surplus services balance suffered a loss of approx. EUR 13.8 billion, compared with 2019 figures, mainly due to tourist industry collections[21], whereas the diachronically deficient balance of goods improved by EUR 4.3 billion, with reductions in both exports and imports of goods[22]. In total, the exports of goods and services dropped by almost 29% and imports by 15.4%, and as a result, the CAB deficit more than quadrupled.

Already since 2021, the aforementioned compression in Greek international trade had been completely restored, actually exceeding 2019 figures. The course of the overall exports was particularly encouraging, and not only did this course continue the pre-pandemic trend, but it also accelerated significantly, thus achieving historically high levels in 2021 and 2022, in both absolute terms (EUR 74.4 billion and EUR 101.5 billion, respectively) and GDP terms (at 41% and 49.1%, respectively). This is unprecedented in the modern history of the Greek economy. These performances of Greek exports are surely a strongly encouraging development for the Greek economy, especially if we also consider that the substantial increase in exports over the last years—the difficult 2020 excluded—has not relied exclusively on the development of the exports of services, but its crushingly biggest part (approximately three-quarters of the total alteration since 2019) derives from the export of goods. As a matter of fact, even if we exclude fuels—the raised price of which artificially increases the value of fuel exports—the rest of the goods continue having a significantly larger share of services in the rise in overall exports (at 44.3% of the total change, as opposed to 26.3%). This fact proves that, after so many years, the Greek economy is regaining powerful developmental support from both its primary and secondary sectors, thanks to, at least a part, these sectors, which are highly energetic, healthy and extroverted.

On the other hand, at the same time as the successive export records in recent years, there were equivalent or even more powerful successive records in imports as well, either in absolute terms (EUR 88.3 billion in 2021 and EUR 121.7 billion in 2022) or GDP terms (at 48.6% and 58.9%, respectively), a phenomenon not compatible with a conclusion of improved general competitiveness. As the increase in imports outweighs the increase in exports following 2020, the total impact on CAB is negative and, as a result, Greece is in danger of wasting all the progress in counterbalancing it, a goal achieved by means of great sacrifices during the crisis decade. A lot of people attribute the derailment of imports—and, consequently, of the CAB deficit—to the energy crisis, as Greece is an energy net importer and, therefore, the increased prices of basic energy goods it imports artificially inflate net imports. Nevertheless, by isolating fuel imports, we can observe that solely 35.3% of the total increase in imports since 2019 can be attributed to fuels, and by extension, partially, to the energy crisis (Figure 7). Even if we completely exclude the change in fuel imports, the remaining 64.7% of the import increase since 2019 (EUR 30.6 billion) is enough to continue overbalancing the whole increase in total exports (EUR 28.9 billion).

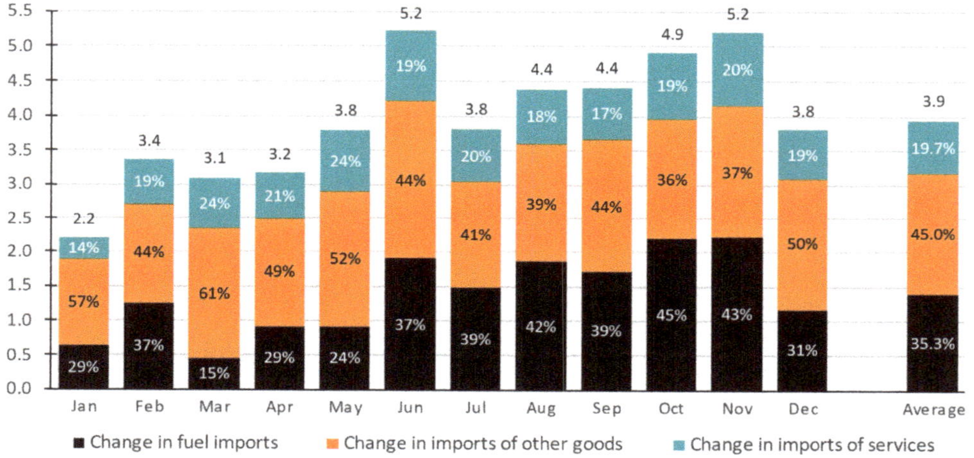

Figure 7. Change in imports per month in 2022 compared to 2019 (EUR, billion). Fuel shares on total change are represented in label percentages. Source: Bank of Greece, diaNEOsis editing.

5.2. International Trade in Goods

As already mentioned, if we focus on exports and imports of goods, Greece is a net importer. This is due to many factors, such as the focus of the Greek economy on the tertiary sector, especially tourism, and reversely, the very limited focus on high-tech goods, the limited interconnection between Greek businesses and international value chains and, more generally, the low competitiveness of Greek manufacturing. Not all of these factors necessarily have negative connotations, nor is it necessary for an economy to have a balanced or surplus balance of goods, as potential surpluses in the services balance might as well fill the gap.

However, the problem arises when we include two important elements. The first is the inherent volatility in tourist traffic and its revenue, because of external and unpredictable factors.[23] This volatility should be taken for granted and into consideration in private citizens' business choices, as well as in the development policy options. If tourism is the Greek "economic locomotive", it should be known that this "locomotive" does not have particularly stable power. It is obvious that political and business actions are necessary for the reduction in this volatility to the highest degree (extension of the tourist season, creation of alternative tourist products, accession into more tourist markets, etc.)[24]; however, what is perhaps more necessary is the development of other sectors of the Greek economy as well, so that it does not rely solely on tourism. The other element is the broader tertiary sector. The Greek tertiary sector focuses to a high degree on the provision of end services (B2C), that is, on end consumers. As we already explained in an earlier section, the domestic disposable income leaves no margin for the stimulation of consumption expenditure and, therefore, the tertiary sector of end services has no substantial margin for growth. On the contrary, as is also the case with the strongest developed economies, the tertiary sector focusing on the provision of interim services (B2B) and the support of the other sectors of the economy (businesses of the primary and secondary sector) has significant advantages not only for itself but also for the supported sectors. However, the development of a tertiary sector of this type requires that the primary and secondary sectors be relatively healthy and thriving.

Therefore, it is worth using data on the international trade of goods as evidence of the competitiveness, extroversion and, thus, the health of the particular sections of the primary and secondary sectors. Figures 8–11 depict the diachronic progress of Greek exports and imports of goods for seven individual categories of goods, according to the Standard International Trade Classification (SITC).[25]

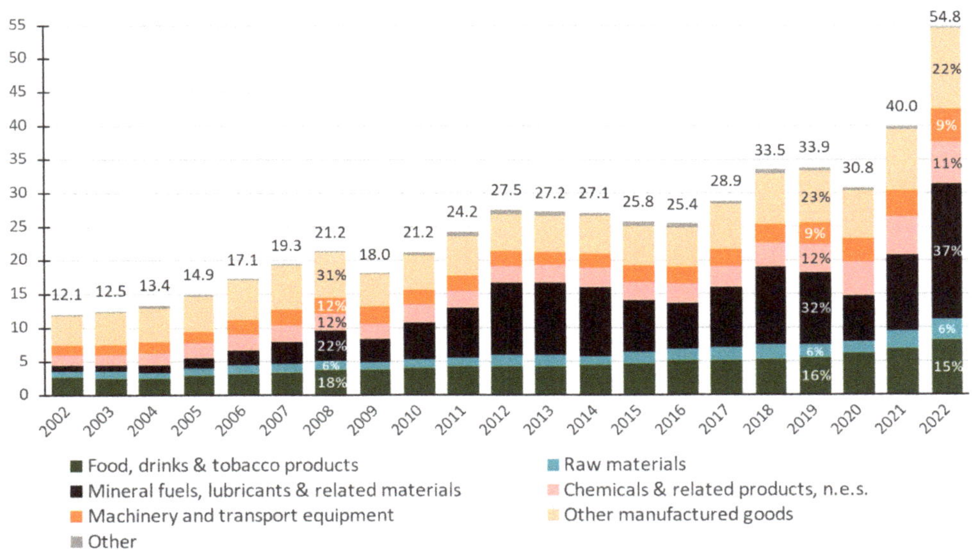

Figure 8. Exports of goods: progress and composition of Greek exports of goods (EUR, billion, current values) Source: Eurostat.

The restriction on the imports of goods becomes obvious once more from the aforementioned data in the first years of the Greek economic crisis, obviously due to the compression in consumption expenditure. At the same time, exports seem to have grown significantly during the 2010–2012 period but then remained stagnant until the imposition of capital controls. Capital controls, especially during the first phase of their imposition (2015–2016) seem to have considerably influenced the total value of the international trade of goods, but this influence was not at all symmetrical regarding the type of goods. On the contrary, the international trade of mineral fuels and lubricants fully determined the progress of the total value of goods exports and imports (almost entirely). Subsequently, both aspects of Greek international trade developed rapidly until the beginning of the pandemic, which is when they were disrupted.

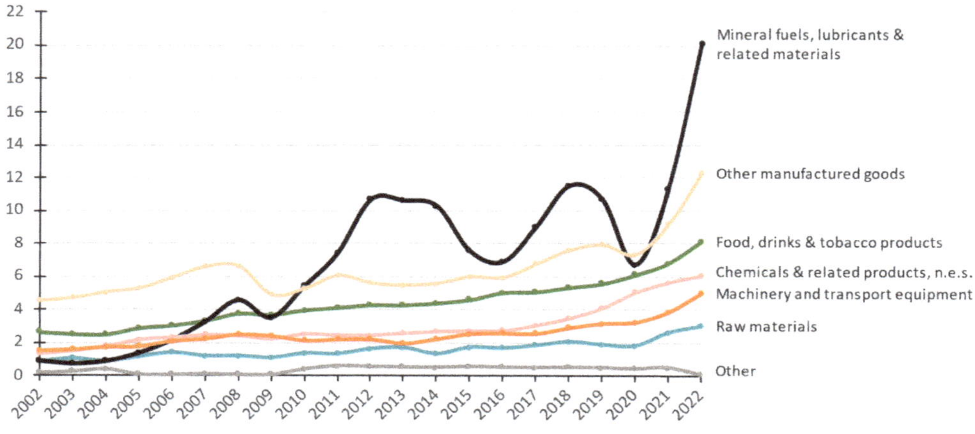

Figure 9. Exports of goods: evolution of individual SITC categories of Greek exports of goods (EUR, billion, current values). Source: Eurostat.

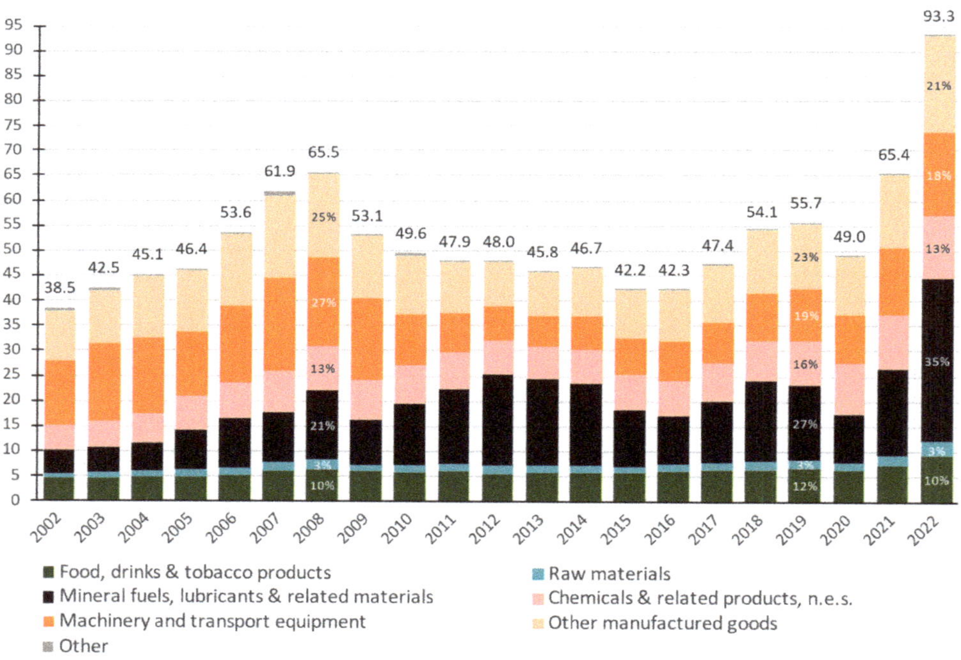

Figure 10. Imports of goods: progress and composition of Greek imports of goods (EUR billion, current values). Source: Eurostat.

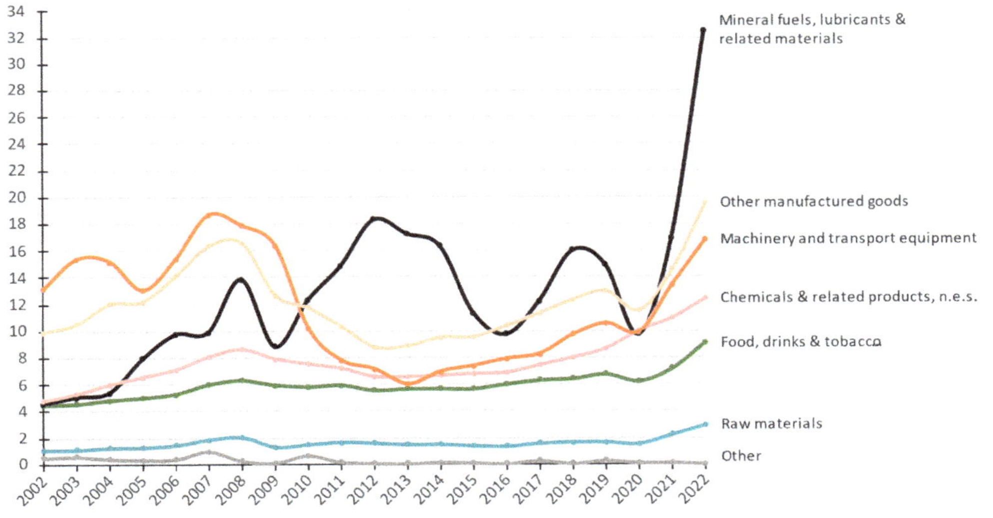

Figure 11. Imports of goods: evolution of individual SITC categories of Greek imports of goods (EUR, billion, current values). Source: Eurostat.

The first fact worth commenting on is the significant contribution of "mineral fuels, lubricants and related materials" to both the imports and exports of goods in Greece. Although Greece is a net energy importer, in the form of mainly crude oil and natural gas, it is also an important junction in the value chain of oil products (diaNEOsis and IOBE 2021). The country imports much larger quantities of crude oil than those required by its energy needs and then these quantities are refined so that oil products can be produced. The products that do not cover domestic needs are exported to neighbor, mainly Balkan, economies. This activity, which yields a share on added value for Greece (see Section 4), was significantly intensified during the crisis years, with the exception of the years 2015–2016, during which it was significantly disrupted by capital controls. During the 2008–2009 period, the exports of "mineral fuels, lubricants and related materials" increased by 133.1% and their share in the total exports of goods reached 32% in 2019, whereas their imports increased by only 7.7% and their share in the total imports of goods reached 27% in 2019. Surely, due to the energy crisis after the pandemic, the value of the international trade of mineral fuels, lubricants and related materials in current values skyrocketed in 2022. This reveals a broader problem of analysis arising from the significant volatility, exhibited by the international trade of energy goods in Greece. This significant volatility is mainly due to purely external factors in the case of Greece and that is why our following analysis will focus on the rest of the categories of international trade goods.

With reference to the other exports, the performance of "chemicals and related products, n.e.s." is particularly positive, with exports increasing by 68.6% in the 2008–2019 period and by an additional 48% in the 2019–2022 period. In fact, these products also had excellent export performance in 2020, in the midst of the pandemic, when they had an increase of 22.9% compared to 2019. The total alteration in their exports from 2008 to 2022 was 149.5% (CAGR: 6.75%). Respectively, large percentage changes were also seen in raw materials exports, the value of which in 2022 came to be higher by 147.8% in comparison with the one in 2008 (CAGR: 6.7%) and higher by 58.9% in comparison to the one in 2019. Exports of the category "food, drinks and tobacco products" are also significantly higher than those of the pre-crisis levels and have been increasing steadily since after 2009, without demonstrating any slowdown due to the imposition of capital controls or the pandemic crisis. Specifically, their export value in 2019 was 47.7% higher than the 2008 level and they further increased by 45.6% by 2022 (a total change in the period 2008–2022: 115%, CAGR: 5.6%). Two categories of manufactured goods also had positive performance but only in recent years (after 2016): "machinery and transport equipment" and "other manufactured goods", the exports of which in 2022 increased by 93% and 107.1% compared to their 2016 level, respectively (total changes since 2008: 98.9% and 86.2%, respectively).

With reference to imports, if we exclude "mineral fuels, lubricants and related materials", the peculiar behavior of which has been analyzed previously, all other categories suffered decreases in the first phase of the Greek economic crisis, in the period 2009–2013. The most significant changes during this period were the 66.4% decrease in imports of "machinery and transport equipment" and the 46.7% decrease in imports of "other manufactured goods". Subsequently, and until 2019, all categories except for "food, drinks and tobacco products" and "chemicals and related products, n.e.s." only partially recovered. The imports of the "food, drinks and tobacco products" category had already fully recovered since 2018. The "chemicals and related products, n.e.s." category had fully recovered by 2019 and was also the only product category with a 15.3% indeed increase in imports in 2020, while the rest of the imports trade in goods suffered significant losses. All goods import categories had significant increases henceforth, with "raw materials" (a 75.8% change in the 2019–2022 period), "machinery and transport equipment" (a 59.3% change) and "other manufactured goods" (a 51.2% change) being the main protagonists.

Overall, from the behavior of the international trade in goods, we can distinguish some encouraging elements and some elements of concern. Among the encouraging elements we have, first of all, to include the extremely positive trend in exports of "food, drinks and tobacco products". These products, produced by both the primary and the secondary sector, seem to be gaining more and more recognition from abroad and improving their competitiveness. What is also particularly encouraging is the increase in exports of two categories of manufactured goods: "chemicals and related products, n.e.s." and "other manufactured goods". These sectors, especially after 2016, demonstrate strong export dynamics, which is a good indication of the competitiveness course of Greek industry. On the negative side, we should firstly mention the significantly reduced import share of the category "machinery and transport equipment", despite its significantly increasing trend in recent years. These tradable items are pure capital goods, and their imports follow the trend in investment expenditure, the importance of which will be discussed in detail in the next chapter. A second negative element emerging from the aforementioned data is that the country continues to export more raw materials than it imports. The exported raw materials do not generate significant export revenues, nor do they offer significant added value to an economy, both of which could certainly be enhanced if processed domestically. This fact highlights, in a more general way, a limited manufacturing sector in Greece, unable to use domestic and international raw materials in significant quantities for the creation of additional added value.

In conclusion, the CAB deficit is a long-standing problem of the Greek economy, indicating its long-standing inability to remain competitive. The competitiveness of an economy is not a static issue and does not depend only on labor costs. On the contrary, first the improvement in and then preservation of competitiveness require increases in the productivity of resources—not only labor—and the efficiency of production at a rate initially higher and then at least equivalent to the rest of the world. In a rapidly changing technological world, the economy of Greece will have to "run" even faster and smarter in order to cover the competitiveness deficit and continue at a sustainable competitive pace. This can only be achieved by the immediate adoption of more advanced technologies, by rapidly training the labor force on them, by magnifying the average business size, by stimulating R&D and innovation[26] and by fostering a more business-friendly environment for entrepreneurship—not only for international and established entrepreneurship, but especially for domestic and new entrepreneurship.[27] The benefits of this will be multiple. The consolidation of a competitive and dynamic productive base will stabilize the Greek economy and decouple it from the domestic demand, whereas the increase in real incomes will allow for a better standard of living, higher levels of investment expenditure and improved public debt sustainability. However, as long as this does not happen and the competitiveness of Greek businesses remains limited, the Greek economy will maintain and possibly intensify its diachronic ease of covering a significant part of domestic demand with imports without being able to finance them with equivalent exports. As a result, there will be a new expansion in CAB deficits, which implies further accumulation of external debt and, inevitably, new bankruptcy.

6. The Problem of Investment in the Greek Economy

6.1. The Investment Gap

During the Greek economic crisis, in the first years due to high recession rates and then due to poor policy followed and the accumulation of significant sources of risk, there was a drastic reduction in investment expenditure in the Greek economy. The gross fixed capital formation (GFCF)—from a historically high level of EUR 55.7 billion in 2007, in constant 2015 values (in current values it was EUR 60.5 billion)—reached a level of EUR 19.6 billion in 2012 (Figure 12) and remained at that level until 2020. That is to say, for a series of 9 consecutive years, the investments of the Greek economy were about one-third of 2007 investments. In relative GDP terms, the GFCF had stood at 21.9% of GDP until 2008[28] and then fell to a level of around 11.1% of GDP in the 2012–2019 period, an undoubling documenting that the decrease in investment expenditure is not only due to income reduction, but also to additional discouraging factors. From 2020 onwards, we have observed the share of GDP directed towards investment increasing significantly, thus reaching an estimated (by EC (European Commission and Directorate-General for Economic and Financial Affairs (2023b))) 14.7% in 2023, which on the one hand can be attributed to fund inflows from the very strong European NGEU program[29], but also indicates a clear shift in investment climate.

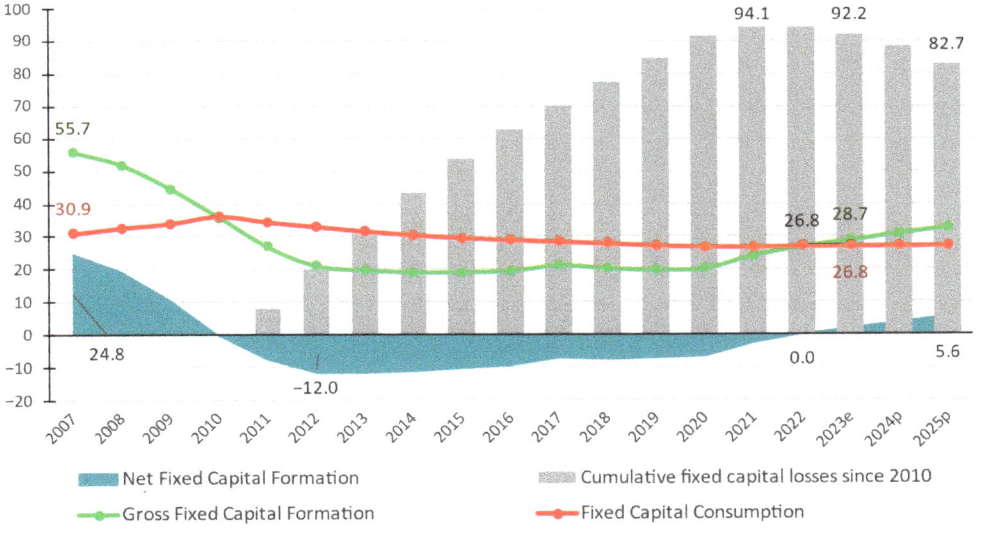

Figure 12. Fixed capital formation (EUR, billion, constant 2015 values). e = estimation; p = forecast. Source: European Commission (AMECO).

As fixed capital investment expenditure was so dramatically reduced, since 2010, it has not only lost the ability to counterbalance fixed capital consumption (FCC), but it has stabilized at a much lower level than the FCC, resulting in a consistently and strongly negative net fixed capital formation (NFCF) for a very long period of time (12 years). More specifically, whereas in 2007 the NFCF amounted to EUR 24.8 billion in 2015 value, by 2010, it had been reduced to zero; in 2012, it reached its minimum point of -EUR 12 billion and then slowly increased until 2020. This slow growth was not due to the improvement in GFCF, but to the decrease in FCC, due to the reduction in fixed capital stock. Therefore, the Greek economy was in a continuous, and indeed intensive, state of decumulation of its physical capital stock for 12 consecutive years, with the cumulative loss of fixed capital exceeding EUR 94 billion—in 2015 values—by the end of 2021. The significant increase in investment expenditures since 2021 has resulted in capital consumption being counterbalanced in 2022, thus stopping this decumulation of capital stock. In fact, according to EC estimates and predictions, a process of covering the losses of previous years already began in 2023, a process which will continue to accelerate in the following years.

The growth in Greece's GDP in recent years has certainly freed up some resources for investment purposes. However, it is clear from the data on disposable domestic income and savings, analyzed in a previous chapter, that there is no significant space for the required investment expenditure to be financed by domestic means. The gap between the demand for resources for investment purposes and the supply of financing reinforces the importance of incoming financial resources for the Greek economy, such as European, NGEU and National Strategic Reference Framework (NSRF) resources, as well as FDI. And indeed, incoming FDI has emerged in recent years as a very important reinforcement factor for domestic investments, having reached unprecedented heights (Figure 13). Significant benefits from FDI also arise at the levels of (a) the partnership with international entrepreneurship and the integration of domestic production with international chains, (b) the transfer of modern know-how and cutting-edge technologies and (c) the practical creation of a climate of trust, which is a prerequisite for growth. For these reasons, a sustained policy of attracting further FDI is useful, particularly in targeted sectors.[30]

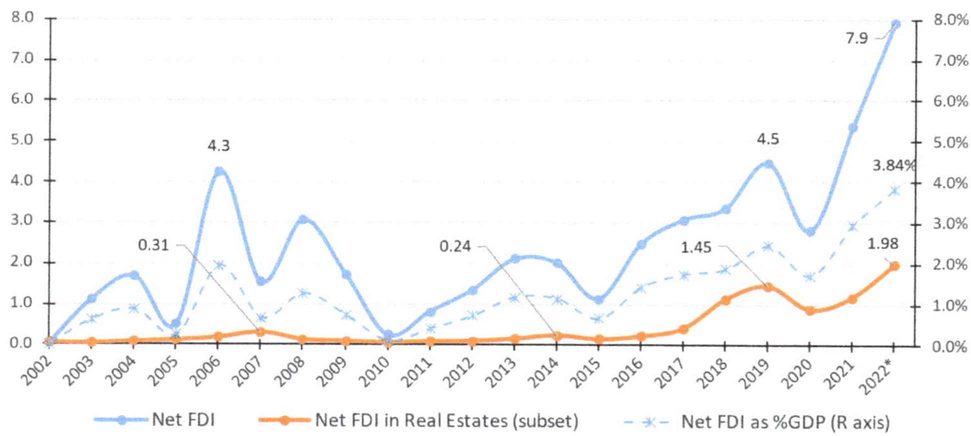

Figure 13. Foreign direct investment (EUR, million, current values). Source: Bank of Greece. *: provisional data.

In any case, despite the big improvement in the Greek economy's investment rate in recent years, capital stock remains at a much lower level than that before the economic crisis, and its restoration will take many more years. The re-accumulation of physical capital is perhaps the most crucial factor for the achievement of sustainable growth. Only through it can potential GDP and labor productivity be increased and therefore sustainable growth in GDP, employment and real wages be achieved. Moreover, the economic growth of an economy by stimulating aggregate supply enhances its competitiveness, unlike what happens by stimulating aggregate demand. It is therefore clearly necessary, on the one hand, to make the best use of the very significant European resources of the NGEU and, on the other hand, to take advantage of the opportunity of the change in climate brought about by these resources, with policies to actively attract further investment and mitigate all the discouraging factors that still exist.

6.2. The Critical Factor of Banking Sector Robustness

One of the main factors that contributed to the negative trend in investment expenditures in the Greek economy is the difficult position of the banking sector, which resulted in a very limited supply of loans to businesses and the subsequent increase in their borrowing costs.

During the crisis years, banking institutions faced significant difficulties in accessing international markets, due to the overall classification of Greece as a high-risk country and market doubts about the capital adequacy of the banks themselves. The capital adequacy of the banks had been affected, as a very large part of their assets (in particular, mainly loans to the private sector and Greek public sector bonds) had an increased degree of risk and therefore reduced financial value. Moreover, Greek citizens' very low disposable income was putting strong pressure on the stock of deposits. To cover this liquidity gap, the banks were forced to resort to increasingly expensive funding sources, including emergency liquidity reinforcement from the Bank of Greece—under the supervision of the European Central Bank (ECB)—through the ELA ("Emergency Liquidity Assistance") mechanism and reduced credit provision to the private sector to the maximum degree. This situation is illustrated in a highly characteristic way in Figure 14.

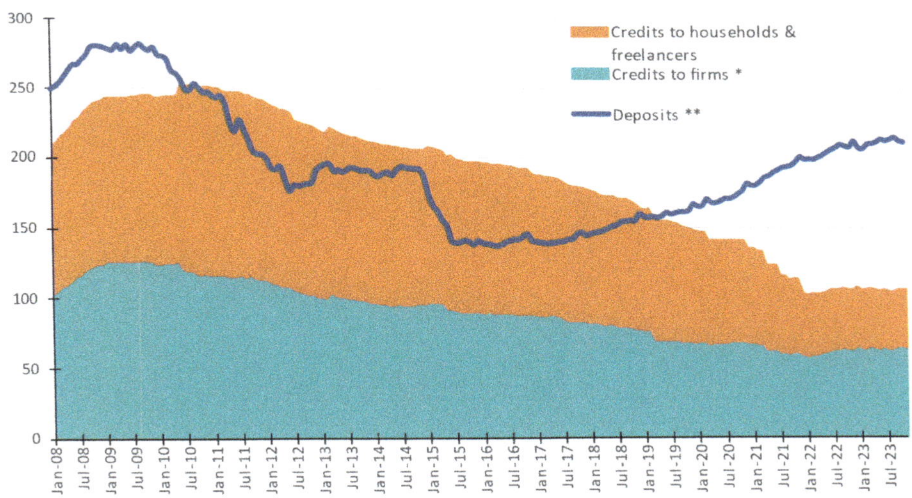

Figure 14. Deposits and credits to the private economy (EUR, billion). * excluding financial and insurance firms. ** excluding the "liabilities related to transferable assets" account. Source: Bank of Greece.

The viability of the banking sector in Greece had become practically impossible. In order to stay alive, it took a total of three rounds of recapitalization,[31] two of which after its bankruptcy,[32] and a cosmogenic restructuring, which has led to 96% of total assets being concentrated in just four large banks today, the so-called "systemic" banks. The worst period of the banking sector started at the end of 2014 (the time of the failed Hellenic Republican presidential election), with the sum of deposits plummeting by EUR 52.7 billion (a 27.5% decrease) over eight months (from December 2014 to July 2015) and balancing at a level below EUR 140 billion only due to the imposition of capital controls and the signing of a third memorandum (Memorandum of Understanding). By the imposition of capital controls, which limited the "bleeding" of deposits, and the latest round of recapitalization, the banking sector was able to "stand on its own two feet", although it continued to be weak. The fundamental problem that remained unsolved was the huge volume of non-performing loans (NPLs) in the banks' portfolios.

As shown in Figure 15, in December 2015, total NPLs were close to EUR 120 billion, whereas their share of total loans was over 48%.[33] Dealing with this problem proved an extremely difficult exercise, as the sale of NPLs can only be carried out at a much lower price than their nominal value, which implies additional capital needs.[34] The much-needed solution seems to have been finally found in the "Hellenic Asset Protection Scheme", with the code name "Hercules"[35]. This scheme contributed to a drastic acceleration in NPL reduction pace during its implementation (from December 2019 to April 2021), resulting in the EC's approval of two more phases of its extension: "Hercules II" (from April 2021 to October 2022) and "Hercules III" (from November 2023 to December 2024), which included some improvements/additions. The results are quite evident in the figures. According to the latest available data, in September 2023, the total NPLs had fallen to EUR 12.1 billion, at one-sixth of their level before the implementation of the first "Hercules" scheme (EUR 77.6 billion, at the end of September 2019), and their share had reached 7.3% (from 41.9% at the end of September 2019).

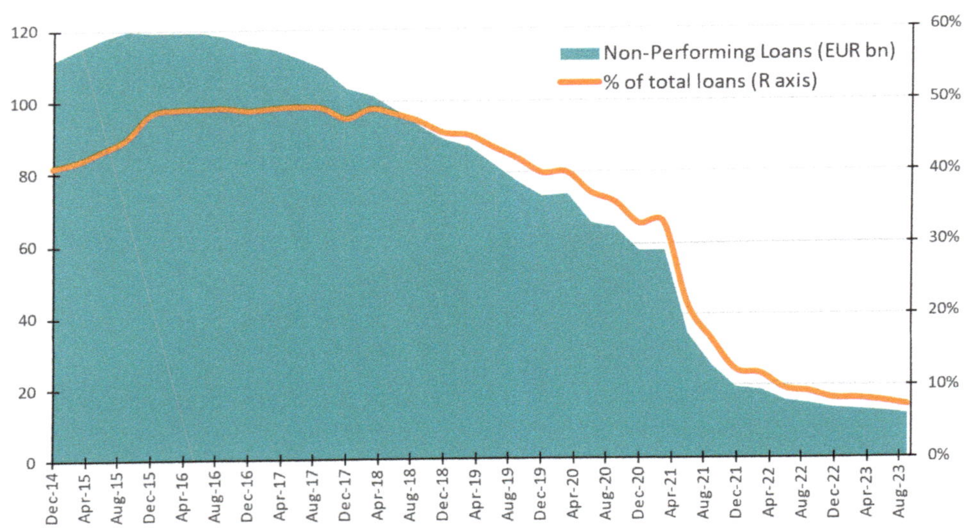

Figure 15. Non-performing loans. Source: Bank of Greece; figures on a consolidated basis, on-balance sheet and before provisions.

The "purge" of the banking system was a necessary objective for one more reason, as it plays a key role under the loan part of the RRF, which includes part of the accompanying financing and supervision. In particular, according to the Greek recovery and resilience plan (RRP) "Greece 2.0", a portion of 20–40% of the budget of each investment project selected in the RRF loan program is financed by domestic or international financial institutions. These authors have argued over time (See: Makantasi and Valentis (2021) and Makantasi and Valentis (2020)) for the significant benefits that would arise if public and European funds directed to support private investments were given through private specialized financial institutions, which would both leverage these funds with additional resources of their own and provide a more efficient mechanism for the management and screening of applications, initially, and the supervision and accountability later on. An important positive element is that these loans will not be guaranteed by the Greek public sector, so the public sector comes to assist the private investment, not to eliminate its risk, whereas the private investor maintains the incentive to make every effort so that the investment pays off and the co-financing banking institution maintains the incentive of strict and integral supervision.

6.3. The Investment Model of the Greek Economy

Apart from the quantitative issue of the necessary investments, analyzed above, there is also the issue of their qualitative structure. Figures 16 and 17 show the diachronic structure of the GFCF according to the type of fixed capital created and the sector making the investment (in accordance with the corresponding previous grouping), respectively.

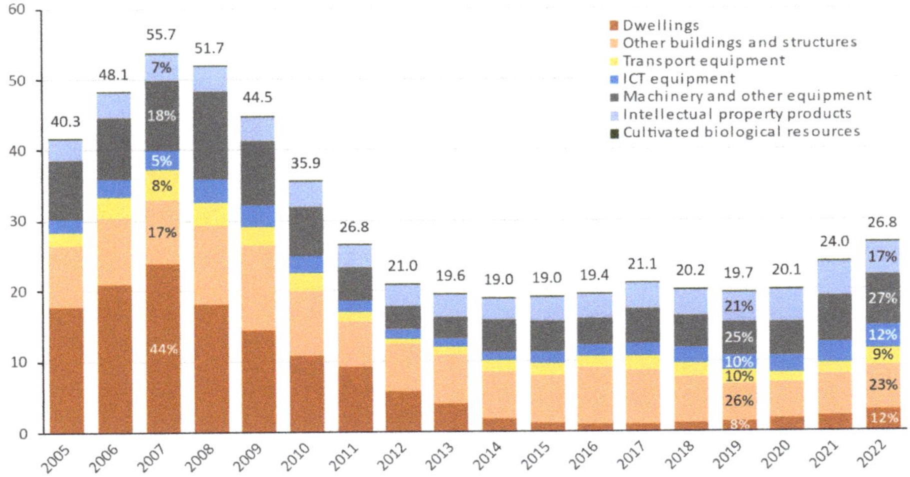

Figure 16. The mixture of fixed capital formation in Greece: by capital type (EUR, billion, constant 2015 prices). Source: Eurostat, diaNEOsis editing.

To a large extent, observation of the investment structure in Greece before the economic crisis points out the specific characteristics of the country's development model at that time. In particular, more than 61% of investment expenditure in 2007 was directed to the construction sector, with a ratio of 5:7 for residential construction and 2:7 for other constructions. On the contrary, net productive investments, such as investment in equipment (ICT, machinery, transport equipment, etc.) and intellectual property products[36], were the minority, with a share of only 38.4%. Constructions that are not residences may have some productive footprint, as their main part is the infrastructure constituting public goods with large positive externalities in production as well, but residence construction does not contribute significantly to the expansion of the productive potential of an economy. As a result, the country's investment model has had a limited efficiency in increasing its potential GDP from the beginning.

It is extremely interesting to see which sectors of the economy made these investments. In perfect accordance with the aforementioned analysis, we note that the real estate management sector accounted for 45% of the total GFCF consistently until 2007. It should be recalled that this particular sector generated only 10.4% of the total GVA in 2007. The second largest contributor to the GFCF was the narrow public sector ("public administration, defense and compulsory social security") with a share of 14%. Out of a total of 14 sector groups, 2 of them alone accounted for almost 60% of total fixed capital investment, as all other sector groups had an individual share of less than 6%. It is indicative that the industry sector, which is by definition a capital-intensive—and thus highly investment-dependent—sector, with a share of total GVA of 11.9%, had a GFCF share of only 4%.

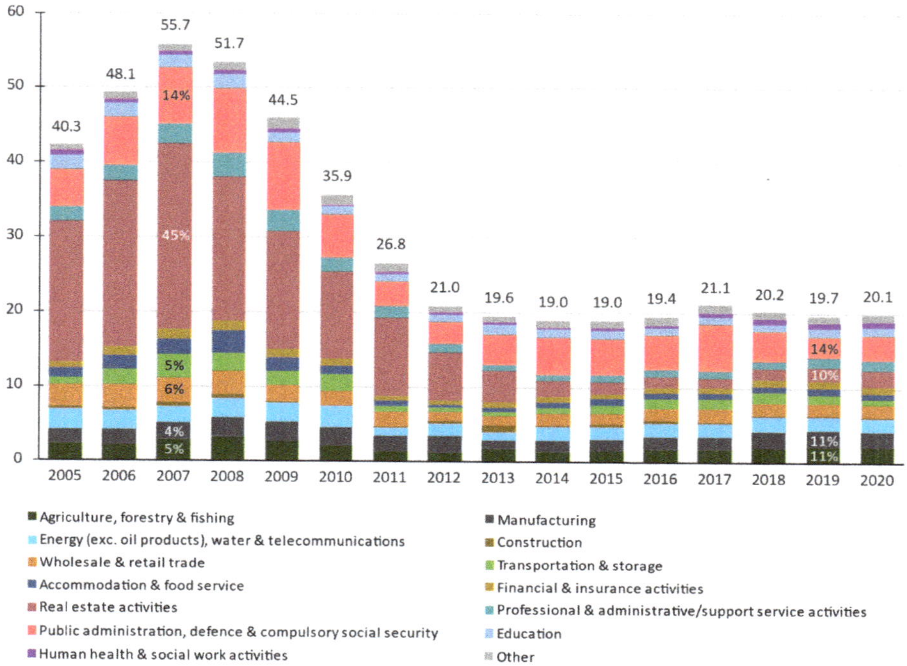

Figure 17. The mixture of fixed capital formation in Greece: by sector (EUR, billion, constant 2015 prices). Source: Eurostat, diaNEOsis editing.

The advent of the economic crisis created an environment of severe income constraints and uncertainty that made the aforementioned—in any way unsustainable—investment behavior impossible to maintain. The inevitable reduction in investment expenditure was not at all symmetrical, but instead focused primarily on investments that were abnormally high. In this way, the economic crisis has contributed to the rationalization of the country's investment model to a certain extent, without it being certain whether this is genuine or out of necessity. More specifically, whereas the total GFCF was reduced in 2019 compared to 2007 by 65% in real terms, the reduction in GFCF dedicated to residential construction in the same period was 93.5% (from EUR 23.9 billion to just EUR 1.5 billion, both in 2015 values). This was the main factor of the reduction in total GFCF, as investments directed at other types of fixed capital had significant, but comparatively smaller, reductions. The subsequent distribution of GFCF in 2019 was clearly more balanced. The expansion of investment opportunities in recent years has reversed the aforementioned trend, with investments towards the residential sector being more than double by 2022 (+102.6% from 2019, in constant values). Two other categories of fixed capital had a higher change in investment than the total GFCF (+35.9%): ICT equipment (+63.1%) and "machinery and other equipment" (+50.5%), resulting in an increase in their shares.

With reference to the subject of investment expenditure, the two dominant sectoral groups accounting for almost 60% of the GFCF in 2007 also had the largest decreases until 2019. The real estate management sector reduced its investment expenditure by 92.5% in real terms (from EUR 25 billion to EUR 1.9 billion, in 2015 values) and the narrow public sector by around two-thirds (from EUR 7.6 billion to EUR 2.7 billion). Almost all of the remaining sector groups also suffered significant decreases in investment expenditure, the largest of which were in construction (−72.3%), accommodation and food services (−69%), and professional and administrative/support services (−62.6%). The exceptions to this rule were the health and social work sector, which had a marginal in absolute terms but significant percentage increase (by EUR 154 million or 27.9%), and the industry sector, which had a marginal increase in investment expenditure of 3.4%. The subsequent distribution of the GFCF in 2019 was also much more balanced at subject level. The sectoral group with the largest investment expenditure is now the narrow public sector, which has experienced a significantly decreasing share in recent years (from 30% in 2017 to 14.1% in 2019) and the vast majority of other sectors, including the real estate management sector, now hold investment shares of 5–10%.

6.4. The Need for a Strategic Focusing of Investments

As noted by these authors (Makantasi and Valentis (2020)), a long-standing problem in the management of European funds in Greece is the pursuit of the greatest possible fragmentation of funds into many small projects or many individual beneficiaries, most probably as a result of the Greek political culture. The result is the almost horizontal funding of all economy sectors, with small funds to each of them, funds not capable of providing significant benefit to any of them. The absence of strategic targeting leads to the non-maximization of overall productive benefit and a loss of opportunities, as equal resources are arbitrarily allocated to all sectors instead of prioritizing sectors with potentially multiplicative benefits or comparative advantages. In this way, European funds turn into a mere tool for boosting demand in a country diachronically characterized as a "demand-driven economy", rather than being used as a lever for growth. This tactic has further negative consequences, such as the failure to achieve critical mass of reinforcement in any sector, the non-exploitation of the significant economies of a scale inherent in the management of European resources, the excessive increase in administrative and bureaucratic costs, and the creation of ideal conditions for the incubation of opacity and corruption.

So, what are some of the characteristics of the optimal targeting strategy in the case of Greece?

6.4.1. Priority to Investments in Labor-Intensive Sectors

As described in detail in a previous section, the Greek economic crisis brought about a huge increase in unemployment in its first years. The unemployment rate may have been slowly de-escalating in recent years, but by the end of 2023, it was still at a much higher level than the pre-crisis one (9.2% in December 2023, compared to an annual percentage of 7.8% in 2008), and the level of the pre-crisis unemployment rate cannot be described as low. In macroeconomic terms, the already high pre-crisis unemployment level implies nothing else but a great waste of resources. In terms of resources, unemployment is a twofold problem: the labor force who—against their will—are not put to good use, do not participate in the production process and therefore do not produce any products (reduction in aggregate supply), on the one hand, and create the need for the economy to incur inelastic consumption expenditure to maintain them (decrease in choices in the allocation of product use), on the other hand.

Particularly interesting conclusions can also be drawn from analysis at the level of relative abundance of resources. If we combine the data on the course of the labor force with the data on the course of the stock of physical capital during the economic crisis, as described in this section, a clear shift in the Greek economy (in relation to the rest of the world) emerges, in relative abundance terms, between physical capital and labor. In particular, by using EC estimates of the total amount of physical capital installed in Greece,[37] we come across the fact that during the 2009–2022 period, there was an actual reduction of almost 12.1% in capital stock. In the same period, once again based on EC measurements, the total labor force in Greece had a marginal growth of 0.72%. Therefore, the ratio of available physical capital to available labor decreased during the economic crisis (by 12.7%, according to EC estimates), and the Greek economy is thus characterized today by more relative abundance of labor, compared to the one before the crisis. This shift in the Greek economy implies a corresponding shift in terms of comparative advantage (in relation to the rest of the world) towards labor-intensive sectors.[38] As a result, the relatively higher growth of labor-intensive sectors compared to capital-intensive sectors at this stage would maximize the overall competitiveness and the benefits of international trade.

A focus of investments on labor-intensive sectors has the potential to bring about a double benefit. On the one hand, it is in line with the shift in comparative advantages of the Greek economy and therefore has a benefit in terms of competitiveness. On the other hand, any investment in a labor-intensive sector has by definition a greater impact on the employment level against an equivalent investment in a capital-intensive sector. Thus, a focus of investments on labor-intensive sectors implies significant benefits in terms of employment as well and can help reduce unemployment more rapidly.

Given the aforementioned information, apart from the obvious necessary policy actions that should be adopted to stimulate employment, considerable scope for adapting an investment policy arises, giving priority and stronger incentives to investments in existing and new business activities that are relatively more labor-based. In this way, each unit of additional physical capital will create more job positions, more quickly decreasing the stock of untapped resources called unemployment. This policy has advantages over the opposite strategy (that is, a policy of focusing investment on capital-intensive sectors) or a strategy of non-focusing of private investments at all, as it entails significant benefits at a social level, but also at macroeconomic and competitiveness levels.

6.4.2. Priority to Investments That Enhance the Competitiveness and Openness of the Economy

The need to improve the competitiveness of the Greek economy and the benefits resulting from such a process have been explained in detail in the previous chapter. At this point, we will try to analyze some fields where a strategically targeted investment policy can contribute to achieving this goal.

One of the main aggravating factors on the competitiveness of the Greek economy is the relatively small average size of its businesses, as a result of the strong presence of self-employment and micro-entrepreneurship, which dominate the structure of the Greek productive system. Particularly indicative of the structure of the Greek economy are the EC data in its latest annual report on small and medium enterprises (SMEs) in the EU[39], with estimates for 2022. From these data, listed in Table 1, it becomes obvious that SMEs constitute almost the totality of Greek businesses in the non-financial business sector (NFBS)[40]. However, while they employ 83.5% of the productive labor force, they produce only 57% of the total GVA (always, with respect to the NFBS). On the contrary, large businesses, although they occupy a near-zero percentage in terms of their number, employ about 16.5% of employed persons and produce 43% of the total GVA in Greece. This implies, on the one hand, the difference in efficiency in value-added production per employee between SMEs and large businesses and, on the other hand, the margin of macroeconomic efficiency benefit that exists from a relative expansion of the share of large businesses, or else an increase in the average production scale, at least up to the point observed in the EU as a whole.

The relatively small average size of Greek businesses creates multiple problems. Firstly, it does not allow for businesses to develop economies of scale, which would reduce average production costs and make them more competitive. In addition, the small size of businesses is associated with low labor productivity, inefficient management, difficulty in adopting new technologies, inability to carry out R&D activities[41], increased likelihood of tax evasion and an underground economy, difficulties in financing and an inability to efficiently promote its products. The resulting competitiveness deficit of micro-enterprises excludes them from international markets and limits them to the provision of services for domestic consumption.

Table 1. The structure of Greek entrepreneurship.

	Businesses			Persons Employed			Value Added		
	Greece		EU-27	Greece		EU-27	Greece		EU-27
	#	Share	Share	#	Share	Share	EUR Billion	Share	Share
SMEs (0–249 persons employed)	731,829	99.9%	99.8%	2,180,534	83.5%	64.4%	34.8	57.0%	51.8%
Large businesses (250+ persons employed)	471	0.1%	0.2%	429,679	16.5%	35.6%	26.2	43.0%	48.2%

Note: Figures limited to the non-financial business sector. Estimations for 2022, produced by JRC, based on 2008–2020 figures from national and Eurostat databases. Source: European Commission, 2023 SME Country Fact Sheet for Greece and EU-27.

What keeps Greek businesses small? As the report of the so-called "Pissarides Committee" (Pissarides et al. (2020)) characteristically concludes, "The small size of Greek businesses is a consequence of rigidities in the economy that create incentives for businesses to remain small and make their development difficult". To address this phenomenon, the report suggests creating incentives for the encouragement of mergers and other partnerships. In this context, the Greek government has moved to the enactment of significant tax incentives for SME mergers, transformations and partnerships (Law 4935/2022), whereas the "business scale up through partnerships, acquisitions and mergers" has been identified as one of the five pillars of the loan component in "Greece 2.0". These initiatives are particularly encouraging; however, there is still room for further incentives in this direction, such as special provisions in the Development Law for investment projects aimed at the significant maximization of the existing business activities.

Another aggravating factor for the competitiveness of Greek businesses is the higher taxation compared to the rest of the world—and especially the EU—with regard to indirect taxes that burden the cost of their inflows, and the higher non-wage labor costs. Greek businesses are challenged to compete in the international market with businesses that do not have to face a VAT of 24%[42], the particularly high excise duties on energy burdening the cost of raw materials of every business activity, and the particularly high non-wage costs of Greece. As a result, they are required to make an even bigger effort and even smaller profit margins are required in order for them to be competitive. Unfortunately, the need to generate increased public revenues, combined with the fact that the collection of indirect taxation has significantly increased efficiency in comparison with other forms of taxation, does not allow for a significant reduction in VAT and excise duties. The situation is similar for social security contributions, for which, however, the state's efforts in recent years to limit them as much as possible should be acknowledged. A similar effort should also be made on the indirect taxation front, to a possible degree, since the reduction in taxation affecting productive activities should be a priority over the reduction in taxation not affecting them. With particular reference to excise duties on energy goods, it should be stressed that, apart from the impact on business costs, these taxes also create a negative chain effect, as energy is an influx in all links in a value chain.

Given the aforementioned difficult position of Greek export companies,[43] it is expected that investments in sectors producing goods and services not directed to the domestic market are discouraged. Therefore, in addition to the effort to reduce the aforementioned tax and insurance burdens, there is a need to implement, as a counterweight, special care of privileged treatment for investment projects creating or reinforcing extroverted activities. In addition to this, the political authorities must be aware of the pressure on businesses managing to be exporters and, as a counterweight, there must be a systematic effort to facilitate them at every possible level (e.g., priority and simplification in terms of bureaucracy, more favorable financing, cash facilities for paying taxes/contributions, tax clearance).

In conclusion, one of the major problems of the Greek economic crisis was the deep and lasting shrinkage in investment expenditure. This problem arose as a consequence of the crisis, due to a decrease in domestic income and the emergence of increased risk factors, but at the same time was the cause of its further prolongation. The pandemic crisis that started in 2020 aggravated the discouraging factors, but it was also the reason for the creation of a giant European investment program, which aimed not only to restart the European economy after the pandemic, but also to push it on a new course of faster and more sustainable growth in the coming decades. The NGEU resources, together with the rest of the European resources and the mobilized private resources, have already shown a visible impact on Greek investments and represent a unique opportunity to redirect the Greek economy towards a better development model. Neither the optimal use of these resources—which remains an issue—nor the final result they will have is self-evident. Further optimization of their allocation is required towards productive and appropriately targeted investments, in order to ensure not only that the investment gap is fully covered, but also that the Greek economy moves forward on a course of long-term sustainable development.

7. Challenges and Risk Factors for the Future

The COVID-19 pandemic found the global economy of early 2020 in a state of relative stability. As the SARS CoV-2 virus followed its predestined evolutionary course, by less and less pathogenic strains, the disease became significantly milder and its direct impact on economic activity was nullified. The global economy after the pandemic, however, was nothing like it was before the pandemic. A series of problems and disruptions, which arose as a result of the pandemic and the necessary restrictive measures imposed, continued to have a tangible impact on economies for quite a long time. Some of the main problems were the observed shortages and delays in critical raw materials and necessary inflows (e.g., microchips), the disruption of international freight routes and subsequent depletion of global transport capacity, and the disruption in the energy market.

The disruption suffered by the energy market from the pandemic shock had perhaps the most significant impact on the Greek economy, as well as the global economy. The commodity we call "energy" is not a mere consumer good, but it is, on the contrary, a practically irreplaceable intermediate good used in the production of all other goods. The major changes in global energy demand due to the pandemic (a sharp and unexpected reduction in 2020 and a milder increase in 2021–2022) were not reflected by supply changes of a corresponding rate, initially resulting in a significant drop in the price of all energy goods in 2020[44], followed by a much larger increase, already before the outbreak of the war in Ukraine (February 2022), which intensified the situation even more. As a result, there were very high prices for all energy commodities, which, to a significant degree, still exist. Indicatively, the average monthly price of crude oil in Brent exchange reached USD 117.69/Bbl in June 2022, 103.5% above the average level in the five years prior to the pandemic (USD 57.83/Bbl), whereas in the natural gas (NG) market in Europe, things were even worse, with the average monthly price in the Dutch TTF Spot reaching EUR 235.22/MWh in August 2022, 13.6 times the pre-pandemic average level (EUR 17.25/MWh).

The impact of such a high energy cost on every economy is easy to understand. In a relevant study by diaNEOsis, a theoretical estimate is made of the overall impact on the Greek economy of a reverse and much smaller change: a 10% reduction in the final price of electricity and NG.[45] According to the results, the overall impact on GDP would be an increase of EUR 941 million (a percentage impact of +0.5%) and the overall impact on employment would be 21,500 additional jobs. Unfortunately, the change in the actual prices of NG and electricity is not only completely far off from the aforementioned theoretical hypothesis but is opposite in direction and many times more pronounced in terms of magnitude. We cannot use the quantitative findings of this exercise to proportionally extrapolate quantitative estimates of the effects of the energy crisis on GDP and employment, but we can consider the extent of these effects.

Apart from the energy crisis and the rest of the disruptions caused directly or indirectly by the pandemic, Greece has recently been close to or even within the "epicenters" of several other hotspots of risk and uncertainty. First of all, the proximity of Greece to the geopolitical space of the Russo-Ukrainian war is clear, with whatever this implies in terms of geopolitical risk, defense needs and refugee influxes. Greece, however, faces similar problems regardless of the war in Ukraine. In the summer of 2020, a particularly serious crisis with Turkey was triggered and an independent threat of war is still being maintained by Turkey (an active "casus belli" and, at times, aggressive actions), thus forcing the Greek state to undertake significant rearmament expenditures, after a long period of underfunding of defense needs due to the economic constraints. Also, since the beginning of the last decade, there has been a steady flow of migrants and refugees from the eastern and southern borders of the country, which at times has had significant spikes (both spontaneous and artificial[46]), creating significant social and economic problems in the country. Greece is also in close proximity to the war between Hamas and Israel that started in October 2023, which obviously creates similar pressures to the war in Ukraine. Moreover, however, as the country's freight transit role and much of its international maritime trade is catalytically dependent on the Suez Canal, further strain arises from Houthi attacks on the Bab al-Mandab Strait, which drastically restrict the flow of goods from the Red Sea and Suez. Consequently, the Greek economy is in a challenging environment with a high degree of regional uncertainties, which undoubtedly affect it significantly.

7.1. The Global Inflation Wave

One of the main effects of the energy crisis, that the world has experienced and continues to experience to a smaller degree, has been cost inflation, as the increased energy cost is injected into all links of every value chain. The energy crisis, however, was not the only factor exacerbating production costs, but instead came to reinforce already existing inflationary factors, most of which also had their origins in the pandemic and the problems it caused to the global supply chain and thus on the global aggregate supply side. At the same time, the recovery of global economic activity after the pandemic was mainly driven on the demand side, as, due to the restrictive measures, households had accumulated both a stock of—obligatory—savings and a stock of deferred consumption. The common factor of all these was the highly excessive aggregate demand internationally, which led to strong upward trends in price levels.

In addition to the aforementioned information, mainly due to the climate, but also reinforced by disruptions in the supply chain of agricultural activity, significant upward trends in international prices of cereals (including wheat) and oil seeds were observed in 2020 and 2021. These trends were further enhanced by the Russo-Ukrainian war. On the one hand, both warring sides are major global producers and exporters of these particular agricultural products. On the other hand, the war has also placed considerable burden on agricultural production in the rest of the world through the cost of energy and fertilizers.[47] As cereals are a major inflow in the stock-breeding sector as well (animal feed), it is clear that their very high costs were eventually passed on to the whole range of foodstuffs.

The combination of all these factors created an exogenous inflationary wave that hit all the world's economies to varying degrees. This wave found the Greek economy in a multiannual situation of practically constant prices. As illustrated in Figure 18, the inflation in Greece remained below 1.1% after 2012, by any calculation method. In fact, in the 2013–2016 period (2013–2015, based on the harmonized index of consumer prices—HICP), it was negative.[48] The cumulative price change between 2012 and 2019 was −1.3% according to the national consumer price index (CPI) and almost zero according to the HICP, meaning that the average price level in Greece in 2019 was marginally lower than the 2011 level. The pandemic and the necessary containment measures also led the Greek economy to deflation again in 2020, with the rate of reduction in price level being 1.25% (or 1.3% according to the HICP). In mid-2021, as economic activity restarted after the lockdowns, the price level returned to marginally positive change rates. Then, however, mainly due to the skyrocketing in international energy prices and in combination with all the aforementioned factors, there was a skyrocketing in inflation, which reached 12.1% in September 2022 (similarly by HICP), having, since January of that year, already exceeded any historical level the Greek economy had shown after its accession into the eurozone.

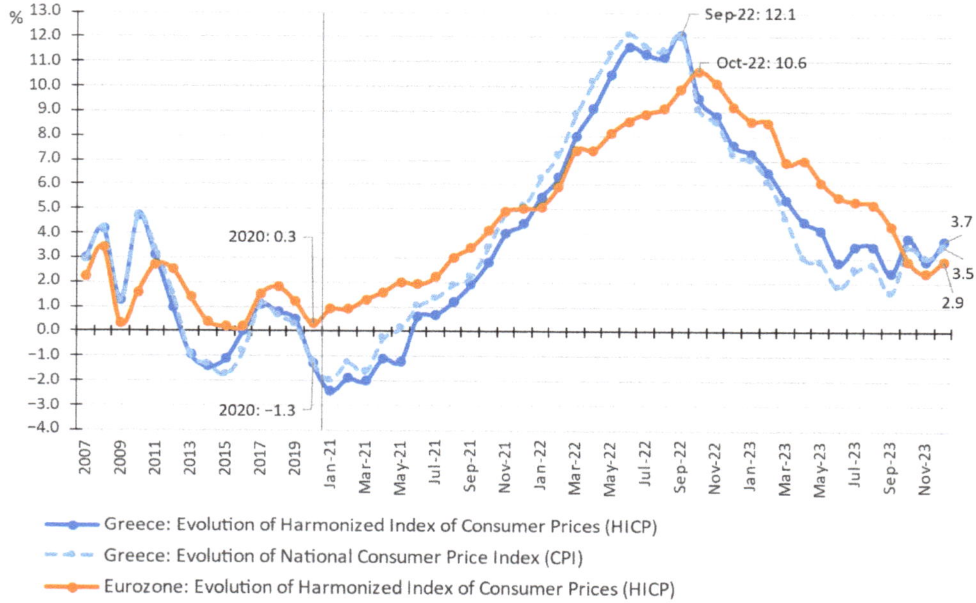

Figure 18. Inflation in Greece vs eurozone. Source: Eurostat and ELSTAT.

For the same period (after 2012), the average inflation rate in the eurozone has remained consistently higher than that in Greece,[49] but also consistently below the ECB's stated target of an average long-term rate of 2%. Indeed, particularly during the 2014–2016 period, the eurozone's inflation was only marginally positive, a phenomenon not due to the reduced economic activity of that period, but rather to the recession of the immediately preceding period. In general, there was a time lag in the reaction of inflation in the eurozone to changes in the real economy or in the ECB's expansionary policy, mainly attributed to the strong persistence of expectations for price change at very low levels, combined with other factors.[50] The pandemic led to a very low inflation rate of only 0.3% for the eurozone as a whole in 2020. The resurgence in demand in early 2021 combined with the lagging supply led to an unusually rapid rise in inflation to 2% by mid-2021, whereas the energy market crisis together with the other factors—which we have described—led to its spike later on. The peak recorded was at 10.6% in October 2022, having already surpassed all previous historical high levels since its creation a year earlier (Oct 2021).

What is the impact on the Greek economy of the soaring inflation in Greece and the eurozone?

The direct answer to this question is "it depends". Mild inflation in Greece, in the range of 2–3%, would be beneficial to the Greek economy, especially after a long period of deflation, provided that it is not higher than the current average inflation in the euro.[51] The reasons mainly have to do with the flexibilization of the real wage so that it better reflects the changes in labor productivity, as the nominal wage shows significant stickiness. An additional benefit for the case of Greece is that the average inflation of the eurozone countries constitutes the overtime loss in real value of the common currency and therefore implies a reduction in the real value of Greek public debt.

However, problems begin at higher inflation levels, which go beyond the range we call "mild". The prolonged occurrence of inflation rates significantly above mild creates a feedback inflationary dynamic that is extremely difficult to stop, mainly because of its integration in the expectations of economic agents. When the vicious cycle of inflationary expectations acts in an economy, it both multiplies any preexisting inflationary trend, creating an unstable system of accelerating inflation, and makes it extremely difficult to counteract the phenomenon. Blocking this vicious cycle, or at least slowing it down, requires a systematic effort over a long period of time combined with a significant level of credibility from the monetary authority, as expectations are always reshaped with a time lag.

Perhaps the most important risk from the international inflationary wave for the Greek economy arises from the pressure on the ECB to pursue a drastically restrictive monetary policy. In mid-2022, as the inflation rate in the eurozone had been well above the target level of 2% for almost a year, and even on an upward trend, the ECB was forced to suspend both active quantitative easing programs (the asset purchase program (APP), which had been active since late 2014 (European Central Bank (n.d.a)), and the pandemic emergency purchase program (PEPP), which was urgently set up to stimulate the eurozone economy during the pandemic (European Central Bank (n.d.b))) and embark on a process of successive and significant increases in key interest rates (Figure 19, European Central Bank (n.d.c))—from virtually zero to the highest levels recorded after 2001. Both these moves were not good news for the Greek economy. On the one hand, Greek government bonds never had time to be included in the APP (especially in the public sector purchase program—PSPP),[52] whereas the emergency PEPP, in which Greece was included by exception,[53] had a very limited duration. On the other hand, a significantly restrictive monetary policy inevitably limits the investment pace and the development speed of all eurozone economies, whereas the Greek economy maintains the greatest (among the euro economies) need for investment and rapid development. Moreover, the increase in the key interest rate of the euro creates significant upward trends in government bond yield rates, which again will asymmetrically affect Greece more, the country maintaining the highest debt in terms of GDP. In this way, the scope for a development-oriented fiscal policy is limited, whereas the monetary policy is—necessarily—recessionary.

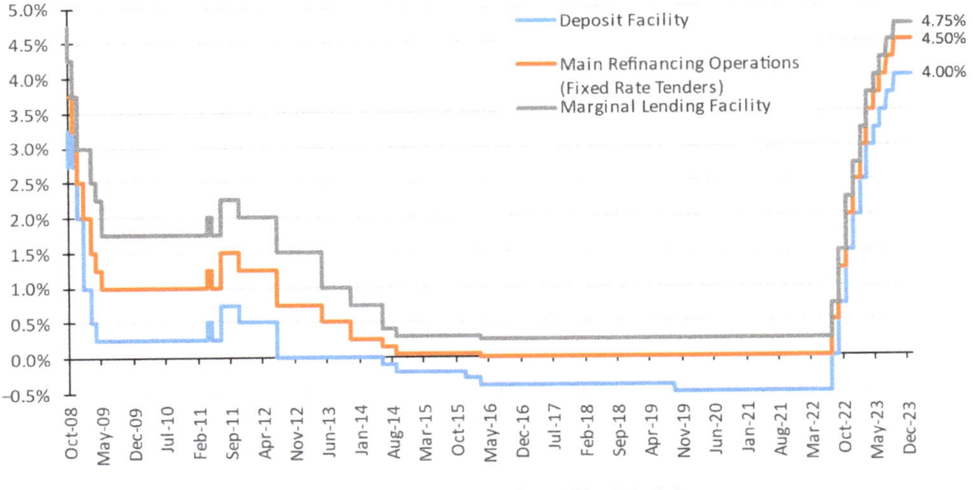

Figure 19. Key ECB interest rates. Source: European Central Bank (n.d.c).

In this context, a major opportunity arising from the skyrocketing in global inflation is also pointed out: the possibility of a rapid improvement in the competitiveness of the Greek economy.[54] The largely imported inflation could be seen as a kind of currency devaluation, as the cost of imported goods, both final and intermediate, suddenly increased. A currency devaluation brings about an immediate improvement in the competitiveness of domestic businesses, through an immediate deterioration in terms of trade, at the cost of a reduction in the real value of domestic incomes and monetary wealth (in domestic currency). As the global inflationary wave raises the prices of all imported goods, it implies about half of the effects of currency devaluation: a reduction in the real value of incomes and monetary wealth, and a potential deterioration in trade terms. In other words, the Greek economy is already paying the costs of a currency devaluation, but in order to collect the benefits, the potential deterioration in trade terms would have to become actual. For this to happen, the increase in the cost of imported goods needs not to be balanced by a corresponding increase in the cost of exported goods. Or, respectively, the domestic inflation needs to remain at lower levels than the international inflation and especially the inflation of the main trading partners of Greece, that is the EU countries. In order to pursue this objective, given the concession of the monetary policy to the ECB, only instruments of fiscal policy, labor market policy and policy to monitor and enforce the proper functioning of markets and competition can be used. There is therefore significant feasibility for using all these instruments in a way that will limit the vicious feedback cycle of all price increases as far as possible.

The main criticism against the proposed deflationary policy is that it does not allow for the full protection of the citizens' real incomes from international inflation. However, "in reality, there is no way and no possibility of fully protecting the citizens of a small open economy from (imported) global inflation" (translated by Gatsios and Ioannou 2022). All efforts to safeguard real income inevitably reinforce the vicious inflationary cycle, with the end result being low or zero efficiency in terms of real income and at the same time generating high costs to the productive economy. Therefore, a major risk is also pointed out: not only of missing the opportunity of a rapid improvement in the competitiveness of the Greek economy, but also of resulting in the further deterioration of its competitiveness. This is not difficult, as the rapid increase in price level creates plausible political incentives for expansionary fiscal policy and the reinforcement of nominal minimum wages. On the one hand, an expansionary fiscal policy is by definition inflationary, as it stimulates the aggregate demand. However, between fiscal expansion through more government expenditure (subsidies to combat price increases) and fiscal expansion through less indirect tax revenue, it is clear that the latter is preferable, as it partially counterbalances cost inflation. On the other hand, reckless increases in nominal wages, whether they are the product of negotiations among social partners or are defined ad hoc by law, pose twice the risk. If they are not covered by a corresponding change in nominal labor productivity, then, apart from reinforcing the vicious cycle of price increases, they will cause a direct reduction in the competitiveness of Greek businesses and, additionally, they could make a part of labor unprofitable. This is the reason why it is essential that any intervention in the labor market is carried out following a thorough study that accurately calculates the actual situation of labor productivity and the potential impact of this intervention.

7.2. The Excessive Level of Public Debt

In recent years, the issue of Greece's large public debt has become a secondary matter. The debt remains very high (in both absolute and GDP-relative terms), but its very high weighted average maturity, combined with the very favorable interest rate conditions of the debt held by the official sector (states and international organizations) and the ECB's previously loose monetary policy, made it easily manageable. Debt servicing costs remain quite low, despite the very large fiscal expansion required in 2020 and 2021, due to exogenous needs arising from the pandemic and Turkey's aggression. At the same time, credit ratings for the Greek state are becoming better and better and, in fact, since 2023, an investment grade has been issued by three of the four major rating agencies.[55] Nevertheless, the very high level of public debt is, in itself, an inactive but extremely important risk factor, which, under certain circumstances, can be triggered and create major problems for the Greek economy.

More specifically, as shown in Figures 20 and 21, Greece after 2015 and until 2019 managed to achieve not only sufficient primary fiscal surpluses and a breakeven fiscal balance (FB), as it was obliged to do, but also notable fiscal surpluses. During the same period, however, public debt did not decrease, as would be expected with current fiscal surpluses, but marginally increased, as the Greek state accumulated a generous level of cash reserves (reaching EUR 32 billion at the end of 2019) (Hellenic Republic and PDMA (Public Debt Management Agency) (2019)). The need that arose in 2020 for significant, urgent government expenditure turned the 2019 primary fiscal surplus of EUR 7.1 billion (3.9% of GDP) into a primary fiscal deficit of EUR 11.1 billion (6.7% of GDP), a change of around EUR 18.2 billion (10.6 pp of GDP). The result of all these changes was an increase in nominal debt by EUR 10.4 billion and the skyrocketing in the debt-to-GDP ratio from 180.6% to 207% of GDP, also due to the major recession in 2020 (9.3%, in real terms). The situation in nominal terms deteriorated further, reaching EUR 356.6 billion by the end of 2022, a level that exceeded the previous historical high level of EUR 356.2 billion in 2011, while the EC estimates that public debt continued to increase in nominal terms in 2023 as well. However, the significant real GDP growth in recent years, combined with strong inflation, resulted in GDP-relative debt drastically decreasing in the 2021–2022 period (to 172.6% of GDP at the end of 2022, reduced by 34.4 pp), which is estimated to have continued in 2023 as well (a reduction by 11.7 pp to 160.9% of GDP). The restoration of the fiscal constraints of the revised Stability and Growth Pact from 2024 is a sufficient guarantee that further de-escalation of Greek public debt in nominal terms will follow, whereas together with the continuation of the course of real growth in the Greek economy and the maintenance of relatively high inflation rates, a further significant reduction in debt is expected in GDP-relative terms as well.

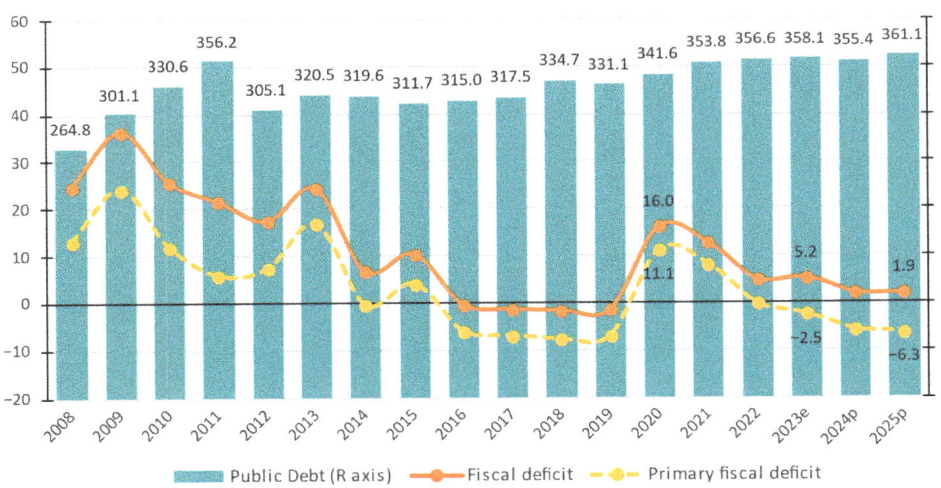

Figure 20. Public debt in current values (EUR, billion). e = estimation; p = forecast. Source: Eurostat and the European Commission (AMECO).

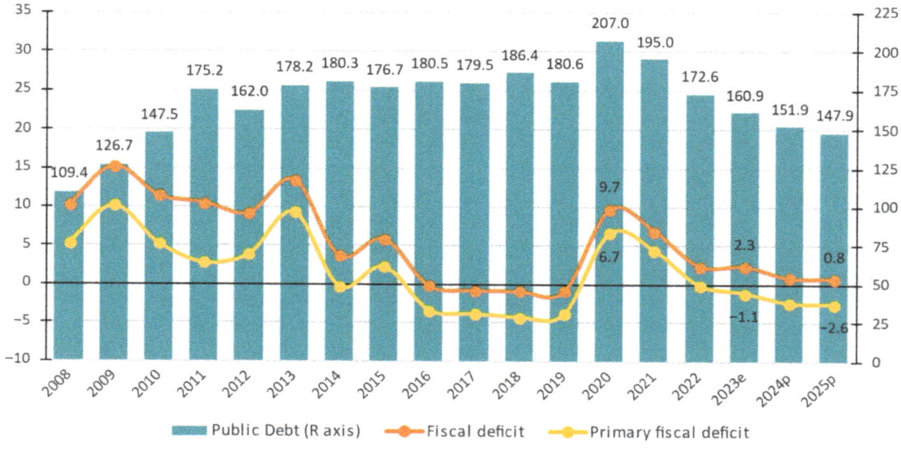

Figure 21. Public debt in GDP terms (%GDP). e = estimation; p = forecast. Source: Eurostat and the European Commission (AMECO).

The current state of Greek debt, despite its large size, seems to be quite good. According to official data, the weighted average maturity currently remains at a very high level of 20 years (Hellenic Republic and PDMA (Public Debt Management Agency) (2023)); the average effective interest rate (the interest paid-to-debt ratio) in 2022 was around 1.45%, whereas it is estimated to have risen to 2.16% in 2023;[56] debt servicing costs were 2.5% of GDP in 2022, whereas in 2023, they reached 3.5% of GDP; 71% of the total debt is held by official sector creditors; and the cash reserves held by the Greek government at the end of 2023 amounted to EUR 30 billion, a figure that would cover the gross refinancing needs of the Hellenic Republic for around 3 years. Because of all these factors, international markets are demonstrating practical confidence in the Greek public sector's credit, documented by the yield rates offered at the issuance of new Greek bonds as well as the yields of Greek government bonds in the secondary market, especially compared to the yield rates of the strongest EU economy (Greece–Germany yield spread, Figure 22).

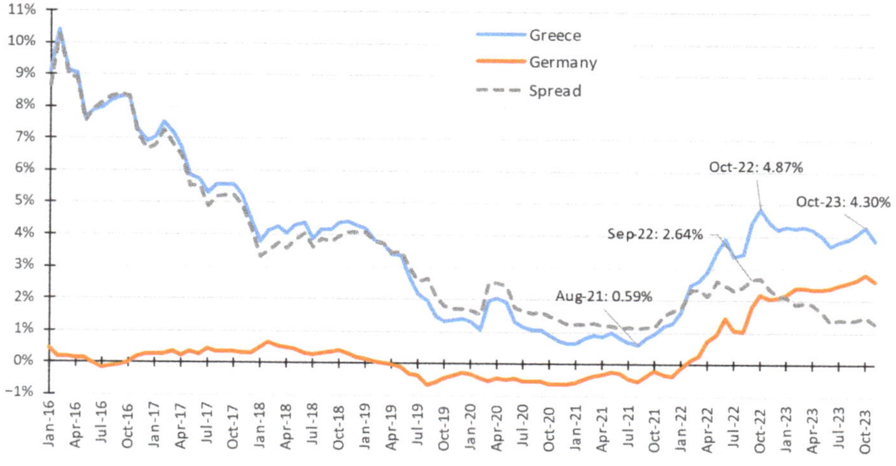

Figure 22. Secondary market: 10y gov. bond yields of Greece vs. Germany. Source: Federal Reserve Bank of St. Louis.

The secondary market may not directly affect the cost of Greek public sector borrowing, but it is a very good indication of the valuation of previously issued bonds of a certain maturity by international markets in a continuous, indeed, time. Greek bond yields, therefore, showed a significant downward trend in the 2016–2017 period, from the very high levels of early 2016 to a level between 4% and 4.5%. At this lower level, which continued to be quite high, they fluctuated steadily from early 2018 to mid-2019, and thereafter showed a new downward trend until the onset of the pandemic. The pandemic initially halted the decrease in Greek bond yield rates, in a transient market reaction specifically to Greece's idiosyncratic risk (a reaction that fully captures the changes in the spread). But the downward trend resumed soon enough, certainly due to the integration of Greek bonds in the ECB's emergency PEPP program. As a result, in August 2021, a historical low level of 0.533% was reached (August 5) with the average monthly yield at 0.59%. Subsequently, however, for about a year (until October 2022), there was a significant upward trend in Greek yields, which reflected both the general upward trend in yields in all eurozone countries and a more specific increase in the risk premium of the Greek state (a positive trend in the spread as well). This behavior can be explained by the increasing likelihood of discount by markets of the reversal in the ECB's hitherto highly expansionary monetary policy. Since then, Greek yields have shown relative stability, around the 4.1% level, with the spread having a significantly decreasing trend.

The behavior of the yield spread between Greek and German government bonds is of particular interest. In every critical circumstance in recent years (the outbreak of the pandemic, the expectation of a change in monetary policy and the outbreak of the war in Ukraine), it seems that markets initially react more quickly and more sharply to Greek public sector securities, whereas subsequently they probably turn out to have overreacted and proceed to a counterbalancing correction. The only exception to this rule, at least on the basis of the data so far, is the crisis in the Middle East, following the Hamas attack on southern Israel in October 2023. In times of crisis, this behavior is not unprecedented for markets, as investors are agitated and try to determine the extent of their exposure, usually taking short positions on the issuers they regard as the weakest links. This highlights how precarious the position of the Greek state becomes because of the amount of public debt, the credit rating it receives, and the idiosyncratic risk that the markets themselves assign to it.

So, despite the fact that the most important part of the decrease in Greek yields in recent years—according to the price signals given by international markets—is due to the drastic reduction in the idiosyncratic risk of the Greek state vis-à-vis the German state, with a secondary part being due to the ECB's highly expansionary monetary policy, the same markets show greater sensitivity/concern towards Greek securities in times of general turmoil. For the time being, the Greek state is quite protected from extreme volatility in the yield rates that markets demand to hold its debt, given that the vast majority of it is held by the official sector and has a fixed rate, whereas market yields only affect new issues. However, the relative participation of the official sector will decline over time, as the public debt of Greece will be refinanced with new issues from markets. And, according to the current amortization schedule, the upcoming 2026–2033 period has particularly demanding refinancing needs. This implies that (a) the Greek government will need to issue more new bonds in a period of relatively high yields; (b) as a result, the average cost of servicing the debt will increase quite rapidly; (c) at the same time, the pace at which public debt is transferred to private sector creditors will have accelerated. Thus, the characteristics of Greek debt that currently make it sound, despite its size, may be quite different at the end of this period and the sensitivity of its sustainability to the faith of markets will be significantly higher. If for some reason, then, a significant increase in Greece's idiosyncratic risk or in the systematic risk of the eurozone/EU occurs, it is not impossible that an unintended overreaction of markets (like those observed in recent years) or a voluntary mistrust by them could lead to a feedback loop of higher and higher risk premia and lower and lower credit, with the inevitable result of a new debt crisis.[57]

Therefore, the size of Greek debt, as long as it remains particularly high in relation to Greece's economic capacity (i.e., in GDP terms), in itself constitutes a risk factor for the Greek economy, threatening it as a "sword of Damocles", already limiting its developmental prospects in the present. Seeking to neutralize this threat as soon as possible is therefore a one-way street. Over time, there have been three alternative methods for decreasing public debt: firstly, through a policy of fiscal austerity for the creation of a budget surplus; secondly, through debt restructuring or partial debt cancellation; and thirdly, through a "mild adjustment", i.e., a gradual decrease in the importance of debt due to economic growth (a reduction in the debt-to-GDP ratio) and inflation (a reduction in the real value of debt)[58]. The only realistic option is the third. On the one hand, after ten years (2010–2019) of harsh fiscal austerity, there is no margin for further reduction in public expenditure and the increase in taxes will have a negative impact on the restart of the economy. On the other hand, the current creditors of the Greek state are mainly European institutions and eurozone member states, which would not consent, under any circumstances—and especially not unanimously—to the restructuring or cancellation of the Greek debt.[59] The "mild adjustment" option essentially requires the Greek economy to "move forward" rapidly, achieving significant and sustainable growth rates in the following years. As discussed in a relevant policy paper by diaNEOsis (Christodoulakis et al. (2020)), this implies the adoption of front-loaded policies for the rapid growth in domestic income that will prevent the debt-to-GDP ratio from increasing and keep it at serviceable levels. It remains to convince both European institutions and international markets of the adequacy of the "mild adjustment" in addressing the debt problem, which makes the need to achieve immediate and strong rates of economic growth even more urgent.

8. Conclusions

Despite the significant rates of investment and growth in the Greek economy since the pandemic crisis, there is still a long way to go for Greece to enter sustainable economic, social and political development orbit. And, as Sharma Ruchir aptly points out in his book *The Rise and Fall of Nations, Forces of Change in the Post-Crisis World* (Sharma (2016)), periods of long-term economic development occur because leaders avoid the excesses that produce debt and investment bubbles, currency and financial crises, and hyperinflation. With this in mind, in order to avoid a new Greek fiscal derailment, it is important that the significant European financial resources that enter the Greek economy do not create the illusion that "money is there" and thus lead to inertia, but that they mobilize us so that the "money will be put to good use". They should be directed towards productive and innovative investments that will increase the country's exports, create new jobs and have the maximum development footprint. And to achieve this, the public sector and market reforms are a one-way street, as is the addressing of major challenges that mine development, such as Greece's rapidly ageing demographic.[60]

Author Contributions: Conceptualization, E.M. and H.V.; methodology, E.M. and H.V.; validation, E.M. and H.V.; formal analysis, E.M. and H.V.; investigation, H.V.; resources, E.M. and H.V.; data curation, H.V.; writing—original draft preparation, H.V.; writing—review and editing, E.M. and H.V.; visualization, H.V.; supervision, E.M.; project administration, E.M. All authors have read and agreed to the published version of the manuscript.

Funding: This research received no external funding.

Conflicts of Interest: The authors declare no conflict of interest.

Notes

1 The entire analysis contained in this paper is based on open data from as late as 15 February 2024.

2 Throughout this paper, we use estimates and predictions by the European Commission, available in the AMECO database. There are a multitude of other estimates/forecasts, using macroeconomic models specific to Greece, from domestic institutions, e.g., the Bank of Greece, the systemic banks, the Centre of Planning and Economic Research (KEPE) and academic research groups. AMECO was selected on the basis of the open access of all estimated variables and indicators necessary for the present analysis.

3 It should be noted that these three bailout programs were not undertaken for the benefit of Greece alone. The official default of a Eurozone member state would set a very negative precedent for the edifice of the monetary union, with obvious implications in terms of trust in the common currency and the EU and would expose other member states with high debt/GDP ratios or significant external imbalances to similar risks. A destabilization of the euro area could also have repercussions for the global economy as a whole. For these reasons, Greece should have been rescued, but at the same time, Greece should also have set an example to be avoided. These factors led to "bitter" bailout programs, combined with very strict fiscal austerity that inevitably resulted in a deepening of the economic recession.
For a very comprehensive chronology of Greece's bailout programs, and the underlying factors that shaped them, see Dallara (2024).

4 For a general overview of the current assessment of the Greek economy by international organizations, see European Commission and Directorate-General for Economic and Financial Affairs (2023a, 2023c), and OECD (2023).

5 Regarding the other three periods of great recession of the UK's in modern history, its recession during the period of the "Great Depression" did not exceed 5.4% cumulatively and had been overcome by 1934; during the war and post-war period of 1944–1951, it did not exceed 12.2% cumulatively and lasted 7 years; and during the financial crisis of 2007–2008, it did not exceed 4.9% cumulatively and lasted 5 years.

6 According to the latest data by ELSTAT (the Hellenic Statistical Authority) and Eurostat, Greek GDP in the third quarter of 2023, with a calendar and seasonal correction and in 2015 values, was EUR 48.7 billion. This amount is equivalent to an annual GDP of EUR 194.8 billion in 2015 values, which is approximately equal to 81.5% of 2008 GDP in 2015 values.

7 For a more detailed analysis of the Ireland case, see the relevant case study by diaNEOsis: Mitsos and Linardatou (2019).

8 For a very comprehensive description of the chronic problems that led to the Greek economic crisis, see Kostis (2018).

9 This reference focuses only on the depreciation due to the underemployment and/or the preservation in an inactive state. The constant and usual depreciation and decrease in physical and human capital is not included here.

10 As an indicative example regarding employment, according to the annual data of the Labor Force Survey of ELSTAT, in 2019, the labor force of the country was smaller by approximately 311 thousand people in comparison with the 2009 level, an alteration of 6.2%.

11 Data from the diaNEOsis research: Matsaganis et al. (2018).

12 As this analysis seeks a diachronic comparison of the consumption expenditure with the disposable income, we have chosen to ignore—and therefore, not to exclude—the share of social security contributions that is not returned to the private economy as pensioners' income. The reason is that it would significantly increase the complexity of the analysis, without any real benefit. The same applies to the inclusion of urgent state aid to the insurance funds, which is of course a net flow from taxes to pensions. These calculations are therefore only of value in a diachronic comparison and not as absolute amounts.

13 In fact, in 2022, the share of per capita consumption in per capita disposable income (with contributions) reached an all-time high of 99% and the remaining per capita savings reached an all-time low of EUR 127.

14 These 14 categories correspond to the NACE rev.2 classification as follows ([group]: [NACE rev.2 codes]): agriculture, forestry and fishing: A; manufacturing: C; energy (excluding oil products), water and telecommunications: D, E and J61; construction: F; wholesale and retail trade: G; transportation and storage: H; accommodation and food service: I; financial and insurance activities (excluding social security): K; real estate activities: L; professional and administrative/support service activities: M and N; public administration, defense and compulsory social security: O; education: P; human health and social work activities: Q; other: B, J58-J60, J62, J63, R, S, T and U.

15 This analysis as a whole has been conducted at constant prices (2015) and is therefore about real changes.

16 The entire air transport sector—including freight transport—which depends on tourism to a higher degree, has a GVA that does not exceed EUR 771 million or 0.48% of total GVA (the highest achieved in 2018).

17 See Figure 13 in the next section.

18 We exclude from this phrase the trade policy instruments that have been used over time for CAB improvement, such as import duties and export subsidies, as their use is not free in member countries of customs or economic unions, as is the case of Greece.

19 According to the balance of payment statistics (BOP) methodology by the Bank of Greece. This does not apply on a national accounting basis.

20 In all election years of this specific period, that is, 1981, 1985, 1989, 1990, 1996 and 2000, except for the year 1993, the CAB deteriorated significantly.

21 From travel collections from abroad alone, there was a loss of EUR 13.9 billion compared to 2019 (−76%). Of course, travel payments to foreign countries also decreased by around EUR 2 billion (−71%). Therefore, the travel balance showed a loss of almost EUR 12 billion in 2020 compared to 2019 (−77%).

22 Exports of goods decreased by EUR 3.5 billion compared to 2019 (−10.9%), whereas imports of goods decreased by EUR 7.8 billion (−14.2%).

23 Examples of such factors can be the recent pandemic and previous, less severe pandemics (e.g., SARS in 2004, the bird flu in 2007), various international developments (such as wars or turmoil in nearby or competitive—from a tourism point of view—countries, and financial difficulties in countries of origin), international or domestic terrorism, migration crises, etc.

24 For a more detailed analysis of this issue and relevant proposals, see relevant studies by diaNEOsis: diaNEOsis and ISPM (2019) and Vaggelas et al. (2021).

25 Specifically, "food, drinks and tobacco products": SITC0 and SITC1; "raw materials": SITC2 and SITC4; "mineral fuels, lubricants and related materials": SITC3; "chemicals and related products, n.e.s.": SITC5; "machinery and transfer equipment": SITC7; "other manufactured goods": SITC6 and SITC8; and "other": SITC9.

26 Specifically on the issue of R&D and innovation in the Greek economy, see the relevant study by diaNEOsis: Kalogirou et al. (2021).

27 For a detailed mapping of the current situation in the Greek startup ecosystem, see a relevant study by diaNEOsis: Pepelasis et al. (2022).

28 The average of the three-year period of 2006–2008. We avoid counting the years until 2004, as investment expenditure was increased due to an exogenous need, the preparation of the Olympic Games. We also avoid counting the year 2005, as the reduced investment in this year is partly caused by investment "fatigue", after a long period of exogenously increased investment, and cautiousness about the course of the Greek economy in the post-Olympic Games era.

29 Of the total NGEU resources (EUR 750 billion in 2018 constant values), Greece was allocated EUR 29.1 billion from the recovery and resilience facility (RRF—EUR 16.5 billion in grants and EUR 12.6 billion in loans), as well an additional amount of EUR 3 billion from the other NGEU funds.

30 For the benefits that a well-designed and targeted FDI attraction policy can have, see the case study on Ireland as a role model for Greece, by diaNEOsis: Mitsos and Linardatou (2019).

31 The first round of recapitalizations was completed in 2013, as a result of private sector involvement (PSI), with EUR 25.5 billion from the Hellenic Financial Stability Fund (HFSF) and EUR 3 billion from private investors. The second round took place in 2014, with EUR 8.3 billion from private investors. The third round took place in late 2015, in the shadow of the referendum, with EUR 5.4 billion from the HFSF and EUR 9 billion from private investors.

32 The value of the equity capital of the banks was zeroed out twice: in February 2012 and November 2015.

33 For a better understanding of this level, we indicatively note that the corresponding share at the end of 2008 was 5.7%.

34 For a more detailed analysis of this, see Hardouvelis (2021).

35 The "Hercules" scheme provided for the creation of a special-purpose vehicle (SPV), which would purchase the non-performing exposures with resources derived from the issuance of securities of three quality grades. The low-rated securities would be transferred to an investor for a fee and the high-rated securities would be retained by the bank and guaranteed by the Greek public sector for a royalty.

36 This reference focuses on intellectual property products that constitute a fixed capital and are therefore used in the production process.

37 AMECO database, accessed on: 24 January 2024. The capital stock in this database is estimated by using historical fixed capital flows (GFCF and FCC) with an initial level defined as three times the GDP in 1960.

38 As there are no significant differentiations from the rest of the world in terms of relative changes in production technology and productivity of individual sectors during the same period.

39 European Commission et al. (2023). *Annual report on European SMEs 2022/2023* and its accompanying documents: "2023 SME Country Fact Sheet. Greece" and "2023 SME Country Fact Sheet. EU27".

40 The non-financial business sector includes industry, construction, trade and services (NACE rev. 2, divisions B to J, L, M and N), but excludes agriculture, forestry and fishing as well as services that do not participate in the market to a high degree, such as education and health.

41 See the relevant information in the study by diaNEOsis: Kalogirou et al. (2021).

42 The fifth highest VAT coefficient in the EU, after Hungary (27%), Denmark, Croatia and Slovenia (25% for all three of them), whereas Finland also has a 24% coefficient.

43 For a detailed description of what happened in all energy markets in 2020, see IEA (2021).

44 For a detailed inventory of the issues faced by Greek export businesses, see Kalyvitis et al. (2018).

45 diaNEOsis and IOBE (2021). This analysis focused on electricity and NG, as the prices of these energy sources determine the competitiveness of the energy-intensive industry to a significant degree.

46 See the crisis at the Evros border in March 2020, within the framework of asymmetrical operations by Turkey.

47 One of the main raw materials for the production of fertilizers is NG (70–90% methane), which is used to mass-produce the ammonia contained in fertilizers. In addition, Russia is one of the main producers of fertilizers internationally, and together with its partner Belarus, they have a significant share in the global production of another important raw material for fertilizers: potassium.

48 Conventionally, unless otherwise stated, the calculation basis of the reported item will be the national consumer price index (CPI).

49 Based on the HICP, on the basis of which the interstate comparison should be made.

50 See the relevant ECB study: Koester et al. (2021).

51 In order to avoid a loss of competitiveness in the Greek economy vis-à-vis its main trading partners. It also implies the additional assumption that the monetary policy will be such that it will not allow for a loss of competitiveness vis-à-vis the rest of the world.

52 Since the Greek public sector had not had time to be rated by at least one rating agency (out of the four main agencies recognized by the ECB) with an investment grade.

53 While, in general, the eligibility requirements for eligible debt instruments set out in the APP were maintained, an exemption was granted specifically regarding securities issued by the Greek public sector. The total amount of the Greek debt purchased by the ECB under the PEPP exceeds EUR 39.2 billion.

54 See the relevant paper: Gatsios and Ioannou (2022).

55 S&P: BBB (20 October 2023, Standard & Poor's (2023)); Fitch Ratings: BBB (1 December 2023, Fitch Ratings (2023)); and DBRS: BBB (low) (8 September 2023, DBRS Ratings (2023)); whereas only Moody's rates Greek state bonds at one step below its lower investment grade (Baa3): Ba1 (15 September 2023, Moody's (2023)).

56 According to Eurostat figures (as of January 2024) and EC estimates (November 2023).

57 See Calvo (1988) for such a feedback mechanism.

58 On the condition that government bond yields remain below the sum of GDP growth and inflation.

59 See Alogoskoufis (2021) for a more detailed analysis of these available options and the arguments in favor of the third of them.

60 For a comprehensive analysis of Greece's demographic problem, see the relevant study by diaNEOsis: Balourdos et al. (2019).

References

Alogoskoufis, George. 2021. Το *χρέος και η αντιμετώπισή του μετά την πανδημία* [Debt and How to Deal with It after the Pandemic]. *Οικονομικός Ταχυδρόμος*. June 6. Available online: https://www.ot.gr/2021/06/06/academia/hellenic-observatory-lse/to-xreos-kai-i-antimetopisi-tou-meta-tin-pandimia (accessed on 15 February 2024).

Balourdos, Dionyssis, Nicolas Demertzis, George Pierrakos, and Elias Kikilias. 2019. *Η χαμηλή γονιμότητα στην Ελλάδα, δημογρ αφική κρίση και πολιτικές ενίσχυσης της οικογένειας [Low Fertility in Greece, Demographic Crisis and Family Support Policies]*. Athens: diaNEOsis. Available online: https://www.dianeosis.org/research/demography (accessed on 15 February 2024).

Calvo, Guillermo Antonio. 1988. Servicing the Public Debt: The Role of Expectations. *American Economic Review* 78: 647–61.

Christodoulakis, Nikos, Miltiadis Nektarios, Helias Valentis, and Christos Axioglou. 2020. *Η Επανεκκίνηση Της Ελληνικής Οικονομίας. Ταμείο Ανάκαμψης Και Δημοσιονομικές Προοπτικές [The Restart of the Greek Economy. RRF and Fiscal Outlook]*. Athens: diaNEOsis. Available online: https://www.dianeosis.org/research/epanekkinisi-ellinikis-oikonomias (accessed on 15 February 2024).

Dallara, Charles. H. 2024. *Euroshock: How the Largest Debt Restructuring in History Helped Save Greece and Preserve the Eurozone*. New York: Rodin Books.

DBRS Ratings. 2023. DBRS Morningstar Upgrades the Hellenic Republic to BBB (Low), Stable Trend. September 8. Available online: https://dbrs.morningstar.com/research/420362/dbrs-morningstar-upgrades-the-hellenic-republic-to-bbb-low-stable-trend (accessed on 15 February 2024).

diaNEOsis, and IOBE [Foundation for Economic & Industrial Research]. 2018. *Η Φορολογία Εισοδήματος Στην Ελλάδα [Income Tax in Greece]*. Athens: diaNEOsis. Available online: https://www.dianeosis.org/research/i-forologia-eisodimatos-stin-ellada (accessed on 15 February 2024).

diaNEOsis, and IOBE [Foundation for Economic & Industrial Research]. 2021. *Ο Τομέας Ενέργειας Στην Ελλάδα: Τάσεις, Προοπτικές και Προκλήσεις [The Energy Sector in Greece: Trends, Prospects and Challenges]*. Athens: diaNEOsis. Available online: https://www.dianeosis.org/research/i-energeia-stin-ellada (accessed on 15 February 2024).

diaNEOsis, and ISPM [Institute of Social & Preventive Medicine]. 2019. *Η Ανάπτυξη Του Τουρισμού Τρίτης Ηλικίας Στην Ελλάδα Και Η Συμβολή Του Τουρισμού Υγείας [The Development of Third Age Tourism in Greece and the Contribution of Health Tourism]*. Athens: diaNEOsis. Available online: https://www.dianeosis.org/research/tourismos-tritis-ilikias (accessed on 15 February 2024).

European Central Bank. n.d.a. Asset Purchase Programmes. Retrieved 30 January 2023. Available online: https://www.ecb.europa.eu/mopo/implement/app/html/index.en.html (accessed on 30 January 2023).

European Central Bank. n.d.b. Key ECB Interest Rates. Retrieved 30 January 2023. Available online: https://www.ecb.europa.eu/stats/policy_and_exchange_rates/key_ecb_interest_rates/html/index.en.html (accessed on 30 January 2023).

European Central Bank. n.d.c. Pandemic Emergency Purchase Programme (PEPP). Retrieved 30 January 2023. Available online: https://www.ecb.europa.eu/mopo/implement/pepp/html/index.en.html (accessed on 30 January 2023).

European Commission, and Directorate-General for Economic and Financial Affairs. 2023a. 2023 Country Report–Greece. June 14. Available online: https://www.data.europa.eu/doi/10.2765/450492 (accessed on 15 February 2024).

European Commission, and Directorate-General for Economic and Financial Affairs. 2023b. *European Economic Forecast: Autumn 2023*. Luxembourg: Publications Office of the European Union. Available online: https://data.europa.eu/doi/10.2765/325116 (accessed on 15 February 2024).

European Commission, and Directorate-General for Economic and Financial Affairs. 2023c. *Post-Programme Surveillance Report: Greece, Autumn 2023*. Luxembourg: Publications Office of the European Union. Available online: https://data.europa.eu/doi/10.2765/900936 (accessed on 15 February 2024).

European Commission, and Directorate-General for Economic and Financial Affairs. 2024. *European Economic Forecast: Winter 2024 (Interim)*. Luxembourg: Publications Office of the European Union. Available online: https://data.europa.eu/doi/10.2765/01964 (accessed on 15 February 2024).

European Commission, Directorate-General for Internal Market, Industry, Entrepreneurship and SMEs, Joint Research Centre, Laura Di Bella, Anastasis Katsinis, and Jaime Lagüera-González. 2023. *Annual Report on European SMEs 2022/2023: SME Performance Review 2022/2023*. Luxembourg: Publications Office of the European Union. Available online: https://data.europa.eu/doi/10.2760/028705 (accessed on 15 February 2024).

Fitch Ratings. 2023. Fitch Upgrades Greece to 'BBB-'; Outlook Stable. December 1. Available online: https://www.fitchratings.com/research/sovereigns/fitch-upgrades-greece-to-bbb-outlook-stable-01-12-2023 (accessed on 15 February 2024).

Gatsios, Konstantine, and Dimitris A. Ioannou. 2022. Ο πληθωρισμός ως ευκαιρία βελτίωσης της ανταγωνιστικότητας της ελληνικής οικονομίας [Inflation As an Opportunity to Improve the Competitiveness of the Greek Economy]. *Το Βήμα της Κυριακής*. February 13. Available online: https://www.tovima.gr/printed_post/o-plithorismos-os-eykairia-veltiosis-crtis-antagonistikotitas-crtis-ellinikis-oikonomias (accessed on 15 February 2024).

Hardouvelis, Gikas A. 2021. Κρίση και χρηματοπιστωτικά ανοίγματα στην Ελλάδα [Crisis and financial exposures in Greece]. In *Υποχρεώσεις Χρηματοπιστωτικών Φορέων [Obligations of Financial Institutions]*. Edited by Association of Greek Commercialists. Athens: Νομική Βιβλιοθήκη, pp. 245–97. Available online: https://hardouvelis.gr/el/gikas-hardouvelis-quot-krisi-kai-chrimatopistotika-anoigmata-stin-ellada-quot-meleti-gia-to-mellon-ton-trapezon (accessed on 15 February 2024).

Hellenic Republic, and PDMA (Public Debt Management Agency). 2019. Funding Strategy for 2020. December. Available online: https://www.pdma.gr/en/?view=article&id=5901:funding-strategy-for-2020 (accessed on 15 February 2024).

Hellenic Republic, and PDMA (Public Debt Management Agency). 2023. Funding Strategy for 2024. December 21. Available online: https://www.pdma.gr/en/?view=article&id=5901:funding-strategy-for-2024 (accessed on 15 February 2024).

IEA. 2021. *Global Energy Review 2021*. Paris: IEA. Available online: https://www.iea.org/reports/global-energy-review-2021 (accessed on 15 February 2024).

Kalogirou, Giannis, Aggelos Tsakanikas, Aimilia Protogerou, Panagiotis Panagiotopoulos, Evangelos Siokas, Georgios Siokas, and Dimitrios Stamatopoulos. 2021. *Η Ελλάδα που Μαθαίνει, Ερευνά, Καινοτομεί και Επιχειρεί [Greece That Learns, Researches, Innovates and Does Business]*. Athens: diaNEOsis. Available online: https://www.dianeosis.org/research/research_policy (accessed on 15 February 2024).

Kalyvitis, Sarantis, Margarita Katsimi, and Thomas Moutos. 2018. *Εξαγωγές και Εξαγωγικές Επιχειρήσεις στην Ελλάδα [Exports and Export Businesses in Greece]*. Athens: diaNEOsis. Available online: https://www.dianeosis.org/2018/12/eksagoges-kai-eksagogikes-epixeiriseis-stin-ellada (accessed on 15 February 2024).

Koester, Gerrit, Frank Smets, and Chiara Osbat. 2021. *Understanding Low Inflation in the Euro Area from 2013 to 2019: Cyclical and Structural Drivers*. Frankfurt: European Central Bank. Available online: https://data.europa.eu/doi/10.2866/869984 (accessed on 15 February 2024).

Kostis, Kostas. 2018. *History's Spoiled Children: The Story of Modern Greece*. Oxford: Oxford University Press.

Makantasi, Evmorfia (Fay), and Helias Valentis. 2020. *ΕΣΠΑ-Ένα Εν Μέρει Ανεκμετάλλευτο Αναπτυξιακό Κοινοτικό Εργαλείο [NSRF-A Partly Unutilized EU Development Instrument]*. Athens: diaNEOsis. Available online: https://www.dianeosis.org/2020/07/espa-ena-anekmetaleyto-anaptyksiako-ergaleio (accessed on 15 February 2024).

Makantasi, Evmorfia (Fay), and Helias Valentis. 2021. *Η "Χρηματοδότηση Βάσει Αποτελεσμάτων" Ως Εργαλείο Κοινωνικής Πολιτικής [Results-Based Funding as a Social Policy Tool]*. Athens: diaNEOsis. Available online: https://www.dianeosis.org/2021/02/i-xrimatodotisi-vasei-apotelesmatwn (accessed on 15 February 2024).

Matsaganis, Manos, Andrea Parma, and Alexandros Karakitsios. 2018. *Όψεις Κοινωνικής Κινητικότητας στην Ελλάδα της Κρίσης [Aspects of Social Mobility in Crisis Greece]*. Athens: diaNEOsis. Available online: https://www.dianeosis.org/2018/11/oi-epiptoseis-tis-krisis-sta-eisodimata-twn-ellinwn (accessed on 15 February 2024).

Mitsos, Michalis, and Odin Linardatou. 2019. *Ξένες Επενδύσεις, Παιδεία και Εξωστρέφεια: Πώς Σώθηκε Η Ιρλανδία [Foreign Investment, Education and Openness: How Ireland Was Saved]*. Athens: diaNEOsis. Available online: https://www.dianeosis.org/research/ameses-ksenes-ependyseis (accessed on 15 February 2024).

Moody's. 2023. Government of Greece-Ba1 Stable: Annual Credit Analysis. October 11. Available online: https://www.moodys.com/research/Government-of-Greece-Ba1-stable-Annual-credit-analysis-Issuer-In-Depth--PBC_1376383 (accessed on 15 February 2024).

OECD. 2020. *OECD Tourism Trends and Policies 2020*. Paris: OECD Publishing. [CrossRef]

OECD. 2023. *OECD Economic Outlook, Volume 2023 Issue 2*. Paris: OECD Publishing. [CrossRef]

Pepelasis, Ioanna Sapfo, Ioannis Spyropoulos, Georgios Kokkotas, Dimitris Zisis, and Ioannis Besis. 2022. *Χαρτογράφηση Ελληνικού Οικοσυστήματος Νεοφυών Επιχειρήσεων [Mapping the Greek Start-up Business Ecosystem]*. Athens: diaNEOsis. Available online: https://www.dianeosis.org/2022/01/oi-neofyeis-epixeiriseis-stin-ellada (accessed on 15 February 2024).

Pissarides, Christopher A., Dimitri Vayanos, Nikolaos Vettas, and Costas Meghir. 2020. Σχέδιο Ανάπτυξης για την Ελληνική Οικονομία [A Growth Strategy for the Greek Economy]. Available online: https://www.government.gov.gr/schedio-anaptixis-gia-tin-elliniki-ikonomia (accessed on 15 February 2024).
Sharma, Ruchir. 2016. *The Rise and Fall of Nations: Forces of Change in the Post-Crisis World*. New York: W. W. Norton & Company.
Standard & Poor's. 2023. Greece Upgraded To 'BBB-/A-3' On An Improved Budgetary Position; Outlook Stable. October 20. Available online: https://www.disclosure.spglobal.com/ratings/en/regulatory/article/-/view/type/HTML/id/3074450 (accessed on 15 February 2024).
Vaggelas, George. K., Athanasios Pallis, Christina Kontaxi, Giannis Soultanis, Vicky Loizou, Zoe Rimpa, Marios Nakas, and Panagiotis Markantonatos. 2021. *Διαμόρφωση Στρατηγικής Ανάπτυξης Τουριστικών Λιμένων [Formulation of a Strategy for the Development of Tourist Ports]*. Athens: diaNEOsis. Available online: https://www.dianeosis.org/research/cruise_industry_in_greece (accessed on 15 February 2024).

economies

MDPI

Article

The Relationship between Credit Rating and Environmental, Social, and Governance Score in Banking

Dimitrios Vortelinos [1,*], Angeliki N. Menegaki [2] and Spyros Alexiou [2]

1 Department of Accounting and Finance, Hellenic Mediterranean University, 71410 Heraklion, Greece
2 Department of Economic and Regional Development, Agricultural University of Athens, Amfissa Campus, 33100 Amfissa, Greece; amenegaki@aua.gr (A.N.M.); salexiou@aua.gr (S.A.)
* Correspondence: dvortelinos@hmu.gr

Abstract: The present paper investigates the relationship between stock prices, credit ratings, and ESG scores for banks internationally. First, it describes stock prices and ESG scores at an annual frequency, as well as stock price and credit risk at a daily frequency. The relationships between (a) stock price and credit rating returns with ESG score returns and (b) among ESG scores are examined by pairwise annual correlation, and daily correlations are examined between price and credit rating returns. Furthermore, Granger causality is used to examine the relationships between the following: (a) price and ESG score annual returns; (b) price and credit rating daily returns; and (c) total and pillar annual ESG scores. This study makes a significant contribution to the literature by providing a detailed temporal analysis using both annual and daily data frequencies, which is relatively rare in the field. There is evidence of statistically and empirically important relations in the form of pairwise correlations. The regressions reveal a low significance of few ESG score changes in explaining credit rating changes. A unique aspect of this paper is the comprehensive analysis of 16 granular ESG scores, including overall scores, pillar scores, and sub-scores, allowing for a multi-faceted understanding of how specific ESG factors impact financial metrics. We found evidence of the significance of COVID-19 in all research questions. Additionally, this paper highlights the impact of the COVID-19 pandemic on the relationships between ESG scores, credit ratings, and stock prices, offering timely insights into the heightened importance and volatility of ESG factors during crisis periods. Future research needs to shed more light on this relationship, however.

Keywords: banks; ESG; credit ratings; stock prices; inter-relation; COVID-19

1. Introduction

Credit ratings estimate the creditworthiness of an entity and are provided by a few major agencies, such as Standard & Poor's, Fitch, and Moody's, all approved by the Securities and Exchange Commission (SEC). Credit ratings affect entities in numerous ways, including cost of capital and stock prices. These ratings offer a unique information set that is as critical for corporations as financial statements. Credit ratings concern the probability of either a default (default risk) or a credit event (credit risk), whereas financial statements refer to the economic condition and performance of an entity. In the banking sector, credit ratings are determined differently than in other sectors. Market anomalies and high information asymmetry significantly influence the effects of financial ratios on credit ratings in the banking sector (Shen et al. 2012). Additionally, the location of banks affects credit ratings through a monetary union effect (van Loon and Haan 2015).

The banking sector is influenced by both credit ratings and Environmental, Social, and Governance (ESG) scores (Jang et al. 2020). Credit ratings impact banks' capital structure, with banks close to a credit rating upgrade often having a higher capital-to-assets ratio. Furthermore, "too-big-to-fail" banks nearing an upgrade tend to have lower capital relative to assets, and credit ratings have a relatively minor economic effect on the speed at which a bank's capital is adjusted (Wojewodzki et al. 2020). The credit ratings of banks are also affected by the solicitation status and financial profile of the banks (Poon et al. 2009). An important issue in bank credit ratings is whether there is enforcement action due to credit-rating changes from entities such as the Federal Deposit Insurance Corporation (FDIC), the Office of the Comptroller of the Currency (OCC), or the Federal Reserve Bank (FRB) in the USA, or other international or regional authorities (Apergis et al. 2012).

ESG factors are increasingly recognized as crucial for the banking sector. Europe has led in requiring ESG disclosures from banks since the Non-Financial Reporting Directive (2014/95/EU). ESG practices can enhance financial wealth and ensure financial stability for banking shareholders (Houston and Shan 2022). ESG factors should be integrated into the EU banking regulatory and supervisory framework (European Banking Authority 2023). ESGs affect main banking operations and nonperforming loans (Liu et al. 2023). It has been found that a bank's high performance in all three pillars of ESG evaluation reduces its ratio of nonperforming loans, and also that a bank's favorable ESG performance improves its loan quality and provides archival evidence of the importance of all three pillars of ESG. Other parameters are stock value (Azmi et al. 2021), stability (Chiaramonte et al. 2022), financial distress (Citterio and King 2022), and financial performance (Zhou et al. 2021). The ESG role in financial performance has been examined for different regions, including Europe (Batae et al. 2020), the Middle East, North Africa, and Turkey (MENT) (El Khoury et al. 2023). ESG features foster an investing culture focused on long-term growth in an entity's value and prioritize management targets for stakeholders and entity sustainability. Few studies have examined the relationship between ESGs and financial performance in the banking sector (Cornett et al. 2016; La Torre et al. 2021).

Despite the growing body of literature on ESG factors, credit ratings, and financial performance, there is limited research that comprehensively examines the relationships between these variables using both annual and daily data frequencies. Furthermore, the impact of specific ESG sub-scores on financial metrics has not been thoroughly explored. Additionally, while the COVID-19 pandemic has significantly influenced financial markets, its specific effects on the relationship between ESG scores, credit ratings, and stock prices in the banking sector require further investigation. Note that the first major wave of COVID-19 was from January to May 2020. Thus, the primary goal of this paper is to fill these research gaps by providing a detailed analysis of the relationships between stock prices, credit ratings, and ESG scores for banks internationally, using both annual and daily data frequencies. This study aims to offer a comprehensive understanding of how specific ESG factors impact financial metrics and to highlight the role of the COVID-19 pandemic in these relationships. This paper addresses questions such as the following:

What is the relationship between stock price returns and ESG score returns in the banking sector?

How do ESG score changes influence credit rating changes for banks?

What is the relationship between daily credit rating returns and daily stock price returns?

How has the COVID-19 pandemic affected the relationships between ESG scores, credit ratings, and stock prices?

This paper contributes to the literature in several ways. Firstly, it targets the banking sector internationally, providing insights into how ESG scores, credit ratings, and stock prices interact in different economic environments. Secondly, it examines the relationship between various ESG scores, offering a granular analysis that distinguishes between overall scores, pillar scores, and sub-scores. Thirdly, it investigates the effect of annual ESG score returns on credit rating changes and their relations, as well as the impact of daily credit rating returns on daily stock price returns. Finally, it highlights the significance of the COVID-19 pandemic in all research questions, providing timely insights into the heightened importance of ESG factors during crisis periods.

In addition to these noted contributions, this paper also considers the impact of fintech development on ESG performance, as discussed by Wang et al. (2022). The integration of fintech in banking operations is shown to alleviate financing constraints and enhance ESG practices, particularly in emerging markets. This perspective provides a modern dimension to the analysis, emphasizing the role of digital technology in improving corporate sustainability. Galeone et al. (2024) further explore the relationship between fintech and sustainability, showing that social influence reinforced by ESG factors encourages technology adoption in the banking sector. The study by Dospinescu et al. (2021) highlights the importance of fintech in promoting ESG performance by reducing information asymmetry and transaction costs, thereby providing a comprehensive view of how technological advancements can bolster sustainable finance in the banking sector.

The rest of the paper is structured as follows: after this Introduction (part 1), Section 2 contains the literature review, Section 3 presents the tested hypotheses with a theoretical framework, Section 4 is the Methodology, Section 5 is the Discussion, and Section 6 provides concluding remarks.

2. Literature Review

The integration of Environmental, Social and Governance (ESG) factors into financial and credit risk assessments has gained increasing research attention in recent years. ESG considerations are becoming crucial for investors, credit rating agencies, and regulatory bodies as they strive to understand their impact on financial performance, credit risk, and overall market stability. This literature review synthesizes findings from up-to-date studies that examine the relationship between ESG factors and various aspects of financial risk, particularly credit ratings and default risk, across different markets and sectors. We have identified four main strands of literature on this topic (Table 1): the first strand deals with the relationship between ESGs and credit ratings, the second deals with ESGs and default risk, the third deals with ESGs and stock volatility, and the fourth deals with ESGs and the financial sector.

Table 1. Identified literature review groupings with a short summary of each reviewed paper.

ESGs and Credit Ratings	ESGs and Default Risk	ESGs and Stock Volatility	ESGs in the Financial Sector
Chodnicka-Jaworska (2021) investigates the impact of ESG measures on credit ratings for non-financial institutions. The study finds that ESG factors significantly influence credit ratings, particularly during periods of financial instability like the COVID-19 pandemic.	Michalski and Low (2024) use machine learning models to evaluate the predictive power of ESG variables on corporate credit ratings. Their results demonstrate that ESG factors, especially environmental and social responsibility variables, are significant predictors of corporate credit ratings, particularly post-financial crisis.	Singh and Jaiwani (2023) analyze the influence of ESG factors on share price volatility (SPV) in energy sector firms, considering the development phase of countries. They find that ESG factors reduce SPV in developing economies, while increasing SPV in developed economies, suggesting that the impact of ESG varies depending on the economic context.	Hau et al. (2013) examine the quality of bank ratings and identify determinants of rating quality. Their study reveals that larger banks receive more favorable ratings due to conflicts of interest, particularly those providing significant business to rating agencies. This bias highlights the need for enhanced transparency and improved public disclosure to ensure accurate and unbiased ratings.
Kiesel and Lücke (2022) analyze the incorporation of ESG factors into credit rating reports and their impact on financial markets. Their findings indicate that while governance issues are prominently considered, the overall integration of ESG factors remains limited.	Penikas (2022) explores the relationship between credit risk and climate risk, finding that this relationship varies significantly by industry and region. While certain sectors benefit from positive climate–credit risk correlations, the majority exhibit negative correlations, implying that green finance initiatives need to be carefully tailored to avoid financial instability.	Liu et al. (2022) identify the causal effect of ESG performance on stock idiosyncratic volatility in the Chinese market. They find that ESG performance significantly reduces stock idiosyncratic volatility by promoting high-quality information disclosure and enhancing transparency, thereby reducing firm-specific risk.	Grigorieva and Vukovic (2020) analyze the methodologies of credit rating assessments used by major rating agencies, with a focus on Fitch Ratings. They highlight the importance of qualitative measures such as risk appetite and economic and operational conditions in credit risk assessment.

Table 1. *Cont.*

ESGs and Credit Ratings	ESGs and Default Risk	ESGs and Stock Volatility	ESGs in the Financial Sector
Devalle et al. (2017) examine the effect of ESG performance on the credit ratings of Italian and Spanish public firms. The study finds a positive association between ESG performance and higher credit ratings, with social and governance scores having a significant impact. This suggests that ESG factors enhance transparency and reduce information asymmetry, leading to better credit evaluations.	Liu et al. (2023) investigate the volatility risk premium (VOLRP) in China and its relationship with ESG sentiment. They find a positive correlation between ESG sentiment and VOLRP, suggesting that investors perceive ESG investments as potentially risky in the short term. This contrasts with developed markets and indicates unique dynamics in emerging markets like China.	Burger et al. (2022) examine the impact of ESG ratings on both the implied and historical volatility of companies' stock prices. They find that better ESG performance leads to lower stock price volatility, both historical and implied. The combined ESG rating has the strongest impact on reducing volatility compared to individual ratings from each agency.	Ruddy (2021) compares Bank Financial Strength Ratings (BFSRs) with general credit ratings from different agencies. The study finds that BFSRs are more conservative and provide earlier indications of financial distress compared to general credit ratings, highlighting their importance for standalone creditworthiness assessment.
Pineau et al. (2022) analyze the importance of ESG factors in sovereign credit ratings. They find that governance is the most crucial ESG factor for advanced economies, while non-ESG factors are more significant for emerging markets.	Arif et al. (2024) examine the global association between ESG disclosures and future earnings risk, finding that higher ESG disclosures are linked to reduced earnings risk.		
	Li et al. (2022) explore the relationship between ESG practices and default risk among Chinese listed firms. Their findings indicate that higher ESG ratings are associated with lower default risk, particularly over longer periods.		
	Brogi et al. (2022) investigate the impact of ESG awareness on credit risk using a sample of global firms. They find that higher ESG awareness is strongly associated with better creditworthiness, as indicated by a reduction in credit risk proxied by the Altman Z-score. The social dimension of ESG scores is particularly significant in reducing credit risk		

Source: Authors' compilation.

Apparently, based on Table 1, there are various research articles on the topic, reflecting the diverse approaches to studying the impact of ESG factors on financial metrics such as credit ratings, default risk, and stock volatility. Common methodologies include regression models, panel data analysis, machine learning techniques, and qualitative assessments. Many studies, such as those by Chodnicka-Jaworska (2021) and Kiesel and Lücke (2022), employ regression models to analyze the impact of ESG factors on financial outcomes. Devalle et al. (2017) also use ordered logistic regression models to assess the relationship between ESG performance and credit ratings. In contrast, Michalski and Low (2024) utilize machine learning models to evaluate the predictive power of ESG variables, highlighting the increasing use of advanced techniques in this field. Panel data analysis is another common approach, as seen in Liu et al. (2022) and Abdul Abdul Razak et al. (2020), who use dynamic panel models to control for time-invariant characteristics and enhance the robustness of their findings. Qualitative assessments, like those conducted by Grigorieva and Vukovic (2020), provide a detailed understanding of the methodologies and factors used by rating agencies, emphasizing the importance of qualitative measures such as management quality and operational environment. Moreover, hybrid approaches are seen in studies like Brogi et al. (2022) and Singh and Jaiwani (2023), which combine multiple techniques to provide a more comprehensive analysis. These approaches often enhance the reliability of findings by incorporating robustness checks and multi-dimensional models. Comparing these methodologies with those used in our paper reveals several similarities and differences. Our paper employs a combination of descriptive statistics, pairwise correlations, Granger causality tests, and OLS regressions to analyze the relationships between stock prices, credit ratings, and ESG scores for banks internationally. This comprehensive approach is similar to the hybrid methodologies used in some of the up-to-date reviewed literature. However, our unique focus on both annual and daily data frequencies, as well as a detailed analysis of the COVID-19 period, provides additional insight into the short-term dynamics of these relationships.

In terms of the variables used in the literature, our paper examines annual and daily stock prices, credit ratings, and a comprehensive set of 16 ESG scores, including overall scores, pillar scores, and sub-scores. This detailed breakdown of ESG scores provides a more granular analysis compared to the broader ESG metrics used in many other studies. The impact of COVID-19 is a significant focus of our paper, aligning with studies like Demir and Danisman (2021) and Yuen et al. (2022), who also highlight the effects of the pandemic on financial performance and ESG practices. Our detailed comparative analysis of pre- and post-pandemic periods offers valuable insights into how COVID-19 altered the relationships between ESG scores, credit ratings, and stock prices.

When comparing our results with those of the up-to date literature, our findings of significant relationships in the form of pairwise correlations are similar to those of Chodnicka-Jaworska (2021) and Devalle et al. (2017), who report significant impacts of ESG on credit ratings. However, the limited explanatory power of ESG score on credit rating changes in our regressions contrasts with the stronger predictive power found in some other studies. Our finding that better ESG performance reduces stock price volatility aligns with the results of Liu et al. (2023) and Burger et al. (2022), although the latter report a stronger negative relationship.

Overall, our paper adds valuable insight to the existing literature by highlighting the various relationships between ESG scores, credit ratings, and stock prices, particularly under the influence of COVID-19. The detailed analysis of both annual and daily data frequencies, combined with a comprehensive set of ESG scores, provides a robust examination of these relationships. Future research can build on these findings by employing more advanced methodologies like machine learning and expanding the dataset to include more banks and regions, enhancing the generalizability and depth of the analysis.

3. The Research Hypotheses with a Brief Theoretical Framework

The primary aim of this study is to investigate the relationship between stock prices, credit ratings, and ESG scores for banks internationally, with a specific focus on the impact of the COVID-19 pandemic. This brief theoretical framework outlines our hypotheses together with the theories that support them. These theories are important as background knowledge in order to understand the hypotheses investigated in this paper.

Hypothesis 1: *There is a significant relationship between stock price and ESG score in the banking sector.*

This hypothesis is grounded in Stakeholder Theory and the Efficient Market Hypothesis, suggesting that improved ESG performance is associated with better stock market performance. Stakeholder Theory proposes that companies are accountable to a broad range of stakeholders, including investors, customers, employees, and the community. Incorporating ESG factors is seen as a way to manage these relationships better and achieve long-term sustainable growth. The Efficient Market Hypothesis (EMH) asserts that stock prices reflect all available information, including ESG disclosures and credit ratings. Any new information about ESG performance or credit ratings should be quickly incorporated into stock prices. Furthermore, we could base this hypothesis on the Resource-Based View (RBV), which suggests that firms can achieve competitive advantage by utilizing resources and capabilities, such as robust ESG practices, which are valuable, rare, inimitable, and non-substitutable.

Hypothesis 2: *ESG scores significantly affect credit ratings for banks.*

Based on Credit Risk Theory and Information Asymmetry Theory, this hypothesis posits that higher ESG scores contribute to better credit ratings by reducing risk and providing additional relevant information. Credit Risk Theory suggests that credit ratings assess the creditworthiness of an entity, reflecting the probability of default and credit risk. Ratings are influenced by financial ratios, economic conditions, and qualitative factors such as management quality and governance practices. The Information Asymmetry Theory suggests that credit ratings reduce information asymmetry between borrowers and lenders by providing an independent assessment of credit risk. ESG disclosures can further reduce asymmetry by providing additional non-financial information relevant to credit risk.

Hypothesis 3: *Credit ratings and stock prices are significantly related.*

This hypothesis is derived from the Efficient Market Hypothesis and Behavioral Finance, proposing that changes in credit ratings are reflected in stock prices, as they provide critical information about the risk and financial health of a firm. The former theory has been explained under Hypothesis 1. The Behavioral Finance field recognizes that investor behavior and market sentiment can also influence stock prices. ESG factors can affect investor perceptions and behavior, leading to changes in stock prices.

Hypothesis 4: *The COVID-19 pandemic had a significant impact on the relationships between stock prices, credit ratings, and ESG scores.*

This hypothesis is informed by the recent literature highlighting the impact of COVID-19 on financial markets and the increased importance of ESG factors during crises.

4. Methodology

This paper follows a hybrid methodology to analyze the relationships between ESG scores, credit ratings, and stock prices, given the banking sector's financial dynamics and the impact of global crises like COVID-19. More specifically, we employ descriptive statistics to summarize data and provide an initial understanding of the trends and distributions of the variables; pairwise correlations such as Pearson correlation to examine the relationships (strength and direction) between stock price returns, credit rating changes, and ESG score changes; annual correlations to examine the relationships between stock price returns and ESG score returns, credit rating returns and ESG score returns, and among different ESG scores; and daily correlations to examine the relationships between daily stock price returns and daily credit rating returns.

Foremost, we use annual and daily data Granger causality tests to determine whether one time series can predict another, thereby exploring the directional relationships between variables. The annual causality tests are between stock price returns and ESG score returns, and between total and pillar ESG scores. The daily causality tests are between daily stock price returns and daily credit rating returns. Afterwards, we use annual and daily data Ordinary Least Squares (OLS) Regressions to assess the explanatory power of ESG scores on credit rating changes and stock prices, making allowance for multicollinearity, heteroskedasticity, and autocorrelation issues. In the annual regressions, ESG score changes as a predictor of credit rating changes, and in the daily regressions, the daily credit rating changes as a predictor of daily stock price changes. Lastly, we employ Vector Autoregression (VAR) to analyze the dynamic relationships among the variables and test the robustness of the model's results with sensitivity analysis.

4.1. Data

Data include stock prices, ESG scores, and credit ratings (Table 2, Panel A). They include a sample of both annual and daily data for the years 2012–2022. The banking sector is represented by six banks from Brazil, Canada, and the UK. In addition to reasons of data availability, they were selected under various criteria, with the most important being the data consistency and strength of internationalization of the banks, as well as their willingness to comply with ESG internationally. Data were retrieved from the Refinitiv Eikon database (previously known as Thomson Reuters Eikon). Regarding the COVID-19 period, we denoted the first major wave of COVID-19 from January to May 2020 (following Demir and Danisman 2021).

Table 2. Data.

Panel A. Firm selection.

	1	2	3	4	5	6
Country	Brazil	Brazil	Canada	Canada	UK	UK
Sector/ Industry	Banks	Banks	Investment Management and Fund Operators	Investment Management and Fund Operators	Banks	Investment Management and Fund Operators
Symbol	BBDC3_SA	SANB11_SA	CIX_TO	ONEX_TO	STAN_L	III_L
Name	Banco Bradesco SA	Banco Santander Brasil SA	CI Financial Corp	Onex Corp	Standard Chartered PLC	3i Group PLC

Panel B. ESG scores.

ESG	Score
Total combined ESG score	D_A1
Total ESG score	D_A2
Environmental pillar score (Weight 16.8%)	D_B1
Resource use (Weight 4.8%)	D_B2
Emissions (Weight 6.0%)	D_B3
Innovation (Weight 6.0%)	D_B4
Social pillar score (Weight 47.3%)	D_C1
Workforce (Weight 9.0%)	D_C2
Human rights (Weight 12.0%)	D_C3
Community (Weight 12.0%)	D_C4
Product responsibility (Weight 14.4%)	D_C5
Governance pillar score (Weight 35.9%)	D_D1
Management (Weight 24.0%)	D_D2
Shareholders (Weight 7.2%)	D_D3
CSR Strategy (Weight 4.8%)	D_D4
Controversies	D_E1

Panel C. ESG metrics.

Level of Metrics	
AAA+	100
AAA	96.30
AAA-	92.59
AA+	88.89
AA	85.19
AA-	81.48
A+	77.78
A	74.07

Table 2. *Cont.*

Level of Metrics	
A-	70.37
BBB+	66.67
BBB	62.96
BBB-	59.26
BB+	55.56
BB	51.85
BB-	48.15
B+	44.44
B	40.74
B-	37.04
CCC+	33.33
CCC	29.63
CCC-	25.93
CC+	22.22
CC	18.52
CC-	14.81
C+	11.11
C	7.41
C-	3.70

Source: Authors' compilation (Panel A), Refinitiv Eikon database (Panels B and C).

To further justify the selection of the data sample, we applied standard data filtration methods. Following the Bankscope database by Bureau van Dijk, we targeted only individual, profit-maximizing banks. All state-owned, worldwide and central banks were omitted because their selection would have changed the scope of the paper from the corporate finance area to the macroeconomic finance area. Also, we left out banks with a large number of gaps in their time series, considering the large number of variables employed. In particular, it was mostly ESG scores that were not fully available for such a lengthy period of time for banks. We also put a further restriction upon bank selection. This was that the bank should have a rating grade by at least one of the main rating agencies—Moody's, Standard & Poor's, or Fitch—continuously, and for the entire sample period.

This paper examines 16 ESG scores (Table 2, Panel B): two overall ESG scores, three pillars (E, S, G) scores, one controversies score, three environmental pillar (E) sub-scores, five social pillar (S) sub-scores, and four governance pillar (G) sub-scores. Both credit ratings and ESG scores were reported in a qualitative form. They were then transformed in numerical terms in order to be quantitatively examined (Table 2, Panel C). The data analysis was mostly performed at an annual frequency. It was also performed at a daily frequency for stock price and credit rating returns. The ESG metrics in Table 2, Panel C refer to a standard list, as suggested by the Refinitiv Eikon database. This list was employed in the present paper. These metrics do not differentiate because the dataset concerns banks; they are usual metrics for any type of company.

4.2. Empirical Findings

The section provides a descriptive analysis of the data and our empirical findings, namely via the examination of pairwise correlations, Granger causalities, and regressions. The results are reported for both the full sample and the COVID-19 period.

4.2.1. Descriptive Analysis

The descriptive analysis of the data examined in this paper is reported in Table 3. This analysis consists of the mean, standard deviation, and the Jarque–Bera statistic of the first differences of the ESG scores. In the annual frequency of analysis and across all banks, the ESG score with the highest average was the human rights score (D_C3), with the governance pillar, management, and controversies scores (D_D1, D_D2 and D_E1) having a negative mean. For COVID-19, the highest and lowest (negative) ESG change originated from the human rights (D_D3) and workforce (D_C2) fields, respectively. Moreover, returns in full and COVID-19 samples had negative means. The controversies (D_E1) score was the one with the highest dispersion in both samples. This indicates the importance of its inclusion in ESG analyses. This also indicates that there should be a way for these controversies to be incorporated into ESG scores to make them more accurate. Looking at the remaining scores, the highest dispersions were for the human rights (D_C3) and emissions (D_B3) scores in full and COVID-19 samples, respectively. The normality null hypothesis (joint hypothesis of the skewness being zero and the excess kurtosis being zero) of the Jarque–Bera test could not be rejected for most of the ESG scores in both samples. More specifically, it was rejected for six and two scores in the full and COVID-19 samples, respectively. The normality was rejected for returns in both the annual and the daily frequencies, as well as in both samples (full and COVID-19). The daily credit rating change also rejected the normality hypothesis in both samples.

Table 3. Descriptive statistics.

	Mean		**Std. Dev.**		**Jarque–Bera (prob.)**	
	Full sample	COVID-19	Full sample	COVID-19	Full sample	COVID-19
			Annual			
ret	-4×10^{-4}	-1×10^{-4}	0.0011	3×10^{-4}	6.27×10^{-5} **	6.08×10^{-5} **
D_A1	0.0148	0.0228	0.0490	0.0733	0 **	0.9757
D_A2	0.0148	0.0228	0.3544	0.0733	0.7791	0.9757
D_B1	0.0127	0.0074	0.0832	0.1901	0.8781	0.9357
D_B2	0.0421	9×10^{-11}	0.0985	0.2620	0.0063 **	0.0145 **
D_B3	0.0146	0.0203	0.0790	0.2713	0.8603	0.4198
D_B4	0.0116	0.0369	0.1052	0.1788	0.0012 **	0.3352
D_C1	0.0275	−0.0046	0.0911	0.1278	0 **	0.9673
D_C2	0.0036	−0.0121	0.1248	0.1074	0.7159	0.6336
D_C3	0.1500	0	0.3418	0	0.0175 **	-
D_C4	0.0307	0.0148	0.2031	0.1139	0.2277	0.8635
D_C5	0	0	0	0	-	-
D_D1	−0.0221	0.0228	0.1276	0.2048	0.8623	0.5634
D_D2	−0.0148	0.0189	0.0794	0.2394	0.8520	0.1570
D_D3	0	0.0457	0.0845	0.2604	0.9858	0.3743
D_D4	0.0214	0.0203	0.1050	0.1390	0.0111 **	9×10^{-4} **
D_E1	−0.0305	0	0.8217	0.3023	0.9271	0.4311
			Daily			
ret	-6.67×10^{-13}	-6.08×10^{-5}	0.0168	0.0101	0 **	0 **
Credit risk	1.65×10^{-4}	-7.50×10^{-5}	0.0268	0.0184	0 **	0 **

Source: Authors' compilation. ** indicates statistical significance in 5% significance level.

Comparing only the overall (i.e., D_A1 and D_A2) and the three pillar (E, S, G) scores (i.e., D_B1, D_C1, and D_D1), the social pillar score (D_C1) had the highest return, while the lowest and highest dispersions (st.deviations) were for the total combined ESG score (D_A1) and governance pillar score (D_D1), respectively. These results hold for both samples.

From a descriptive analysis point of view, COVID-19 has affected ESGs in two ways. First, it has changed the scores with the highest and lowest changes. Second, the standard deviation of most ESG scores has increased.

4.2.2. Pairwise Correlations

The inter-relation of stock prices and credit ratings with ESG scores is firstly examined via the pairwise annual correlations (a) between stock price and credit rating returns with ESG score returns (Table 4A), and (b) among ESG scores (Table 4B) and, the daily correlations between price and credit rating returns are also examined (Table 4C). Table 4A–C contain an indication of statistical significance in pairwise correlations.

Regarding Table 4A and the full sample, most of the pairwise correlations between credit rating and ESG score changes are positive and insignificant. Most of the statistically significant correlations are also negative. These scores are for the governance pillar (D_D1), management (D_D2), and controversies (D_E1). This is an important result as it indicates a possible different information set between these ESG scores and credit ratings. In the COVID-19 subsample, there is no correlation that is statistically significant, however, despite the fact that there are four correlations with negative values.

Concerning Table 4B, 24.2% (29 out of 120) of the pairwise annual correlations among the ESG scores are statistically significant (at either the 10% or 5% level) in the full sample. This decreases to 16.7% (20 out of 120) in the COVID-19 subsample. The number of statistically significant correlations that are negative more than doubles from 17% (5 out of 29) in the full sample to 35% (7 out of 20) in the COVID-19 subsample. Also, the number of statistically significant and negative correlations is higher in the COVID-19 subsample than in the full sample (seven compared to five).

The total combined ESG score (D_A1) is the score that has the most statistically significant correlations with the remaining scores in both the full sample and the COVID-19 subsample. In the full sample, the human rights (D_C3) and the community (D_C4) scores are the scores with the second most significant correlations. In the COVID-19 subsample, the second most statistically significant correlations are for all sub-scores of the governance pillar (D). These are management (D_D2), shareholders (D_D3) and corporate social responsibility (CSR) strategy (D_D4).

All daily correlations between price and credit rating returns are positive and statistically insignificant in both the full sample and the COVID-19 subsamples (Table 4C).

Table 4. (**A**) Pairwise annual correlations of credit rating with ESG score annual returns.

	Full Sample	COVID-19
D_A1	−0.3633	0.1622
D_A2	−0.3633	−0.1413
D_B1	0.1857	0.1371
D_B2	0.7200 **	0.1833
D_B3	0.2477	0.1286
D_B4	−0.0052	0.1510
D_C1	0.2412	0.1622
D_C2	0.1298	−0.1556
D_C3	–	0.0760
D_C4	−0.1372	0.0910
D_C5	–	–
D_D1	−0.6455 **	0.2683
D_D2	−0.6804 **	0.0320
D_D3	−0.4351	0.0941
D_D4	0.4171	−0.1096
D_E1	−0.7294 **	−0.1323

Source: Authors' compilation. ** indicate statistical significance at 5% significance levels.

Table 4. *Cont.*

(**B**) Pairwise annual correlations among ESG scores.

	Panel A. Full sample															
	D_A1	D_A2	D_B1	D_B2	D_B3	D_B4	D_C1	D_C2	D_C3	D_C4	D_C5	D_D1	D_D2	D_D3	D_D4	D_E1
D_A1	1															
D_A2	−0.4212	1														
D_B1	0.5887 *	−0.0498	1													
D_B2	−0.1416	−0.0196	0.4402	1												
D_B3	0.6118 **	−0.2577	0.6574 **	0.4523	1											
D_B4	0.9165 **	−0.1948	0.5355 *	−0.0518	0.5607 *	1										
D_C1	1	−0.4212	0.5887 *	−0.1416	0.6118 **	0.9165 **	1									
D_C2	0.4165	−0.3588	−0.2208	−0.4052	0.0275	0.3550	0.4165	1								
D_C3	0.8651 **	−0.2800	0.6232 **	−0.0104	0.5293 *	0.8185 **	0.8651 **	0.1742	1							
D_C4	0.7608 **	−0.6499 **	0.4459	−0.0709	0.6346 **	0.4807	0.7608 **	0.5061	0.5906 *	1						
D_C5	-	-	-	-	-	-	-	-	-	-	-					
D_D1	0.0573	−0.2824	0.3223	−0.1289	−0.1901	−0.1685	0.0573	−0.3976	0.0143	0.1269	-	1				
D_D2	0.0617	0.2144	0.4257	−0.2030	−0.2735	0.0226	0.0617	−0.2570	−0.0027	−0.1374	-	0.7240 **	1			
D_D3	0.5244 *	−0.4609	0.3048	−0.2609	0.0412	0.4544	0.5244 *	0.4063	0.2942	0.3442	-	0.4026	0.5565 *	1		
D_D4	−0.0676	−0.3605	−0.2580	−0.5014	−0.2769	−0.4283	−0.0676	0.1875	−0.0899	0.4040	-	0.4465	0.0417	0.0000	1	
D_E1	−0.5948 *	0.9604 **	−0.1265	0.0174	−0.3639	−0.3982	−0.5948 *	−0.5484 *	−0.3948	−0.7531 **	-	−0.1409	0.2261	−0.5480 *	−0.2570	1
	Panel B. COVID-19															
	D_A1	D_A2	D_B1	D_B2	D_B3	D_B4	D_C1	D_C2	D_C3	D_C4	D_C5	D_D1	D_D2	D_D3	D_D4	D_E1
D_A1	1															
D_A2	1	1														
D_B1	0.2275	0.2275	1													
D_B2	0.1514	0.1514	0.5961 *	1												
D_B3	−0.2239	−0.2239	0.4861	0.4254	1											
D_B4	0.4811	0.4811	0.7845 **	0.4892	0.5772 *	1										
D_C1	0.5506 *	0.5506 *	0.4715	0.4154	0.1321	0.4995	1									
D_C2	0.4417	0.4417	0.2636	0.3463	−0.1578	0.1855	0.1908	1								

Table 4. *Cont.*

D_C3	-	-	-	-	-	-	-	-	-							
D_C4	0.6743 **	0.6743	0.2971	0.1567	−0.2025	0.4173	0.6773 **	−0.1614	-	1						
D_C5	-	-	-	-	-	-	-	-	-	-	-					
D_D1	0.4405	0.4405	0.2081	−0.2171	−0.1441	0.1436	−0.2499	0.4596	-	−0.0445	-	1				
D_D2	0.5590 *	0.5590 *	0.1669	−0.2153	−0.1273	0.1658	−0.1354	0.4334	-	0.0392	-	0.9723 **	1			
D_D3	0.7653 **	0.7653 **	−0.1877	−0.2210	−0.6257 **	0.1188	0.1968	0.4105	-	0.4067	-	0.3212	0.3893	1		
D_D4	−0.7299 **	−0.7299 **	0.0930	0.2030	0.2722	−0.2847	−0.4524	0.0182	-	−0.6245 **	-	−0.1006	−0.2486	−0.7587 **	1	
D_E1	0.1238	0.1238	−0.4701	−0.7675 **	−0.2935	−0.4469	−0.2578	−0.0319	-	−0.1587	-	0.5494 *	0.6090 **	0.1874	−0.2243	1

Source: Authors' compilation. ** and * indicate statistical significance at 5% and 10% significance levels, respectively.

Table 4. *Cont.*

(**C**) Pairwise daily correlations among the returns of prices and credit ratings.

		Credit Rating Returns	
		Full sample	COVID-19
Price returns	Full sample	0.0245	-
	COVID-19	-	0.0210

Source: Authors' compilation. ** and * indicate statistical significance at 5% and 10% significance levels, respectively.

4.2.3. Granger Causality

The inter-relations were also examined via Granger causality relations between (a) price and ESG score annual returns (Table 5A); (b) price and credit rating daily returns (Table 4A); and total and pillar ESG scores (Table 5B).

Table 5. (**A**) Granger causality between price and ESG score annual returns, and between price and credit rating daily returns.

	Full Sample	COVID-19
	Panel A. Price returns causing ESG score changes	
D_A1	0.6057	1.09
D_A2	0.6057	0.6250
D_B1	0.2786	0.1692
D_B2	1.43	0.2809
D_B3	1.38	0.3377
D_B4	0.7574	1.59
D_C1	0.0629	1.09
D_C2	0.4628	1.52
D_C3	-	1.27
D_C4	0.1807	2.34
D_C5	-	-
D_D1	2.46	2.46
D_D2	4.67 **	0.3171
D_D3	0.1133	1.43
D_D4	0.3474	0.2568
D_E1	0.9162	1.00
	Panel B. ESG score changes causing price returns	
D_A1	0.1535	0.1778
D_A2	0.2176	0.1778
D_B1	0.3504	0.5203
D_B2	0.2069	0.3578
D_B3	0.2100	0.9001
D_B4	1.98	0.2656
D_C1	0.1535	0.0707
D_C2	4.65 *	4.46 *
D_C3	0.6406	-
D_C4	0.8079	0.5813
D_C5	-	-
D_D1	0.7357	0.2819
D_D2	0.2748	0.3813
D_D3	0.2303	1.86
D_D4	1.25 **	1.25
D_E1	0.2131	0.9945
	Panel C. Relationship between price (P) and credit rating (CR) returns	
P causing CR	0.0663	0.0544
CR causing P	0.0754	0.0329

Source: Authors' compilation. Notes. The table reports the F-statistic value of the Granger causality test with 1 lag. ** and * indicate statistical significance at 5% and 10% significance levels, respectively.

Table 5. *Cont.*

(**B**) Granger causality between total and pillar ESG scores.

	D_A1	D_A2	D_B1	D_C1	D_D1	D_E1
Panel A. Full Sample						
D_A1	-	-	0.0765	0.5807	0.5859	0.5929
D_A2	-	-	0.0765	0.5807	0.5859	0.5929
D_B1	0.9078	0.9078	-	0.5523	1.80	0.3681
D_C1	0.5565	0.5565	0.1294	-	0.7397	0.8755
D_D1	2.65	6.49 *	0.2570	1.47	-	2.02
D_E1	0.8043	0.8043	0.7707	0.0219	23.07 **	-
Panel B. COVID-19						
	D_A1	D_A2	D_B1	D_C1	D_D1	D_E1
D_A1	-	0.2832	2.94	-	5.77 *	0.1447
D_A2	3.1×10^{-16}	-	3.36	0.0000	6.20 *	0.3219
D_B1	2.52	1.66	-	2.52	3.37	1.68
D_C1	-	0.2832	2.94	-	1.77	0.1447
D_D1	0.7261	5.34 *	0.5551	0.7261	-	2.75
D_E1	0.0036	1.03	3.28	0.0036	0.3866	-

Source: Authors' compilation. Notes. The table reports the F-statistic value of the Granger causality test with 1 lag between total and pillar ESG scores. Test whether each ESG score in column Granger-causes each ESG score in rows. ** and * indicate statistical significance at 5% and 10%.

Regarding Table 5A and the full sample, price returns Granger-cause only management (D_D2), across all scores. Moreover, the score changes only for workforce (D_C2) and CSR strategy (D_D4) Granger-cause price returns. In the COVID-19 subsample, there is only one case of statistically significant Granger causality. This is that workforce (D_C2) changes Granger-cause price returns. Price returns do not Granger-cause ESG changes for any score in the COVID-19 subsample. Also, there is no Granger causality relationship between price and credit-rating daily returns in either the full or the COVID-19 sample.

Concerning Table 5B, most of the ESG scores do not have any (in any direction) Granger causality among them in either the full sample or the COVID-19 subsample. An important result is that the governance pillar score (D_D1) Granger-causes the total ESG score (D_A2), and this also holds in both the full sample and the COVID-19 subsample. Moreover, the statistical significance of ESGs' Granger causality increased from 6.3% (2 out of 32) in the full sample to 9.4% (3 out of 32) in the COVID-19 subsample.

4.2.4. Regressions

The explanatory power of ESG score change upon credit-rating change is also examined with an OLS regression (Table 6A). Moreover, the explanatory power of daily credit-rating returns upon price returns is examined at a daily frequency (Table 6B). Both OLS regressions concern the full sample and the COVID-19 subsample.

Regarding Table 6A, the α- and β-coefficients reveal the effect of ESG changes and COVID-19, respectively. Values and *p*-values concern the coefficient values and the level of statistical significance, respectively. The direct explanatory power of ESGs on credit ratings is around 25% (for 4 out of 16 scores, there is a statistically significant α-coefficient). The statistical significance of the COVID-19 explanatory (dummy) variable is higher at around 44% (for 7 out of 16 scores there is a statistically significant β-coefficient). This indicates that COVID-19 reveals some of the explanatory power of ESG scores upon credit ratings. The overall joint significance of both β- and γ-coefficients (i.e., R-squared) across ESGs is high, ranging from 5.9% to 54.5%. Here, we have to consider that we have employed only two explanatory variables without any control variables. The reason for such a choice is to target the explanatory power of each ESG score at a time, as well as COVID-19 (as a dummy variable).

The explanatory power of daily credit-rating returns and COVID-19 (as a dummy variable) upon price returns at a daily frequency is reported in Table 6B. The former and latter effects are revealed by the γ- and δ-coefficients, respectively. The impact of credit ratings on price returns was statistically insignificant. COVID-19 has negatively (and in a statistically significant way) affected price returns, though. The low joint explanatory power of the variables on price returns was also revealed by the low R-squared value (3.8%).

Table 6. (**A**) OLS regressions between ESG score, credit rating annual changes, and COVID-19.

	α-Coefficient		β (COVID-19)-Coefficient		R-Squared
	Value	*p*-Value	Value	*p*-Value	
D_A1	−0.0016	0.2721	2.01×10^{-5}	0.9481	13.2%
D_A2	−0.0016	0.2721	2.01×10^{-5}	0.9481	13.2%
D_B1	2.98×10^{-4}	0.5846	2.67×10^{-4} *	0.0185	9.4%
D_B2	9.04×10^{-4} **	0.0125	2.64×10^{-4} **	0.0132	51.8%
D_B3	3×10^{-4}	0.4628	2.71×10^{-4} *	0.0214	12.3%
D_B4	-9.63×10^{-6}	0.9878	3×10^{-4}	0.1362	6.6%
D_C1	6.21×10^{-4}	0.4749	5.37×10^{-4} *	0.0063	23.8%
D_C2	3.98×10^{-4}	0.7037	2.59×10^{-4} *	0.0284	7.3%
D_C3	-	-	-	-	-
D_C4	-3.96×10^{-4}	0.6874	2.55×10^{-4}	0.2556	5.9%
D_C5	-	-	-	-	-
D_D1	−0.0011 **	0.0320	2.36×10^{-4} **	0.0308	41.7%
D_D2	-9.35×10^{-4} *	0.0212	1.12×10^{-4}	0.2552	47.3%
D_D3	-5.50×10^{-4}	0.1810	2.83×10^{-5}	0.8566	18.9%
D_D4	0.0010	0.2019	-9.95×10^{-4} *	0.0056	30.3%
D_E1	-7.94×10^{-4} *	0.0002	1.28×10^{-4}	0.1344	54.5%

Source: Authors' compilation. Notes. The OLS regression estimates the explanatory power of annual ESG score returns upon credit-rating changes at an annual frequency. The coefficient covariance estimation method is HAC (Newey–West). ** and * indicate statistical significance at 5% and 10%.

(**B**) OLS regressions between credit rating, daily price returns, and COVID-19.

	Coefficient	*p*-Value	R-Squared
γ	0.0389	0.1549	0.0377
δ (COVID-19)	−0.0030	0.0678 *	

Source: Authors' compilation. Notes. The OLS regression estimates the explanatory power of daily credit-rating returns upon price returns at a daily frequency. The coefficient covariance estimation method is HAC (Newey–West). * indicates statistical significance at 5%.

5. Discussion

The results of our paper provide a comprehensive analysis of the relationships between ESG scores, credit ratings, and stock prices in the banking sector, with a unique focus on both annual and daily data frequencies. This dual-frequency approach offers a detailed temporal perspective that is not commonly found in the existing literature. Our findings highlight significant pairwise correlations between stock price returns and ESG score returns, especially during the COVID-19 pandemic, indicating a positive relationship where improved ESG performance is associated with better stock market outcomes. This aligns with the studies by Devalle et al. (2017) and Liu et al. (2023), which also report that better ESG performance reduces stock price volatility and enhances returns. However, the results of our paper diverge from these studies in the context of the explanatory power of ESG scores on credit rating changes, which our regressions suggest is limited. This contrasts with the findings of Chodnicka-Jaworska (2021) and Devalle et al. (2017), who observed significant impacts of ESG factors on credit ratings. This discrepancy may stem from differences in sample size, methodology, or the specific ESG sub-scores considered.

Our paper finds significant daily correlations and Granger causality between credit rating changes and stock price returns, suggesting that credit rating changes are promptly reflected in stock prices. This is consistent with the results of Hau et al. (2013) and Wojewodzki et al. (2020), who highlight the influence of credit ratings on stock prices and capital structures, reinforcing the critical role of credit ratings in financial markets. The significant impact of the COVID-19 pandemic on the relationships among ESG scores, credit ratings, and stock prices is a key finding of our study, echoing insights from Demir and Danisman (2021) and Yuen et al. (2022). These studies similarly find that the pandemic has heightened the relevance of ESG considerations and altered financial dynamics.

Methodologically, our paper uses a robust combination of descriptive statistics, pairwise correlations, Granger causality tests, and OLS regressions. This comprehensive approach, coupled with the analysis of both annual and daily data, provides a more detailed understanding of these relationships. This contrasts with many of the reviewed studies, which typically focus on annual data alone. The detailed breakdown of ESG scores into 16 sub-scores in our paper allows for a comprehensive analysis, distinguishing our work from others that use broader ESG metrics. This granularity provides deeper insights into specific ESG factors, contributing uniquely to the literature.

In conclusion, our paper corroborates many findings from the reviewed literature while also presenting unique insights due to its detailed ESG breakdown, dual-frequency analysis, and focus on the COVID-19 pandemic. The mixed results regarding the influence of ESG scores on credit ratings highlight the complexity of these relationships and the need for further research. Our methodological rigor and comprehensive approach significantly advance the understanding of the relationships between ESG factors, credit ratings, and stock prices in the banking sector.

The results of our paper differ from the results of the 20 reviewed articles in several key areas. Firstly, our study finds a limited explanatory power of ESG scores on credit rating changes, as indicated by the low significance in the regression models. This contrasts with studies by Chodnicka-Jaworska (2021) and Devalle et al. (2017), which report significant impacts of ESG factors on credit ratings. The difference may be due to the granularity of the ESG scores used in our analysis or the specific sample of banks studied.

Secondly, while our paper highlights the significant impact of the COVID-19 pandemic on the relationships between ESG scores, credit ratings, and stock prices, this focus on the pandemic's effects is less emphasized in some of the reviewed studies. Although studies like Demir and Danisman (2021) and Yuen et al. (2022) also recognize the pandemic's influence, they do not explore it to the same depth or with the same methodological rigor as our study.

Additionally, our detailed breakdown of ESG scores into 16 sub-scores provides a more comprehensive analysis than most other studies, which typically use broader ESG metrics. This granularity allows our paper to identify specific ESG factors that impact financial metrics, offering insights that are not captured in studies that use more aggregated ESG data.

In summary, the primary differences lie in the detailed granularity of ESG scores, the limited explanatory power of these scores on credit ratings in our findings, and the extensive focus on the COVID-19 pandemic's impact. These distinctions highlight the unique contributions and insights provided by our research, setting it apart from the existing literature. Overall, based on these results, the hypotheses examined in this paper and stated in Section 3 are all validated.

6. Conclusions

This paper provides evidence of the inter-relations among ESGs, stock prices, and credit ratings in the banking sector. In the descriptive analysis, concentrating only on the overall and pillar scores, the highest mean score change was for the social pillar, while the lowest and highest dispersions were for the total combined and governance pillar scores. Most of the changes in ESG scores were normally distributed. Price returns and credit rating changes were non-normally distributed, however. All the above results hold in the full sample as well as the COVID-19 subsample.

The significant inter-relation is expressed in the form of pairwise annual correlations (a) between credit rating returns with ESG score returns, and (b) among ESG scores. Most of the ESG scores are positively correlated with credit ratings with low statistical significance, however. Most of the ESG pillar and total scores are negatively and statistically significantly correlated. This result is very promising, as it indicates the different information captured by the different total and pillar scores. On the other hand, there is clear evidence that there is no Granger causality between (a) price and ESG score annual returns, (b) price and credit rating daily returns, or (c) total and pillar ESG scores. Furthermore, our regression findings revealed a limited explanatory power of ESGs on credit ratings. COVID-19 increased the overall explanatory power of credit ratings, however. Moreover, credit ratings could not explain price returns.

These results reveal that COVID-19 had an important role in price returns, credit ratings, and ESGs in the banking sector. Firstly, COVID-19 appears to have affected ESGs based on the descriptive statistics analysis. More specifically, it caused a change in the scores with the highest and lowest changes. Also, the standard deviation of most ESG scores increased. Secondly, COVID-19 affected the statistical significance of the pairwise correlations between credit ratings and ESG scores, as well as between ESG scores. Even though, in the latter case (among ESG scores), the number of statistically significant correlations that were negative more than doubled, this may indicate that COVID-19 revealed distinct informational content among ESG scores. Thirdly, COVID-19 decreased the Granger causality between prices and ESGs. Fourthly, COVID-19 increased the statistical significance of the ESGs' Granger causality. Finally, COVID-19 revealed some of the explanatory power of ESG scores upon credit ratings (as indicated by more statistically significant coefficients and higher R-squared values). Moreover, COVID-19 positively and negatively affected credit-rating changes and price returns, respectively.

Future research should place emphasize on other forms of inter-relations between stock prices and credit ratings with ESG scores, as well as between credit rating changes and price returns.

Our paper finds that the explanatory power of ESG scores on credit rating changes is relatively low. This might be due to the complexity of credit ratings, which are influenced by a wide range of financial and non-financial factors. ESG scores, while important, may not capture all the aspects that credit rating agencies consider. Also, this low performance might be attributed to data limitations, because the use of data from only six banks, while carefully selected taking into consideration data availability, may limit the generalizability and robustness of the findings. The sample size might be too small to capture the full variability and impact of ESG scores across a more diverse set of banks and market conditions. In addition to possible data limitations, we also understand that linear models may oversimplify interactions and miss important dynamics, and thus other model approaches could be tried in future research. Last but not least, the pandemic has introduced high volatility and uncertainty in financial markets. Thus, the model performance during such a period might be affected by factors such as sudden policy changes, economic shutdowns, and changes in investor behavior which were not accounted for in the current study. Future research could possibly address all the aforementioned aspects by enlarging the dataset, differentiating the econometric approach, and controlling external factors.

Author Contributions: Conceptualization, D.V.; Methodology, D.V.; Software, A.N.M.; Validation, A.N.M.; Formal analysis, A.N.M.; Investigation, A.N.M.; Resources, D.V.; Data curation, D.V.; Writing—original draft, A.N.M.; Writing—review & editing, A.N.M. and S.A.; Visualization, A.N.M.; Supervision, D.V.; Project administration, A.N.M.; Funding acquisition, A.N.M. All authors have read and agreed to the published version of the manuscript.

Funding: This research received no external funding.

Informed Consent Statement: Informed consent was obtained from all subjects involved in the study.

Data Availability Statement: Restrictions apply to the availability of these data. Data were obtained from Refinitiv Eikon, Reuters, and are available [from the authors/at https://eikon.refinitiv.com/] with the permission of Refinitiv Eikon, Reuters.

Conflicts of Interest: The authors declare no conflict of interest.

References

Abdul Razak, Lutfi, Mansor H. Ibrahim, and Adam Ng. 2020. Which Sustainability Dimensions Affect Credit Risk? Evidence from Corporate and Country-Level Measures. *Journal of Banking & Finance* 113: 105772.

Apergis, Nicholas, James E. Payne, and Chris Tsoumas. 2012. The Impact of Credit Rating Changes on U.S. Banks. *Banking and Finance Review* 4: 1–50.

Arif, Muhammad, Christopher Gan, and Hussein Ahmed Betaineh. 2024. Global evidence on the association between environmental, social, and governance disclosures and future earnings risk. *Business Strategy and the Environment* 33: 2497–517. [CrossRef]

Azmi, Wajahat, M. Kabir Hassan, Reza Houston, and Mohammad Sydul Karim. 2021. ESG activities and banking performance: International evidence from emerging economies. *Journal of International Financial Markets, Institutions and Money* 70: 101277. [CrossRef]

Batae, Oana-Marina, Voicu D. Dragomir, and Liliana Feleaga. 2020. Environmental, social, governance (ESG), and financial performance of European banks. *Journal of Accounting and Management Information Systems* 19: 480–501. [CrossRef]

Brogi, Marina, Valentina Lagasio, and Pasqualina Porretta. 2022. Be Good to Be Wise: Environmental, Social, and Governance Awareness as a Potential Credit Risk Mitigation Factor. *Journal of International Financial Management & Accounting* 33: 522–47.

Burger, Eric, Fabian Grba, and Thomas Heidorn. 2022. The Impact of ESG Ratings on Implied and Historical Volatility. Frankfurt School—Working Paper Series, no. 230, Frankfurt School of Finance & Management, March 2022. Available online: http://hdl.handle.net/10419/251516 (accessed on 1 January 2024).

Chiaramonte, Laura, Alberto Dreassi, Claudia Girardone, and Stefano Piserà. 2022. Do ESG strategies enhance bank stability during financial turmoil? Evidence from Europe. *The European Journal of Finance* 28: 1173–211. [CrossRef]

Chodnicka-Jaworska, Patrycja. 2021. ESG as a Measure of Credit Ratings. *Risks* 9: 226. [CrossRef]

Citterio, Alberto, and Timothy King. 2022. The role of Environmental, Social, and Governance (ESG) in predicting bank financial distress. *Finance Research Letters* 51: 103411. [CrossRef]

Cornett, Marcia Millon, Otgontsetseg Erhemjamts, and Hassan Tehranian. 2016. Greed or good deeds: An examination of the relation between corporate social responsibility and the financial performance of US commercial banks around the financial crisis. *Journal of Banking and Finance* 70: 137–59. [CrossRef]

Demir, Ender, and Gamze Ozturk Danisman. 2021. Banking sector reactions to COVID-19: The role of bank-specific factors and government policy responses. *Research in International Business and Finance* 58: 101508. [CrossRef]

Devalle, Alain, Simona Fiandrino, and Valter Cantino. 2017. The Linkage between ESG Performance and Credit Ratings: A Firm-Level Perspective Analysis. *International Journal of Business and Management* 12: 53–65. [CrossRef]

Dospinescu, Octavian, Nicoleta Dospinescu, and Daniela-Tatiana Agheorghiesei. 2021. Fintech Services and Factors Determining the Expected Benefits of Users: Evidence in Romania for Millennials and Generation Z. *Finance* 2: 101–18. [CrossRef]

El Khoury, Rim, Nohade Nasrallah, and Bahaaeddin Alareeni. 2023. ESG and financial performance of banks in the MENAT region: Concavity–convexity patterns. *Journal of Sustainable Finance and Investment* 13: 406–30. [CrossRef]

European Banking Authority. 2023. On the Role of Environmental and Social Risks in the Prudential Framework. Report 34. Available online: https://www.eba.europa.eu/sites/default/files/document_library/Publications/Reports/2023/1062711/Report%20on%20the%20role%20of%20environmental%20and%20social%20risks%20in%20the%20prudential%20framework.pdf (accessed on 1 January 2024).

Galeone, Graziana, Simona Ranaldo, and Antonio Fusco. 2024. ESG and FinTech: Are they connected? *Research in International Business and Finance* 69: 102225. [CrossRef]

Grigorieva, Elena, and Darko Vukovic. 2020. Assessing Methodology of Banks' Ratings and Their Competitive Positions: Overview of Main Rating Agencies. *RUDN Journal of Economics* 28: 23–30. [CrossRef]

Hau, Harald, Sam Langfield, and David Marques-Ibanez. 2013. Bank Ratings: What Determines Their Quality? *Economic Policy* 28: 289–333. [CrossRef]

Houston, Joel F., and Hongyu Shan. 2022. Corporate ESG profiles and banking relationships. *The Review of Financial Studies* 35: 3373–417. [CrossRef]

Jang, Ga-Young, Hyoung-Goo Kang, Ju-Yeong Lee, and Kyounghun Bee. 2020. ESG Scores and the Credit Market. *Sustainability* 12: 3456. [CrossRef]

Kiesel, Florian, and Felix Lücke. 2022. ESG in Credit Ratings and the Impact on Financial Markets. *Journal of International Financial Markets, Institutions and Money* 77: 101547. [CrossRef]

La Torre, Mario, Sabrina Leo, and Ida Claudia Panetta. 2021. Banks and environmental, social and governance drivers: Follow the market or the authorities? *Corporate Social Responsibility and Environmental Management* 28: 1620–34. [CrossRef]

Li, Hao, Xuan Zhang, and Yang Zhao. 2022. ESG and Firm's Default Risk. *Finance Research Letters* 47: 1027. [CrossRef]

Liu, Dayong, Kaiyuan Gu, and Wenhua Hu. 2023. ESG Performance and Stock Idiosyncratic Volatility. *Finance Research Letters* 58: 104393. [CrossRef]

Liu, Zhaohua, Susheng Wang, Siyi Liu, Haixu Yu, and He Wang. 2022. Volatility Risk Premium, Return Predictability, and ESG Sentiment: Evidence from China's Spots and Options' Markets. *Complexity* 2022: 6813797. [CrossRef]

Michalski, Lachlan, and Rand Kwong Yew Low. 2024. Determinants of Corporate Credit Ratings: Does ESG Matter? *International Review of Financial Analysis* 94: 103228. [CrossRef]

Penikas, Henry. 2022. The Interrelationship of Credit and Climate Risks (Working Paper No. 100). Bank of Russia. Available online: https://www.cbr.ru (accessed on 1 January 2024).

Pineau, Édouard, Phuong Le, and Rémy Estran. 2022. Importance of ESG Factors in Sovereign Credit Ratings. *Finance Research Letters* 49: 102966. [CrossRef]

Poon, Winnie, Junsoo Lee, and Benton Gup. 2009. Do solicitations matter in bank credit ratings? Results from a study of 72 countries. *Journal of Money, Credit and Banking* 41: 285–314. [CrossRef]

Ruddy, John A. 2021. An Analysis of Bank Financial Strength Ratings and Credit Rating Data. *Risks* 9: 155. [CrossRef]
Shen, Chung-Hua, Yu-Li Huang, and Iftekhar Hasan. 2012. Asymmetric benchmarking in bank credit rating. *Journal of International Financial Markets, Institutions and Money* 22: 171–93. [CrossRef]
Singh, Kuldeep, and Megha Jaiwani. 2023. ESG and Share Price Volatility in Energy Sector Firms: Does the Development Phase of Countries Matter? *International Journal of Energy Sector Management* 17: 489–512. [CrossRef]
van Loon, Eric, and Jakob de Haan. 2015. Location of banks and their credit ratings. *Journal of Risk Finance* 16: 220–30. [CrossRef]
Wang, Deli, Ke Peng, Kaiye Tang, and Yewei Wu. 2022. Does Fintech Development Enhance Corporate ESG Performance? Evidence from an Emerging Market. *Sustainability* 14: 16597. [CrossRef]
Wojewodzki, Michal, Agyenim Boateng, and Sanjukta Brahma. 2020. Credit rating, banks' capital structure and speed of adjustment: A cross-country analysis. Journal of International Financial Markets. *Institutions and Money* 69: 101260. [CrossRef]
Yuen, Mui Kuen, Thanh Ngo, Tu D Le, and Tin H Ho. 2022. The environment, social and governance (ESG) activities and profitability under COVID-19: Evidence from the global banking sector. *Journal of Economics and Development* 24: 345–64. [CrossRef]
Zhou, Guangyou, Yongkun Sun, Sumei Luo, and Jiayi Liao. 2021. Corporate social responsibility and bank financial performance in China: The moderating role of green credit. *Energy Economics* 97: 105190. [CrossRef]

economies

MDPI

Article

Crises and Contagion in Equity Portfolios

Christos Floros, Dimitrios Vortelinos * and Ioannis Chatziantoniou

Department of Accounting and Finance and Laboratory of Accounting and Financial Management (LAFIM), Hellenic Mediterranean University, 71410 Heraklion, Greece; cfloros@hmu.gr (C.F.); yanhatzi@hmu.gr (I.C.)
* Correspondence: dvortelinos@hmu.gr

Abstract: We examine the international impact of recent financial crises on contagion dynamics within international equity portfolios. First, we highlight the importance of macroeconomics for portfolio weighting for each region, and then we examine contagion via a structural regime-switching model and a contagion test. We also examine sources of contagion using regime variables, crisis events, and macroeconomic variables. In particular, we study the Argentine debt crisis, the US financial crisis, and the EU sovereign debt crisis. The macroeconomic variables include changes in market capitalization, trade integration, GDP growth, inflation rate, and interest rate. We also employ two classifications, one relating to the portfolio weighting scheme and another one that considers implied global and regional betas. The empirical findings reveal the existence of financial contagion for all the crises that we investigate. Both methods produce similar results. Stronger contagion is evident for global rather than regional betas. Europe is the region with the highest level of contagion and the one mostly affected by the crises. As far as macroeconomic variables are concerned, they are very important in two ways. They statistically significantly explain contagion, while they also reveal contagion under various portfolio weighting schemes. Both methods suggest that the Argentinian crisis mainly contributes to contagion. The research implications suggest that asset allocation and portfolio management should consider both the global and the regional aspects of contagion as differences can occur.

Keywords: contagion; financial crises; portfolios; equity; macroeconomics

1. Introduction

The international impact of the recent financial crises raises issues concerning the contagion (integration and comovements). Financial integration offers welfare gains; it may also carry substantial risks. This becomes more evident in crises (Devereux and Yu 2020). There is a transmission of crisis effects from one market to another (see, among others, Baele and Inghelbrecht 2010). Each crisis has different causes and consequences to financial markets. (Ehrmann et al. 2011) and (Gunay and Can 2022) researched the existence of contagion and spillovers in the global financial crisis.

The global financial crisis refers to the 2008 subprime crisis starting in the United States and having global consequences for a few years (Raddant and Kenett 2021). The 2010 EU sovereign debt crisis had similar international consequences (Shen et al. 2015). Contagion in the European Union during the global financial crisis and the European debt crisis were examined via ADCC-GJR-GARCH and Markov-switching models citepALEXAKIS2018222. The role of national governments (via the evolution of macroeconomics and policy making) in the EU debt crisis was also researched (Kosmidou et al. 2019).

In line with Corbet and Goodell (2022), we also opine that both financial contagion and systemic risk pose major considerations when it comes to financial market operations, while the investigation of interconnectedness dynamics has become one of major importance. Globalization dynamics and technological advancements have resulted in increased interconnectedness across financial markets and affect investments all over the world. In this paper, we consider cross-border investments and international portfolio contagion by looking into international equity markets (i.e., 4 regions/containments, 67 countries) and by further applying weights based on a set of macroeconomic variables that affect contagion dynamics.

The present paper makes a number of contributions to the literature. It extends the empirical findings provided by Cho et al. (2015) to the international stock markets. The augmented structural factor model of Cho et al. (2015) is employed to model shifts in integration and incorporate crisis dummies. It examines sixty international stock indices from sixty respective national stock exchanges instead of firm level data. The second contribution is whether certain portfolios based on national macroeconomic variables provide different contagion evidence than others. Moreover, the paper determines the value of the stock indices, either emerging or developed, and with different values of country characteristics (macroeconomic variables), on a regional and global level.

As far as the theoretical contributions of the paper are concerned, we add to the existing literature by considering various crises periods across the globe and by adopting different portfolio frameworks. For instance, we employ different weights for portfolio construction depending on the underlying macroeconomic variable. Moreover, we show that portfolio contagion is stronger in the global rather than the regional framework. In turn we find that market capitalization is the most appropriate macroeconomic variable to use in order to reveal contagion, compared to all other macroeconomic variables. We also show that Europe is the region mostly affected by crises and that the Argentinian crisis had a very pronounced effect across global economies. In this respect, we offer fresh insights regarding contagion in international equity portfolios, and we further provide fertile ground for future research on the relevant topic.

The remainder of the paper is organized as follows. Section 2 presents the literature review. Section 3 describes the dataset. In turn, Section 4 outlines methodology. Section 5 presents the empirical findings and the discussion, and Section 6 concludes.

2. Literature Review

Many scholars have recently been involved in research relating to the dynamics of contagion and financial interdependence. For instance, Corbet and Goodell (2022) stress the importance of investigating interconnectedness dynamics across firms, industries, and markets and provide evidence by considering reputational contagion. Furthermore, Corbet et al. (2022) offer valuable insights with regard to contagion dynamics by looking into the implications of the COVID-19 pandemic for stock market performance. In turn, Bouzzine and Lueg (2020) look into the impact of contagion dynamics stemming from environmental violations on the stock market performance.

Different methods have been employed to study contagion in financial crises. A part of the literature employed the DCC-GARCH methodology to quantify the impact of a global financial crisis in the interdependence of the markets (Nguyen et al. 2022). The literature has also employed a Markov-switching Bayesian vector autoregression (MSBVAR) model to research contagion for the global financial crisis (Troug and Murray 2021). It is expected that a trade-off emerges between the probability of crises and the severity of crises (Devereux and Yu 2020). The importance of national or regional exposures to contagion was evident and increased due to the global financial crisis, however. These effects have not been researched a lot in the literature. There was evidence for the banking sector, however (Park and Shin 2020), as well as in equity markets (Trihadmini and Falinaty 2020).

Another stream of the literature examined the role of macroeconomics in the international impact of the recent financial crises in contagion (Jiang et al. 2022). The Mexican and Asian crises, originating in emerging markets, were considered to have mostly a regional impact, whereas the recent US and EU debt crises had a global impact. The global impact of global financial crisis and the European sovereign debt crisis were examined in BenSaïda and Litimi (2021). They found an increased degree of dependence for each crisis, suggesting strong evidence of contagion for both the global financial crisis and EU sovereign debt crisis. The strong impacts depend on the role of macroeconomics. This is because controlling the impact of macro variables that capture real or financial linkages on stock correlations is crucial for determining market overreactions to shocks (Pineda et al. 2022).

The internationalization of the impact of the financial crises was expressed in both trading as well as asset allocation. The literature examined such impact for the recent global and EU financial crises in an asset allocation framework. Such regional and global impacts affect portfolio diversification and asset allocation. Financial crises create international portfolio diversification opportunities as the extent of the contagion increases (Akhtaruzzaman et al. 2014). Cho et al. (2015) examined whether crises have different effects on style portfolios. Others researched international contagion (the transmission of financial shocks internationally) for US downturns and the global financial crisis (Akhtaruzzaman and Shamsuddin 2016). The literature attempted to conceptualize this impact in a portfolio framework (e.g., Shen and Li 2020).

The methodology employed is a regime-switching GARCH model in accordance with a world–regional–local CAPM, similar to Cho et al. (2015) and Baele and Inghelbrecht (2010). More of the recent studies include Shruthi and Shijin (2020), Dua and Tuteja (2021), and Bouker and Mansouri (2022), among others. This is a joint hypothesis problem of an appropriate factor specification of comovements. Moreover, Baele and Inghelbrecht (2010) and Ehrmann et al. (2011) contagion tests are employed to discover whether international equity portfolios experienced contagion effects through increased comovements during periods of financial crises. Ehrmann et al. (2011) examined the additional impact on comovement represented by a multi-factor model with global, regional, and country factors. The US and EU financial crises are expected to have a high global impact in international equity portfolios. Cho et al. (2015) found signs of contagion with a global impact for the US crisis (also evident in Bekiros 2014; Dungey and Gajurel 2014). Cho et al. (2015) also found a regional impact for the Mexican and Asian crises (also evident in Ehrmann et al. 2011), and a limited impact for the EU debt crisis. Similar evidence is expected for the international equity portfolios in the present paper.

3. Dataset

The dataset begins on 3 January 2000 and ends on 31 December 2016, for a total of 4264 trading days. All of the data have been extracted from Datastream. We have employed data only up to 2016, because we targeted only the examination of financial crises. A wider dataset should have included data within the COVID-19 pandemic. This would have affected our results, as the literature provided evidence that COVID-19 affected contagion (Akhtaruzzaman et al. 2021). After cleaning the dataset for common trading days in an international setting; the trading days were reduced to 3906. All of the stock market data are in US dollars. Table 1 reveals the countries (split in regions/continents) and their respective stock exchanges and indices. The symbols, as well as the regional and global weights based on trade integration, GDP, and stock market capitalization, are also provided. In terms of trade integration, the Americas and Europe have the highest and lowest weightings, respectively. In terms of GDP, USA and Africa have the highest and lowest weightings, respectively. In terms of stock market capitalization, Europe and Africa have the highest and lowest weightings, respectively. We may conclude that USA and Europe are the regions with the highest portfolio weightings. The region with the lowest portfolio weightings is Africa. Sixty-seven countries are researched across four regions.[1]

The countries selected are the countries with the most significant economies and stock markets in their regions/continents. The three financial crisis periods, following Cho et al. (2015), are: the Argentine debt crisis (1 December 2001–29 November 2002), the US financial crisis (18 July 2007–27 August 2009), and the EU debt crisis (8 December 2010–31 December 2011). Table 1 also reveals the regional (local) and the international significance of each country's trade integration, gross domestic product (GDP), inflation rate, interest rate, and stock market capitalization of each country. A quarterly or monthly macro data series is retrieved by the Economic Outlook Database of the International Monetary Fund. For quarterly data, a linear interpolation based on the monthly ones is implemented.[2]

Table 1. Description of the dataset.

				Weights					
				Trade Integration		GDP		Stock Market Capitalization	
Country	**Stock Exchange**	**Index**	**Symbol**	**Regional**	**International**	**Regional**	**International**	**Regional**	**International**
AFRICA			AFR		9.70%		0.92%		7.19%
Botswana	Botswana stock exchange	Botswana Gaborone Index (BGSMDC)	BWA	35.56%	3.45%	2.26%	0.02%	29.32%	2.11%
Egypt	Egyptian exchange	Egypt Stock Market (EGX30)	EGY	−7.88%	−0.76%	33.67%	0.31%	16.32%	1.17%
Kenya	Nairobi stock exchange	Nairobi Securities Exchange 20 share index (N20I)	KEN	51.28%	4.97%	6.81%	0.06%	15.70%	1.13%
Mauritius	Mauritius stock exchange	Mauritius Stock Exchange Semdex Index (SEMDEX)	MUS	−44.42%	−4.31%	1.73%	0.02%	21.85%	1.57%
South Africa	Johannesburg stock exchange	FTSE/JSE Africa All Shares Index (JALSH)	ZAF	65.45%	6.35%	55.52%	0.51%	16.80%	1.21%
AMERICAS			AME		66.54%		36.05%		15.47%
Argentina	Argentina stock exchange	Argentina Merval Index (MERVAL)	ARG	17.53%	11.66%	1.96%	0.71%	7.46%	1.15%
Brazil	Brazil Stock Market (BOVESPA)	Ibovespa Brasil Sao Paulo Stock Exchange Index (IBOV)	BRA	5.70%	3.80%	7.50%	2.70%	7.51%	1.16%
Canada	Toronto stock exchange (TMX)	S&P/Toronto Stock Exchange Composite Index (SPTSX)	CAN	6.42%	4.27%	7.11%	2.56%	9.50%	1.47%
Chile	Santiago stock exchange	Santiago Stock Exchange Ipsa Index (IPSA)	CHL	13.12%	8.73%	0.89%	0.32%	9.40%	1.45%
Colombia	Bolsa de Valores de Colombia (BVC)	IGBC index	COL	11.64%	7.75%	1.18%	0.42%	8.90%	1.38%
Jamaica	Jamaica stock exchange	Jamaica Stock Exchange Market Index (JMSMX)	JAM	1.65%	1.10%	0.06%	0.02%	10.04%	1.55%
Mexico	Mexico Stock Market (IPC)	Mexican Stock Exchange Mexican Bolsa Ipc Index (MEXBOL)	MEX	0.84%	0.56%	5.19%	1.87%	9.40%	1.45%
Panama	Panama Stock Market (BVPSI)	Bolsa de Valores de Panama General Index (BVPSBVPS)	PAN	0.02%	0.02%	0.12%	0.04%	9.85%	1.52%
Peru	Bolsa de Valores de Lima (BVL)	Bolsa de Valores de Lima General Sector Index (IGBVL)	PER	12.04%	8.01%	0.61%	0.22%	9.20%	1.42%
United States	NASDAQ Stock Market	Nasdaq Composite Index (CCMP)	USA	−1.57%	−1.04%	74.32%	26.80%	8.80%	1.36%
Venezuela	Venezuela Stock Market (IBVC)	Caracas Stock Exchange Stock Market Index (IBVC)	VEN	32.61%	21.70%	1.04%	0.38%	9.95%	1.54%
ASIA			ASI		22.63%		30.19%		32.90%
Australia	Australian Securities Exchange (ASE)	Australian Stock Exchange All Ordinaries Index (AS30)	AUS	27.89%	6.31%	6.09%	1.84%	5.37%	1.77%
Bangladesh	Dhaka stock exchange (DSE)	Dhaka Stock Exchange Index (DHAKA)	BGD	−25.81%	−5.84%	0.63%	0.19%	5.12%	1.68%
China	Shanghai stock exchange (SSE)	Shanghai Stock Exchange Composite Index (SHCOMP)	CHN	−4.17%	−0.94%	28.84%	8.71%	8.55%	2.81%
Hong Kong SAR	Hong Kong Stock Exchange (HKEx)	Hang Seng CSI Shanghai-Hong Kong AH Smart Index (HSI)	HKG	−1.57%	−0.36%	1.36%	0.41%	4.61%	1.52%
India	National Stock Exchange of India Limited (NSE)	S&P Bse Sensex Index (SENSEX)	IND	−20.30%	−4.59%	7.64%	2.31%	6.36%	2.09%
Indonesia	Indonesia Stock Exchange (IDX)	Jakarta composite index (JCI)	IDN	48.93%	11.07%	3.13%	0.95%	5.50%	1.81%
Israel	Tel Aviv Stock Exchange (TASE)	Tel Aviv 25 Index (TA-25)	ISR	−4.67%	−1.06%	1.23%	0.37%	3.90%	1.28%
Japan	Japan Exchange Group (JPX)	Nikkei 225 (NKY)	JPN	−8.16%	−1.85%	30.86%	9.32%	4.37%	1.44%
Jordan	Amman Stock Exchange (ASE)	Amman Stock Exchange General Index (JOSMGNFF)	JOR	−25.79%	−5.84%	0.13%	0.04%	4.87%	1.60%
Malaysia	Bursa Malaysia (KLSE)	Ftse Bursa Malaysia Klci Index Kuala Lumpur Composite Index (FBMKLCI)	MYS	10.19%	2.30%	1.26%	0.38%	4.68%	1.54%
New Zealand	New Zealand Stock Market (NZX)	New Zealand Exchange 50 Gross Index (NZSE50FG)	NZL	14.27%	3.23%	0.78%	0.23%	4.31%	1.42%
Oman	Muscat Securities Market (MSM)	Muscat Securities Msm 30 Index (MSM30)	OMN	54.00%	12.22%	0.29%	0.09%	5.08%	1.67%
Pakistan	Islamabad Stock Exchange (ISE)	Karachi Stock Exchange Kse100 Index (KSE100)	PAK	−4.17%	−0.94%	0.98%	0.30%	3.14%	1.03%
Philippines	Philippine Stock Exchange (PSE)	Philippines Stock Exchange Ps Ei Index (PCOMP)	PHL	-26.35%	−5.96%	1.01%	0.31%	3.96%	1.30%
Saudi Arabia	Saudi Stock Exchange (Tadawul)	Tadawul All Share Index (TASI)	SAU	67.28%	15.23%	2.82%	0.85%	4.93%	1.62%
Singapore	Singapore Exchange (SGX)	Singapore exchange market index (SGX)	SGP	−1.47%	−0.33%	1.17%	0.35%	5.24%	1.72%

Table 1. *Cont.*

Country	Stock Exchange	Index	Symbol	Weights: Trade Integration Regional	Trade Integration International	GDP Regional	GDP International	Stock Market Capitalization Regional	Stock Market Capitalization International
South Korea	Korea stock exchange (KRX)	Korea Stock Exchange Kospi Index (KOSPI)	KOR	−4.61%	−1.04%	6.15%	1.86%	6.23%	2.05%
Taiwan Province of China	Taiwan Stock Exchange (TWSE)	Taiwan Stock Exchange Weighted Index (TWSE)	TWN	−27.74%	−6.28%	2.51%	0.76%	4.19%	1.38%
Thailand	Thailand Stock Market (SET)	Stock Exchange Of Thailand Set Index (SET)	THA	5.87%	1.33%	1.56%	0.47%	5.24%	1.72%
United Arab Emirates	United Arab Emirates Stock Market (ADX)	Dubai Financial Market General Index (DFMGI)	ARE	26.39%	5.97%	1.56%	0.47%	4.37%	1.44%
EUROPE			EUR		1.13%		32.84%		44.43%
Austria	Austria Stock Market (WBI)	Vienna Stock Exchange130245 Austrian Traded Index (ATX)	AUT	−148.60%	−1.68%	1.97%	0.65%	3.29%	1.46%
Belgium	Brussels Stock Exchange (BSE)	Bel 20 Index (BEL20)	BeA	−39.74%	−0.45%	2.41%	0.79%	3.11%	1.38%
Bulgaria	Bulgaria Stock Market (SOFIX)	Bulgaria Stock Exchange Sofix Index (SOFIX)	BGR	−228.25%	−2.58%	0.22%	0.07%	3.65%	1.62%
Croatia	Zagreb Stock Exchange (ZSE)	Croatia Zagreb Stock Exchange Crobex Index (CRO)	CRO	−124.08%	−1.40%	0.29%	0.09%	3.64%	1.62%
Cyprus	Cyprus Stock Exchange (CSE)	Cyprus Stock Exchange General Index (CYSMMAPA)	CYP	30.67%	0.35%	0.11%	0.04%	2.60%	1.15%
Czech Republic	Prague Stock Exchange (PSE)	Prague Stock Exchange Index (PX)	CZE	−188.59%	−2.13%	0.91%	0.30%	3.87%	1.72%
Denmark	Copenhagen Stock Exchange (CSE)	OMX Copenhagen 20 index (KFX)	DNK	166.65%	1.88%	1.61%	0.53%	2.88%	1.28%
Estonia	Tallinn Stock Exchange (TSE)	Omx Tallinn Index (TALSE)	EST	200.38%	2.27%	0.10%	0.03%	4.49%	2.00%
Finland	OMX Helsinki (OMXH)	Omx Helsinki Index (HEX)	FIN	141.38%	1.60%	1.30%	0.43%	3.36%	1.49%
France	Euronext Paris	Cac 40 Index (CAC)	FRA	114.39%	1.29%	13.79%	4.53%	3.28%	1.46%
Germany	Frankfurt Stock Exchange (FWB)	Deutsche Boerse Ag German Stock Index Dax (DAX)	DEU	-188.26%	−2.13%	17.63%	5.79%	2.68%	1.19%
Greece	Greece Stock Market (ASE)	Athens Stock Exchange General Index (ASE)	GRE	−466.40%	−5.28%	1.43%	0.47%	2.98%	1.32%
Hungary	Budapest Stock Exchange (BUX)	Budapest Stock Exchange Budapest Stock Index (BUX)	HUN	−214.57%	−2.43%	0.65%	0.21%	3.24%	1.44%
Ireland	Irish Stock Exchange (ISE)	Irish Stock Exchange Overall Index (ISEQ)	IRL	−158.80%	−1.80%	1.21%	0.40%	3.26%	1.45%
Italy	Italian stock exchange (MIB)	Ftse Mib Index (FTSEMIB)	ITA	−141.16%	−1.60%	10.81%	3.55%	2.95%	1.31%
Latvia	Riga Stock Exchange (RSE)	OMX Riga (OMXR)	LVA	−62.84%	−0.71%	0.13%	0.04%	4.05%	1.80%
Lithuania	Vilnius Stock Exchange (VSE)	OMX Vilnius (OMXV)	LTU	−100.11%	−1.13%	0.19%	0.06%	3.08%	1.37%
Luxembourg	Luxembourg Stock Exchange (LUX)	Luxembourg Stock Exchange Lux X Index (LUXXX)	LUX	38.58%	0.44%	0.26%	0.08%	3.07%	1.37%
Malta	Malta Stock Exchange (MALTEX)	Malta Stock Exchange (MALTEX)	MLT	−66.73%	-0.75%	0.04%	0.01%	2.80%	1.24%
Netherlands	Amsterdam Stock Exchange (AMX)	Amsterdam Stock Exchange Amsterdam Midkap Index (AMX)	NLD	−82.38%	−0.93%	4.27%	1.40%	3.05%	1.36%
Norway	Norway Stock Market (OBX)	Oslo Stock Exchange All Share Index (OSEAX)	NOR	629.64%	7.12%	2.10%	0.69%	3.31%	1.47%
Portugal	Lisbon Stock Exchange (LSE)	Portugal PSI 20 Index (PSI20)	PRT	−636.74%	−7.20%	1.17%	0.38%	3.21%	1.42%
Romania	Bucharest Stock Exchange (BSE)	Bucharest Stock Exchange Trading Index (BET)	ROU	380.70%	4.31%	0.76%	0.25%	3.62%	1.61%
Russia	Moscow Interbank Currency Exchange (MICEX)	Micex Index (INDEXCF)	RUS	1372.99%	15.53%	6.88%	2.26%	3.13%	1.39%
Slovak Republic	Bratislava Stock Exchange (BSE)	Slovak Share Index (SKSM)	SVK	−266.50%	−3.01%	0.38%	0.13%	3.61%	1.61%
Spain	Madrid Stock Exchange (MSE)	Madrid Stock Exchange IBEX 35 Index (IBEX)	ESP	−151.99%	−1.72%	6.94%	2.28%	3.70%	1.65%
Sweden	Stockholm Stock Exchange (SSE)	OMX Stockholm 30 Index (OMX)	SWE	−57.17%	−0.65%	2.43%	0.80%	2.70%	1.20%
Switzerland	Swiss Exchange (SIX)	Swiss Exchange (SIX)	CHE	−115.91%	−1.31%	2.74%	0.90%	3.15%	1.40%
Turkey	Istanbul Stock Exchange (ISE)	Borsa Istanbul 100 Index (XU100)	TUR	−161.64%	−1.83%	3.28%	1.08%	2.87%	1.27%
Ukraine	Ukrainian Stock Exchange (PFTS)	Ukrainian Equities Index (UX)	UKR	658.62%	7.45%	0.65%	0.21%	3.00%	1.33%
United Kingdom	London stock exchange (LSE)	FTSE 100 Index (UKX)	GBR	−33.55%	−0.38%	13.36%	4.39%	2.40%	1.07%
ALL			ALL		100.00%		100.00%		100.00%

Notes: Table 1 describes the dataset. It includes the countries examined, their respective stock exchanges, main stock indices, and symbols. It also includes the average values of the international and regional significance of each country and region (for international significance) for different weighting schemes (e.g., trade integration, GDP, and stock market capitalization).

Table 2 presents the portfolio descriptive statistics. In terms of average portfolio values, the Americas and Europe have the highest values. In terms of portfolio standard deviations, Africa and Europe have the lowest values. In terms of portfolio Sharpe ratios, Europe and Asia have the highest values. In terms of cumulative return, the Americas with Europe second have the highest values, across all portfolio types. Regarding the overall portfolio performance by considering all portfolio descriptive estimates; Europe first and the Americas second are the best performers, with Africa last. By comparing portfolio types, the market capitalization seems to provide the best portfolio weighting scheme in terms of portfolio performance.

Table 2. Portfolio performance.

	Average				Standard Deviation				Sharpe Ratio				Cumulative Return			
	Africa	Americas	Asia	Europe	Africa	Americas	Asia	Europe	Africa	Americas	Asia	Europe	Africa	Americas	Asia	Europe
Market Capitalization	0.0039	0.0460	0.0055	3.8×10^{-4}	0.0221	0.3747	0.0441	0.0038	0.9745	1.31	1.20	1.49	0.1967	5.06	1.09	0.1166
Trade Integration	3.7×10^{-4}	0.0249	0.0073	0.0109	0.0021	0.2030	0.0588	0.1104	0.8965	0.1242	0.2281	0.2823	0.0187	2.74	1.46	3.39
GDP	0.0029	0.0107	0.0079	0.0148	0.0164	0.0871	0.0641	0.1494	0.9522	0.9709	1.78	2.21	0.1458	1.18	1.59	4.58
Inflation Rate	2.9×10^{-4}	0.0024	0.0182	0.0068	0.0017	0.0199	0.1470	0.0683	0.8948	0.0977	0.1794	0.2220	0.0147	0.2681	3.64	2.10
Interest Rate	0.0014	0.0066	0.0097	0.0156	0.0079	0.0537	0.0779	0.1580	0.9192	0.4696	0.8620	1.07	0.0705	0.7248	1.93	4.85

Notes: Table 2 presents the portfolio performance measures (average, standard deviation, Sharpe ratio, and cumulative return) of the different types of international equity portfolios.

4. Methods

4.1. Structural Regime-Switching Factor Model

The present paper employs the Cho et al. (2015) structural regime-switching factor model in an asset (non-portfolio) CAPM model. The present paper's model, as employed in Cho et al. (2015), concerns regional and international results and targets to capture key stylized facts like time varying betas, volatility clustering, volatility regimes, financial crises, and structural economic variables.

$$r_{i,t}=\mu_{i,t-1} + \beta^{w}_{i,t}e_{w,t} + \beta^{reg}_{i,t}e_{reg,t} + e_{j,t} \tag{1}$$

where $r_{i,t}$ is the excess return on country i with $\mu_{i,t}$ its time-varying mean (expected return); $r_{reg,t}$ is the regional market return; $e_{w,t}$ is the global market shock ($r_{w,t} = \mu_{w,t-1} + e_{w,t}$); $e_{i,t}$ is the country specific idiosyncratic shock; $e_{reg,t}$ is the regional market shock (obtained from the regression $r_{reg,t} = \mu_{reg,t-1} + \beta^{w}_{reg,t}e_{w,t} + e_{reg,t}$);

Time varying betas are explained from both structural economics variables, a regime variable, and crisis dummies.

$$\beta^{w}_{i,t}=\beta^{w}_{0,i}(S_{i,t}) + \beta^{w}_{1,t}X^{w}_{reg,t-1} + \sum_{j=1}^{5}\gamma^{w}_{j,i}D_{j,t} \tag{2}$$

$$\beta^{reg}_{i,t}=\beta^{reg}_{0,i}(S_{i,t}) + \sum_{j=1}^{5}\gamma^{reg}_{j,i}D_{j,t} \tag{3}$$

where $\beta^{w}_{i,t}$ and $\beta^{reg}_{i,t}$ are the time-varying exposures of country i to the world and regional shocks; $S_{i,t}$ is a latent regime variable different for each country; $X^{w}_{reg,t-1}$ are structural variables like trade integration (TI), gross domestic product (GDP), and stock market capitalization (MC) that are regionally or internationally aggregated; $D_{j,t}$ is a crisis dummy variable.

Following the specifications of Cho et al. (2015), the regional shocks $(e_{reg,t})$ are estimated by an asymmetric GARCH(1,1) t-student model, and the world (global) shocks $(e_{w,t})$ by a regime-switching asymmetric GARCH(1,1) Normal model, respectively.

The model is estimated in three steps: First, the world shock is estimated; second, the regional shock is computed using the first step's world shock, and finally, the full model is estimated for each country.

4.2. Contagion Test

Ehrmann et al. (2011) consider contagion as the excess comovement beyond fundamental linkages and suggest the following test for contagion:

$$\hat{e}_{i,t} = v_0 + \sum_{j=1}^{3} v_j D_{j,t} + u_{i,t} \quad (4)$$

where $\hat{e}_{i,t}$ is the estimated idiosyncratic return shocks of portfolio i, $D_{j,t}$ is a crisis dummy variable, and v_j captures the contagion crisis effect.

5. Empirical Findings and Discussion

Empirical findings concern (i) the portfolio performance (different measures); (ii) the stylized facts of volatility regimes, financial crises, and structural economics variables (in a structural regime-switching model); and (iii) the contagion test (following Ehrmann et al. 2011) results.

5.1. Portfolio Performance

In the present subsection, the results concern the portfolio time-varying betas. These are indicated by the implied global and implied regional betas (see Table 3). They are also reported for various portfolio weighting schemes (market capitalization, trade integration, GDP, inflation, and interest rates). In terms of implied global betas, the highest and lowest concern Botswana and the United Arab Emirates. An interesting result is that the countries in the Americas have low average values of implied global betas. It is also noticeable that most of the countries, even in Africa or Asia, that should have been expected to have exceptionally high global betas did not. All regions had average implied global betas compatible with most of the countries of other regions; with the single exception of Africa. Moreover, there is a lot of dispersion among countries of the same region. This is why we provided the average implied regional betas.

Table 3. Average implied global and regional betas.

	Implied Global Betas					Implied Regional Betas				
	MC	TI	GDP	INF	INT	MC	TI	GDP	INF	INT
AFRICA										
Botswana	1.29	2.12	0.0123	0.1170	0.1999	17.99	21.82	1.39	16.16	5.75
Egypt	0.3687	0.2395	0.0977	0.0544	0.1295	5.14	2.48	10.61	7.52	3.72
Kenya	0.0223	0.0982	0.0012	0.0016	0.0090	0.3101	1.01	0.1345	0.2163	0.2600
Mauritius	0.1739	0.4773	0.0022	0.0025	0.2052	2.42	4.92	0.1916	0.3414	5.90
South Africa	0.0836	0.4389	0.0352	0.0179	0.0297	1.16	4.52	3.84	2.47	0.8541
AMERICAS										
Argentina	0.3807	3.86	0.2350	0.0087	0.1082	2.47	5.80	0.6488	0.2473	1.13
Brazil	0.1662	0.5444	0.3868	0.0328	0.0402	1.08	0.8167	1.07	0.9294	0.4221
Canada	0.3869	1.12	0.6738	0.2054	0.4628	2.50	1.69	1.87	5.83	4.86
Chile	0.0177	0.1065	0.0039	0.0057	0.0118	0.1147	0.1601	0.0109	0.1618	0.1238
Colombia	0.0169	0.0950	0.0051	0.0039	0.0077	0.1090	0.1426	0.0145	0.1095	0.0806
Jamaica	0.0034	0.0024	4.4×10^{-5}	2.5×10^{-5}	7.7×10^{-4}	0.0220	0.0036	1.3×10^{-4}	7.1×10^{-4}	0.0080
Mexico	0.1138	0.0440	0.1468	0.0268	0.0499	0.7380	0.0660	0.4075	0.7598	0.5240
Panama	0.0069	9.1×10^{-5}	1.8×10^{-4}	2.2×10^{-4}	0.0077	0.0447	9.1×10^{-5}	5.4×10^{-4}	0.0062	0.0810
Peru	0.0780	0.4400	0.0121	0.0310	0.0605	0.5054	0.6614	0.0335	0.8784	0.6352
United States	0.0074	0.0057	0.1464	0.0036	0.0087	0.0481	0.0086	0.4059	0.1016	0.0913
Venezuela	0.1423	2.01	0.0351	0.0081	0.0178	0.9195	3.01	0.0961	0.2284	0.1864
ASIA										
Australia	0.3238	1.15	0.3366	0.0048	0.1542	0.9824	5.10	1.11	0.0064	0.3856
Bangladesh	0.5042	1.75	0.0570	0.0564	0.1624	1.54	7.75	0.1891	0.0747	0.4062
China	0.1986	0.0664	0.6155	0.0426	0.0469	0.6042	0.2947	2.04	0.0565	0.1173
Hong Kong SAR	0.0022	5.2×10^{-4}	5.9×10^{-4}	0.0011	0.0019	0.0066	0.0023	0.0020	0.0015	0.0048
India	0.0148	0.0325	0.0164	9.4×10^{-4}	0.0043	0.0450	0.1437	0.0541	0.0012	0.0108
Indonesia	0.0032	0.0196	0.0017	2.8×10^{-4}	8.6×10^{-4}	0.0097	0.0866	0.0055	3.7×10^{-4}	0.0022
Israel	0.0780	0.0646	0.0225	0.0432	0.0653	0.2376	0.2846	0.0749	0.0573	0.1634
Japan	0.0312	0.0401	0.2021	1.46	0.3133	0.0948	0.1769	0.6691	1.94	0.7837
Jordan	0.0033	0.0121	8.3×10^{-5}	5.9×10^{-5}	0.0016	0.0101	0.0532	2.7×10^{-4}	7.8×10^{-5}	0.0040

Table 3. *Cont.*

	Implied Global Betas					Implied Regional Betas				
	MC	**TI**	**GDP**	**INF**	**INT**	**MC**	**TI**	**GDP**	**INF**	**INT**
Malaysia	0.0920	0.1374	0.0227	0.0382	0.0796	0.2797	0.6089	0.0753	0.0507	0.1992
New Zealand	0.0307	0.0697	0.0050	0.0046	0.0173	0.0931	0.3081	0.0168	0.0061	0.0432
Oman	0.0197	0.1442	0.0011	4.7×10^{-4}	0.0256	0.0600	0.6373	0.0034	6.2×10^{-4}	0.0642
Pakistan	0.0469	0.0428	0.0136	0.0080	0.0172	0.1429	0.1897	0.0446	0.0105	0.0429
Philippines	0.0216	0.0988	0.0051	0.0059	0.0112	0.0657	0.4369	0.0167	0.0078	0.0281
Saudi Arabia	0.0054	0.0503	0.0028	0.0015	0.0039	0.0163	0.2223	0.0093	0.0020	0.0099
Singapore	0.1223	0.0235	0.0249	0.0513	0.3539	0.3726	0.1045	0.0832	0.0681	0.8853
South Korea	0.0143	0.0073	0.0130	0.0036	0.0078	0.0435	0.0322	0.0429	0.0048	0.0196
Taiwan Province of China	0.0676	0.3075	0.0372	0.0695	0.0904	0.2051	1.36	0.1229	0.0922	0.2261
Thailand	0.1119	0.0865	0.0306	0.0359	0.1081	0.3409	0.3819	0.1015	0.0476	0.2705
United Arab Emirates	9.9×10^{-4}	0.0041	3.3×10^{-4}	2.3×10^{-4}	0.0021	0.0030	0.0183	0.0011	3.0×10^{-4}	0.0053
EUROPE										
Austria	0.1004	0.1156	0.0447	0.0513	0.1224	0.2263	10.22	0.1355	0.2525	0.2604
Belgium	0.0930	0.0303	0.0532	0.0500	0.1226	0.2096	2.68	0.1624	0.2460	0.2608
Bulgaria	0.1385	0.2206	0.0060	0.0290	0.1527	0.3121	19.51	0.0189	0.1427	0.32470
Croatia	0.0155	0.0134	8.6×10^{-4}	0.0059	0.0045	0.0349	1.19	0.0028	0.0289	0.0096
Cyprus	0.0238	0.0072	8.3×10^{-4}	0.0012	0.0374	0.0537	0.6340	0.0023	0.0057	0.0796
Czech Republic	0.0036	0.0044	6.2×10^{-4}	0.0014	0.0041	0.0080	0.3921	0.0019	0.0067	0.0088
Denmark	0.0072	0.0106	0.0030	0.0045	0.0105	0.0163	0.9437	0.0091	0.0219	0.0223
Estonia	0.0444	0.0505	6.7×10^{-4}	0.0092	0.0412	0.0998	4.45	0.0022	0.0451	0.0876
Finland	0.0331	0.0355	0.0095	0.0087	0.0411	0.0745	3.14	0.0288	0.0428	0.0874
France	0.0321	0.0284	0.0997	0.0205	0.0408	0.0722	2.52	0.3035	0.1007	0.0868
Germany	0.0262	0.0469	0.1275	0.0223	0.0462	0.0590	4.14	0.3881	0.1099	0.0868
Greece	0.0291	0.1162	0.0103	0.0138	0.0207	0.0656	10.27	0.0315	0.0679	0.0868
Hungary	0.0070	0.0118	0.0010	0.0031	0.0025	0.0157	1.04	0.0031	0.0150	0.0054
Ireland	0.0292	0.0362	0.0080	0.0155	0.0373	0.0655	3.19	0.0243	0.0763	0.0792
Italy	0.0263	0.0322	0.0714	0.0155	0.0431	0.0593	2.84	0.2173	0.0761	0.0793
Latvia	0.0302	0.0119	6.7×10^{-4}	0.0058	0.0311	0.0680	1.05	0.0022	0.0285	0.0661
Lithuania	0.0099	0.0082	4.4×10^{-4}	0.0039	0.0084	0.0223	0.7255	0.0014	0.0192	0.0179
Luxembourg	0.0296	0.0095	0.0017	0.0148	0.0401	0.0664	0.8339	0.0056	0.0729	0.0852
Malta	0.0268	0.0163	2.2×10^{-4}	0.0154	0.0150	0.0606	1.44	8.7×10^{-4}	0.0758	0.0319
Netherlands	0.0273	0.0187	0.0281	0.0150	0.0373	0.0613	1.66	0.0858	0.0739	0.0792
Norway	0.0194	0.0939	0.0091	0.0105	0.0161	0.0437	8.31	0.0277	0.0519	0.0343
Portugal	0.0240	0.1219	0.0064	0.0119	0.0314	0.0544	10.78	0.0198	0.0585	0.0667
Romania	0.4531	1.21	0.0704	0.0500	0.1465	1.02	107.15	0.2139	0.2460	0.3115
Russia	0.0332	0.3715	0.0541	0.0034	0.0138	0.0749	32.84	0.1646	0.0166	0.0294
Slovak Republic	0.0230	0.0430	0.0019	0.0059	0.0265	0.0516	3.81	0.0054	0.0289	0.0564
Spain	0.0242	0.0252	0.0334	0.0091	0.0272	0.0543	2.23	0.1018	0.0446	0.0578
Sweden	0.0409	0.0221	0.0272	0.0377	0.0518	0.0919	1.95	0.0827	0.1855	0.1103
Switzerland	0.0411	0.0384	0.0264	0.0845	0.1019	0.0925	3.40	0.0804	0.4160	0.2168
Turkey	0.0340	0.0490	0.0289	0.0047	0.0053	0.0769	4.33	0.0878	0.0230	0.0112
Ukraine	0.0265	0.1485	0.0042	0.0031	0.0081	0.0598	13.13	0.0130	0.0153	0.0173
United Kingdom	0.0245	0.0087	0.1005	0.0147	0.0255	0.0549	0.7681	0.3059	0.0725	0.0543

Notes: Table 3 presents the average values of implied global (internationally aggregated) and regional (regionally aggregated) betas of all countries. MC, IT, GDP, INF, and INT refer to the respective portfolio weighting schemes: changes in market capitalization, trade integration , GDP growth, inflation rate, and interest rate, from which the betas are estimated.

Next, the average implied regional betas indicate the relative market risk of national stock indices within the region they belong to, and these are reported for various portfolio types (i.e., portfolio weighting schemes). Africa first with the Americas second are the regions where most of their regional countries have high implied regional betas. Europe has the lowest. The results are robust across most of the portfolio weighting schemes. A single exception is trade integration, for which the implied regional betas change a lot, with most of the countries having average implied regional betas higher than 1.

5.2. Stylized Facts

Tables 4–7, as well as, Table 8, report the estimated coefficients for all types of international equity portfolios. The results from such a model are retrieved regionally and internationally and concern the stylized facts of volatility regimes, financial crises, and structural macroeconomic variables. The differences between the portfolio types are signified via their differences in the magnitude and statistical significance of the coefficients in the structural regime-switching factor models. The magnitude and statistical significance results are not contradictory. This is why we mostly concentrate on statistical significance.

The statistical significance in the structural regime-switching factor model is high for both global and regional betas. This result concerns all regions and most of the portfolio weighting schemes.

The single exception was market capitalization, for which the results for most of regions were statistically significant only for regional betas. This exception concerns the statistical significance of all coefficients (regime variables, crises, and macroeconomic variables) and the overall model significance (adjusted R-squared and F-test).

The following results concern most portfolio weighting schemes. By considering the majority of the countries within a region with statistically significant latent regime variables. Regarding crisis-coefficients (ARG, US, and EU), Europe was affected by all crises, Africa was affected only by the US crisis, the Americas region was affected by the Argentinian and US crises, and Asia was affected mostly by the Argentinian and US crises (and in some weighting schemes, from the EU crisis as well). The macroeconomic variables indicated a significantly greater affect (where most of the countries had statistically significant macro-coefficients (MC, TI, GDP, INF, INT)) for all regions, as well as for all portfolio weighting schemes (the single exception is the market capitalization scheme for global betas). The overall significance (F-stat) was impressively high and was mostly concentrated on the Americas and Europe. The adjusted R-squared values are not impressively high, however.

5.3. Contagion Test

Tables 9–12, as well as Table 13, report the Ehrmann et al. (2011) contagion test results of all international equity portfolios while splitting them between the implied global and implied regional betas. The differences between the portfolio types are signified via their differences in the magnitude and statistical significance of the coefficients in the structural regime switching factor models. The magnitude and statistical significance results are not contradictory. This is why we mostly concentrate on statistical significance. The contagion effect is assessed by the v_0 coefficient, whereas the contagion from each crisis is indicated by the (Arg cr., US cr., and EU cr.) coefficients. They are all reported in Table 5A–E.

The most important result of the Ehrmann et al. (2011) contagion test was the indication of strong contagion. There were 3–4 regions with most of their countries having statistically significant contagion. This result holds for all portfolio weighting schemes. Specifically, across the portfolio weighting schemes, the presence of contagion was evident in all regions (in descending order): Europe (7 cases), Asia (5 cases), the Americas (3 cases), and Africa (2 cases). Furthermore, across all regions, the presence of contagion was evident in all portfolio weighting schemes (in a descending order): MC, GDP, and INT first with 4 cases per each scheme and TI and INF with 3 cases per each scheme. Moreover, across all regions and portfolio weighting schemes, the implied global betas had stronger indications of contagion compared to the implied regional betas (11 compared to 7 cases).

Table 4. Structural regime-switching factor model on market-capitalization-based portfolios.

	Global Betas												Regional Betas											
	β_0^{tw}	β_1^{tw}	ARG Crisis	US Crisis	EU Crisis	MC	TI	GDP	INF	INT	adj. R^2	$F-Stat$	β_0^{tw}	β_1^{tw}	ARG Crisis	US Crisis	EU Crisis	MC	TI	GDP	INF	INT	adj. R^2	$F-Stat$
AFRICA																								
Botswana	−27.634	−34.292	−34.292	23.372	−47.175 **	−14.236	−0.878	1.476 **	−1.266	−0.550	0.068	1.135	−0.499 **	−0.389 **	0.671	1.067 *	0.129 **	−0.256 **	−0.065 **	−0.055 **	0.087 **	0.019 **	0.112	1.961 **
Egypt	0.4865 **	−0.374 **	1.027 **	0.973	−0.740	−2.632	−0.375 **	0.027 **	0.960 *	0.040	0.055	0.915	0.031	1.184	1.379	−1.854 **	−1.959	0.608	−0.338 *	0.094 **	0.094 **	0.242 **	0.058	0.957
Kenya	18.900	15.396	35.040 **	−16.909	−27.446	−5.818	93.566 **	2.253 *	−26.874 **	12.245 *	0.180	0.179 **	0.809 **	1.069 **	−0.094	1.077	−0.026	0.772 *	−0.867	−0.011 **	0.320 **	−0.170 **	0.098	1.700 *
Mauritius	3.413	0.949	−9.760 *	−3.297	5.806	−4.812	4.311	−1.299 *	−0.435	2.676	0.065	1.084	−0.184 *	0.133	−0.028	−0.228 **	−0.669 **	−0.105	−0.329 **	0.065 **	0.016 **	0.028 **	0.050	0.815 *
South Africa	−1.706 *	−2.130	0.129	2.807 **	−1.196	−3.528	5.402	0.094 **	−1.200	0.070	0.049	0.820	1.474 **	1.932 **	1.136 **	−0.976 **	−0.562	3.306 **	−1.488	−0.023 **	−0.675	−0.320 **	0.137	2.478 **
AMERICAS																								
Argentina	0.820	2.516	−2.504	−2.165	−1.723	−6.689	0.022	10.878	−1.341 *	1.629 **	0.039	0.632	−0.655	−1.588 **	−2.046 **	−1.537 **	1.097	0.657	−0.035	−2.340	−0.132	−0.058 *	0.067	1.125
Brazil	−0.977 **	−0.977 **	1.075 **	0.748 **	0.769 *	−0.546	−0.117 **	0.080 **	−0.157 *	0.028 **	0.115	2.028 **	−0.280	−0.713 **	−1.012	−0.905 **	0.644	−0.381	−0.026	−0.104 **	−0.367 **	−0.050 **	0.063	1.049
Canada	7.615	2.131	−1.123	−1.123 *	3.765	2.214	2.482	−1.355	3.669 *	−0.911	0.039	0.039	−0.501 **	−0.667 **	−0.848 **	−1.248 **	0.091	0.054	0.173 **	−0.113 **	0.311 **	0.154 **	0.072	1.201
Chile	−3.104	−10.182	3.070	−16.019	−7.192	−15.022	13.432	0.186	−18.776 *	6.780	0.024	0.392	−0.024 **	−0.092 **	−0.086 **	−0.153 **	0.171 **	0.116 **	−0.076 **	−0.019 **	0.375 **	−0.046 **	0.050	0.824
Colombia	−5.982 **	−3.139 *	0.298	0.298	−6.174 *	−4.005	−0.865 **	0.475	−0.056 *	0.421	0.065	1.090	−0.236 **	−0.204 **	−0.199 **	−0.297 **	0.085	−0.019 **	0.020 **	−0.011 **	−0.714 **	0.025 **	0.060	0.989
Jamaica	46.184	4.877	−19.652	20.257	−6.063	4.735	19.386	19.386	−0.108	30.973	0.025	0.395	−0.059 **	0.201 **	−0.406 **	−0.028	1.641 **	−0.759 **	0.016 **	0.008 *	0.081	−0.090 **	0.249	5.162 **
Mexico	−1.423	−1.423	−0.909	−2.069	1.019	−4.791	−0.251	0.077 **	−4.809 **	1.121 **	0.062	1.037	−0.186	−0.332 **	−0.762 **	−1.542 **	0.223	0.299	−0.063 **	−0.080 **	1.263 **	0.188 **	0.161	2.985 **
Panama	−9.605	0.772	−13.944	−11.056	−13.053	0.311	4.225	3.650	0.645	2.752	0.024	0.379	0.443 **	0.173 **	−0.711 **	−0.142 **	0.152	−0.263	0.202	−0.104 **	0.302 **	0.094 **	0.092	1.582
Peru	−0.083	−0.778	0.712	−1.540	−0.332	−4.935 **	0.695	3.763 **	−0.045	0.362 **	0.106	1.886 **	−0.333 **	−0.220 **	−0.191 **	−0.296 **	−0.123 **	0.084 **	0.062 **	−0.020 **	0.076 **	−0.017 **	0.065	1.093
United States	−3.083	−1.261 *	2.010	0.145	−0.920	0.166	3.043 *	0.109 **	−0.661 **	0.015	0.075	1.268	0.510 **	−0.117 **	−1.420	−0.779	0.234	0.780	−1.419	−0.075 **	−0.244 **	0.165 **	0.125	2.227 **
Venezuela	−0.425 **	−0.093	−0.185	−0.185 *	0.242	0.713 **	−0.111	−0.044 **	−0.278 **	−0.035 **	0.039	0.039	−0.087 **	−0.309 **	−0.144 **	−0.571 **	−0.134 **	0.030	−0.498 **	0.006 **	0.454 **	0.090 **	0.067	1.126
ASIA																								
Australia	−1.452	−4.301	−1.233	−6.066	−13.007 **	12.287 *	−2.383	0.749 **	0.749	−0.391	0.065	1.086	0.024	−0.087 *	−0.131 **	−0.180 **	0.129 **	−0.455 **	0.110 **	−0.071 **	−0.075 **	0.088 **	0.095	1.630 *
Bangladesh	0.817	1.284	1.007	−1.734	−1.708	1.811	−1.704	−1.228	1.479	−0.777 *	0.020	0.313	1.780 **	1.796 **	−0.122 **	−0.389 **	−0.168 **	−0.036 **	−0.101 **	0.049 **	−0.454 **	0.002	0.159	2.952 **
China	−4.142	−3.168	−0.758	1.726	−1.992	1.290	−5.952 *	0.158	−4.896 **	−1.786 **	0.106	0.106 **	3.656 **	3.406 **	−0.789 **	−0.996 *	−0.090	0.356	−0.192	−0.014 *	0.051	0.267 **	0.130	2.339 **
Hong Kong SAR	1.903	1.401	−1.846 **	1.397 **	0.948	4.703 **	−2.633	−0.029 **	−2.084 **	−0.441 **	0.062	1.023	6.972 *	6.922 *	−0.195	−1.961	−0.619	−1.574	1.771	0.014 **	0.078	0.542 **	0.154	2.834 **
India	−43.779	−52.495	−2.343	−20.970	−12.942	−56.845 *	50.272	0.255	−5.771	2.768	0.040	0.649	1.282 **	0.813 **	−0.390 *	−1.608	−0.903	−1.611	−0.385	0.068 **	−0.054	0.531	0.077	1.308
Indonesia	1.435	2.740	4.379	−1.167	−6.984 *	−4.394	−3.319	0.372 **	0.135 *	0.522	0.042	0.676	1.912 **	1.525 **	−0.100 *	−0.586 **	0.004	0.814 **	−0.057	−0.012 **	0.095 **	−0.157 **	0.124	2.215 **
Israel	−3.248	−1.490	−3.394 *	−0.325	0.210	−0.117	−7.674	−0.088	−1.096 *	−0.307	0.037	0.599	2.561 **	2.310 **	0.033	−0.844 **	0.089 *	−0.372	2.950	0.066 **	−0.014 **	0.175 **	0.180	3.416 **
Japan	5.177	2.906	4.802	2.611	−5.324 **	−5.088	−8.796	0.556 **	4.395 *	0.810 **	0.073	1.227	8.437 **	8.055 **	−0.092	−0.745 **	−0.281 **	0.764 *	−1.817 **	−0.035 **	−0.218 **	−0.104 **	0.240	4.919 **
Jordan	28.346	18.577	−4.986	−34.331 **	0.718	37.840 **	9.022 *	−0.333 **	8.443 **	3.022	0.153	2.813 **	−0.032 **	−0.043 **	0.065 **	−0.067 **	−0.206 **	−0.156 **	0.076 **	0.023 **	−0.058 **	0.031 **	0.120	2.127 **
Malaysia	−2.037	−3.726	−7.148	−3.180	−5.377	−19.308 *	−2.289	0.300 *	0.288	0.915	0.032	0.514	0.666 **	0.541 **	0.066 *	−0.327 **	−0.052 **	−0.602 **	0.018 **	0.015 **	−0.055 **	0.120 **	0.080	1.364
New Zealand	13.148	11.159	1.283	−1.466	−14.293 *	12.527 **	−33.315 **	0.577	−13.415 **	−2.451	0.205	4.024 **	0.943 **	0.763 **	−0.054	0.127 **	0.549 **	0.583 **	0.575 **	−0.047 **	0.042 **	−0.104 **	0.148	2.708 **
Oman	38.748 **	38.937 **	−5.425	1.257	−2.595	5.243	2.038	−0.311	3.139	−0.763	0.084	1.427	3.956 **	3.812 **	−0.080 **	−0.155 **	−0.031 **	0.341 **	−0.038 **	−0.017 **	0.035 **	−0.034 **	0.315	7.164 **
Pakistan	−2.453	−3.324	−3.074	−1.877	−0.421	1.712	2.763	−0.081	−5.863	−0.137	0.021	0.339	1.783 **	1.637 **	0.344 **	−0.319 **	−0.162 **	0.064	−0.174 **	−0.002 **	0.1834 **	0.030	0.151	2.782 **
Philippines	−0.399	−0.400	−29.569 **	−29.569	−9.525	−6.610	19.407 **	15.843	−0.423	3.019	0.074	0.074	1.111 **	0.769 **	1.033 **	−0.516 **	−0.469 **	0.345 **	0.380 **	−0.431 **	0.019 **	−0.032 **	0.126	2.254 **
Saudi Arabia	13.927	15.432	−7.392 *	1.027	3.800	−0.465	−2.696 *	0.016 **	0.777	3.746	0.033	0.528	−0.352 **	−0.313 **	0.092 **	−0.106 **	0.126 **	0.091 **	0.012 **	−0.004 **	−0.032 **	−0.035 **	0.082	1.402

Table 4. *Cont.*

	Global Betas												Regional Betas											
	β_0^w	β_1^w	ARG Crisis	US Crisis	EU Crisis	MC	TI	GDP	INF	INT	adj. R^2	$F-Stat$	β_0^w	β_1^w	ARG Crisis	US Crisis	EU Crisis	MC	TI	GDP	INF	INT	adj. R^2	$F-Stat$
Singapore	−3.920	−3.719	−2.273	−3.019 *	2.508	−4.741 *	1.973	0.463	−0.087	1.518 **	0.050	0.819	3.538 **	3.324 **	−0.398 **	−0.984 **	−0.402 **	1.061 **	−0.196 **	−0.160 **	−0.017 **	0.087 **	0.159	2.948 **
South Korea	−6.866	−7.869	−1.929	−1.545	−6.082 *	−3.300	0.012	1.426 *	−0.194	−0.455 *	0.045	0.727	9.806 *	9.462 *	−0.375	−0.965 **	0.237	0.941 *	−0.312 **	−0.273 **	0.051 **	0.044 **	0.186	3.574 **
Taiwan Province of China	−0.279	0.223	1.704 *	5.135 **	−2.464	0.803 *	1.815 **	−0.083	1.855 **	−1.163 **	0.107	1.894 **	4.926 **	4.700 **	−0.011	−1.426 **	−0.196	0.102	−0.195	0.198 *	−0.183 **	0.254 **	0.151	2.764 **
Thailand	−3.796	1.115	−6.950	−2.116	4.590	28.333 **	−7.722 *	−9.261 **	−4.396	−4.935 **	0.090	1.547	1.662 **	1.356 **	−0.352 **	−0.848 **	−0.466 **	−0.308	0.176 *	0.226 **	−0.058	0.199 *	0.117	2.059 **
United Arab Emirates	−13.047	−12.159	1.278	10.542 **	−4.110	−8.980 *	17.659 *	0.355	0.507	−2.382 *	0.123	2.190 **	0.222 **	0.168 **	0.082 **	−0.088 **	−0.058 **	0.076 **	−0.123 **	0.038 **	0.033 **	−0.019 **	0.102	1.766 *
EUROPE																								
Austria	−7.253	−8.223	0.298	5.069 *	−3.733	1.992	−2.165	0.201	1.319	2.765	0.040	0.643	0.479 **	0.532 **	−0.239 **	−0.413 **	−0.390 **	−0.652 **	−0.123 **	0.034 **	−0.048 **	0.512 **	0.137	2.485 **
Belgium	−1.429	−1.052	−0.709 *	0.303	−1.018	−0.320	−0.741	0.701	−0.291 **	−0.188 **	0.018	0.282	0.479 **	0.234 **	−0.146 *	−0.542 **	−0.690 **	0.514 **	0.751 **	0.829	−0.028	0.273 **	0.127	2.272 **
Bulgaria	−1.873	−3.518	−0.402	−0.389	−5.728 **	1.410	2.245	4.516	0.328 *	−0.144	0.030	0.474	−0.146	0.287	−0.533	−1.795 **	−1.169	5.325	2.024	−2.409	−0.050	−0.370	0.072	1.216
Croatia	−4.797	3.990	53.029 **	0.990	1.673	−5.405	3.361	0.034 **	−7.348	0.539	0.082	1.402	−0.353 **	−0.656 **	−0.704 **	−0.825 **	−0.825	0.971	1.585	−0.082 **	−0.027	0.071 **	0.114	2.006 **
Cyprus	−3.995	−2.229	0.447	−7.248 **	−6.017 *	−12.041 **	−1.114	0.255	−0.823	2.950 **	0.036	0.578	0.417 **	0.536 **	−1.080 **	−1.080 **	−1.241 **	−1.295	−0.091	0.027 **	−0.255 **	0.350 **	0.102	1.779 *
Czech Republic	−3.475 **	−1.823 **	4.626 **	−1.022	−1.050 **	0.790	−1.018 *	0.133 **	1.323	0.229	0.075	1.263	−1.137 **	−1.36 **	−0.311 **	−1.479 **	−0.906 **	−0.699 **	−0.024	0.134 **	0.208 **	0.261 **	0.151	2.775 **
Denmark	−1.530	−2.123 **	0.715	0.655	3.088	5.956	−0.355	−0.316	−3.072 *	−0.562	0.025	0.401	0.067 *	−0.110 **	−0.086 **	−0.212 **	0.119	1.204 **	0.458 **	−0.047 **	−0.066 **	−0.164 **	0.185	3.536 **
Estonia	−4.232 **	−3.756 **	1.026	−3.357	−4.431	−2.136	0.663 *	0.119	0.314 **	0.504	0.033	0.536	−0.277 **	−0.346 **	−0.211 **	−0.845 **	0.415 **	0.692 **	−0.168 **	−0.154 **	0.048 **	−0.582 **	0.213	4.216 **
Finland	−2.062 *	−3.560 *	0.606	4.440 *	−2.142 *	−4.815	0.729	0.101 **	−1.103 **	0.407 **	0.086	0.086	2.839 **	3.109 **	−0.323	−1.804 **	0.469	1.301	1.982	−0.049 **	−0.258 **	−0.173 **	0.239	4.890 **
France	−0.298	−0.729 *	0.017	−0.382 *	−0.503 *	1.437	−0.193 **	−0.649	0.165 **	0.199 **	0.077	1.296	0.117	−0.259 **	−1.179 **	−0.592 **	−0.273 *	−0.389 **	−0.089 **	−0.089 **	−0.076 **	0.084 **	0.075	1.257
Germany	−0.957 **	−0.643 **	0.137 **	0.230 **	0.051	0.059	−0.011	−0.063 **	−0.197 **	0.045 **	0.041	0.666	1.601 **	1.226 **	−1.035 **	−1.280 **	−1.116 **	−0.790 **	0.044 *	0.017 **	0.645 **	0.204 **	0.093	1.618 *
Greece	−1.115	−0.883	−2.295	2.191 *	1.835	2.026	0.564	−0.081	−2.346 **	0.019	0.044	0.718	−0.869 **	−1.142 **	−0.319 **	−0.910 **	−0.735 **	−0.835	−0.215 *	0.039 *	0.126 *	0.046 **	0.140	2.536 **
Hungary	11.534	8.376	0.948	−6.221	−15.865 *	0.994	−7.753	0.994	−1.307	−0.695	0.043	0.695	−0.808 **	−0.547 **	−0.632 **	−1.585 **	−0.275	0.476	0.970 *	0.056 **	0.157 **	0.267 **	0.084	1.436
Ireland	0.168	−1.349 **	0.390	2.529 **	−0.043	1.573	−0.618	−0.282 **	−0.847 **	−0.024	0.075	1.257	−1.639 **	−1.775 *	1.139 **	−0.446 **	−1.172 **	−6.659	1.545 **	0.440 **	0.130 **	0.571 **	0.075	0.188 **
Italy	−4.031 **	−3.436 **	−0.010	0.074	0.337 **	−1.093	0.4620 **	−0.018 **	0.355 **	0.419 **	0.058	0.965	−1.009 **	−1.160 **	−0.653 **	−0.649 **	−0.107 **	−1.365 **	0.325 **	−0.001 **	−0.194 **	0.222 **	0.076	1.284
Latvia	−6.288	−1.859	−5.190	−1.209	3.804	2.356	−1.497	−0.293 *	2.758	−2.124 *	0.081	1.371	8.323 **	7.399 **	0.377	−0.412 *	−2.463	2.185	0.023	0.036 **	−0.995 **	−0.575 **	0.255	5.350 **
Lithuania	−3.449 **	−2.264 **	0.224	3.004	−1.682	−1.988 **	−1.420	0.193 **	0.293	1.972 **	0.137	2.483 **	0.785 **	0.732 **	−0.050 **	−0.177 **	−0.053 **	−0.095 **	0.141 **	0.083 **	0.032 **	0.150 **	0.169	3.182 **
Luxembourg	−6.387	−6.587	−1.542	−3.787	−1.672	−5.655 *	2.400	0.498	−0.123	2.494 *	0.024	0.388	0.844 **	0.687 **	−0.475 **	−0.142 **	−0.405 **	0.563 **	0.161 **	−0.040 **	−0.058 **	−0.232 **	0.200	3.791 **
Malta	−15.354	−11.309	−5.249	−3.260	−16.529 *	14.302	7.076	0.293	−0.017	0.137	0.059	0.985	0.332 **	0.354 **	−0.212 **	−0.369 **	−0.026	0.230	−0.061 **	−0.031 **	0.077 **	−0.026 **	0.088	1.496
Netherlands	0.746	−0.815	9.499 **	−0.257	−2.482	6.038	−5.730 *	0.029 **	−0.633	0.085	0.046	0.746	0.877 **	0.552 **	−0.820 **	−0.761 **	−0.761 **	1.240	0.594	0.062 **	−0.337	0.089	0.082	1.395
Norway	−0.556	−0.901	−0.265	0.069	1.772	−0.547	1.991	0.030	−1.633 **	−0.154	0.076	1.275	0.806 **	0.585 **	−0.430 **	−0.052 *	0.024	0.467 **	0.703 **	−0.019 **	0.123 **	−0.233 **	0.159	2.956 **
Portugal	−1.627 **	−1.176 **	1.384 **	0.287 **	0.774 **	0.774 *	0.682	−0.058 **	−0.140	−0.235	0.059	0.975	−0.376 **	−0.342 **	−0.582 **	−0.919 **	−0.785 **	0.603 **	1.715 **	−0.020 **	0.093 **	−0.165 **	0.135	2.424 **
Romania	−1.217	2.849 **	−0.019	2.716	2.838	1.952	3.885	−0.059	−2.101	−1.728	0.029	0.469	−0.721 **	−0.708 **	−1.033 **	−0.445 **	−0.486 **	0.872 *	−1.382 *	−0.026 **	−0.298 **	−0.364 **	0.153	2.817 **
Russia	0.034	−0.452 **	2.303	0.815 **	0.758 **	0.564 *	1.119 **	−0.026 **	0.349 **	−0.036	0.064	1.068	2.289 **	2.082 **	−1.439 **	−1.336 **	−1.432 **	0.734 **	−1.735 **	−0.009 **	0.014	−0.711 **	0.148	2.699 **
Slovak Republic	−1.963 *	−2.830 **	4.654 **	−1.976 *	−1.778	0.067	−0.288	0.055 **	0.770	0.672 **	0.101	1.747 *	−0.042	−0.068 **	−0.685 **	−0.803 **	−0.272 **	0.283 **	−0.359 **	−0.014 **	0.025 *	0.155 **	0.137	2.484 **
Spain	−2.991 **	−3.004 **	−1.857	1.078	−2.417 *	0.603	0.133	0.090 **	0.868 *	0.146 **	0.107	1.960 **	−0.152	−0.234	0.280	−0.397	−0.212	2.162 **	−0.399 **	−0.057 **	−0.067	−0.059 **	0.183	3.497 **

Table 4. *Cont.*

	Global Betas												Regional Betas											
	β_0^w	β_1^w	ARG Crisis	US Crisis	EU Crisis	MC	TI	GDP	INF	INT	adj. R^2	$F-Stat$	β_0^w	β_1^w	ARG Crisis	US Crisis	EU Crisis	MC	TI	GDP	INF	INT	adj. R^2	$F-Stat$
Sweden	−2.227 **	−2.227 **	1.135 *	0.446	0.336	0.118	0.175 **	0.161 **	0.715 **	0.043 **	0.060	1.001	0.924 *	0.719 *	−0.645 **	−1.358 **	−1.869 **	−0.407	0.813 **	−0.016 **	0.531 **	−0.049 **	0.158	2.931 **
Switzerland	−0.584	−0.292	0.872	−1.549 *	−2.121 **	−0.782	−1.729 **	−0.031 **	−0.892 *	3.753 *	0.189	3.657 **	0.735 **	0.659 **	−0.634 **	−0.560 **	−0.245 **	−0.218 **	0.212 **	0.011 **	0.631 **	−0.306 **	0.134	2.418 **
Turkey	−0.075 **	−0.075 **	0.076 **	0.031 *	0.396 **	−0.462 **	−0.098	0.034 **	−0.128 **	0.012 **	0.148	2.706 **	−1.697	−1.932	−0.408 **	−2.397 **	−0.129	−4.365 **	−0.277	0.019 **	0.012	0.226	0.119	2.097 **
Ukraine	0.906	0.986 **	3.860 *	2.617	0.410 **	2.542 *	−2.351	−0.030 **	1.193	−0.302 **	0.062	1.032	0.271 **	0.136 *	−0.647 **	−0.477 **	−0.116 *	1.152	−0.771	−0.013 **	0.111 *	−0.218 **	0.147	2.68 **
United Kingdom	−0.123	−0.489 *	−2.423 *	−2.410 **	−2.142 *	−1.295	0.542 **	0.195 **	0.106	0.439 **	0.262	5.545 **	−0.038 **	0.407 **	−0.120 **	−0.521 **	−0.351 **	0.025	0.224 **	−0.018 **	0.074 **	−0.038 **	0.118	0.118 **

Notes: Table 4 reports the estimated coefficients for all types of international equity market-capitalization-based portfolios from the structural regime-switching factor model. Coefficients are retrieved regionally and internationally and concern the stylized facts of volatility regimes, financial crises, and structural economic variables. β_0^w and β_1^w are the estimates of the latent regime variables. The three crises concern the coefficients of the three respective dummy variables. MC, IT, GDP, INF, and INT concern the coefficients of the respective structural macroeconomic variables (i.e., changes in market capitalization, trade integration , GDP growth, inflation rate, and interest rate). Then, the adjusted R^2 (adj. R^2) and the joint significance hypothesis F test ($F - stat$) are reported. ** and * indicate statistical significance in 5% and 10%, respectively.

Table 5. Structural regime-switching factor model on trade-integration-based portfolios.

	Global Betas												Regional Betas											
	β_0^{tw}	β_1^{tw}	ARG Crisis	US Crisis	EU Crisis	MC	TI	GDP	INF	INT	adj. R^2	$F-Stat$	β_0^{tw}	β_1^{tw}	ARG Crisis	US Crisis	EU Crisis	MC	TI	GDP	INF	INT	adj. R^2	$F-Stat$
AFRICA																								
Botswana	−0.352 **	−0.241 **	−0.093	0.176 **	0.028	−0.230 **	−0.011 **	−0.008 **	0.006 **	0.015 **	0.081	1.370	−0.415 **	−0.556 **	0.775	0.560 **	0.152 *	−0.226 **	−0.064 **	0.002 **	0.027 **	0.010 **	0.069	1.169
Egypt	1.783	3.275	0.371	−2.402 **	−2.844	−0.088	−0.326	0.016 **	0.267 **	−0.343 **	0.088	1.513	0.950	1.049	−0.523	−2.641 **	−1.961	0.678	−0.737 *	0.014 **	0.230	−0.070	0.039	0.650
Kenya	1.219 **	1.377 **	−0.222	0.874	−0.147	0.654	−0.773	−0.015 **	0.312 **	−0.260 **	0.048	0.781	1.071 **	1.246 **	−0.873	1.559	0.259	1.605	−2.011	−0.040 **	0.336 *	−0.344 **	0.067	1.123
Mauritius	−0.559	0.103	−0.491 **	−0.707 **	−1.338 **	0.074	−0.541	0.102 **	0.016 **	0.051 **	0.033	0.538	−0.016	0.295	−0.183 **	−0.321 **	−0.702 **	0.220	−0.515 **	0.051 **	0.024 **	0.013 *	0.047	0.766
South Africa	1.632 **	2.483 **	0.560	−1.587 *	−1.518	3.463	1.741	−0.079 **	−1.345	−0.462 **	0.152	2.803 **	2.317	2.176 *	0.507	−1.872	−1.477	7.246	5.454	−0.079 **	−0.308	−0.990 **	0.125	2.226 **
AMERICAS																								
Argentina	−0.933	−2.147 **	−3.430	−1.550	0.337	0.166	−0.223	−4.410	0.186	−0.281 **	0.071	1.193	−2.032 *	−2.404 **	−2.363 **	−1.410 *	1.153	0.269	−0.226 **	−1.472	0.295	−0.117 **	0.061	1.020
Brazil	−0.272	−0.434	−1.716 *	−1.168 **	0.485	−1.986	0.077	−0.099 **	−0.492 **	0.088	0.101	1.748 *	−1.081 **	−1.180 **	−0.931 *	−0.909 **	−0.064	−0.604	0.073	−0.011 **	−0.414 **	0.062 **	0.052	0.849
Canada	−0.462 *	−0.690 **	−1.734 *	−2.907	−0.291	−0.291	−0.158	−0.182 *	0.580 **	0.476 *	0.059	0.975	−0.649	−0.763	−0.729	−1.015 **	0.143	0.428	0.159	−0.191 **	0.179	−0.021	0.079	1.331
Chile	0.201 **	0.138 **	−0.201 **	−0.298 **	0.125 **	0.347 **	−0.075 **	−0.046 **	0.075 **	−0.032 **	0.064	1.062	−0.133 **	−0.221 **	−0.018 *	−0.127 **	0.107 **	−0.036 *	0.088	0.005 **	0.088 **	−0.016 **	0.044	0.715
Colombia	−0.076 **	−0.050 **	−0.365 **	−0.411 **	−0.411 **	0.148 **	0.021 **	−0.013 **	−0.125 **	−0.011 **	0.089	1.527	−0.345 **	−0.298 **	−0.115 **	−0.260 **	−0.071 **	−0.071 **	0.038 **	0.061 **	−0.045 **	0.026 **	0.051	0.834
Jamaica	0.804 **	0.923 **	−0.463 **	−0.190 **	0.998 **	−0.507 **	−0.013	0.003 **	0.112 **	−0.091 **	0.200	3.905 **	0.089	0.059 *	−0.241 **	−0.070 *	1.231 **	−0.397 *	0.013 **	0.004 **	0.130 **	−0.074 **	0.290	6.374 **
Mexico	−0.015	0.174	−1.432 **	−2.221 **	−0.215	0.248	−0.119 **	−0.019 **	1.505	0.215 **	0.155	2.869 **	−0.351 **	−0.561 *	−0.559 **	−1.239 **	0.475 **	0.472	−0.069 **	−0.020 **	0.648	0.117 **	0.099	1.723 *
Panama	0.933 **	0.583 **	−0.881 *	−0.444 **	0.065	−0.111	0.105	−0.094 **	0.427 **	0.149 **	0.084	1.438	0.148 **	−0.094	−0.523 *	−0.213 **	0.130	−0.149	0.192 *	−0.082 **	0.181 **	0.054 **	0.070	1.181
Peru	−0.388 **	−0.206 **	−0.369 **	−0.377 **	−0.039	0.330 **	0.069 **	−0.225 **	0.011 **	−0.090 **	0.087	1.485	−0.445 **	−0.326 **	−0.202 **	−0.331 **	−0.235 **	0.079 **	0.062 **	0.049 **	−0.015 **	−0.025	0.051	0.843
United States	1.232 **	0.280 **	−1.937 *	−0.632	0.269	1.587	−3.713	−0.207 **	−0.212	−0.044	0.120	2.132 **	0.011	−0.523 **	−0.986 **	−0.687 **	−0.282 **	0.431 *	−0.801	−0.031 **	−0.140 **	0.117	0.115	2.017 **
Venezuela	0.195 **	−0.058 **	−0.316 **	−0.772 **	−0.346 **	−0.037 **	−0.203	0.002 **	0.040 *	0.104 **	0.098	1.691 *	−0.371 **	−0.662 **	0.265	−0.319	−0.204 **	0.069	−0.700 *	0.015 **	−0.035	0.072 **	0.027	0.439
ASIA																								
Australia	2.939 **	2.843 **	−0.455 **	−0.236 **	0.271 **	−1.003 **	0.429 **	−0.043 **	−0.110 **	0.033 **	0.210	4.154 **	0.121 **	0.037	0.439 **	−0.089 **	0.312 **	−0.630 **	0.030 **	0.037 **	0.037 **	0.116 **	0.124	2.217 **

Table 5. *Cont.*

	Global Betas												Regional Betas											
	β_0^w	β_1^w	ARG Crisis	US Crisis	EU Crisis	MC	TI	GDP	INF	INT	adj. R^2	$F-Stat$	β_0^w	β_1^w	ARG Crisis	US Crisis	EU Crisis	MC	TI	GDP	INF	INT	adj. R^2	$F-Stat$
Bangladesh	2.707 **	2.853 **	−0.423 **	−0.216 **	−0.402 **	−0.037	0.056	−0.022	−0.047 **	−0.166 **	0.156	2.878 **	0.654 **	0.731 **	2.217 **	−0.257 **	0.196 **	0.159 **	−0.189 **	−0.111 **	−0.043 **	−0.061 **	0.103	1.798 *
China	6.008 **	5.502 **	−1.450 **	−0.506	0.175	2.447	−0.248	−0.150 **	0.361	−0.286 **	0.109	1.902 **	1.698 **	1.615 **	−0.387 **	−0.534 **	0.130 *	0.903 **	0.343 **	−0.052 **	0.096 **	0.021	0.135	2.438 **
Hong Kong SAR	9.573 *	9.596 *	−0.594 **	−2.000 **	−0.953 **	−1.380	−1.379	0.012 **	0.249	0.207 **	0.222	4.459 **	3.100 **	3.084 **	−0.059	−0.749 **	0.490 *	0.846	0.895	−0.041 **	0.516 **	0.016	0.120	2.127 **
India	6.987 **	6.595 **	−1.511 **	−1.456	−0.779	−1.082	−0.985	0.040 **	−0.552	0.331	0.122	2.165 **	1.135 **	0.925 **	−0.126	−0.546 **	0.132	0.766	−0.219	−0.027 **	−0.090 *	−0.025	0.075	1.261
Indonesia	3.142 **	2.546 **	−0.837 **	−0.965 **	−0.271	1.404 *	0.105	−0.066 **	0.182 **	−0.429 **	0.091	1.568	1.283 **	0.764 **	0.421 **	−0.236	0.436 *	1.999 **	−0.171 *	−0.051 **	0.151 **	−0.556 **	0.144	2.614 **
Israel	9.546 **	9.385 **	−0.842 **	−1.352 **	−0.200 **	−1.569 **	−8.612	0.205 **	−0.032 **	0.258 **	0.249	5.165 **	1.870 **	1.638 **	0.435 **	0.474 **	0.574 **	0.440 **	−3.069 **	0.010	0.027 **	0.048 **	0.171	3.218 **
Japan	25.886 **	25.265 **	−0.242	−1.663 **	−1.232 *	2.811	−6.639	−0.087 **	−0.334 **	−0.489 **	0.300	6.688 **	4.941 **	4.677 **	−0.163 **	−0.393 **	0.546 **	1.000 **	−0.856	−0.070 **	−0.042 **	−0.138 **	0.213	4.221 **
Jordan	−0.049 **	−0.022	−0.055 **	−0.059 **	−0.300 **	−0.168 **	0.111 **	0.030 **	−0.030 **	0.049 **	0.118	2.082 **	−0.108 **	−0.154 **	0.043 **	−0.046 **	−0.090 **	−0.150 **	0.051 **	0.020 **	0.030 **	0.012 **	0.114	2.002 **
Malaysia	1.179 **	1.030 **	−0.808 **	−0.524 **	−0.617 **	−1.638	−0.012 *	0.038 **	−0.083 **	0.142 **	0.058	0.962	−0.126	−0.218 *	0.101	−0.330 **	0.201	−0.934 **	−0.040 **	0.022 **	0.036 **	0.089 **	0.088	1.502
New Zealand	2.911 **	2.686 **	−0.128 **	0.419 **	1.370 **	0.898 **	2.181 **	−0.062 **	−0.099 **	−0.300 **	0.240	4.929 **	0.543 **	0.377 **	0.360 **	0.069 *	0.561 **	0.585 **	0.331 **	−0.047 **	0.111 **	−0.131 **	0.182	3.464 **
Oman	5.289 **	5.109 **	−0.325 **	−0.375 **	−0.163 **	0.301 **	−0.239 **	−0.013 **	0.153 **	−0.026 **	0.252	5.259 **	1.420 **	1.304 **	0.140 **	−0.196 **	0.275 **	0.154 **	−0.057 **	−0.015 **	0.034	−0.025 **	0.108	1.881 *
Pakistan	3.645 **	3.590 **	−0.196	−0.022	−0.500 **	0.809	−1.126 **	−0.072 **	0.222	−0.210 **	0.165	3.071 **	0.980 **	0.817 **	0.522 **	−0.114 **	0.361 **	0.668 **	−0.200 **	−0.042 **	0.043	−0.092 **	0.130	2.338 **
Philippines	2.589 **	2.253 **	−0.280 **	−0.928 **	−0.790 **	0.888 *	0.297 **	−0.765	0.082 **	−0.136 **	0.103	1.792 *	0.807 *	0.020	5.062	−0.273	−0.046	0.294	0.155 **	−1.001	0.083 **	−0.045 **	0.108	1.895 **
Saudi Arabia	−0.423 **	−0.360 **	−0.101 *	−0.161 *	0.094 *	0.167 *	0.034 *	−0.006 **	0.016	−0.450 **	0.130	2.320 **	−0.161 **	−0.167 **	0.333 **	−0.130 **	0.175 **	0.038 **	0.051 **	−0.002 **	0.085 **	0.037 **	0.159	2.939 **
Singapore	10.203 **	9.830 **	−0.011	−1.364 **	−0.526 *	2.168 **	0.269 **	−0.146 **	0.058 **	−0.111 **	0.332	7.767 **	1.835 **	1.818 **	−0.286 *	−0.554 **	−0.076	0.360 **	−0.096 **	−0.173 **	−0.015 **	−0.017 *	0.120	2.123 **
South Korea	15.759 **	15.411 **	−1.030	−1.715 *	−0.274	1.573	−0.030	−0.296 **	0.166 **	−0.036	0.243	4.997 **	4.283 **	3.951 **	0.679	−0.464 **	0.701 **	0.766 **	−0.455 **	−0.280 **	−0.069 **	0.019 **	0.152	2.788 **
Taiwan Province of China	15.636 **	15.509 **	−0.632 **	−1.515 **	0.172	0.953 **	−0.558 *	−0.098	−0.092 *	−0.252 **	0.353	8.517 **	3.161 **	2.906 **	0.947 **	−1.378 **	−0.292	0.039	0.027	0.378 **	−0.139 **	0.228 **	0.113	1.981 **
Thailand	4.871 **	4.430 **	−0.514 **	−1.088 **	−0.706 **	2.081 *	−0.538	−0.479 **	−0.125 **	−0.326 **	0.154	2.828 **	0.679 **	0.679 **	−0.026	−0.742 **	−0.526 **	−0.837 **	0.448 **	0.352 **	−0.028 **	−0.028 **	0.142	2.582 **
United Arab Emirates	0.384 **	0.307 **	−0.076 **	−0.071 **	−0.117 **	0.071 **	−0.047	−0.019 **	0.034 **	−0.048 **	0.033	0.526	0.169 **	0.103 **	0.076 **	−0.063 **	−0.053 **	0.127 **	−0.124 **	−0.067 **	0.045 **	−0.021 **	0.091	1.568
EUROPE																								
Austria	0.871 **	1.009 **	−0.254 **	−0.524 **	−0.524 **	−1.080 **	−0.065 **	−0.039 **	−0.027 **	0.698 **	0.190	3.668 **	0.087	−0.051	−0.321 **	−0.544 **	−0.511 **	−0.561	−0.068 *	0.075 **	0.075	0.374 **	0.101	1.747 *
Belgium	0.829 **	0.441 **	−0.277	−0.613 **	−0.692	0.760 **	0.973 **	0.363	0.093 *	0.390 **	0.111	1.953 **	0.622 **	0.194 *	−0.490 **	−1.026 **	−0.482 **	−0.482 **	1.132 *	−0.051	−0.033 **	−0.054	0.134	2.411 **
Bulgaria	0.884	1.283	−0.183	−3.038	−0.647	8.143	4.287	−2.919	−0.115	−0.013	0.067	1.112	−1.418	−1.122	−2.073	−1.868 **	−2.046	1.446	0.033	−2.399	0.411 **	−1.067 **	0.073	1.227
Croatia	−0.219	−0.542	−1.060 **	−1.002 **	0.412	1.470	2.857	−0.027 **	−0.379 **	0.148 **	0.127	2.278 **	−0.985 **	−1.516 **	−0.833 **	−1.242 **	−0.285	2.693	2.660	−0.020 **	−0.292	−0.010	0.101	1.746 *
Cyprus	1.098 **	1.395 **	−1.551 **	−1.832 **	−1.168 **	−0.481	0.522	0.014 **	−0.496 **	0.280 **	0.107	1.859 *	0.232	−0.082	−0.983 **	−2.157 *	−1.706 **	−2.634	−1.196	0.054 **	0.250	0.774 **	0.091	1.556
Czech Republic	−0.964 **	−1.110 **	−0.656 **	−1.740 **	−0.751 **	−0.415	−0.055	0.093 **	0.220 *	0.298 **	0.153	2.824 **	−1.708 **	−2.403 **	−0.181 **	−1.989 **	−1.579 **	−1.184	0.085	0.228 **	0.228	0.358 **	0.130	2.330 **
Denmark	0.438 **	0.149 **	−0.136 **	−0.186 **	0.492 **	1.754 **	0.686 **	−0.078 **	0.086 **	−0.217 **	0.201	3.913 **	−0.245 **	−0.679 **	−0.064 **	−0.324 **	−0.144	1.159 **	0.365 **	−0.047 **	0.140 **	−0.223 **	0.127	2.262 **
Estonia	−0.150 **	−0.192 **	−0.281 **	−1.105 **	0.907 **	1.058 **	−0.241 **	−0.263 **	0.046 **	−0.685 **	0.203	3.973 **	−0.529 **	−0.795 **	−0.248 **	−1.019 **	0.152	0.702 **	−0.253 **	−0.111 **	0.058 **	−0.693 **	0.157	2.909 **
Finland	3.700 **	4.177 **	0.735	−1.929 **	1.589 **	−1.973	4.399 **	−0.150 **	−0.344	−0.059 **	0.289	6.330 **	2.737	2.325 **	−1.989	−3.093	0.079	5.962	0.236	−0.023 **	0.181	−0.439	0.111	1.940 **
France	0.523 **	0.166 *	−1.463 **	−0.745 **	0.263	−0.219	−0.285 **	0.022	−0.132 **	0.104 **	0.083	1.407	−0.449 *	−1.051 **	−1.553 **	−0.824 **	−1.122 **	−0.910 **	0.145 **	0.604 **	−0.015 **	0.120 **	0.066	1.098
Germany	2.589 **	2.175 **	−1.486 **	−1.491 **	−0.944 **	−1.174	−0.059	−0.048	0.704 **	0.269 **	0.095	1.646 *	0.123	−0.654 **	−1.143 **	−1.839 **	−1.839 **	−0.731 *	0.211 **	0.043 **	0.398 **	0.261 **	0.080	1.353
Greece	−0.623 **	−0.855 **	−0.619 **	−1.246 **	−0.751 **	−1.112	−0.264 **	0.017 **	0.370 **	0.084 **	0.103	1.781 *	−1.197 **	−1.886 **	−0.684 **	−1.536 **	−1.173 **	−0.864	0.031	0.018 **	0.145	−0.062 **	0.094	1.615 *

Table 5. *Cont.*

	Global Betas												Regional Betas											
	β_0^w	β_1^w	ARG Crisis	US Crisis	EU Crisis	MC	TI	GDP	INF	INT	adj. R^2	$F-Stat$	β_0^w	β_1^w	ARG Crisis	US Crisis	EU Crisis	MC	TI	GDP	INF	INT	adj. R^2	F $Stat$
Hungary	−0.706 **	−0.478 **	−1.01 **	−1.550 **	0.065	0.368	1.160	0.0107 **	0.109 *	0.064 **	0.084	1.430	−0.750 **	−0.853 **	−0.547 **	−2.426 *	−0.943 **	−1.591	1.050 *	0.137 **	0.556 **	0.656 **	0.110	1.936 **
Ireland	−2.148 *	−2.299	1.694 *	−0.692 *	−1.559 *	−10.049	2.212 **	0.664 **	0.300 **	0.902 **	0.162	3.007 **	−1.064 **	−1.093 **	0.718 **	−1.110 **	−1.223 **	−3.471	1.069 **	0.310 **	0.039	0.404 **	0.226	4.562 **
Italy	−0.611	−0.906	−0.992 **	−0.751 **	−0.068	−1.134	0.328 **	−0.037 **	−0.320 **	0.216 **	0.060	0.987	−1.436 **	−1.671 **	−0.593 **	−0.823 **	−0.279 **	−2.319 **	0.496 **	0.039 **	−0.118 **	0.290 **	0.133	2.382 **
Latvia	13.930 *	13.244 *	0.040	−0.533 **	−1.655 *	1.608	0.194 **	0.022 **	−0.758 **	−0.394 **	0.372	9.231 **	0.873	−0.818	0.962	−0.484	−4.302	3.635	−0.177	0.065 **	−1.542	−0.958 **	0.144	2.627 **
Lithuania	1.155 **	1.112 **	−0.117 **	−0.244 **	−0.093 **	−0.077 **	0.185 **	0.042 **	−0.021 **	0.164 **	0.184	3.513 **	0.336 **	0.147 **	−0.080	−0.196 **	−0.124 **	−0.148 **	−0.036	0.017 **	0.051 **	0.257 **	0.099	1.719 *
Luxembourg	1.174 **	0.988 **	−0.689 **	0.069	−0.220 **	0.955 **	0.171 **	−0.113 **	−0.030 **	−0.385 **	0.241	4.956 **	1.150 **	0.752 **	−0.567 **	−0.359 **	−0.771 **	0.849 **	0.259 **	−0.081 *	−0.146 **	−0.307 **	0.167	3.132 **
Malta	0.543 **	0.622 **	−0.218 **	−0.323 **	0.093 **	0.110 **	−0.083	−0.051 **	0.024 **	−0.026 **	0.086	1.458	−0.065	−0.151 **	−0.255 **	−0.671 **	−0.064	0.671	−0.268 **	−0.010 **	−0.022	−0.046 **	0.067	1.118
Netherlands	1.444 **	1.106 **	−1.252 **	−0.892 **	−1.290 **	2.409	0.913	−0.044 **	−0.746 *	−0.065	0.072	1.209	−0.220	−0.696 **	−1.139 **	−0.984 **	−1.406 **	−0.657	1.035 **	0.019 **	−0.281	0.433 **	0.095	1.630 *
Norway	1.476 **	1.166 **	−0.599 **	0.012	0.258 *	0.958 *	0.893 **	−0.061 **	0.225 **	−0.346 **	0.185	3.546 **	0.445 **	−0.119	−0.537 **	0.029	0.014	0.793	0.999 **	−0.033 **	0.321 **	−0.419 **	0.146	2.674 **
Portugal	−0.086	−0.063	−0.798 **	−0.993 **	−0.569 **	1.239 **	1.702 **	−0.041 **	0.035	−0.224 **	0.083	1.412	−0.895 **	−1.024 **	−0.741 **	−1.454 **	−1.193 **	0.504	3.132 **	−0.012 **	0.309 **	−0.118 **	0.183	3.487 **
Romania	−0.531 **	−0.515 **	−1.329 **	−0.488	−0.070	1.516 **	−1.590	−0.045 **	−0.146 **	−0.489 **	0.161	2.994 **	−1.366 **	−1.565 **	−0.979 **	−0.703 **	−1.177 **	0.142	−1.806 **	−0.066 **	−0.469 **	−0.288 **	0.138	2.487 **
Russia	3.671 **	3.505 **	−1.948 **	−1.685 **	−1.270 **	1.348 **	−2.329 **	−0.052 **	0.065 **	−0.893 **	0.215	4.272 **	1.299 **	0.467	−2.531 **	−2.203 **	−2.573 **	0.951	−3.319	−0.014 **	0.071	−1.508 **	0.467	1.979 **
Slovak Republic	0.134	0.227 **	−0.825 **	−0.873 **	0.054	0.637 **	−0.584 **	−0.030 **	0.042 **	0.116 **	0.176	3.338 **	−0.370 **	−0.629 **	−0.835 **	−1.061 **	−0.545 **	0.303	−0.393 **	−0.013 **	0.073 **	0.271 **	0.111	1.946 **
Spain	−0.090	−0.077	0.443 *	−0.419 **	−0.057	3.243 **	−0.587 **	−0.088 **	−0.185 **	−0.085 **	0.207	4.070 **	−0.377 **	−0.625 **	0.030	−0.610 **	−0.675 **	2.099 **	−0.260 **	−0.041 **	−0.026	−0.046 **	0.157	2.908 **
Sweden	1.873	1.731 **	−0.974 **	−1.935	−1.999 **	0.198	0.922 **	−0.055 **	0.656 **	−0.073 **	0.168	3.144 **	−0.101	−0.486	−0.586	−1.438 *	−2.520 **	−1.351	1.163 **	−0.076	0.706 **	−0.054 **	0.134	2.408 **
Switzerland	1.333 **	1.299 **	−0.774 **	−0.642 **	−0.178 **	−0.161 **	0.177 **	0.037 **	0.804 **	−0.357 **	0.107	1.875 *	−0.057	−0.338 **	−0.964 **	−0.833 **	−0.102	−0.231 **	0.451 **	0.011 **	0.695 **	−0.482 **	0.130	2.338 **
Turkey	−1.548 **	−1.460 **	−0.514 **	−0.514 **	−0.461	−2.615	−2.855	0.075 **	−0.424 **	0.120 **	0.140	2.543 **	−1.437 **	−2.805 **	−0.499	−3.909	0.925	−7.876	3.182	0.042 **	0.870	0.662 *	0.114	2.007 **
Ukraine	−0.411	−2.461	−1.584	−10.414 **	−3.307	5.363	−12.590 **	−0.087 *	0.753	−0.443	0.093	1.592	−3.511	−13.557	2.904	−33.024 **	−19.302 *	−5.018	−35.661 **	−0.028	5.625	−0.269	0.089	1.532
United Kingdom	1.098 **	0.872 **	0.028	−0.572 **	−0.152	0.178	0.302 **	−0.038 **	0.053 **	−0.013 **	0.152	2.799 **	0.419	−0.114	−0.108 *	−0.769 **	−0.987 **	−0.192	0.123 **	0.016 **	−0.007	−0.018 **	0.110	1.933 **

Notes: Table 5 reports the estimated coefficients for all types of international equity international-trade-based portfolios from the structural regime-switching factor model. Coefficients are retrieved regionally and internationally and concern the stylized facts of volatility regimes, financial crises, and structural economics variables. β_0^w and β_1^w are the estimates of the latent regime variables. The three crises concern the coefficients of the three respective dummy variables. MC, IT, GDP, INF, and INT concern the coefficients of the respective structural macroeconomic variables (i.e., changes in market capitalization, trade integration, GDP growth, inflation rate, and interest rate). Then, the adjusted R^2 (adj. R^2) and the joint significance hypothesis F test ($F-stat$) are reported. ** and * indicate statistical significance in 5% and 10%, respectively.

Table 6. Structural regime-switching factor model on GDP-based portfolios.

	Global Betas												Regional Betas											
	β_0^w	β_1^w	ARG Crisis	US Crisis	EU Crisis	MC	TI	GDP	INF	INT	Adj. R^2	$F-Stat$	β_0^w	β_1^w	ARG Crisis	US Crisis	EU Crisis	MC	IT	GDP	INF	INT	Adj. R^2	$F-Stat$
AFRICA																								
Botswana	−0.087 **	−0.102 **	0.074 **	−0.059 **	−0.165 **	−0.024 **	−0.081 **	0.046 **	−0.041 **	−0.029 **	0.058	0.962	−0.773 **	−0.741 **	−0.434 **	0.207 **	−0.233 **	−0.386 **	0.035 **	0.037 **	0.043 **	0.021 **	0.053	0.869
Egypt	0.092 **	−0.059 **	0.158 **	0.064 **	−0.070	−0.450 **	−0.084 **	0.050 **	0.148 **	−0.012 **	0.043	0.705	−1.892	−0.888	0.743	−2.333 **	−2.607	0.314	−0.282	0.017 **	0.277	−0.433	0.052	0.852
Kenya	0.628 **	0.533 **	1.043 *	−0.540 *	−0.777	−0.221	2.837 **	0.069 **	−0.861 **	0.381 **	0.174	3.293 **	0.478 **	0.613 **	−0.212	0.574	−0.044	0.527 **	−0.728	−0.011	−0.048	−0.125 **	0.063	1.046
Mauritius	0.027 **	0.073 **	−0.035 **	−0.024 **	0.035 **	−0.029 **	0.038 **	−0.067 **	−0.036 **	0.015 **	0.074	1.247	−0.318 **	−0.079	−0.103 **	−0.197 **	−0.572 **	−0.404 **	−0.248 **	0.080 **	−0.016 **	0.052 **	0.086	1.473
South Africa	−0.493 **	−0.568 **	−0.011	0.609 **	−0.097	−0.681 **	0.978	0.012 **	−0.191 **	−0.069 **	0.050	0.828	0.610	1.227 *	0.734	−1.156	−0.884	4.268	3.300	−0.044 **	−0.757	−0.592 **	0.109	1.905 **
AMERICAS																								
Argentina	0.926 *	−0.022	−0.674	−0.382	−0.657	−1.343	−0.017	2.908	−0.399 **	0.461 **	0.038	0.615	−6.474	−8.041 *	−5.249	−2.094	−0.990	−5.184	0.278	−3.519	0.852	−0.899	0.100	1.738 *
Brazil	−1.579 **	−0.852	1.285 **	1.117 **	1.176	−2.004	−0.216 **	0.018 **	−0.290	0.042 **	0.119	2.100 **	−1.350	−1.477	−3.480	−3.070	−1.900	−6.110	1.118 **	0.004	−1.778	0.321 **	0.127	2.278 **
Canada	6.820	2.180	−1.981	10.119	2.991	3.304	1.604	−1.983	3.051	−1.358	0.036	0.576	−0.287	−0.379 *	−3.786 **	−4.591 **	0.772	3.005 **	0.336 *	−1.244 **	0.255 *	−0.034	0.164	3.052 **
Chile	−0.376	−1.729	0.655	−3.288	−2.080	−4.692	2.601	0.054 **	−3.410	1.515	0.022	0.352	0.500 *	0.214	−0.745 **	−0.931 **	−0.381	0.235	0.016	−0.011 **	−0.058	0.101 **	0.074	1.254
Colombia	−1.268	−0.673 **	0.106 **	−0.618 **	−1.290 **	−0.877 **	−0.144 **	0.098 **	0.098	0.093	0.061	1.016	−0.240	−0.174	−1.036 **	−1.117 **	−0.879 **	−0.022	0.132 **	0.030 **	−0.308 **	0.049 **	0.086	1.477
Jamaica	0.342 **	0.083	−0.144 *	0.185	−0.060 **	0.022	0.149 **	−0.008 **	0.030	0.271 **	0.026	0.409	2.274 **	2.206 **	−1.200 **	−0.342 *	1.461 **	−1.127	−0.590 **	0.008 **	0.249 **	−0.375 **	0.148	2.708 **
Mexico	−1.175	1.355	−0.908	−3.214	0.230	−9.309 *	−0.316	0.205 **	−4.936 **	1.503 **	0.070	1.182	−0.296	−0.477	−4.128 **	−3.918 **	−1.175	4.290	0.252 **	−0.199 **	0.466	−0.045	0.107	1.864 **
Panama	−0.119 **	0.079 **	−0.298 **	−0.276 **	−0.256 **	0.062 **	0.110 **	0.064 **	0.025 **	0.025 **	0.026	0.415	1.389 **	1.001 **	−1.806 **	−1.792 **	−0.286	1.162	0.697	0.041	0.424	0.036	0.061	1.014
Peru	0.021	0.021	0.026 **	−0.112 **	−0.012	−0.346 **	0.030 **	0.196 **	0.036 **	0.072 **	0.077	1.296	−0.720 **	−0.343 **	−1.288 **	−1.361 **	−0.281	1.093 **	0.511 **	−0.253 **	−0.118 **	−0.175 **	0.109	1.910 **
United States	−39.942	−16.488	15.708	1.057	−9.594	−4.763	40.778	1.238	−9.155	0.443	0.068	1.145	2.242	−0.136	−2.375	−1.929	−2.358	3.941	−16.487	−0.416 **	−1.283	−0.466	0.160	2.970 **
Venezuela	−0.071 **	−0.071 **	−0.034 **	0.098 **	0.036 **	0.091 **	−0.077 **	−0.010 **	−0.036 **	−0.018 **	0.073	1.231	0.653 **	0.222 **	−1.440 **	−0.982 **	−0.831 **	0.338 **	1.926	0.005 **	−0.244 **	0.031 **	0.116	2.054 **
ASIA																								
Australia	−0.152	−2.010	−0.349	−3.991	−3.991 **	7.157	−1.746	0.508	1.151	−0.138	0.084	1.427	2.755 **	2.666 **	−0.493 **	−0.221 **	0.484 **	−0.884 **	0.300 **	−0.040 **	−0.116 **	0.058 **	0.177	3.346 **
Bangladesh	0.028	0.063 *	0.030 **	0.030 **	−0.111 **	0.092 **	−0.083 **	−0.086 **	0.079 **	−0.052 **	0.019	0.297	3.222 **	3.248 **	−0.344 **	−0.309 **	−0.089	−0.048	−0.117	−0.090	−0.011	−0.149 **	0.185	3.534 **
China	−5.429	−4.196	0.169	−0.037	−4.411	−5.510	−6.905	0.569 **	−5.915 **	−1.523 *	0.155	2.863 **	6.460 **	5.867 **	−1.624 **	−0.596	0.495	2.338	−0.911	−0.151 **	0.101	−0.157	0.101	1.750 *
Hong Kong SAR	0.149 **	0.148	0.032 **	0.212 **	0.205 **	0.712 **	−0.712 **	−0.059 **	−0.406 **	−0.035 **	0.060	0.997	11.196	11.221	−0.782 *	−2.694	−1.110	−2.195	2.319	0.017 **	0.103	0.531	0.212	4.204 **
India	−14.523	−19.831	−6.716	−3.499	−2.935	−10.792	5.074	0.049	10.808	−1.999	0.047	0.761	6.672 **	6.197 **	−1.585	−2.099	−0.882	−1.963	−1.134	0.073 **	0.129	0.583	0.071	1.192
Indonesia	0.460	0.695 **	0.695 **	−0.350	−1.561	−1.049	−0.727 **	0.086 **	0.027 **	0.141 **	0.141	0.593	3.706 **	3.105 **	−0.621 **	−0.777 **	0.115	1.512 **	−0.253	−0.019 **	0.182 **	−0.343 **	0.102	1.767 *
Israel	−0.552 **	−0.293 **	−0.581 **	−0.096 **	−0.034	−0.016	−0.977	−0.016 **	−0.190 **	−0.056 **	0.037	0.595	9.586 **	9.567 **	−0.674 **	−1.423 **	0.253 **	−0.984 **	−6.239	0.153 **	0.074	0.310 **	0.328	7.615 **
Japan	26.129	15.435	19.415	22.298	−14.103	−32.515	−29.724	0.798	22.329 *	3.999	0.075	1.272	26.750 **	26.141 **	−0.770	−1.721 **	−0.639	1.191	−4.432	−0.069 **	−0.441 **	−0.214 **	0.355	8.577 **
Jordan	0.453 **	0.376 **	−0.015 **	−0.202 **	0.054 **	0.186 **	0.056 **	−0.018 **	0.049 **	0.010 **	0.122	2.172 **	0.006	0.064 **	−0.033 **	−0.074 **	−0.245 **	−0.116 **	0.095 **	0.026 **	−0.028 **	0.056 **	0.086	1.466
Malaysia	−0.075 **	−0.221 *	−0.588 **	−0.268 **	−0.558 **	−1.669	−0.185 **	0.027 **	0.015 **	0.072 **	0.031	0.506	1.391 **	1.305 **	−0.551 **	−0.473 **	−0.092	−1.062 *	0.013	0.029 **	−0.165 **	0.213 **	0.068	1.144
New Zealand	−0.054	−0.205	0.155 **	−0.046	−0.737 **	0.063	−0.756	0.040 **	−0.743 **	−0.076 **	0.082	1.391	2.999 **	2.756 **	−0.345 **	0.491 **	1.487 **	1.180 **	1.654 **	−0.086 **	−0.026	−0.350 **	0.204	3.992 **
Oman	1.220 **	1.227 **	−0.089 **	−0.019 **	−0.049 **	0.033 **	0.078 **	−0.018 **	0.036 **	−0.079 **	0.199	3.875 **	6.204 **	6.019 **	−0.325 **	−0.330 **	−0.096	0.370 **	−0.182 **	−0.021 **	0.152 **	−0.032 **	0.310	7.000 **
Pakistan	−0.644 **	−0.754 **	−0.583 **	−0.410 **	−0.086	0.195	0.567 **	−0.008 **	−1.268	−0.054 **	0.026	0.423	3.898 **	3.755 **	−0.144	0.028	−0.183 *	0.930	−0.979 **	−0.090 **	0.228	−0.208 **	0.151	2.777 **
Philippines	−0.179 **	−0.179 **	−0.272 **	0.531 **	0.178 **	0.671 **	−0.277 **	−0.446 **	−0.043 **	−0.056 **	0.076	1.282	2.662 **	2.373 **	0.361 *	−0.728 **	−0.492 **	0.685 **	0.246 **	−0.974 *	0.070 **	−0.122 **	0.114	2.013 **
Saudi Arabia	3.894 **	3.958 **	−1.438	−0.265	1.069	−0.219 *	−0.418	0.006 **	0.146	−0.019	0.039	0.628	−0.367 **	−0.277 **	−0.095 **	−0.160 **	0.249 **	0.126 **	−0.020 **	−0.006 **	−0.047 **	−0.335 **	0.113	1.996 **
Singapore	−0.389 **	−0.352 **	−0.186 **	−0.301 **	0.052	−0.325 **	0.136 **	0.061 **	−0.018 **	0.084 **	0.054	0.892	10.246 **	9.699 **	0.085	−1.244 **	−1.218	3.587	−0.317	−0.064	−0.014	−0.357	0.285	6.221 **

Table 6. *Cont.*

	Global Betas												Regional Betas											
	β_0^{tw}	β_1^{tw}	ARG Crisis	US Crisis	EU Crisis	MC	TI	GDP	INF	INT	Adj. R^2	$F-Stat$	β_0^{w}	β_1^{w}	ARG Crisis	US Crisis	EU Crisis	MC	IT	GDP	INF	INT	Adj. R^2	$F-Stat$
South Korea	−3.059	−3.453	−0.919	−0.761 **	−2.834	−1.662 **	−0.307	0.773 **	−0.124 **	−0.210 **	0.044	0.719	−0.103	17.276	−1.378	−1.613 **	0.356	2.885	−0.402	−0.432 **	0.108 **	−0.103 **	0.247	5.127 **
Taiwan Province of China	−0.057	0.022	0.590 **	1.407 **	−0.746 **	0.214 **	0.483 **	−0.023	0.499 **	−0.351 **	0.099	1.715 *	15.659 **	15.503 **	−0.536	−1.415 *	0.351	0.923 *	−0.375	−0.130	−0.146 **	−0.185	0.341	8.077 **
Thailand	−0.529	0.035	−0.589	−0.214	0.448	2.013 **	−0.460	−0.634 *	−0.340	−0.359 **	0.073	1.232	4.463 **	4.144 **	−0.671 **	−1.002 **	−0.425 **	1.176	0.179	−0.372 **	0.126 **	0.126 **	0.150	2.760 **
United Arab Emirates	−0.474	−0.587	0.277	0.852 **	−0.819 *	−1.048	3.500	0.148 **	0.075 **	−0.425 **	0.085	1.441	0.448 **	0.385 **	−0.078 **	−0.090 **	−0.067 **	0.093 **	−0.086 **	−0.016 **	0.050 **	−0.033 **	0.048	0.793
EUROPE																								
Austria	−1.209 **	−1.434 **	−0.101	1.728 **	−0.375	1.139	−0.275 *	0.013 **	0.165	0.447	0.077	1.303	−0.283 **	−0.017	−0.244 **	−0.771 **	−0.553 **	−2.059 **	−0.237 **	0.048 **	0.051	1.294 **	0.150	2.743 **
Belgium	−0.445	−0.232	−0.278 **	0.066	−0.316 *	−0.533 **	−0.068	−0.018	−0.091 **	−0.056 **	0.032	0.508	1.065 *	0.596 **	−0.652	−0.890 **	−0.615	1.388 *	1.031	−0.430	0.025 **	0.368 *	0.107	1.871 *
Bulgaria	−0.053 **	−0.087 **	−0.0128 **	−0.034 **	−0.115 **	0.032 **	0.021	0.064 *	0.049 **	−0.013 **	0.021	0.343	−3.270	−1.671	−1.018	−4.166	−0.189	7.098	5.972	−3.926	0.404	−0.388	0.063	1.043
Croatia	−0.077 **	0.137 **	1.337 **	0.025 **	0.078 **	−0.170 **	0.071 **	0.010 **	−0.194 **	0.095 **	0.080	1.357	−0.954 *	−1.494 **	−1.288 **	−1.381 *	0.923	2.710	2.710	−0.037 **	−0.252	0.140 **	0.132	2.380 **
Cyprus	−0.072	−0.042	0.016	−0.151 **	−0.122	−0.247 *	−0.047	0.053 **	−0.015	0.059 **	0.039	0.639	−1.367 **	−0.723	−2.339 **	−3.099 **	−1.460 **	−1.599	0.590	0.039 **	−0.760 *	0.763 **	0.080	1.356
Czech Republic	−0.235 **	−0.187 **	0.272 **	−0.038	−0.133 **	0.105 **	−0.038 **	0.011 **	0.172 **	−0.015 **	0.053	0.871	−1.277 **	−1.681 **	−0.928 **	−2.213 **	−0.880 **	−0.380	0.086	0.120 **	0.692 **	0.372 **	0.137	2.473 **
Denmark	−0.314	−0.480	0.254	0.254	0.868	1.479	−0.080	−0.090	−0.847	−0.227	0.023	0.373	−0.242 **	−0.638 **	−0.089 *	0.175	1.049 *	2.756 **	1.057 **	−0.139 **	−0.226	−0.430 **	0.144	2.632 **
Estonia	−0.028 **	−0.034 **	−0.046 **	−0.043 **	−0.057 **	−0.024 **	−0.003 **	0.051 **	0.054 **	0.082 **	0.036	0.036	−0.488 **	−0.435 **	−0.534 **	−1.038 **	1.395 **	1.336 **	−0.399 **	−0.350 **	0.021 **	−0.876 **	0.235	4.796 **
Finland	−0.238 **	−0.429 **	0.051 **	0.590 **	−0.248 **	−0.689 **	0.098 **	0.072 **	−0.133 **	0.053 **	0.112	1.975 **	−0.370	0.381	0.779	−2.982	3.561 **	0.338	6.002	−0.257 **	−0.736	−0.171 **	0.282	6.137 **
France	0.971	−0.084	−0.186	−1.271 *	−0.323	3.117	−0.390 **	−1.725	0.281 **	0.481 **	0.077	1.303	−0.611	−0.794 **	−2.508 **	−1.076 **	0.457	−0.469	−0.339 **	0.090	−0.184 **	0.218 **	0.085	1.444
Germany	−2.620 **	−1.844 **	0.290	1.469 **	0.153	−0.552	−0.036	0.018	−0.726	−0.123	0.028	0.447	−0.531	−0.896 **	−2.295 **	−2.155 **	−1.223 **	−2.086	0.105	−0.032	0.439	0.504 **	0.088	1.497
Greece	0.520 **	0.526 **	−0.512 **	0.405 **	0.590 **	0.514	0.095 **	−0.018 **	−0.495 **	−0.018 *	0.044	0.716	−0.624 **	−0.951 **	−0.973 **	−1.243 **	−0.280	−0.599	−0.385 **	−0.040	0.7769 **	0.061 **	0.104	1.808 *
Hungary	1.177	0.855 **	0.117	−0.579 *	−1.580	0.034	−0.800	0.100 **	−0.128 **	−0.072 **	0.041	0.672	−1.640 **	−1.276 **	−1.240	−2.605 **	0.597	0.042	2.592	0.040 **	0.370 *	0.237 **	0.097	1.668 *
Ireland	0.231 **	−0.087 **	−0.226 **	0.559 **	0.127 **	0.669 **	−0.337 **	−0.085 **	−0.252 **	−0.032 **	0.079	1.335	−3.078 **	−3.010	2.240 *	−1.475 **	−2.268 **	−13.351	3.053 **	0.951 **	0.568 **	1.313 **	0.185	3.545 **
Italy	−5.650	−4.737	−0.445	−0.515	0.210	0.459	0.158	−0.091 **	0.044	0.044 **	0.036	0.580	−1.022	−1.275	−1.421 *	−0.941 **	0.021	−2.136	0.509 **	−0.035 **	−0.231 **	0.306 **	0.068	1.134
Latvia	−0.042 **	−0.042 **	−0.004	−0.055 **	0.044 **	0.022	−0.019 **	−0.016 **	0.041 **	0.015 **	0.037	0.592	1.028	0.256	−0.015	−0.594 **	−2.336	2.206	0.246 **	0.030 **	−0.942 **	−0.600 **	0.175	3.305 **
Lithuania	−0.084 **	−0.083 **	−0.031 **	0.022 **	−0.060 **	−0.041 **	−0.022 **	0.042 **	0.018 **	0.022 **	0.053	0.867	0.166 **	0.021	−0.092 **	−0.245 **	−0.049 **	−0.173 **	0.153 **	0.015 **	−0.023 **	0.355 **	0.132	2.370 **
Luxembourg	−0.644 **	−0.682 **	−0.015 **	−0.185 **	−0.141 **	−0.542 **	0.105 **	0.031 **	0.020 **	0.134 **	0.134	0.467	0.884 **	0.713 **	−1.032 **	0.266 **	−0.343 **	1.604 **	0.340 **	−0.171 **	−0.031 *	−0.620 **	0.237	4.844 **
Malta	−0.098 **	−0.081 **	−0.025 **	−0.013 **	−0.106 **	0.132 **	0.051 **	0.014 **	−0.013 **	0.015 **	0.058	0.954	−0.214 **	−0.032	−0.655 **	−0.694 **	0.596 **	0.742 **	−0.121 **	−0.030 **	0.144 **	−0.062 **	0.070	1.167
Netherlands	0.752	−0.379	5.653 **	−0.225	−1.332	3.940	−4.010	0.012 **	−0.609	0.044	0.044	0.724	−0.106	−0.260	−2.159 *	−1.357 **	−1.726 **	2.263	1.371	0.003	−0.852	0.236	0.072	1.209
Norway	−0.356 **	−0.511 **	−0.134 **	0.119 *	0.696 **	−0.103	0.577 **	0.036 **	−0.361 **	−0.063 **	0.053	0.877	0.307 **	−0.166	−0.844 **	0.335 **	0.562 **	1.393	1.525 **	−0.098 **	0.334 **	−0.574 **	0.183	3.492 **
Portugal	−0.043 **	−0.034 **	0.146 **	0.013 **	0.169 **	0.154 **	0.143 **	−0.060 **	0.019 **	−0.038 **	0.025	0.397	−1.119 **	−1.103 **	−1.112 **	−1.328 **	−0.560 **	1.719 **	2.497 *	−0.055 **	−0.010	−0.265 **	0.101	1.749 *
Romania	0.358 **	0.608 **	−0.015	0.231 **	0.208 **	0.086	0.387	−0.027 **	−0.118 **	−0.112 **	0.033	0.525	−1.588 **	−1.153 **	−2.301 **	−0.945	−0.185	1.977	−3.461	−0.063 **	−0.848 **	−0.582 **	0.152	2.787 **
Russia	−0.375 **	−0.781 **	1.070 **	0.871 **	0.218	−0.014	0.886 **	0.018 **	0.295 **	−0.087 **	0.071	1.193	1.537 **	1.020 **	−2.838 **	−2.181 **	−1.428 **	2.090 **	−3.225 *	−0.086 **	0.075	−1.373 **	0.184	3.518 **
Slovak Republic	0.063	−0.052 **	0.081 **	−0.110 **	−0.199 **	−0.060 **	0.033 *	0.010 **	0.012 **	0.024 **	0.122	2.158 **	−0.656 *	−0.590 **	−1.331 **	−1.118 **	0.617 **	1.329 **	−1.316 **	−0.066 **	−0.004	0.061	0.137	2.475 **
Spain	−1.703 **	−1.719 **	−0.990	0.267	−1.311	−0.805	0.220	0.072 **	0.535 *	0.084 **	0.056	0.056	−0.360	−0.369 **	0.695	−0.588 **	−0.051	5.821 *	−1.007 **	−0.154 **	−0.193 **	−0.146 **	0.167	3.125 **
Sweden	0.930 **	−0.863 **	0.438 **	0.438	−0.207 **	0.276 *	0.026	0.061 **	0.309 **	0.011 **	0.057	0.935	0.575	0.532	−1.516	−1.967	−2.992 **	−0.555	1.801 *	−0.117 **	0.967 **	−0.076 **	0.116	2.052 **

Table 6. *Cont.*

	Global Betas												Regional Betas											
	β_0^w	β_1^w	ARG Crisis	US Crisis	EU Crisis	MC	TI	GDP	INF	INT	Adj. R^2	$F-Stat$	β_0^w	β_1^w	ARG Crisis	US Crisis	EU Crisis	MC	IT	GDP	INF	INT	Adj. R^2	$F-Stat$
Switzerland	−0.220 **	−0.129 *	0.317 **	−0.339 **	−0.622 **	−0.056	−0.525 **	−0.015 **	−0.291 **	0.935 **	0.161	2.992 **	−0.252 **	−0.249 **	−1.147 **	−0.755 **	0.205 **	−0.211 **	0.273 **	−0.006	1.270 **	−0.573 **	0.118	2.082 **
Turkey	0.065 **	0.136 **	0.042 **	−0.069	0.084 **	−0.421 **	−0.018	0.023 **	−0.070 **	0.023 **	0.116	2.047 **	−3.213 **	−3.202 **	−0.451	−3.868 **	−0.176	−4.585	−5.749	0.013 **	−0.158	0.306	0.091	1.558
Ukraine	0.483 **	0.478 **	0.259 **	0.212 **	−0.047 **	0.061 **	−0.236 **	−0.001 **	0.098 **	−0.039 **	0.049	0.800	2.020	−3.877	0.182	−23.329 **	−7.704	9.997	−30.578 **	−0.017	6.953	−0.952	0.080	1.349
United Kingdom	0.085	−0.954	−6.716	−6.554 **	−6.560 *	−4.063	1.525 *	0.550 **	0.196	1.205 **	0.243	4.994 **	0.447	0.356	−0.036	−0.613 *	−0.076	0.189	0.480 **	−0.072 **	0.120 **	−0.020 **	0.112	1.960 **

Notes: Table 6 reports the estimated coefficients for all types of international equity GDP-based portfolios from the structural regime-switching factor model. Coefficients are retrieved regionally and internationally and concern the stylized facts of volatility regimes, financial crises, and structural economic variables. β_0^w and β_1^w are the estimates of the latent regime variables. The three crises concern the coefficients of the three respective dummy variables. MC, IT, GDP, INF, and INT concern the coefficients of the respective structural macroeconomic variables (i.e., changes in market capitalization, trade integration , GDP growth, inflation rate, and interest rate). Then, the adjusted R^2 (adj. R^2) and the joint significance hypothesis F test ($F-stat$) are reported. ** and * indicate statistical significance in 5% and 10%, respectively.

Table 7. Structural regime-switching factor model on inflation-rate-based portfolios.

	Global Betas												Regional Betas											
	β_0^w	β_1^w	ARG Crisis	US Crisis	EU Crisis	MC	TI	GDP	INF	INT	Adj. R^2	$F-Stat$	β_0^w	β_1^w	ARG Crisis	US Crisis	EU CRISIS	MC	TI	GDP	INF	INT	Adj. R^2	$F-Stat$
AFRICA																								
Botswana	−0.460 **	−0.380 **	−0.071 **	0.061 *	0.658 **	0.004	−0.029 **	0.026 **	0.063 **	−0.079 **	0.066	1.094	−0.683 **	−0.552 **	0.229	0.978 **	−0.037	−0.300 **	−0.062 **	−0.011 **	0.025 **	0.014 **	0.099	1.710 *
Egypt	−0.965	−1.144 **	−0.389	−1.914 **	−0.376	−2.029	−0.166	0.027 **	0.178	0.507 **	0.082	1.401	−1.265	−0.258	0.987	−1.956 **	−1.82	0.834	−0.355	0.083 **	0.203	−0.339 **	0.048	0.786
Kenya	0.082	−0.186 **	−0.611 **	0.388 **	1.219 **	0.439	−0.715 **	−0.024 **	−0.020	−0.109 **	0.065	1.084	0.586 **	0.712 **	0.017	0.530 **	−0.196 *	0.498 **	−0.348	0.057 **	0.048	−0.071 **	0.090	1.543
Mauritius	−0.333 **	−0.302 **	−0.092 **	−0.032 **	0.146 **	0.161 **	−0.379 **	0.059 **	−0.015 **	0.025 **	0.230	4.662 **	−0.144 **	0.087 **	−0.085	−0.099 **	−0.480 **	−0.218 **	−0.269 **	0.056 **	−0.041 **	0.028 **	0.075	1.262
South Africa	−0.823 **	−0.700 **	−0.781 **	−1.367 **	0.620	0.475	1.325	0.017 **	0.715 *	−0.059	0.074	0.270	0.977 *	1.454 **	0.918	−0.816	−0.369	4.236 *	0.465	−0.052 **	−0.680 *	−0.518 **	0.104	1.810 *
AMERICAS																								
Argentina	−2.056 *	−1.925 *	−0.903 *	0.012	−0.360	−1.102	−0.111	−1.307	0.095	−0.334 **	0.118	2.084 **	−1.729	−2.676	−2.245	−1.684 **	−0.429	−0.563	−0.0479	−2.023	−0.151	−0.168 **	0.068	1.132
Brazil	0.525	0.883 **	−1.018 **	−0.835 **	0.056	−0.042	0.047 **	−0.070 **	−0.226 **	−0.083	0.094	1.628 *	−0.327	−0.573 **	−1.292	−1.226 **	0.092	−2.728	0.197 **	−0.074 **	−0.433	0.042	0.103	1.798 *
Canada	0.138	0.575 **	−0.288 **	−1.141 **	−0.210 **	−0.141	−0.022	0.024	0.185 **	0.238 **	0.210	4.158 **	−0.542 **	−0.606 **	−1.440	−2.762	−0.396 *	0.075	−0.144	−0.255 **	0.702 **	0.389	0.075	1.260
Chile	0.618 **	0.637 **	−0.146 **	−0.133 **	−0.029	0.238 **	−0.158 **	−0.026 **	0.035 **	−0.012 **	0.083	1.418	0.142 **	0.053	−0.061	−0.308 **	−0.069	0.264 **	−0.223 **	−0.033 **	0.107 **	−0.025 **	0.074	1.255
Colombia	0.276 **	0.339 **	−0.083 **	−0.150 **	−0.040 **	0.122 **	−0.008	−0.087 **	0.010 **	−0.018 **	0.092	1.582	−0.047 **	−0.018	−0.294 **	−0.409 **	−0.095 **	0.138 **	0.051 **	−0.015 **	−0.144 **	−0.046 **	0.108	1.892 **
Jamaica	1.930 **	2.040 **	−0.148 **	−0.077 **	0.557 **	−0.129 **	−0.019 **	0.002 **	0.015 **	−0.047 **	0.332	7.767 **	0.900 **	0.964 **	−0.413 **	−0.168 **	0.717 **	−0.554 **	−0.024 **	0.004 **	0.137 **	−0.094 **	0.194	3.764 **
Mexico	0.890 **	1.180 **	−0.468 *	−0.505 *	−0.247 *	0.715 *	0.069 **	−0.043 **	0.460 **	−0.048 **	0.101	1.757 *	−0.123	0.101	−1.365 **	−2.296 **	−0.650 **	0.073	−0.131 **	−0.013 **	1.664 *	0.204 **	0.139	2.508 **
Panama	0.953 **	0.999 **	−0.250 **	−0.185 **	0.180 **	0.128 **	0.087 **	−0.046 **	0.028 **	0.013 **	0.077	1.293	0.885 **	0.630 **	−0.811 **	−0.353 **	−0.189	−0.115	0.102	−0.114 **	0.379 **	0.126 **	0.098	1.692 *
Peru	−0.103 **	0.120 **	−0.092 **	−0.176 **	0.017	0.310 **	0.134 **	−0.168 **	−0.078 **	−0.043 **	0.140	2.537 **	−0.514 **	−0.268 **	−0.296 **	−0.412 **	−0.019	0.337 **	0.132 **	−0.206 **	−0.079 **	−0.107 **	0.067	1.116
United States	1.260 **	1.219 **	−0.388 **	0.053	0.091	0.798 **	−2.073 **	−0.098 **	−0.038	−0.161 **	0.171	3.218 **	1.124 **	0.274 **	−1.777 *	−0.899	−0.107	1.210	−2.812	−0.160 **	−0.241 **	0.069	0.140	2.546 **
Venezuela	0.588 **	0.715 **	0.512 **	−0.094 **	−0.113 **	0.122 **	0.363 **	−0.003 **	−0.134 **	−0.095 **	0.142	2.576 **	0.179 **	−0.065 **	−0.115 **	−0.901 **	−0.560 **	0.092	−0.684 **	−0.007 **	0.012	0.099 **	0.127	2.272 **
ASIA																								
Australia	0.053	0.242	−0.734 **	−0.793 **	1.649 **	−1.937 **	0.841 **	−0.118 **	−0.158 **	0.117 **	0.102	1.767 *	18.683	18.657	−1.740 **	−0.601	1.441 **	−2.949	1.782 **	−0.219 **	−0.630 **	0.010	0.366	8.997 **

Table 7. *Cont.*

	Global Betas												Regional Betas											
	β_0^{w}	β_1^{w}	ARG Crisis	US Crisis	EU Crisis	MC	TI	GDP	INF	INT	Adj. R^2	$F-Stat$	β_0^{w}	β_1^{w}	ARG Crisis	US Crisis	EU CRI-SIS	MC	TI	GDP	INF	INT	Adj. R^2	$F-Stat$
Bangladesh	−3.208 **	−2.471 **	−1.380 **	−0.626	0.470	0.079	−0.248	−0.870 **	−0.069	−0.427 **	0.076	1.281	7.128 **	7.376 **	−0.914 **	−0.709	−0.104	0.655	−0.663	−0.541	0.121	−0.455 **	0.135	2.443 **
China	−0.818	−0.959	−2.592 *	−0.319	1.403	5.180	−1.984	−0.395 **	−0.122	−0.647	0.077	1.296	13.348 **	12.713 **	−4.324	−0.594	1.211	9.532	−0.893	−0.570 **	1.371	−1.311 *	0.075	1.273
Hong Kong SAR	−2.915 *	−2.831 **	−0.986	−4.156 **	−0.938	−2.263	7.867	0.011 **	0.792	0.395 **	0.108	1.895 **	14.101 **	14.183 **	−1.210 **	−4.161 **	−1.367	−0.996	8.565	0.015 **	0.616	0.097	0.157	2.914 **
India	−1.882	−2.415	−2.433	−2.692	−0.529	−0.286	−0.679	−0.078 **	−0.009	0.110	0.057	0.947	35.487	34.845	−5.524	−3.778	−1.814	−1.927	−3.099	0.030 **	−4.542	0.650	0.130	2.332 **
Indonesia	−2.161	−2.130 **	−2.437	−1.488	−0.339	3.537	0.5921	−0.155 **	0.317 **	−1.098 **	0.069	1.163	7.958 **	6.650 **	−2.649	−2.975	−0.876	4.507	1.060	0.030	0.239 **	−1.286 *	0.074	1.242
Israel	1.736 **	1.373 **	−0.725	−2.370 **	0.368	−0.385	−14.927	0.179 **	−0.016	0.346 **	0.197	3.832 **	45.088	44.339	−2.527	−3.280 *	−0.651	−5.627	−32.214	0.718 **	−0.380 **	0.737 **	0.289	6.354 **
Japan	2.267	2.805	−1.737	−1.494 **	0.020	3.631	−6.040	−0.390 **	−0.418	−0.588 **	0.122	2.168 **	110.164	108.847	1.308	−4.134	−3.272	19.732	−31.957	−0.403	−0.027	−2.420 **	0.345	8.211 **
Jordan	−1.503 **	−1.525 **	−0.073 **	−0.302 **	−0.933 **	−0.662 **	0.269 **	0.092 **	−0.043 **	0.127 **	0.113	1.977 **	0.212 *	0.338 **	−0.096 **	−0.106	−0.355 **	0.043	0.143 **	0.029 **	−0.018 **	0.059 **	0.046	0.757
Malaysia	−2.241 **	−2.508 **	−0.850	−1.190 **	0.999	−1.585	−0.341 **	0.050 **	−0.075	0.686 **	0.077	1.295	4.327 **	4.261 **	−2.745	−1.267 *	−0.996	−5.076	0.086	0.085 **	−0.134 **	0.168 **	0.052	0.855
New Zealand	−0.665	−1.096 *	−0.675	1.161	3.206 *	3.717 *	3.901	−0.275 **	−0.025	−1.077 **	0.162	3.018 **	13.520	13.059	0.046	1.657	4.758	3.068	7.481	−0.169 **	−0.334	−1.007 **	0.288	6.311 **
Oman	−0.402 **	−1.114 **	−0.751 **	−0.877 **	0.183	0.590	−0.673 **	−0.059 **	0.057	−0.056 **	0.082	1.402	6.016 **	5.4592 **	−0.844 **	−1.069 **	−0.417 *	1.197 *	−0.840 **	−0.063 **	0.341 **	−0.125 **	0.085	1.454
Pakistan	−2.097 *	−1.900 *	−1.018	−1.314 *	0.233	0.808	−0.195	−0.015 *	−0.160	−0.092	0.050	0.829	13.423 *	13.337 *	−1.737	−0.496	−1.142 **	3.800	−2.082 **	−0.023 **	−0.162	−0.482 **	0.115	2.024 **
Philippines	0.600	−0.300	2.640	−2.479 **	−1.027 **	1.496	0.790 **	−0.956	0.158 **	−0.074 **	0.141	2.562 **	11.960	10.535	−0.249	−3.430	−1.692	3.845	0.881	−1.303	0.333 **	−0.337 **	0.105	1.838 *
Saudi Arabia	−1.252 **	−1.269 **	−0.077	−0.660 **	−0.419 **	0.052 **	−0.067 **	−0.007 **	−0.488 **	−0.398 **	0.094	1.691 *	0.342	0.343	−0.275 **	−0.391 **	−0.350	0.356 **	−0.064	−0.003 **	−0.153	−1.715 **	0.145	2.648 **
Singapore	1.341	1.475	0.104	−2.624 **	−1.042	4.493	0.026	−0.740 *	0.093 **	−0.550	0.164	3.061 **	40.310	40.351	−0.849	−4.267 **	1.266	3.231	2.287 **	−1.525 **	0.307 **	0.307	0.321	7.362 **
South Korea	−0.158	−0.585	−2.173	−3.394 **	−0.783	4.976	−0.460	−1.093 **	0.162 **	−0.239 **	0.158	2.929 **	32.372 **	31.917 **	−2.169	−5.582	−1.071	4.194	1.536	−1.348 **	0.755 *	0.156 **	0.154	2.843 **
Taiwan Province of China	1.997	1.266	−1.138	−1.822	−1.229 *	1.087	−0.071	−0.972 **	−0.282 **	−0.126	0.113	1.986 **	67.188	67.085	−1.585	−3.453	1.809	3.446 *	−1.988	−0.754	−0.482	−0.723 **	0.457	13.100 **
Thailand	−1.163 *	−1.720 **	−1.206 **	−2.086 **	−1.568 **	0.874	0.158	−0.668 **	0.153	−0.112 **	0.148	2.717 **	20.523	19.356	−2.044 **	−2.565 **	−0.636	11.369	−4.282	−3.405	−0.647 *	−1.899 **	0.180	3.432 **
United Arab Emirates	−0.070 **	−0.190 **	−0.139 **	−0.244 **	−0.202 **	0.223 **	−0.444 **	−0.049 **	0.105 **	−0.053 **	0.091	1.570	1.816 **	1.655 **	−0.284 **	−0.149 **	−0.189 **	0.227 **	−0.149	−0.067 **	0.025 **	−0.105 **	0.058	0.954
EUROPE																								
Austria	0.151	−0.028	−0.197 **	−0.443 **	−0.395 **	−0.375	−0.104 **	0.017 **	−0.015 *	0.342 **	0.102	1.762 *	0.375 **	0.584 **	−0.200 **	−0.624 **	−0.449 **	−1.482 **	−0.109 **	0.035 **	0.036 **	0.921 **	0.189	3.642 **
Belgium	0.527 **	−0.049	−0.211 **	−0.875 **	−0.626 **	0.629 **	0.692 **	0.949	0.073 **	0.088 **	0.116	2.044 **	0.761 **	0.459 **	−0.430	−0.691 **	−0.600	0.951 **	0.917 **	−0.012	−0.057 **	0.346 **	0.135	2.439 **
Bulgaria	−0.142	−0.085	−0.546	−1.768 **	−0.433	3.090	1.244	−0.210	−0.023	−0.224	0.059	0.971	−0.654	0.757	−0.733	−3.133	−0.832	6.743	4.022	−2.664	0.122	−0.282	0.086	1.461
Croatia	−0.686 *	−1.284 *	−0.455 **	−1.516 **	−0.499	2.589	1.302	0.093 **	0.162	0.106 **	0.090	1.536	−0.477	−0.810 *	−1.102 **	−1.256 **	0.548	2.487	3.373	−0.033 **	−0.413 *	0.099 **	0.138	2.498 **
Cyprus	0.306	−0.041	−0.665 **	−1.989 **	−1.587 **	−2.549	−0.958	0.054 **	0.028	0.607 **	0.092	1.586	0.170	0.562 *	−1.812 **	−1.892 **	−1.212 **	−0.419	0.529	0.012 **	−0.592 **	0.279 **	0.104	1.809 *
Czech Republic	−2.163 **	−2.851 **	−0.049	−2.073 **	−1.791 **	−1.817	0.067	0.260 **	−0.618 **	0.455 **	0.145	2.655 **	−1.343 **	−1.553 **	−0.719 **	−1.970 **	−0.897 **	−0.550	−0.104 **	0.118 **	0.221	0.340 **	0.142	2.585 **
Denmark	−0.255 **	−0.660 **	−0.096 **	−0.422 **	−0.422 **	0.613 **	0.293 **	−0.016 **	0.034	−0.149 **	0.108	1.897 **	0.153 **	−0.139 **	−0.166 **	−0.095	0.620 **	2.091 **	0.841 **	−0.098 **	0.120	−0.293 **	0.171	3.218 **
Estonia	−0.580 **	−0.908 **	−0.217 **	−0.665 **	0.219	0.405 **	−0.068 **	−0.066 **	0.043 **	−0.679 **	0.132	2.374 **	−0.343 **	−0.339 **	−0.276 **	−1.101 **	1.004 **	1.110 **	−0.342 **	−0.267 **	0.046 **	−0.697 **	0.280	6.079 **
Finland	2.670 *	1.869 **	−2.109	−2.199	0.859 **	7.332	−1.050	0.052 **	−0.187 **	−0.634 **	0.124	2.210 **	1.268 **	2.214 **	1.155	−2.333 **	1.978 **	−1.822	5.186 **	−0.170 **	−0.232	−0.033	0.334	7.833 **
France	−0.685 **	−1.439 **	−1.191 **	−0.941 **	−1.177 **	−1.094 **	0.030	0.702 **	0.049 **	0.101 **	0.072	1.215	−0.220	−0.325 **	−1.627 **	−0.813 **	0.352 *	−0.339	−0.342 **	0.086	−0.133 **	0.120 **	0.108	1.892 **
Germany	0.652	−0.206	−0.721 **	−1.663 **	−1.701 **	−1.107 **	0.091 **	0.101 **	0.637 **	0.295 **	0.095	1.643 *	1.461 **	1.289 **	−1.607 **	−1.553 **	−1.038 **	−1.430 *	−0.028	0.099	0.499	0.320 **	0.112	1.968 **
Greece	−1.695 **	−2.389 **	−0.107	−1.442 **	−1.478 **	−1.404 **	−0.137	0.102 **	0.260	0.104 **	0.112	1.974 **	−0.782 **	−0.972 **	−0.829 **	−1.414 **	−0.822 **	−1.250	−0.334 **	0.013 **	0.468 **	0.087 **	0.097	1.669 *

Table 7. *Cont.*

	Global Betas												Regional Betas											
	β_0^w	β_1^w	ARG Crisis	US Crisis	EU Crisis	MC	TI	GDP	INF	INT	Adj. R^2	$F-Stat$	β_0^w	β_1^w	ARG Crisis	US Crisis	EU CRISIS	MC	TI	GDP	INF	INT	Adj. R^2	$F-Stat$
Hungary	−0.476 **	−0.777 **	−0.374 **	−2.044 **	−0.833 **	−1.366	0.804 *	0.120 **	0.395 **	0.557 **	0.100	1.735 *	−1.189 **	−0.717 **	−1.134 **	−1.662 **	0.169	0.404	1.446	0.069 **	0.130 **	0.029	0.120	2.126 **
Ireland	−1.075 **	−1.320 **	0.918 **	−1.054 **	−1.149 **	−4.167	1.135 **	0.356 **	0.156 **	0.437 **	0.167	3.127 **	−2.250 **	−2.184	1.674 **	−0.995 **	−1.671 **	−10.004	2.249 **	0.692 **	0.339 **	0.957 **	0.225	4.536 **
Italy	−1.400	−1.820	−0.566 **	−0.871 **	−0.257 **	−1.902 **	0.411 **	0.044 **	0.153 **	0.242 **	0.098	1.704 *	−0.847	−1.022	−1.091 **	−0.804 **	−0.054	−1.322	0.363 **	−0.035 **	−0.298 **	−0.298 **	0.079	1.332
Latvia	3.493	1.723	1.080 *	−0.440	−4.750	2.317	−0.195 *	0.094 **	−1.624	−0.791 **	0.191	3.678 **	9.621 **	8.879 **	0.037	−0.569 **	−1.894 *	1.707	0.228 **	0.029 **	−1.004 **	−0.422 **	0.288	6.316 **
Lithuania	0.529 **	0.358 **	0.049 **	−0.080 **	−0.096 **	0.112 **	0.023 *	−0.009 **	−0.009	0.234 **	0.122	2.163 **	0.804 **	0.746 **	−0.111 **	−0.240 **	−0.014 **	−0.128 **	0.176 **	0.010 **	−0.044 **	0.244 **	0.151	2.769 **
Luxembourg	0.785 **	0.361 **	−0.343 **	−0.676 **	−0.707 **	0.255	0.081	0.076 **	−0.021 **	−0.045	0.128	2.284 **	0.680 **	0.553 **	−0.855 **	0.178 *	−0.215 **	1.163 **	0.279 **	−0.140 **	−0.067 **	−0.470 **	0.219	4.379 **
Malta	−0.046	−0.111 **	−0.173 **	−0.588 **	0.074	0.572	−0.164 **	0.021 **	0.061 **	−0.023 **	0.080	1.362	0.056	0.239 **	−0.426 **	−0.437 **	0.227 **	0.138 **	−0.024	−0.014 **	0.029	−0.048 **	0.065	1.078
Netherlands	−0.086	−0.695 **	−0.638 **	−1.050 **	−1.278 **	−0.567	0.290	0.022 **	0.010	0.372 **	0.095	1.646 *	0.695 *	0.580 **	−1.376 **	−0.906 **	−1.321 **	2.250	1.077	−0.026 **	−0.587 **	−0.037	0.091	1.558
Norway	0.585 **	0.240 **	−0.437 **	−0.408 **	−0.318 **	0.077	0.918 **	0.062 **	0.207 **	−0.097 **	0.125	2.221 **	0.957 **	0.691 **	−0.723 **	0.024	0.333 **	1.054 *	1.123 **	−0.063 **	0.209 **	−0.403 **	0.181	3.457 **
Portugal	−0.403 **	−0.684 **	−0.444 **	−1.050 **	−0.738 **	0.765 **	2.125 **	−0.017 **	0.053	−0.221 **	0.149	2.722 **	−0.617 **	−0.389 *	−0.958 **	−1.139 **	−0.602 **	1.382 **	1.966	−0.047 **	0.056	−0.256 **	0.112	1.962 **
Romania	−1.080 **	−1.433 **	−0.532 **	−0.521 **	−1.046 **	−0.149	−1.391 **	0.083 **	−0.422 **	−0.327 **	0.109	1.908 **	−0.776 **	−0.534 **	−1.646 **	−0.476	−0.031	1.824 *	−1.768	−0.053 **	−0.516 **	−0.576 **	0.175	3.314 **
Russia	1.149 **	0.467	−2.136 **	−1.811 **	−2.074 **	0.091	−2.717	0.081 **	0.045	−1.164 **	0.096	1.664 *	2.442 **	2.411 **	−2.225 **	−1.909 **	−1.272 **	1.579 **	−2.541 **	−0.064 **	0.179 **	−1.049 **	0.219	4.378 **
Slovak Republic	−0.150	−0.581 **	−0.754 **	−1.231 **	−0.402	−0.170	−0.336 *	−0.034 *	0.092 *	0.435 *	0.121	2.145 **	−0.141	−0.043	−1.008 **	−0.880 **	0.293 **	0.918 **	−0.747 **	−0.040 **	0.022	0.041 *	0.157	2.902 **
Spain	−0.270 **	−0.706 **	0.174	−0.601 **	−0.731 **	1.827 **	−0.270 **	−0.028 **	0.019	−0.036 **	0.144	2.627 **	−0.237 **	−0.216 **	0.5712 *	−0.506 **	−0.103 **	4.097 **	−0.749 **	−0.108 **	−0.168 **	−0.105 **	0.213	4.215 **
Sweden	−0.061	−0.712	−0.535	−1.645 **	−1.937 **	−0.545	0.708 **	0.021 **	0.672 **	−0.071 **	0.111	1.956 **	0.952	1.053	−1.263 *	−2.063	−2.063 **	−0.017	1.229 **	−0.070 **	0.755 **	−0.074 **	0.151	2.778 **
Switzerland	0.150	−0.247 **	−0.584 **	−0.720 **	0.138	−0.404 **	0.323 **	0.027 **	0.525 **	−0.304 **	0.141	2.555 **	0.460 **	0.705 **	−1.021 **	−0.757 **	−0.188 **	−0.187 **	0.161 **	0.021 **	1.077 **	−0.485 **	0.111	1.948 **
Turkey	−2.624 **	−3.740 **	−0.284 *	−2.612	−0.399	−3.712	0.540	0.028 **	0.679	−0.012	0.111	1.927 **	−2.612 **	−2.287 **	−0.382 **	−2.821 **	−1.579	−2.138	−5.745	0.025 **	−0.206	−0.010	0.125	2.237 **
Ukraine	−5.060	−15.256	3.534	−29.829 **	−29.829 *	−6.130	−34.934 **	−0.043	3.372	−1.214	0.107	1.862 *	−1.714	−4.037	−3.099	−9.142 *	−3.582	6.003	−10.750	−0.095 *	0.655	−0.825	0.069	1.163
United Kingdom	0.206	−0.372 *	0.150	−0.769 **	−0.829	0.004	0.083 **	0.025 **	0.012	−0.026 **	0.106	1.854 *	0.532 **	0.443 **	0.037	−0.679 **	−0.135	0.376	0.270 **	−0.046 **	0.029 *	−0.031 **	0.141	2.552 **

Notes: Table 7 reports the estimated coefficients for all types of international equity inflation-rate-based portfolios from the structural regime-switching factor model. Coefficients are retrieved regionally and internationally and concern the stylized facts of volatility regimes, financial crises, and structural economic variables. β_0^w and β_1^w are the estimates of the latent regime variables. The three crises concern the coefficients of the three respective dummy variables. MC, IT, GDP, INF, and INT concern the coefficients of the respective structural macroeconomic variables (i.e., changes in market capitalization, trade integration , GDP growth, inflation rate, and interest rate). Then, the adjusted R^2 (adj. R^2) and the joint significance hypothesis F test ($F - stat$) are reported. ** and * indicate statistical significance in 5% and 10%, respectively.

Table 8. Structural regime-switching factor model on interest-rate-based portfolios.

	Global Betas												Regional Betas											
	β_0^w	β_1^w	ARG Crisis	US Crisis	EU Crisis	MC	TI	GDP	INF	INT	Adj. R^2	$F-Stat$	β_0^w	β_1^w	ARG Crisis	US Crisis	EU Crisis	MC	TI	GDP	INF	INT	Adj. R^2	$F-Stat$
AFRICA																								
Botswana	−0.146 **	−0.245 **	0.183 **	0.050 **	0.311 **	0.035 **	0.037 **	−0.031 **	0.056 **	0.056 **	0.037	0.603	−0.351 **	−0.241 **	−0.093	0.176 **	0.028	−0.230 **	−0.011 **	−0.080 **	0.064 **	0.015 **	0.081	1.370
Egypt	1.610 **	1.391 **	−1.268 **	−1.473 **	0.335	0.535	0.243 **	−0.062 **	−0.102 **	0.178 **	0.076 **	1.290	1.783	3.275	0.371	−2.402 **	−2.844	−0.088	−0.326	0.016 **	0.267 **	−0.343 **	0.088	1.513
Kenya	0.520 **	0.389 **	−0.672 **	0.847 **	0.861 **	0.932 **	−0.933 **	−0.046 **	0.057 **	−0.215 **	0.049	0.809	1.219 **	1.377 **	−0.222	0.874	−0.147	0.654	−0.773	−0.015 **	0.312 **	−0.260 **	0.048	0.781

Table 8. *Cont.*

	Global Betas												Regional Betas											
	β_0^w	β_1^w	ARG Crisis	US Crisis	EU Crisis	MC	TI	GDP	INF	INT	Adj. R^2	$F-Stat$	β_0^w	β_1^w	ARG Crisis	US Crisis	EU Crisis	MC	TI	GDP	INF	INT	Adj. R^2	$F-Stat$
Mauritius	0.325 **	0.289 **	−0.089 **	−0.069 **	0.021	0.092 **	−0.302 **	0.097 **	0.022 **	0.011 **	0.127	2.274 **	−0.559	0.103	−0.491 **	−0.707 **	−1.338 **	0.074	−0.541	0.102 **	0.016 **	0.051 **	0.033	0.538
South Africa	0.287	−0.174	−0.467 **	−0.136	0.331	4.112	6.641	−0.112 **	0.515 *	−0.815 **	0.102	1.764 *	1.632 **	2.483 **	0.560	−1.587 *	−1.518	3.463	1.741	−0.080 **	−1.345	−0.462 **	0.152	2.803 **
AMERICAS																								
Argentina	−0.863	−0.959	−1.266 **	0.400	−0.016	−0.325	−0.489 **	−1.766	0.233	−0.211 **	0.109	1.926 **	−0.933	−2.147 **	−3.430	−1.550	0.337	0.166	−0.223	−4.410	0.186	−0.281 **	0.071	1.193
Brazil	−0.113	0.106 **	−0.274 **	−0.642 **	−0.082	−0.210	0.185 **	−0.050 **	−0.097 **	0.029 **	0.143	2.599 **	−0.272	−0.434	−1.716	−1.168 **	0.485	−1.986	0.077	−0.099 **	−0.492 **	0.088	0.101	1.748 *
Canada	−0.397 **	−0.043 **	−0.148 **	−0.842 **	−0.012	0.324 **	0.014 **	−0.167 **	0.075 **	0.057 **	0.201	3.929 **	−0.462 *	−0.690 **	−1.734 *	−2.907	−0.291	−0.090	−0.158	−0.182 *	0.580 **	0.476 *	0.059	0.975
Chile	0.023 **	0.087 **	0.033	−0.099 **	0.081	0.170 **	0.042 **	−0.022 **	−0.073 **	−0.065 **	0.072	1.208	0.201 **	0.138 **	−0.201 **	−0.298 **	0.125 **	0.347 **	−0.075 **	−0.046 **	0.075 **	−0.032 **	0.064	1.062
Colombia	−0.036 **	0.015 **	−0.034 **	−0.149 **	−0.098 **	0.072 **	0.028 **	−0.063 **	−0.017 **	−0.091 **	0.083	1.404	−0.076 **	−0.050 **	−0.365 **	−0.411 **	−0.056 **	0.148 **	0.021 **	−0.013 **	−0.125 **	−0.011 **	0.089	1.527
Jamaica	0.358 **	0.474 **	−0.150 **	−0.052 **	0.632 **	−0.165 **	−0.059 **	0.007 **	0.064 **	−0.063 **	0.267	5.678 **	0.804 **	0.923 **	−0.463 **	−0.190 **	0.998 **	−0.507 **	−0.013	0.003 **	0.112 **	−0.091 **	0.200	3.905 **
Mexico	0.012	0.082 **	−0.247 **	−0.599 **	0.030	1.446 **	0.111 **	−0.066 **	0.051	−0.031 **	0.150	2.743 **	−0.015	0.174	−1.432 **	−2.221 **	−0.215	0.248	−0.119 **	−0.019 **	1.505	0.215 **	0.155	2.869 **
Panama	0.251 **	0.216 **	−0.338 **	−0.215 **	0.108 **	0.169 **	0.140 **	−0.037 **	−0.024 **	0.061 **	0.033	0.532	0.933 **	0.583 **	−0.881 **	−0.444 **	0.065	−0.111	0.105	−0.094 **	0.427 **	0.149 **	0.084	1.438
Peru	−0.212 **	−0.087 **	−0.087 **	−0.131 **	0.048 **	0.430 **	0.042 **	−0.284 **	−0.052 **	−0.048 **	0.140	2.531 **	−0.388 **	−0.206 **	−0.369 **	−0.377	−0.039	0.330 **	0.069 **	−0.225 **	0.011 **	−0.090 **	0.087	1.485
United States	0.482 **	0.508 **	−0.274 **	0.195	−0.019	0.710	−2.347 **	−0.110 **	0.073 **	−0.181 **	0.177	3.346 **	1.232 **	0.280 **	−1.937 *	−0.632	0.269	1.587	−3.713	−0.207 **	−0.212	−0.044	0.120	2.132 **
Venezuela	0.014	0.120 **	0.247 **	−0.143 **	−0.079	−0.112 **	0.670 **	−0.008 **	−0.204 **	0.060 **	0.102	1.767 *	0.195 **	−0.058 **	−0.316 **	−0.772 **	−0.346 **	−0.037 **	−0.203	0.002 **	0.040 *	0.104 **	0.098	1.691 *
ASIA																								
Australia	−0.193 **	−0.141 **	−0.202 **	−0.327 **	0.383 **	−0.953 **	0.523 **	−0.063 **	−0.067 **	−0.059	0.199	3.875 **	2.939 **	2.843 **	−0.455 **	−0.236 **	0.271 **	−1.026 **	0.430 **	−0.043 **	−0.110 **	0.033 **	0.210	4.154 **
Bangladesh	−0.745 **	−0.628 **	−0.499 **	−0.335 **	−0.154 *	0.116 *	−0.117	−0.258 **	−0.065 **	−0.162 **	0.070	1.165	2.707 **	2.853 **	−0.423 **	−0.216 **	−0.402 **	−0.037	0.056	−0.022	−0.047 **	−0.166 **	0.156	2.878 **
China	0.395 **	0.204	−1.015 **	−0.142	0.287	2.460	−0.423	−0.169 **	−0.083	−0.292 **	0.114	2.006 **	6.008 **	5.502 **	−1.450 **	−0.506	0.175	2.447	−0.248	−0.150 **	0.361	−0.286 **	0.109	1.902 **
Hong Kong SAR	−0.021	−0.122	−0.942 **	−1.805 **	−0.419	0.057	5.163	−0.011 **	0.018	0.081	0.088	1.513	9.573 *	9.596 *	−0.594 **	−2.000 **	−0.953 **	−1.379	2.331	0.012 **	0.249	0.207 **	0.222	4.459 **
India	−0.930 **	−0.806	−1.164 *	−1.611 *	−0.942 **	−0.821	−0.477	0.018 **	−0.295	0.264 *	0.066	1.101	6.987 **	6.595 **	−1.511 **	−1.456	−0.779	−1.082	−0.985	0.040 **	−0.552	0.331	0.122	2.165 **
Indonesia	0.123	−0.281	−1.309 **	−0.838 **	−0.496 **	1.803 *	0.311 **	−0.045 **	0.280 **	−0.532 **	0.108	1.887 **	3.142 **	2.546 **	−0.837 **	−0.965 **	−0.271	1.404 *	0.105	−0.066 **	0.182 **	−0.429 **	0.091	1.568
Israel	0.323 **	0.088	−0.572 **	−1.255 **	−0.390 **	−1.287 **	−10.663	0.180 **	0.073 **	0.267 **	0.237	4.857 **	9.546 **	9.385 **	−0.842 **	−1.352 **	−0.200 **	−1.569 **	−1.569	0.205 **	−0.032 **	0.258 **	0.249	5.165 **
Japan	1.224 **	1.116 **	−0.347 **	−0.657 **	−0.461 **	2.420 **	−4.089 *	−0.164 **	−0.031 **	−0.383 **	0.242	4.991 **	25.886 **	25.265 **	−0.242	−1.663 **	−1.232 *	2.811	−6.639	−0.087 **	−0.334 **	−0.489 **	0.300	6.688 **
Jordan	−0.674 **	−0.672 **	−0.065 **	−0.226 **	−0.484 **	−0.250 **	−0.250 **	0.036 **	−0.011 **	0.074 **	0.125	2.238 **	−0.049 **	−0.022	−0.055 **	−0.059 **	−0.300 **	−0.168 **	0.111 **	0.030 **	−0.030 **	0.049 **	0.118	2.082 **
Malaysia	−0.652 **	−0.917 **	−0.468 *	−0.650 **	−0.032	−0.566	−0.127 **	0.017 **	−0.259 **	0.375 **	0.118	2.090 **	1.179 **	1.030 **	−0.808 **	−0.524 **	−0.617 **	−1.638	−0.012 *	0.038 **	−0.083 **	0.142 **	0.058	0.9623
New Zealand	−0.053	−0.197 **	−0.121	0.496 **	1.555 **	1.426 **	2.554 *	−0.084 **	−0.253 **	−0.330 **	0.183	3.493 **	2.911 **	2.686 **	−0.128 **	0.419 **	1.370 **	0.898 **	2.181 **	−0.062 **	−0.099 **	−0.300 **	0.240	4.929 **
Oman	0.344 **	0.052 **	−0.217 **	−0.312 **	0.163	0.700	−0.291 **	−0.050 **	−0.120 **	−0.099 **	0.057	0.944	5.289 **	5.109 **	−0.325 **	−0.375 **	−0.163 **	0.301 **	−0.239 **	−0.013 **	0.153 **	−0.026 **	0.252	5.259 **
Pakistan	−0.325 **	−0.331 **	−0.369 **	−0.344 **	−0.189 **	0.621	−0.249 **	−0.058 **	0.088	−0.107 **	0.075	1.266	3.645 **	3.590 **	−0.196	−0.022	−0.500 **	0.809	−1.126 **	−0.072 **	0.222	−0.210 **	0.165	3.071 **
Philippines	0.283 *	−0.090	0.944	−1.091 **	−0.740 **	1.166 **	0.276 **	0.102	0.064 **	−0.045 **	0.120	2.133 **	2.589 **	2.253 **	−0.280 **	−0.928 **	−0.790 **	0.888 *	0.297 **	−0.765	0.082 **	−0.136 **	0.103	1.792 *
Saudi Arabia	−0.493 **	−0.504 **	0.049	−0.279 **	−0.321 **	0.099 **	−0.015 **	−0.007 **	−0.188 **	−0.349 **	0.095	1.643 *	−0.423 **	−0.360 **	−0.101 **	−0.161 **	0.094 **	0.167 **	0.034 *	−0.006 **	0.016 **	−0.450 **	0.130	2.320 **
Singapore	0.968 **	0.865 **	0.358	−1.212 **	−0.337	1.825 *	0.262 **	−0.331 **	0.056 **	0.056 *	0.291	6.415 **	10.203 **	9.830 **	−0.011	−1.364 **	−0.526 *	2.168 **	0.269 **	−0.146 **	0.058 **	−0.111 **	0.332	7.767 **
South Korea	0.772 **	0.805 **	−0.970 **	−1.591 **	−0.601 **	1.581	−0.141	−0.141 **	0.119 **	−0.036 **	0.174	3.289 **	15.759 **	15.411 **	−1.030	−1.715 **	−0.274	1.573	−0.030	−0.296 **	0.166 **	−0.036	0.243	4.997 **
Taiwan Province of China	1.795 **	1.417 **	−0.350	−1.338 **	0.131	1.422 **	−0.691 **	−0.624 **	−0.132 **	−0.258 **	0.133	2.395 **	15.636 **	15.509 **	−0.632 **	−1.515 **	0.172	0.953 **	−0.558 *	0.098	−0.092 *	−0.252 **	0.353	8.517 **

Table 8. *Cont.*

	Global Betas												Regional Betas											
	β_0^w	β_1^w	ARG Crisis	US Crisis	EU Crisis	MC	TI	GDP	INF	INT	Adj. R^2	$F-Stat$	β_0^w	β_1^w	ARG Crisis	US Crisis	EU Crisis	MC	TI	GDP	INF	INT	Adj. R^2	$F-Stat$
Thailand	−0.268 **	−0.468 **	−0.409 **	−1.036 **	−0.609 **	1.387 **	−0.603 **	−0.574 **	0.108 **	−0.228 **	0.156	2.890 **	4.871 **	4.430 **	−0.514 **	−1.088 **	−0.706 **	2.081 **	−0.538	−0.479 **	−0.125 **	−0.326 **	0.154	2.828 **
United Arab Emirates	−0.016 **	−0.068 **	−0.050 **	−0.135 **	−0.149 **	0.100 **	0.100 **	−0.002	0.013 **	−0.023 **	0.086	1.460	0.384 **	0.307 **	−0.076 **	−0.071 **	−0.117 **	0.071 **	−0.047	−0.019 **	0.034 **	−0.048 **	0.033	0.526
EUROPE																								
Austria	0.826 **	0.678 **	−0.282 **	−0.429 **	−0.351 **	−0.260	−0.109 *	0.072 **	0.078	0.279 **	0.137	2.474 **	0.871 **	1.009 **	−0.254 **	−0.524 **	−0.330 **	−1.080 **	−0.065 **	−0.039 **	−0.027 **	0.698 **	0.190	3.668 **
Belgium	0.544 **	0.086	−0.161 **	−0.747 **	−0.696 **	0.537 **	0.667 **	1.030	0.049 **	0.171 **	0.128	2.296 **	0.829 **	0.441 **	−0.277	−0.613 **	−0.692	0.760 **	0.973 **	0.363	0.093 *	0.390 **	0.111	1.953 **
Bulgaria	1.094	1.312	−0.608	−1.565 **	−1.581	4.188	1.181	−1.727	−0.054	−0.473	0.080	1.358	0.884	1.283	−0.183	−3.038	−0.647	8.143	4.287	−2.920	−0.115	−0.013	0.067	1.112
Croatia	−0.286	−0.664 **	−0.649 **	−1.253 **	−0.160	−0.160	1.710	−0.019 **	−0.153	0.115 **	0.099	1.730 *	−0.219	−0.542	−1.060 **	−1.002 **	0.412	1.470	2.857	−0.027 **	−0.379 **	0.105 **	0.127	2.278 **
Cyprus	1.162 **	0.961 **	−0.847 **	−1.417 **	−1.417 **	−1.515	−1.042	0.028 **	−0.059 **	0.314 **	0.095	1.639 *	1.098 **	1.395 **	−1.551 **	−1.832 **	−1.168 **	−0.481	0.522	0.014 **	−0.496 **	0.280 **	0.107	1.859 *
Czech Republic	0.257 **	−1.954 **	−0.276 **	−1.515 **	−1.312 **	−0.639	0.171 **	0.168 **	−0.310 **	0.257 **	0.165	3.075 **	−0.964 **	−1.110 **	−0.656 **	−1.740 **	−0.751 **	−0.415	−0.055	0.093 **	0.220	0.298 **	0.153	2.824 **
Denmark	0.251 **	−0.107	−0.079 **	−0.317 **	−0.197	0.824 **	0.342 **	−0.029 **	0.014	−0.160 **	0.174	3.291 **	0.438 **	0.149 **	−0.136 **	−0.186 **	0.492 **	1.754 **	0.686 **	−0.078 **	0.086 **	−0.217 **	0.201	3.913 **
Estonia	−0.255 **	−0.435 **	−0.233 **	−0.695 **	0.290 **	0.514 **	−0.135 **	−0.095 **	0.037 **	−0.612 **	0.182	3.461 **	−0.151 **	−0.192 **	−0.281 **	−1.105 **	0.907 **	1.058 **	−0.241 **	−0.263 **	0.046 **	−0.685 **	0.203 **	3.973 **
Finland	5.119 **	4.990 **	−0.899	−1.738 **	0.252	1.558	1.180	−0.072 **	−0.161 **	−0.285 **	0.199	3.889 **	3.700 **	4.177 **	0.735	−1.929 **	1.589 **	−1.973	4.400 **	−0.150 **	−0.344	−0.059 **	0.289	6.33 **
France	0.280	−0.316	−1.157 **	−0.676 **	−0.801 **	−0.801 **	−0.021	0.594 **	−0.013 **	0.071 **	0.082	1.401	0.523 *	0.166 *	−1.463 **	−0.745 **	0.263	−0.219	−0.285 **	0.022	−0.132 *	0.104 *	0.083	1.407
Germany	2.265 **	1.609 **	−0.787 **	−1.387 **	−1.399 **	−0.977 **	−0.014	0.078 **	0.655 **	0.219 **	0.120	2.128 **	2.589 **	2.175 **	−1.486 **	−1.491 **	−0.944 **	−0.944	−0.060	−0.048	0.704 **	0.269 **	0.095	1.656 *
Greece	−1.106 *	−1.642 **	−0.419 **	−1.310 **	−1.239 **	−0.680	−0.076	0.042 **	0.365 **	−0.058 **	0.120	2.123 **	−0.623 **	−0.855 **	−0.619 **	−1.246 **	−0.751 **	−1.112	−0.264 **	0.017 **	0.370 **	0.084 **	0.103	1.781 *
Hungary	−0.482 **	−0.535 **	−0.488 **	−1.349 **	−0.492 **	−0.555	0.630 **	0.056 **	0.195 **	0.246 **	0.097	1.679 *	−0.706 **	−0.478 **	−1.095 **	−1.550 **	0.065	0.368	1.160	0.011 **	0.109 *	0.064 **	0.084	1.430
Ireland	−1.252 **	−1.465 **	0.933 **	−0.686 **	−1.108 **	−5.164	1.187 **	0.372 **	0.127 **	0.464 **	0.171	3.228 **	−2.148 *	−2.299	1.694 **	−0.692 **	−1.559 **	−10.049	2.212 **	0.664 **	0.300 **	0.902 **	0.162	3.007 **
Italy	0.227 **	−1.575 **	−0.600 **	−0.804 **	−0.200 **	−1.545 **	0.322 **	0.024 **	−0.020	0.227 **	0.094	1.681 *	−0.611	−0.906	−0.992 **	−0.751 **	−0.068	−1.134	0.328 **	−0.037 **	−0.320 **	0.216 **	0.060	0.987
Latvia	11.103	9.623	0.910 **	−0.492	−4.142	2.331	−0.146 *	0.075 **	−1.170 *	−0.759 **	0.261	5.498 **	13.930 *	13.244 **	0.040	−0.533 **	−1.655 *	1.608	0.194 **	0.022 **	−0.758 **	−0.394 **	0.372	9.231 **
Lithuania	1.101 **	1.009 **	−0.056 **	−0.121 **	−0.043 **	−0.086 **	0.110 **	0.085 **	−0.040 **	0.122 **	0.169	3.163 **	1.155 **	1.112 **	−0.117 **	−0.244 **	−0.093 **	−0.077 **	0.185 **	0.042 **	−0.021 **	0.164 **	0.184	3.513 **
Luxembourg	1.470 **	1.139 **	−0.432 **	−0.328 **	−0.546 **	0.569 **	0.270 **	0.078 **	−0.038 **	−0.235 **	0.150	2.754 **	1.174 **	0.988 **	−0.689 **	0.068	−0.220 **	0.955 **	0.171 **	−0.113 **	−0.030 **	−0.385 **	0.241	4.956 **
Malta	0.598 **	0.575 **	−0.136 **	−0.421 **	−0.020	0.223	−0.117 **	0.069 **	0.041 **	−0.011 **	0.098	1.693 *	0.543 **	0.622 **	−0.218 **	−0.323 **	0.093 **	0.109 **	−0.083	−0.051 **	0.024 **	−0.026 **	0.086	1.459
Netherlands	1.175 **	0.705 **	−0.587 **	−0.855 **	−1.239 **	0.497	0.342	0.014 **	−0.127	0.116	0.094	1.691 *	1.444 **	1.106 **	−1.252 **	−0.892 **	−1.290 **	2.409	0.913	−0.044 **	−0.746 *	−0.065	0.072	1.209
Norway	1.373 **	1.009 **	−0.463 **	−0.286 **	−0.150	0.337 *	0.748 **	0.748 **	0.164 **	−0.169 **	0.170	3.187 **	1.476 **	1.166 **	−0.599 **	0.012	0.258 *	0.958 *	0.893 **	−0.061 **	0.225 **	−0.346 **	0.185	3.546 **
Portugal	−0.081	−0.198 *	−0.469 **	−0.955 **	−0.829 **	0.485 **	1.650 **	−0.013 **	0.065 **	−0.173 **	0.145	2.652 **	−0.086	−0.063	−0.798 **	−0.993 **	−0.569 **	1.239 **	1.702 **	−0.041 **	0.035	−0.224 **	0.083	1.412
Romania	−0.655 **	−0.931 **	−0.641 **	−0.391 **	−0.850 **	0.425	−0.700	−0.076 **	−0.076 **	−0.401 **	0.148	2.710 **	−0.531 **	−0.515 **	−1.329 **	−0.488	−0.070	1.516 **	−1.590	−0.045 **	−0.146 **	−0.489 **	0.161	2.994 **
Russia	3.384 **	2.987 **	−1.683 **	−1.362 **	−1.442 **	0.353	−1.657 **	−0.008	0.016	−0.855 **	0.134	2.422 **	3.671 **	3.505 **	−1.948 **	−1.685 **	−1.269 **	1.348 **	−2.329 **	−0.052 **	0.065 **	−0.893 **	0.215	4.272 **
Slovak Republic	0.178 **	−0.045	−0.726 **	−0.977 **	−0.314 **	−0.128 **	−0.157 **	−0.045 **	0.042 **	0.291 **	0.121	2.143 **	0.134	0.227 **	−0.825 **	−0.873 **	−0.873	0.637 **	−0.583 **	−0.030 **	0.042 **	0.116 **	0.176	3.337 **
Spain	−0.041	−0.352 **	0.185 **	−0.458 **	−0.434 **	1.611 **	−0.266 **	−0.035 **	−0.085 **	−0.040 **	0.189	3.645 **	−0.090	−0.077 *	0.443 *	−0.419 **	−0.057	3.243 **	−0.587 **	−0.088 **	−0.185 **	−0.085 **	0.207	4.070 **
Sweden	1.405 **	0.863 **	−0.560 *	−1.399 **	−1.791 **	−0.704	0.731 **	0.061 *	0.543 **	−0.043 **	0.150	2.751 **	1.873	1.731 **	−0.974 **	−1.935	−1.999 **	0.198	0.922 **	−0.055 **	0.656 **	−0.073 **	0.168	3.144
Switzerland	1.136 **	0.899 **	−0.671 **	−0.753 **	−0.252 **	−0.183 **	0.313 **	0.020 **	0.404 **	−0.335 **	0.147	2.697 **	1.333 **	1.299 **	−0.774 **	−0.774 **	−0.178 **	−0.161 **	0.177 **	0.037 **	0.804 **	−0.357 **	0.107	1.875 *

Table 8. *Cont.*

	Global Betas												Regional Betas											
	β_0^w	β_1^w	ARG Crisis	US Crisis	EU Crisis	MC	TI	GDP	INF	INT	Adj. R^2	$F-Stat$	β_0^w	β_1^w	ARG Crisis	US Crisis	EU Crisis	MC	TI	GDP	INF	INT	Adj. R^2	$F-Stat$
Turkey	−1.933 **	−2.568 **	−0.352 **	−2.145 **	−0.836	−2.654	−0.992	0.016 **	0.285	0.285	0.133	2.398 **	−1.548 **	−1.460 **	−0.514 **	−2.426 **	−0.461	−2.615	−2.855	0.075 **	−0.424 **	0.120 **	0.140	2.543 **
Ukraine	−3.925	−10.226	0.442	−16.358	−11.479 *	−4.015	−17.389 *	−0.011	2.384	−0.757	0.098	1.697 *	−0.411	−2.461	−1.584	−10.414 **	−3.307	5.363	−12.590 **	−0.087 *	0.753	−0.443	0.093	1.592
United Kingdom	0.847 **	0.384 **	0.086	−0.623 **	−0.469 **	0.045	0.126 **	−0.037 **	0.080 **	−0.020 **	0.144	2.628 **	1.098 **	0.872 **	0.028	−0.572 **	−0.152	0.178	0.302 **	−0.039 **	0.053 **	−0.013 **	0.152	2.799 **

Notes: Table 8 reports the estimated coefficients for all types of international equity interest-rate-based portfolios from the structural regime-switching factor model. Coefficients are retrieved regionally and internationally and concern the stylized facts of volatility regimes, financial crises, and structural economic variables. β_0^w and β_1^w are the estimates of the latent regime variables. The three crises concern the coefficients of the three respective dummy variables. MC, IT, GDP, INF, and INT concern the coefficients of the respective structural macroeconomic variables (i.e., changes in market capitalization, trade integration , GDP growth, inflation rate, and interest rate). Then, the adjusted R^2 (adj. R^2) and the joint significance hypothesis F test ($F-stat$) are reported. ** and * indicate statistical significance in 5% and 10%, respectively.

Table 9. Ehrmann et al. (2011) contagion test on market-capitalization-based portfolios.

	Implied Global Betas				Implied Regional Betas			
	v_0	Arg cr.	US cr.	EU cr.	v_0	Arg cr.	US cr.	EU cr.
AFRICA								
Botswana	−1.387 *	−1.390	0.517	1.524	0.054	−0.706 **	0.312 *	−0.083
Egypt	−0.011	0.253	−0.022	0.050	−0.076	0.997	0.220	0.047
Kenya	−0.010	−0.481 **	−0.003	0.404 **	−0.063 *	0.156	0.043	0.055
Mauritius	−0.205	−0.465	−0.099	0.687	0.009	0.099	0.018	0.012
South Africa	0.120 *	0.172	−0.463 **	−0.351 *	−0.019	0.372 **	−0.055	0.023
AMERICAS								
Argentina	0.541 *	−0.508	−0.533	−2.091 *	0.042	0.175	0.074	−0.623
Brazil	−0.089	−0.019	0.066	−0.015	0.178	0.025	−0.048	−0.307
Canada	1.592 *	−1.330	−0.912	−1.311	−0.092	0.260	0.153	0.029
Chile	3.287 **	−3.507	−3.482	−3.980	−0.014	0.121 **	0.038	−0.054 *
Colombia	0.244 **	−0.069	−0.087	0.097	−0.043 **	0.098 *	0.067 *	0.020
Jamaica	2.928 **	−5.013	−3.803 *	−2.384	−0.009	0.030	0.020	0.282 **
Mexico	0.539 **	−0.754	−0.839 *	−0.234	0.178	0.068	−0.098	−0.334
Panama	0.110 *	−0.010	0.002	0.356 *	0.085	−0.095	−0.085	−0.193
Peru	−0.040	−0.262 *	−0.056	−0.111	−0.001	0.071	0.035	−0.026
United States	0.009	−0.002	0.032	0.125	0.020	0.044	0.055	−0.002
Venezuela	0.709 **	−1.208	−0.933	−0.449	0.005	0.061	0.070	−0.012
ASIA								
Australia	1.109 **	−1.045	−1.507 **	−1.066	0.004	0.035	0.004	−0.007
Bangladesh	0.210 *	−0.944 *	0.024	0.131	−0.027 *	0.027	0.024	0.025
China	0.046	−0.183	−0.749 *	0.562	0.035	0.038	−0.020	0.011
Hong Kong SAR	−0.221 **	0.475 **	0.323 **	0.280	0.094	0.075	−0.079	−0.032
India	−2.228 **	2.442	1.658	5.270 *	−0.021	0.181	0.054	0.003
Indonesia	−0.414 *	0.238	0.174	0.746	−0.054 *	0.176 *	0.063	0.092
Israel	0.182	−0.471	−0.239	0.229	−0.054	0.222 *	0.075	0.072
Japan	0.169	−0.619 *	0.003	−0.245	−0.099	0.123	0.109	0.053
Jordan	−0.662	0.650	0.555	0.884	0.002	0.035 **	0.004	0.019
Malaysia	−0.816 *	1.001	0.677	1.381	0.011	0.144 *	0.003	0.036
New Zealand	0.004	0.262	−0.039	0.052	−0.050 *	0.160	0.064	0.058
Oman	−0.324 *	0.079	−0.159	0.806	−0.047 **	0.048	0.052	0.053
Pakistan	0.441 **	−0.583	−0.542	−0.683	−0.013	0.098 *	0.010	0.049
Philippines	0.280	0.069	−0.353	−0.341	0.004	0.476 **	0.004	−0.014
Saudi Arabia	0.665 **	−0.846	−1.318 **	0.869 *	0.001	0.045	0.004	0.028
Singapore	−0.192 **	0.228	−0.022	0.623 **	0.044	0.008	−0.030	0.012
South Korea	0.743 **	−0.929 *	−0.632 *	−1.083 **	−1.083 *	0.039	−0.141	−0.237
Taiwan Province of China	−0.225 *	−0.027	0.248	−0.975 **	0.002	0.200	−0.001	−0.094
Thailand	−0.094	0.154	−0.305	−0.872	0.052	0.039	−0.049	−0.041
United Arab Emirates	0.719 **	−0.810	−1.700 **	−0.173	2.21×10^{-4}	0.020	1.29×10^{-4}	−0.001
EUROPE								
Austria	0.741 **	−0.802	−0.849 *	−0.717	−0.057 **	0.065	0.061	0.067
Belgium	0.114 **	−0.119	−0.316 **	0.124	−0.111	0.113	0.136	0.097
Bulgaria	−0.087	0.183	−0.448	1.949 **	−1.174 **	1.169	1.156	1.085
Croatia	0.394	−1.477 **	−0.480	−0.480	0.213 **	0.166	0.198	0.157
Cyprus	−0.481 **	−0.152	0.238	−0.339	−0.104 *	0.103	0.159	0.051
Czech Republic	−0.120 *	−0.806 **	−0.027	−0.066	−0.194 **	0.205	0.224	0.130
Denmark	0.410 *	−0.318	−0.356	−0.506	−0.084 *	0.106	0.097	0.017
Estonia	0.122	−0.671 *	0.083	0.380	−0.150 **	0.159	0.176 *	0.151
Finland	−0.285 **	−0.303	0.316	−0.384	−0.498 **	0.499	0.638 **	0.393
France	−0.171 **	0.201	0.090	0.054	−0.159	0.166	0.209	0.099
Germany	−0.085 *	0.198	−0.007	0.088	−0.125	0.131	0.155	0.082
Greece	−0.063	0.208	−0.611 **	0.152	−0.129 **	0.153	0.157	0.004
Hungary	0.127	−0.157	−0.190	−0.247	−0.198 **	0.208	0.231	0.179
Ireland	0.103 *	−0.339 *	0.145	−0.046	−0.187	0.199	0.221	0.191
Italy	0.123 **	−0.137	−0.295 **	0.075	−0.111	0.113	0.136	0.097
Latvia	0.951 **	−2.051 **	−1.143 *	−0.500	−0.314 **	0.323	0.340	0.299
Lithuania	0.250 **	−0.046	−0.948 **	−0.276	−0.031 *	0.037	0.035	0.034
Luxembourg	−0.157 *	0.009	0.001	0.328	−0.088 **	0.095	0.098 *	0.089
Malta	1.015 **	−1.187	−2.382 **	−0.886	−0.044	0.049	0.050	0.022
Netherlands	−0.225 **	−0.498 *	0.211	0.365	−0.168	0.184	0.223	0.142
Norway	0.149 **	−0.088	−0.175	0.473 **	−0.191 **	0.208	0.220 *	0.143

Table 9. *Cont.*

	Implied Global Betas				Implied Regional Betas			
	v_0	Arg cr.	US cr.	EU cr.	v_0	Arg cr.	US cr.	EU cr.
Portugal	−0.071	−0.014	−0.161	−0.276 *	−0.242 **	0.251	0.270 *	0.222
Romania	0.503 **	0.503 *	−0.497	−0.717	−0.149 *	0.162	0.178	0.136
Russia	−0.033	−0.111	0.437 **	0.168	−0.275 **	0.299	0.337 *	0.276
Slovak Republic	0.145 **	−0.769 **	−0.098	0.350	−0.030	0.028	0.038	0.008
Spain	−0.083	−0.093	−0.533 **	0.352	−0.162 **	0.171	0.185	0.157
Sweden	−0.178 **	0.294	0.071	0.416 *	−0.462 **	0.502	0.506	0.440
Switzerland	−0.249 **	0.082	0.227	0.134	−0.201 **	0.214	0.226	0.156
Turkey	0.114 **	0.160	−0.056	−0.239	−0.181 *	0.201	0.227	−0.015
Ukraine	0.085	−0.362	−0.487	0.114	−0.296	0.299	0.340	0.274
United Kingdom	0.015	−0.275 *	−0.096	−0.079	−0.221 **	0.240	0.230 *	0.133

Notes: Table 9 presents the results of the Ehrmann et al. (2011) contagion test depending on market-capitalization-based portfolios. The v_0 and v_j coefficients (j concerns the crises) are reported with an indication of statistical significance as well. ** and * indicate statistical significance in 5% and 10%, respectively. Results came from either internationally or regionally constructed portfolios. Portfolios are market capitalization weighted portfolios; specifically, the weighting scheme is based upon changes in stock market capitalization.

Table 10. Ehrmann et al. (2011) contagion test on trade-integration-based portfolios.

	Implied Global Betas				Implied Regional Betas			
	v_0	Arg cr.	US cr.	EU cr.	v_0	Arg cr.	US cr.	EU cr.
AFRICA								
Botswana	−0.007 *	0.073 **	−0.013	0.016	0.281	7.368 **	−3.039 **	0.003
Egypt	−0.054	0.213 **	0.049	0.059	−1.239	4.652	1.845	−0.100
Kenya	−0.041 **	0.056 *	0.007	0.043	−0.504	1.096	−2.088	0.384
Mauritius	0.052	−0.044	−0.083	−0.045	0.684 *	0.166	−0.920	−0.378
South Africa	0.003	0.084	−0.020	0.003	2.705 *	2.687	−2.601	−3.716
AMERICAS								
Argentina	−0.459 *	0.653	0.486	0.221	3.136 *	−2.236	0.434	−2.743 **
Brazil	0.127	0.137	−0.077	−0.267	1.406	−0.655	0.447	−6.297 *
Canada	−0.662 **	1.043	0.693	0.591	0.238	1.164	0.395	−3.785 *
Chile	−0.077 **	0.213 **	0.084 *	0.005	0.252	0.833	0.597 *	−2.907 **
Colombia	−0.089 **	0.169 *	0.102 *	0.043	−0.186	0.571	0.890 *	−1.743 **
Jamaica	−0.056 **	0.087	0.061	0.104	−0.034	−0.012	0.383	−5.654 **
Mexico	0.119	0.149	−0.080	−0.221	2.447 **	−0.895	−0.382	−9.325 **
Panama	0.007	0.005	−0.011	−0.126	0.780 *	−1.782	−0.728	−3.093 *
Peru	−0.057 **	0.166 **	0.084 *	−0.020	0.449 *	0.103	0.126	−1.410 *
United States	−0.326 *	0.412	0.362	0.238	0.250	−0.356	1.465	−1.177
Venezuela	−0.081 *	0.175	0.104	0.067	0.542	0.737	4.110 **	−3.565 *
ASIA								
Australia	0.071	−0.315	−0.145	−0.544	0.031	2.160 **	−0.044	0.447
Bangladesh	0.357	−0.649	−0.237	−0.906	−0.456 **	0.669 *	0.423 *	1.174 **
China	−0.036	−0.076	0.059	0.441	−0.155	1.039 *	0.167	0.983
Hong Kong SAR	−0.106	−0.373	0.215	0.152	−0.112	3.633 **	0.082	0.952
India	1.136 *	−1.495	−0.455	−2.212	−0.901 **	3.110 **	0.872	1.897 *
Indonesia	0.101	−0.427	−0.115	0.160	−0.137	4.898 **	0.122	0.594
Israel	0.629	−1.060	−0.921	−1.569	−0.558 *	6.389 **	0.646	0.774
Japan	1.446	−2.327	−1.167	−1.995	−0.591 *	2.741 **	0.558	0.467
Jordan	−0.021	0.021	0.282 *	0.203	0.063 *	0.249 **	−0.085	0.180 *
Malaysia	0.488	−0.504	0.312	−0.480	−0.002	1.653 **	−0.069	1.246 *
New Zealand	−0.465	0.192	0.338	0.708	−0.330 *	4.207 **	0.359	0.281
Oman	−0.490 *	0.273	0.480	0.559	−0.363 **	1.792 **	0.340	1.066 **
Pakistan	−0.051	−0.811	−0.287	3.08×10^{-4}	−0.062	4.412 **	0.134	1.327
Philippines	0.550	−0.983	−0.588	−1.005	−0.456	3.896 **	0.537	0.232
Saudi Arabia	0.225 *	−0.267	−0.320	−0.305	−0.075	1.050 **	0.090	0.101

Table 10. *Cont.*

	v_0	Implied Global Betas Arg cr.	US cr.	EU cr.	v_0	Implied Regional Betas Arg cr.	US cr.	EU cr.
Singapore	0.156	−0.428	−0.208	0.192	−0.202	0.900	0.220	1.309 *
South Korea	−0.059	−1.730	0.757	−1.182	0.623	1.423	−0.738	−1.023
Taiwan Province of China	−0.577	0.132	0.873	−0.122	0.731 *	0.731 **	−0.729	−2.194 **
Thailand	0.017	−0.308	−0.183	−0.084	0.091	−0.589	−0.046	0.294
United Arab Emirates	−0.161 **	0.102	0.147	0.199	−0.006	0.592 **	0.009	0.026
EUROPE								
Austria	−0.282 *	0.333	0.299	0.365	−1.297 *	1.408	1.134	1.596
Belgium	−1.125 *	1.151	1.228	1.077	1.667	−1.556	−1.210	−1.461
Bulgaria	−8.876 **	8.906	8.819	9.369	−7.178 **	7.310	7.820	8.565
Croatia	−1.106 **	1.130	1.245	1.273	−4.463 **	4.638	4.674	4.719
Cyprus	−1.092 **	1.075	1.312	0.764	1.494	−1.462	0.617	−1.311
Czech Republic	−1.121 **	1.218	1.262 *	0.821	−3.182	3.674	4.394	4.044
Denmark	−0.155	0.330	0.211	−0.026	−3.380 **	3.833	3.842	2.883
Estonia	−0.913 **	0.976	1.038 *	0.963	−2.450 **	2.735	2.823	2.822
Finland	−3.312 **	3.387	3.954 *	3.162	−9.881 **	10.430	12.602	8.594
France	−1.560 *	1.655	1.781	1.325	1.179	−1.002	−0.236	−0.370
Germany	−1.695 *	1.745	1.824	1.535	5.040 *	−4.811	−4.550	−5.195
Greece	−0.753 **	0.948	0.875	0.262	−5.067 **	5.489	5.715	4.572
Hungary	−1.566 **	1.664	1.707	1.412	−0.124	0.566	0.536	0.629
Ireland	−1.629 *	1.745	1.788	1.655	0.165	0.061	0.379	0.581
Italy	−1.125 *	1.151	1.228	1.077	1.667	−1.556	−1.210	−1.461
Latvia	−1.461 **	1.196	1.253	1.161	−1.119 *	1.137	1.198	1.132
Lithuania	−0.076	0.118	0.079	0.064	−1.858 **	2.146	1.897	2.264
Luxembourg	−0.515 **	0.577 *	0.568 *	0.550	−1.473 *	1.791	0.960	1.562
Malta	−0.264 **	0.287	0.291 *	0.220	−0.943	1.448	1.196	0.909
Netherlands	−1.722 *	1.853	1.959	1.580	2.111	−1.790	−1.183	−1.421
Norway	−1.015 **	1.165	1.147 *	0.785	−3.867 **	4.310	4.500 *	3.959
Portugal	−1.741 **	1.826	1.848 *	1.758	−3.449 **	3.509	4.442	3.615
Romania	−0.739 *	0.861	0.830	0.689	−5.267 **	6.071	5.613	5.094
Russia	−1.331 **	1.507	1.586 *	1.404	−7.758 **	8.919	10.817	8.351
Slovak Republic	8.351	0.044	0.094	−0.079	0.067	−0.041	−0.282	−0.487
Spain	−0.665 *	0.724	0.775	0.641	−3.855 **	3.999	4.718 *	3.984
Sweden	−1.794 **	2.106	1.986	1.758	−12.048 **	13.583	13.679 *	11.744
Switzerland	−1.466 **	1.561	1.580	1.362	−2.058	2.220	2.664	2.262
Turkey	−0.690 *	0.869	0.845	−0.462	−4.884	5.399	5.391	9.146
Ukraine	−1.832	1.815	1.941	1.728	−3.595	4.368	0.232	3.221
United Kingdom	−0.957 **	1.106	0.986	0.647	−4.388 **	4.757	4.745 *	3.507

Notes: Table 10 presents the results of the Ehrmann et al. (2011) contagion test depending on trade-integration-based portfolios. The v_0 and v_j coefficients (j concerns the crises) are reported with an indication of statistical significance as well. ** and * indicate statistical significance in 5% and 10%, respectively. Results came from either internationally or regionally constructed portfolios. Portfolios are trade integration weighted portfolios; specifically, the weighting scheme is based upon changes in trade integration.

Table 11. Ehrmann et al. (2011) contagion test on GDP-based portfolios.

	v_0	Implied Global Betas Arg cr.	US cr.	EU cr.	v_0	Implied Regional Betas Arg cr.	US cr.	EU cr.
AFRICA								
Botswana	0.074 **	0.188 *	0.087	−0.092	0.115 **	0.324 *	−0.009	−0.138
Egypt	−0.123 **	0.421 **	0.153	0.171	0.124	2.009 *	0.243	−0.487
Kenya	−0.072 **	0.075	−0.152 **	0.255 **	0.255 *	0.213	0.134	−0.041
Mauritius	−0.016	0.004	−0.056 *	0.003	0.030	0.063	0.086	−0.023
South Africa	0.045	0.302 **	−0.030	−0.256 *	0.286	0.939	−0.004	−0.509
AMERICAS								
Argentina	0.099	−0.012	−0.069	−1.658 **	−2.148 **	2.363	2.337	1.853
Brazil	−0.072	−0.069	−0.034	−0.010	−0.556	1.048	0.938	0.201
Canada	1.652 *	−1.403	−1.203	−1.489	−1.228 **	1.553	1.493	1.069

Table 11. *Cont.*

	Implied Global Betas				Implied Regional Betas			
	v_0	Arg cr.	US cr.	EU cr.	v_0	Arg cr.	US cr.	EU cr.
Chile	0.673 **	−0.564	−0.529	−0.771	−0.412 **	0.466	0.403	0.230
Colombia	0.188 **	0.057	0.058 *	0.088 *	−0.268 *	−0.268	0.318	0.170
Jamaica	0.084 **	−0.100	−0.128 **	0.359 **	−0.364 **	0.352	0.375	0.563
Mexico	−0.056	0.519 **	0.308 *	0.044	0.092	0.088	0.090	−0.228
Panama	−0.029	−0.017	−0.037	−0.065	−0.150	0.091	0.116	−0.224
Peru	0.023	0.117	0.171 **	−0.076	−0.416 **	0.467	0.497	0.180
United States	0.534	−4.258 **	−2.681 **	0.624	−2.222 *	2.360	2.435	1.983
Venezuela	−0.027	0.134	0.179 *	0.033	−0.424 **	0.379	0.553	0.399
ASIA								
Australia	0.515 **	−0.376	−0.645 *	−0.515	−0.077	0.035	0.072	−0.107
Bangladesh	−0.076 **	−0.039	0.454 **	0.247 **	−0.025	−0.028	0.015	−0.214
China	−0.100	0.060	−0.435	0.662	−0.294 *	0.324	0.318	0.362
Hong Kong SAR	−0.214 **	0.488 **	0.360 **	0.200	−0.157	0.058	0.193	0.728
India	−1.145 **	1.428	0.924	2.444 *	−0.246	0.254	0.421	−0.259
Indonesia	−0.133 *	0.222	0.217	0.323	−0.224 *	0.130	0.224	0.289
Israel	−0.054	−0.263 *	0.049	0.333 *	−0.178	0.127	0.148	−0.106
Japan	0.311	−1.424 *	1.394 *	0.078	−0.414	0.212	0.457	0.100
Jordan	0.128 **	−0.127 **	−0.099 **	−0.017	−0.036 **	0.048	0.094 **	0.084 *
Malaysia	−0.117 *	0.474 **	0.025	0.555 **	0.031	0.012	0.140	−0.076
New Zealand	0.026	0.213 *	−0.076	−0.032	−0.318 **	0.253	0.317 *	0.325
Oman	−0.110 **	−0.067	−0.054	0.368 **	−0.164 **	0.110	0.188	0.179
Pakistan	0.028	−0.036	−0.034	−0.308 *	−0.162 *	0.014	0.064	0.140
Philippines	−0.071	0.464 **	0.070	−0.181	−0.044	−0.119	0.056	−0.144
Saudi Arabia	0.169 **	−0.203	−0.280 **	0.390 **	−0.012	0.012	0.001	0.005
Singapore	−0.108 **	0.118	0.056	0.012	−0.284	0.274	0.290	0.346
South Korea	0.326 **	0.326 *	−0.157	−0.658 **	−0.324	−0.025	0.478	−0.080
Taiwan Province of China	−0.208 *	−0.029	0.552 *	−0.998 **	−0.353 *	0.315	0.363	0.084
Thailand	0.042	0.092	−0.124	−0.776 **	−0.268 *	0.238	0.218	0.209
United Arab Emirates	0.244 **	−0.149	−0.293 *	−0.079	−0.044 **	0.035	0.041	0.044
EUROPE								
Austria	0.200 **	−0.237 *	−0.200 *	−0.294 *	−0.090	0.102	0.126	0.094
Belgium	0.027	0.004	−0.070	0.092	−0.238	0.241	0.318	0.246
Bulgaria	−0.190	0.373	−0.148	2.033 **	−1.542 *	1.479	1.625	0.603
Croatia	0.118 **	−0.382 **	−0.216 *	−0.151	−0.276 *	0.284	0.362	0.221
Cyprus	−0.150 **	−0.368 *	0.116	−0.708 **	0.083	−0.086	−0.024	0.024
Czech Republic	−0.114 **	0.019	0.085	−0.119	−0.291 *	0.323	0.371	0.142
Denmark	0.060	0.223	0.034	−0.039	−0.074	0.105	0.100	−0.060
Estonia	−0.119 **	0.133	0.457 **	0.196 *	−0.346 **	0.363	0.393 *	0.329
Finland	−0.327 **	−0.185	0.398 *	−0.241	−0.464	0.483	0.720	0.114
France	−0.302 *	0.236	0.143	0.208	−0.093	−0.093	0.234	0.018
Germany	−0.032	0.032	−0.272 *	0.109	−0.124	0.141	0.242	0.173
Greece	−0.078	0.239	−0.131	−0.119	−0.188 *	0.186	0.259	−0.009
Hungary	−0.107 **	0.118	0.139	0.111	−0.699 **	0.713	0.777 *	0.636
Ireland	−0.031	0.211 *	0.306 **	0.015	−0.101	0.106	0.225	0.086
Italy	0.277 **	−0.317	−0.580 **	0.035	−0.238	0.241	0.318	0.246
Latvia	0.151 *	−0.061	−0.056	−0.058	−0.177	0.191	0.251	0.096
Lithuania	−0.078 **	0.265 **	0.053	0.014	0.064	−0.048	−0.080	−0.087
Luxembourg	−0.097 **	0.161 *	0.221 **	−0.028	−0.028	0.079	0.102	0.072
Malta	−0.043	−0.079	0.035	0.097	−0.100	0.114	0.127	0.103
Netherlands	−0.170 **	−0.254	0.184	0.264 *	−0.136	0.160	0.331	0.184
Norway	−0.025	0.138	0.137 *	0.153	−0.363 **	0.386	0.396	0.287
Portugal	−0.126 **	0.278 **	−0.032	−0.119	−0.539 **	0.567	0.615 *	0.453
Romania	0.220 **	−0.633 **	−0.040	−0.275 *	−0.161	0.154	0.266	0.158
Russia	−0.059	0.101	0.458 **	0.187	−0.509 **	0.565	0.653 *	0.444
Slovak Republic	0.043	−0.141	0.170	0.178 *	0.146	−0.156	−0.120	−0.150
Spain	−0.073	−0.036	−0.322 **	0.320 *	0.007	0.005	0.080	−0.045
Sweden	−0.197 **	0.319	0.235	0.403 *	−0.467	0.538	0.593	0.383
Switzerland	−0.154 **	0.113	0.200 *	0.010	−0.405 **	0.422	0.459	0.263
Turkey	0.103 *	0.192	−0.022	−0.229	−0.166	0.170	0.581	−0.490

Table 11. *Cont.*

	Implied Global Betas				Implied Regional Betas			
	v_0	Arg cr.	US cr.	EU cr.	v_0	Arg cr.	US cr.	EU cr.
Ukraine	−0.010	0.172	−0.148	0.140	−1.761	1.760	1.971	1.766
United Kingdom	0.216 *	−1.145 **	−0.508 *	−0.215	−0.254	0.290	0.326	0.075

Notes: Table 11 presents the results of the Ehrmann et al. (2011) contagion test depending on GDP-based portfolios. The v_0 and v_j coefficients (j concerns the crises) are reported with an indication of statistical significance as well. ** and * indicate statistical significance in 5% and 10%, respectively. Results came from either internationally or regionally constructed portfolios. Portfolios are GDP weighted portfolios; specifically, the weighting scheme is based upon changes in GDP growth rate.

Table 12. Ehrmann et al. (2011) contagion test on inflation-rate-based portfolios.

	Implied Global Betas				Implied Regional Betas			
	v_0	Arg cr.	US cr.	EU cr.	v_0	Arg cr.	US cr.	EU cr.
AFRICA								
Botswana	−0.013 *	0.011	0.024	0.027	0.680	0.778 **	−0.259	−0.726
Egypt	−0.012	0.024	0.052	−0.323 **	0.259	1.515 *	3.180	−2.082
Kenya	0.008	−0.008	0.027 *	−0.158 **	−0.563	1.775 *	1.889 *	−0.038
Mauritius	5.14 × 10−4	−3.81 × 10−4	0.012	0.012	0.154	1.034	0.873 *	−0.004
South Africa	−0.022	0.018	0.039	−0.140 *	0.237	0.778 *	−0.696	−0.336
AMERICAS								
Argentina	0.044 *	−0.056	−0.027	−0.113	−0.293	0.668	0.358	0.179
Brazil	0.010	−0.048	−0.005	−0.010	0.909	0.460	−0.061	−0.225
Canada	0.008	−0.070 *	0.004	0.003	−0.665 **	1.336	0.715	0.628
Chile	0.006 *	−0.019	−0.001	−0.006	−0.713 **	0.309 **	0.874 *	0.020
Colombia	0.009 *	−0.009	−0.003	−0.009	−0.758 **	0.222 **	0.971 *	0.365
Jamaica	0.008 *	−0.007	−0.008	−0.042 **	−0.570 **	1.108	0.720	0.316
Mexico	0.036 **	−0.086 *	−0.013	−0.048	0.494	0.454	0.268	−1.221
Panama	0.004	−0.016	−0.004	0.008	0.585	−0.322	−0.573	−0.735
Peru	0.001	−0.001	0.004	−0.001	−0.436 *	0.219	0.874	−0.903
United States	0.032 *	−0.045	−0.021	−0.032	−2.261	4.124	2.883	1.557
Venezuela	0.006	−0.006	0.011	−0.006	−0.407	0.239 *	0.811	0.350
ASIA								
Australia	−0.365 **	0.570 *	0.399 *	1.031 **	1.463 **	−1.686	−1.633	−2.222
Bangladesh	−0.287 **	0.269	0.373	0.808 **	1.419 **	−1.642	−1.248	−2.374
China	−0.676	−1.036	1.455	0.418	3.204 **	−3.389	−3.255	−2.808
Hong Kong SAR	−0.676 **	0.842	0.805 *	1.289 **	1.190	−1.726	−1.128	−1.333
India	−0.473	1.994	0.695	0.746	6.173 **	−6.636	−5.327 *	−7.874 *
Indonesia	−0.232	−0.131	0.330	0.340	2.757 *	−3.176	−2.943	−2.333
Israel	−0.416 **	0.367	0.484	1.067 **	4.212 **	−4.737	−4.763	−5.685
Japan	−0.453 *	0.678	0.686	0.699	1.142 **	−1.209	−1.130	−1.174
Jordan	−1.104 **	0.967	1.762 *	1.843 *	0.874	−1.287	2.449	0.903
Malaysia	−0.453 **	0.496	0.686 *	1.458 **	2.028 *	−2.198	−0.959	−2.257
New Zealand	0.1315	−0.515	−0.842	−0.169	1.171 *	−1.507	−1.424	−0.709
Oman	−0.204 **	0.220	2.333	−0.223	2.034	−3.672	−2.231	−2.691
Pakistan	−0.797	0.484	1.229	2.735	1.621 **	−2.381	−2.223 *	−1.979
Philippines	−0.311 **	1.025 **	0.493	0.356	3.326 **	−3.761	−2.991	−3.495
Saudi Arabia	−0.219 **	0.284	0.239 *	0.212	0.802 **	−0.887	−1.009 *	−1.042
Singapore	−1.398	0.848	0.217	0.566	3.975 **	−4.248	−4.181	−3.792
South Korea	−0.297	1.043	0.488	0.240	2.874 *	−4.455	−1.987	−4.233
Taiwan Province of China	−0.646 **	0.918 *	0.853 *	0.502	1.664	−2.220	−1.233	−1.786
Thailand	−0.261	−0.776	1.011	0.896	2.174 *	−2.474	−2.549	−2.391
United Arab Emirates	−0.669 **	0.919	0.744	0.726	0.265	−0.928	−0.623	0.358
EUROPE								
Austria	−0.062	0.060	0.056	0.177	−0.292	0.417	0.356	0.292
Belgium	0.239 *	−0.214	−0.210	−0.135	−1.342 *	1.430	1.608	1.192
Bulgaria	−1.304 **	1.391	1.384	2.169 *	−0.938 **	0.948	0.945	0.588
Croatia	−0.402 *	0.415	0.425	0.818	−2.119 **	2.194	2.333	1.935
Cyprus	0.098	−0.048	−0.046	0.086	−1.007 *	1.095	1.134	0.500
Czech Republic	−0.278	0.328	0.342	0.393	−2.387 **	2.650	2.595 *	1.602
Denmark	−0.180	0.205	0.197	0.249	−0.438	0.863	0.467	−0.242
Estonia	−0.164	0.166	0.187	0.337	−1.631 **	1.756	1.850 *	1.538
Finland	−0.728 *	0.828	0.947	1.190	−4.677 **	4.940	5.912 *	3.315
France	0.106	−0.044	−0.054	0.102	−1.379	1.604	1.909	0.802

Table 12. *Cont.*

	Implied Global Betas				Implied Regional Betas			
	v_0	Arg cr.	US cr.	EU cr.	v_0	Arg cr.	US cr.	EU cr.
Germany	0.587 *	−0.550	−0.570	−0.449	−1.664 *	1.777	2.051	1.330
Greece	−0.454 *	0.541	0.569	0.581	−1.266 *	1.778	1.572	−0.130
Hungary	−0.156	0.231	0.234	0.249	−2.694 **	2.931	3.028 *	2.197
Ireland	−0.092	0.129	0.161	0.253	−0.978	1.228	1.382	0.897
Italy	0.239 *	−0.214	−0.210	−0.135	−1.342 *	1.430	1.608	1.192
Latvia	−0.471	0.483	0.494	0.528	−1.805 **	1.955	1.961	1.621
Lithuania	−0.165 *	0.165	0.194	0.223	−0.089	0.202	0.020	−0.003
Luxembourg	−0.058	0.083	0.029	0.185	−1.195 **	1.370	1.247 *	1.183
Malta	−0.078	0.103	0.083	0.297	−1.147 **	1.260	1.216 *	0.893
Netherlands	0.134	−0.097	−0.059	−0.008	−1.389	1.676	2.029	1.135
Norway	−0.273 *	0.298	0.371	0.342	−2.030 **	2.393	2.348 *	1.511
Portugal	−0.444 **	0.481	0.542	0.605	−3.422 **	3.609 *	3.595 **	2.983
Romania	−0.329 *	0.416	0.404	0.559	−0.972	1.260	1.094	0.557
Russia	−0.723 *	0.773	0.983	0.977	−2.670 **	3.145 *	3.057 *	2.739
Slovak Republic	0.067	−0.042	−0.085	0.210	0.128	−0.091	−0.105	−0.486
Spain	−0.283 *	0.296	0.324	0.341	−0.396	0.533	0.540	0.211
Sweden	−1.222 **	1.310	1.257	1.430	−2.988 *	3.639	3.144	2.597
Switzerland	−0.400 *	0.412	0.446	0.642	−3.203 **	3.441	3.486 *	2.638
Turkey	−0.206	0.256	0.281	1.290	−2.109 *	2.559	2.819	−2.057
Ukraine	0.362	−0.337	0.042	−0.247	−1.318 *	1.316	1.352	1.291
United Kingdom	−0.345 *	0.370	0.461	0.518	−1.217 *	1.542	1.425	0.305

Notes: Table 12 presents the results of the Ehrmann et al. (2011) contagion test depending on inflation-rate-based portfolios. The v_0 and v_j coefficients (j concerns the crises) are reported with an indication of statistical significance as well. ** and * indicate statistical significance in 5% and 10%, respectively. Results came from either internationally or regionally constructed portfolios. Portfolios are inflation rate weighted portfolios; specifically, the weighting scheme is based upon changes in inflation rates.

Table 13. Ehrmann et al. (2011) contagion test on Interest Rate-based portfolios.

	Implied Global Betas				Implied Regional Betas			
	v_0	Arg cr.	US cr.	EU cr.	v_0	Arg cr.	US cr.	EU cr.
AFRICA								
Botswana	−0.040 **	0.115 **	0.034	0.098 **	−0.198*	2.085 **	−0.373	0.429
Egypt	−0.132 **	0.094	0.178 *	−0.260 *	−1.574	0.616	1.406	1.678
Kenya	−0.028 *	0.025	0.103 **	−0.110 **	−1.185 **	1.535	0.204	1.208
Mauritius	−0.005	0.018	0.022	0.017	1.482	−1.207	−2.353	−1.297
South Africa	−0.188 **	0.200	0.239 *	0.095	0.106	2.382	−0.568	0.148
AMERICAS								
Argentina	0.215 *	−0.190	−0.047	−0.561 *	−0.481 *	0.686	0.509	0.232
Brazil	−0.021	−0.079	0.107	−0.025	1.328	1.434	−0.820	−2.793
Canada	−0.013	−0.037	0.071	0.001	−0.694 *	1.093	0.727	0.620
Chile	0.014	0.036	0.038 *	−0.060 *	−0.807 **	2.244 **	0.888 *	0.068
Colombia	0.001	0.024	0.051 *	−0.013	−0.935 **	1.785 *	1.068 *	0.462
Jamaica	0.008	0.005	−0.002	−0.100 **	−0.586 **	0.923	0.638	1.082
Mexico	0.041	−0.016	0.045	−0.134	1.240	1.572	−0.825	−2.313
Panama	0.030	−0.030	−0.018	−0.064	0.072	0.053	−0.119	−1.319
Peru	−0.005	0.043	0.063	−0.006	−0.595 **	1.720 **	0.872 *	−0.224
United States	0.111 *	−0.086	0.033	−0.146	−3.402 *	4.328	3.800	2.502
Venezuela	1.24×10^{-5}	0.113	0.150 **	−0.012	−0.854 *	1.829	1.102	0.704
ASIA								
Australia	−0.551 **	1.226 **	0.568 *	1.035 **	0.179	−0.779	−0.357	−1.355
Bangladesh	−0.583 **	0.583	0.629 *	0.941 *	0.892	−1.617	−0.604	−2.265
China	−0.790 **	1.265 *	0.773	1.055	−0.089	−0.211	0.141	1.082
Hong Kong SAR	1.082 **	1.813	1.574	1.481	−0.261	−0.939	0.532	0.365
India	−1.210 **	1.260	1.378 *	1.280	0.285	−0.373	−1.137	−0.552
Indonesia	−1.644 **	1.781	1.851 *	1.701	0.247	−1.059	−0.282	0.388
Israel	−1.018 **	1.518	1.023	1.502	1.575	−0.263	−0.233	−0.391
Japan	−1.028 **	1.466 *	1.080 *	1.097	0.362	−0.580	−0.293	−0.498

Table 13. *Cont.*

	Implied Global Betas				Implied Regional Betas			
	v_0	Arg cr.	US cr.	EU cr.	v_0	Arg cr.	US cr.	EU cr.
Jordan	−0.189 **	0.076	0.195	0.235 *	−0.049	0.053	0.713 *	0.511
Malaysia	−0.693 *	1.006	0.699	1.409 *	1.219	−1.257	0.777	−1.196
New Zealand	−0.515 *	1.240	0.838	0.492	−1.161 *	0.461	0.844	1.761
Oman	−0.793 **	0.793	0.804 *	0.412	−1.227 *	0.702	1.204	1.400
Pakistan	−0.242 *	0.454	0.311	0.242	−0.123	−2.027	−0.719	0.007
Philippines	−0.467 *	0.413 **	0.675	0.478	1.372	−2.460	−1.464	−2.491
Saudi Arabia	−0.383 **	0.758 **	0.360 *	0.383	0.572 *	−0.684	−0.808	−0.779
Singapore	−0.806 **	1.668 *	0.829	1.094	0.397	−1.059	−0.536	0.457
South Korea	−0.647 *	2.247 *	0.802	0.554	−0.141	−4.322	1.901	−2.987
Taiwan Province of China	−1.340 **	2.415*	1.570*	1.143	−1.444	0.332	2.189	−0.309
Thailand	−0.540 **	0.816	0.558	0.552	0.041	−0.779	−0.457	−0.203
United Arab Emirates	−0.164 **	0.314 **	0.182 *	0.164	−0.410 *	0.260	0.370	0.525
EUROPE								
Austria	−0.080	0.130	0.103	0.323	−0.600 *	0.713	0.629	0.773
Belgium	0.091	−0.041	0.031	0.071	−2.393 *	2.442	2.612	2.289
Bulgaria	−0.337 **	0.352	0.355	0.360	−1.887 **	1.891	1.875	1.994
Croatia	−0.506 *	0.568	0.777	1.406	−2.349 **	2.399	2.637	2.694
Cyprus	−0.230	0.330	0.623	0.473	−2.324 **	2.298	2.798 *	1.632
Czech Republic	−0.387	0.487	0.606	0.560	−2.383 **	2.583	2.683 *	1.749
Denmark	−0.087	0.124	0.162	0.214	−0.326	0.701	0.459	−0.066
Estonia	−0.191	0.229	0.353	0.457	−1.936 **	2.061	2.190 *	2.040
Finland	−0.697	0.960	1.799 *	1.308	−0.704 **	0.719	0.843 *	0.673
France	0.056	0.119	0.279	0.406	−3.324*	3.536	3.785	2.828
Germany	0.270	−0.133	−0.138	−0.155	−3.606 *	3.719	3.890	3.261
Greece	−0.224	0.374	0.489	0.328	−1.604*	2.016	1.857	0.565
Hungary	−0.349	0.574	0.661	0.453	−3.329 **	3.542	3.629 *	3.017
Ireland	−0.409	0.609	0.657	0.651	−3.468 *	3.705	3.803	3.537
Italy	0.091	−0.041	0.031	0.071	−2.393 *	2.442	2.612	2.289
Latvia	−0.084	0.122	0.297	0.211	−2.415 **	2.541	2.658 *	2.474
Lithuania	−0.080	0.155	0.155	0.184	−0.156	0.255	0.154	0.144
Luxembourg	−0.102	0.152	0.206	0.402	−1.103 **	1.228*	1.230 *	1.184 *
Malta	−0.050	0.113	0.079	0.397	−0.568 **	0.618	0.625 **	0.464
Netherlands	−0.047	0.184	0.370	0.312	−3.665 *	3.939	3.167	3.365
Norway	−0.385 *	0.473	0.668 *	0.605	−2.165 **	2.477	2.442	1.657
Portugal	−0.683 **	0.883	0.908 *	0.775	−3.705 **	3.917	3.930 *	3.728
Romania	−0.072	0.360	0.372	0.234	−1.571*	1.821	1.756	1.467
Russia	−0.763 *	0.863	1.398 *	1.536	−2.836 **	3.198 *	3.378*	2.997 *
Slovak Republic	2.997	0.077	0.107	0.522	−0.105	0.105	0.209	−0.149
Spain	−0.335 *	0.397	0.525	0.450	−1.417 *	1.542	1.648	1.360
Sweden	−1.351 **	1.614	1.634	1.640	−3.812 **	3.487	3.226	3.741
Switzerland	−0.614 **	0.677	0.810	1.041	−3.116 **	3.315	3.357	2.907
Turkey	0.158	−0.070	0.033	1.054	−1.473 *	1.873	1.796	−0.973
Ukraine	3.329	−3.317	−2.301	−3.156	−3.894	3.843	4.125	3.686
United Kingdom	−0.345 *	0.420	0.553	0.691	−2.025 **	−2.025	2.088	1.356

Notes: Table 13 presents the results of the Ehrmann et al. (2011) contagion test. The v_0 and v_j coefficients (j concerns the crises) are reported with an indication of statistical significance as well. ** and * indicate statistical significance in 5% and 10%, respectively. Results came from either internationally or regionally constructed portfolios. Portfolios are interest rate weighted portfolios; specifically, the weighting scheme is based upon changes in interest rates.

Overall, there was no strong evidence in favor of crises causing contagion on a regional level with either global or regional implied betas. There were many countries from all regions with statistically significant crisis-coefficients, however, on a country level. The Argentinian crisis was the crisis that affected mostly contagion, with EU second and US third. The Argentinian crisis caused contagion in three cases: in Africa (on trade-integration- and GDP-based portfolios for implied global betas) and Asia (on trade-integration-based portfolios for implied regional betas). The EU crisis was responsible for contagion in a few cases only: in Africa (on inflation-rate- and interest-rate-based portfolios for the implied global betas) and the Americas (on trade-integration-based portfolios for implied regional betas). The US crisis was responsible for contagion in a single case only: in the Americas on GDP-based portfolios for implied global betas.

6. Concluding Remarks

The Americas and Europe had the highest portfolio weights across the weighting schemes. Furthermore, they were the regions with the best portfolio performance across the portfolio weighting schemes. The market capitalization was the best portfolio weighting scheme in terms of portfolio performance. It revealed the inter-relation of market capitalization (via liquidity) that drives portfolio performance. For the average values of the implied global betas, Europe and Africa were the regions with the lowest and highest dispersion in either implied global or implied regional betas across regional countries. The results in average implied global or regional betas are robust across most of the portfolio weighting schemes. The single exception is the trade integration portfolio weighting scheme, for which both the implied global and regional betas increased across all regions and all countries.

The structural regime-switching factor model revealed strong evidence of contagion across all regions, portfolio types, and for both global and regional betas. Regime variables, crises variables, and macroeconomic variables revealed contagion (were statistically significant). Europe was the region that was mostly affected by the crises. The macroeconomic variables statistically significantly explained betas. Moreover, the overall model significance was high. The Argentinian crisis first and the US crisis second mostly affected contagion across all regions and portfolio types, as well as both global and regional implied betas.

The Ehrmann et al. (2011) contagion test revealed strong contagion across all regions and portfolio types (weighting schemes) and for both global and regional betas. Europe was the region with the strongest evidence of contagion. Stronger contagion was evident for the implied global rather than regional betas. There was no strong evidence of crisis contagion on a regional level. There was on a country level, however. The Argentinian crisis was the most contagion influential crisis, however.

The research implications suggest that asset allocation and portfolio management should consider both the global and the regional aspect of contagion, as differences can occur. In addition, portfolio construction should involve a careful consideration of the underlying impact of the macroeconomic variables considered in this study, as some macroeconomic variables appear to reveal contagion better than others. Finally, it is also important to consider which macroeconomic variable is mainly affected by a given crisis event in order to better understand the impact of contagion on portfolio performance. It is also evident that market capitalization is a very important macroeconomic variable to consider in both the Americas and Europe as it leads to both stronger contagion and portfolio performance. Finally, trade integration is a more important variable to consider in emerging economies.

Turning to the limitations and the future work related to the study, indeed, important events that happened in the years following 2016 cannot be captured; this is due to the data availability at present. Nonetheless, we intend to investigate more recent events in the near future in order to further include events such as the COVID-19 pandemic and the Russia–Ukrainian war.

These results should be considered by investors and risk managers. The use of macroeconomic variables as the main driver of a portfolio weighting scheme reveals their importance in asset allocation. This is true on both the international and regional levels. Higher importance comes for the regional portfolios as the dispersion of results is higher on a regional than international level.

Author Contributions: C.F.: project administration, supervision, formal analysis, writing—original draft, D.V.: conceptualization, methods, data curation, formal analysis, writing—original draft, I.C.: supervision, validation, formal analysis, writing—original draft. All authors have read and agreed to the published version of the manuscript.

Funding: This research received no external funding.

Informed Consent Statement: Not applicable.

Data Availability Statement: The data can be available upon request.

Conflicts of Interest: The authors declare no conflicts of interest.

Notes

1. **(i)** Americas: Argentina (ARG), Brazil (BRA), Canada (CAN), Chile (CHL), Colombia (COL), Jamaica (JAM), Mexico (MEX), Panama (PAN), Peru (PER), United States of America (USA) and Venezuela (VEN); **(ii)** Asia: Australia (AUS), Bangladesh (BGD), China (CHN), Hong Kong SA (HKG), India (IND), Indonesia (IDN), Israel (ISR), Japan (JPN), Jordan (JOR), Malaysia (MYS), New Zealand (NZL), Oman (OMN), Pakistan (PAK), Philippines (PHL), Saudi Arabia (SAU), Singapore (SGP), South Korea (KOR), Taiwan Province of China (TWN), Thailand (THA), and United Arab Emirates (ARE); **(iii)** Europe: Austria (AUT), Belgium (BEL), Bulgaria (BGR), Croatia (CRO), Cyprus (CYP), Czech Republic (CZE), Denmark (DEN), Estonia (EST), Finland (FIN), France (FRA), Germany (DEU), Greece (GRC), Hungary (HUN), Ireland (IRL), Italy (ITA), Latvia (LVA), Lithuania (LTU), Luxembourg (LUX), Malta (MLT), Netherlands (NLD), Norway (NOR), Portugal (PRT), Romania (ROU), Russia (RUS), Slovak Republic (SVK), Spain (ESP), Sweden (SWE), Switzerland (CHE), Turkey (TUR), Ukraine (UKR), and United Kingdom (GBR); and **(iv)** Africa: Botswana (BWA), Egypt (EGY), Kenya (KEN), Mauritius (MUS), and South Africa (ZAF).
2. Trade integration is measured as the ratio of international trade (import plus exports) of a country over the country's GDP.

References

Akhtaruzzaman, Md, and Abul Shamsuddin. 2016. International contagion through financial versus non-financial firms. *Economic Modelling* 59: 143–63. [CrossRef]

Akhtaruzzaman, Md, Abul Shamsuddin, and Steve Easton. 2014. Dynamic correlation analysis of spill-over effects of interest rate risk and return on australian and us financial firms. *Journal of International Financial Markets, Institutions and Money* 31: 378–96. [CrossRef]

Akhtaruzzaman, Md, Sabri Boubaker, and Ahmet Sensoy. 2021. Financial contagion during covid–19 crisis. *Finance Research Letters* 38: 101604. [CrossRef] [PubMed]

Baele, Lieven, and Koen Inghelbrecht. 2010. Time-varying integration, interdependence and contagion. *Journal of International Money and Finance* 29: 791–818. [CrossRef]

Bekiros, Stelios D. 2014. Contagion, decoupling and the spillover effects of the us financial crisis: Evidence from the bric markets. *International Review of Financial Analysis* 33: 58–69. [CrossRef]

BenSaïda, Ahmed, and Houda Litimi. 2021. Financial contagion across g10 stock markets: A study during major crises. *International Journal of Finance and Economics* 26: 4798–21. [CrossRef]

Bouker, Sawsen, and Faysal Mansouri. 2022. Sovereign contagion risk measure across financial markets in the eurozone: A bivariate copulas and markov regime switching arma based approaches. *Review of World Economics* 158: 615–711. [CrossRef]

Bouzzine, Yassin Denis, and Rainer Lueg. 2020. The contagion effect of environmental violations: The case of dieselgate in germany. *Business Strategy and the Environment* 29: 3187–202. [CrossRef]

Cho, Sungjun, Stuart Hyde, and Ngoc Nguyen. 2015. Time-varying regional and global integration and contagion: Evidence from style portfolios. *International Review of Financial Analysis* 42: 109–31. [CrossRef]

Corbet, Shaen, and John W. Goodell. 2022. The reputational contagion effects of ransomware attacks. *Finance Research Letters* 47: 102715. [CrossRef]

Corbet, Shaen, Yang (Greg) Hou, Yang Hu, and Les Oxley. 2022. Financial contagion among covid-19 concept-related stocks in china. *Applied Economics* 54: 2439–52. [CrossRef]

Devereux, Michael B., and Changhua Yu. 2020. International financial integration and crisis contagion. *The Review of Economic Studies* 87: 1174–212. [CrossRef]

Dua, Pami, and Divya Tuteja. 2021. Regime shifts in the behaviour of international currency and equity markets: A markov-switching analysis. *Journal of Quantitative Economics* 19: 309–36. [CrossRef] [PubMed]

Dungey, Mardi, and Dinesh Gajurel. 2014. Equity market contagion during the global financial crisis: Evidence from the world's eight largest economies. *Economic Systems* 38: 161–77. [CrossRef]

Ehrmann, Michael, Marcel Fratzscher, Arnaud Mehl, and Geert Bekaert. 2011. *Global Crises and Equity Market Contagion*. Working Paper Series 1381. Frankfurt: European Central Bank.

Gunay, Samet, and Gokberk Can. 2022. The source of financial contagion and spillovers: An evaluation of the covid-19 pandemic and the global financial crisis. *PLoS ONE* 17: e0261835. [CrossRef] [PubMed]

Jiang, Hai, Shenfeng Tang, Lifang Li, Fangming Xu, and Qian Di. 2022. Re-examining the contagion channels of global financial crises: Evidence from the twelve years since the us subprime crisis. *Research in International Business and Finance* 60: 101617. [CrossRef]

Kosmidou, Kyriaki, Dimitrios Kousenidis, Anestis Ladas, and Christos Negkakis. 2019. Do institutions prevent contagion in financial markets? evidence from the european debt crisis. *The European Journal of Finance* 25: 632–46. [CrossRef]

Nguyen, Thi Ngan, Thi Kieu Hoa Phan, and Thanh Liem Nguyen. 2022. Financial contagion during global financial crisis and covid–19 pandemic: The evidence from dcc–garch model. *Cogent Economics & Finance* 10: 2051824. [CrossRef]

Park, Cyn-Young, and Kwanho Shin. 2020. Contagion through national and regional exposures to foreign banks during the global financial crisis. *Journal of Financial Stability* 46: 100721. [CrossRef]

Pineda, Julián, Lina M. Cortés, and Javier Perote. 2022. Financial contagion drivers during recent global crises. *Economic Modelling* 117: 106067. [CrossRef]
Raddant, Matthias, and Dror Y. Kenett. 2021. Interconnectedness in the global financial market. *Journal of International Money and Finance* 110: 102280. [CrossRef]
Shen, Peilong, and Zhinan Li. 2020. Financial contagion in inter-bank networks with overlapping portfolios. *Journal of Economics and International Cooperation* 15: 845–65. [CrossRef]
Shen, Pei-Long, Wen Li, Xiao-Ting Wang, and Chi-Wei Su. 2015. Contagion effect of the european financial crisis on china's stock markets: Interdependence and pure contagion. *Economic Modelling* 50: 193–99. [CrossRef]
Shruthi, Rajan, and Santhakumar Shijin. 2020. Investigating liquidity constraints as a channel of contagion: A regime switching approach. *Financial Innovation* 6: 24. [CrossRef]
Trihadmini, Nuning, and Telisa Aulia Falinaty. 2020. Stock market contagion and spillover effects of the global financial crisis on five asean countries. *Institutions and Economies* 12: 91–119.
Troug, Haitem, and Matt Murray. 2021. Crisis determination and financial contagion: An analysis of the hong kong and tokyo stock markets using an msbvar approach. *Journal of Economic Studies* 48: 1548–72. [CrossRef]

economies

Article

Governance and Fiscal Decentralisation in Latin America: An Empirical Approach

Diego E. Pinilla-Rodríguez * and Patricia Hernández-Medina

Faculty of Political and Administrative Sciences, National University of Chimborazo, Campus Norte, Av. Antonio José de Sucre Km 1 1/2 via a Guano, Riobamba 060110, Ecuador; patricia.hernandez@unach.edu.ec
* Correspondence: dpinilla@unach.edu.ec

Abstract: The objective of this study was to establish the relationship between certain institutional variables and the effectiveness of fiscal decentralisation in Latin America. To fulfil this objective, we took a sample of 15 Latin American countries for the years 1996 to 2020 to estimate the logarithm of GDP per capita based on the level of fiscal decentralisation, as well as its interaction with six institutional variables plus three control variables. The results show that institutional variables always modulate the effects of fiscal decentralisation, in most cases significantly and negatively, the exceptions being accountability with a positive result and government effectiveness with a non-significant result. It was concluded that in the presence of weak regulations, political conflicts, and corruption, fiscal decentralisation can worsen social or economic circumstances in Latin America.

Keywords: governance; fiscal decentralisation; economic growth; accountability; corruption; panel data

1. Introduction

The normative thesis of fiscal federalism suggests that a decentralised form of government offers higher economic efficiency by providing a diversified set of goods and services that better match the preferences of geographically clustered consumers (Oates 1977). It is also undeniable that there are public goods that are limited to a specific jurisdiction, where their benefits, the expenditure they entail, and the revenue they require have an impact only in that jurisdiction. Thus, the benefit principle presents a territorial variable, where each jurisdiction is more efficient in terms of the spatial dimension of the services it provides.

On this basis, there is a whole economic tradition in favour of the implementation of decentralised models under the assumption of their greater capacity to respond to citizens' needs more efficiently, which, in the long run, may result in higher economic growth and better social outcomes (Pinilla-Rodríguez et al. 2014, 2016). However, not all the literature share this idea. There is a significant body of work that gives a negative account of the relationship between decentralisation and efficiency, stating that in certain circumstances (economies of scale, competency confusion, corruption, soft budget constraints, and others), centralised provision may be more efficient (Rodríguez-Pose and Bwire 2005).

In a representative study, Prud'homme (1995) was among the first to point out that the benefits of decentralisation are not as evident as classical theory would have it, and that its implementation has serious drawbacks that must be considered. The problem should not exclusively revolve around the opposites of centralise or decentralise. Consideration should be given to the concrete objectives to be achieved, which sectors and for which regions or jurisdictional levels. Bahl (1999) argued that the literature has focused too much on evaluating decentralising experiences in contrast to practice versus theory and has given little importance to implementation strategies.

However, only a comprehensive understanding of the process, including its institutional framework, allows for the evaluation of a decentralisation strategy. As Rodden (2003) put it, the effects of decentralisation are conditioned by the governance framework in which the process takes place, so that the potential benefits of decentralisation are not based on decentralisation per se but rather on the institutional features that accompany it. It is necessary to integrate political and economic institutions to understand how and in what circumstances decentralisation can be beneficial, which depends significantly on circumstances such as authority structures or the arrangement of intergovernmental relations (Hankla 2009).

Fiscal decentralisation is not a "magic recipe". It requires the presence of an adequate institutional framework, especially at a local level. It has been evident for several years now that a wide range of variables affects decentralisation efforts. More attention needs to be paid to institutions in the design of decentralisation processes, with a greater focus on accountability, governance, and administrative capacity (Litvack et al. 1998). A crucial factor separating successful and unsuccessful examples of decentralisation is the quality of institutional design, especially at a sub-national level (Hankla 2009).

From an empirical perspective, the evidence also points to demystifying decentralisation and shows that its potential advantages are possible only under certain conditions. Decentralisation by itself is not a possibility (Sharma 2006). It depends on the existing governance creating the right incentive environment. In this respect, Enikolopov and Zhuravskaya (2003) argued that the lack of empirical findings on the effects of decentralisation is because numerous studies do not consider the importance of political institutions. As Voigt and Blume (2012) pointed out, attempts to estimate the economic effects of decentralisation cannot ignore potentially important institutional details. More needs to be known about the transmission mechanisms that decentralisation promotes.

This is especially true for developing countries, where institutional characteristics constitute a challenge to the classical normative theory and have implied the advance of new theoretical proposals or controversial models and empirical results. In this respect, it is important to point out how, without further questioning, many Latin American countries modified their fiscal structures on the conceptual categories and instruments of fiscal federalism, which were developed for industrialised countries with a long federal tradition, ignoring that many of the expected stimuli and incentives would not be realised under certain prevailing conditions (a centralist tradition, limited capacity for displacement, reduced levels of public goods, low tax burden, poor democratic performance, weak local administrative structures, etc.) (González 1994).

As Litvack et al. (1998) point out, much of the literature on decentralisation (normative and empirical) focuses on developed countries and assumes the existence of institutions that do not exist or are very weak in developing countries. Governments in many developing countries are often unresponsive to their citizens, and decision-making is rarely transparent and predictable. Opportunities for participation, punishment, or exit are limited due to weak institutions. Democratic systems are often fragile, making the electoral system a highly problematic method of achieving accountability. Strong, broad-based local participation can overcome weak, formal electoral systems, but local elites make this difficult in many places. Mobility is often constrained by a lack of information, infrastructure, and legal frameworks, resulting in weak markets for land, labour, and capital. There is no doubt that the special characteristics of developing countries represent a challenge for decentralisation, and the theory must be modified to take them into account to realise the advantages of decentralised government (Ahmad and Brosio 2006).

In the presence of weak institutions and political conflict, decentralisation might even worsen social circumstances. The benefits or detriments of decentralisation have conflicting formulations and evidence, depending on the characteristics of the process and the governance framework in which it takes place. In the end, the likelihood of being more responsive to local preferences depends on various incentives and how policy decisions are made. These incentives depend on the institutional structures that facilitate or hinder actors' behaviour. In this regard, it is increasingly evident that explaining decentralisation processes requires the inclusion of governance. Rules and structures matter (Stein 1999). The question is as follows: what are the rules and structures that "matter"?

Initially, a large body of literature highlighted the importance of democratic intensity in decentralised public action (Tanzi 1995). Most of the benefits derived from decentralisation are in some way related to increased accountability and transparency in local governments (Hankla 2009; Hankla and Downs 2010). Democratic institutions are required to ensure that the community exercises control over government affairs at a local level. Giving powers to local governments that are not accountable to their populations may not improve outcomes but rather worsen them. If accountability is incomplete, decentralisation creates powerful incentives for local elites to capture the local political process and divert public resources to satisfy their own aspirations, rather than those of the wider community (Eckardt 2008).

In this respect, it is often assumed that the geographical proximity between those who govern and those who are governed, which increases with decentralisation, favours citizen participation and accountability. In the long run, this makes it more likely that sub-national authorities will provide citizens with the level of quality and governance they desire. But this will only be possible if each jurisdiction takes responsibility for its competencies, is explicit about its institutional relations with other jurisdictions, and is democratically elected in a competitive regime (Roubini and Sachs 1989; Grilli et al. 1991; Bird and Vaillancourt 1998; Manor 1999; Franzese 2002).

Transparent budgetary processes and public procurement procedures, or the distribution of fiscal powers that link tax levels to the quality of locally provided services, are also valued positively (Litvack et al. 1998). In this respect, Huther and Shah (1998) empirically confirmed that citizen participation promotes public sector accountability, which in turn creates the enabling environment for optimal decentralisation.

However, it is necessary to accept, especially in the case of Latin America, that many sub-national political processes are characterised by a low democratic quality, where representative methods of decision-making are weak or are co-opted by local elites who do not promote the public interest and hijack resources in the absence of transparency and accountability (Narayan 1998). Closeness also brings personalism to relationships, and when this occurs, the public interest is often sacrificed in favour of individuals or groups (Tanzi 1995). Perhaps for this reason, the literature assessing the relationship between decentralisation and corruption stresses the need to include in the analysis factors such as inter-jurisdictional mobility and competition, the effective possibility of monitoring and accountability, the degree of dispersion of decision-making powers, and bureaucratic competence and quality (Shleifer and Vishny 1993; Jin et al. 1999).

A strong rule of law would be a further positive institutional factor. The presence of a certain framework of compliance with and trust in social rules and respect for rights can also be a reason for effective decentralisation. The precise allocation of the revenue and expenditure rights of jurisdictions, a rational transfer system, and effective decentralisation and restraint mechanisms would enhance the benefit of the decentralisation process.

The quality of public administration can also be a determinant of the positive impact of a fiscal decentralisation process. If the civil service in general, but especially the local civil service, is of high quality and is exercised in a technical and independent manner with modern planning and control systems, fiscal decentralisation can achieve better results. The fiscal responsiveness of sub-national governments is related to their administrative competence (Manor 1999). Building strong administrative structures is vital for effective decentralisation (Hankla 2009). Of course, if the quality of local bureaucracies is poor and if the public interest is not the guiding principle for local officials, independence and experimentation by local jurisdictions may not achieve the desired results (Tanzi 1995).

In this respect, it must be highlighted how in Latin America, sub-national governments have received new competencies without renewing their administrative structures. This often generates levels of inefficiency in day-to-day operations (Cabrero Mendoza et al. 1997), aggravated by the shortage of trained civil servants (monopolised by central governments that offer better working conditions), something that impedes decentralisation efforts (Murphy et al. 1991; Prud'homme 1995). In general terms, Latin American governments have advanced fiscal decentralisation without considering the conditions in which their sub-national governments find themselves and, even worse, without implementing any consistent and systematic policy to strengthen their administrative and managerial capacities (Campbell et al. 1991). As Nickson (2023) states, the transfer of new powers and financial resources to local governments does not guarantee an increase in the efficiency and effectiveness of local service delivery if administrative practices are not improved. The first pending challenge would be the constitution of true municipal career systems that break with the current caudillismo and the high bureaucratic turnover.

Likewise, the quality of regulation, especially of fiscal institutions, can make the difference between successful and unsuccessful decentralisation. It is presumed that the government has formulated and implemented sound, effective, coherent, and simple fiscal policies and regulations that are consistent with other regulations and are implemented in an equitable, transparent and proportional manner as part of the decentralisation process. However, Latin American countries are characterised by weak regulations that encourage fiscal indiscipline. Countries in the region have not paid sufficient attention to strengthening institutional capacity in the budgetary framework (Shah 1998; Stein et al. 1998; Alesina et al. 1999).

In addition to the institutional factors outlined above, in empirical terms, a variety of factors have been identified as determinants of an effective decentralisation process: optimal allocation of public expenditures across regions, appropriate coordination channels, instruments such as training and adequate financial planning (Robalino et al. 2001); political and bureaucratic leadership of the central sector (Robalino et al. 2001; Heywood and Choi 2010); income level, democratic and institutional quality, ethnic tensions and ethno-linguistic fragmentation (Khaleghian 2003; Nana 2009); informal governance and political culture (Atkinson and Haran 2004); the effective level of political decentralisation (James et al. 2004); the degree of local voters' political education, social homogeneity, and coordination of preferences (Ahmad et al. 2006); the proper design of intergovernmental transfers and local fiscal autonomy (Uchimura and Jütting 2009); and the decentralisation of revenue sources (Nana 2009; Akpan 2011; Jiménez 2011).

Kyriacou et al. (2015) found that decentralisation promotes regional convergence in environments of high government quality and leads to wider regional disparities in countries with poor governance. Hanif et al. (2020) showed that the impact of fiscal decentralisation on economic growth is attenuated in the presence of corruption, weak institutions, and/or political instability. Arif and Ahmad (2020) presented evidence regarding the positive effect of fiscal decentralisation on economic growth, provided it is complemented by a strong institutional structure in terms of rule of law (RLaw), low corruption, high bureaucratic quality, and democratic accountability.

In short, decentralisation is a process whose evaluation must be conducted by defining the governance context in which it is being implemented. Institutional details are important. Empirical results can be quite different if aspects of the governance structure are included (Voigt and Blume 2012). It is hypothesised that the process will show better efficiency results if constitutional and legal frameworks are clearly defined and enforced; if political and administrative processes are transparent and oriented towards the public interest; if participation, freedom of expression, and accountability are enhanced; if a framework of political stability is present; and if the government is administratively efficient, accountable, and independent. The success of the process hinges on institutional components such as inter-jurisdictional competence or coordination, effective monitoring and accountability, dispersed decision-making powers, and bureaucratic capacity and quality.

There is a need to focus on the relationship between specific political institutions and the efficient provision of local public goods in fiscally decentralised systems. Few scholars have examined how government institutions support the social welfare gains expected from decentralising processes. An attempt should be made to construct a more robust "decentralisation theorem" (Ponce-Rodríguez et al. 2020).

For this purpose, it is necessary to analyse decentralisation as a specific process, which requires contextual and extensive information for building knowledge in this field. By identifying the institutions that are important for decentralisation and that may be fragile in developing countries, it is also possible to identify ways to compensate for weak institutions in the short term and build key elements of important institutions in the long term.

In this way, the goal is to account for the growing decentralising experience by identifying governance variables beneficial to the decentralising process. To be sure, much of the discussion on fiscal federalism has revolved around a curious combination of strong preconceived beliefs and limited empirical evidence. However, there are now well-established processes and precise effects to assess. It is no longer a debate confined to institutional description or ideology but can be based on results and new theoretical horizons and available data, which recognise that the best design will vary according to circumstances and institutions and that this complexity has sometimes been overlooked.

This is especially true for Latin America in the period under study (1996–2020), as it presents some circumstances that make it productive in validating these hypotheses. Decentralisation in Latin America has been one of the most significant economic and political developments in the last three decades. It has undoubtedly redefined public policies, especially distributive ones. For years now, many components of social policy have been left to sub-national governments in the belief that they will achieve better social welfare outcomes.

Decentralisation in Latin America was first a political and structural reform process driven by the idea that a system of local governments was economically and politically more profitable. This idea, adopted without questioning the institutional framework within which it was to develop, turned decentralisation into an end rather than the means that it really is, under the political motivation of transforming a centralised and authoritarian state into a decentralised and democratic one (Burki et al. 1999; Mascareño 2009). The autonomy of local jurisdictions was promoted with the guarantee of transferring large fiscal resources from the central government, where the transfers became the main instrument of decentralisation.

In the end, the mismatch between local spending and tax effort widened the gap between the institutions and citizens, contrary to the promise of decentralisation. In states such as Oaxaca and Chiapas (Mexico); in municipalities in the northeast of Brazil, such as Alagoas and Maranhão; in provinces such as Formosa and Santiago del Estero (Argentina); or in regions such as Huancavelica and Apurímac (Peru), low-tax-collection Local governments have contributed to dependence on transfers from the central government, which has created the perception that public services are financed and controlled by an external agent, reducing responsibility and accountability at the local level. The dependence on national funds has led citizens to see local services as external services and managed by a distant level of government (Cabrero Mendoza 2004; Hernandez-Trillo and Jarillo-Rabling 2008; Rezende and Afonso 2006; Shah 2004; Porto and Sanguinetti 2001; Ahmad and Garcia-Escribano 2006).

Achieving efficiency in the management of resources by subjecting public services to more direct public scrutiny is not possible if they do not see them as a collective patrimony. Citizen participation in public management did not occur in the terms and at the levels announced because real incentives to encourage participation were lacking. Sub-national governments were fiscally strengthened, but political practices were not transformed. As the drawbacks became evident, central governments adopted a more cautious attitude towards reforms, imposing stricter regulatory frameworks for intergovernmental finances and monitoring systems and evaluating the fiscal performance of sub-national entities. A "comprehensive strategy" that considered public sector governance was required.

In this framework, the objective of this research was to verify the impact that decentralisation processes have had in Latin America and identify which governance determinants modulate their effectiveness and how they do so. In other words, the aim was to estimate the level of economic efficiency of fiscal decentralisation for a set of Latin American countries and to establish the interaction that certain institutional factors have in this respect. We aimed to find which governance variables correct the social efficiency of fiscal decentralisation processes and how intensely they do so. In concrete terms for the case of Latin America, is the quality of accountability or the rule of law the institutional characteristic that has promoted effective fiscal decentralisation? Or are political stability, government effectiveness, regulatory quality, and corruption control the key institutional variables that explain successful fiscal decentralisation processes? Or, on the contrary, some of these institutional variables cause fiscal decentralisation to present negative results.

2. Materials and Methods

To establish the modulating role of certain institutional variables on the possible positive impact of fiscal decentralisation in Latin America, a panel-data-modelling approach was used for a sample of 15 Latin American countries for the years 1996 and 2020. Economic growth was taken as the dependent outcome variable. That is, this variable was adopted as a proxy for the level of economic efficiency that fiscal decentralisation has had in Latin America. The proposal was conducted through a static analysis, in which fixed effects or random effects estimations were developed according to the origin of the unobserved heterogeneity.

Under this modelling system, we intended to estimate a socio-economic outcome variable (logarithm of GDP per capita) by considering the decentralisation variable (sub-national public expenditure as a percentage of general government public expenditure), as well as its interaction with six governance variables. Also included were three control variables, namely social expenditure, gross capital formation, and the degree of openness of the economy, as indicated in Equation (1):

$$GDPpC_{it} = \alpha + \beta_1 FD_{it} + \beta_2 IG_{it} + \beta_3 (FD_{it} * IG_{it}) + \beta_4 X_{it} + \varepsilon_{it} \quad (1)$$

where i refers to countries and t to years; α is a constant; *GDPpC* is economic output (economic growth); *DF* is a fiscal decentralisation variable; *GI* is an institutional governance variable; X is a vector of control variables; and ε is the error term.

The *GDPpC* variable is the logarithm of GDP per capita in US dollars at constant 2018 prices. The data were taken from the World Bank's World Development Indicators (WGI) database. As Baskaran et al. (2016) point out, the theoretical literature on fiscal federalism has identified several channels through which decentralisation affects economic growth. Efficiency is the decentralised provision of public services or the increasing capacity of the political system to innovate and conduct reforms. Other authors argue that decentralisation increases corruption or inefficiency and thus decreases economic growth.

Despite the theoretical ambiguity, and the fact that the results may depend on the characteristics of the empirical models and the sample used, the literature generally finds a positive and significant relationship between levels of decentralisation and the volume of output per capita (Xie et al. 1999; Lin and Liu 2000; Akai and Sakata 2002; Feld et al. 2004; Iimi 2005; Qiao et al. 2008; Gemmell et al. 2013; Blöchliger and Égert 2013). Particularly for Latin America, Pinilla-Rodríguez et al. (2016) provided evidence of the positive, long-term impact of fiscal decentralisation on economic growth. Other authors such as Bojanic (2018) established for the case of 10 Latin American countries, and without the inclusion of institutional variables, that fiscal decentralisation on the income side exerts a negative influence on growth, but the decentralisation indicator of the spending seems to show a positive influence.

With respect to fiscal decentralisation, it is important to point out that its dimensions are multiple since the instruments on which it plays out are the volumes of fiscal resources spent or received by sub-national governments. The concrete autonomy these governments have for managing resources can be diverse. The practical inconveniences derived from the availability of information to construct a valid measure of physical decentralisation in Latin America are also well known (Martner 2005).

In our case, the variable sub-national public expenditure as a percentage of total general government expenditure (FDExp) was adopted. This measure captures regional and local governments' share of expenditures as a proportion of total general government spending. The measure excludes the portion of spending that is transferred to other levels of government, foreign governments, and international organisations. Measuring only subnational spending may not fully capture fiscal autonomy and responsibility, especially if subnational governments depend largely on transfers from the central government. On the other hand, subnational governments may have different responsibilities in terms of services and functions, which are not adequately reflected through expenditure alone, and in some cases, central governments may impose financial mandates, distorting the real picture of decentralisation. However, despite its limitations, this variable is considered to represent, in a comprehensible way, how fiscal decentralisation has evolved in Latin America in the period under study; although, it is noted that the results are closely linked to the decentralisation variable that has been chosen. The data were taken from the fiscal decentralisation database of the International Monetary Fund (IMF).

Regarding the exogenous variables, Table 1 details those related to the quality of institutions or governance, which were extracted from the WGI database, which reports aggregate and individual governance indicators for more than 200 countries.

Table 1. Description of governance variables.

Participation and accountability (PA): This variable captures perceptions of the extent to which a country's citizens can participate in the selection of their governments as well as freedom of expression, freedom of association, and free media.
Political stability and the absence of violence (PS): This variable measures perceptions of the likelihood of political instability and/or politically motivated violence, including terrorism.
Government Effectiveness (GovEffec): This captures perceptions of the quality of public services, the civil service and its degree of independence from political pressures, and policy formulation and implementation, as well as the credibility of the government's commitment to such policies.
Regulatory quality (RQ): This variable captures perceptions of the government's ability to formulate and implement sound policies and regulations that enable and promote private sector development.
Rule of law (RLaw): This variable captures perceptions of the extent to which agents have confidence in and abide by the rules of society and the quality of contract enforcement, property rights, the police, and the courts, as well as the likelihood of the presence of crime and/or violence.
Control of corruption (Corr): This variable captures perceptions of the extent to which public power is exercised for private gain, including petty and expansive forms of corruption, as well as the 'capture' of the state by elites and private interests.

Source: authors' own, based on Kaufmann et al. (2011).

All governance indicator scores have been re-scaled to values of 1 (lowest perception of a governance dimension) and 6 (highest perception).

The control variables are central government social public expenditure (GPS, measured as % of GDP), gross fixed capital formation (GFCF, measured as % of GDP) and the openness rate of the economy (OPEN), represented by the sum of imports and exports as a percentage of GDP. The choice of control variables was guided by the need to consider factors that may affect the relationship between fiscal decentralisation, institutional quality, and economic growth, and whose omission could bias the estimated relationships between these variables. The values for public social expenditure were taken from ECLAC's Cepalstat database, while the values for OPEN and GFCF were taken from the World Bank's national accounts database.

To analyse these data, which merge temporal elements with cross-subject comparisons, it was necessary to apply panel data analysis techniques. This approach recognises the need to address the inherent heterogeneity in the data, both across subjects (such as countries) and over time. This uncaptured heterogeneity is reflected in the error term, which is composed of the standard estimation error, random noise, and the error arising from unexplained heterogeneity, which remains constant over time.

When estimating, this heterogeneity can be assumed to be related to the explanatory variables, indicating differences between subjects, or it can be considered as random. In the first scenario, fixed effects methods are employed, while in the second, random effects are chosen. If a correlation is confirmed, the estimation may be biased. To mitigate this, the fixed effects approach adjusts variables and errors to their means, eliminating the impact of unobserved heterogeneity.

Random effects estimation, on the other hand, assumes that there is no correlation between the explanatory variables and the unobserved error and adjusts for differences weighted by a factor related to error variance and heterogeneity. The choice between fixed and random effects is guided by the Hausman test, which determines the appropriateness of random versus fixed effects. As regards selecting fixed effects, it is necessary to validate the absence of heteroskedasticity and its corresponding adjustment using generalised least squares (GLS), which allows an efficient estimation of coefficients considering both autocorrelation and heteroskedasticity.

An initial model was estimated, in which the economic growth variable was a function of the control variables and the decentralisation variable. Similarly, and for each institutional variable, two models were estimated: (a) an unrestricted model in which only the control variables, decentralisation variable, and institutional variable were introduced as determinants and (b) a restricted model in which the interaction between the decentralisation variable and the institutional variable was also introduced.

The results must be interpreted with due caution, as in most of the literature. Firstly, the decentralisation variable is limited, in that it does not capture all of the multiple dimensions of a decentralisation process. Secondly, the GDP per capita variable may not fully reflect the underlying level of a society's social welfare, others being more informative and conclusive. Thirdly, environmental variables have been adopted as determinants of the realisation of certain social outcomes, as well as of the efficiency of decentralising processes. Yet, it is possible that other variables, for which we do not have a complete or homogeneous series, may be even more relevant.

3. Results

Economic Growth, Decentralisation and Governance

As can be seen in Figure 1, from 1996 to 2020, Latin America experienced various stages of economic growth. In the late 1990s, the region suffered economic turbulence due to the Asian financial crisis that affected several Latin American countries, especially those with more vulnerable economies dependent on external capital flows.

There were external imbalances, falling exports, and capital flight in a scenario of macroeconomic imbalances. However, some strengths moderated these negative effects (1998–2003). Starting in the first decade of the 21st century, many Latin American countries benefited from rising commodity prices, such as oil, metals, and agricultural products. There was strong recovery driven by an improvement in the terms of trade. The region enjoyed a higher utilisation rate of productive factors that were underutilised in the previous recessionary period. This boosted economic growth in countries such as Brazil, Chile, and Peru, which are major commodity exporters (2004–2008).

In 2008, the global financial crisis had a significant impact on Latin America, although the region was not as severely affected as other parts of the world due to the possibility of activating contracyclical fiscal policies and controlling exchange rate depreciations. However, there was an economic slowdown in several countries and a fall in foreign investment flows and international trade. Finally, the fall in commodity prices in 2014–2015 and the COVID-19 pandemic in 2020 affected the GDP of all countries across the world, but the swings in Latin American economies were significantly more pronounced. Importantly, economic performance has been heterogeneous across the region. Some countries, e.g., Chile, Peru, and Colombia, achieved strong economic growth and macroeconomic stability, while others, such as Venezuela and Argentina, faced severe economic crises and recessions.

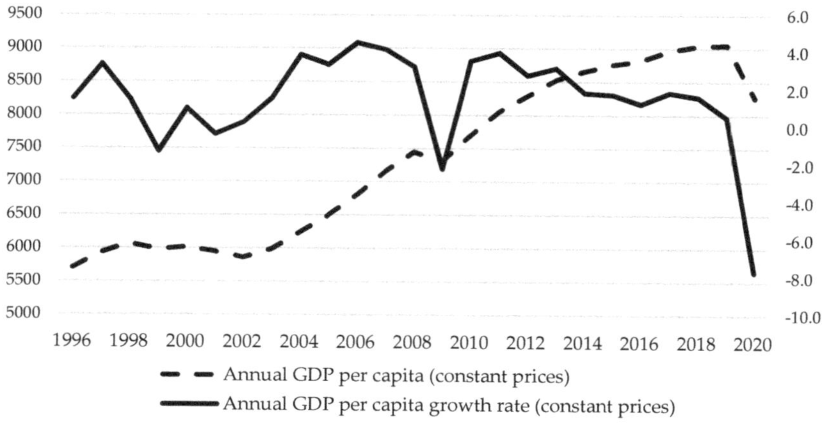

Figure 1. 15 Latin American countries: GDP per capita and its average rate of change (1996–2020). Source: created by the authors based on ECLAC (2024).

As can be seen in Figure 2, regarding the fiscal decentralisation variable, sub-national expenditure (as a percentage of general government expenditure) shows an average decrease of 0.83%. This slight decrease or stabilisation in decentralisation levels responds to the fact that after a period of increasing sub-national expenditure, a set of reforms at the end of the 1990s put an end to quantitative expansion through transfers, with the aim of imposing new priorities (sound local finances, moderate indebtedness, local tax effort, the promotion of market mechanisms, and a justification of the number of administrative levels) (Restrepo 2004).

In the end, the countries with the highest ratios (as an average for the period) are Argentina (42%), Mexico (41%), and Brazil (39%), followed by Colombia, Bolivia, and Peru, with percentages of 30 to 34%. Lower ratios were observed for Ecuador, Guatemala, Chile, and Honduras, with percentages of 15 to 10 percent. Finally, El Salvador, Paraguay, Costa Rica, and Panama had ratios of less than 10%.

With respect to the governance variables, with values of 1 (lowest perception) and 6 (highest perception), the values range between 3.0 and 3.8, which indicates that the level of governance in Latin America is low, especially for rule of law. In contrast, accountability had the highest perception. In temporal terms, there is no evidence of any progress or regression in the governance dimensions in the period studied, with persistent challenges in areas such as democracy, corruption, institutional fragility, and state management capacities.

Table 2 presents the descriptive statistics of all variables. The participation and accountability variable stands out for its highest average value among all institutional variables. It is also true that all these variables present low average values and little progress in the period under study, which denotes very little institutional progress in Latin America in the period under study.

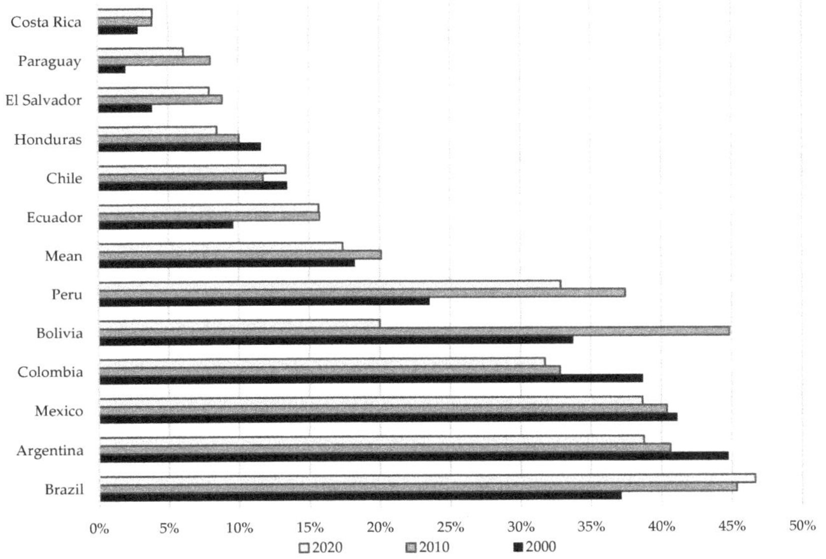

Figure 2. 12 Latin American countries: sub-national public expenditure (% of general government public expenditure) (2000, 2010, and 2020). Source: created by the authors based on the IMF's fiscal decentralisation database.

Table 2. Descriptive statistics of variables: Logarithm of GDP per capita, control variables, and governance variables (1996–2020).

Variable	**N**	**Period**		**1996**		**2020**		**Max. Value**	**Min. Value**
		Average	*SD*	*Average*	*SD*	*Average*	*SD*		
Log. GDP per capita	375	8.729	0.603	8.507	0.571	8.862	0.601	9.360	7.485
Government social public expenditure (%GDP)	375	9.920	3.135	7.381	2.608	14.092	3.935	22.488	2.562
GFCF (%GDP)	297	20.446	4.754	19.603	4.475	17.705	2.819	40.632	11.687
OPEN (%GDP)	297	64.587	32.189	60.011	40.272	51.954	18.724	166.698	15.635
FDExp	256	23.416	14.313	25.755	13.668	19.104	14.699	46.650	1.111
PA	375	3.733	0.494	3.620	0.469	3.784	0.543	4.807	2.861
RLaw	375	3.144	0.645	3.200	0.647	3.131	0.625	4.849	2.255
RQ	375	3.562	0.603	3.695	0.587	3.474	0.561	5.042	2.240
PS	375	3.261	0.650	3.191	0.701	3.368	0.506	4.588	1.124
GovEffec	375	3.350	0.522	3.433	0.596	3.310	0.467	4.838	2.386
Corr	375	3.260	0.711	3.237	0.789	3.190	0.762	5.043	2.063

Source: created by the authors.

Table 3 presents the results of the regression models specified in Equation 1 for the logarithm of GDP per capita as a function of sub-national public expenditure (% of general government public expenditure), the institutional variables (accountability, rule of law, and quality of regulation), the institutional variables in interaction with the sub-national expenditure variable, plus the control variables. The goodness of fit of the models is appreciable if we consider the significance of the variables and of the estimates in general.

Table 3. Logarithm of GDP per capita, fiscal decentralisation, and governance variables (accountability, rule of law, and regulatory quality) in interaction with the decentralisation variable. Random and fixed effects estimation were corrected for heteroskedasticity.

	Model 1. Random	Model 2. Fixed—Robust	Model 3. Fixed—Robust	Model 4 Fixed—Robust	Model 5 Fixed—Robust	Model 6 Fixed-Robust	Model 7 Fixed—Robust
GSP	0.040 *** (0.003)	−0.006 *** (0.001)	−0.0005 (0.004)	−0.004 (0.006)	0.003 (0.005)	0.027 *** (0.004)	0.018 *** (0.004)
GFCF	0.010 *** (0.003)	0.011 *** (0.003)	0.011 *** (0.003)	0.0001 *** (0.005)	0.006 (0.004)	−0.003 (0.005)	0.002 (0.006)
OPEN	−0.00004 (0.0009)	−0.006 *** (0.0007)	−0.006 *** (0.0008)	−0.006 *** (0.001)	−0.008 *** (0.0009)	−0.002 ** (0.001)	−0.004 *** (0.001)
FDExp	0.006 *** (0.002)	0.006 *** (0.001)	0.014 * (0.007)	0.007 *** (0.002)	0.087 *** (0.012)	0.006 *** (0.001)	0.101 *** (0.010)
PA		0.862 *** (0.027)	0.893 *** (0.040)				
FDExp * PA			0.011 *** (0.003)				
RLaw				0.570 *** (0.035)	0.858 *** (0.051)		
FDExp * RLaw					−0.025 *** (0.003)		
RQ						0.444 *** (0.001)	0.844 *** (0.064)
FDExp * RQ							−0.026 *** (0.002)
Constant	7.901 *** (0.197)	5.534 *** (0.131)	5.368 *** (0.188)	7.146 *** (0.110)	6.161 *** (0.188)	6.939 *** (0.133)	5.538 *** (0.227)
Wald (chi2)	38.96 ***	1602.95 ***	1606.96 ***	901.57 ***	1042.91 ***	555.69 ***	558.42 ***
Hausman	2.98	39.50 ***	11.29 *	19.95 ***	68.34 ***	19.72 ***	11.75 *
Homoskedasticity (Wald)	N/A	790.26 ***	733.35 ***	915.97 ***	812.01 ***	841.42 ***	827.17 ***

Note: Values in brackets are standard errors. Significant up to 1% (***), between 1% and 5% (**), and between 5% and 10% (*). N/A Not applicable. Source: created by the authors.

Model 1 includes only the control variables and the decentralisation variable. All control variables appear to be significant and with the expected sign, except for OPEN. This would indicate that, without considering the governance framework, public social spending, GFCF, and the level of sub-national spending may be explanatory variables for economic growth in Latin America in the period under study.

Models 2 and 3 include the institutional variable of citizen participation and accountability (PA) and its interaction with the decentralisation variable. The results suggest that fiscal decentralisation and especially the institutional variable of accountability promote economic growth (Model 2). The inclusion of the accountability variable maintains the coefficients and significance of the fiscal decentralisation variable, suggesting that there is no omitted variable bias with respect to the accountability variable.

Nonetheless, the role of accountability becomes clear when it interacts with fiscal decentralisation (Model 3). It had been argued that decentralisation could achieve better efficiency gains in the presence of better democratic quality. This expectation is supported by the fact that the interaction term between fiscal decentralisation and the participation and accountability variable is positive and statistically significant. Even the value of the coefficient could indicate that, in the case of Latin America, institutional conditions of accountability have promoted a greater positive impact of fiscal decentralisation.

These results provide evidence of how certain improvements in democratic conditions in Latin America in the period under study have been able to reinforce the positive effects of a certain level of fiscal decentralisation. It is noteworthy that of all the governance conditions analysed, accountability had the highest perception in the period under study, which would indicate the presence of certain conditions that promote the efficiency sought in fiscal decentralisation processes: public control over local public affairs, jurisdictions responsible for their competencies, and competitive local electoral processes. Accountability, or increased information about local government activities, has created incentives for elected officials and civil servants to reduce opportunistic behaviour and improve their performance, which has promoted better local services.

Models 4 and 5 include the institutional variable RLaw and its interaction with the decentralisation variable. The results again suggest that fiscal decentralisation and rule of law promote economic growth (Model 4). However, the role of the quality of RLaw modulates the effects of fiscal decentralisation differently from that of accountability. The negative and significant interaction term between decentralisation and RLaw (Model 5) indicates that, for Latin America, low trust and compliance with rules have limited the efficiency gains expected from decentralisation in relation to economic growth.

It may be that for Latin America, revenue and expenditure entitlements have not been correctly allocated to local authorities. Or it might be that the transfer systems, the main instrument of decentralisation in Latin America, are not very transparent, have poorly defined allocation criteria, or are not adapted to local conditions, which makes the general transfer system an unreliable set of rules or with a high component of discretion.

Models 6 and 7 include the institutional variable of regulatory quality (RQ) and its interaction with the decentralisation variable. The results again suggest that greater fiscal decentralisation and RQ promote economic growth (Model 6). However, the negative and significant interaction term between decentralisation and RQ (Model 7) indicates that, for Latin America, low government capacity to formulate and implement sound policies and regulations has made decentralisation processes harm economic growth.

This is an expected result that is in line with the findings on the interaction with the quality of the RLaw. It is evident that the regulatory quality of sub-national fiscal institutions has been low, which has hampered the potential efficiency gains of decentralisation processes. Such a regulation plays a key role in promoting fiscal discipline and stability, and hence, economic growth. Nevertheless, the processes may not have been adequately designed in consideration of the circumstances of each country or jurisdiction or may not adequately balance fiscal responsibilities between central and sub-national governments.

As seen in Table 4, models 8 and 9 include the institutional variable of political stability and its interaction with the decentralisation variable. The coefficients of Model 8 and their significance indicate that fiscal decentralisation and the perception of political stability promote economic growth, especially on the part of the institutional variable. However, the negative and significant interaction term between decentralisation and political stability (Model 9) indicates that political instability in Latin America has caused decentralisation processes to harm economic growth. Weak national or sub-national political institutions or the presence of politically motivated violence mean that further fiscal decentralisation has limited rather than promoted economic growth.

Table 4. Logarithm of GDP per capita, fiscal decentralisation, and governance variables in interaction with the decentralisation variable. Random and fixed effects estimation were corrected for heteroskedasticity.

	Model 8 Random	Model 9 Fixed—Robust	Model 10 Random	Model 11 Random	Model 12 Random	Model 13 Fixed—Robust
GSP	0.040 *** (0.003)	0.027 *** (0.006)	0.040 *** (0.003)	0.041 *** (0.003)	0.040 *** (0.003)	−0.001 (0.005)
GFCF	0.008 *** (0.003)	0.016 *** (0.005)	0.009 ** (0.003)	0.008 ** (0.003)	0.010 *** (0.003)	0.004 (0.004)
OPEN	0.0002 (0.0009)	−0.009 *** (0.011)	−0.00007 (0.0009)	0.0002 (0.001)	−0.0003 (0.0009)	−0.008 *** (0.0008)
FDExp	0.005 ** (0.002)	0.068 *** (0.008)	0.006 *** (0.002)	−0.003 (0.009)	0.006 *** (0.002)	0.111 *** (0.011)
PS	0.076 *** (0.002)	0.868 *** (0.063)				
FDExp ∗ PS		−0.018 *** (0.002)				
GovEffec			0.036 (0.047)	−0.016 (0.075)		
FDExp ∗ GovEffec				0.002 (0.002)		
Corr					−0.009 (0.045)	0.955 *** (0.052)
FDExp ∗ Corr						−0.032 *** (0.003)
Constant	7.671 *** (0.194)	5.629 *** (0.229)	7.801 *** (0.203)	7.963 *** (0.263)	7.935 *** (0.206)	5.836 *** (0.171)
Wald (chi2)	168.78 ***	571.36 ***	149.34 ***	146.56 ***	147.37 ***	1322.64 ***
Hausman	−12.50	45.66 ***	−13.59	−24.20	−44.05	250.61 ***
Homoskedasticity (Wald)	N/A	779.74 ***	N/A	N/A	N/A	390.16 ***

Note: Values in brackets are standard errors. Significant up to 1% (***), between 1% and 5% (**), and between 5% and 10% (*). N/A Not applicable. Source: created by the authors.

Models 10 and 11 include the institutional variable of government effectiveness (GovEffec)—i.e., the quality of public services and of public policy formulation and implementation—and its interaction with the decentralisation variable. The coefficients of Model 10 and their significance indicate that government effectiveness does not explain economic growth, while fiscal decentralisation retains its explanatory power. However, the non-significant term of the interaction between decentralisation and government effectiveness (Model 11) indicates that the low quality of public services in Latin America makes decentralisation processes less effective in terms of the overall efficiency of the economic system. This confirms what Cabrero Mendoza et al. (1997) established, that the administrative competencies of sub-national governments in Latin America have not been completely updated, which has nullified the expected efficiency effects of decentralisation.

Finally, Models 12 and 13 include the institutional variable of corruption perception (Corr) and its interaction with the decentralisation variable. The results suggest that corruption does not affect economic growth (Model 12). The inclusion of the corruption variable maintains the coefficients and significance of the fiscal decentralisation variable, suggesting that there is no omitted variable bias with respect to the corruption variable. However, the effect of controlling corruption becomes evident when interacting with fiscal decentralisation (Model 13). The interaction term between these variables is negative and statistically significant. This indicates that, given the level of corruption control in Latin America, decentralisation processes have hindered rather than boosted economic growth.

An overview of the estimated models shows that in all of them, the decentralisation variable appears positive and with a positive sign. Although it is accepted that the relationship between fiscal decentralisation and economic growth is complex and varies according to the context, in Latin America, our evidence shows that fiscal decentralisation can be a robust explanatory variable of economic growth in the long run. Greater autonomy may have promoted efficiency, the promotion of collective goods, and the utilisation of productive resources.

Nonetheless, what is also evident is that this relationship is negatively affected by the governance framework in which decentralisation takes place. Most of the governance variables in interaction with decentralisation appear significant and with a negative sign, except for accountability (which appears with a positive sign) and government effectiveness (which appears to be non-significant). This provides empirical evidence on how the governance framework, in most of its dimensions, modulates the possible effects of decentralisation in the region under analysis. If we stick to the value of the coefficients, we can identify corruption as the most determinant institutional factor in reducing the positive impact that decentralisation can have. This is followed by regulatory quality and rule of law.

4. Conclusions

As has been shown, there are many important theoretical and common-sense reasons to expect a productive relationship between decentralisation and the achievement of various social and economic outcomes. Nevertheless, these positive outcomes are linked to an appropriate institutional design and environment. Emphasising the institutional aspects of intergovernmental fiscal relations is, of course, not new. However, there has been a scarcity of empirical exploration into the role of the institutional environment in the success of decentralisation processes and specifically which institutional determinants matter and how they matter.

To help bridge this gap, the links between fiscal decentralisation (local spending as a % of general government spending) and economic growth have been explored for the Latin American case by considering six institutional factors that may determine the effectiveness and direction of this relationship. The structural variables included central government social public expenditure (% of GDP), gross fixed capital formation (% of GDP), and the openness of the economy, represented by the sum of imports and exports as a percentage of GDP. Several models integrating all of these variables were estimated using data from 15 developing countries for the years 1996 to 2020 by means of fixed or variable effects general least squares. Broadly speaking, the fit of the models is sufficient.

We independently estimated that fiscal decentralisation, accountability, rule of law, regulatory quality, and political stability are variables that positively and significantly explain economic growth in Latin America in the period under study. This is especially true for the institutional variables if we consider the value of their coefficients.

Nevertheless, when verifying their interaction, that is, when evaluating the effect of fiscal decentralisation on economic growth by considering the institutional variables at the same time, we obtained, in all cases, significant coefficients with a negative sign. In this way, it was firstly empirically proven that the institutional framework, regardless of the dimension considered, is always relevant in establishing the effects of a decentralisation process. Importantly, our evidence showed that any evaluation of decentralisation processes must consider the governance framework in which they have been developed. It does not seem possible to consider this without considering the overall public action structure in which it has evolved. The theoretical underpinning and the empirical evidence presented do not cast any doubt upon this.

Concerning the question of which rules matter, it is worth noting that the effect of interaction is not the same for all institutional conditionalities. Specifically, for Latin

America in the period under study, fiscal decentralisation has a greater positive impact if we consider the framework of democratic quality and accountability, which was the governance dimension that had the highest level of perception. In contrast, low levels of compliance with the rule of law and regulatory quality, political instability, or corruption not only hinder the positive results of fiscal decentralisation but also create negative results. In other words, considering the present level of these institutional factors, decentralisation has reduced rather than promoted economic growth.

Finally, it must be stressed that the level of government effectiveness, i.e., the quality of the bureaucracy and public services, eliminates the positive or negative effect that fiscal decentralisation may have on economic growth. This may confirm for the Latin American case what Murphy et al. (1991) or Prud'homme (1995) stated about how central bureaucracies attract more skilled people, while sub-national governments maintain a low-skilled workforce. If individuals with optimal qualifications are in short supply, it is difficult for sub-national governments to recruit and retain staff who are as qualified as central government personnel. Local talent shortages will undoubtedly hamper fiscal decentralisation efforts. The effectiveness of decentralisation processes is also hampered by cultural factors and a lack of adequate public expenditure management structures.

In this way and in terms of economic policy, the results and their possible interpretations point out the need for Latin America to make progress in improving local democracy and promote the strengthening of local capacities, developing municipal career systems, increasing subnational fiscal transparency, and promoting citizen participation mechanisms in budget decision-making. It would also be optimal to implement performance evaluation systems that measure the efficiency and effectiveness of public spending at the local level.

All these actions to strengthen subnational governments could constitute new lines of research, on more complex theoretical models to explain the mechanisms involved. It is also necessary to build more precise fiscal decentralisation indicators and contrast their effectiveness with respect to other institutional variables other than those used in this research.

Author Contributions: Conceptualization, D.E.P.-R.; methodology, D.E.P.-R. and P.H.-M.; software, P.H.-M.; validation, D.E.P.-R. and P.H.-M.; formal analysis, D.E.P.-R.; investigation, D.E.P.-R.; data curation, D.E.P.-R. and P.H.-M.; writing—original draft preparation, D.E.P.-R.; writing—review and editing, D.E.P.-R. and P.H.-M. All authors have read and agreed to the published version of the manuscript.

Funding: The authors confirm that this research received no external funding.

Informed Consent Statement: Not applicable.

Data Availability Statement: The original data presented in the study are openly available in IMF's Fiscal Decentralization Dataset at https://data.imf.org/ (accessed on 12 February 2024) and World Bank's Worldwide Governance Indicators | DataBank at https://databank.worldbank.org/source/worldwide-governance-indicators (accessed on 12 February 2024).

Conflicts of Interest: The authors declare no conflict of interest.

References

Ahmad, Ehtisham, and Giorgio Brosio. 2006. Introduction: Fiscal federalism—A review of developments in the literature and policy. In *Handbook of Fiscal Federalism*. Cheltenham: Edward Elgar Publishing.

Ahmad, Ehtisham, and Mercedes Garcia-Escribano. 2006. *Fiscal Decentralization and Public Subnational Financial Management in Peru*. Working Paper No. 2006/120. Washington, DC: International Monetary Fund.

Ahmad, Junait, Shantayanan Devarajan, Stuti Khemani, and Shekhar Shah. 2006. Decentralization and Service Delivery. In *Handbook of Fiscal Federalism*. Edited by E. Ahmad and G. Brossio. Gloucestershire: Edward Elgar Publishing.

Akai, Nobuo, and Masayo Sakata. 2002. Fiscal decentralization contributes to economic growth: Evidence from state-level cross-section data for the United States. *Journal of Urban Economics* 52: 93–108. [CrossRef]

Akpan, Eme O. 2011. Fiscal Decentralization and Social Outcomes in Nigeria European. *Journal of Business and Management* 3: 167–83.

Alesina, Alberto, Ricardo Hausmann, Rudolf Hommes, and Ernesto Stein. 1999. *Budget Institutions and Fiscal Performance in Latin America*. Working Paper 394. Washington, DC: Inter-American Development Bank (IADB).

Arif, Umaima, and Eatzaz Ahmad. 2020. A framework for analysing the impact of fiscal decentralization on macroeconomic performance, governance and economic growth. *The Singapore Economic Review* 65: 3–39. [CrossRef]

Atkinson, Sarah, and Dave Haran. 2004. Back to basics: Does decentralization improve health system performance? Evidence from Ceará in north-east Brazil. Bulletin of the World Health Organization. *The International Journal of Public Health* 82: 822–27.

Bahl, Roy W. 1999. *Implementation Rules for Fiscal Decentralization*. Working Paper No. 10. Atlanta: International Studies Program, School of Policy Studies, Georgia State University.

Baskaran, Thushyanthan, Lars P. Feld, and Jan Schnellenbach. 2016. Fiscal federalism, decentralization, and economic growth: A meta-analysis. *Economic Inquiry* 54: 1445–63. [CrossRef]

Bird, Richard M., and François Vaillancourt. 1998. Fiscal decentralization in developing countries: An overview. In *Fiscal Decentralization in Developing Countries*. Edited by Richard M. Bird and Francois Vaillancourt. New York: Cambridge University Press.

Blöchliger, Hansjörg, and Balázs Égert. 2013. *Decentralisation and Economic Growth—Part 2: The Impact on Economic Activity, Productivity and Investment*. OECD Working Papers on Fiscal Federalism, No. 15. Paris: OECD Publishing.

Bojanic, Antonio N. 2018. The Impact of Fiscal Decentralization on Growth, Inflation, and Inequality in the Americas. *Cepal Review* 124: 57–77. [CrossRef]

Burki, Shahid Javed, Guillermo E. Perry, and William R. Dillinger. 1999. *Beyond the Center, Decentralizing the STATE*. Washington, DC: World Bank.

Cabrero Mendoza, Eduardo, Laura Flamand Gómez, Claudia Santizo Rodall, and Alejandro Vega Godínez. 1997. Claroscuros del nuevo federalismo mexicano: Estrategias en la descentralización federal y capacidades en la gestión local. *Gestión y Política Pública* VI: 329–87.

Cabrero Mendoza, Enrique. 2004. Capacidades institucionales en gobiernos subnacionales de México ¿Un obstáculo para la descentralización fiscal? *Gestión y Política Pública* XIII: 753–84.

Campbell, Tim, George Peterson, and José Brakarz. 1991. *Decentralization in LAC: National Strategies and Local Response in Planning, Spending and Management*. LACTD Dissemination Note No. 5. Latin America and the Caribbean Technical Dept., Regional Studies Program. Washington, DC: World Bank.

Eckardt, Sebastian. 2008. Political accountability, fiscal conditions, and local government performance—Cross-sectional evidence from Indonesia. *Public Administration and Development* 28: 1–17. [CrossRef]

Enikolopov, Ruben, and Ekaterina Zhuravskaya. 2003. *Decentralization and Political Institutions*. Discussion Papers 3857. London: Center for Economic Policy Research (CEPR).

Feld, Lars P., Horts Zimmermann, and Thomas Döring. 2004. Federalism, decentralization, and economic growth (No. 2004, 30). In *Marburger Volkswirtschaftliche Beiträge, No. 2004, 30*. Marburg: Philipps-Universität Marburg, Fachbereich Wirtschaftswissenschaften.

Franzese, Robert J., Jr. 2002. *Macroeconomic Policies of Developed Democracies*. Ann Arbor: University of Michigan Press.

Gemmell, Norman, Richard Kneller, and Ismael Sanz. 2013. Fiscal decentralization and economic growth: Spending versus revenue decentralization. *Economic Inquiry* 51: 1915–31. [CrossRef]

González, Jorge Ivan. 1994. Un ordenamiento territorial de corte fiscalista, en A. Cifuentes Noyes (coord.). In *Diez años de descentralización, Resultados y perspectivas*. Bogotá: Fundación Friedrich Ebert de Colombia.

Grilli, Vittorio, Donato Masciandaro, and Guido Tabellini. 1991. Political and monetary institutions and public financial policies in the industrial democracies. *Economic Policy* 6: 341–92. [CrossRef]

Hanif, Imran, Sally Wallace, and Pilar Gago-de-Santos. 2020. Economic growth by means of fiscal decentralization: An empirical study for federal developing countries. *Sage Open* 10: 1–12. [CrossRef]

Hankla, Charles R. 2009. When is fiscal decentralization good for governance? *Publius: The Journal of Federalism* 39: 632–50. [CrossRef]

Hankla, Charles, and William Downs. 2010. Decentralization, Governance, and the Structure of Local Political Institutions: Lessons for Reform? *Local Government Studies* 36: 759–83. [CrossRef]

Hernandez-Trillo, Fausto, and Brenda Jarillo-Rabling. 2008. Is local beautiful? Fiscal decentralization in Mexico. *World Development* 36: 1547–58. [CrossRef]

Heywood, Peter, and Yoonjoung Choi. 2010. Health system performance at the district level in Indonesia after decentralization. *BMC International Health and Human Rights* 10: 3. [CrossRef]

Huther, Jeff, and Anwar Shah. 1998. *Applying a Simple Measure of Good Governance to the Debate on Fiscal Decentralization*. Policy Research Paper, 1894. Washington, DC: World Bank.

Iimi, Atsushi. 2005. Decentralization and economic growth revisited: An empirical note. *Journal of Urban Economics* 57: 449–61. [CrossRef]

James, K. S., Klaus Frohberg, Abay Asfaw, and Johannes P. Jütting. 2004. *Modeling the Impact of Fiscal Decentralization on Health Outcomes: Empirical Evidence from India*. ZEF Discussion Papers on Development Policy, No. 87. Bonn: University of Bonn, Center for Development Research (ZEF).

Jiménez, Rubio Dolores. 2011. The impact of fiscal decentralization on infant mortality rates: Evidence from OECD countries. *Social Science and Medicine* 73: 1401–7. [CrossRef]

Jin, Hehui, Yingyi Qian, and Barry R. Weingast. 1999. *Regional Decentralization and Fiscal Incentives: Federalism, Chinese Style*. Working Paper. Stanford: Hoover Institution, Stanford University.

Kaufmann, Daniel, Aart Kraay, and Massimo Mastruzzi. 2011. The worldwide governance indicators: Methodology and analytical issues. *Hague Journal on the Rule of Law* 3: 220–46. [CrossRef]

Khaleghian, Peyvand. 2003. *Decentralization and Public Services: The Case of Immunization*. World Bank Policy Research Working Paper no. 2989. Washington, DC: Development Research Group (DECRG) World Bank.

Kyriacou, Andreas P., Leonel Muinelo-Gallo, and Oriol Roca-Sagalés. 2015. Fiscal decentralization and regional disparities: The importance of good governance. *Papers in Regional Science* 94: 89–107. [CrossRef]

Lin, Justin Yifu, and Zhiqiang Liu. 2000. Fiscal decentralization and economic growth in China. *Economic Development and Cultural Change* 49: 1–21. [CrossRef]

Litvack, Jennie, Junaid Ahmad, and Richard Bird. 1998. *Rethinking Decentralization in Developing Countries (English)*. World Bank Sector Studies Series; Washington, DC: World Bank Group. Available online: http://documents.worldbank.org/curated/en/938101468764361146/Rethinking-decentralization-in-developing-countries (accessed on 12 February 2024).

Manor, James. 1999. *The Political Economy of Democratic Decentralization*. Washington, DC: The World Bank.

Martner, Ricardo. 2005. *Indicadores fiscales en América Latina y el Caribe. Documento preparado para la Reunión de la Red de Gestión y Transparencia de la Política Pública: Efectividad del Desarrollo y Gestión Presupuestaria por Resultados, mayo de 2005*. Washington, DC: Instituto Latinoamericano y del Caribe de Planificación Económica y Social (ILPES).

Mascareño, Carlos. 2009. Descentralización y democracia en América Latina, ¿una relación directa? Revisión conceptual del estado del arte. *Reforma y Democracia* 45: 63–98.

Murphy, Kevin M., Andrei Shleifer, and Robert W. Vishny. 1991. The allocation of talent: Implications for growth. *The Quarterly Journal of Economics* 106: 503–30. [CrossRef]

Nana, Nketcha. 2009. *Expenditure Decentralization and Outcomes: Some Determinant Factors for Success from Cross Country Evidence*. París: Economica.

Narayan, Deepa. 1998. Participatory rural development. In *Agriculture and the Environment: Perspectives on Sustainable Rural Development*. Edited by E. Lutz. Washington, DC: World Bank.

Nickson, Andrew. 2023. Decentralization in Latin America After 40 Years: Work in Progress; A Commentary Essay. *Public Organiz Rev* 23: 1017–34. [CrossRef]

Oates, Wallace. E. 1977. *Federalismo Fiscal*. Colección nuevo urbanismo. No. 25. Versión en ingles. Madrid: Instituto de Estudios de Administración Local.

Pinilla-Rodríguez, Diego. E., Juan de Dios Jiménez-Aguilera, and Roberto Montero-Granados. 2014. Descentralización fiscal en América Latina: Impacto social y determinantes. *Investigación Económica* 73: 79–110. [CrossRef]

Pinilla-Rodríguez, Diego. E., Juan de Dios Jiménez Aguilera, and Roberto Montero Granados. 2016. Descentralización fiscal y crecimiento económico. La experiencia reciente de América Latina. *Desarrollo y Sociedad* 77: 11–52. [CrossRef]

Ponce-Rodríguez, Raúl A., Charles R. Hankla, Jorge Martinez-Vazquez, and Eunice Heredia-Ortiz. 2020. The politics of fiscal federalism: Building a stronger decentralization theorem. *Journal of Theoretical Politics* 32: 605–39. [CrossRef]

Porto, Alberto, and Pablo Sanguinetti. 2001. Political determinants of intergovernmental grants: Evidence from Argentina. *Economics & Politics* 13: 237–56.

Prud'homme, Rémy. 1995. *On the Dangers of Decentralization*. Washington, DC: The World Bank Research Observer, vol. 10.

Qiao, Baoyun, Jorge Martinez-Vazquez, and Yongsheng Xu. 2008. The trade-off between growth and equity in decentralization policy: China's experience. *Journal of Development Economics* 86: 112–28. [CrossRef]

Restrepo, Juan Camilo. 2004. La segunda generación de las reformas descentralistas en América Latina. Paper presented at Conferencia Anual de Ejecutivos Competitividad y Desarrollo en la Democracia, Panamá City, Panamá, March 18–20.

Rezende, Fernando, and José Roberto Afonso. 2006. The Brazilian federation: Facts, challenges, and perspectives. In *Federalism and Economic Reform: International Perspectives*. Edited by Jessica Wallack and T. N. Srinivasan. Cambridge: Cambridge University Press, pp. 143–88.

Robalino, David A., Oscar F. Picazo, and Al Voetberg. 2001. *Does Fiscal Decentralization Improve Health Outcomes? Evidence from a Cross-Country Analysis*. Policy Research Working Paper 2565. Washington, DC: World Bank.

Rodden, Jonathan. 2003. Reviving Leviathan: Fiscal Federalism and the Growth of Government. *International Organization* 57: 695–729. [CrossRef]

Rodríguez-Pose, Andres, and Adala P. Bwire. 2005. La ineficiencia económica en los procesos de descentralización. *Ekonomiaz: Revista Vasca de Economía* 58: 146–75.

Roubini, Nouriel, and Jeffrey Sachs. 1989. *Government Spending and Budget Deficits: Industrial Democracies*. Working Paper 2919. Cambridge, MA: National Bureau of Economic Research.

Shah, Anwar. 1998. *Fiscal Federalism and Macroeconomic Governance: For Better or For Worse?* Washington, DC: World Bank.

Shah, Anwar. 2004. *Fiscal Decentralization in Developing and Transition Economies: Progress, Problems, and the Promise*. Washington, DC: World Bank Publications, vol. 3282.

Sharma, Chanchal Kumar. 2006. Decentralization Dilemma: Measuring the Degree and Evaluating the Outcome. *Indian Journal of Political Science* 67: 49–64.

Shleifer, Andrei, and Robert. W. Vishny. 1993. Corruption. *The Quarterly Journal of Economics* 108: 599–617. [CrossRef]

Stein, Ernesto, Ernesto Talvi, and Alejandro Grisanti. 1998. Institutional arrangements and fiscal performance: The Latin American experience. In *Fiscal Institutions and Fiscal Performance*. Chicago: University of Chicago Press, pp. 103–34.

Stein, Robert. M. 1999. Devolution and challenge for state and local governance. In *American State and Local Politics: Directions for the 21st Century*. Edited by Ronald E. Weber and Paul Brace. New York: Chatham House, pp. 21–37.

Tanzi, Vito. 1995. Fiscal federalism and decentralization: A review of some efficiency and macroeconomic aspects. In *Annual World Bank Conference on Development Economics 1995*. Edited by Michael Bruno and Boris Pleskovic. Washington, DC: World Bank, pp. 295–316.

Uchimura, Hiroko, and Johannes. P. Jütting. 2009. Fiscal Decentralization, Chinese Style: Good for Health Outcomes? *World Development* 37: 1926–34. [CrossRef]

Voigt, Stefan, and Lorenz Blume. 2012. The economic effects of federalism and decentralization—A cross-country assessment. *Public Choice* 151: 229–54. [CrossRef]

Xie, Danyang, Heng-fu Zou, and Hamid Davoodi. 1999. Fiscal decentralization and economic growth in the United States. *Journal of Urban Economics* 45: 228–39. [CrossRef]

economies

MDPI

Article

Technological Innovation and Agricultural Productivity in Nigeria Amidst Oil Transition: ARDL Analysis

Joel T. Adeyemo [1], Adel Ahmed [2], Dominic T. Abaver [3], Hosam Alden Riyadh [4], Mosab I. Tabash [5] and Adedoyin Isola Lawal [1,*]

[1] Department of Economics, Bowen University, Iwo 23401, Nigeria; joel.adeyemo@bowen.edu.ng
[2] Amity Business School, Amity University Dubai, Dubai International Academic City, Dubai P.O. Box 345019, United Arab Emirates; aahmed1@amityuniversity.ae
[3] Department of Laboratory Medicine and Pathology, School of Medicine, Faculty of Medicine and Health Sciences, Walter Sisulu University, Eastern Cape 5117, South Africa; dabaver@wsu.ac.za
[4] Department of Accounting, School of Economics and Business, Telkom University, Bandung 40257, Indonesia; hussam_19860@yahoo.com
[5] Department of Business Administration, College of Business, Al Ain University, Al Ain P.O. Box 64141, United Arab Emirates; mosab.tabash@aau.ac.ae
* Correspondence: adedoyin.lawal@bowen.edu.ng or l.adedoyin@yahoo.com; Tel.: +234-8035233567

Abstract: In contemporary discourse, Nigeria's reliance on its oil sector is proving insufficient for sustained economic growth. The volatility of oil prices, geopolitical tensions, technological advancements, and environmental sustainability concerns have exposed the vulnerabilities of an oil-dependent economy, emphasizing the need for diversification and a renewed focus on agriculture. This study investigates the relationship between technological innovation and agricultural productivity in Nigeria, contrasting it with the oil sector. Using the ARDL estimation technique, our findings reveal a significant negative influence of immediate lagged agricultural productivity (AGTFP(−1)), indicating technological constraints. Technological innovation, proxied by TFP, shows a substantial impact on agricultural productivity, with a negative long-term effect (−90.71) but a positive, though insignificant, impact on agricultural output (0.0034). The comparative analysis underscores that the agricultural sector tends to benefit more from technological innovation than the oil sector. This highlights the critical need to prioritize technological advancements in agriculture to drive sustainable growth and economic resilience in Nigeria.

Keywords: technological innovation; agricultural productivity; oil; ARDL; Nigeria

1. Introduction

In contemporary discourse, it is evident that Nigeria's once-thriving oil sector is insufficient for ensuring sustained economic growth (Ben Salem et al. 2022; Tabe-Ojong et al. 2023). The previous belief that oil was the key to national prosperity has given way to a harsh reality: relying heavily on oil revenues cannot guarantee long-term stability and development. This shift is driven by several challenges, among which are price volatility, geopolitical tensions, technological advancements, and the call for environmental sustainability (Chatziantoniou et al. 2021; Lawal et al. 2015; Ben Salem et al. 2022; Jacal et al. 2022). As highlighted by Yilanci et al. (2021), the susceptibility of oil-dependent economies like Nigeria to global market fluctuations emphasizes the necessity for diversification, emphasizing the revival of the nation's original economic backbone—agriculture—as an increasingly imperative course of action.

The ascent of non-fossil-fuel technologies further looms as an ominous specter over Nigeria, an economy intricately tethered to its oil sector. Precise projections and compelling statistics accentuate the gravity of this impending dilemma. The International Energy Agency (IEA)'s World Energy Outlook predicts an exponential growth trajectory for electric vehicles (EVs), estimating that by 2030, global EV sales could reach a staggering 250 million. This seismic shift threatens to eviscerate the demand for traditional hydrocarbon fuels, and for Nigeria, a prominent oil exporter, the ramifications are dire. The Nigerian National Petroleum Corporation (NNPC) underscores this concern, projecting a conspicuous decline in crude oil demand as nations galvanize their commitment to cleaner energy alternatives. The traditional modus operandi of oil extraction and exploration, reliant on outdated technologies, is proving to be steadily costly and environmentally detrimental (Jacal et al. 2022). The emergence of advanced drilling techniques, the rise of electric vehicles, and the global push for decarbonization have collectively led to a decreased global appetite for oil, rendering Nigeria's oil-centric economy progressively precarious (Kayode et al. 2022; Djoumessi 2022). Adding to the fray is the plummeting cost of renewable energy technologies; solar energy costs, for instance, have diminished by over 80% since 2010, setting the stage for a pivotal transition away from fossil fuels. Reflecting this transformative trajectory, the International Renewable Energy Agency (IRENA) estimates that renewable capacity could surge by 50% globally by 2030. In this shifting landscape, Nigeria's entrenched dependency on oil could precipitate an economic abyss, necessitating a paradigm shift towards diversification, innovation, and a resurgent focus on sectors like agriculture.

Interestingly, while technological evolution casts a shadow of uncertainty over Nigeria's oil sector, it also ushers in a promising era of prosperity for Nigeria's agriculture industry. This transformative shift can be a beacon not only for Nigeria but for the entirety of Africa (Tabe-Ojong et al. 2023). The convergence of cutting-edge technologies, from precision agriculture to data-driven decision-making, holds the potential to encourage large-scale farming and unlock the latent possibilities of agriculture (Adeagbo et al. 2023). For Nigeria, where a significant portion of the population is engaged in farming, innovative tools such as smart sensors, drone-assisted crop monitoring, and digital platforms for market access can catalyze a modern agricultural revolution. These advancements not only enhance productivity but also mitigate the challenges of climate change, enabling more efficient water usage and soil management (Mandal et al. 2022; Balana and Oyeyemi 2022; Ejem et al. 2023). Technology-driven agriculture has the potential to uplift smallholder farmers, a cornerstone of Nigeria's agrarian landscape, by elevating their access to vital resources and markets, ultimately fostering sustainable rural development (Etuk and Ayuk 2021; Akinola et al. 2023).

Before the oil boom of the 1970s, Nigeria's economy was predominantly driven by its agricultural sector. In the 1960s, agriculture accounted for nearly 50% of government revenue, 65% of GDP, and over 80% of export earnings. However, over time, the significance of agriculture to Nigeria's economic growth has diminished, with agriculture contributing approximately 26.84% to the GDP in 2021. This decline in agricultural contributions has negatively impacted the welfare of low-income earners. Additionally, the recent decline in global oil prices has raised concerns about the sustainability of the country's economy (Ojo and Baiyegunhi 2023).

Uji (2020) highlights corruption as a major issue affecting development in many developing nations, including Nigeria. The agricultural sector, a key component of national development, is significantly hindered by corruption, despite government efforts to enhance agricultural production through projects and research institutes (Sarimiento 2000). This challenge has led to diminished agricultural output, limiting Nigeria's potential despite its rich resources (Ani and Nuhu 2010). Although measures like the Economic and Financial Crimes Commission (EFCC), the Independent Corrupt Practices Commission (ICPC), and Nigerian Transparency International have been established to combat corruption, the issue persists, partly due to the involvement of those meant to fight it (Uji 2020; Abah et al. 2024). This entrenched corruption continues to undermine efforts to revitalize the agricultural sector and, by extension, the overall development of the country.

Over the years, Nigeria's agricultural sector has undergone several reform efforts, starting with initiatives like Operation Feed the Nation, the Structural Adjustment Program for agriculture, and the Green Revolution. The most recent initiative, the Agricultural Transformation Agenda (ATA), was introduced by the government around 2015 to modernize the sector through the promotion of digital technologies (Federal Ministry of Agriculture and Rural Development (FMARD) 2015). As part of this agenda, grassroots farmers were provided with free mobile phones to facilitate their participation in e-agriculture. Although the concept of e-agriculture was initially unfamiliar to many farmers, its growing acceptance was driven by the convenience it offered, such as the delivery of fertilizers and farming tools through digital means.

To further support this transition, the National Information Technology Development Agency (NITDA) established an e-portal to help farmers leverage digital tools for better productivity (National Information Technology Development Agency (NITDA) 2015). However, despite these advancements, many farmers remained unaware of the portal and its potential benefits, resulting in underutilization of the available resources. Adoption of e-agriculture before the year 2000 was notably slow, as the technology and its applications were poorly understood by the farming community (Mwangi and Kariuki 2015; Eweoya et al. 2021). Thus, while there have been efforts to modernize farming practices, there is still much work to be done to ensure widespread awareness and adoption of digital solutions for agricultural development in Nigeria.

In tandem with these challenges, the COVID-19 pandemic has also exacerbated vulnerabilities in Nigeria's oil sector, notably in the oil industry itself (Chiaramonti and Maniatis 2020; Valadkhani et al. 2021). Ongoing geopolitical tensions between Russia and Ukraine have further heightened the situation, causing an unprecedented surge in crude oil prices. The apprehensions of major oil-importing nations that conflict could disrupt global oil markets led to pre-emptive actions, propelling oil prices to a 14-year peak of USD 140 per barrel on 7 March 2022. Russia, contributing about 14% of global production, grapples with these ramifications. For Nigeria, heavily reliant on oil exports, escalating oil prices due to geopolitical turmoil offer temporary relief but do not resolve deeper sectoral issues. The global oil market's volatility, coupled with shifts to renewable energy sources, underscores Nigeria's fragile oil revenue dependency (Ben Salem et al. 2022).

Rapid population growth exacerbates food insecurity in Nigeria, with predictions indicating a population of 400 million by 2050, emphasizing the urgent need to address this issue for improved food security (Otekunrin et al. 2019; Amzat et al. 2020). This aligns with the African Union's Malabo Declaration, underscoring the vital role of agriculture in achieving inclusive growth and food security across the continent by 2025. The exponential growth of mobile technology penetration in Africa, as indicated by the International Telecommunication Union (ITU), paves the way for digital platforms to reach even the most remote farming communities, providing them with critical information on weather patterns, market prices, and best agricultural practices. The success stories from countries like Kenya, where mobile payment systems have revolutionized small-scale farming, inspire optimism for Africa's agricultural future (Parlasca et al. 2022; Andati et al. 2023). Thus, as suggested in the research of Rongjian et al. (2019) and Djoumessi (2022), technological innovations have the potential to leapfrog traditional barriers, amplifying agricultural productivity and forging a sustainable development trajectory for both Nigeria and the broader African continent.

Nigeria stands at a pivotal juncture as it grapples with the challenges posed by its heavy dependence on the volatile oil sector. The vulnerabilities inherent in relying on oil revenues for economic stability have become increasingly evident, necessitating a crucial shift back to the agricultural sector, historically the nation's economic backbone (Eleke et al. 2019; Yilanci et al. 2021). While existing literature has extensively examined the effects of technological practices on various aspects of agriculture, such as output, crop yields, food security, and economic development in certain regions of Nigeria, Africa, and around the world (Olayide et al. 2016; Balana and Oyeyemi 2022; Djoumessi 2022; Edafe et al.

2023; Ejem et al. 2023; Wang and Qian 2024), there has been limited focus on agricultural productivity, particularly within Nigeria. Furthermore, few studies have delved into the potential trade-offs between the oil and agricultural sectors based on technological progress. As such, there is a noticeable gap in the literature, highlighting the imperative for an investigation into the aggregate impact of technological innovation on agricultural productivity in the country.

Given the precarious state of the Nigerian economy and the significant role the agricultural sector plays in sustaining growth, it is crucial to meticulously examine and measure the intricate relationship between technological innovation and agricultural productivity. Therefore, this study seeks to understand the nature of the relationship between technological innovation and agricultural productivity in Nigeria, assess the impact of agricultural innovation on agricultural output, and compare the effects of technological innovation on the oil and agricultural sectors within Nigeria's context. To address these objectives, the study will be guided by the following research questions: What is the relationship between technological innovation and agricultural productivity in Nigeria? How does agricultural innovation affect agricultural output in Nigeria? How do the effects of technological innovation differ between the oil and agricultural sectors in Nigeria? This implies conducting a national analysis, a sectoral analysis, and a comparative analysis between the two sectors. Anchored on the Solow–Swan Growth model, the study will utilize the Autoregressive Distributed Lag (ARDL) model for estimation. This thorough exploration is essential for providing valuable insights and guiding strategic decisions aimed at strengthening agricultural technology. By doing so, we can enhance growth and food security not only in Nigeria but also extend the positive impact across Africa.

2. Empirical Review

An in-depth examination of the extant literature underscores the enduring importance of the nexus between technological innovation and agricultural growth, especially in the Nigerian economy. In the ever-evolving landscape of agriculture, technology has emerged as a transformative force, capable of shaping the trajectory of productivity, food security, and economic progress in Nigeria.

This literature review is organized into four distinct strands. The first strand explored the dynamic intersections between energy considerations and agriculture. From mechanization to the adoption of renewable energy, this section uncovered the varied ways in which technological innovations affect efficiency, yield, and the overall agricultural landscape. Transitioning to the second strand, we delved into the connection between climate change and technological agricultural practices, as it brings to light how innovative solutions contribute to adaptive and resilient farming techniques.

Furthermore, the third strand addressed the foundational elements of agriculture: land and soil-related issues. Here, we dissected the effects of technological interventions on soil selection and sustainable land management with the aim of underpinning their crucial role in influencing overall productivity. Lastly, the fourth strand placed governmental and non-governmental agriculture programs into focus. Through an examination of their design, implementation, and outcomes, the review sought to unravel the collective impact of technological innovation on large-scale agricultural initiatives.

2.1. *Energy Diversification and Agricultural Development*

Nigeria's economy faces challenges stemming from its heavy dependence on the oil sector, a vulnerability that has been underscored by external crises. Recognizing the need for diversification, there is a growing emphasis on revitalizing the agricultural industry, which historically served as the country's backbone (Eleke et al. 2019). Aye and Odhiambo (2021) conducted a threshold analysis to identify critical tipping points where fluctuations in oil prices negatively impact agricultural growth. Their findings underscored the importance of reducing reliance on fossil fuels in the agricultural sector to enhance energy and food security, especially in contexts like that of South Africa, where oil reserves are not as abundant, rendering the economy vulnerable to external shocks.

While the threshold analysis provides valuable insights, one of its weaknesses lies in its reliance on predetermined thresholds, which can be arbitrary and subjective. In a related study, Olujobi et al. (2023) delved into the availability of low-carbon energy sources in Nigeria to ensure a reliable electricity supply and foster industrial sustainability. Their research included a comparative analysis of legal frameworks for low-carbon energy adoption in China, Spain, Germany, and Nigeria. The study highlighted the importance of establishing robust legal structures that leverage Nigeria's abundant renewable energy resources to maximize low-carbon energy adoption, drawing insights from the legal frameworks of other countries.

Furthermore, Aworunse et al. (2023) conducted exploratory research on the prospects of building a sustainable bioeconomy in Nigeria. They identified biomass energy as a promising avenue for fostering resilience in the bioeconomy, driven by environmental concerns, climate change, municipal solid waste management, and the imperative of energy diversification (Okafor et al. 2022). These studies collectively underscore the importance of transitioning towards sustainable energy sources, such as low-carbon and biomass energy, to mitigate environmental impacts, enhance energy security, and promote economic resilience in Nigeria's agricultural sector.

2.2. Climate Change, Technology, and Food Security

Rongjian et al. (2019) conducted a comprehensive review across three distinct economic contexts—China, Pakistan, and Nigeria—revealing contrasting scenarios in agricultural technological advancements. While China has made strides in introducing technological innovations to enhance agriculture, Pakistan, despite being agriculturally self-sufficient, has harnessed such advances effectively. In stark contrast, Nigeria, despite its vast farmland endowment, lags due to backwardness in agricultural technology. Weak institutional support, a deficient educational system, brain drain, underfunded educational systems, and inadequate infrastructure were identified as significant barriers hindering technological advancements in Nigeria (Balana and Oyeyemi 2022; Edafe et al. 2023). Notably, communication emerged as a major obstacle to agricultural innovations among rural farmers in Nigeria, prompting Ejem et al. (2023) to advocate for a more effective two-way communication approach within Nigeria's extension system to disseminate global agricultural practices.

In Sub-Saharan Africa, Djoumessi (2022) employed the stochastic frontier analysis (SFA) to unveil positive and statistically significant production elasticity regarding land, capital, and machinery, while labor appeared insignificantly positive. This finding seemingly contradicts the region's labor-intensive agricultural practices, potentially influenced by the SFA estimation approach's functional-form choices, which could impact the analysis's robustness and interpretation. Conversely, Amare and Balana (2023) underscored climate change's adverse impact on agricultural productivity and farmers' revenue distribution. However, Olayide et al. (2016) and Tabe-Ojong et al. (2023) showcased climate-smart agriculture (CSA)'s effectiveness in mitigating climate change's adverse effects, thereby enhancing crop yields and promoting food security. Awolala et al. (2023) delved into weather and climate-information consumption, estimating a significant market value in Nigeria. They identified institutional and socioeconomic conditions as pivotal determinants of climate change-adaptation technologies. Moreover, factors such as performance expectancy, effort expectancy, and social effort were found to influence the usage intention of adopting e-agriculture (Adeagbo et al. 2023; Eweoya et al. 2021; Babatunde et al. 2021).

Isukuru et al. (2023) explored bamboo's ecological benefits, highlighting its renewable nature and versatility across various sectors, including construction and paper production. Bamboo's ability to grow in diverse climatic conditions and soil types positions it as an effective tool for erosion control and soil conservation, contributing significantly to climate-change mitigation. Conservation efforts in agriculture were also emphasized by Kolapo and Kolapo (2023), who employed multinomial endogenous switching regression (MESR) models to underscore the importance of conservation practices in mitigating climate change and enhancing crop productivity. They identified gender, age, farm size and experience, formal education, access to extension services, and association membership as significant factors influencing the adoption of conservation agricultural practices and crop yields among farmers.

Studies focusing on smallholder farmers highlighted the pivotal role of improved practices and ICT in enhancing income distributions and value-chain processes, reducing gender disparities, ensuring food security, influencing consumption patterns, and driving economic growth (Ayanwale et al. 2023; Matthew et al. 2023; Ndaghu et al. 2023; Melesse et al. 2023; Eke et al. 2019). Melesse et al. (2023) employed endogenous switching regression models to assess the relationship between improved groundnut varieties and household food security, demonstrating that adoption increases groundnut consumption and reduces vulnerability to food insecurity. Similarly, Ayanwale et al. (2023) utilized instrumental variable quantile treatment effects (IV-QTEs) to examine the distributional effects of improved practices adoption on the income of smallholder maize farmers, revealing significant influences on revenue distributions, particularly among impoverished households. Matthew et al. (2023) identified farmgate collectors as pivotal actors in the agricultural value chain, with ICT deployment significantly impacting their roles. Ogunsolu (2021) explored the potential impact of digitizing the Nigerian agricultural industry, offering insights into its ability to remedy economic recessions, albeit with sustainability concerns. Moreover, technological adoption exhibited varied effects in Africa, with factors such as data availability, region, model specification, and sample size identified as being responsible for such variations (Habtewold and Heshmati 2023).

2.3. Sustainable Land Management and Agricultural Productivity

The study conducted by Kayode et al. (2022) investigated the relationship between soil parameters and agricultural productivity, focusing on a commercial farm in Omu-Aran, Nigeria. Utilizing vertical electrical sounding (VES) and 2D resistivity inversion models, the research revealed the prevalence of gravelly and sandy soils within the area. The findings suggest potential challenges related to soil quality that could impact agricultural productivity. In response to identified nutrient deficiencies, the authors recommended regular fertilization practices as a means to enhance soil fertility and ultimately improve agricultural productivity (Kianguebene-Koussingounina et al. 2023). These recommendations align with the broader consensus within agricultural research regarding the importance of soil management practices, such as fertilization, in optimizing crop yields and ensuring sustainable agricultural development.

Maertens et al. (2023) further support the significance of site-specific nutrient management (SSNM), particularly in soil fertilization, for fostering gradual and sustainable agricultural development in Nigeria. Their research emphasizes the importance of tailored approaches to soil fertility management, considering the specific needs and characteristics of individual agricultural sites. By implementing SSNM practices, farmers can optimize nutrient use efficiency, minimize environmental impacts, and achieve more sustainable increases in agricultural productivity over the long term. These findings contribute to a growing body of literature highlighting the potential for a more gradual and sustainable intensification of smallholder agriculture in Sub-Saharan Africa (SSA), in contrast to the rapid intensification observed during the Asian Green Revolution. The emphasis on increased fertilizer use accompanied by improved fertilizer management underscores the importance of precision agriculture techniques in optimizing resource utilization and promoting sustainable agricultural growth in the region.

Mandal et al. (2022) conducted a study employing 300 paired soil and rice plants, which identified Bisalayi as the most suitable rice type for cultivation on polluted farmlands in Nigeria. This finding sheds light on potential solutions for addressing agricultural challenges in areas affected by land pollution, offering insights into crop-resilience and -adaptation strategies. Furthermore, Adenle et al. (2022) revealed that human activities, migration, and land tenure issues significantly contribute to land degradation in the country. Understanding these underlying factors is crucial for implementing effective land management policies and practices to mitigate degradation and ensure sustainable agricultural development.

On a positive note, the maize sector in Nigeria has experienced notable improvements in productivity over recent decades. Wossen et al. (2023) attributed this growth to tailored policies and institutional arrangements that promote access to modern inputs and expand markets for maize grain. Additionally, the surge in productivity is further explained by the adoption of improved maize varieties (IMVs), crop diversification (CD), and sustainable land management practices (SLMPs), as demonstrated by studies conducted by Baiyegunhi et al. (2022) and Kolapo et al. (2022). These findings underscore the importance of policy support and agricultural innovations in driving productivity gains in staple crops like maize, contributing to food security and economic development in the country.

However, challenges persist in ensuring widespread adoption of sustainable agricultural practices (SAPs) across communities. Oyetunde-Usman et al. (2021) found that household head characteristics, including size, wealth status, education, gender, and access to extension services, collectively influence the adoption of multiple SAPs. This highlights the need for targeted interventions and capacity-building efforts to promote sustainable farming methods among diverse farming households. In contrast, Edafe et al. (2023) demonstrated that communities with land investments have a lower probability of achieving food security compared to those without land investments, pointing to potential trade-offs between land ownership and food security outcomes that warrant further investigation and policy consideration.

2.4. Agricultural Programs and Gender-Based Disparities

Etuk and Ayuk (2021) conducted a comprehensive analysis using various poverty measures to evaluate the impact of the Commercial Agricultural Development Project (CADP) in Nigeria. Employing the Average Treatment effect on the Treated (ATT), Foster–Greer–Thorbecke (FGT) poverty measures, and the Poverty Equivalent Growth Rate (PEGR) pro-poor measure, their study revealed that CADP effectively mitigates poverty and substantially enhances commercialization, particularly benefiting its beneficiaries. The research highlighted that almost 43% of the sample data consisted of non-beneficiaries who experienced lesser improvements. As a result, the authors emphasized the importance of ensuring that development intervention programs effectively target the poor, stressing the need for focused efforts to address poverty alleviation.

Akinola et al. (2023) delved into the factors influencing tomato yields in rural Nigeria, uncovering the significant impact of membership in agricultural cooperatives under equal circumstances. Their findings underscored the pivotal role of cooperative membership in enhancing agricultural productivity, particularly in the tomato sector. However, Balana and Oyeyemi (2022) shed light on a major obstacle faced by smallholder farmers: insufficient collateral hindering their access to necessary credit facilities for adopting agricultural technologies and improving yields. This highlights the need for supportive policies and financial mechanisms tailored to the specific needs of smallholder farmers to facilitate their adoption of modern agricultural practices.

In a related context, Ikuemonisan et al. (2022) explored the determinants influencing individuals' decisions to pursue a career in agribusiness. Their study identified teaching quality, learning environment, and course difficulty as significant factors shaping individuals' career choices in the agricultural sector. Conversely, Bello et al. (2021) found gender disparities among rice farmers, with men outperforming women by 11%. Furthermore, Ojo and Baiyegunhi (2023) identified key drivers of gender inequality in agricultural productivity, including marital status, farm size, education, and market access. These studies collectively underscore the multifaceted nature of challenges and opportunities within the agricultural sector, highlighting the importance of addressing systemic barriers and promoting inclusive policies to foster sustainable agricultural development.

2.5. Theoretical Review of Literature

This study examines a few relevant theories, offering an analysis of those deemed most pertinent. However, the primary theory underpinning this research is the Solow–Swan growth model due to its emphasis on technological progress, capital accumulation, and long-run equilibrium analysis, all of which align closely with the research objectives. This model provides a robust framework for understanding how technological advancements contribute to sustained growth in the agricultural sector.

2.5.1. Solow–Swan Growth Model

The Solow–Swan Growth (SSG) model, formulated by Robert Solow and Trevor Swan during the 1950s and 1960s, stands as a fundamental concept in economic theory. It extends the Harrod–Domar model by incorporating labor as a factor of production and allowing for variable capital-output ratios. The model aims to elucidate the factors driving long-term economic growth, emphasizing the contributions of capital accumulation and technological progress (Solow 1956).

At its core, the SSG model posits that economic growth is a function of increases in capital (both physical and human) and technological advancements. Mathematically, this can be expressed as follows:

$$Y = f(K, H, A, L)$$

where Y represents output or GDP, K denotes the stock of physical capital, H represents the stock of human capital, A signifies technological progress or total factor productivity (TFP), and L denotes the labor force.

In the absence of technological breakthroughs, the model predicts that economies will eventually reach a steady state where further accumulation of capital ceases to significantly impact growth. Mathematically, this steady state can be represented by the following condition:

$$sY = (n + \delta)K$$

where s denotes the savings rate, n represents the rate of population growth, and δ signifies the depreciation rate of capital.

Technological progress, considered an external force, becomes imperative for breaking out of this equilibrium and achieving sustained economic growth (Frey 2017). Endogenous growth theory further extends the Solow model by emphasizing the role of knowledge and human capital (Romer 1990). It posits that technological advancements are endogenously determined by factors such as research and development (R&D) investments, and human capital is considered a critical driver of growth.

Critics argue that endogenous growth theory lacks empirical evidence and may not fully explain observed growth patterns. Additionally, convergence theory suggests that poorer countries tend to catch up with richer ones over time. Empirical studies, however, have found mixed evidence regarding convergence, with some countries converging while others diverging. Critics argue that convergence may not occur uniformly due to differences in institutions, policies, and technological adoption.

The Solow model's assumptions about exogenous technological growth have also been challenged by economists like Robert Gordon, who argue that the pace of technological progress has slowed significantly. Gordon's thesis suggests that recent technological advancements may not be as impactful as transformative innovations of the past (Gordon

2012). Critics highlight the importance of institutions and policy frameworks in shaping economic growth, factors which the Solow model abstracts from.

The relevance of this model to the study of technological innovation's impact on agricultural productivity in Nigeria lies in its recognition of the transformative potential of technological progress. While initial investments in capital, such as modern machinery and infrastructure, may yield short-term gains in agricultural productivity, the model suggests that the sustained impact comes from exogenous technological innovation (Olayide et al. 2016; Tabe-Ojong et al. 2023). This implies that for long-term and sustained growth in the agricultural sector in Nigeria, the adoption of cutting-edge technologies like precision farming, genetic modifications, and data-driven decision-making is paramount.

In summary, the SSG model offers a solid theoretical foundation for understanding the interplay between technological progress, capital accumulation, and economic growth. Applied to agriculture, it highlights the crucial role of technological innovation in enhancing productivity and achieving sustainable agricultural practices, making it a pertinent guide for examining the impact of technological innovation on agricultural productivity in Nigeria.

2.5.2. Endogenous Growth Theory

The endogenous growth theory (EGT) represents a significant advancement in economic thought, addressing limitations observed in traditional models such as the neoclassical growth theory. Unlike conventional viewpoints that attribute growth solely to external factors, EGT redirects attention towards internal elements within an economy, particularly emphasizing the significance of human capital, innovation, and knowledge in propelling long-term growth (Romer 1990). In contrast to the perspective that regards technological advancements as externally driven forces, EGT asserts that purposeful activities within an economy, such as research and development, serve as primary drivers of technological innovation, thereby fueling economic growth (Romer 1987; Latzer et al. 2019). It places crucial emphasis on human capital—the skills, knowledge, and expertise possessed by individuals—arguing that investments in education and training play a pivotal role in fostering economic growth by enhancing productivity and stimulating innovation.

Human capital augmented endogenous growth theory further emphasizes the role of human capital accumulation in driving long-term economic growth. Developed by Lucas (1988), Romer (1990), and others, this theory posits that investments in education, training, and skills development can enhance labor productivity, technological innovation, and overall economic performance. The mathematical representation of this theory can be depicted by the following production function:

$$Y = A(K, H)F(L, E)$$

where Y represents output or GDP, A denotes total factor productivity (TFP), which captures technological progress and efficiency, K denotes physical capital, H represents human capital, L denotes labor input, E represents the level of technology, and F is the production function indicating the relationship between inputs and output.

The inclusion of human capital (H) as a determinant of output reflects the key tenet of human capital augmented endogenous growth theory, emphasizing the importance of education and knowledge accumulation in fostering economic growth.

Another supporting theory of endogenous growth is based on the idea of innovation and technological spillovers. Pioneered by Romer (1990), Grossman and Helpman (1991), and Aghion and Howitt (1992), this theory argues that technological progress can be driven by knowledge spillovers and externalities arising from innovation activities. The mathematical formulation of this theory often involves incorporating a knowledge production function, where technological progress is endogenously determined by investments in research and development (R&D), knowledge creation, and diffusion processes. One such representation is given by the following:

$$A^{\cdot} = \gamma \cdot A(K, H) \cdot R$$

where $A^{\cdot}$ represents the rate of technological progress, γ denotes the effectiveness of R&D investments, $A(K, H)$ represents the level of TFP, and R denotes R&D expenditure.

This formulation highlights the self-sustaining nature of technological progress, where investments in R&D lead to the creation of new knowledge and innovations, which, in turn, drive further economic growth.

Critics of EGT often target its reliance on the assumption of increasing returns to scale, commonly utilized in models like that of Romer (1990) and Lucas (1988) to generate sustained endogenous growth. They argue that this assumption may lack empirical support in many industries and could lead to unrealistic predictions about the long-term behavior of the economy. Additionally, the presence of increasing returns to scale might exacerbate income inequality and market distortions, undermining market efficiency and potentially impeding economic growth. Consequently, proponents of alternative theories, such as neoclassical growth theory, highlight the importance of diminishing returns to scale in driving convergence to steady-state levels of output per capita.

While EGT extends its relevance to various sectors, including agriculture, where intentional technological advancements enhance practices, its application serves as a secondary focus in this research. EGT provides a comprehensive framework for understanding economic growth dynamics, particularly within agriculture, emphasizing the role of innovation and human capital. By employing EGT as a guide, this study aims to delve into the impact of technological innovation on agricultural productivity in Nigeria, offering insights into strategies for fostering sustainable economic growth in the agricultural sector.

2.5.3. Innovation Diffusion Theory

Everett Rogers introduced the Innovation Diffusion Theory (IDT) in 1962 as a framework for comprehending how technological innovations are embraced within a social framework over time. Within the agricultural sector, innovations encompass new technologies and methodologies aimed at enhancing productivity. These innovations are disseminated through various channels, including agricultural extension services, research entities, and mass media. Over time, farmers progress through stages of awareness, interest, evaluation, trial, and adoption regarding these innovations. Adoption rates are influenced by social factors such as resource accessibility, cultural norms, and governmental policies (Ejem et al. 2023). Farmers are often categorized into groups based on their inclination to adopt new technologies. The characteristics of innovations, including their advantages and compatibility with existing practices, significantly influence their adoption trajectory. Utilizing this theory, researchers can discern factors driving or hindering adoption and devise strategies to facilitate widespread adoption of agricultural innovations, thereby bolstering agricultural productivity and sustainability.

The contemporary literature further supports the validity of the IDT in the agricultural context. Recent studies have highlighted its efficacy in explaining the adoption patterns of various agricultural innovations, ranging from precision farming technologies to sustainable agricultural practices. For instance, research by Teklu et al. (2023) demonstrated how the principles of the IDT can be applied to understand the adoption of climate-smart agricultural practices among smallholder farmers in developing countries. The authors also found that social networks play a crucial role in facilitating the diffusion of agricultural innovations among farmers, corroborating the central tenets of the theory.

However, while the IDT remains a widely accepted framework, some scholars have raised concerns regarding its applicability in contemporary agricultural contexts. Critics argue that the theory may oversimplify the complex socio-economic dynamics influencing technology adoption in agriculture (Mardiana and Kembauw 2021). They suggest that factors such as institutional barriers, market structures, and power dynamics among stakeholders may not be adequately addressed within the framework of the Innovation Diffusion Theory. Additionally, the rapid pace of technological change and globalization in the agricultural sector may necessitate a more dynamic and nuanced approach to understanding innovation adoption processes.

Despite these critiques, the IDT continues to provide valuable insights into the adoption and diffusion of agricultural innovations. By integrating contemporary perspectives and addressing emerging challenges, researchers can further enhance the applicability and robustness of this theoretical framework in driving agricultural development and sustainability agendas.

3. Data and Estimation Techniques

3.1. Data

The study draws data from five reputable sources: The World Development Indicators (WDIs), the United States Department of Agriculture (USDA), the Penn World Table (PWT), the World Intellectual Property Organization (WIPO), and the Central Bank of Nigeria (CBN) statistical bulletin. Total factor productivity (TFP), gross fixed capital formation (GFCF), agricultural credit guarantee scheme fund (ACGSF), trade (TRADE), and exchange rate (EXR) serve as independent variables.

TFP, the core independent variable, acts as the primary proxy for technological innovation, indicating advancements in technology and innovation that lead to higher output levels without a corresponding increase in input usage. GFCF serves as a proxy for investment in agricultural infrastructure and equipment, which can influence the adoption and effectiveness of technological innovations in farming practices. ACGSF reflects a government lending scheme to encourage large-scale farming. TRADE facilitates access to new technologies and markets for agricultural products, thereby influencing productivity and innovation. This is particularly significant for Nigeria, as the country heavily relies on imports for technology. EXR affects agricultural exports and imports, influencing technology adoption and competitiveness.

Dependent variables include agricultural total factor productivity (AGTFP), agricultural output (AGO), agricultural value added (AGVA), and oil rents (OLRs). The use of AGTFP and AGO as dependent variables for assessing the impact of technological innovation on the Nigerian agricultural sector is justified because AGTFP captures efficiency improvements resulting from innovation within the sector, while AGO represents the quantitative increase in agricultural production facilitated by technological advancements. These variables offer a comprehensive view of the sector's performance and the effectiveness of innovation strategies in enhancing productivity and output levels.

The basis for using AGVA and OLR in comparing the effects of technological advancements on both sectors lies in how they capture more precisely the sector-specific economic contributions. AGVA represents the net value created within the agricultural sector, reflecting its economic significance and productivity. Conversely, OLR represents the income generated specifically from the oil sector, indicating its importance to the overall economy. By analyzing both AGVA and OLR, we can assess how technological advancements impact the economic performance and productivity of each sector independently, providing valuable insights for policymakers and stakeholders seeking to promote balanced economic development and innovation strategies across both agriculture and oil industries.

Patent applications (PATs), scientific and technical published articles (SCIs), credit to the private sector (CPS), foreign direct investment (FDI), and interest rate (INR) are included as additional control variables in the analysis to account for their potential impacts on the relationship between technological innovation and agricultural productivity. PAT represents the level of innovation and technological advancement, which can directly influence agricultural productivity through new methods and tools. SCI measures the dissemination of knowledge and research, which can enhance agricultural practices and productivity. CPS indicates the availability of domestic financial resources for investment in agricultural technologies and infrastructure. FDI reflects the inflow of capital and expertise from abroad, potentially introducing advanced technologies and practices into the agricultural sector. INR affects the cost of borrowing and investment decisions, influencing the ability of farmers and agribusinesses to invest in new technologies. By including these control variables, this analysis aims to mitigate potential confounding factors and ensure a more robust assessment of the relationship between technological innovation and agricultural productivity.

The study focuses on the period from 1981 to 2021 due to strategic considerations and data availability. This timeframe encompasses significant events relevant to the study's objectives. Firstly, it includes the initial oil boom in Nigeria, extending into the early 1980s, a pivotal period for economic development. Additionally, it covers the establishment of the Federal Ministry of Science and Technology on 1 January 1980, indicating a shift towards prioritizing technological innovation. The study also spans the era when mobile technological devices, such as Global Systems for Mobile Communications (GSMs), and various forms of Information and Communication Technology (ICT) gained prominence in Nigeria in the early 2000s. Moreover, this timeframe captures the integration of smart agriculture in the country and the COVID-19 period.

3.2. Estimation Technique

This study employs the Autoregressive Distributed Lag (ARDL) model, contingent upon the time-series data meeting essential criteria following preliminary tests such as correlation, stationarity, causality, and cointegration, conducted using the EViews Statistical Software Package. These tests ensure the suitability of the data for ARDL modelling, which is effective when the variables are stationary and exhibit cointegrated relationships, thus producing reliable estimates. The appropriateness of employing ARDL is supported by its ability to incorporate variables with differing timeframes, capture both short-term dynamics and long-term equilibrium relationships, and provide insights into temporal interdependencies between variables (Lawal et al. 2016; Apraku et al. 2021; Aragie et al. 2023; Jiaduo et al. 2023). The ARDL bounds test requires that the order of integration of all variables does not exceed I (1), given that the presence of I (2) among the considered variables may likely result in spurious results. In the presence of I(2) variables, the computed F-statistic provided by the ARDL bound test becomes invalid, for the ARDL bound test is based on the assumption that the variables are either I(0), I(1) or a mixture of both (Lawal et al. 2018; Lawal et al. 2016). Augmented Dickey–Fuller and Philip–Perron (PP) were employed to validate the order of integration of the employed variables.

To measure the adequacy of the model specification, the study conducted some diagnostic and stability tests. While we employed the Cumulative Sum test (CUSUM) and Cumulative Sum of Squares (CUSUMSQ) to test for model stability, we employed a diagnostic test to address problems associated with non-normality, functional form, serial correlation, and heteroscedasticity (Tabash et al. 2024).

Moreover, ARDL accommodates both stationary and non-stationary variables and has seen limited application in examining the nexus between technological innovation and agricultural productivity in Nigeria.

The ARDL model equations are specified as follows in the unrestricted form to achieve our objectives:

$$\Delta AGTFP_t = \alpha_{01} + \sum_{i=1}^{p} \alpha_{1i}\Delta AGTFP_{t-i} + \sum_{i=1}^{q} \alpha_{2i}\Delta TFP_{t-i} + \sum_{i=1}^{q} \alpha_{3i}\Delta GFCF_{t-i} + \sum_{i=1}^{q} \alpha_{4i}\Delta ACGSF_{t-i} + \sum_{i=1}^{q} \alpha_{5i}\Delta TRADE_{t-i} + \sum_{i=1}^{q} \alpha_{6i}\Delta EXR_{t-i} + \lambda \mathrm{ECT}_{t-1} + \mu_t \quad (1)$$

$$\Delta AGO_t = \beta_{01} + \sum_{i=1}^{p} \beta_{1i}\Delta AGO_{t-i} + \sum_{i=1}^{q} \beta_{2i}\Delta TFP_{t-i} + \sum_{i=1}^{q} \beta_{3i}\Delta GFCF_{t-i} + \sum_{i=1}^{q} \beta_{4i}\Delta ACGSF_{t-i} + \lambda ECT_{t-1} + \eta_t \quad (2)$$

$$\Delta OLR_t = \gamma_{01} + \sum_{i=1}^{p} \gamma_{1i}\Delta OLR_{t-i} + \sum_{i=1}^{q} \gamma_{2i}\Delta TFP_{t-i} + \sum_{i=1}^{q} \gamma_{3i}\Delta GFCF_{t-i} + \sum_{i=1}^{q} \gamma_{4i}\Delta TRADE_{t-i} + \sum_{i=1}^{q} \gamma_{5i}\Delta EXR_{t-i} + \varepsilon_{1t} \quad (3)$$

$$\Delta AGVA_t = \delta_{01} + \sum_{i=1}^{p} \delta_{1i}\Delta AGVA_{t-i} + \sum_{i=1}^{q} \delta_{2i}\Delta TFP_{t-i} + \sum_{i=1}^{q} \delta_{3i}\Delta GFCF_{t-i} + \sum_{i=1}^{q} \beta_{4i}\delta TRADE_{t-i} + \sum_{i=1}^{q} \delta_{5i}\Delta EXR_{t-i} + \varepsilon_{2t}$$

where Δ is the difference operator, indicating changes in the variables from one period to the next; t is time period; $\sum$ is the summation symbol, indicating the sum over specified lags; α_{01}, β_{01}, γ_{01}, and δ_{01} are the constant terms for their respective models; α_{1i}, β_{1i}, γ_{1i}, and δ_{1i} are the coefficients for the respective lagged differences of variables; p and q are the lag orders of the dependent and independent variables, respectively; λ is the coefficient of the error correction term (ECT); ECT_{t-1} is the error-correction term at lag $t-1$; and μ_t, η_t, ϵ_{1t}, and ϵ_{2t} are the error terms.

The study employs the Akaike Information Criterion (AIC) for selecting the appropriate lag order in its time series analysis. The AIC is a widely used statistical measure that helps identify the model that best fits the data while balancing model complexity and goodness of fit. By minimizing the AIC value, the study ensures that the chosen lag length captures the underlying data patterns without overfitting, thereby enhancing the reliability and validity of the results. This criterion is particularly useful in a time-series analysis, as it aids in determining the optimal number of lagged observations to include, which is crucial for accurate model specification and subsequent interpretation of the relationships among the variables.

4. Results

4.1. Descriptive Statistics

The descriptive statistics in Table 1 reveal key insights into the characteristics and distribution of the variables examined in our study. The means and medians of variables related to agricultural productivity, such as agricultural total factor productivity (AGTFP), logarithm of agricultural output (LOG(AGO)), and agricultural value added (AGVA), indicate relatively stable central tendencies. This stability suggests consistency in agricultural performance over the study period. However, the standard deviations for AGTFP (11.27) and AGVA (4.59) highlight notable fluctuations, indicating some degree of variability in agricultural productivity and value added. These fluctuations may be influenced by factors such as technological advancements, policy interventions, and external market dynamics.

Turning to the variables associated with economic indicators and innovation, such as oil rents (OLRs), total factor productivity (TFP), gross fixed capital formation (GFCF), logarithm of agricultural credit guaranteed scheme fund (LOG(ACGSF)), trade volume (TRADE), exchange rate (EXR), logarithm of patents (LOG(PAT)), logarithm of scientific publications (LOG(SCI)), credit to the private sector (CPS), foreign direct investment (FDI), and interest rates (INRs), we observe a wider range of values, indicating greater variability. For instance, the standard deviations of OLR, GFCF, and EXR suggest considerable dispersion around their respective means, highlighting heterogeneity in oil sector revenue and investment patterns over time. The presence of skewness and kurtosis in some variables further underscores deviations from normal distribution, indicating potential asymmetry and peakiness in their distributions.

The Jarque–Bera test results provide additional insights into the distributional properties of the variables. While some variables exhibit p-values that fail to reject the null hypothesis of normality, indicating relatively normal distributions, others such as AGVA, GFCF, EXR, CPS, FDI, and INR display significant departures from normality, with p-values below the conventional significance level of 0.05. This deviation from normality suggests that certain variables may be influenced by non-normal factors or exhibit non-linear relationships, warranting further investigation into their underlying dynamics.

Table 1. Descriptive statistics.

	AGTFP	LOG(AGO)	AGVA	OLR	TFP	GFCF	LOG(ACGS)	TRADE	EXR	LOG(PAT)	LOG(SCI)	CPS	FDI	INR
Units of Measurement	**Index, 2015 = 100**	**Naira**	**% of GDP**	**% of GDP**		**% of GDP**	**Naira**	**% of GDP**	**Local Currency per USD**	**Count of Patent Applications**	**Count of Scientific Publications**	**% of GDP**	**% of GDP**	**%**
Mean	96.38836	7.300383	22.88138	11.51401	0.363506	35.63058	13.46867	31.67436	108.0868	6.200730	7.136119	9.387385	1.476171	0.453578
Median	99.78920	7.608584	22.23471	11.14464	0.372391	33.10736	13.49881	33.71975	111.2313	6.143809	6.954143	8.234514	1.087951	4.310292
Maximum	111.0581	10.62440	36.96508	28.70544	0.695784	89.38613	16.38023	53.27796	401.1520	7.022868	8.974612	19.62560	5.790847	18.18000
Minimum	75.15485	2.836278	12.24041	1.573876	0.115230	14.16873	10.11273	9.135846	0.617708	5.459586	5.290134	4.957522	0.183822	−65.85715
Std. Dev.	11.26548	2.535542	4.589772	6.173340	0.181204	18.96943	2.115533	12.42937	109.9700	0.408439	0.947922	3.559186	1.235819	14.25917
Skewness	−0.759089	−0.403899	0.440302	0.477526	0.215744	1.087484	−0.046453	−0.260245	0.978891	0.138853	0.045019	1.039979	1.766764	−2.717477
Kurtosis	2.335507	1.735150	4.732787	2.875631	1.677406	3.924531	1.413048	2.128483	3.189257	2.012887	2.104805	3.625500	6.193077	12.91104
Jarque–Bera	4.691796	3.847817	6.454107	1.584635	3.145085	9.541464	4.317038	1.760356	6.609079	1.752519	1.349135	8.059020	38.74765	218.2694
Probability	0.095761	0.146035	0.039674	0.452794	0.207517	0.008474	0.115496	0.414709	0.036716	0.416337	0.509377	0.017783	0.000000	0.000000
Sum	3951.923	299.3157	938.1364	472.0742	14.17674	1460.854	552.2154	1298.649	4431.558	248.0292	285.4448	384.8828	60.52301	18.59670
Sum Sq. Dev.	5076.444	257.1590	842.6402	1524.405	1.247721	14,393.57	179.0193	6179.566	483736.1	6.506085	35.04373	506.7123	61.08993	8132.960
Observations	41	41	41	41	39	41	41	41	41	40	40	41	41	41

4.2. Correlation Matrix

The correlation coefficients presented in Table 2 above are suggestive of the direction and strength of relationships among the selected variables, shedding light on the impact of technological innovation on agricultural productivity in Nigeria. A notable finding is the weak negative correlation between agricultural total factor productivity (AGTFP) and total factor productivity (TFP) (−0.3957). This suggests that advancements in technological innovation across sectors may not necessarily translate into immediate improvements in agricultural productivity, indicating potential challenges in aligning agricultural practices with broader technological trends in the country. TFP, as a measure of technological innovation, exhibits moderate negative correlations with agricultural value added (AGVA) (−0.630) and oil rents (OLRs) (−0.638), suggesting that increased technological innovation may coincide with reduced agricultural value added and oil revenues. However, TFP shows weak positive correlations with agricultural credit (LOG(ACGSF)) (0.268) and exchange rate (EXR) (0.381), implying potential links between technological progress and agricultural credit availability, as well as exchange rate dynamics.

Table 2. Correlation matrix.

	AGTFP	LOG(AGO)	AGVA	OLR	TFP	GFCF	LOG(ACGSF)	TRADE	EXR	LOG(PAT)	LOG(SCI)	CPS	FDI	INR
AGTFP	1													
LOG(AGO)	0.760	1												
AGVA	0.727	0.468	1											
OLR	0.383	−0.000	0.362	1										
TFP	−0.395	0.095	−0.630	−0.638	1									
GFCF	−0.718	−0.929	−0.520	−0.114	0.036	1								
LOG(ACGSF)	0.605	0.952	0.322	−0.100	0.267	−0.900	1							
TRADE	0.759	0.567	0.623	0.556	−0.499	−0.538	0.452	1						
EXR	0.476	0.875	0.176	−0.252	0.380	−0.764	0.853	0.267	1					
LOG(PAT)	0.418	0.659	0.307	−0.033	0.189	−0.580	0.666	0.435	0.541	1				
LOG(SCI)	0.623	0.967	0.328	−0.042	0.181	−0.922	0.944	0.463	0.913	0.624	1			
CPS	0.413	0.741	0.170	−0.209	0.284	−0.696	0.808	0.237	0.675	0.512	0.749	1		
FDI	0.304	0.0741	0.357	0.685	−0.419	−0.140	0.037	0.293	−0.119	−0.011	0.046	0.087	1	
INR	0.296	0.462	0.342	−0.035	−0.077	−0.559	0.459	0.227	0.379	0.331	0.490	0.421	−0.049	1

Moving to gross fixed capital formation (GFCF), a key indicator of investment, its strong negative correlations with agricultural output (LOG(AGO)) (−0.930) and agricultural credit (LOG(ACGSF)) (−0.900) highlight the inverse relationship between capital formation and agricultural credit or output. Additionally, GFCF demonstrates moderate-to-strong negative correlations with trade volumes (TRADE) (−0.538) and exchange rates (EXR) (−0.765), indicating potential impacts of investment activities on trade volumes and exchange rate fluctuations. The matrix also reveals that patent counts (LOG(PAT)) and scientific publications (LOG(SCI)) (0.659 and 0.967, respectively) are positively associated with agricultural output, suggesting a strong connection between scientific and technological advancements and agricultural output, albeit not as directly with productivity.

Considering agricultural credit (ACGSF), the correlation matrix indicates very strong positive associations with agricultural output (LOG(AGO)) (0.952) and scientific publications (LOG(SCI)) (0.945), emphasizing the intertwined nature of agricultural credit with agricultural output and scientific advancements. Moreover, ACGSF displays strong positive correlations with exchange rates (EXRs) (0.853) and credit to the private sector (CPS) (0.808), suggesting connections between credit availability, exchange rates, and financial sector performance.

There is a moderate negative correlation between technological advancement (TFP) and oil rents (OLRs) (−0.638), indicating a potential trade-off between technological progress and revenues from the oil sector. Additionally, weak correlations between oil rents (OLRs) and exchange rates (EXRs) (−0.252) and the moderate positive relationship between OLRs and trade volume (TRADE) (0.557) suggest the influence of global market dynamics on the oil sector in Nigeria. Moreover, the weak negative relationship between investment in fixed assets (GFCF) and the oil sector (−0.114) implies limited impact of capital investment on oil sector performance. EXR displays notable positive correlations with agricultural output (LOG(AGO)) (0.876) and scientific publications (LOG(SCI)) (0.913), suggesting interdependencies between exchange rates and agricultural organizations or scientific innovations.

Finally, positive correlations between real interest rates (INRs) and agricultural productivity and output (0.297 and 0.463) indicate potential benefits of higher real interest rates on agricultural performance, highlighting the importance of monetary policy in shaping agricultural productivity dynamics. Foreign direct investment (FDI), however, depicts weak positive correlations with agricultural performance indicators, suggesting a nuanced and possibly indirect relationship between foreign investment and agricultural productivity.

The unit root test results offer crucial information about the stationarity properties of the variables examined in this study. Employing both the Augmented Dickey–Fuller (ADF) and Philips–Perron (PP) tests, we assessed whether the variables possess a unit root and thereby determine their stationarity status.

The results of the unit root tests is presented in Table 3, the table is divided into two distinct categories based on the null hypothesis: 'level' and 'first difference'. Our analysis reveals that most of the variables (AGTFP, AGO, AGVA, OLR, TFP, ACGSF, TRADE, EXR, PAT, SCI, and CPS) demonstrate signs of non-stationarity in their level form, with p-values exceeding the conventional threshold of 0.05 for both the ADF and PP tests.

Table 3. Unit root tests.

Variables	ADF		PP	
	Level	First Difference	Level	First Difference
AGTFP	0.2375	0.0362	0.3344	0.0000
LOG(AGO)	0.2182	0.0035	0.2182	0.0030
AGVA	0.1096	0.0000	0.0726	0.0000
OLR	0.3749	0.0000	0.0640	0.0000
TFP	0.3495	0.0000	0.3328	0.0000
GFCF	0.0064	0.0012	0.0086	0.0017
LOG(ACGSF)	0.6497	0.0029	0.7382	0.0029
TRADE	0.1541	0.0000	0.1821	0.0000
EXR	1.0000	0.0032	1.0000	0.0043
LOG(PAT)	0.7455	0.0090	0.5506	0.0000
LOG(SCI)	0.9208	0.0061	0.9083	0.0071
CPS	0.2186	0.0000	0.5362	0.0000
FDI	0.0049	0.0000	0.0059	0.0000
INR	0.0000	0.0000	0.0000	0.0001

However, exceptions exist, notably GFCF, FDI, and INR, which exhibit stationarity at the level for both tests. For instance, AGTFP yields p-values of 0.2375 and 0.3344 in its level form for the ADF and PP tests, respectively, indicating non-stationarity.

Yet, upon differencing, the p-values reduce significantly to 0.0362 and 0.000, signifying the attainment of stationarity. Similar patterns are observed across other variables, underscoring the effectiveness of differencing in rendering the variables stationary for subsequent analysis.

Evidence from this test indicates that the regression model used to examine the impact of technological innovation on agricultural productivity in Nigeria is appropriate and consistent with the ARDL estimation technique. This is because the variables under consideration exhibit a mixed stationarity form, comprising both levels and first differences. This supports the validity and reliability of the conclusions regarding the impact of technological innovation on agricultural productivity amidst oil transition in Nigeria.

The Granger causality test in Table 4 assesses the directional relationship between two key variables: AGTFP and TFP, with the latter representing technological innovation. The results show a statistically significant unidirectional causality from TFP to AGTFP, with a p-value of 0.0009, indicating that technological innovation has a strong predictive influence on agricultural productivity at the 1% significance level. However, AGTFP does not Granger Cause TFP, as reflected by the non-significant p-value of 0.1280. This suggests that while technological innovation drives changes in agricultural productivity, the reverse is not true, indicating no evidence of feedback effects or endogeneity concerns between the variables. These findings underscore the role of technological progress in shaping agricultural outcomes in Nigeria.

Table 4. Causality test.

Null Hypothesis	Obs	F-Statistic	Prob.
AGTFP does not Granger Cause TFP	37	2.19377	0.1280
TFP does not Granger Cause AGTFP		8.79471	0.0009

4.2.1. Objectives 1: Impact of Technological Innovation on Agricultural Productivity

The results of the ARDL bounds test is presented in Table 5, it assesses the presence of a long-run equilibrium relationship among the variables of interest. With an F-statistic value of 6.28, exceeding the critical values of the lower and upper bounds at a 5% significance level, we find evidence supporting the existence of long-run relationships among the variables under consideration. Therefore, there is sufficient evidence to reject the null hypothesis and conclude that a long-run equilibrium relationship exists between agricultural productivity (AGTFP) and technological innovation (TFP, GFCF, LNACGSF, TRADE, and EXR) in Nigeria.

Table 5. Results of bounds test.

	F-Statistic	I0 Bound	I1 Bound
Values	6.277068	2.62	3.79

The ARDL regression analysis offers valuable insights into the short and long-run relationships between AGTFP and its determinants, focusing on technological innovation (TFP), GFCF, ACGSF, TRADE, and EXR from 1981 to 2021.

In Table 6, we present the results of the short run, lagged values of agricultural productivity (AGTFP) show a mixed impact: a one-period lag exhibits a statistically significant negative effect of −0.4856 on its current value, while a two-period lag shows a positive but weaker impact of 0.3132. This is suggestive of a complex relationship between AGTFP and its lagged values, likely associated with technological constraints within the sector and market dynamics, particularly input prices, considering the high inflationary pressures in the country over time (Rongjian et al. 2019; Djoumessi 2022).

TFP and its lags exhibit statistically significant positive coefficients and consistent with a priori expectations, indicating that increased technological innovation leads to higher agricultural productivity. For instance, a 1% rise in technological innovation (TFP) induces approximately a 13% increase in agricultural productivity in the short term. However, significance diminishes with lagged values, with TFP(−1) not being significant and TFP(−2) being marginally significant. These lagged values are likely to capture the adjustments and adaptations in agricultural practices preceding the gradual unfolding of technological adoption effects (Ndaghu et al. 2023).

Table 6. Results of regression analysis.

Dep. Variable: AGTFP	Short-Run ARDL	Long-Run ARDL
AGTFP(−1)	−0.485642 *** (0.162660)	
AGTFP(−2)	0.313153 * (0.153593)	
TFP	12.996919 ** (6.129376)	−90.705103 *** (29.133142)
TFP(−1)	1.704428 (6.549078)	
TFP(−2)	10.250378 * (5.824857)	
GFCF	0.132536 (0.124183)	−0.741846 (0.723579)
GFCF(−1)	−0.415371 *** (0.127285)	
GFCF(−2)	0.305549 *** (0.085259)	
LOG(ACGSF)	−0.243834 (1.071571)	−1.158985 (5.282161)
TRADE	−0.177887 *** (0.049887)	−1.171365 * (0.596564)
EXR	−0.009330 (0.010459)	−0.044347 (0.062212)
CointEq(−1)	−0.210386 ** (0.085558)	
Constant		219.468117 * (109.461685)

Note: Standard errors are reported in parenthesis; *, **, and *** represent 10%, 5%, and 1%, respectively.

GFCF and its lags show mixed effects on AGTFP, with both positive and negative impacts, indicating a nuanced relationship. The coefficients of ACGSF, TRADE, and EXR (−0.2438, −0.1779, and −0.0093, respectively) do show negative impacts on AGTFP in the short run, with only TRADE being significant. This implies that the ACGSF might not be effectively directed toward fostering technological innovation (Balana and Oyeyemi 2022).

The presence of a significant error correction term (CointEq(−1)) with a negative coefficient (−0.2104) at the 5% level indicates the presence of a stable long-run equilibrium relationship between the variables, with adjustments occurring at a rate of approximately 21% per period when the system experiences disequilibrium.

Transitioning to the long run, TFP exhibits a significant negative coefficient, suggesting that increased technological innovation leads to decreased agricultural productivity over time. That is, a 1% increase in nation-wide total factor productivity will induce a 90.71% decrease in agricultural total factor productivity. This is suggestive of the fact that the initial positive effects may diminish or reverse over time. Conversely, the coefficient for GFCF in the long run is negative (−0.7419), although not statistically significant, suggesting a potential but uncertain impact on AGTFP over time.

ACGSF, TRADE, and EXR do not exhibit significant impacts on AGTFP in the long run, with coefficients close to zero and statistically insignificant. The constant term (C) suggests an expected AGTFP of approximately 219.47 units when all other variables are zero, albeit marginally significant.

Comparing the long-run coefficients with the short-run ones from the ARDL model, differences in significance and magnitude are apparent. In the short term, lagged AGTFP, TFP, and GFCF exhibit significant impacts on AGTFP, while others may lack statistical significance or show mixed effects. However, in the long run, the influence of TFP becomes more pronounced and significant, indicating its dominant role in shaping agricultural productivity over time. Thus, we reject the null hypothesis and affirm a significant relationship between technological innovation and agricultural productivity in Nigeria. Conversely, the effects of variables such as GFCF, ACGSF, TRADE, and EXR are less prominent in the long run, suggesting their impacts may be more transient or influenced by unaccounted factors.

4.2.2. Objectives 2: Impact of Agricultural Innovation on Agricultural Output

The ARDL bounds test aimed to ascertain the existence of long-run relationships among the analyzed variables (AGO, AGTFP, GFCF, and ACGSF), (see Tables 7 and 8). In this instance, the calculated F-statistic (1.2291) falls below the critical value bounds provided for the conventional 5% threshold, leading us to fail to reject the null hypothesis. This indicates insufficient evidence to assert the presence of long-run relationships among the variables in the model at standard levels of significance. In essence, it suggests a lack of a long-term relationship between output and technological innovation within the agricultural sector.

Table 7. Results of bounds test.

	F-Statistic	I0 Bound	I1 Bound
Values	1.229078	3.23	4.35

Source: Author's computation (2024).

Table 8. Results of regression analysis.

Dep. Variable: LOG(AGO)	Short-Run ARDL
LOG(AGO(−1))	1.438718 *** (0.185242)
LOG(AGO(−2))	−0.757006 ** (0.287187)
LOG(AGO(−3))	0.257262 (0.169151)
AGTFP	0.003439 (0.004408)
GFCF	−0.013607 * (0.006737)
GFCF(−1)	0.018206 ** (0.008529)
GFCF(−2)	−0.012603 ** (0.005767)
LOG(ACGSF)	0.083087 (0.113581)
LOG(ACGSF(−1))	0.034489 (0.154148)
LOG(ACGSF(−2))	−0.344734 ** (0.152554)
LOG(ACGSF(−3))	0.209129 * (0.110472)
Constant	0.775767 (1.290656)

Note: Standard errors are reported in parentheses; *, **, and *** represent 10%, 5%, and 1%, respectively. Source: Author's computation (2024).

The short-run coefficients provide valuable insights into the immediate impacts of the dynamic regressors on LOG(AGO). Firstly, lagged values of AGO exhibit significant effects, with AGO(−1) showing a strong positive coefficient (1.4387) and AGO(−2) displaying a negative coefficient (−0.757). This suggests a persistent positive influence from the previous period's agricultural output, with a negative impact from two periods ago, indicating a short-term correction effect. The coefficient for AGO(−3) is positive (0.2573), albeit not statistically significant, implying a weaker but still present influence from three periods ago.

Moving to the dynamic regressors, AGTFP's coefficient (0.0034) is positive but not statistically significant, indicating a minor immediate effect on AGO. However, GFCF's coefficients show more pronounced impacts, with GFCF and its lagged values exhibiting significant effects. Specifically, GFCF has a negative coefficient (−0.0136), indicating that an increase in gross fixed capital formation leads to a decrease in agricultural output in the short run. As observed with AGTFP, the lagged values of GFCF display both positive and negative coefficients, suggesting varied short-term impacts from previous periods' investment levels.

The coefficients associated with ACGSF offer interesting observations. Although the coefficient for ACGSF in the current period is positive (0.083), it fails to reach statistical significance, implying a minor immediate impact on AGO. However, the lagged values of ACGSF demonstrate more pronounced impacts, with ACGSF(−2) and ACGSF(−3) exhibiting statistically significant negative and positive coefficients, respectively, suggesting that agricultural credit guarantee scheme fund levels from two and three periods ago have a significant short-term influence on agricultural output.

In conclusion, the short-run coefficients highlight a dynamic and intricate relationship between agricultural output and innovation in Nigeria. Lagged output values notably influence current output levels, indicating persistence over time. However, the immediate effects of innovation, investment, and credit guarantee scheme funds vary both in significance and direction, with agricultural innovation showing insignificance. Consequently, based on this outcome, we uphold the null hypothesis, suggesting that agricultural innovation has no significant influence on agricultural output in Nigeria.

4.2.3. Objective 3: Comparison of the Impact of Technological Innovation on Oil and Agriculture

In Table 9, we present the results of the ARDL bounds test for the impact of technological innovation on oil and agriculture. The ARDL bounds test examines whether a long-run equilibrium relationship exists among the variables of interest. With F-statistic values of 2.98 and 2.82, below the critical values of their respective lower and upper bounds at a 5% significance level, there is no substantiating evidence for the presence of long-run relationships among the variables being studied. Consequently, there is insufficient evidence to reject the null hypothesis, indicating no long-run equilibrium relationship between technological innovation and oil rents, as well as technological innovation and agricultural value added.

Table 9. Results of bounds test.

	F-Statistic	I0 Bound	I1 Bound
Model 1	2.974503	2.86	4.01
Model 2	2.816324	2.86	4.01

Source: Author's computation (2024).

The ARDL analysis as presented in Table 10 provides insights into the relationships between technological innovation, represented by TFP, GFCF, TRADE, and EXR, and the oil sector (OLR) and agricultural sector (AGVA) in Nigeria.

Table 10. (Results of Regression Analysis).

Explanatory Variables	Dep. Variable: OLR	Dep. Variable: AGVA
OLR(−1)/AGVA(−1)	0.411624 ** (0.170837)	0.483405 *** (0.136338)
TFP	−5.549463 (6.229909)	−9.723358 ** (3.945871)
GFCF	−0.006840 (0.081175)	−0.026433 (0.048159)
TRADE	0.249432 ** (0.101562)	−0.070126 (0.060587)
TRADE(−1)	−0.137314 (0.098422)	0.085395 (0.054002)
EXR	−0.011688 (0.016411)	0.004699 (0.008887)
Constant	6.742564 (6.670831)	15.50906 *** (5.116708)

Note: standard errors are reported in parentheses; **, and *** represent 5%, and 1%, respectively. Source: Author's computation (2024).

Starting with the oil sector, the coefficient for lagged OLR (−1) is positive and statistically significant (0.4116), indicating that past levels of oil sector revenues positively influence current revenues. Conversely, the coefficients for all the explanatory variables are not statistically significant in explaining variations in OLR, except for TRADE in its current levels. This suggests that changes in technological innovation, investment, trade volume, and exchange rates have limited short-term impacts on oil sector revenues.

In contrast, for the agricultural sector (AGVA), the coefficients present a different picture. Lagged AGVA (−1) has a positive and significant coefficient (0.4834), indicating that past levels of agricultural value added positively affect current levels. Interestingly, TFP exhibits a negative but statistically significant coefficient (−9.7234), implying that increases in technological innovation induce decreases in agricultural value added. This suggests that the relationship between technological innovation and agricultural productivity may be more nuanced than initially anticipated. However, the coefficients for GFCF, TRADE, and EXR are not statistically significant in explaining variations in AGVA.

The effects of technological innovation differ between Nigeria's oil and agricultural sectors. While past revenues significantly influence current revenues in the oil sector, technological innovation and other factors show no immediate significant effects. In contrast, in agriculture, past agricultural value added significantly impacts current levels, and technological innovation (TFP) shows a significant negative impact on agricultural productivity. This leads us to reject the null hypothesis and emphasize the need for sector-specific policies and interventions (Aye and Odhiambo 2021).

To explore the robustness of our model for the core objective, we conducted two additional regression analyses. The results are presented in Table 11. The first analysis measured technological innovation using PAT and SCI instead of TFP. The second analysis measured investments in fixed assets, using the product of CPS and FDI instead of GFCF. Both analyses incorporated other explanatory variables and maintained ARDL as the estimation technique.

In comparing the first regression with the original model, TFP remains significant in both the short and long run, while PAT*STCI is only significant in the long run (−23.79). The consistent significance of TFP supports the robustness of the initial estimates. The long-run significance of PAT*STCI, despite its short-run insignificance, suggests that while TFP has an immediate impact, the effect of patents and scientific innovation is more complex and may require further exploration.

Table 11. Robustness checks.

Dep. Variable: AGTFP	Short-Run ARDL	Long-Run ARDL
LOG(PAT*SCI)	0.615223 (2.146106)	−23.789149 ** (9.786836)
LOG(PAT*SCI(−1))	1.815923 (3.157214)	
LOG(PAT*SCI(−2))	3.649458 (3.235388)	
CPS*FDI	−0.011452 (0.035115)	−0.310681 (0.182384)

Note: Standard errors are reported in parentheses; ** represent 5%.

In examining GFCF and CPS*FDI, the first model shows a long-run coefficient of −0.7418 for GFCF, indicating an insignificant effect. The second model, replacing GFCF with CPS*FDI, yields a long-run coefficient of -0.3107, which is also insignificant. This consistent insignificance suggests that financial capital investments (GFCF or CPS*FDI) may not have a robust impact on agricultural productivity. However, the consistent significance of TFP across both models reaffirms its crucial role in determining agricultural productivity in Nigeria.

The two models for the robustness checks exhibit a long-run equilibrium relationship among the variables, with significant error-correction terms. The consistent significance of TFP in both models further supports its robustness as a critical factor. Thus, our model is consistent, appropriate, and reliable for policy implications.

The CUSUM (Cumulative Sum) test in Figure 1 assesses the stability of the relationship between technological innovation and agricultural productivity in Nigeria over time. The CUSUM line shows the cumulative sum of the residuals from the regression model, with horizontal lines representing the 5% significance level bounds. Since the CUSUM line remains within these critical bounds, the test confirms the regression model's stability, indicating that the relationship between technological innovation and agricultural productivity was consistent from 1981 to 2021.

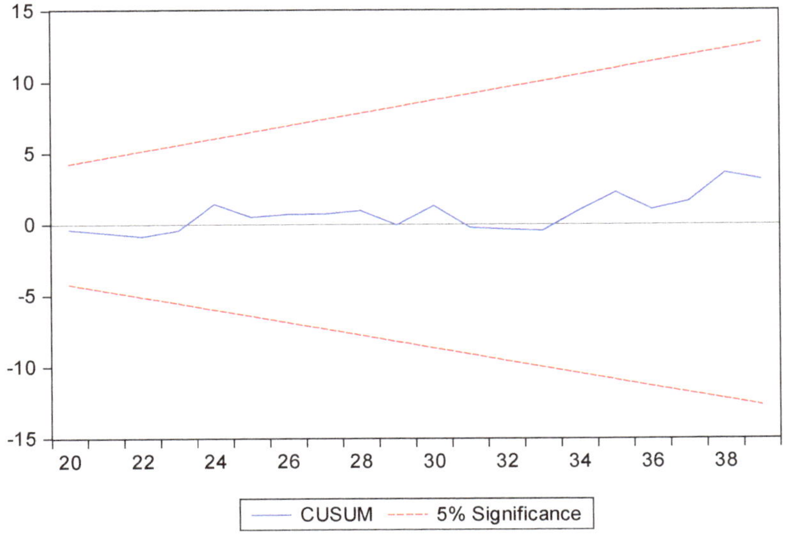

Figure 1. CUSUM test assessing the nature of the relationship between technological innovation and agricultural productivity in Nigeria.

Figure 2 illustrates the CUSUM of Squares test, a diagnostic tool for detecting systematic changes in the regression model's variance over time. This test plots the cumulative sum of squared residuals against the 5% significance bounds. Since the CUSUM of Squares line stays within the critical limits, it confirms that the variance in the relationship between technological innovation and agricultural productivity is stable throughout the study period, ensuring the reliability of the regression model's predictions and conclusions.

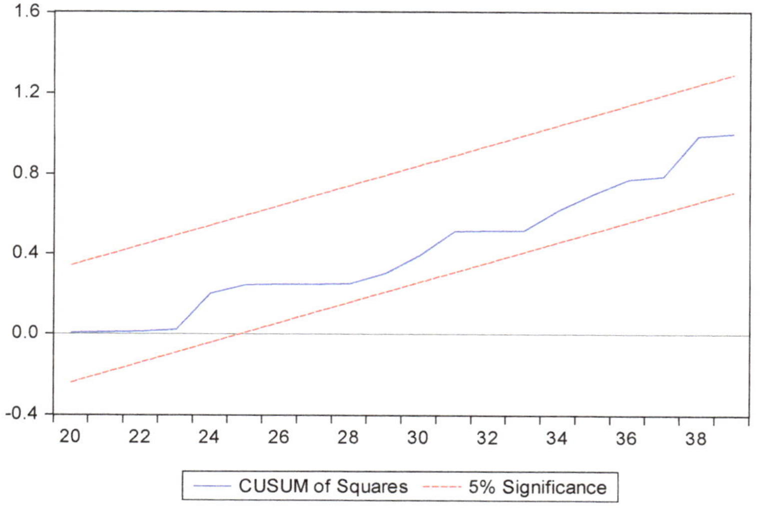

Figure 2. CUSUM of Squares test assessing the nature of the relationship between technological innovation and agricultural productivity in Nigeria.

4.3. Discussion of Results

The regression analyses provide crucial insights into the intricate relationship between technological innovation and agricultural productivity amidst Nigeria's transition away from oil dependence. Notably, the findings underscore a significant and negative influence of immediate lagged agricultural productivity (AGTFP(−1)), indicative of prevailing technological constraints within the sector. Moreover, the study reveals the substantial impact of technological innovation, proxied by total factor productivity (TFP), on agricultural productivity both in the short and long term. The lagged values of technological innovation suggest a gradual realization of its positive effect on agricultural productivity over time (Ndaghu et al. 2023). However, the long-run coefficient depicting a more pronounced, yet negative impact raises concerns. This negative correlation could be attributed to several factors, such as diminishing returns on technological investments, elevated costs of technology due to currency weakness, and a lack of skilled manpower to effectively implement technological practices, thereby limiting their productivity-enhancing potential (Akinola et al. 2023; Ejem et al. 2023).

To address these challenges, a multi-faceted policy approach is needed. First, the government should invest in capacity-building programs to equip farmers with the skills needed to effectively use new technologies, while promoting agricultural education to develop a skilled workforce. Subsidies and tax incentives for technology adoption can help reduce costs, especially in the context of currency depreciation, which local farmers may find difficult to manage. Encouraging public–private partnerships will also facilitate the development of affordable, locally suited technologies for Nigeria's agricultural sector. Also, improving infrastructure and expanding access to finance for smallholder farmers will support wider and more sustainable technology adoption, ensuring long-term productivity gains. Notably, the consistent coefficient estimates of TFP highlight its crucial role in determining agricultural productivity, as demonstrated by its impact on both AGTFP and AGVA.

The mixed findings regarding investment in fixed assets (GFCF) vis-à-vis agricultural productivity (AGTFP) and output (AGO) underscore the complexities inherent in the relationship and underscore the inadequacy of investment in agricultural-related infrastructure. Furthermore, our results indicate that agricultural innovation yields a positive albeit insignificant impact on agricultural output. This suggests that agricultural output in Nigeria is predominantly labor-induced rather than capital-induced (Ojo and Baiyegunhi 2023). The extant literature affirms this notion, with over 90% of non-mechanized production systems relying on human labor, and mechanized systems still requiring 50–60% of tasks to be performed manually (Edohen and Ikelegbe 2018; Ogunsolu 2021). It is worth noting, however, that Djoumessi's (2022) position, where the estimated elasticity of production to labor is positive but not significant, may differ due to a larger study area and distinct model specifications (Habtewold and Heshmati 2023).

Furthermore, the agricultural credit guarantee scheme funds (ACGSFs) exhibit a negative relationship with agricultural productivity in both short-run and long-run analyses. However, while their current and lagged values mostly display insignificant positive relationships with agricultural output in the short run, this may signal potential misappropriation of funds (Rongjian et al. 2019).

Given the stark disparities observed between the oil and agricultural sectors through our comparative analysis, it becomes increasingly clear that the agricultural sector stands to gain more from technological innovation compared to the oil sector. This deduction is drawn from the significant negative coefficient of TFP on AGVA, implying that technological advancements lead to decreased agricultural productivity. This underscores the potential for improvement in the agricultural sector through the adoption of advanced technologies such as precision agriculture, improved irrigation techniques, mechanization, and digital farming practices (Rongjian et al. 2019; Balana and Oyeyemi 2022; Ndaghu et al. 2023). Conversely, the oil sector, characterized by an insignificant negative coefficient estimate, may not experience significant short-term benefits from technological innovation. Therefore, given the transformative potential of technological innovation to positively impact productivity and output in the agricultural sector, prioritizing advancements in agriculture emerges as a strategic imperative to propel growth, sustainability, and resilience in Nigeria's economy.

4.4. Recommendations

The study's findings lead to the following recommendations:

1. Invest in agricultural technology infrastructure: The government and relevant stakeholders should prioritize substantial investment in agricultural infrastructure. This includes funding for advanced irrigation systems, precision agriculture tools, and mechanized farming equipment. These investments can help mitigate the diminishing returns and high technology costs currently limiting agricultural productivity.
2. Enhance agricultural education and training: To address the lack of the skilled manpower necessary for effective implementation of technological practices, educational programs and vocational training in agricultural technology should be expanded. Universities and technical institutions should collaborate with agricultural technology companies to ensure that farmers and agricultural professionals are well-trained in the latest innovations.
3. Strengthen agricultural credit schemes: Revise the Agricultural Credit Guarantee Scheme Fund (ACGSF) to ensure the proper allocation and utilization of funds. Implement robust monitoring and evaluation frameworks to prevent misappropriation of funds and ensure that financial support is effectively enhancing technological adoption and productivity in the agricultural sector.
4. Promote research and development in agriculture: Increase funding and support for research and development (R&D) in agriculture to foster innovation. Partnerships

between government agencies, research institutions, and private sector entities should be encouraged to develop and disseminate new agricultural technologies tailored to Nigeria's specific climatic and soil conditions.

5. Implement favorable trade policies: Reform trade policies to support the agricultural sector. Reducing trade barriers and providing incentives for agricultural exports can enhance market access for farmers, allowing them to benefit from economies of scale and better integrate into global value chains, which can incentivize the adoption of technological innovations.
6. Encourage private sector participation: Foster a conducive environment for private sector investments in agricultural technology. This includes creating favorable tax policies, providing subsidies for technology adoption, and establishing public-private partnerships to facilitate the development and distribution of agricultural technologies. Enhanced collaboration with technology firms can drive innovation and efficiency in the agricultural sector.

5. Conclusions

Based on our objectives and study findings, we conclude that there is a meaningful relationship between technological innovation and agricultural productivity in Nigeria. Technological innovation is a significant factor in enhancing agricultural productivity, highlighting the critical role of modern technologies in the sector. Conversely, agricultural innovation, in terms of new methods and practices, appears to have an insignificant impact on overall output, indicating that Nigeria's agricultural sector relies more heavily on labor than on capital investments. This reliance underscores the predominance of manual labor over mechanized or technologically driven agricultural processes.

Additionally, our comparative analysis reveals that the agricultural sector benefits more from technological innovation than the oil sector. While technological advancements in agriculture have the potential to significantly boost productivity and efficiency, the same level of impact is not observed in the oil sector. This disparity suggests that targeted technological interventions can yield substantial gains in agriculture.

Furthermore, variables such as gross fixed capital formation (GFCF) and trade have proven significant in determining agricultural productivity. Investments in fixed assets and the expansion of trade activities play crucial roles in supporting agricultural development. These findings underscore the importance of creating policies that enhance technological adoption, promote investment in agricultural infrastructure, and facilitate trade to drive growth in Nigeria's agricultural sector.

Limitations of the Study

This study acknowledges significant limitations due to data availability and accuracy issues. Missing and inconsistent data may have influenced the analysis and interpretation of results, potentially introducing biases and errors. These limitations could impact variable selection, model specification, and result interpretation, ultimately affecting the reliability and applicability of the findings. Future research should focus on addressing data-quality issues through improved collection methods and validation procedures to enhance the credibility of empirical analyses.

Author Contributions: J.T.A., Conceptualization, Writing the original draft, Literature review, Methodology, Validation; A.I.L., Conceptualization, Writing the original draft, Literature review, Methodology, Results, Validation, Supervision; D.T.A., Conceptualization, Literature review, Methodology, Validation; A.A., Literature review, Validation, resources; H.A.R., Literature review, methodology, validation; M.I.T., Resources, supervision, validation, literature review. All authors have read and agreed to the published version of the manuscript.

Funding: This research received no external funding.

Informed Consent Statement: Not applicable.

Data Availability Statement: Available upon reasonable demand.

Conflicts of Interest: The authors declared no conflict of interest.

References

Abah, Esther Enuwa, Clement Owoicho Momoh, and Samuel Olushola Fadairo. 2024. Endogenous measures for stifling corruption within selected agricultural and food development projects in Benue State, North Central, Nigeria. *Journal of Economic Criminology* 4: 100060. [CrossRef]

Adeagbo, O. A., A. S. Bamire, A. A. Akinola, A. D. Adeagbo, T. S. Oluwole, O.A. Ojedokun, T. O. Ojo, H. S. Kassem, and C. U. Emenike. 2023. The level of adoption of multiple climate change adaptation strategies: Evidence from smallholder maize farmers in Southwest Nigeria. *Scientific African* 22: e01971. [CrossRef]

Adenle, Ademola A., Sébastien Boillat, and Chinwe Ifejika Speranza. 2022. Key dimensions of land users' perceptions of land degradation and sustainable land management in Niger State, Nigeria. *Environmental Challenges* 8: 100544. [CrossRef]

Aghion, Philippe, and Peter Howitt. 1992. A growth model with creative destruction. *Econometrica* 60: 323–51. [CrossRef]

Akinola, Adebayo, Ayodeji Kehinde, Akeem Tijani, Adeolu Ayanwale, Felicia Adesiyan, Victoria Tanimonure, Ayodeji Ogunleye, and Temitope Ojo. 2023. Impact of membership in agricultural cooperatives on yield of smallholder tomato farmers in Nigeria. *Environmental and Sustainability Indicators* 20: 100313. [CrossRef]

Amare, Mulubrhan, and Bedru Balana. 2023. Climate change, income sources, crop mix, and input use decisions: Evidence from Nigeria. *Ecological Economics* 211: 107892. [CrossRef]

Amzat, Jimoh, Kafayat Aminu, Victor I. Kolo, Ayodele A. Akinyele, Janet A. Ogundairo, and Maryann C. Danjibo. 2020. Coronavirus outbreak in Nigeria: Burden and socio-medical response during the first 100 days. *International Journal of Infectious Diseases* 98: 218–24. [CrossRef]

Andati, P., E. Majiwa, M. Ngigi, R. Mbeche, and J. Ateka. 2023. Effect of climate-smart agriculture technologies on crop yields: Evidence from potato production in Kenya. *Climate Risk Management* 41: 100539. [CrossRef]

Ani, R. A., and B. Nuhu. 2010. Impact of corruption on farm production and profit. *Russian Journal of Agricultural and Socio-Economic Sciences* 2: 3.

Apraku, Amos, John F. Morton, and Benjamin Apraku Gyampoh. 2021. Climate change and small-scale agriculture in Africa: Does indigenous knowledge matter? Insights from Kenya and South Africa. *Scientific African* 12: e00821. [CrossRef]

Aragie, E., Jean Balié, C. Morales, and Karl Pauw. 2023. Synergies and trade-offs between agricultural export promotion and food security: Evidence from African economies. *World Development* 172: 106368. [CrossRef]

Awolala, David, Joseph Mutemi, Elijah Adefisan, Philip Antwi-Agyei, Andrea Taylor, Richard Muita, Emily Bosire, Bethwel Mutai, and Elias Nkiaka. 2023. Economic value and latent demand for agricultural drought forecast: Emerging market for weather and climate information in Central-Southern Nigeria. *Climate Risk Management* 39: 100478. [CrossRef]

Aworunse, Oluwadurotimi Samuel, Honey Aanu Olorunsola, Eze Frank Ahuekwe, and Olawole Odun Obembe. 2023. Towards a sustainable bioeconomy in a post-oil era Nigeria. *Resources, Environment and Sustainability* 11: 100094. [CrossRef]

Ayanwale, A. B., T. O. Ojo, and A. A. Adekunle. 2023. Estimating the distributional impact of innovation platforms on income of smallholder maize farmers in Nigeria. *Heliyon* 9: e16026. [CrossRef]

Aye, Goodness C., and Nicholas M. Odhiambo. 2021. Oil prices and agricultural growth in South Africa: A threshold analysis. *Resources Policy* 73: 102196. [CrossRef]

Babatunde, Abdulhammed Opeyemi, Ahmad Abdullateef Abdulkareem, Foluso Olugbenga Akinwande, Aminat Olaitan Adebayo, Ebelechukwu Tabitha Omenogor, Yusuff Adebayo Adebisi, and Esther Bosede Ilesanmi. 2021. Leveraging mobile health technology towards achieving universal health coverage in Nigeria. *Public Health in Practice* 2: 100120. [CrossRef] [PubMed]

Baiyegunhi, L. J. S., F. Akinbosoye, and L. O. Bello. 2022. Welfare impact of improved maize varieties adoption and crop diversification practices among smallholder maize farmers in Ogun State, Nigeria. *Heliyon* 8: e09338. [CrossRef]

Balana, Bedru B., and Motunrayo A. Oyeyemi. 2022. Agricultural credit constraints in smallholder farming in developing countries: Evidence from Nigeria. *World Development Sustainability* 1: 100012. [CrossRef]

Bello, Lateef Olalekan, Lloyd J. S. Baiyegunhi, Gideon Danso-Abbeam, and Abiodun A. Ogundeji. 2021. Gender decomposition in smallholder agricultural performance in rural Nigeria. *Scientific African* 13: e00875. [CrossRef]

Ben Salem, Leila, Ridha Nouira, Khaled Jeguirim, and Christophe Rault. 2022. The determinants of crude oil prices: Evidence from ARDL and nonlinear ARDL approaches. *Resources Policy* 79: 103085. [CrossRef]

Chatziantoniou, Ioannis, Michail Filippidis, George Filis, and David Gabauer. 2021. A closer look into the global determinants of oil price volatility. *Energy Economics* 95: 105092. [CrossRef]

Chiaramonti, David, and Kyriakos Maniatis. 2020. Security of supply, strategic storage and COVID-19: Which lessons learnt for renewable and recycled carbon fuels, and their future role in decarbonizing transport? *Applied Energy* 271: 115216. [CrossRef] [PubMed]

Djoumessi, Yannick Fosso. 2022. New trend of agricultural productivity growth in Sub-Saharan Africa. *Scientific African* 18: e01410. [CrossRef]

Edafe, Oluwatosin D., Evans Osabuohien, Oluwatoyin Matthew, Isaiah Olurinola, Joel Edafe, and Romanus Osabohien. 2023. Large-scale agricultural land investments and food security in Nigeria. *Heliyon* 9: e19941. [CrossRef]

Edohen, O. P., and O. O. Ikelegbe. 2018. Labour use types, agricultural income of farm households in Nigeria: An evidence from rural Benin. *Knowledge Review* 37: 1–9.

Ejem, Agwu Agwu, Charity Aremu, Olanrewaju O. P. Ajakaiye, Charity Ben-Enukora, Oluwakemi E. Akerele-Popoola, T. I. Ibiwoye, and A. F. Olaniran. 2023. Perspectives on communicating 21st-century agricultural innovations to Nigerian rural farmers. *Journal of Agriculture and Food Research* 11: 100511. [CrossRef]

Eke, Ihuoma Chikulirim, F Felix Awara Eke, and Awara Emeng Edom. 2019. Technological advancement and economic growth in Nigeria. *African Journal of Applied and Theoretical Economics* 5: 124–45.

Eleke, P. N., M. Jibril, and J. M. Nte. 2019. A review of the effect of crude oil exploration on agriculture: A case study of the Niger Delta region. *Journal of Agricultural Economics, Environment, and Social Sciences* 5: 87–98.

Etuk, Ekanem Abasiekong, and Josephine Oluwatoyin Ayuk. 2021. Agricultural commercialisation, poverty reduction, and pro-poor growth: Evidence from Commercial Agricultural Development Project in Nigeria. *Heliyon* 7: e06818. [CrossRef]

Eweoya, Ibukun, Senanu R. Okuboyejo, Oluwole A. Odetunmibi, and Babafemi O. Odusote. 2021. An empirical investigation of acceptance, adoption, and the use of e-agriculture in Nigeria. *Heliyon* 7: e07588. [CrossRef]

Federal Ministry of Agriculture and Rural Development (FMARD). 2015. Growth Enhancement Scheme. Available online: http://www.fmard.gov.ng/Growth-Enhancement-Scheme (accessed on 15 October 2023).

Frey, Eric. 2017. The Solow model and standard of living. *Undergraduate Journal of Mathematical Modeling: One + Two* 7: 5. [CrossRef]

Gordon, Robert J. 2012. *Is U.S. Economic Growth Over? Faltering Innovation Confronts the Six Headwinds*. NBER Working Paper No. 18315. Cambridge: National Bureau of Economic Research.

Grossman, Gene M., and Elhanan Helpman. 1991. Trade, knowledge spillovers, and growth. *European Economic Review* 35: 517–26. [CrossRef]

Habtewold, Tsegaye Mulugeta, and Almas Heshmati. 2023. Impacts of improved agricultural technologies on food security and child nutrition in rural Ethiopia. *Cogent Food & Agriculture* 9: 2276565. [CrossRef]

Ikuemonisan, Edamisan Stephen, Adebayo B. Abass, Shiferaw Feleke, and Igbekele Ajibefun. 2022. Influence of agricultural degree programme environment on career in agribusiness among college students in Nigeria. *Journal of Agriculture and Food Research* 7: 100256. [CrossRef]

Isukuru, Efe Jeffery, Akinyemi Olufemi Ogunkeyede, Adedoyin Ayorinde Adebayo, and Matthew Freedom Uruejoma. 2023. Potentials of bamboo and its ecological benefits in Nigeria. *Advances in Bamboo Science* 4: 100032. [CrossRef]

Jacal, Samara, Franziska Brigitte Straubinger, Emmanuel Olatunbosun Benjamin, and Gertrud Buchenrieder. 2022. Economic costs and environmental impacts of fossil fuel dependency in Sub-Saharan Africa: A Nigerian dilemma. *Energy for Sustainable Development* 70: 45–53. [CrossRef]

Jiaduo, Erti, Md. Golam Kibria, Nazhat Nury Aspy, Ehsan Ullah, and Md. Emran Hossain. 2023. The impact of agricultural employment and technological innovation on the environment: Evidence from BRICS nations considering a novel environmental sustainability indicator. *Sustainability* 15: 15083. [CrossRef]

Kayode, Olusola Titilope, A. P. Aizebeokhai, and A. M. Odukoya. 2022. Geophysical and contamination assessment of soil spatial variability for sustainable precision agriculture in Omu-Aran Farm, Northcentral Nigeria. *Heliyon* 8: e08976. [CrossRef]

Kianguebene-Koussingounina, Chrisfanel E., Jerry O. Olajide-Kayode, Ibrahim A. Oyediran, Raymond Webrah Kazapoe, Ebenezer Ebo Yahans Amuah, Bawa Naziru, Aliyu Ohiani Umaru, and Millicent Obeng Addai. 2023. Geostatistical assessment of soils in Ibadan, Southwest Nigeria: Focus on agricultural lands. *Environmental and Sustainability Indicators* 19: 100287. [CrossRef]

Kolapo, Adetomiwa, Adekunle John Didunyemi, Oluwatoba John Aniyi, and Oluwatosin Emmanuel Obembe. 2022. Adoption of multiple sustainable land management practices and its effects on productivity of smallholder maize farmers in Nigeria. *Resources, Environment and Sustainability* 10: 100084. [CrossRef]

Kolapo, Adetomiwa, and Adeyera James Kolapo. 2023. Implementation of conservation agricultural practices as an effective response to mitigate climate change impact and boost crop productivity in Nigeria. *Journal of Agriculture and Food Research* 12: 100557. [CrossRef]

Latzer, Hélène, Kiminori Matsuyama, and Mathieu Parenti. 2019. *Reconsidering the Market Size Effect in Innovation and Growth*. Global Poverty Research Lab Working Paper. Brussels: BrusselsL Universite Libre de Bruxelles, pp. 19–106. [CrossRef]

Lawal, Adedoyin Isola, Abiola John Asaleye, Joseph Iseolorunkanmi, and Olabisi Popoola. 2018. Economic Growth, Agricultural Output and Tourism Development in Nigeria: An Application of the ARDL Bound Testing Approach. *Journal of Environmental Management and Tourism* 9: 786–794. [CrossRef]

Lawal, Adedoyin Isola, Awolusi Frank, and Babalola Kehinde Leke. 2015. Can Nigeria achieve millennium development goals? *The Journal of Social Sciences Research*. Available online: http://eprints.lmu.edu.ng/3065/ (accessed on 11 May 2024).

Lawal, Lawal, Adedoyin Isola, Tony I. Nwanji, Abiola Asaleye, Victor Ahmed, and Mariam Camarero, eds. 2016. Economic growth, financial development and trade openness in Nigeria: An application of the ARDL bound testing approach. *Cogent Economics & Finance* 4: 1258810. [CrossRef]

Lucas, Robert E., Jr. 1988. On the mechanics of economic development. *Journal of Monetary Economics* 22: 3–42. [CrossRef]

Maertens, Miet, Oyakhilomen Oyinbo, Tahirou Abdoulaye, and Jordan Chamberlin. 2023. Sustainable maize intensification through site-specific nutrient management advice: Experimental evidence from Nigeria. *Food Policy* 121: 102546. [CrossRef]

Mandal, Jajati, Waheed Ariyo Bakare, Mohammad Mahmudur Rahman, Md Aminur Rahman, Abu Bakkar Siddique, Effiom Oku, Michael D. Wood, Simon M. Hutchinson, and Debapriya Mondal. 2022. Varietal differences influence arsenic and lead contamination of rice grown in mining impacted agricultural fields of Zamfara State, Nigeria. *Chemosphere* 305: 135339. [CrossRef]

Mardiana, Harisa, and Esther Kembauw. 2021. The Role of Diffusion of Innovation in Agricultural to Compete in Asean Community. *IOP Conference Series: Earth and Environmental Science* 755: 012074. [CrossRef]

Matthew, Oluwatoyin A., Romanus Osabohien, Olanrewaju Olaniyi Omosehin, Nasreen Jawaid, Timothy Aderemi, Opeyemi Olanrewaju, and Patience N. Evans-Osabuohien. 2023. Information and communication technology deployment and agricultural value chain nexus in Nigeria. *Heliyon* 9: e19043. [CrossRef]

Melesse, Mequanint B., Philip Miriti, Geoffrey Muricho, Chris O. Ojiewo, and Victor Afari-Sefa. 2023. Adoption and impact of improved groundnut varieties on household food security in Nigeria. *Journal of Agriculture and Food Research* 14: 100817. [CrossRef]

Mwangi, Margaret, and Samuel Kariuki. 2015. Factors determining adoption of new agricultural technology by smallholder farmers in developing countries. *Journal of Economics and Sustainable Development* 6: 215–232.

National Information Technology Development Agency (NITDA). 2015. eAgriculture Portal. Available online: http://www.eagriculture.org.ng/eAgricPortal/ (accessed on 11 May 2024).

Ndaghu, Ndonkeu Nathanel, Tahirou Abdoulaye, Amina Mustapha, Djomo Choumbou Raoul Fani, Rayner Tabetando, Ukpe Udeme Henrietta, and Sahbong Lucy Kamsang. 2023. Gender differentiation on the determinants and intensity of adoption of Purdue Improved Cowpea Storage (PICS) bags in Northern Nigeria. *Heliyon* 9: e23026. [CrossRef]

Ogunsolu, Olamide. 2021. *Technological Transformation of the Agricultural Sector in Nigeria: An Antidote for Economic Recession*. Tallinn: Tallinn University of Technology, School of Business and Governance.

Ojo, Temitope O., and Lloyd JS Baiyegunhi. 2023. Gender differentials on productivity of rice farmers in Southwestern Nigeria: An Oaxaca-Blinder decomposition approach. *Heliyon* 9: e22724. [CrossRef]

Okafor, Chukwuebuka C., Chinelo A. Nzekwe, Charles C. Ajaero, Juliet C. Ibekwe, and Festus A. Otunomo. 2022. Biomass utilization for energy production in Nigeria: A review. *Cleaner Energy Systems* 3: 100043. [CrossRef]

Olayide, Olawale Emmanuel, Isaac Kow Tetteh, and Labode Popoola. 2016. Differential impacts of rainfall and irrigation on agricultural production in Nigeria: Any lessons for climate-smart agriculture? *Agricultural Water Management* 178: 30–36. [CrossRef]

Olujobi, Olusola Joshua, Uchechukwu Emena Okorie, Elizabeta Smaranda Olarinde, and Adetutu Deborah Aina-Pelemo. 2023. Legal responses to energy security and sustainability in Nigeria's power sector amidst fossil fuel disruptions and low carbon energy transition. *Heliyon* 9: e17912. [CrossRef]

Otekunrin, Olutosin A., Oluwaseun A. Otekunrin, S. Momoh, and Idris A. Ayinde. 2019. How far has Africa gone in achieving the zero-hunger target? Evidence from Nigeria. *Global Food Security* 22: 1–12. [CrossRef]

Oyetunde-Usman, Zainab, Kehinde Oluseyi Olagunju, and Oyinlola Rafiat Ogunpaimo. 2021. Determinants of adoption of multiple sustainable agricultural practices among smallholder farmers in Nigeria. *International Soil and Water Conservation Research* 9: 241–8. [CrossRef]

Parlasca, Martin C., Constantin Johnen, and Matin Qaim. 2022. Use of mobile financial services among farmers in Africa: Insights from Kenya. *Global Food Security* 32: 100590. [CrossRef]

Romer, Paul M. 1987. Growth based on increasing returns due to specialization. *The American Economic Review* 77: 56–62.

Romer, Paul M. 1990. Endogenous technological change. *Journal of Political Economy* 98: S71–S102. [CrossRef]

Rongjian, Yu, Ikpe-etim Nathan Obomufok, and N. Khan. 2019. The role of advanced technology in agricultural innovation. *Modern Concepts in Developmental Agronomy* 4: MCDA.000576. [CrossRef]

Sarimiento, Prime. 2000. Agriculture Weighed Down by Corruption and Waste. Philippine Centre for Investigative Journalism. Available online: http://www.pcij.org/stories/2000/agri.html (accessed on 12 October 2009).

Solow, Robert M. 1956. A contribution to the theory of economic growth. *The Quarterly Journal of Economics* 70: 65–94. [CrossRef]

Tabash, Mosab I., Ezekiel Oseni, Adel Ahmed, Yasmeen Elsantil, Linda Nalini Daniel, and Adedoyin Isola Lawal. 2024. Pathway to a Sustainable Energy Economy: Determinants of Electricity Infrastructure in Nigeria. *Sustainability* 16: 2953. [CrossRef]

Tabe-Ojong, Martin, Ghislain BD Aihounton, and Jourdain C. Lokossou. 2023. Climate-smart agriculture and food security: Cross-country evidence from West Africa. *Global Environmental Change* 81: 102697. [CrossRef]

Teklu, Abyiot, Belay Simane, and Mintewab Bezabih. 2023. Multiple adoption of climate-smart agriculture innovation for agricultural sustainability: Empirical evidence from the Upper Blue Nile Highlands of Ethiopia. *Climate Risk Management* 39: 100477. [CrossRef]

Uji, Wilfred Terlumun. 2020. Corruption and national development in Nigeria: An appraisal. *Global Journal of Human-Social Science: Sociology and Culture* 15: 9.

Valadkhani, Abbas, Arezoo Ghazanfari, Jeremy Nguyen, and Amir Moradi-Motlagh. 2021. The asymmetric effects of COVID-19 on wholesale fuel prices in Australia. *Economic Analysis and Policy* 71: 255–66. [CrossRef]

Wang, Yun, and Yuhao Qian. 2024. Driving factors to agriculture total factor productivity and its contribution to just energy transition. *Environmental Impact Assessment Review* 105: 107369. [CrossRef]

Wossen, Tesfamicheal, Abebe Menkir, Arega Alene, Tahirou Abdoulaye, Sam Ajala, Baffour Badu-Apraku, Melaku Gedil, Wendie Mengesha, and Silvestro Meseka. 2023. Drivers of transformation of the maize sector in Nigeria. *Global Food Security* 38: 100713. [CrossRef]

Yilanci, Veli, Ilham Haouas, Onder Ozgur, and Samuel Asumadu Sarkodie. 2021. Energy diversification and economic development in emergent countries: Evidence from Fourier function-driven bootstrap panel causality test. *Frontiers in Energy Research* 9: 632712. [CrossRef]

economies

MDPI

Article

Business Efficiency: Insights from Visegrad Four Before, During, and After the COVID-19 Pandemic

Pavol Durana [1,*], Erika Kovalova [1], Roman Blazek [1] and Klaudia Bicanovska [2]

[1] Department of Economics, Faculty of Operation and Economics of Transport and Communications, University of Zilina, Univerzitna 1, 010 26 Zilina, Slovakia; erika.kovalova@uniza.sk (E.K.); roman.blazek@uniza.sk (R.B.)
[2] Sungwoo Hitech Slovakia s.r.o., Cestarska 1, 010 01 Zilina, Slovakia
* Correspondence: pavol.durana@uniza.sk

Abstract

Efficiency is one of the tenets in assessing the financial health of an enterprise. Ultimately, the form of asset management has a major impact on growth but also on the decline of profit. It also reveals how the enterprises are positioned within the competitive market environment. For this reason, the aim of this article is to define the level of business activity in the Visegrad Four in the pre-crisis, during-crisis and post-crisis periods of the COVID-19 pandemic. The investigation included 48,650 enterprises from Slovakia, Czechia, Poland, and Hungary over the period 2017–2023. We determined the median values of eleven business efficiency indicators separately for each country and sector. The Friedman test and Kruskal–Wallis test confirmed significant differences between years and countries. Furthermore, multiple pairwise comparisons revealed analogies between the pre-crisis and post-crisis periods, as well as similarities between the two pandemic years for the tested ratios. One can observe that the results serve as the foundation for regional and international benchmarks, particularly for enterprises from former Eastern Bloc countries.

Keywords: activity ratios; assets; COVID-19; efficiency; Visegrad Four

1. Introduction

Changes in the global market have posed critical challenges for industrial and services industries (Capestro et al., 2024). Especially, the COVID-19 pandemic, which started in the first quarter of 2020, triggered unprecedented economic challenges, prompting governments worldwide to implement intervention measures to mitigate its impacts on business and employment (Svabova et al., 2024). During negative pandemic years, 2020 and 2021, several companies have come to believe in the importance of continuous analysis of the financial situation (Atayah et al., 2022; Derco, 2022). Business continuity and sustainability of business operations, especially for managing any turbulent situation like the COVID-19 pandemic, are necessary (Chatterjee et al., 2024). Identification of threats and business weaknesses, but also preparation for unexpected and crisis situations (Lukac et al., 2022), were the most important areas of interest for the company's management (Gajdosikova et al., 2022; Adamowicz, 2022). Despite the partial improvement in the situation, global stabilization has not yet taken place. The ongoing energy crisis also corresponds to the current development (Harantova et al., 2022). Particularly, considering the mentioned rationale, it is crucial to persist in monitoring the financial well-being of the company through the use of appropriate tools (Bartos et al., 2022). Effective monitoring of financial health is essential in the financial management of enterprises (Valaskova et al., 2023a). Financial managers must implement a mechanism for analysing the financial situation that will effectively respond to all stimuli threatening the very existence of the company and its further operation in the market (Mijoc, 2024; Bizjak et al., 2024).

One of the most important steps in financial analysis, apart from the preparation of financial statements and the collection of data from around the company (Chambost & Praquin, 2021), is the process of choosing an appropriate method (Michalkova et al., 2022). Businesses use various procedures and techniques that bring relevant results. Currently, various statistical analysis methods are gaining prominence, while, at the same time, "traditional" methods like ratio analysis continue to receive constant application (Kovalchuk & Verhun, 2019). The analysis includes several groups of indicators that represent the basic elements of various professional studies, due to their simple applicability in business practice (Gonchar, 2016). This paper primarily focuses on one of these indicator groups, revealing the effectiveness of individual property components in the operational process (Goldmann, 2020).

Activity indicators, together with recommendations resulting from the achieved results, represent an important part of analysing the financial health of the company (Hiadlovsky et al., 2016). Ultimately, the form of asset management has a major impact on growth but also on the decline of profit (Amoa-Gyarteng, 2021). It also indicates the position of the company in the environment of market competition (Kristof & Virag, 2022). Thus, the aim of this article is to define the level of business activity in the Visegrad Four in the pre-crisis, during-crisis, and post-crisis periods of the COVID-19 pandemic.

In addition, the bibliometric analysis was realised by VOSviewer version 1.6.20 to prove the significance of the solved issue. The method is used to provide quantitative analysis of published documents (Eger & Žižka, 2024). This search query was used in Web of Science: "business efficiency" (Topic) or "business activity" (Topic) or "activity ratio" (Topic) and Economics (Web of Science Categories) or Business (Web of Science Categories) or Management (Web of Science Categories) or Business Finance (Web of Science Categories) and Article (Document Types). The targeted issue yielded 1385 related articles. Figure 1 represents a bibliometric map of 32 dominant countries involved in this issue (each country published at least 15 articles). This led to the creation of four clusters of cooperating countries within business efficiency. Hungary, as a part of the Visegrad Four, is not included, but Slovakia, Czechia, and Poland are included. The red cluster dominates the map, connecting the USA, China, Australia, Germany, Canada, Brazil, Portugal, South Korea, Switzerland, Finland, Japan, and Russia. The green cluster includes the remaining developed European countries that are historically or economically connected to themselves or with others from the cluster, including England, France, Italy, Spain, Scotland, New Zealand, India, and Pakistan. Malaysia, Indonesia, Vietnam, and Taiwan represent close Asian cooperation in the yellow cluster. Slovakia, Czechia, and Poland, along with Ukraine, Lithuania, Croatia, Serbia, and Bosnia and Herzegovina, form a blue cluster of post-Soviet cooperation.

VOSviewer also created the bibliometric map of keyword occurrence (Figure 2). Each keyword must be marked at least 20 times in used articles. Four clusters were detected. The red cluster concentrates on the overall management and performance of business efficiency, encompassing aspects such as returns, governance, models, risk, and market. The blue one illustrates the financial aspect of business efficiency, encompassing factors such as profitability, financial performance, capital structure, and productivity. Business potential is defined by a yellow cluster that includes strategy, innovation, knowledge, sustainability, technology, etc. The last cluster is the green one that is related to this article and maps business activity through entrepreneurship, the effect of economic growth, foreign direct investments, and crisis periods, as well as COVID-19 consequences.

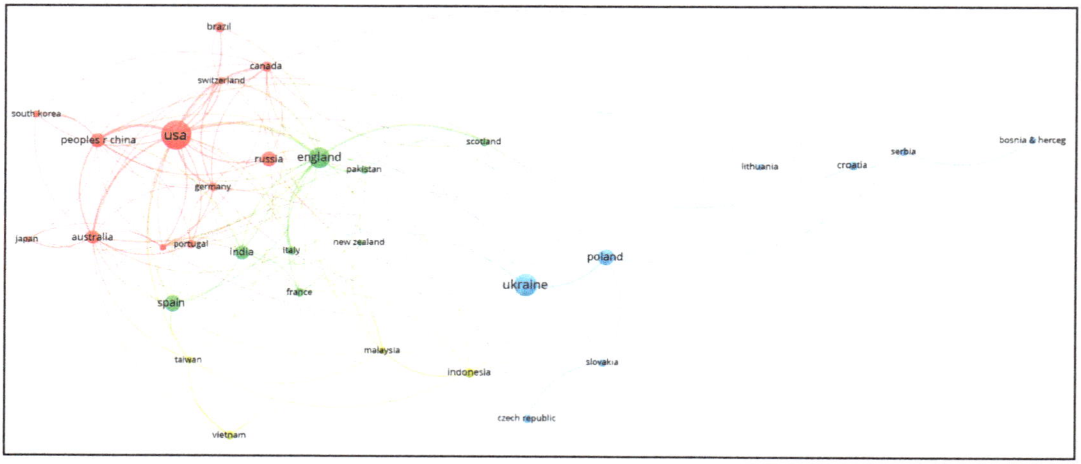

Figure 1. Bibliometric map of cooperating countries. Own processing.

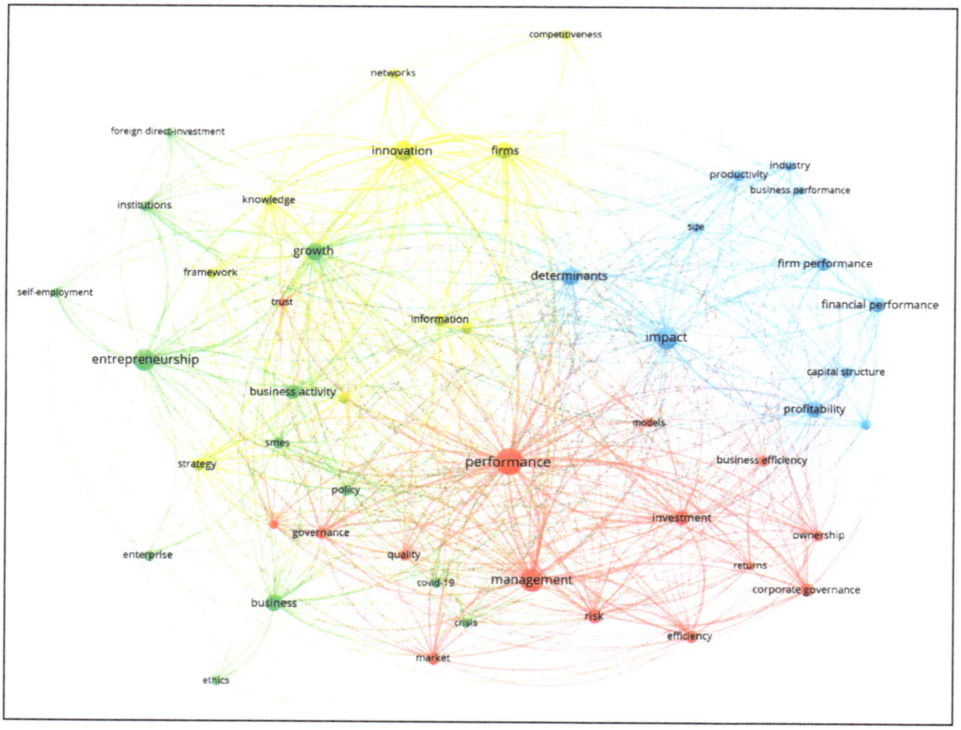

Figure 2. Bibliometric map of co-occurrence of keywords. Own processing.

The article is organised as follows: A literature review covers the theoretical background of business efficiency. The paper then proceeds to explain the creation of the sample from V4, calculate activity ratios, and identify the preferred tests. The results illustrate the median values of eleven ratios and test the set hypotheses. The discussion compares the results. The conclusions outline potential focuses for future research and identify the limitations of the current study.

2. Literature Review

Svabova et al. (2022); Kramolis and Dobes (2020) define seven initial goals, which are as follows: evaluation of the impact of internal and external factors on the existence of the company, assessment of changes in the management of the business entity, sectoral comparison of financial indicators, monitoring of mutual relationships between the analysed indicators, creation of a relevant information source for the needs of managerial decision-making, prediction of the future financial situation of the enterprise in various variations, and defining recommendations for planning and management (Rahman & Sharma, 2020).

Mirza et al. (2020) consider information available from financial statements to be the primary element of financial analysis. This statement is further supplemented by Pech et al. (2020), who describe the financial statement as a source of information about the business activity of the accounting unit. Sacer et al. (2018); Demirhan and Anwar (2014) state that each financial statement contains specific data. In the case of the profit and loss statement, it is mainly a display of the achieved performance of the business entity during a defined period. On the other hand, the balance sheet captures the state of the company's financial situation as of a specified date. Notes are also an important part. The last part of the financial statements is supplementary to the previous statements. It also presents changes in cash flows, which are found in the cash flow statement (Makoji et al., 2021).

Welc (2016) and Fitriani (2023) consider the method of ratio analysis, which is based on the quantification of ratios of selected data from accounting statements, to be the main method of assessing the financial health of a company. This method consists of indicators aimed at assessing the profitability, liquidity, indebtedness, activity, and market value of the company (Priya & Sharma, 2023). According to Hunjra et al. (2011), ratio indicators are considered important metrics for determining the performance but also the growth of the company. Jones and Godday (2015) further highlight the importance of ratio indicators in investment decision making but also in taking measures to improve the financial performance of the company (Batrancea, 2021).

Activity indicators monitor the company's ability to use assets (its assets)—they indicate how efficiently the company uses its individual assets, i.e., whether the company has enough productive assets or not (Hyrslova et al., 2017). It is important for a business to find a reasonable ratio between the assets the business has acquired to achieve its sales and the sales of the business. If the company has high assets compared to sales, it can be said that the company is using its assets economically (Yousaf et al., 2021). If, on the other hand, it has a lack of assets, it prepares itself for the revenues that would arise from potential orders. In other words, the acceleration of asset turnover is a positive trend because it means higher sales for businesses. However, excessive acceleration of turnover can threaten the flow of production and sales (Tian & He, 2016).

Susellawati et al. (2022) characterise the meaning of the quantification of activity indicators as the ability to define the level of asset efficiency in the operational process. The contribution of selected asset items in the process of revenue generation is also assessed, as is the number of investments in current and non-current assets. To determine the competitiveness of the analysed entity, the activity indicators are also used to compare companies within the respective industries. As individual branches of the national economy are characterised by a different structure of assets and, consequently, turnover, Kovalchuk and Verhun (2019) draw attention to the diversity of the results of activity indicators depending on the characteristics of the branch.

For this reason, they consider it important to adequately adapt and improve the applied methods and procedures of financial analysis in view of the specific circumstances of the business activity of the analysed entity (Rep, 2021). The authors subsequently state in their article that effective management of corporate assets will be reflected in the growth of turnover indicators but also in the growth of the company's competitiveness (Belas et al., 2022). According to Mia et al. (2014), among the most used activity indicators that we can include are accounts receivable turnover, asset turnover, and inventory turnover.

Information on the collection of receivables from corporate customers can be determined using the receivables turnover indicator. To evaluate the proportionality of assets in relation to sales production, on the other hand, the turnover of total assets is used, which, according to Purwanto and Bina (2016), is considered one of the most important indicators of company evaluation. The last indicator of activity is inventory turnover, which Farooq (2018) perceives as a tool for determining the number of conversions of inventory sales during the year. Zisoudis et al. (2020) claim that a high inventory turnover will ensure a faster process of revenue generation but also a lower probability of depreciation of the company's inventory.

In several studies, we record the analysis of activity indicators in connection with the assessment of the impact of property items on the profitability of the company (Gazi et al., 2022; Hunjra et al., 2011). While Pham et al. (2020) concluded that there is a positive relationship between receivables turnover time, inventory turnover time, liability maturity period, and profitability, Rezai and Pourali (2015), on the contrary, identified the inverse nature of the mutual connection between the mentioned activity indicators and profitability. Different results were also achieved by Tahir and Anuar (2016), who, based on the evaluation of 127 companies in the textile industry, confirmed the existence of a negative relationship between receivables turnover time and profitability.

On the other hand, they established a positive relationship between profitability and the turnover period of liabilities and the turnover period of receivables. Activity indicators are also included in the analysis of bankruptcy models as variables involved in predicting the future financial situation of the company. One of the studies focused on the issue was also published by Kliestik et al. (2020), who dealt with prediction models of transitive economies. The result of the investigation was the identification of financial indicators with the greatest frequency of occurrence in the given models. Out of a set of 917 indicators, asset turnover ranked third. A similar study was carried out by Kovacova et al. (2019), in which they used constructed bankruptcy prediction models in the territory of the Visegrad Four countries. From the group of activity indicators, the ratio of sales to total assets was also most often used, but it was part of only the Czech and Polish prediction models. In the case of the Slovak Republic and Hungary, the occurrence of the indicator is zero (Gundova & Medvedova, 2016; Valaskova et al., 2021).

We can also identify the use of activity indicators when assessing the financial performance of selected business entities (Valaskova et al., 2019). For example, Shukla and Roopa (2017) deal with the mentioned issue, whose aim was to determine the financial performance of Indian telecommunication service providers. Podhorska and Siekelova (2020) compared the financial situation of companies from the IT sector. Selected activity indicators can also be found in the article by Rafaqat and Rafaqat (2020), who analysed the impact of mergers and acquisitions on the financial performance of technology companies. In their conclusions, they stated that it was based on activity indicators that they identified the significant effects of the mentioned forms of direct foreign investment on the financial performance of business entities. In the company's management system, the evaluation of the company's efficiency occupies a prominent place, since the adoption of strategically important managerial decisions depends on its results.

Since business efficiency is a multidimensional phenomenon, its evaluation involves the use of many indicators, which complicates management (Kliestik et al., 2020). The integrated approach as a modern, progressive, methodical apparatus makes it possible to systematise indicators into sub-indices and thus obtain one integrated indicator of the business efficiency of enterprises (Balaniuk et al., 2020).

Activity indicators, together with recommendations arising from the achieved results, represent an important part of the analysis of the company's financial health. Ultimately, the form of asset management has a major impact on growth, but also on profit decline (Istok & Kanderova, 2019; Purwanto & Bina, 2016). It also indicates the company's position in the environment of market competition. Business efficiency of a business is the most important sign of its viability. Business efficiency is primarily the ability of a business to generate income and profit even under the most adverse external and internal conditions.

In this case, there are also external conditions that do not directly depend on the company's actions, especially market demand, business conditions, the overall state of the company, and the state of the financial and credit system (Valaskova et al., 2021). There are also internal conditions that are created because of the enterprise, especially value-added production, resource potential, production capacity, innovation, etc. In this regard, the assessment of the business efficiency of the enterprise is a multifaceted component of management, which includes a significant number of absolute or monetary indicators and indicators, their dynamics, and criteria (Gajdosikova et al., 2022).

The results from the Visegrad Four region assessing efficiency are as follows: Kliestik et al. (2020) emphasised that structural economic factors heavily influence asset efficiency and financial health. Similarly, Gajdosikova and Pavic Kramaric (2023) highlighted the role of divergent national policies in shaping financial health indicators across industries.

Analysing the efficiency of corporate assets and fixed assets utilization highlights notable regional differences among Visegrad Group countries. Indicators analysing asset efficiency recorded the best results in Polish and Czech companies. However, Svabova et al. (2020), who analysed financial data from 400 Slovak firms, argue that insufficient reinvestment in capital assets significantly contributes to inefficiency in Slovak companies. Despite these shortcomings, Slovak firms demonstrate exceptional performance in managing warehouse stocks. This finding aligns with Vavrek et al. (2021), who analysed 469 Slovak agricultural enterprises and emphasised the importance of inventory management in mitigating financial instability. Mazanec (2022) notes that success in optimization in collection period ratio can be gained through the implementation of strict credit management policies.

Jencova et al. (2024) add that they applied multicriteria evaluation methods (MCEM) and nonmetric multidimensional scaling (NMDS) to assess hospital performance in Slovakia during pre-crisis, crisis, and post-crisis periods. Their research demonstrates how temporal changes in performance rankings can highlight strengths and weaknesses in operational and financial strategies.

Papikova and Papik (2022) further expand the scope by examining the role of intellectual capital in determining profitability. Their analysis of 24,351 Slovak SMEs highlights the positive relationship between intellectual capital and profitability before the pandemic, as well as the challenges faced during the crisis. Restrictions primarily affected sectors like tourism and gastronomy, where structural capital and capital-employed efficiencies had a negative impact on profitability. This sector-specific vulnerability highlights the broader theme of the pandemic's disproportionate impact on industries with limited adaptability.

Valaskova et al. (2023b) contribute to the understanding of how corporate debt influences financial health and resilience. Using the Friedman test to analyse Slovak firms from 2018 to 2021, they identified significant shifts in financial indicators, particularly in self-financing and equity leverage ratios. Their findings underscore the pandemic's adverse effects on corporate indebtedness while emphasizing the need for robust debt policies to ensure long-term financial stability.

In the service sector, Bacik et al. (2020) examined 585 hotel businesses across the V4 region to investigate the impact of industry characteristics on financial stability and activity indicators. Their study revealed that Polish firms outperformed their Slovak counterparts in generating consistent returns from fixed assets, attributed to better capital utilization strategies. Similarly, Vitéz-Durgula et al. (2023) analysed healthcare SMEs across the V4 countries and noted that Polish and Czech firms showcased superior asset management efficiency compared to Slovak enterprises, which face challenges in reinvestment.

Between 2020 and 2021, activity indicators across the V4 countries demonstrated a predominantly negative trend. Simionescu et al. (2021) observe that the adoption of digital tools during the COVID-19 pandemic improved financial performance in key sectors across the V4 region, particularly in Poland and Hungary.

3. Materials and Methods

The origin data were gained from Database Orbis, provided by Moody's (Moody's, 2024). The sample after removing missing values consisted of 48,650 enterprises from the Visegrad Group. This group of countries represents the political grouping of Central European states, specifically the regional cooperation of Slovakia (SK), the Czech Republic (CZ), Hungary (HU), and Poland (PL). The largest number of assessed business entities have Polish nationality. In total, the sample comprises 20,479 Polish enterprises, accounting for a 42.09% share. Furthermore, 16,901 business entities, holding a 34.74% share, represent the Slovak Republic. The sample also includes 5,354 enterprises from the Czech Republic and 5,916 enterprises from Hungary that are analysed. It was evaluated over seven years (2017–2023), covering the period before (2017–2019), during (2020–2021), and after (2022–2023) the COVID-19 pandemic.

Table 1 shows the structure of the final sample according to the NACE (statistical classification of economic activities in the European community).

Table 1. Structure of the sample according to NACE.

Sector	NACE Description	Number of Enterprises	Share
A	Agriculture, forestry, and fishing	2411	4.96%
B	Mining and quarrying	240	0.49%
C	Manufacturing	11,110	22.84%
D	Electricity, gas, steam, and air conditioning supply	1042	2.14%
E	Water supply, sewerage, waste management, and remediation activities	1150	2.36%
F	Construction	3558	7.31%
G	Wholesale and retail trade; repair of motor vehicles and motorcycles	12,614	25.93%
H	Transporting and storage	2424	4.98%
I	Accommodation and food service activities	821	1.69%
J	Information and communication	1608	3.31%
K	Financial and insurance activities	675	1.39%
L	Real estate activities	4454	9.16%
M	Professional, scientific, and technical activities	3086	6.34%
N	Administrative and support service activities	1709	3.51%
O	Public administration and defence, compulsory social security	29	0.06%
P	Education	245	0.50%
Q	Human health and social work activities	777	1.60%
R	Arts, entertainment, and recreation	441	0.91%
S	Other service activities	256	0.53%

Source: own processing.

There are three groups into which the activity ratios fall. Turnover ratios (Equations (1)–(3) determine the number of conversions of a particular asset over the year. Then, the inverted values of these ratios express the level of commitment (Equations (4)–(6). Finally, the turnover period ratios (Equations (7)–(11) represent the duration of a single conversion in days (Zagita et al., 2024). The coefficients of commitment are based on the same principle as for the turnover period ratios, but the difference is in the use of a time interval (Bartosova & Kral, 2016). The calculation of ratios is as follows, and it is based on Aqil et al. (2019); Bărbuță-Mișu et al. (2019); Kwak (2019); Lian et al. (2021); Yousaf et al. (2021).

$$\text{Asset turnover} = \frac{\text{sales}}{\text{average total assets}} \tag{1}$$

$$\text{Fixed asset turnover} = \frac{\text{sales}}{\text{average fixed assets}} \tag{2}$$

$$\text{Inventory turnover} = \frac{\text{sales}}{\text{average inventory}} \tag{3}$$

$$\text{Asset to sales ratio} = \frac{\text{average total assets}}{\text{sales}} \tag{4}$$

$$\text{Fixed asset to sales ratio} = \frac{\text{average fixed assets}}{\text{sales}} \tag{5}$$

$$\text{Inventory turnover period} = \frac{\text{average inventory}}{\text{sales}} \tag{6}$$

$$\text{Inventory to sales ratio} = \frac{\text{average total assets}}{\text{sales}} \tag{7}$$

$$\text{Fixed asset turnover period} = \frac{\text{average fixed assets}}{\text{sales}} \cdot 365 \tag{8}$$

$$\text{Inventory turnover period} = \frac{\text{average inventory}}{\text{sales}} \cdot 365 \tag{9}$$

$$\text{Collection period ratio} = \frac{\text{average current trade receivables}}{\text{sales}} \cdot 365 \tag{10}$$

$$\text{Credit period ratio} = \frac{\text{average current trade liabilities}}{\text{sales}} \cdot 365 \tag{11}$$

Verification of a normal distribution is the basic premise of the application of several statistical methods. It involves testing the normal distribution of the analysed set. If the sample of the data set includes at least 50 measurements, the Kolmogorov–Smirnov test is preferred (Linares-Mustaros et al., 2022). Based on pre-processing, the final sample of all calculated ratios for each year in this research cannot confirm the normal distribution of data.

That is why non-parametric tests were applied for testing. The Friedman test, the first mentioned statistical procedure, identifies differences between dependent samples. The rejection of the null hypothesis indicates significant differences between the distributions. In addition, it was necessary to run pairwise comparisons (Liu & Xu, 2022). The following hypotheses were tested:

H_{0a}. *The distributions of activity ratios (asset turnover, fixed asset turnover, inventory turnover, asset to sales ratio, fixed asset to sales ratio, inventory to sales ratio, asset turnover period, fixed asset turnover period, inventory turnover period, collection period ratio) are not influenced by the specific year.*

H_{1a}. *The distributions of activity ratio (asset turnover, fixed asset turnover, inventory turnover, asset to sales ratio, fixed asset to sales ratio, inventory to sales ratio, asset turnover period, fixed asset turnover period, inventory turnover period, collection period ratio) are influenced by the specific year. The activity ratio differs between at least one pair of years.*

Secondly, the Kruskal–Wallis test was also used to compare at least three independent samples. As with the Friedman test, we also perform a post-hoc analysis when rejecting the null hypothesis with the Kruskal–Wallis test. Multiple comparisons are made using the Dunn–Bonferroni corrections. The mentioned method identifies files that show significant differences between distributions (Kwak, 2019). The following hypotheses were tested for each year (2016, 2017, 2018, 2019, 2020, 2021, 2022, 2023):

H_{0b}. *The distributions of activity ratios (asset turnover, fixed asset turnover, inventory turnover, asset to sales ratio, fixed asset to sales ratio, inventory to sales ratio, asset turnover period, fixed asset turnover period, inventory turnover period, collection period ratio) are not influenced by the country.*

H_{1b}. *The distributions of activity ratios (asset turnover, fixed asset turnover, inventory turnover, asset to sales ratio, fixed asset to sales ratio, inventory to sales ratio, asset turnover period, fixed asset turnover period, inventory turnover period, collection period ratio) are influenced by country. The activity ratio differs between at least one pair of countries.*

All hypotheses were tested on a significant level of alpha 0.05 by IBM SPSS Statistics version 28.0.

4. Results

Firstly, this chapter provides a description of the median values of the analysed activity ratios, both from the perspective of the assessed country and each individual year. The assessment of the development per individual indicator and per country during pandemic years is presented below according to three groups: turnover ratios (Table 2), asset to sales ratios (Table 3), and turnover period ratios (Table 4).

Table 2. Median values of turnover ratios according to countries.

V4				**Asset Turnover [Coefficient]**			
	2017	**2018**	**2019**	**2020**	**2021**	**2022**	**2023**
SK	0.87	0.87	0.86	0.80	0.83	0.85	0.89
CZ	1.40	1.38	1.35	1.27	1.31	1.35	1.39
PL	1.40	1.39	1.38	1.27	1.33	1.37	1.41
HU	1.29	1.30	1.27	1.17	1.17	1.23	1.26
V4				**Fixed asset turnover [coefficient]**			
	2017	2018	2019	2020	2021	2022	2023
SK	2.76	2.74	2.72	2.52	2.70	2.73	2.75
CZ	3.82	3.88	3.85	3.66	3.92	3.85	3.81
PL	4.41	4.45	4.35	4.12	4.52	4.40	4.39
HU	3.52	3.55	3.47	3.20	3.36	3.49	3.50
V4				**Inventory turnover [coefficient]**			
	2017	2018	2019	2020	2021	2022	2023
SK	7.06	7.09	6.91	6.45	6.34	7.01	7.05
CZ	8.14	7.98	7.95	7.73	7.43	7.99	8.12
PL	9.45	9.33	9.36	9.07	8.64	8.93	9.32
HU	8.41	8.27	8.56	8.27	7.95	8.17	8.44

Source: own processing.

Table 3. Median values of asset to sales ratios according to countries.

V4	2017	2018	2019	2020	2021	2022	2023
				Asset to Sales Ratio [Coefficient]			
SK	1.14	1.14	1.17	1.25	1.21	1.16	1.13
CZ	0.72	0.72	0.74	0.79	0.76	0.73	0.70
PL	0.72	0.72	0.73	0.79	0.75	0.72	0.72
HU	0.78	0.77	0.79	0.85	0.86	0.80	0.77
				Fixed asset to sales ratio [coefficient]			
V4	2017	2018	2019	2020	2021	2022	2023
SK	0.32	0.32	0.33	0.35	0.33	0.32	0.31
CZ	0.25	0.25	0.25	0.26	0.24	0.25	0.25
PL	0.22	0.22	0.23	0.24	0.21	0.22	0.20
HU	0.28	0.27	0.28	0.30	0.28	0.28	0.26
				Inventory to sales ratio [coefficient]			
V4	2017	2018	2019	2020	2021	2022	2023
SK	0.03	0.03	0.03	0.03	0.03	0.03	0.03
CZ	0.06	0.06	0.06	0.06	0.06	0.06	0.06
PL	0.05	0.05	0.05	0.05	0.05	0.05	0.05
HU	0.06	0.06	0.06	0.06	0.06	0.06	0.06

Source: own processing.

Table 4. Median values of turnover period ratios according to countries.

V4	2017	2018	2019	2020	2021	2022	2023
				Asset Turnover Period [Day]			
SK	417	417	426	455	440	418	413
CZ	261	263	270	287	277	269	262
PL	262	263	265	289	273	263	260
HU	283	281	287	312	312	295	289
				Fixed asset turnover period [day]			
V4	2017	2018	2019	2020	2021	2022	2023
SK	118	118	120	129	119	119	116
CZ	90	90	90	95	87	91	90
PL	82	81	82	87	78	80	82
HU	101	99	102	111	104	102	100
				Inventory turnover period [day]			
V4	2017	2018	2019	2020	2021	2022	2023
SK	10	10	10	11	12	10	10
CZ	22	21	21	22	23	20	21
PL	18	18	18	18	20	18	18
HU	22	22	22	21	22	22	22
				Collection period ratio [day]			
V4	2017	2018	2019	2020	2021	2022	2023
SK	47	45	43	43	43	44	46
CZ	42	41	39	39	38	40	41
PL	49	47	45	44	44	46	46
HU	31	31	28	27	26	29	30
				Credit period ratio [day]			
V4	2017	2018	2019	2020	2021	2022	2023
SK	39	38	35	35	35	37	38
CZ	28	27	26	26	27	29	28
PL	29	28	26	24	26	26	28
HU	21	22	20	19	20	22	22

Source: own processing.

4.1. Turnover Ratios

The asset turnover ratio in Slovakia decreased to 0.80 in 2020, a significant decrease compared to previous years (2017–2019, where it was around 0.86–0.87). In 2021, it increased slightly to 0.83, indicating some stabilization after the initial decline. In the Czech Republic, the ratio decreased to 1.27 in 2020 (from 1.35 in 2019), which is a significant decrease in performance. However, in 2021, there was a partial improvement to 1.31, indicating some return to pre-pandemic values. In Poland, there was a decrease to 1.27 in 2020 from 1.38 in 2019, which is a similar trend to the Czech Republic. In 2021, it increased to 1.33, showing signs of recovery in Poland. This indicator decreased to 1.17 in Hungary in 2020, which represents a significant decrease from the previous value of 1.27. In 2021, it remained at the same level of 1.17, indicating the absence of a significant recovery during this period.

The value of the fixed asset turnover indicator in Slovakia decreased to 2.52 in 2020 (compared to 2.72 in 2019), which indicates a less efficient use of fixed assets. The increase in 2021 to 2.70 indicates an improvement in efficiency, which may be associated with the recovery of sales and better adaptation of enterprises to pandemic conditions. In 2020, the fixed asset turnover indicator decreased to 3.66 (compared to 3.85 in 2019), which signals a temporary weakening of revenue generation from fixed assets. Enterprises were able to increase the efficiency of using their fixed assets in 2021, as evidenced by an increase to 3.92, surpassing the pre-pandemic level. In 2020, the fixed asset turnover decreased to 4.12 from 4.35 in 2019 in Poland, indicating a weakening of performance. The increase to 4.52 in 2021 indicates a significant recovery and even better performance than before the pandemic in Poland. The median value of fixed asset turnover in Hungary decreased in 2020 to 3.20 (compared to 3.47 in 2019), indicating a significant weakening of the efficiency of the use of fixed assets. We identify an increase to 3.36 in 2021, suggesting a slight recovery, but the value remains below the pre-pandemic level, indicating a lack of full efficiency restoration.

Slovakia in 2020 reported a decrease in inventory turnover to 6.45 (compared to 6.91 in 2019), indicating a slowdown in inventory turnover, which may be a result of reduced demand or distribution issues during the pandemic. In 2021, there was a further decrease to 6.34, indicating continued challenges in inventory management and maintaining efficiency. In 2020, the Czech Republic recorded a decrease in inventory turnover to 7.73 from 7.95 in 2019, indicating a slight weakening of turnover. A further decrease in 2021 to 7.43 indicates that the challenges associated with effective inventory management persisted into the second year of the pandemic. In 2020, Poland also recorded a decrease to 9.07 (compared to 9.36 in 2019), indicating a slowdown in inventory turnover. A further decline in 2021 to 8.64 suggests that problems with effective inventory management persisted into the second year of the pandemic. Hungary identified a decline in 2020 to 8.27 (from 8.56 in 2019) and shows a slight decrease in inventory turnover efficiency. The value fell to 7.95 in 2021, indicating a continued weakening of inventory management, likely due to ongoing restrictions and reduced demand.

4.2. Asset to Sales Ratios

The asset to sales ratio in Slovakia in 2020 increased to 1.25 (compared to 1.17 in 2019), indicating reduced efficiency of asset use. In 2021, the value decreased to 1.21, indicating a partial improvement in efficiency. In the Czech Republic in 2020, the indicator increased to 0.79 (compared to 0.74 in 2019), reflecting a weakening of the efficiency of asset use. In 2021, it decreased to 0.76, indicating a slight improvement in efficiency. The analysed indicator increased in Poland in 2020 to 0.79 from the pre-pandemic 0.73, indicating lower efficiency of asset use. In 2021, it decreased to 0.75. In Hungary, the asset to sales ratio increased to 0.85 in 2020 (compared to 0.79 in 2019). In 2021, another slight increase to 0.86 signals that the efficiency of asset use has not continued to improve.

The fixed asset to sales ratio in Slovakia increased to 0.35 in 2020 from 0.33 in 2019, reflecting lower efficiency. The decrease to 0.33 indicates a slight improvement in 2021. In the Czech Republic, the fixed asset to sales ratio recorded a slight increase to 0.26 in 2020, signalling a temporary weakening of efficiency. The value of 0.24 in 2021 indicates an improvement and a return to pre-pandemic values. In Poland, there was an increase to 0.24 in 2020 from 0.23 in 2019. In 2021, there was a decrease to 0.21, indicating a significant recovery in fixed asset efficiency. In Hungary, there was an increase to 0.30 in 2020, indicating lower efficiency. In 2021, a drop to 0.28 signals a slight improvement but not a return to pre-pandemic levels.

The median values of the inventory to sales ratio remained unchanged throughout the analysed period: in Slovakia, 0.03; in the Czech Republic, 0.06; in Poland, 0.05; and in Hungary, 0.06.

4.3. Turnover Period Ratios

The asset turnover period in Slovakia increased from 426 to 455 days in 2020. In 2021, there was an improvement to 440 days, which indicates a partial recovery of economic activity. In the Czech Republic in 2020, there was also an increase from 270 to 287 days. In 2021, there was an improvement to 277 days, which indicates a recovery of efficiency but still slightly below the pre-pandemic level. In Poland, the asset turnover period in 2020 increased from 265 to 289 days, indicating temporary difficulties with asset turnover. In 2021, there was a decrease to 273 days, which signals a faster return to pre-crisis levels compared to other countries. In Hungary, the indicator increased from 287 to 312 days in 2020, which indicates a significant deterioration in the efficiency of asset use. Stagnation at 312 days in 2021 points to ongoing problems in the economy.

The fixed asset turnover period in Slovakia in 2020 extended from 120 to 129 days, reflecting a decline in the efficiency of fixed asset use. In 2021, there was an improvement to 119 days, indicating a return to the pre-crisis level. In the Czech Republic, there was an extension from 90 to 95 days in 2020. In 2021, there was a significant improvement, reaching 87 days, the highest efficiency in the V4. In Poland, there was an extension from 82 to 87 days in 2020, indicating a temporary decline in efficiency. In 2021, there was a significant improvement to 78 days, indicating the most efficient use of fixed assets in the region. In Hungary, there was an extension from 102 to 111 days in 2020, indicating significant efficiency problems. The situation improved to 104 days in 2021, yet it remained worse than before the pandemic.

The inventory turnover period in Slovakia in 2020 increased from 10 to 11 days. In 2021, there was an additional rise to 12 days. In 2020, there was a noted increase from 21 to 22 days in the Czech Republic, and this trend continued in 2021 with an increase to 23 days. In Poland, we detected stability at 18 days in 2020, indicating a smaller impact of the pandemic on inventory turnover. However, 2021 saw an increase to 20 days. In Hungary, we observed a decrease from 22 to 21 days in 2020, suggesting more effective inventory management during the pandemic. In 2021, the inventory returned to its pre-crisis level, returning to 22 days.

The collection period ratio decreased compared to pre-pandemic values. This ratio was stable at 43 days in 2020 and 2021, indicating that companies effectively manage receivables. The Czech Republic also shows stability at 39 days in 2020. In 2021, there was an enhancement to 38 days, which validates efficient management of receivables. In Poland, a decrease from 45 to 44 days occurred in 2020, indicating a slight improvement in receivables management. In 2021, the value remained consistent at 44 days. Receivables management in Hungary improved from 28 to 27 days in 2020, making it the best in the V4 region. In 2021, there was an additional enhancement to 26 days, which remains the lowest value for the analysed countries.

The credit period ratio for Slovakia in 2020 is stable at 35 days, indicating consistency in payment terms, the same in 2021. In the Czech Republic in 2020, the stability value was 26 days, the shortest credit terms in the V4. In 2021, there was a slight increase to 27 days, reflecting flexibility in credit terms. In Poland, we identified a decrease from 26 to 24 days in 2020, indicating stricter credit terms during the pandemic. The return to 26 days in 2021 signifies the relaxation of terms following the economic stabilization. In Hungary in 2020, there was a decrease from 20 to 19 days. In 2021, we recorded a 20-day credit period ratio.

Secondly, to comprehensively explain the issue of business activity and provide the possibility of international cross-sectoral benchmark median values of asset turnover (Table A1), the fixed asset turnover (Table A2), inventory turnover (Table A3), asset to sales ratio (Table A4), fixed asset to sales ratio (Table A5), inventory to sales ratio (Table A6), asset turnover period (Table A7), fixed asset turnover period (Table A8), inventory turnover period (Table A9), collection period ratio (Table A10), credit period ratio (Table A11) according to NACE are provided in Appendix A.

5. Discussion

The Friedman test was run to identify differences between the years for all activity ratios. If the computed p-value is lower than the significance level alpha (Table 5), one should reject the null hypothesis and accept that all activity ratios (asset turnover, fixed asset turnover, inventory turnover, asset to sales ratio, fixed asset to sales ratio, inventory to sales ratio, asset turnover period, fixed asset turnover period, inventory turnover period, collection period ratio) are different over the analysed period of years.

Table 5. Friedman test.

Ratio	p-Value
Asset turnover 2017–2023	<0.05
Fixed asset turnover 2017–2023	<0.05
Inventory turnover 2017–2023	<0.05
Asset to sales ratio 2017–2023	<0.05
Fixed asset to sales ratio 2017–2023	<0.05
Inventory to sales ratio 2017–2023	<0.05
Asset turnover period 2017–2023	<0.05
Fixed asset turnover period 2017–2023	<0.05
Inventory turnover period 2017–2023	<0.05
Collection period ratio 2017–2023	<0.05
Credit period ratio	<0.05

Source: own processing.

We also ran a post hoc (ph) test of pairwise comparison between the years.

H_{ph0a}. *There is not a difference between two selected years in specific activity ratios.*

H_{ph1a}. *There is a difference between two selected years in specific activity ratios.*

If the computed p-value is higher than the significance level alpha (Table 6), one cannot reject the null hypothesis. This explains why only the years listed in Table 6 did not exhibit significant differences in activity ratios. In summary, there is no significant difference in inventory turnover, inventory to sales ratio, or inventory turnover period between the pre-crisis and post-crisis years (2017, 2018, 2019, 2022, and 2023). Additionally, the credit period ratio does not significantly differ between pandemic years (2020 and 2021). In all other pairwise comparisons over the years, significant differences have occurred.

The Kruskal–Wallis test was run to detect that the activity ratios are influenced by the country for each year of investigation. If the computed p-value is lower than the significance level alpha (Table 7), one should reject the null hypothesis and accept that all activity ratios (asset turnover, fixed asset turnover, inventory turnover, asset to sales ratio, fixed asset to sales ratio, inventory to sales ratio, asset turnover period, fixed asset turnover period, inventory turnover period, collection period ratio) are different within the countries. Each year, there are differences in the activity ratios between countries.

Table 6. Pairwise comparison of years for activity ratios.

Ratio	Compared Years	*p*-Value	Compared Years	*p*-Value
Asset turnover	–	–	–	–
Fixed asset turnover	–	–	–	–
Inventory turnover	2017–2018 2017–2022 2018–2019 2018–2023 2019–2023	0.960 0.087 0.089 0.092 0.221	2017–2019 2017–2023 2018–2022 2019–2022 2022–2023	0.099 0.093 0.087 0.103 0.378
Asset to sales ratio	–	–	–	–
Fixed asset to sales ratio	–	–	–	–
Inventory to sales ratio	2017–2018 2017–2022 2018–2019 2018–2023 2019–2023	0.921 0.091 0.059 0.084 0.218	2017–2019 2017–2023 2018–2022 2019–2022 2022–2023	0.074 0.065 0.076 0.115 0.391
Asset turnover period	–	–	–	–
Fixed asset turnover period	–	–	–	–
Inventory turnover period	2017–2018 2017–2022 2018–2019 2018–2023 2019–2023	0.923 0.077 0.060 0.099 0.261	2017–2019 2017–2023 2018–2022 2019–2022 2022–2023	0.074 0.083 0.099 0.133 0.303
Collection period ratio	–	–	–	–
Credit period ratio	–	–	2020–2021	0.247

Source: own processing.

Table 7. Kruskal–Wallis test.

Ratio	*p*-Value						
	2017	2018	2019	2020	2021	2022	2023
Asset turnover	<0.05	<0.05	<0.05	<0.05	<0.05	<0.05	<0.05
Fixed asset turnover	<0.05	<0.05	<0.05	<0.05	<0.05	<0.05	<0.05
Inventory turnover	<0.05	<0.05	<0.05	<0.05	<0.05	<0.05	<0.05
Asset to sales ratio	<0.05	<0.05	<0.05	<0.05	<0.05	<0.05	<0.05
Fixed asset to sales ratio	<0.05	<0.05	<0.05	<0.05	<0.05	<0.05	<0.05
Inventory to sales ratio	<0.05	<0.05	<0.05	<0.05	<0.05	<0.05	<0.05
Asset turnover period	<0.05	<0.05	<0.05	<0.05	<0.05	<0.05	<0.05
Fixed asset turnover period	<0.05	<0.05	<0.05	<0.05	<0.05	<0.05	<0.05
Inventory turnover period	<0.05	<0.05	<0.05	<0.05	<0.05	<0.05	<0.05
Collection period ratio	<0.05	<0.05	<0.05	<0.05	<0.05	<0.05	<0.05
Credit period ratio	<0.05	<0.05	<0.05	<0.05	<0.05	<0.05	<0.05

Source: own processing.

We also ran a post hoc test of pairwise comparison between the countries.

H_{ph0b}. *There is not a difference between two selected countries in specific activity ratios.*

H_{ph1b}. *There is a difference between two selected countries in specific activity ratios.*

If the computed *p*-value is higher than the significance level alpha (Table 8), one cannot reject the null hypothesis. This explains why only the countries listed in Table 8 did not exhibit significant differences in activity ratios.

The Czech Republic and Poland have similar developments throughout the analysed period (2017–2023) in asset turnover, asset to sales ratio, asset turnover period, and collection period ratio.

The fixed asset to sales ratio and fixed asset turnover period show no differences between the Czech Republic and Poland, except for in the year 2021.

The Czech Republic and Poland have no differences in inventory to sales ratio and inventory turnover period in the years 2017, 2018, 2022, and 2023.

Table 8. Pairwise comparison of countries for activity ratios.

Ratio	2017		2018		2019		*p*-Value 2020		2021		2022		2023	
Asset turnover	CZ-PL CZ-HU	0.999 0.179	CZ-PL CZ-HU	0.999 0.328	CZ-PL CZ-HU	0.999 0.183	CZ-PL -	0.999 -	CZ-PL -	0.999 -	CZ-PL CZ-HU	0.999 0.115	CZ-PL CZ-HU	0.999 0.272
Fixed asset turnover	CZ-HU	0.999	CZ-HU	0.999	CZ-HU	0.663	CZ-HU	0.200	-	-	CZ-HU	0.059	CZ-HU	0.158
Inventory turnover	CZ-HU	0.717	CZ-HU	0.951	CZ-HU	0.334	CZ-HU	0.312	CZ-HU	0.068	CZ-HU	0.263	CZ-HU	0.294
Asset to sales ratio	CZ-PL CZ-HU	0.999 0.126	CZ-PL CZ-HU	0.999 0.279	CZ-PL CZ-HU	0.999 0.153	CZ-PL -	0.999 -	CZ-PL -	0.999 -	CZ-PL CZ-HU	0.999 0.102	CZ-PL CZ-HU	0.999 0.196
Fixed asset to sales ratio	CZ-PL CZ-HU	0.921 0.126	CZ-PL CZ-HU	0.410 0.162	CZ-PL CZ-HU	0.451 0.070	CZ-PL -	0.525 -	- -	- -	CZ-PL CZ-HU	0.776 0.074	CZ-PL CZ-HU	0.792 0.108
Inventory to sales ratio	CZ-PL - CZ-HU	0.444 - 0.999	CZ-PL - CZ-HU	0.103 - 0.999	- - CZ-HU	- - 0.999	- HU-PL CZ-HU	- 0.230 0.999	- HU-PL CZ-HU	- 0.786 0.999	CZ-PL - CZ-HU	0.139 - 0.999	CZ-PL - CZ-HU	0.217 - 0.999
Asset turnover period	CZ-PL CZ-HU	0.999 0.126	CZ-PL CZ-HU	0.999 0.279	CZ-PL CZ-HU	0.999 0.153	CZ-PL -	0.999 -	CZ-PL -	0.999 -	CZ-PL CZ-HU	0.999 0.102	CZ-PL CZ-HU	0.999 0.196
Fixed asset turnover period	CZ-PL CZ-HU	0.921 0.126	CZ-PL CZ-HU	0.410 0.162	CZ-PL CZ-HU	0.451 0.070	CZ-PL -	0.525 -	- -	- -	CZ-PL CZ-HU	0.776 0.074	CZ-PL CZ-HU	0.792 0.108
Inventory turnover period	CZ-PL - CZ-HU	0.444 - 0.999	CZ-PL - CZ-HU	0.103 - 0.999	- - CZ-HU	- - 0.999	- HU-PL CZ-HU	- 0.230 0.999	- HU-PL CZ-HU	- 0.786 0.999	CZ-PL - CZ-HU	0.139 - 0.999	CZ-PL - CZ-HU	0.217 - 0.999
Collection period ratio	CZ-PL	0.060	CZ-PL	0.999	CZ-PL	0.093	CZ-PL	0.999	CZ-PL	0.999	CZ-PL	0.999	CZ-PL	0.999
Credit period ratio	-	-	-	-	-	-	SK-PL	0.753	SK-PL	0.999	-	-	-	-

Source: own processing.

The Czech Republic and Hungary have the same values during each year (2017–2023) analysed for inventory turnover, inventory to sales ratio and inventory turnover period.

There are no differences in the fixed asset turnover ratio values between the Czech Republic and Hungary, except for in the year 2021.

The Czech Republic and Hungary also have similar developments in asset turnover, asset to sales ratio, fixed asset to sales ratio, asset turnover period, and fixed asset turnover period, except for the pandemic years 2020 and 2021.

The values of the inventory to sales ratio and inventory turnover period do not differ in the pandemic years for Poland and Hungary.

The credit period ratio does not differ in the pandemic years for Poland and Slovakia.

In all other pairwise comparisons of countries, significant differences have occurred.

6. Conclusions

The aim of this article was to define the level of business activity in the Visegrad Four in the pre-crisis, during-crisis, and post-crisis periods of the COVID-19 pandemic. The analysis covered the period from 2017 to 2023. Eleven activity ratios (asset turnover, fixed asset turnover, inventory turnover, asset to sales ratio, fixed asset to sales ratio, inventory to sales ratio, asset turnover period, fixed asset turnover period, inventory turnover period, collection period ratio, credit period ratio) were computed for 48,650 enterprises.

Median values for all activity ratios according to countries were set. All V4 countries experienced a decline in asset turnover, fixed asset turnover, and inventory turnover and an increase in asset to sales ratio, fixed asset to sales ratio, and inventory to sales ratio during the pandemic, reflecting a lower ability to generate revenue from assets due to restrictions and the economic downturn. Slovakia and the Czech Republic had a partial recovery in 2021 in increasing asset turnover, fixed asset turnover, and inventory turnover, which they attributed to growing sales or asset optimization. Poland noted an upward trend in asset turnover and fixed asset turnover. In contrast, Hungary showed stagnation, indicating more persistent difficulties in increasing asset turnover, fixed asset turnover, and a downward trend in asset to sales ratio, fixed asset to sales ratio, and inventory to sales ratio. Asset to sales ratio and fixed asset ratio increased in all countries in 2020, reflecting lower sales and lower asset utilization efficiency. There was an improvement in 2021, although some countries (e.g., Hungary) still showed weaker results. The asset turnover period and fixed asset turnover period increased in all V4 countries during the pandemic. During the asset turnover period, Slovakia and Hungary experienced the most significant fluctuations, while the Czech Republic and Poland showed a smaller deterioration. In the post-pandemic period, the situation in Slovakia, Czechia, and Poland improved, while Hungary stagnated. After the pandemic subsided, the Czech Republic and Poland recovered quickly, while Hungary showed a slower return and Slovakia returned to the pre-crisis level. In the Czech Republic and Slovakia, the inventory turnover period increased during the pandemic. On the other hand, Poland and Hungary maintained stability, while Hungary showed a slight improvement. During the second year of the pandemic and the post-pandemic period, Hungary and Poland experienced stability in their values, whereas Slovakia and Czechia experienced further deterioration, with an increase in these values during the post-pandemic period. The collection period ratio remained relatively stable in all countries during the pandemic. Slovakia, the Czech Republic, and Poland showed only minimal changes, while Hungary maintained the most efficient receivables management. Hungary maintained the best results in the V4. The credit period ratio remained largely stable during the pandemic, with a slight decrease in Poland and Hungary, indicating tighter credit conditions. The values of credit period ratio remained stable, with no significant changes in Slovakia and Czechia.

The Friedman test proved the significant differences in development over the period for all ratios, but in addition, pairwise comparison detected similarities between pre-crisis and post-crisis periods within inventory turnover, inventory to sales ratio, and inventory turnover period. The credit period ratio did not show differences between the two pandemic years. The Kruskal–Wallis test detected significant differences between all ratios throughout all involved countries.

Theoretical implications of the research may be derived as follows. We confirmed that the pandemic significantly impacted business efficiency. The COVID-19 pandemic significantly impacted business activity across several countries. The article develops knowledge about economic crises and their impact on business activity indicators, thereby improving the understanding of the dynamics of business activity in times of crisis. We also identified differences between economically and politically related countries. The analysis reveals that the impact of the pandemic varied among the V4 countries (Slovakia, the Czech Republic, Poland, and Hungary), potentially serving as a foundation for future research on the diverse responses of economies and sectors to the crisis. Several performance-related indicators have demonstrated sensitivity to economic shifts, making them valuable tools for evaluating the crisis resilience of enterprises. Future research could also focus on disclosure of specific business tools that caused similarities between 2017, 2018, 2019, 2022, and 2023 within inventory turnover, inventory to sales ratio, and inventory turnover period and similarities between credit period ratio in 2020 and 2021 in general.

Practical implications of the research may be set as follows. Findings on differences between countries and sectors can be useful for governments and policymakers in designing support for businesses during future crises to support economic policy. Businesses can use this knowledge to better prepare for crises. Findings on the importance of inventory optimization and efficient asset utilization can serve as a guide for managers to improve financial stability and performance. Businesses can use the indicators as tools for monitoring their own financial performance and benchmarking. Businesses can use the values as reference points to compare their own developments and pinpoint areas for enhancing their business efficiency. The next investigation could analyse the sizes of enterprises, expanding the scope from the V4 region to the Bucharest Nine (B9) and incorporating all ratios related to liquidity, profitability, and indebtedness.

We address the limitations by using no-balance samples based on countries and NACE and include ratios with zero values to maintain the robustness of the samples. We calculate the ratios annually, but monitoring data quarterly or monthly could potentially capture development, trends, and seasonality more systematically. This approach could have led to a smaller sample size, but it would have yielded more accurate results. This paves the way for future collaborations between governments, municipalities, business agencies, and enterprises to comprehensively monitor business activity, thereby enhancing the efficiency of policymakers and recipients of these decisions.

Author Contributions: Conceptualization, P.D. and K.B.; methodology, P.D.; software, K.B.; validation, R.B. and E.K.; formal analysis, R.B. and E.K.; investigation, R.B. and E.K.; resources, R.B. and K.B.; data curation, P.D.; writing—original draft preparation, E.K.; writing—review and editing, R.B.; visualization, E.K.; supervision, P.D.; project administration, P.D.; funding acquisition, P.D. All authors have read and agreed to the published version of the manuscript.

Funding: This research received no external funding.

Institutional Review Board Statement: Not applicable.

Informed Consent Statement: Not applicable.

Data Availability Statement: The data presented in this study are available upon request from the corresponding author.

Acknowledgments: This research was financially supported by the Slovak Research and Development Agency—Grant VEGA 1/0677/22: Quo Vadis, Bankruptcy Models? Prospective Longitudinal Cohort Study with Emphasis on Changes Determined by COVID 19.

Conflicts of Interest: Author Klaudia Bicanovska was employed by the company Sungwoo Hitech Slovakia s.r.o. The remaining authors declare that the research was conducted in the absence of any commercial or financial relationships that could be construed as a potential conflict of interest.

Appendix A

Table A1. Median values of asset turnover according to NACE.

		Asset Turnover [Coefficient]						
Sector	Country	2017	2018	2019	2020	2021	2022	2023
A	SK	0.65	0.65	0.65	0.64	0.71	0.70	0.68
	CZ	0.62	0.62	0.60	0.60	0.61	0.61	0.62
	PL	0.58	0.58	0.57	0.59	0.62	0.61	0.61
	HU	0.82	0.80	0.82	0.78	0.80	0.80	0.81
B	SK	0.94	1.50	0.82	0.80	0.80	0.84	0.87
	CZ	0.78	0.79	0.74	0.73	0.79	0.79	0.77
	PL	1.20	0.97	1.4	0.97	0.94	1.00	1.02
	HU	0.92	1.1	1.3	0.79	0.92	0.92	0.96
C	SK	1.33	1.31	1.3	1.19	1.23	1.31	1.33
	CZ	1.55	1.49	1.47	1.40	1.46	1.49	1.53
	PL	1.50	1.49	1.48	1.37	1.46	1.44	1.49
	HU	1.39	1.39	1.35	1.22	1.25	1.26	1.31
D	SK	0.41	0.40	0.40	0.42	0.46	0.45	0.43
	CZ	0.55	0.55	0.57	0.58	0.63	0.60	0.58
	PL	0.68	0.68	0.73	0.70	0.77	0.74	0.72
	HU	0.91	0.87	0.97	0.86	0.96	0.92	0.90

Table A1. *Cont.*

		Asset Turnover [Coefficient]						
Sector	**Country**	**2017**	**2018**	**2019**	**2020**	**2021**	**2022**	**2023**
E	SK	0.79	0.83	0.82	0.76	0.86	0.82	0.82
	CZ	1.19	1.28	1.25	1.29	1.18	1.20	1.18
	PL	0.57	0.60	0.62	0.63	0.68	0.64	0.62
	HU	1.19	1.14	1.15	1.18	1.21	1.17	1.18
F	SK	1.12	1.13	1.1	0.98	0.96	0.99	1.01
	CZ	1.50	1.54	1.45	1.43	1.44	1.46	1.51
	PL	1.33	1.43	1.39	1.21	1.25	1.28	1.31
	HU	1.21	1.39	1.41	1.25	1.24	1.21	1.23
G	SK	1.25	1.26	1.2	1.13	1.15	1.18	1.21
	CZ	1.96	1.93	1.93	1.81	1.93	1.91	1.91
	PL	2.13	2.13	2.10	1.94	2.70	2.03	2.07
	HU	1.97	1.98	2.00	1.90	1.86	1.91	1.99
H	SK	1.38	1.41	1.33	1.31	1.31	1.36	1.34
	CZ	1.88	1.85	1.84	1.73	1.67	1.78	1.81
	PL	1.93	1.90	1.84	1.69	1.77	1.81	1.88
	HU	1.31	1.36	1.34	1.25	1.32	1.33	1.33
I	SK	0.39	0.39	0.42	0.32	0.31	0.33	0.34
	CZ	0.45	0.47	0.49	0.32	0.33	0.34	0.36
	PL	0.74	0.75	0.76	0.46	0.59	0.62	0.72
	HU	0.77	0.74	0.69	0.48	0.59	0.63	0.71
J	SK	1.50	1.50	1.00	0.94	0.94	1.04	1.05
	CZ	1.47	1.51	1.67	1.49	1.49	1.46	1.51
	PL	1.31	1.31	1.33	1.24	1.32	1.31	1.31
	HU	1.33	1.29	1.25	1.22	1.17	1.20	1.23
K	SK	0.71	0.74	0.78	0.88	0.87	0.84	0.78
	CZ	1.11	1.16	1.20	1.15	1.21	1.18	1.17
	PL	0.86	0.91	1.50	0.93	0.98	0.94	0.92
	HU	0.63	0.60	0.69	0.63	0.64	0.63	0.63
L	SK	0.15	0.15	0.15	0.14	0.15	0.15	0.15
	CZ	0.12	0.12	0.13	0.12	0.13	0.13	0.13
	PL	0.27	0.28	0.28	0.29	0.32	0.31	0.30
	HU	0.18	0.19	0.19	0.20	0.18	0.18	0.18
M	SK	0.43	0.42	0.43	0.42	0.43	0.42	0.43
	CZ	1.25	1.17	1.20	1.11	1.16	1.20	1.23
	PL	1.25	1.30	1.30	1.22	1.18	1.18	1.23
	HU	0.97	0.97	1.00	0.91	0.95	0.97	0.98
N	SK	0.55	0.54	0.56	0.50	0.54	0.54	0.55
	CZ	1.74	1.77	1.71	1.53	1.49	1.60	1.69
	PL	1.83	1.89	1.82	1.52	1.51	1.69	1.78
	HU	1.47	1.48	1.70	1.38	1.24	1.42	1.49
O	SK	1.39	1.45	1.70	1.75	1.32	1.42	1.44
	CZ	1.70	0.83	0.50	0.59	0.31	0.52	0.80
	PL	0.90	0.86	0.84	0.87	0.79	0.79	0.93
	HU	0.79	0.57	0.76	0.52	0.59	0.60	0.63
P	SK	0.41	0.48	0.45	0.32	0.31	0.36	0.40
	CZ	0.83	0.77	0.85	0.85	0.80	0.84	0.82
	PL	0.66	0.67	0.68	0.64	0.64	0.65	0.66
	HU	1.41	0.52	0.66	0.52	1.50	1.46	1.26
Q	SK	1.80	1.12	1.50	1.50	1.14	1.12	1.14
	CZ	1.21	1.50	1.37	1.40	1.53	1.49	1.46
	PL	1.16	1.14	1.23	1.17	1.33	1.28	1.26
	HU	1.62	1.55	1.37	1.34	1.36	1.49	1.58
R	SK	0.46	0.42	0.41	0.35	0.34	0.40	0.43
	CZ	0.92	0.97	1.70	0.91	1.30	1.05	1.02
	PL	0.68	0.67	0.66	0.57	0.53	0.62	0.66
	HU	1.11	0.95	1.00	0.78	0.77	0.80	0.84
S	SK	0.72	0.69	0.69	0.58	0.73	0.72	0.72
	CZ	1.27	1.80	1.21	1.13	1.10	0.99	1.01
	PL	1.40	0.98	1.50	0.97	0.94	0.96	1.02
	HU	0.82	0.89	1.30	0.74	0.81	0.83	0.87

Source: own processing.

Table A2. Median values of fixed asset turnover according to NACE.

		Fixed Asset Turnover [Coefficient]						
Sector	**Country**	**2017**	**2018**	**2019**	**2020**	**2021**	**2022**	**2023**
A	SK	1.80	1.14	1.12	1.10	1.27	1.31	1.26
	CZ	1.00	1.10	0.94	0.96	0.97	1.01	1.03
	PL	0.75	0.73	0.72	0.80	0.91	0.88	0.85
	HU	1.39	1.37	1.35	1.31	1.34	1.36	1.38
B	SK	1.59	1.82	1.38	1.44	1.46	1.49	1.53
	CZ	1.39	1.59	1.37	1.30	1.49	1.51	1.58
	PL	1.74	2.20	1.95	1.76	1.98	2.03	1.91
	HU	1.96	2.19	1.97	1.79	1.94	1.95	1.95
C	SK	3.60	3.59	3.59	3.31	3.70	3.69	3.69
	CZ	3.60	3.51	3.52	3.32	3.71	3.55	3.69
	PL	3.98	3.88	3.90	3.72	4.13	3.98	3.83
	HU	3.10	3.20	2.90	2.70	2.89	3.02	3.11
D	SK	0.49	0.51	0.58	0.66	0.69	0.71	0.70
	CZ	0.61	0.64	0.63	0.63	0.74	0.79	0.77
	PL	0.82	0.82	0.86	0.84	0.93	0.90	0.89
	HU	1.26	1.15	1.23	1.16	1.48	1.44	1.36
E	SK	1.81	1.83	1.99	1.97	2.55	2.43	2.26
	CZ	2.79	2.53	2.70	2.43	2.65	2.62	2.84
	PL	0.61	0.62	0.64	0.68	0.71	0.69	0.69
	HU	2.28	2.53	2.63	2.75	2.82	2.62	2.55
F	SK	5.92	5.74	5.55	5.12	4.77	5.85	6.22
	CZ	6.47	7.15	6.91	6.24	6.70	7.11	7.11
	PL	7.33	7.74	7.39	6.82	6.90	7.11	7.65
	HU	6.55	6.58	6.80	5.69	6.15	6.63	7.11
G	SK	7.27	7.30	7.19	6.52	6.96	8.29	8.29
	CZ	10.87	10.87	10.53	10.71	11.56	12.44	12.44
	PL	12.58	12.90	12.67	11.99	13.16	14.21	12.44
	HU	11.84	11.84	12.8	11.35	11.79	12.44	12.44
H	SK	3.39	3.60	3.55	3.73	4.10	4.33	4.15
	CZ	4.63	4.60	4.80	4.51	4.16	4.74	5.24
	PL	5.22	5.28	5.18	4.92	5.43	5.85	5.53
	HU	2.42	2.54	2.65	2.81	2.86	2.69	2.76
I	SK	0.44	0.44	0.47	0.34	0.34	0.40	0.43
	CZ	0.59	0.64	0.73	0.58	0.69	0.74	0.72
	PL	0.69	0.74	0.75	0.45	0.61	0.64	0.73
	HU	0.63	0.56	0.63	0.44	0.52	0.60	0.61
J	SK	6.45	5.56	5.62	5.16	4.73	6.63	7.65
	CZ	12.20	13.68	11.45	12.31	13.68	14.21	14.21
	PL	7.52	8.27	7.78	7.58	7.40	8.29	7.65
	HU	7.68	7.68	6.72	5.97	5.89	6.63	7.65
K	SK	4.44	3.76	3.46	2.88	2.52	5.24	6.63
	CZ	1.22	3.24	2.37	1.69	2.10	2.21	2.62
	PL	3.30	3.81	3.70	2.95	3.14	3.98	3.98
	HU	2.11	1.52	2.60	1.59	1.70	2.21	2.26
L	SK	0.18	0.18	0.19	0.18	0.18	0.19	0.19
	CZ	0.13	0.14	0.15	0.14	0.15	0.15	0.15
	PL	0.25	0.27	0.27	0.27	0.31	0.32	0.33
	HU	0.20	0.21	0.21	0.21	0.20	0.22	0.22
M	SK	1.27	1.20	1.13	1.14	1.16	1.66	1.69
	CZ	7.20	6.63	7.30	5.88	6.11	7.11	8.29
	PL	6.24	6.44	6.40	6.14	6.76	7.11	6.63
	HU	4.90	3.89	3.98	4.24	4.16	4.52	4.33
N	SK	1.55	1.35	1.37	1.23	1.25	2.12	2.12
	CZ	6.72	5.80	6.37	5.76	4.81	8.29	7.65
	PL	11.53	11.44	11.30	10.69	10.23	12.44	12.44
	HU	4.68	5.11	5.17	3.96	3.73	4.74	5.24
O	SK	9.73	9.46	12.97	10.22	5.42	8.29	9.05
	CZ	2.81	1.36	1.65	1.80	0.53	0.80	1.02
	PL	2.59	2.45	2.58	2.79	2.63	2.76	2.76
	HU	1.99	2.20	2.23	1.44	2.00	1.88	2.03
P	SK	0.76	0.72	1.11	0.92	0.91	1.00	1.09
	CZ	2.60	1.46	1.26	1.20	1.23	1.18	1.28
	PL	0.69	0.75	0.70	0.77	0.81	0.75	0.72
	HU	8.77	8.48	8.95	6.4	12.37	9.95	8.29
Q	SK	3.61	3.91	3.77	3.82	4.39	3.98	4.33
	CZ	2.38	2.67	2.85	2.96	3.33	3.32	3.02
	PL	2.67	2.75	2.86	2.68	3.28	2.69	2.84
	HU	2.68	2.42	2.90	3.13	3.51	3.32	3.11

Table A2. *Cont.*

Sector	Country	2017	2018	2019	2020	2021	2022	2023
		Fixed Asset Turnover [Coefficient]						
R	SK	0.61	0.51	0.47	0.37	0.44	0.48	0.56
	CZ	2.17	2.10	3.9	3.53	3.43	3.43	3.69
	PL	0.57	0.58	0.62	0.52	0.54	0.56	0.63
	HU	1.77	1.84	2.13	1.54	1.76	2.07	2.26
S	SK	2.71	2.54	3.28	2.23	2.34	2.49	2.84
	CZ	6.54	7.12	5.42	7.42	6.98	6.63	7.11
	PL	1.85	1.96	1.94	1.69	1.88	1.84	1.91
	HU	0.64	1.40	0.78	0.60	0.54	0.60	0.65

Source: own processing.

Table A3. Median values of inventory turnover according to NACE.

Sector	Country	2017	2018	2019	2020	2021	2022	2023
		Inventory Turnover [Coefficient]						
A	SK	3.75	3.79	3.53	3.58	3.99	4.09	4.12
	CZ	3.53	3.72	3.55	3.46	3.62	3.65	3.70
	PL	3.33	3.28	3.27	3.36	3.31	3.33	3.38
	HU	4.18	3.98	4.20	4.58	4.21	4.26	4.30
B	SK	15.20	15.76	15.63	18.18	14.42	14.59	14.98
	CZ	14.24	17.30	13.94	12.54	13.29	14.05	14.33
	PL	14.48	14.72	12.85	12.28	12.49	13.02	14.07
	HU	9.51	10.57	10.70	7.93	9.10	9.45	10.15
C	SK	9.50	9.10	9.26	8.66	7.76	8.10	8.86
	CZ	7.83	7.77	7.76	7.25	6.47	6.74	7.12
	PL	8.75	8.72	8.8	8.32	7.46	7.89	8.11
	HU	7.76	7.53	7.56	7.36	6.70	7.12	7.62
D	SK	10.87	11.99	12.63	11.32	14.31	13.15	12.66
	CZ	26.59	23.87	20.92	23.33	33.18	28.17	27.54
	PL	13.85	11.90	11.70	13.84	15.57	14.96	13.59
	HU	24.43	24.30	24.15	31.49	26.17	25.53	24.93
E	SK	42.05	42.78	42.05	39.29	44.50	43.08	44.20
	CZ	44.53	52.74	51.37	45.61	47.82	48.86	49.77
	PL	75.42	76.27	72.67	75.29	73.97	74.62	74.98
	HU	44.81	45.28	47.79	50.8	53.53	50.13	49.11
F	SK	16.00	16.94	17.78	15.35	12.18	13.13	14.87
	CZ	15.50	18.20	19.28	19.46	15.17	16.25	17.84
	PL	12.83	13.70	14.00	12.41	10.77	11.27	12.98
	HU	14.25	14.72	16.47	22.25	21.66	18.22	20.14
G	SK	7.66	7.56	7.51	6.98	7.21	7.26	7.54
	CZ	7.84	7.66	7.50	7.33	7.80	7.80	7.76
	PL	8.89	8.85	8.74	8.70	8.58	8.81	8.85
	HU	8.91	8.80	9.90	8.86	8.81	8.87	9.03
H	SK	59.14	66.49	74.76	64.84	66.32	66.87	64.15
	CZ	56.03	57.56	62.45	60.73	57.04	57.19	59.81
	PL	42.02	44.36	45.20	43.02	42.30	44.77	45.38
	HU	98.14	94.74	91.76	100.61	99.04	100.93	100.04
I	SK	39.03	36.85	42.02	34.73	32.52	34.55	36.89
	CZ	49.44	73.44	74.60	60.42	52.98	56.48	58.93
	PL	71.89	77.51	79.14	66.52	66.31	69.11	72.57
	HU	73.61	76.72	71.13	52.60	68.15	72.24	74.63
J	SK	11.56	11.70	9.92	9.22	7.68	8.44	10.17
	CZ	17.00	15.53	17.15	18.73	19.45	18.14	18.99
	PL	17.19	19.16	15.42	16.11	14.42	16.42	18.31
	HU	11.40	5.75	6.66	7.51	5.60	5.74	6.22
K	SK	0	0	0	0	0	0	0
	CZ	0	0	0	0	0	0	0
	PL	0	0	0	0	0	0	0
	HU	0	0	0	0	0	0	0
L	SK	0	0	0	0	0	0	0
	CZ	0	0	0	0	0	0	0
	PL	0	0	0	0	0	0	0
	HU	0	0	0	0	0	0	0
M	SK	0	0	0.04	0.12	0.19	0.17	0.13
	CZ	7.54	6.60	6.69	6.71	6.72	6.76	6.69
	PL	3.34	3.37	2.82	1.67	2.97	3.36	3.32
	HU	3.51	4.16	3.86	2.35	2.49	2.67	3.11

Table A3. *Cont.*

Sector	Country	2017	2018	2019	2020	2021	2022	2023
		Inventory Turnover [Coefficient]						
N	SK	0.52	0.85	1.23	0.92	1.13	0.96	1.05
	CZ	10.40	22.20	14.59	12.20	15.47	16.13	14.65
	PL	11.90	13.57	12.40	14.10	12.41	13.52	14.03
	HU	20.98	23.60	20.63	17.33	17.13	19.48	20.36
O	SK	103.09	46.67	295.46	391.47	180.77	195.45	130.11
	CZ	2.56	4.67	5.12	2.32	1.62	2.94	4.06
	PL	0.18	0	0.05	0	0.48	0	0
	HU	11.49	11.52	12.26	10.67	13.44	12.68	11.97
P	SK	7.10	7.60	8.58	5.66	6.54	7.16	7.90
	CZ	44.82	18.53	9.69	2.83	10.26	19.67	13.52
	PL	84.78	84.24	67.88	76.7	85.54	86.88	84.29
	HU	36.61	87.19	71.31	95.06	35.82	36.51	74.10
Q	SK	50.78	49.43	50.10	34.31	41.51	45.13	50.23
	CZ	59.53	60.13	62.83	52.61	60.25	60.54	61.57
	PL	80.16	84.63	89.25	54.86	68.38	77.16	80.97
	HU	93.93	99.05	90.09	58.75	56.75	90.35	93.20
R	SK	41.76	67.01	65.46	52.09	26.50	41.86	54.46
	CZ	133.97	119.33	102.77	77.88	89.94	90.96	102.37
	PL	103.51	102.28	98.93	75.57	70.17	84.27	97.21
	HU	102.56	90.03	114.53	69.37	88.47	91.40	98.67
S	SK	20.61	16.60	18.18	13.11	18.91	19.12	18.30
	CZ	18.94	25.20	14.20	20.72	19.96	20.04	22.57
	PL	22.98	21.55	18.15	19.46	17.84	19.46	21.07
	HU	63.71	61.65	59.56	51.78	71.16	62.49	61.23

Source: own processing.

Table A4. Median values of asset to sales ratio according to NACE.

Sector	Country	2017	2018	2019	2020	2021	2022	2023
		Asset to Sales Ratio [Coefficient]						
A	SK	1.53	1.53	1.53	1.55	1.42	1.43	1.46
	CZ	1.60	1.63	1.67	1.66	1.64	1.64	1.61
	PL	1.71	1.73	1.75	1.69	1.60	1.63	1.64
	HU	1.22	1.24	1.22	1.29	1.25	1.24	1.23
B	SK	1.70	0.96	1.22	1.26	1.25	1.19	1.15
	CZ	1.29	1.26	1.35	1.36	1.26	1.26	1.29
	PL	0.98	1.30	0.96	1.30	1.70	1.00	0.98
	HU	1.90	0.99	0.97	1.26	1.80	1.08	1.04
C	SK	0.75	0.77	0.77	0.84	0.81	0.76	0.75
	CZ	0.65	0.67	0.68	0.71	0.68	0.67	0.65
	PL	0.67	0.67	0.68	0.73	0.69	0.69	0.67
	HU	0.72	0.72	0.74	0.82	0.80	0.79	0.76
D	SK	2.44	2.52	2.48	2.38	2.17	2.21	2.34
	CZ	1.83	1.83	1.77	1.73	1.58	1.66	1.71
	PL	1.47	1.48	1.37	1.42	1.31	1.34	1.38
	HU	1.10	1.15	1.30	1.16	1.40	1.08	1.10
E	SK	1.27	1.21	1.23	1.32	1.17	1.21	1.22
	CZ	0.84	0.78	0.80	0.78	0.85	0.83	0.84
	PL	1.74	1.68	1.62	1.58	1.48	1.55	1.60
	HU	0.84	0.88	0.87	0.85	0.83	0.85	0.84
F	SK	0.89	0.88	0.91	1.20	1.50	1.01	0.99
	CZ	0.66	0.65	0.69	0.70	0.69	0.68	0.66
	PL	0.75	0.70	0.72	0.82	0.80	0.78	0.76
	HU	0.83	0.72	0.71	0.80	0.80	0.82	0.81
G	SK	0.80	0.80	0.84	0.88	0.87	0.84	0.82
	CZ	0.51	0.52	0.52	0.55	0.52	0.52	0.52
	PL	0.47	0.47	0.48	0.51	0.48	0.49	0.48
	HU	0.51	0.51	0.5	0.53	0.54	0.52	0.50
H	SK	0.72	0.71	0.75	0.76	0.76	0.73	0.74
	CZ	0.53	0.54	0.54	0.58	0.60	0.56	0.55
	PL	0.52	0.53	0.54	0.59	0.56	0.55	0.53
	HU	0.76	0.73	0.74	0.80	0.76	0.75	0.75
I	SK	2.59	2.55	2.37	3.15	3.18	3.03	2.89
	CZ	2.23	2.13	2.60	3.13	3.20	2.91	2.73
	PL	1.35	1.33	1.32	2.17	1.69	1.60	1.38
	HU	1.29	1.35	1.44	2.70	1.69	1.57	1.41

Table A4. *Cont.*

		Asset to Sales Ratio [Coefficient]						
Sector	**Country**	**2017**	**2018**	**2019**	**2020**	**2021**	**2022**	**2023**
J	SK	0.95	0.95	1.00	1.60	1.60	0.96	0.95
	CZ	0.68	0.66	0.60	0.67	0.67	0.68	0.66
	PL	0.76	0.76	0.75	0.81	0.76	0.76	0.76
	HU	0.75	0.78	0.80	0.82	0.85	0.83	0.81
K	SK	1.41	1.24	1.27	1.14	1.14	1.19	1.27
	CZ	0.90	0.87	0.83	0.87	0.83	0.84	0.85
	PL	1.16	1.80	0.94	1.70	1.10	1.06	1.08
	HU	1.58	1.67	1.44	1.58	1.57	1.57	1.58
L	SK	6.47	6.57	6.56	6.99	6.84	6.72	6.57
	CZ	8.11	8.2	7.49	7.94	7.52	7.67	7.74
	PL	3.69	3.59	3.52	3.41	3.13	3.24	3.29
	HU	5.56	5.13	5.33	5.70	5.47	5.48	5.47
M	SK	2.34	2.36	2.34	2.35	2.35	2.36	2.33
	CZ	0.80	0.85	0.83	0.90	0.86	0.83	0.81
	PL	0.80	0.77	0.77	0.82	0.85	0.84	0.81
	HU	1.30	1.30	1.00	1.10	1.60	1.03	1.02
N	SK	1.83	1.87	1.77	2.10	1.83	1.83	1.81
	CZ	0.58	0.56	0.58	0.65	0.67	0.62	0.59
	PL	0.55	0.53	0.55	0.66	0.66	0.59	0.56
	HU	0.68	0.68	0.59	0.72	0.81	0.70	0.67
O	SK	0.72	0.69	0.59	0.57	0.76	0.70	0.69
	CZ	0.93	1.21	2.00	1.70	3.21	1.93	1.25
	PL	1.80	1.10	0.96	1.15	1.27	1.26	1.07
	HU	1.54	2.45	2.92	2.40	1.82	1.66	1.57
P	SK	2.42	2.70	2.21	3.80	3.20	2.76	2.48
	CZ	1.23	1.30	1.18	1.18	1.25	1.18	1.22
	PL	1.51	1.48	1.47	1.57	1.55	1.54	1.51
	HU	0.71	1.93	1.51	1.93	0.67	0.68	0.79
Q	SK	0.93	0.89	0.95	0.95	0.87	0.89	0.87
	CZ	0.83	0.67	0.73	0.71	0.65	0.67	0.68
	PL	0.86	0.88	0.81	0.85	0.75	0.78	0.79
	HU	0.62	0.64	0.73	0.75	0.73	0.67	0.63
R	SK	2.16	2.39	2.42	2.87	2.92	2.48	2.33
	CZ	1.80	0.99	0.90	1.30	0.92	0.95	0.98
	PL	1.46	1.50	1.53	1.76	1.88	1.61	1.50
	HU	0.90	1.50	1.00	1.28	1.31	1.24	1.18
S	SK	1.39	1.46	1.44	1.75	1.39	1.39	1.38
	CZ	0.80	1.20	0.83	0.92	1.00	1.01	0.99
	PL	0.96	1.20	0.95	1.30	1.70	1.04	0.98
	HU	1.22	1.13	0.97	1.36	1.24	1.20	1.15

Source: own processing.

Table A5. Median values of fixed asset to sales ratio according to NACE.

		Fixed Asset to Sales Ratio [Coefficient]						
Sector	**Country**	**2017**	**2018**	**2019**	**2020**	**2021**	**2022**	**2023**
A	SK	0.90	0.87	0.88	0.90	0.78	0.76	0.79
	CZ	1.00	0.98	1.60	1.50	1.40	0.99	0.97
	PL	1.33	1.36	1.38	1.24	1.10	1.13	1.17
	HU	0.72	0.73	0.74	0.76	0.74	0.73	0.72
B	SK	0.63	0.55	0.72	0.69	0.69	0.67	0.65
	CZ	0.72	0.63	0.73	0.77	0.67	0.66	0.63
	PL	0.58	0.5	0.51	0.56	0.49	0.49	0.52
	HU	0.51	0.46	0.51	0.56	0.52	0.51	0.51
C	SK	0.27	0.27	0.27	0.29	0.26	0.27	0.27
	CZ	0.27	0.28	0.28	0.3	0.27	0.28	0.27
	PL	0.25	0.26	0.26	0.27	0.24	0.25	0.26
	HU	0.32	0.33	0.34	0.37	0.34	0.33	0.32
D	SK	2.4	1.96	1.70	1.49	1.41	1.40	1.43
	CZ	1.51	1.45	1.53	1.51	1.25	1.26	1.29
	PL	1.21	1.21	1.16	1.17	1.70	1.10	1.12
	HU	0.79	0.87	0.81	0.86	0.64	0.69	0.73
E	SK	0.52	0.54	0.48	0.5	0.39	0.41	0.44
	CZ	0.34	0.38	0.36	0.41	0.37	0.38	0.35
	PL	1.65	1.6	1.57	1.47	1.4	1.45	1.44
	HU	0.43	0.4	0.38	0.36	0.35	0.38	0.39

Table A5. *Cont.*

		Fixed Asset to Sales Ratio [Coefficient]						
Sector	Country	2017	2018	2019	2020	2021	2022	2023
F	SK	0.16	0.16	0.17	0.18	0.19	0.17	0.16
	CZ	0.15	0.14	0.14	0.15	0.15	0.14	0.14
	PL	0.13	0.13	0.13	0.14	0.14	0.14	0.13
	HU	0.15	0.14	0.14	0.17	0.16	0.15	0.14
G	SK	0.12	0.12	0.12	0.13	0.12	0.12	0.12
	CZ	0.08	0.08	0.09	0.09	0.08	0.08	0.08
	PL	0.08	0.08	0.08	0.08	0.07	0.07	0.08
	HU	0.08	0.08	0.08	0.08	0.08	0.08	0.08
H	SK	0.27	0.26	0.27	0.26	0.23	0.23	0.24
	CZ	0.19	0.21	0.19	0.19	0.22	0.21	0.19
	PL	0.19	0.18	0.19	0.19	0.17	0.17	0.18
	HU	0.41	0.39	0.38	0.36	0.35	0.37	0.36
I	SK	2.23	2.22	1.99	2.8	2.84	2.50	2.34
	CZ	1.68	1.57	1.37	1.71	1.39	1.34	1.38
	PL	1.44	1.35	1.33	2.22	1.59	1.56	1.36
	HU	1.57	1.61	1.47	2.19	1.88	1.66	1.64
J	SK	0.12	0.14	0.15	0.15	0.16	0.15	0.13
	CZ	0.08	0.07	0.08	0.07	0.07	0.07	0.07
	PL	0.13	0.12	0.13	0.13	0.12	0.12	0.13
	HU	0.13	0.13	0.14	0.16	0.16	0.15	0.13
K	SK	0.12	0.11	0.17	0.17	0.22	0.19	0.15
	CZ	0.30	0.31	0.42	0.41	0.5	0.45	0.38
	PL	0.27	0.23	0.23	0.25	0.26	0.25	0.25
	HU	0.46	0.59	0.45	0.54	0.46	0.45	0.44
L	SK	5.34	5.38	5.5	5.44	5.24	5.21	5.27
	CZ	7.57	7.23	6.80	6.90	6.53	6.49	6.73
	PL	3.86	3.68	3.60	3.62	3.14	3.08	3.02
	HU	5.30	4.76	4.72	4.46	4.54	4.49	4.60
M	SK	0.60	0.66	0.63	0.70	0.62	0.60	0.59
	CZ	0.12	0.12	0.14	0.14	0.14	0.14	0.12
	PL	0.16	0.15	0.15	0.15	0.13	0.14	0.15
	HU	0.24	0.24	0.23	0.22	0.20	0.22	0.23
N	SK	0.44	0.52	0.49	0.47	0.45	0.47	0.47
	CZ	0.13	0.13	0.11	0.13	0.14	0.12	0.13
	PL	0.08	0.08	0.09	0.09	0.09	0.08	0.08
	HU	0.18	0.18	0.18	0.24	0.23	0.21	0.19
O	SK	0.10	0.11	0.08	0.10	0.18	0.12	0.11
	CZ	0.36	0.73	0.60	0.56	1.89	1.25	0.98
	PL	0.37	0.36	0.38	0.36	0.38	0.36	0.36
	HU	0.54	0.59	0.48	0.72	0.51	0.53	0.49
P	SK	0.92	0.89	0.89	0.82	1.10	1.00	0.91
	CZ	0.49	0.73	0.83	0.83	0.81	0.84	0.78
	PL	1.45	1.32	1.42	1.29	1.24	1.33	1.38
	HU	0.11	0.12	0.11	0.16	0.08	0.10	0.12
Q	SK	0.27	0.25	0.27	0.26	0.23	0.25	0.23
	CZ	0.42	0.37	0.35	0.34	0.30	0.30	0.33
	PL	0.37	0.36	0.35	0.37	0.30	0.37	0.35
	HU	0.37	0.41	0.35	0.32	0.29	0.30	0.32
R	SK	1.56	1.88	1.98	2.55	2.22	2.08	1.79
	CZ	0.43	0.46	0.29	0.27	0.26	0.29	0.27
	PL	1.76	1.72	1.62	1.93	1.86	1.79	1.59
	HU	0.45	0.53	0.44	0.56	0.53	0.48	0.44
S	SK	0.37	0.33	0.29	0.39	0.38	0.40	0.35
	CZ	0.15	0.14	0.19	0.14	0.14	0.15	0.14
	PL	0.54	0.51	0.51	0.59	0.53	0.54	0.52
	HU	1.56	0.97	1.29	1.67	1.85	1.65	1.54

Source: own processing.

Table A6. Median values of inventory to sales ratio according to NACE.

		Inventory to Sales Ratio [Coefficient]						
Sector	Country	2017	2018	2019	2020	2021	2022	2023
A	SK	0.23	0.24	0.25	0.25	0.23	0.23	0.24
	CZ	0.26	0.25	0.26	0.26	0.25	0.25	0.25
	PL	0.28	0.27	0.27	0.25	0.27	0.27	0.27
	HU	0.24	0.25	0.24	0.22	0.23	0.23	0.24

Table A6. *Cont.*

Inventory to Sales Ratio [Coefficient]								
Sector	**Country**	**2017**	**2018**	**2019**	**2020**	**2021**	**2022**	**2023**
B	SK	0.06	0.06	0.06	0.05	0.06	0.06	0.06
	CZ	0.07	0.06	0.07	0.08	0.08	0.07	0.07
	PL	0.05	0.04	0.04	0.05	0.04	0.04	0.05
	HU	0.08	0.09	0.08	0.08	0.08	0.08	0.09
C	SK	0.08	0.09	0.09	0.09	0.10	0.10	0.09
	CZ	0.12	0.12	0.12	0.13	0.15	0.12	0.13
	PL	0.11	0.11	0.11	0.11	0.12	0.11	0.12
	HU	0.12	0.13	0.12	0.13	0.14	0.13	0.13
D	SK	0	0	0	0	0	0	0
	CZ	0	0	0	0	0	0	0
	PL	0.05	0.07	0.06	0.06	0.05	0.05	0.05
	HU	0.01	0.01	0.01	0.01	0.01	0.01	0.01
E	SK	0.01	0.01	0.01	0.01	0.01	0.01	0.01
	CZ	0.02	0.02	0.02	0.02	0.02	0.02	0.02
	PL	0.01	0.01	0.01	0.01	0.01	0.01	0.01
	HU	0.02	0.02	0.02	0.02	0.02	0.02	0.02
F	SK	0.01	0.01	0.01	0.02	0.02	0.01	0.01
	CZ	0.04	0.04	0.04	0.04	0.05	0.04	0.04
	PL	0.04	0.03	0.03	0.04	0.05	0.04	0.03
	HU	0.04	0.04	0.04	0.02	0.02	0.04	0.04
G	SK	0.08	0.08	0.09	0.09	0.09	0.08	0.08
	CZ	0.10	0.10	0.10	0.10	0.10	0.10	0.10
	PL	0.10	0.10	0.10	0.10	0.10	0.10	0.10
	HU	0.10	0.10	0.10	0.10	0.10	0.10	0.10
H	SK	0	0	0	0	0	0	0
	CZ	0	0	0	0	0	0	0
	PL	0	0	0	0	0	0	0
	HU	0	0	0	0	0.01	0.01	0.01
I	SK	0.02	0.02	0.01	0.01	0.02	0.02	0.02
	CZ	0.01	0.01	0.01	0.01	0.01	0.01	0.01
	PL	0.01	0.01	0.01	0.01	0.01	0.01	0.01
	HU	0.01	0.01	0.01	0.01	0.01	0.01	0.01
J	SK	0	0	0	0	0	0	0
	CZ	0	0	0	0	0	0	0
	PL	0	0	0	0	0	0	0
	HU	0	0	0	0	0	0	0
K	SK	0	0	0	0	0	0	0
	CZ	0	0	0	0	0	0	0
	PL	0	0	0	0	0	0	0
	HU	0	0	0	0	0	0	0
L	SK	0	0	0	0	0	0	0
	CZ	0	0	0	0	0	0	0
	PL	0	0	0	0	0	0	0
	HU	0	0	0	0	0	0	0
M	SK	0	0	0	0	0	0	0
	CZ	0.01	0	0	0	0	0	0.01
	PL	0	0	0	0	0	0	0
	HU	0	0	0	0	0	0	0
N	SK	0	0	0	0	0	0	0
	CZ	0	0	0	0	0	0	0
	PL	0	0	0	0	0	0	0
	HU	0	0	0	0	0	0	0

Table A6. *Cont.*

		Inventory to Sales Ratio [Coefficient]						
Sector	**Country**	**2017**	**2018**	**2019**	**2020**	**2021**	**2022**	**2023**
O	SK	0	0	0	0	0	0	0
	CZ	0.07	0.05	0.06	0.02	0.42	0.07	0.08
	PL	0	0	0	0	0	0	0
	HU	0.09	0.09	0.09	0.09	0.08	0.09	0.09
P	SK	0	0	0	0	0	0	0
	CZ	0	0	0	0	0	0	0
	PL	0	0	0	0	0	0	0
	HU	0.01	0.01	0.01	0	0	0	0.01
Q	SK	0.01	0.01	0.01	0.01	0.01	0.01	0.01
	CZ	0.01	0.02	0.01	0.02	0.01	0.02	0.01
	PL	0	0	0	0.01	0	0.01	0.01
	HU	0.01	0.01	0.01	0.01	0.01	0.01	0.01
R	SK	0	0	0	0.01	0	0	0
	CZ	0	0	0	0	0	0.01	0.01
	PL	0.01	0.01	0	0.01	0.01	0.01	0.01
	HU	0	0	0	0	0	0	0
S	SK	0.01	0.01	0.02	0.01	0.01	0.01	0.01
	CZ	0.03	0.03	0.04	0.03	0.03	0.04	0.03
	PL	0	0	0	0.01	0.01	0	0
	HU	0.01	0.01	0.01	0.02	0.01	0.01	0.01

Source: own processing.

Table A7. Median values of asset turnover period according to NACE.

		Asset Turnover Period [Day]						
Sector	**Country**	**2017**	**2018**	**2019**	**2020**	**2021**	**2022**	**2023**
A	SK	560	558	559	567	517	522	534
	CZ	586	593	608	607	600	598	588
	PL	625	630	637	616	584	594	598
	HU	447	454	446	469	456	452	448
B	SK	389	349	447	459	455	433	420
	CZ	471	461	492	498	461	460	472
	PL	357	374	349	375	390	366	359
	HU	396	360	355	461	395	395	381
C	SK	275	279	280	307	296	278	274
	CZ	236	244	249	260	250	246	237
	PL	243	245	247	267	251	251	244
	HU	263	264	271	299	292	290	276
D	SK	892	918	905	868	792	805	854
	CZ	667	667	645	630	578	606	624
	PL	536	539	501	520	476	488	502
	HU	402	419	375	424	379	396	401
E	SK	465	442	447	481	426	441	447
	CZ	307	285	291	284	310	302	305
	PL	637	613	592	576	538	567	583
	HU	306	320	317	310	301	309	306
F	SK	326	322	330	371	382	370	363
	CZ	240	238	250	256	253	247	242
	PL	274	255	263	301	291	286	279
	HU	302	263	259	292	293	300	296

Table A7. *Cont.*

Asset Turnover Period [Day]								
Sector	**Country**	**2017**	**2018**	**2019**	**2020**	**2021**	**2022**	**2023**
G	SK	292	290	305	322	318	305	299
	CZ	186	189	189	202	189	189	189
	PL	172	172	174	188	176	180	174
	HU	186	184	183	192	196	190	184
H	SK	264	258	274	278	279	268	271
	CZ	194	197	199	211	218	205	199
	PL	189	192	198	216	206	200	193
	HU	278	268	272	291	277	274	272
I	SK	946	930	864	1148	1159	1106	1054
	CZ	813	776	751	1143	1104	1063	998
	PL	494	486	481	790	617	584	502
	HU	471	492	525	757	619	573	516
J	SK	349	347	363	386	388	350	347
	CZ	248	241	219	246	245	249	240
	PL	279	279	275	294	276	279	279
	HU	274	283	291	298	311	304	295
K	SK	514	451	465	417	415	433	462
	CZ	329	316	303	318	302	308	310
	PL	422	395	342	391	370	387	396
	HU	578	609	527	576	572	572	578
L	SK	2361	2396	2394	2552	2497	2453	2397
	CZ	2960	2928	2734	2898	2746	2798	2824
	PL	1347	1312	1283	1246	1142	1182	1201
	HU	2029	1872	1945	1850	1998	2002	1996
M	SK	852	863	856	859	857	860	852
	CZ	291	310	303	329	312	303	296
	PL	291	282	282	300	309	306	294
	HU	377	376	365	401	386	377	373
N	SK	667	681	647	735	669	667	659
	CZ	210	206	213	238	245	228	217
	PL	200	193	201	239	242	216	205
	HU	249	247	215	265	295	255	243
O	SK	262	251	215	209	277	254	251
	CZ	340	441	731	621	1171	705	456
	PL	394	401	349	418	463	460	390
	HU	562	895	1064	874	666	605	574
P	SK	884	754	805	1124	1169	1006	904
	CZ	448	476	430	431	458	430	446
	PL	551	541	535	572	567	562	550
	HU	259	704	552	704	244	249	288
Q	SK	339	325	347	347	319	325	319
	CZ	302	243	266	260	238	246	248
	PL	313	320	296	311	275	284	287
	HU	225	235	267	273	268	243	231
R	SK	787	874	884	1048	1066	907	851
	CZ	396	363	327	375	336	348	359
	PL	534	546	557	642	685	589	547
	HU	328	384	365	468	476	453	432
S	SK	507	533	527	637	508	508	505
	CZ	291	371	304	334	366	370	361
	PL	350	371	347	375	390	378	356
	HU	444	412	356	495	452	437	421

Source: own processing.

Table A8. Median values of fixed asset turnover period according to NACE.

Sector	Country	Fixed Asset Turnover Period [Day]						
		2017	2018	2019	2020	2021	2022	2023
A	SK	330	319	322	329	284	276	289
	CZ	364	359	387	382	378	362	353
	PL	486	497	505	453	402	412	428
	HU	262	266	270	277	270	265	261
B	SK	230	200	264	253	250	243	236
	CZ	262	229	267	281	244	240	231
	PL	210	181	187	204	180	180	189
	HU	186	167	186	204	188	186	186
C	SK	100	100	100	107	97	100	100
	CZ	100	102	102	109	97	102	98
	PL	92	94	93	98	87	93	94
	HU	118	120	125	135	125	120	116
D	SK	745	715	620	542	516	510	523
	CZ	551	528	559	549	456	460	472
	PL	443	441	424	427	391	402	410
	HU	290	317	296	315	232	253	268
E	SK	191	197	174	182	142	148	162
	CZ	125	139	131	148	133	137	129
	PL	602	582	572	536	512	530	526
	HU	157	144	139	133	129	137	141
F	SK	58	58	62	66	70	63	57
	CZ	55	49	52	56	54	52	50
	PL	48	47	48	52	51	52	49
	HU	54	52	52	61	57	55	52
G	SK	43	44	45	48	44	42	42
	CZ	30	30	31	31	28	30	28
	PL	29	28	28	30	27	27	28
	HU	30	30	29	31	29	30	29
H	SK	100	95	99	93	85	84	88
	CZ	71	76	70	69	79	75	70
	PL	69	67	69	70	63	63	67
	HU	150	141	138	130	128	135	130
I	SK	814	811	727	1023	1035	912	854
	CZ	614	573	499	624	506	490	502
	PL	524	494	485	810	579	569	498
	HU	572	587	536	798	686	606	597
J	SK	45	50	53	55	58	55	48
	CZ	29	25	29	27	26	26	24
	PL	47	44	46	48	44	44	46
	HU	47	46	52	60	59	56	49
K	SK	44	40	62	62	81	69	55
	CZ	109	113	154	150	182	165	139
	PL	97	84	84	93	94	90	93
	HU	168	215	164	196	167	164	160
L	SK	1949	1962	1844	1987	1913	1902	1923
	CZ	2763	2639	2483	2519	2382	2368	2457
	PL	1409	1342	1313	1323	1145	1124	1102
	HU	1838	1736	1722	1629	1657	1638	1678
M	SK	218	242	230	254	225	220	217
	CZ	44	45	50	51	50	50	44
	PL	57	56	55	56	49	52	55
	HU	87	88	85	79	74	79	83

Table A8. *Cont.*

		Fixed Asset Turnover Period [Day]						
Sector	**Country**	**2017**	**2018**	**2019**	**2020**	**2021**	**2022**	**2023**
N	SK	159	189	178	173	165	170	173
	CZ	47	47	40	47	50	45	47
	PL	29	31	31	33	33	30	31
	HU	67	65	67	86	85	77	68
O	SK	38	39	28	36	67	43	39
	CZ	130	268	221	203	692	456	357
	PL	133	131	138	131	139	131	133
	HU	195	216	174	262	185	195	179
P	SK	336	325	326	298	400	365	331
	CZ	177	266	302	305	297	305	284
	PL	530	484	518	471	452	487	503
	HU	42	43	41	57	29	35	42
Q	SK	99	93	97	94	83	90	85
	CZ	153	137	128	123	110	110	121
	PL	135	133	128	134	110	135	128
	HU	136	151	126	117	104	109	115
R	SK	570	686	723	932	811	758	654
	CZ	157	169	105	100	93	105	100
	PL	642	628	593	704	678	652	581
	HU	163	192	162	205	195	174	160
S	SK	135	120	106	143	137	145	127
	CZ	56	51	69	49	52	55	50
	PL	197	186	188	216	194	197	188
	HU	571	352	471	611	674	602	563

Source: own processing.

Table A9. Median values of inventory turnover period according to NACE.

		Inventory Turnover Period [Day]						
Sector	**Country**	**2017**	**2018**	**2019**	**2020**	**2021**	**2022**	**2023**
A	SK	86	87	92	92	84	85	87
	CZ	93	90	94	94	91	90	90
	PL	101	97	98	92	98	100	97
	HU	87	92	87	79	85	83	88
B	SK	23	22	21	19	21	22	21
	CZ	26	21	25	29	27	25	24
	PL	18	15	16	17	14	15	17
	HU	31	33	29	30	31	30	33
C	SK	31	32	32	34	38	36	32
	CZ	45	45	45	48	53	45	46
	PL	39	39	39	40	45	41	43
	HU	45	47	46	47	51	47	49
D	SK	0	0	0	0	0	0	0
	CZ	1	1	1	2	1	1	1
	PL	18	24	22	21	17	18	20
	HU	4	4	4	4	4	4	4
E	SK	4	5	4	5	4	5	5
	CZ	6	5	6	6	6	6	6
	PL	4	4	4	4	4	4	4
	HU	6	6	7	6	6	6	6

Table A9. *Cont.*

Inventory Turnover Period [Day]								
Sector	**Country**	**2017**	**2018**	**2019**	**2020**	**2021**	**2022**	**2023**
F	SK	4	4	5	5	7	5	4
	CZ	14	14	13	14	17	14	14
	PL	14	13	12	13	17	13	12
	HU	15	16	13	8	9	14	15
G	SK	31	31	31	32	32	31	31
	CZ	35	36	36	37	35	36	36
	PL	37	37	38	38	39	37	37
	HU	36	37	36	36	36	36	36
H	SK	1	1	1	1	1	1	1
	CZ	1	1	2	1	1	1	1
	PL	1	1	1	1	1	1	1
	HU	1	2	2	2	2	2	2
I	SK	6	6	5	5	6	6	6
	CZ	4	4	3	5	4	5	5
	PL	4	4	4	4	4	4	4
	HU	4	4	4	4	4	4	4
J	SK	0	0	0	0	0	0	0
	CZ	2	1	1	1	1	1	1
	PL	1	1	1	1	1	1	1
	HU	1	1	0	0	0	1	1
K	SK	0	0	0	0	0	0	0
	CZ	0	0	0	0	0	0	0
	PL	0	0	0	0	0	0	0
	HU	0	0	0	0	0	0	0
L	SK	0	0	0	0	0	0	0
	CZ	0	0	0	0	0	0	0
	PL	0	0	0	0	0	0	0
	HU	0	0	0	0	0	0	0
M	SK	0	0	0	0	0	0	0
	CZ	2	1	2	2	2	1	2
	PL	0	0	0	0	0	0	0
	HU	1	0	0	0	0	0	0
N	SK	0	0	0	0	0	0	0
	CZ	0	0	0	0	1	0	0
	PL	0	0	0	0	0	0	0
	HU	1	1	1	1	1	1	1
O	SK	1	0	0	0	0	0	0
	CZ	27	19	22	6	153	25	31
	PL	0	0	0	0	0	0	0
	HU	34	34	32	34	31	34	34
P	SK	0	1	0	1	0	1	0
	CZ	1	1	0	0	0	0	0
	PL	1	1	1	1	1	1	1
	HU	3	3	2	1	1	1	2
Q	SK	2	3	3	4	3	3	3
	CZ	5	6	5	6	5	6	5
	PL	2	2	2	2	2	2	2
	HU	3	2	2	4	4	3	2

Table A9. *Cont.*

		Inventory Turnover Period [Day]						
Sector	**Country**	**2017**	**2018**	**2019**	**2020**	**2021**	**2022**	**2023**
R	SK	1	1	1	2	1	1	1
	CZ	1	2	2	2	2	2	2
	PL	2	2	2	2	2	2	2
	HU	1	1	1	1	1	1	1
S	SK	3	4	6	4	4	4	4
	CZ	13	12	14	11	12	13	12
	PL	1	1	2	2	1	1	1
	HU	5	5	5	6	5	5	5

Source: own processing.

Table A10. Median values of collection period ratio according to NACE.

		Collection Period Ratio [Day]						
Sector	**Country**	**2017**	**2018**	**2019**	**2020**	**2021**	**2022**	**2023**
A	SK	31	29	30	29	29	30	31
	CZ	32	30	28	28	30	28	28
	PL	61	63	61	53	47	51	56
	HU	21	22	23	21	18	22	22
B	SK	47	43	38	36	40	41	42
	CZ	44	40	39	40	39	39	39
	PL	55	51	49	47	47	48	50
	HU	24	26	22	19	21	21	22
C	SK	49	45	42	42	43	42	44
	CZ	44	43	40	42	41	44	43
	PL	54	52	50	48	49	50	53
	HU	35	34	32	31	31	33	34
D	SK	35	40	41	36	40	40	39
	CZ	21	21	19	17	20	22	21
	PL	52	53	53	52	56	54	56
	HU	19	20	18	17	14	18	20
E	SK	46	50	45	47	49	49	48
	CZ	34	33	30	31	33	34	34
	PL	43	43	43	42	39	41	43
	HU	59	58	57	50	47	55	56
F	SK	75	72	73	74	74	74	74
	CZ	65	59	58	57	58	60	53
	PL	68	60	63	62	61	62	65
	HU	60	53	50	46	50	50	54
G	SK	40	38	35	35	34	36	36
	CZ	39	36	36	34	35	35	36
	PL	40	39	37	35	34	35	35
	HU	29	30	28	24	25	28	30
H	SK	57	56	54	57	54	56	57
	CZ	27	28	23	27	25	27	28
	PL	60	58	55	57	55	59	55
	HU	44	45	41	41	42	42	41
I	SK	20	21	17	20	19	20	20
	CZ	19	17	15	15	20	19	50
	PL	22	19	16	21	17	22	20
	HU	11	10	10	5	8	10	11

Table A10. *Cont.*

		Collection Period Ratio [Day]						
Sector	**Country**	**2017**	**2018**	**2019**	**2020**	**2021**	**2022**	**2023**
J	SK	69	62	63	58	56	59	63
	CZ	54	55	51	48	48	50	50
	PL	69	66	62	60	59	62	66
	HU	36	40	40	33	36	40	40
K	SK	39	39	38	40	37	39	39
	CZ	41	37	40	37	31	35	37
	PL	50	47	50	49	46	50	49
	HU	11	10	10	16	18	16	16
L	SK	38	36	36	39	41	38	39
	CZ	30	29	26	32	27	29	31
	PL	32	30	29	28	27	27	30
	HU	14	14	11	10	9	11	14
M	SK	64	62	61	60	60	60	60
	CZ	59	62	58	53	55	58	60
	PL	73	72	72	71	69	74	71
	HU	39	39	36	32	29	35	29
N	SK	51	51	51	53	48	50	51
	CZ	44	47	48	45	43	46	46
	PL	60	58	54	55	55	57	55
	HU	32	31	28	27	30	30	32
O	SK	62	72	66	63	89	75	77
	CZ	25	42	43	59	72	66	60
	PL	31	31	34	36	39	36	35
	HU	13	13	18	6	7	10	14
P	SK	44	37	33	33	32	35	35
	CZ	23	22	18	24	18	20	22
	PL	11	11	11	12	11	11	11
	HU	23	23	38	24	27	23	24
Q	SK	41	36	32	42	41	40	41
	CZ	30	28	28	28	26	28	28
	PL	34	34	33	35	36	33	34
	HU	40	34	36	33	21	29	30
R	SK	25	24	28	30	26	25	25
	CZ	19	14	12	16	12	16	14
	PL	17	16	15	17	18	17	17
	HU	5	6	4	2	4	5	4
S	SK	50	57	57	42	39	45	50
	CZ	27	30	34	37	28	30	29
	PL	24	26	25	27	28	28	25
	HU	21	16	14	7	12	13	19

Source: own processing.

Table A11. Median values of credit period ratio according to NACE.

		Credit Period Ratio [Day]						
Sector	**Country**	**2017**	**2018**	**2019**	**2020**	**2021**	**2022**	**2023**
A	SK	46	46	49	48	44	46	46
	CZ	25	27	28	26	29	27	28
	PL	21	20	21	16	19	20	21
	HU	19	22	23	20	18	20	20

Table A11. *Cont.*

		Credit Period Ratio [Day]						
Sector	**Country**	**2017**	**2018**	**2019**	**2020**	**2021**	**2022**	**2023**
B	SK	30	27	24	18	23	25	24
	CZ	34	28	29	27	27	27	30
	PL	27	24	21	22	21	21	22
	HU	12	24	20	15	19	20	18
C	SK	39	38	35	35	37	35	38
	CZ	30	29	27	27	31	30	30
	PL	32	31	29	28	31	30	31
	HU	25	25	23	24	26	25	25
D	SK	29	33	32	32	32	33	32
	CZ	16	15	17	14	13	15	15
	PL	30	29	31	26	30	29	30
	HU	19	21	17	17	15	15	17
E	SK	34	31	28	29	26	29	30
	CZ	24	24	22	22	23	24	24
	PL	18	17	17	17	18	18	18
	HU	29	33	32	28	29	30	32
F	SK	53	52	51	46	48	50	50
	CZ	41	39	36	36	36	36	36
	PL	41	35	35	33	35	35	35
	HU	47	47	40	38	39	40	38
G	SK	41	39	36	35	36	35	36
	CZ	31	31	28	28	29	30	31
	PL	32	31	30	27	28	28	31
	HU	20	20	17	16	16	20	20
H	SK	32	32	30	29	29	30	29
	CZ	51	51	48	51	49	51	51
	PL	28	29	26	25	27	27	28
	HU	22	23	20	19	22	23	22
I	SK	31	30	28	30	30	30	30
	CZ	13	14	13	8	12	13	13
	PL	17	15	14	16	17	15	16
	HU	18	16	16	18	19	18	16
J	SK	34	35	34	31	30	33	34
	CZ	22	22	21	19	21	20	20
	PL	28	26	24	24	24	24	26
	HU	21	18	20	17	18	17	20
K	SK	33	25	25	21	20	25	22
	CZ	23	17	17	15	16	17	17
	PL	20	20	17	17	18	17	18
	HU	9	8	9	7	10	10	10
L	SK	40	36	35	36	32	35	37
	CZ	16	16	13	13	15	16	16
	PL	26	26	24	23	24	26	24
	HU	11	12	11	9	10	11	11
M	SK	40	39	35	35	32	33	35
	CZ	21	22	21	19	23	20	22
	PL	24	24	23	21	21	21	23
	HU	18	15	14	15	15	15	15
N	SK	31	30	28	31	29	30	30
	CZ	20	22	20	19	16	17	16
	PL	15	14	13	13	14	14	14
	HU	14	12	11	11	12	11	11

Table A11. *Cont.*

		Credit Period Ratio [Day]						
Sector	**Country**	**2017**	**2018**	**2019**	**2020**	**2021**	**2022**	**2023**
O	SK	12	12	11	7	6	10	12
	CZ	35	27	17	57	40	35	32
	PL	14	13	18	32	27	24	26
	HU	18	17	22	27	30	25	24
P	SK	27	20	24	23	18	20	19
	CZ	14	16	13	13	9	11	15
	PL	7	7	6	6	7	6	7
	HU	11	18	20	19	17	18	20
Q	SK	18	17	16	15	13	16	16
	CZ	17	15	15	13	14	15	13
	PL	17	17	17	17	17	17	17
	HU	13	13	15	11	10	14	12
R	SK	27	32	27	29	34	30	28
	CZ	15	14	17	16	19	18	16
	PL	11	11	10	8	10	11	10
	HU	11	11	9	8	13	10	11
S	SK	26	21	21	21	25	26	24
	CZ	15	17	18	18	17	15	15
	PL	8	6	6	5	8	6	6
	HU	16	21	23	23	25	22	23

Source: own processing.

References

Adamowicz, M. (2022). COVID-19 pandemic as a change factor in the labour market in Poland. *Sustainability, 14*(15), 9197. [CrossRef]

Amoa-Gyarteng, K. (2021). Corporate financial distress: The impact of profitability, liquidity, asset productivity, activity and solvency. *Journal of Accounting, Business and Management (JABM), 28*(2), 104–115. [CrossRef]

Aqil, M., Ahmed, R. R., Vveinhardt, J., & Streimikiene, D. (2019). Factors influencing the profitability of heavy vehicle industry: A case of Pakistan. *Montenegrin Journal of Economics, 15*(1), 61–72. [CrossRef]

Atayah, O. F., Dhiaf, M. M., Najaf, K., & Frederico, G. F. (2022). Impact of COVID-19 on financial performance of logistics firms: Evidence from G–20 countries. *Journal of Global Operations and Strategic Sourcing, 15*(2), 172–196. [CrossRef]

Bacik, R., Fedorko, R., Gavurova, B., Ivankova, V., & Rigelsky, M. (2020). Differences in financial performance between various categories of hotels in the Visegrad Group countries. *Journal of International Studies, 13*(2), 279–290. [CrossRef]

Balaniuk, I. F., Shelenko, D. I., Biloshkurskyi, M. V., Povorozniuk, I. M., & Slatvinska, L. A. (2020). An integrated approach to the enterprises' business efficiency assessment. *Management Theory and Studies for Rural Business and Infrastructure Development, 42*(4), 486–495. [CrossRef]

Bărbuță-Mișu, N., Madaleno, M., & Ilie, V. (2019). Analysis of risk factors affecting firms' financial performance—Support for managerial decision-making. *Sustainability, 11*(18), 4838. [CrossRef]

Bartos, V., Vochozka, M., & Skopkova, K. (2022). Assessment of financial health of service sector companies in the Central European region. *Entrepreneurship and Sustainability Issues, 10*(2), 375–393. [CrossRef] [PubMed]

Bartosova, V., & Kral, P. (2016, September 21–23). *A methodological framework of financial analysis results objectification in the Slovak Republic*. BE-ci 2016: 3rd International Conference on Business and Economics (pp. 189–197), Mara, Malaysia. [CrossRef]

Batrancea, L. (2021). The influence of liquidity and solvency on performance within the healthcare industry: Evidence from publicly listed companies. *Mathematics, 9*(18), 2231. [CrossRef]

Belas, J., Gavurova, B., Dvorsky, J., Cepel, M., & Durana, P. (2022). The impact of the COVID-19 pandemic on selected areas of a management system in SMEs. *Economic Research-Ekonomska Istrazivanja, 35*(1), 3754–3777. [CrossRef]

Bizjak, J. M., Kalpathy, S. L., Mihov, V. T., & Ren, J. (2024). COVID-19 vaccinations, business activity, and firm value. *Journal of Financial and Quantitative Analysis*, 1–29. [CrossRef]

Capestro, M., Rizzo, C., Kliestik, T., Peluso, A. M., & Pino, G. (2024). Enabling digital technologies adoption in industrial districts: The key role of trust and knowledge sharing. *Technological Forecasting and Social Change, 198*, 123003. [CrossRef]

Chambost, I., & Praquin, N. (2021). Spotlights and shadows of financial analysis: History of the making of one of its devices: The funds-flow statement. *Comptablite Controle Audit, 27*(3), 41–69. [CrossRef]

Chatterjee, S., Chaudhari, R., & Shams, R. (2024). Applications of Industry 4.0 for pandemic responses and business continuity: A TOE-DCV integrated approach. *IEEE Transactions on Engineering Management*, *71*, 13240–13250. [CrossRef]

Demirhan, H. G., & Anwar, W. (2014). Factors affecting the financial performance of the firms during the financial crisis: Evidence from Turkey. *Ege Strategic Research Journal*, *5*(2), 65–80. [CrossRef]

Derco, J. (2022). The impacts of the COVID-19 pandemic on the tour operator market: The case of Slovakia. *Journal of Risk and Financial Management*, *15*(10), 466. [CrossRef]

Eger, L., & Žižka, M. (2024). Industry 4.0, digital transformation and human resource management: Emerging themes and research trends in the context of the Visegrad countries. *Oeconomia Copernicana*, *15*(3), 1021–1065. [CrossRef]

Farooq, U. (2018). Impact of inventory turnover on the profitability of non-financial sector firms in Pakistan. *Journal of Finance and Accounting Research*, *1*(1), 34–51. [CrossRef]

Fitriani, F. (2023). Analysis of the effect of financial ratios on firm value in pharmaceutical sector companies listed on the Indonesia Stock Exchange 2016–2021. *Journals of Economics and Business*, *3*(1), 43–52. [CrossRef]

Gajdosikova, D., & Pavic Kramaric, T. (2023). Debt structure and its impact on financial performance: An empirical study on the enterprises operating in the Visegrad Group countries. *Ekonomicko-manazerske spektrum*, *17*(2), 107–124.

Gajdosikova, D., Valaskova, K., Kliestik, T., & Machova, V. (2022). COVID-19 pandemic and its impact on challenges in the construction sector: A case study of Slovak enterprises. *Mathematics*, *10*(7), 3130. [CrossRef]

Gazi, M. A. I., Nahiduzzaman, M., Harymawan, I., Masud, A. A., & Dhar, B. K. (2022). Impact of COVID-19 on financial performance and profitability of banking sector in special reference to private commercial banks: Empirical evidence from Bangladesh. *Sustainability*, *14*(10), 6260. [CrossRef]

Goldmann, K. (2020). Use of financial analysis in operational and strategic management in practise of Polish business. *Eurasian Business Perspectives*, *12*(2), 115–125. [CrossRef]

Gonchar, O. I. (2016). Increasing of business activity in management of innovative and investment potential of the company. *Scientific Bulletin of Polissia*, *4*(8), 262–267. Available online: http://ir.stu.cn.ua/123456789/15092 (accessed on 11 November 2024).

Gundova, P., & Medvedova, M. (2016, May 17). *Methods of financial analysis in Slovak companies as a tool for increasing of competitiveness*. 8th Annual International Scientific Conference on Competition 2016 (pp. 130–143), Jihlava, Czech Republic.

Harantova, V., Kalasova, A., Skrivanek Kubikova, S., Mazanec, J., & Jordova, R. (2022). The impact of mobility on shopping preferences during the COVID-19 Pandemic: The evidence from the Slovak Republic. *Mathematics*, *10*(9), 1394. [CrossRef]

Hiadlovsky, V., Rybovicova, I., & Vinczeova, M. (2016). Importance of liquidity analysis in the process of financial management of companies operating in the tourism sector in Slovakia: An empirical study. *International Journal for Quality Research*, *10*(4), 799–812. [CrossRef]

Hunjra, A. I., Niazi, G. S. K., Majid, N. R., Akbar, S. W., & Akhtar, M. N. (2011). Practices of working capital policy and performance assessment financial ratios and their relationship with organization performance. *World Applied Sciences Journal*, *12*(10), 1967–1973.

Hyrslova, J., Beckova, H., & Beranova, K. (2017, September 14–16). *Financial analysis of urban transport companies*. 11th International Days of Statistics and Economics 2017 (pp. 548–556), Prague, Czech Republic.

Istok, M., & Kanderova, M. (2019). Debt/asset ratio as evidence of profit-shifting behaviour in the Slovak Republic. *Technological and Economic Development of Economy*, *25*(6), 1293–1308. [CrossRef]

Jencova, S., Vasanicova, P., & Miskufova, M. (2024). Comprehensive assessment of Slovakian hospitals using financial and non-financial criteria in the COVID-19 context. *Economies*, *12*(9), 255. [CrossRef]

Jones, A. S., & Godday, O. O. (2015). Accounting ratios as a veritable tool for corporate Investment decisions: A study of selected organizations in Delta State. *Journal of Policy and Development Studies*, *9*(5), 38–49. [CrossRef]

Kliestik, T., Valaskova, K., Lazaroiu, G., Kovacova, M., & Vrbka, J. (2020). Remaining financially healthy and competitive: The role of financial predictors. *Journal of Competitiveness*, *12*(1), 74–92. [CrossRef]

Kovacova, M., Kliestik, T., Valaskova, K., Durana, P., & Juhaszova, Z. (2019). Systematic review of variables applied in bankruptcy prediction models of Visegrad group countries. *Oeconomia Copernicana*, *10*(4), 743–772. [CrossRef]

Kovalchuk, T., & Verhun, A. (2019). Improvement of the method of analysis of asset management efficiency. *Baltic Journal of Economic Studies*, *5*(5), 61–66. [CrossRef]

Kramolis, J., & Dobes, K. (2020). Debt as a financial risk factor in SMEs in the Czech Republic. *Equilibrium. Quarterly Journal of Economics and Economic Policy*, *15*(1), 87–105. [CrossRef]

Kristof, T., & Virag, M. (2022). What drives financial competitiveness of industrial sectors in Visegrad Four countries? Evidence by use of machine learning techniques. *Journal of Competitiveness*, *14*(4), 117–136. [CrossRef]

Kwak, J. K. (2019). Analysis of inventory turnover as a performance measure in manufacturing industry. *Processes*, *7*(10), 760. [CrossRef]

Lian, Z., Su, Z., & Zheng, T. (2021, December 3–5). *Analysis and research on credit risk factors of listed companies in China based on CVM-MLP*. 3rd International Conference on Machine Learning, Big Data and Business Intelligence (MLBDBI) (pp. 542–547), Taiyuan, China. [CrossRef]

Linares-Mustaros, S., Farreras-Noguer, M. A., Arimany-Serrat, N., & Coenders, G. (2022). New financial ratios based on the compositional data methodology. *Axioms*, *11*(12), 694. [CrossRef]

Liu, J., & Xu, Y. B. (2022). T-Friedman test: A new statistical test for multiple comparison with an adjustable conservativeness measure. *International Journal of Computational Intelligence Systems*, *15*, 29. [CrossRef]

Lukac, J., Oleova, C., & Kudlova, Z. (2022). Factors predicting companies' crisis in the engineering industry from the point of view of financial analysis. *Plos One*, *17*(2), e0264016. [CrossRef] [PubMed]

Makoji, E. E., Orugun, F. I., & Adelakun, A. (2021). Exploration of cash flow management for enterprise's business performance. *Asian Journal of Economics Business and Accounting*, *21*(10), 97–105. [CrossRef]

Mazanec, J. (2022). Working capital management as a crucial tool for corporate performance in the transport sector: A case study of Slovakia and the Czech Republic. *Mathematics*, *10*(15), 2584. [CrossRef]

Mia, M. A., Uddin, M. S., & Chowdhury, M. A. I. (2014). Evaluation of operational performance-A case study on Summit Power Limited (SPL). *IOSR Journal of Business and Management*, *16*(9), 45–51. [CrossRef]

Michalkova, L., Kovacova, M., Cepel, M., & Belas, J. (2022). Insolvency prediction and corporate bankruptcy model in Visegrad group countries. *Transformations in Business & Economics*, *21*(2A), 529–548.

Mijoc, I. (2024). Determinants of profitability of the IT industry in Croatia. *Ekonomski Vjesnik*, *37*(1), 45–62. [CrossRef]

Moody's. (2024). *Orbis*. Available online: https://www.moodys.com/web/en/us/capabilities/company-reference-data/orbis.html (accessed on 1 October 2022).

Mirza, N., Rahat, B., Naqvi, B., & Rizvi, S. K. A. (2020). Impact of COVID-19 on corporate solvency and possible policy responses in the EU. *Quarterly Review of Economics and Finance*, *87*, 181–190. [CrossRef] [PubMed]

Papikova, L., & Papik, M. (2022). Intellectual capital and its impacts on SMEs profitability during COVID-19 Pandemic. *Journal of Eastern European and Central Asian Research*, *9*(3), 521–531. [CrossRef]

Pech, M., Prazakova, J., & Pechova, L. (2020). The evaluation of the success rate of corporate failure prediction in a five-year period. *Journal of Competitiveness*, *12*(1), 108–124. [CrossRef]

Pham, K. X., Nguyen, Q. N., & Nguyen, C. V. (2020). Effect of working capital management on the profitability of steel companies on Vietnam Stock Exchanges. *The Journal of Asian Finance, Economics and Business*, *7*(10), 741–750. [CrossRef]

Podhorska, I., & Siekelova, A. (2020). Enterprises financial performance in a globalized world. *SHS Web of Conferences*, *74*, 05018. [CrossRef]

Priya, P., & Sharma, C. (2023). COVID-19 related stringencies and financial market volatility: Sectoral evidence from India. *Journal of Financial Economic Policy*, *15*(1), 16–34. [CrossRef]

Purwanto, A., & Bina, C. R. (2016). Analysis of Financial ratio towards earning growth in mining companies. *Universal Journal of Industrial and Business Management*, *4*(3), 81–87. [CrossRef]

Rafaqat, S., & Rafaqat, S. (2020). The impact of merge and acquisition on the financial performance of the NASDAQ listed small size technology company. *Economics and Finance Letters*, *7*(2), 200–217. [CrossRef]

Rahman, A., & Sharma, R. B. (2020). Cash flows and financial performance in the industrial sector of Saudi Arabia: With special reference to Insurance and Manufacturing Sectors. *Investment Management & Financial Innovations*, *17*(4), 76. [CrossRef]

Rep, A. (2021). Notes to the financial statements: Current state and improvement. *Business Systems Research Journal*, *12*(2), 60–78. [CrossRef]

Rezai, M., & Pourali, M. R. (2015). The relationship between working capital management components and profitability: Evidence from Iran. *European Online Journal of Natural and Social Sciences*, *4*(1), 342–351. Available online: https://european-science.com/eojnss_proc/article/view/4237/1959 (accessed on 11 November 2024).

Sacer, I. M., Deccan, N., & Rep, A. (2018, May 24–26). *Practical problems in understanding accounting terminology used in the preparation of general purpose financial statements—Evidence from Croatia*. 7th International Scientific Symposium on Economy of Eastern Croatia—Vision And Growth (pp. 1077–1085), Osijek, Croatia.

Shukla, S., & Roopa, T. N. (2017). Financial behaviour of selected telecom companies in India: A comparative analysis. *International Journal of Indian Culture and Business Management*, *14*(2), 141–161. [CrossRef]

Simionescu, M., Wojciechowski, A., Tomczyk, A., & Rabe, M. (2021). Revised environmental Kuznets curve for V4 countries and Baltic states. *Energies*, *14*(11), 3302. [CrossRef]

Susellawati, Sari, D. P., Nabella, S. D., & Fadlilah, A. H. (2022). The effect of profitability, liquidity, leverage, and activity ratios on dividend policy in manufacturing companies in the food and beverage industry sector listed on the Indonesia Stock Exchange in the 2016–2020 period. *Jurnal Mantik*, *6*(2), 1365–1375.

Svabova, L., Valaskova, K., Durana, P., & Kliestik, T. (2020). Dependency analysis between various profit measures and corporate total assets for Visegrad group's business entities. *Organizacija*, *53*(1), 80–90. [CrossRef]

Svabova, L., Kramarova, K., & Chabadova, D. (2022). Impact of the COVID-19 pandemic on the business environment in Slovakia. *Economies*, *10*(10), 244. [CrossRef]

Svabova, L., Stefunova, D., Kramarova, K., Durica, M., & Gabrikova, B. (2024). Would it have been cheaper to let them become unemployed? Costs and benefits of First Aid intervention for companies in Slovakia during the COVID-19 pandemic. *Equilibrium. Quarterly Journal of Economics and Economic Policy*, *19*(1), 139–169. [CrossRef]

Tahir, M., & Anuar, M. B. A. (2016). The determinants of working capital management and firms performance of textile sector in Pakistan. *Quality & Quantity*, *50*(2), 605–618. [CrossRef]

Tian, J. Y., & He, S. J. (2016, August 27–28). *Financial analysis: Current situation and development trend-review and evaluation of corporate financial analysis*. International Conference on Education, E-learning and Management Technology (EEMT) 2016 (pp. 77–81), Xi'an, China. [CrossRef]

Valaskova, K., Lazaroiu, G., Olah, J., Siekelova, A., & Lancova, B. (2019). How capital affects business valuation: A case study of Slovakia. *Central European Business Review*, *8*(3), 1–17. [CrossRef]

Valaskova, K., Kliestik, T., & Gajdosikova, D. (2021). Distinctive determinants of financial indebtedness: Evidence from Slovak and Czech enterprises. *Equilibrium. Quarterly Journal of Economics and Economic Policy*, *16*(3), 639–659. [CrossRef]

Valaskova, K., Gajdosikova, D., & Belas, J. (2023a). Bankruptcy prediction in the post-pandemic period: A case study of Visegrad Group countries. *Oeconomia Copernicana*, *14*(1), 253–293. [CrossRef]

Valaskova, K., Gajdosikova, D., & Lazaroiu, G. (2023b). Has the COVID-19 pandemic affected the corporate financial performance? A case study of Slovak enterprises. *Equilibrium. Quarterly Journal of Economics and Economic Policy*, *18*(4), 1133–1178. [CrossRef]

Vavrek, R., Kravcakova Vozarova, I., & Kotulic, R. (2021). Evaluating the financial health of agricultural enterprises in the conditions of the Slovak Republic using bankruptcy models. *Agriculture*, *11*(3), 242. [CrossRef]

Vitéz-Durgula, J., Dunay, A., Thalmeiner, G., Vajai, B., & Pataki, L. (2023). Financial analysis and survival research of the Visegrad countries' health industries. *Sustainability*, *15*(16), 12360. [CrossRef]

Welc, J. (2016). Empirical safety thresholds for liquidity and indebtedness ratios on the Polish capital market. *European Financial and Accounting Journal*, *11*(3), 37–50. Available online: https://ssrn.com/abstract=2876477 (accessed on 11 November 2024). [CrossRef]

Yousaf, M., Bris, P., & Haider, I. (2021). Working capital management and firm's profitability: Evidence from Czech certified firms from the EFQM excellence model. *Cogent Economics & Finance*, *9*(1), 1–16. [CrossRef]

Zagita, T., Novalia, N., & Suhada, S. (2024). Analysis of solvency ratio and activity ratio in the financial performance of Pt Bukit Asam Tbk. *Jemasi: Jurnal Ekonomi Manajemen Dan Akuntansi*, *20*(1), 28–38. [CrossRef]

Zisoudis, N., Karelakis, C., Theodossiou, C., & Loizou, E. (2020). Financial analysis of major retail chains within a turbulent economic environment. *Studies in Business and Economics*, *15*(3), 208–222. [CrossRef]

economies

MDPI

Article

Divergence Between New and Existing FDI in Times of Sustained Inflation Post the COVID-19 Pandemic: The Case of a Subnational Economy in the U.S.

Roxana Wright and Chen Wu *

School of Business, Plymouth State University, MSC 27, 17 High Street, Plymouth, NH 03264, USA; rwright01@plymouth.edu
* Correspondence: cwu@plymouth.edu; Tel.: +1-603-535-3241

Abstract

The relationship between inflation and foreign direct investment (FDI) is not clear-cut in theory. In the U.S., rising inflation coupled with increased economic recovery boosted FDI immediately after the COVID-19 pandemic but suppressed it afterwards. To shed light on the relationship between inflation and the resulting contractionary monetary policy and FDI, three key propositions were put forth for investigation. The propositions rely on relevant scientific literature showing that (1) although the connection between FDI and inflation is complex, a high and sustained inflation depresses incoming FDI due to increases in uncertainty and guarding government policies; (2) there exist significant location-based differences in how this connection manifests; and (3) high inflation and subsequent policies motivate FDI-related strategic action. Thus, we propose that new FDI is expected to be negatively affected by the rising entry cost associated with an inflationary economy that adopts anti-inflationary policies. Second, there exists heterogeneity in the effects of inflation on new FDI across subnational economies with various local characteristics. Third, existing FDI demonstrates strategic actions and expansion at the subnational location and beyond, even under inflationary pressure. We employ a positive comparative analysis based on descriptive statistics and qualitative interpretation of data to examine the status and activities of both new FDI (using subnational aggregated data) and existing foreign businesses (using firm-level data) in the state of New Hampshire during the recent inflation surge of 2022–2023. Our analysis provides empirical evidence supporting our propositions. Key implications are that, during challenging times of inflation and recovery, business leaders and economic development professionals should anticipate strategic actions to expand markets, products, operations, and partnerships. Leaders and professionals should act to take advantage of business actions outside the subnational location, as more companies look to strengthen and diversify their national and international networks.

Keywords: foreign direct investment; inflation; subnational economy; business strategy

1. Introduction

The world is facing unprecedented challenges emerging from dealing with a pandemic, addressing disruptions, and grappling with economic times that have rarely been seen in the past. As economists and businesspeople are charged with finding the best adjustments to the current situation, it is timely to investigate and report on current realities, such as the status and characteristics of foreign direct investment (FDI) and FDI-related business activities (Tabash et al., 2024). We take on such an endeavor. Our findings shed light on how FDI fared at a subnational location in comparison to national data and investigates FDI-related actions to uncover how foreign companies handle a period of high inflation.

The present research focuses on the subnational location to identify patterns in new and existing FDI. The selected subnational location is the U.S. state of New Hampshire (NH). It was chosen because, first of all, as a relatively small state, New Hampshire benefits from FDI in a more than proportionate manner. It ranks third among all states in the share of private sector employment accounted for by foreign companies: 8.7 percent compared to 6.2 percent for the country (U.S. Bureau of Economic Analysis, 2023). Second, New Hampshire experienced a significant inflation surge. Its prices of goods and services went up by nearly 18 percent between January 2021 and September 2024 (Granite State Times, 2024). Lastly, New Hampshire is a typical subnational economy that possesses key factors for the FDI location choice suggested by the literature (Wu & Rogers, 2018). To name some of these factors, it is situated at the border with Canada, considered as the gateway to the East Coast, and displays stability in economic fundamentals as well as physical and institutional infrastructure. These characteristics make the state of New Hampshire a suitable location for evaluating FDI during inflation (Wright & Wu, 2024).

Our study starts by providing an understanding of the relationship between FDI and inflation and reveals how contractionary monetary policy relates to foreign investments. This puts our investigation into the larger context of how rising inflation coupled with increased economic recovery stimulated FDI immediately after the pandemic but suppressed it afterwards (Agudze & Ibhagui, 2021). With this understanding of inflationary pressure, we then evaluate new FDI in New Hampshire and identify that, during the period of high inflation in 2022 and 2023, new FDI in the state at an aggregate level underperformed in comparison to the national level.

Once we realize the significant impact of inflation and related policies on FDI throughout 2022 to the end of 2023, we then investigate the firm-level responses that followed in 2023 and at the start of 2024. We took a broad view in this investigation and considered any FDI or FDI-related action or strategic action that involved foreign-affiliated companies that related to businesses in our state. We drew conclusions based on a sample of companies that pursued such actions and were able to find some notable patterns. We intentionally attempted to view all nuances of foreign business and how it may play a role in the local economy. We acknowledge that there were many negative effects and pivoting actions that most companies, domestic and non-domestic, had to undertake as a result of inflation, rising costs, uncertainty, and policy responses. Nevertheless, based on the information and analysis in this study, these negative impacts may not have been large enough to derail all strategic actions.

Kojima (1973) and the following studies (Kojima, 1982; Kojima & Ozawa, 1984; Kojima & Ozawa, 1985) propose two approaches to FDI, namely the macroeconomic approach and the international business approach. Our study uses the macroeconomic approach to examine new FDI and the effects that inflation and inflation-responding policies have on it. We expect that, just as is the case for the national level, the subnational impact of inflation on local FDI has a negative effect (Boateng et al., 2015). However, we posit that the effects vary with the location, given differences in economic environment characteristics. We use the international business approach and contend that the impact of inflation on existing FDI and FDI-related activities is less foreseeable, with many companies originating FDI-pursuing expansionary strategies during the inflationary period.

Our study makes meaningful contributions to both the macroeconomic perspective and the international business perspective of FDI by going beyond the traditional quantity-based conceptualization of FDI to consider presence and related activities. In previous research, FDI theory has been related to the theory of multinational enterprise and its transfer of resources and orchestration of activities across different locations (Jha et al., 2024). We take a different perspective on FDI that aims to understand it both as a quantitative concept and as an outcome of the actions of the subsidiary and its management of resources. By focusing on subnational location, the present paper contributes to the research on location strategies and adds to the relatively recent literature looking to understand the multinational enterprise's post-entry actions (Belderbos et al., 2024).

As we expand in the literature review section, extant literature found the relationship between inflation and FDI to be a prolific topic and recognized the importance of the subnational location when investigating the relationship. Existing studies provided evidence on the importance of the subnational location factors in determining FDI amounts and related business activities.

Our study contributes to the debated topic of the relationship between inflation and FDI by adding meaningful evidence from both the sub-national and even firm-level perspectives, which are the intrinsic foundations for the observed macroeconomic relationship between inflation and FDI. Specifically, it provides a timely investigation at the intersection of three important strands of literature: the theory of the multinational enterprise and on foreign subsidiary expansion, the investigation of the foreign companies' actions at the subnational level, and the study of how inflation impacts business activities at a particular location.

The present work contributes to the international business field on the importance of the subnational dimension of the multinational enterprise and its subsidiaries (Ghemawat, 2003). In alignment with other literature (Chidlow et al., 2015), we ground our investigation on the understanding that there are regional differences in how subsidiaries at different subnational locations develop.

Our research heeds the call to place subnational-level analysis in the national context, by comparing data at the two levels. This study contributes to research on regional expansion of foreign subsidiaries and intraregional geographic subsidiary activities. First, it theorizes how inflation may be associated with FDI as well as actions of foreign companies during inflationary times. Most of the previous studies have built upon a theory of post-entry expansion from the perspective of the multinational enterprise (e.g., Arregle et al., 2016). The understanding of the expansion of the subsidiary from and at the location of operation is underdeveloped (Ando, 2024). Our study provides the overall picture of how subsidiaries expand and grow under the circumstances of the local environment.

Second, extant empirical studies used data at the parent, multinational enterprise level, or data related to FDI projects at a subnational location. They did this to explore how companies use spatial proximity to ensure efficient communication, coordination, and knowledge sharing (Qian et al., 2010). Our work takes a different approach by collecting and analyzing data focused on the presence and actions of the subsidiaries, with no preset agenda of what these may be during inflation. This approach allows us to keep an open mind about the types of activities subsidiaries may undertake in the more unusual times of inflation.

Our study matches international business research avenues theorizing the impact of inflation on business performance and activities. A recent study (Cevik et al., 2024) found that inflation affects productivity, profitability, and net fixed investment in the short and medium term, and at a dissipating rate. Companies' actions during inflation include substituting inputs to adjust costs and increasing prices. The literature contended that firms raise prices and reduce capital spending (Coibion et al., 2020), while large firms increase net investments after inflation shocks and may even benefit from inflation (Yotzov et al., 2024). While the factors driving company actions are outside the boundaries of our paper, many of the actions we have discovered may be determined by the motivations for agile resource reallocations and cost-reducing financial adjustments. What is within our scope of discovery represents the propensity of companies to pursue long-term strategic action. In this regard, our work fits the literature expecting investments during inflationary times.

While the present analysis draws from known theories and research avenues about FDI, inflation, and the activities of multinational enterprise and its subsidiaries, we take a different approach by describing and contrasting data. Our investigation is about describing the evolution of FDI during the latest inflationary period. We also employ a qualitative approach to the examination of a sample of instances of FDI-related business actions. Our exploratory analysis is grounded in the context of a chosen subnational location; however, the larger national setting is still relevant. We are able to draw meaningful conclusions by contrasting the subnational with national-level situations. The country and international levels also remain relevant for the FDI-related actions considered, as many foreign firms engage in activities with a larger scope than the subnational location where they operate. Inflation remains an applicable background for our analysis. Given the descriptive and qualitative methodologies, we are not concerned with testing the relationship between FDI and inflation. Rather, we seek to provide specific and rich examples of how the two concepts may be associated, and how the association may differ depending on the national versus subnational levels, and when contrasting new versus existing FDI.

2. Literature Review

The theoretical foundation of our research is the model of Kojima (1973, 1982), which states that FDI is originated from the investing country's comparatively disadvantaged industry, which happens to be a comparatively advantaged industry in the host country. This is also known as the Kojima Theorem, and it is the first in the literature to distinguish the macroeconomic approach to FDI from the prevailing international business approach that is based on the classical profit maximization assumption in microeconomics and the Heckscher–Ohlin–Samuelson theoretical framework of international trade (Kastratović, 2020). While Kojima's research focuses on Japanese and American multinational enterprises, his macroeconomic perspective for FDI has been adopted by studies of different countries, such as Korea (Lee & Jung, 2015), India (Banga, 2006), and the least-developed countries (Tekin, 2012). Our study purposefully follows both approaches to FDI and provides nuanced empirical evidence for the two lines of FDI theories. Specifically, our macroeconomic perspective examines the impact of new FDI on a subnational economy, and our international business angle investigates the strategic activities of foreign firms during the inflation surge of 2022–2023.

The theoretical exploration of the relationship between inflation and FDI has been founded on the models of Mundell (1965) and Tobin (1965). They forecast a positive link between inflation and capital accumulation because the increased price levels lower the purchasing power of money balances and cause a shift in portfolio allocation from money balances to real tangible assets, including FDI (Mensah et al., 2024). Existing studies that consider inflation as a relevant determinant of FDI are predominantly at the country level and report mixed findings for the relationship between inflation and FDI inflow volume. Most research has found that the inflation rate plays a significant and negative role in a country's inward FDI volume due to elevated economic uncertainty and business operation costs (Tabash et al., 2024; Boateng et al., 2015). Some research, contrarily, has provided evidence on a positive role of moderate inflation as a signal of the adequate rate of return for foreign investments (Mason & Vracheva, 2017). More interestingly, some research has revealed heterogeneity in this relationship between developed and developing countries (Sabir et al., 2019), and even non-linearity in the link between inflation and FDI (Agudze &

Ibhagui, 2021). Meanwhile, the lack of any significant relationship is also seen mainly in the research of developing countries (Sabir et al., 2019; Alshamsi et al., 2015).

Looking at the literature examining FDI by employing large data sets, for example, there is a long-standing understanding that the FDI and inflation connection is complex but important to elucidate. For example, based on research in ASEAN countries during 2007 and 2016, FoEh et al. (2020) found that the inflation rate has a negative impact on foreign direct investment, which should inform economic growth policy in the region. The connection between FDI and inflation may depend on the location of study. Using time series data from 1970 to 2016, Musyoka and Ocharo (2018) concluded that, in Kenya, inflation does not have a significant effect on FDI. A study using data from 74 countries clustered into industrialized and developing economies showed that the relationship between inflation and FDI can be nonlinear. Agudze and Ibhagui (2021) concluded that inflation reduces FDI in industrialized countries after reaching a threshold, whereas in developing countries, inflation's impact on FDI is negative even before reaching its threshold. These authors purported that the mixed results documented in the literature may be explained by the presence of previously overlooked threshold effects. Thus, according to the literature, the relationship between inflation and FDI continues to be a topic requiring investigation that recognizes differences depending on the context in which the relationship is examined. The present study adds to the evidence on this relationship.

Extant literature has long acknowledged that foreign subsidiary development at a location is determined to a significant extent by the local environment (Birkinshaw & Hood, 1998). There has also been much evidence on how the subnational location is important for the competitive advantage of multinational enterprises (Buckley & Ghauri, 2004). Hence, there is agreement on the key roles that the economy and other factors at the location of the subsidiary's operations play in determining company performance. The current study is grounded in the subnational dimension of FDI.

Previous work has confirmed repeatedly that subnational regions matter for understanding business development and actions, due to differences in culture, institutions, and level of economic development. With this observation across world economies, scholars have noted that international investment appears to be concentrated in a few subnational regions and global cities (Beaudouin et al., 2018). Hutzschenreuter et al. (2020) noted that the international business field may need to dedicate more study to the "conceptual advancement of subnational level research", beyond quantitative analysis and statistical modeling. These researchers posited that companies' international strategies can be understood better by combining national- and subnational-level analyses. Extant literature thus emphasized the importance of a strong local business climate in attracting FDI, and the idea that FDI determinants and activities can be best understood by analyzing both the national and subnational settings in which they occur.

Previous studies (Ando, 2024) showed that local partners enhance the benefits of intraregional expansion of the foreign subsidiary. Our methodology provides us with an opportunity to discover to what extent foreign subsidiaries enter contracts and partnerships, both at and outside their subnational location. Ando (2024) found that "geographically isolated and small subsidiaries and those co-owned by local partner firms gain large benefits from intraregional expansion". Thus, recent literature demonstrated that there are patterns in how foreign subsidiaries expand intraregionally.

The recession that followed the COVID-19 pandemic in 2020 was brief, but it revealed the importance of making meaningful strategic choices for decisionmakers. Surowiecki (2024) found that some growing companies became stronger during this time, improving how their products were appealing to existing and new customers. Drawing from a previous period of inflation in the 1970s, when some of the most successful companies started, this analyst predicted that the inflation of recent years may also be the time when highly successful companies arise. It is therefore important to examine the actions taken by firms during the most recent period of inflation, as they may represent the hallmark of future strength.

The relationship between inflation and FDI is highly complicated, as revealed by both theoretical and empirical research. Understanding of this complex relationship would benefit from being put in a broader context, including how inflation impacts a firm's strategic behavior in general and how inflation varies across locations. As the business world aimed to deal with the effects of inflation, it was expected that companies would adjust prices and find new sources of growth, while also cutting costs. Strategists were advised to choose to support strategic initiatives and distinguish them from nonstrategic moves. In a difficult economic environment, investing in core businesses should be maintained, and broad cost-cutting initiatives should be avoided. According to Heinrich et al. (2021), companies were expected to do better if their decisionmakers focused on "signature customer and employee experiences" and continued to invest in growth with high potential return on investment.

Past studies (e.g., Ridhwan, 2016) investigated regional inflation variability. It was determined that national factors like common monetary policy, exchange rate movements, and changes in commodity prices impact inflation. Regional inflation differentials are specifically determined by "differences in sectoral specialization, asynchronous business cycles, degree of openness, nominal wage rigidities, and local (spatial) specific factors". Although the research pointing out these phenomena was outside the U.S., the findings were meaningful, suggesting that weakness in local institutions and governance could delay the inflation convergence that appears to happen eventually. Ultimately, when taking inflation into account, the subnational level is important.

The literature has also found that inflation does not manifest itself in the same way across subnational regions. Price changes in the housing sector, for instance, were found to be a key determinant of regional differences in inflation in the U.S. in recent periods. Residents across subnational locations may also have different purchasing patterns, which may also lead to regional variations in inflation. The U.S. northeast was determined as an example of an area where lower transportation expenditure contributed to lower inflation readings. Notable differences were observed in the recent inflationary period, although inflation levels appear to move together. These works (Gupta & McGranahan, 2023) indicate that it is imperative to evaluate inflation and its effects not only at the national level, but also in consideration of how it is experienced at the subnational level.

3. Propositions on New and Existing FDI During Inflation

Inflation is defined as a sustained increase in the average price of goods and services. It reduces consumers' and businesses' purchasing power. A moderate inflation rate is an indicator of economic stability and a factor of economic growth that benefits foreign direct investors. The U.S. Federal Reserve Bank targets a two percent inflation rate over time. However, high levels of inflation cause economic uncertainty and negatively affect foreign investors by reducing the value of assets pegged to the local currency, which tends to be depreciated in relation to foreign currency. Therefore, the relationship between FDI and inflation is not clear-cut.

Since the Great Economic Recession of 2008–2009, unconventional monetary policy tools have been used more powerfully and widely than ever before. Specifically, expansionary monetary policy gives central banks the opportunity to swiftly respond to various crises of economic downturns by increasing liquidity. In response to the unprecedented disruptions to economies brought about by the COVID-19 pandemic that started in 2020, countries continued to implement expansionary monetary policies and the abundance of liquidity decreased interest rates and increased stock market indexes at a global level until the end of the pandemic (Karahan & Bayır, 2022). In the U.S., the Fed decreased its administered rates (the interest rate on reserve balances, the discount rate, etc.) as an expansionary policy tool, which pushed the rate in the federal funds market and interest rates on other investment options lower for all types of financial institutions. These lower market interest rates were aimed at boosting the overall borrowing and lending needed for more consumption and investment spending. As illustrated in Figure 1, the U.S. federal funds rate went down from around 2 percent in 2019 to 0.25 percent between March 2020 and February 2022.

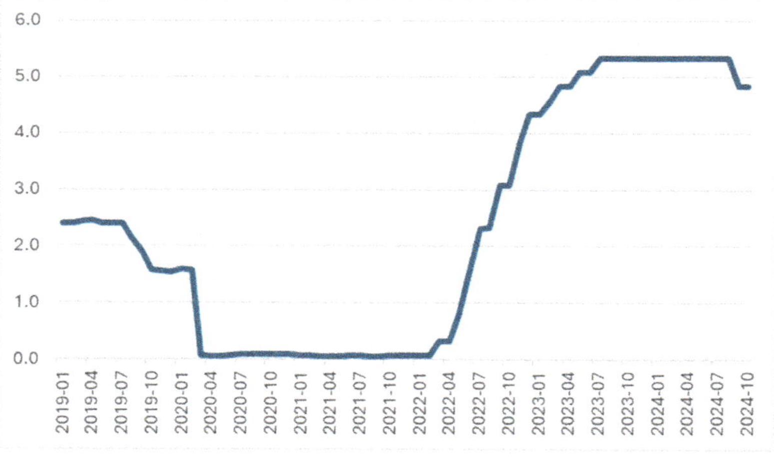

Figure 1. End-of-month effective federal funds rate in the U.S., 2019–2024. Data source: Federal Reserve Bank of St. Louis.

Due to supply chain disruptions and the lockdown of economies, prices in the U.S. went up moderately in the first year of the COVID-19 outbreak, and the 12-month change in the Consumer Price Index (CPI) increased from 0.1 percent in May 2020 to 2.6 percent in March 2021. The price hike, however, sustained since the spring of 2021 and the 12-month change in CPI, surged to 9.1 percent in June 2022, a record-high inflation rate for the past four decades. It then went down every month, to between three percent and four percent by the summer of 2023, and became stable for one year until July 2024, when it dropped below three percent in the following months. As of November 2024, the inflation rate is still around its peak value between 2014 and when the surge occurred in 2021. This is illustrated in Figure 2.

In response to surging inflation pressure, the U.S. Federal Reserve started raising interest rates in March 2022. Afterwards, the effective federal funds rate continuously climbed, hitting 1 percent in May, 2.5 percent in July, 3.25 percent in September, 4 percent in November, 5 percent in March 2023, and maintained a 23-year high of 5.5 percent from July 2023 until September 2024. Figure 1 captures the "U" shape of the interest rate scatterplot corresponding to the period 2019–2022. Similar contractionary monetary policy was also carried out in this period by the central banks of major economies, including the Bank of England, the European Central Bank, etc., to combat inflation (Caon, 2022).

Figure 2. 12–month percentage change in the Consumer Price Index in the U.S., January 2014–October 2024. Data source: U.S. Bureau of Labor Statistics.

In theory, the monetary tightening that boosts interest rates may curb rising prices through the following channels: First, higher interest rates discourage borrowing and encourage saving, and thus reduce aggregate demand and total spending. Second, within the context of open economies, the interest rate measures the expected rate of return, and elevated interest rates attract more foreign investment, which boosts the demand for local currency. This will appreciate the value of the exchange rate and make the goods/services labeled in the local currency more expensive, which reduces exports, further lowers domestic production, and lowers import prices, contributing to lower inflation (Horwich, 2023). It is worth noting that empirical findings on the relationship between exchange rates and trade balance, however, reveal significant variances owing to the heterogeneity in trade portfolios across countries (Hong Nga et al., 2024).

Did worldwide contractionary monetary policy stimulate more foreign investment flowing into these countries? Although there were worldwide recessionary fears, global foreign direct investment (FDI) flows in 2023 reached $1.37 trillion, a three percent increase over 2022. This increase, however, was concentrated in a few European Union (EU) countries, such as Luxembourg and the Netherlands. FDI inflows to the rest of the EU and in other developed countries either stagnated or declined. Even in developing Asia, normally the engine of FDI growth, FDI inflows fell by 12 percent. China reported a decline of six percent in its FDI inflows, which was rare after a couple decades of continued growth. In total, developing countries saw a nine percent drop (UNCTAD, 2024). The economic uncertainty and higher interest rates did affect global investment.

In addition to worldwide evidence, in the United States, the largest FDI recipient, FDI inflows also went down by three percent from 2022 to 2023. Quarterly inward FDI transactions reveal a downward trend throughout 2023, as shown in Figure 3. A breakdown of FDI inflows by country of origin uncovers that FDI from Canada declined significantly in 2023 while FDI from the Middle East and Asia and Pacific was relatively stable. However, inward FDI was seen climbing up throughout 2022 until the last quarter, a period in which U.S. inflation reached its 40-year high, although it started to go downhill. This may suggest that rising inflation caused by the economic recovery from the global pandemic stimulated FDI from 2021 to 2022, but high and sustained inflation discouraged foreign investors in 2023. During this period, another important external shock to the global economy was Russia's invasion of Ukraine in March 2022 and the war that has continued since then.

This war heightened global inflation by diverting supply chains for vital food, energy, and industrial products. The United States has not been immune to this crisis (Ronaghi & Scorsone, 2023).

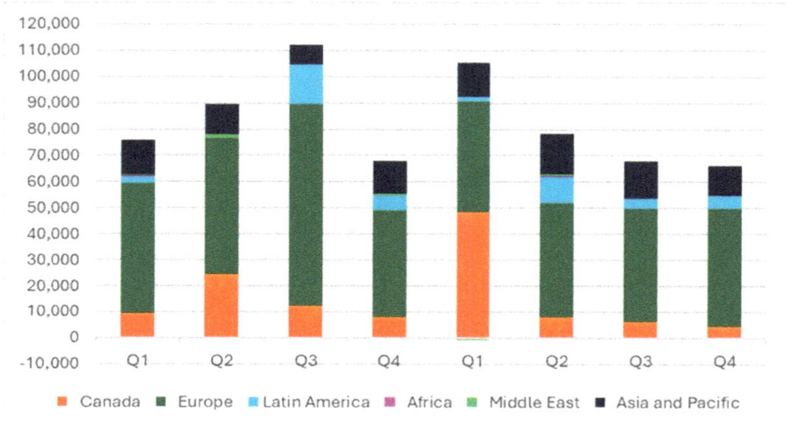

Figure 3. Quarterly transactions for inward FDI in the U.S., 2022–2023, by country of origin (million USD). Data source: U.S. Bureau of Economic Analysis, data on U.S. international financial transactions for direct investment.

Given the predictable negative effects of inflation on global and national new FDI, we submit that inflation will also have a profound and negative effect on new FDI at the subnational level. Hence, we propose the following:

Proposition 1. *At the subnational level, new FDI is expected to be negatively influenced by inflation.*

Furthermore, as our literature review suggests, location-specific characteristics such as comparative advantage determine variations in FDI, both in the amount and in how the new FDI occurs. The literature also suggests that the effects of inflation on key factors of FDI location choices vary across locations and, accordingly, the inflation impact on FDI will be mitigated by the specifics of the subnational location. Therefore, following the macroeconomic approach to FDI, we posit that the amount of new FDI and how it evolves throughout the inflationary period might also be expected to be different from the national level and, potentially, from other subnational location trends. Thus, we submit the following:

Proposition 2. *The effect of inflation on new FDI across subnational economies is heterogenous.*

As extant studies have shown, multinational companies and their subsidiaries are expected to respond to inflation and monetary policy, as well as to the specific conditions at the subnational locations where they operate. Studies adopting the international business approach to FDI have suggested that foreign subsidiaries may attempt cost-cutting measures but also investments in core business areas or in expanding market power or competitive position for the purpose of maximizing long-run profits. We thus posit that foreign subsidiaries in New Hampshire will act with significant strategic actions to expand or strengthen existing FDI. Concurrently, foreign-affiliated companies outside New Hampshire may also take actions that affect state businesses. We contend that, although inflation destabilized new FDI and caused a period of turbulence and variability, it did not significantly negatively impact existing FDI and respective companies' strategies of growth and stability. Therefore, we propose the following:

Proposition 3. *Existing FDI at the subnational location is not always deterred by inflation and can demonstrate significant strategic actions to increase scale and value.*

4. Data and Findings

4.1. New FDI Under High Inflation: New Hampshire Compared with the Country

The analysis of new FDI aims to identify patterns. We selected a subnational location in the U.S. that is a relatively small but distinct state with relatively significant FDI inflows and international activities. This selection allows us to evaluate FDI and to juxtapose the analysis with an inflation surge, which this state experienced during the timeframe of our investigation. We conducted a positive analysis based on descriptive statistics. To understand the new FDI, we examined the investment expenditures, employment, sales revenue, and net income of newly acquired, established, and expanded U.S. businesses by foreign enterprises at the chosen location within the context of evolving inflation measured by the regional Consumer Price Index (CPI). Both the new FDI data and CPI data are explored descriptively and compared to national levels for the purpose of evaluating the dynamics stated in the first and second propositions. The sources of our data are credible and our methods are fully replicable for studying the propositions at a different subnational location or contrasting several subnational locations, if investment activities and inflation data can be obtained at those locations.

We started by examining the investment activities and revenue performances of the newly acquired, established, or expanded U.S. businesses by foreign enterprises (new FDI, hereafter) in New Hampshire within the context of high inflation pressure in 2022. In this analysis, we used U.S. Bureau of Economic Analysis data on new FDI in the United States to construct tables and figures, and 2023 is their most recent available data as of November 2024. Four measures (investment expenditure, employment, sales revenue, and net income) are the only variables accessed via this data, and the beginning year is 2014, which is when the Bureau of Economic Analysis reinstated its Survey of New Foreign Direct Investment in the United States after ending the series in 2008 due to budget cuts. It is also worth noting that the Bureau of Economic Analysis suppresses some data to avoid disclosure of individual companies and rounds some small nonzero values to zero. This operation mainly appears in the data for New Hampshire. Therefore, we tried to draw the best information as possible from this limited data associated with a credible source.

Because CPI data for New Hampshire alone are not available, we adopted U.S. Bureau of Labor Statistics data for the northeast region, which is comprised of Connecticut, Maine, Massachusetts, New Hampshire, New Jersey, New York, Pennsylvania, Rhode Island, and Vermont. As shown in Figure 4, the 12-month percentage change in all-item CPI for this region surged from February 2021 until it reached a four-decade high of 7.5 percent in the summer of 2022. It trended down but remained at a high position of between 6 and 7.5 percent throughout 2022. The downward trend went sharper in the first half of 2023 and stabilized after the summer in the two to three percent range.

During this period, new FDI in New Hampshire was weaker than in 2021. As shown in Table 1, both newly acquired and newly expanded U.S. businesses in New Hampshire did not make any investment expenditures in 2022. This happened during the COVID-19 pandemic in 2020. One newly established business made an investment expenditure, but the data were suppressed to avoid disclosure of the individual company. Therefore, it is possible that the investment expenditure of new FDI in 2022 was even lower than

2020, when it was $2 million, not to mention that it had an average of $148 million per year between 2016 and 2019 (Wright & Wu, 2024). This figure remained low in 2023 because, although one newly acquired business made an investment expenditure, the expenditure by the newly established business was negligible. Further scrutiny by type of investment reveals that greenfield FDI (i.e., newly established businesses and newly expanded businesses combined) in New Hampshire has been the state's driving power for FDI growth. This type of FDI poses greater risks and longer-term commitment of capital than other types of FDI. In exchange, the parent company owns a greater degree of control of the foreign subsidiaries.

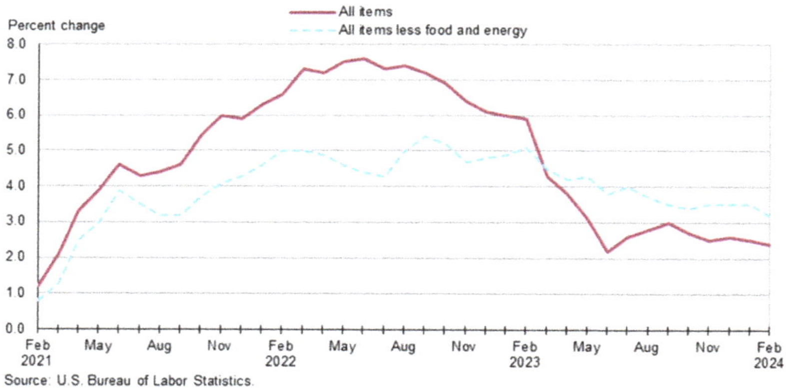

Figure 4. 12-month percentage change in the Consumer Price Index for the northeast region, February 2021–February 2024.

Table 1. First-year investment expenditures of new FDI in New Hampshire by type of investment (million USD).

	Acquired	Established	Expanded	Total
2018	(D)	(*)	2	(D)
2019	(D)	(*)	(D)	131
2020	0	2	0	2
2021	2	1	2	5
2022	0	(D)	0	(D)
2023	(D)	(*)	0	(D)

Note: (D) means data are suppressed to avoid disclosure of data on individual companies. (*) means a nonzero value that rounds to zero. (Data source: U.S. Bureau of Economic Analysis).

New Hampshire seemed to follow the national trend in investment expenditures with respect to new FDI. As illustrated in Figure 5, new FDI investment expenditures at the national level bounced up in 2021 to be above pre-pandemic levels, but then dropped sharply in 2022, when inflation pressures kept accumulating, and dropped further in 2023 at the tail end of the inflation surge. This is consistent with empirical findings that temporary increases in inflation are not likely to have a significant relationship with FDI, while sustained rising inflation tends to lower FDI due to its impact on a country's economic and business climate (ResearchFDI, 2022). Looking into the type of investment reveals that the cut in investment expenditures was solely from newly acquired businesses, which has been the dominant source of new FDI in the U.S. On the positive side of the story, the U.S. had more greenfield FDI in 2022 and 2023, because both newly established and newly expanded businesses increased their investment expenditures in comparison to 2021 and the years before it.

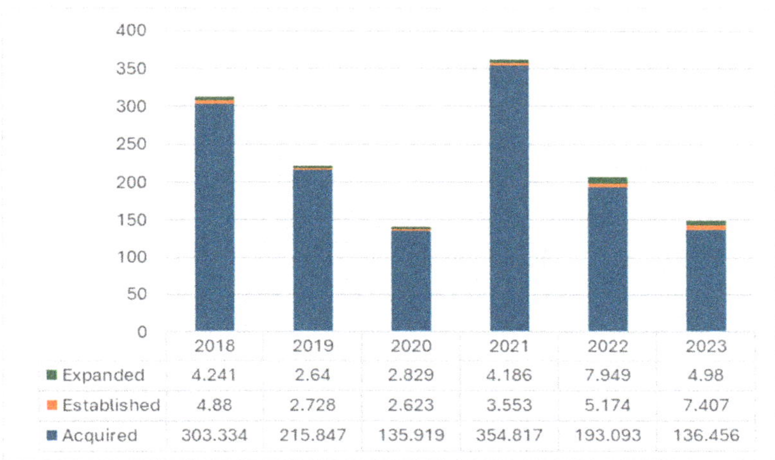

Figure 5. First-year investment expenditures of new FDI in the U.S. by type of investment (billion USD). Data source: U.S. Bureau of Economic Analysis.

Job creation is an important contribution of inward FDI to local economies. In the U.S., FDI directly and indirectly supports over 15 million jobs across the country (U.S. Department of Commerce, 2024). For the state of New Hampshire, FDI-related jobs were added solely by newly acquired businesses. According to Table 2, 800 jobs were added by new FDI in New Hampshire in 2020; the number went up to 1100 jobs in 2021 but fell to 800 in 2022 and then experienced a major decline to only 300 jobs in 2023. A similar dynamic was uncovered at the national level, illustrated in Figure 6. From 2021 to 2023, the number of American jobs added by new FDI decreased every year, and was cut in half owing to a reduction in employment in newly acquired U.S. businesses. Newly established and expanded businesses provided more jobs after 2021, but job creation by greenfield FDI in the U.S. was still weaker than the year of the pandemic and prior years.

Table 2. Current employment from new FDI in New Hampshire by type of investment (1000 employees).

	Acquired	Established	Expanded	Total
2018	1.8	(*)	0	1.8
2019	G	0	0	G
2020	0.8	0	0	0.8
2021	1.1	0	0	1.1
2022	0.8	0	0	0.8
2023	0.3	0	0	0.3

Note: (*) means fewer than 50 employees. Size ranges are given in employment cells that are suppressed, and G means a range from 1000 to 2499. Data source: U.S. Bureau of Economic Analysis.

Sales revenue from new FDI in New Hampshire is dominated by acquired local businesses over greenfield FDI. As shown in Table 3, newly established and newly expanded businesses in New Hampshire have shown negligible sales revenue in the past decade. It is notable that the scale of sales revenue from new FDI in New Hampshire follows a downward trend since 2014. Revenue dropped from $148 million in 2019 to nearly $0 in 2020 due to the COVID-19 pandemic, and then sales from both newly acquired and newly expanded FDI bounced up in the post-pandemic year of 2021. In the following year, when inflation pressures continued to rise, all (but the newly acquired) types of new FDI reported a total sales revenue that rounds to zero. At the tail end of the inflation surge in 2023, the sluggish revenues from new FDI in New Hampshire were improved by new establishments.

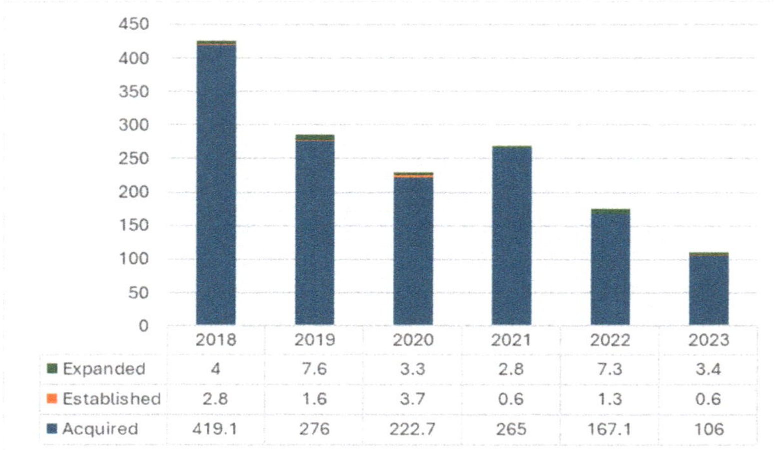

Figure 6. Current employment from new FDI in the U.S. by type of investment (1000 employees). Data source: U.S. Bureau of Economic Analysis.

Table 3. Sales from new FDI in New Hampshire by type of investment (million USD).

	Acquired	Established	Expanded	Total
2014	(D)	0	(D)	213
2015	(D)	0	0	(D)
2016	220	0	0	220
2017	77	(*)	0	77
2018	(D)	2	0	(D)
2019	(D)	(*)	(D)	148
2020	0	(*)	0	(*)
2021	(D)	(*)	2	(D)
2022	(D)	(*)	0	(D)
2023	(D)	5	0	(D)

Note: (D) means data are suppressed to avoid disclosure of data on individual companies. (*) means a nonzero value that rounds to zero. Data source: U.S. Bureau of Economic Analysis.

Similar to the case of New Hampshire, Figure 7 illustrates that sales revenue from new FDI at the U.S. national level also primarily came from acquired businesses and seemed to follow a downward trend between 2014 and 2020. The post-pandemic economic recovery almost doubled sales revenue from new FDI in 2021 and 2022. Different from the case of New Hampshire, both newly established and newly expanded businesses at the national level reported the highest sales revenues in 2022. The strong performance of greenfield FDI in the U.S. released a positive signal on the resilience of FDI in terms of recovery from the disruptions caused by the global pandemic. This resilience, however, was challenged by sustained increases in prices and costs, such that, in 2023, sales figures from new FDI in the U.S. declined by almost half to pandemic levels.

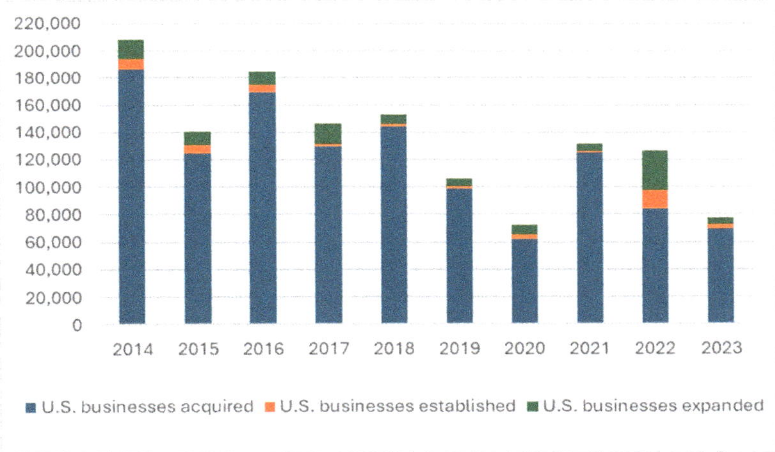

Figure 7. Sales from new FDI in the U.S. by type of investment (million USD). Data source: U.S. Bureau of Economic Analysis.

By subtracting all costs and expenses from gross income, which includes revenue and income from other sources, net income measures a firm's profitability. Table 4 below reports net income for new FDI in New Hampshire. Newly acquired businesses, the dominant type of FDI, experienced a downward trend in their net income, similar to their sales revenue. They remained profitable every year until the COVID-19 economic lockdown in 2020. They bounced up immediately after the pandemic, but the data were suppressed for the years of the inflation surge, making it difficult to compare the post-pandemic and pre-pandemic years. In contrast, as illustrated in Figure 8, net income from new FDI at the national level was rather stable until the pandemic, when newly acquired businesses suffered from negative net incomes. The condition was reversed in 2021 and further improved in 2022, when net incomes from newly acquired businesses restored their pre-pandemic levels of $7 billion and, more surprisingly, greenfield FDI reported a record-high net income of over $4 billion. In 2023, however, net incomes from new FDI in the country drastically fell by more than half in response to the sustained increase in prices and costs and its cumulated negative impact on the profitability of businesses.

Table 4. Net incomes from new FDI in New Hampshire by type of investment (million USD).

	NH Businesses Acquired	NH Businesses Established	NH Total
2014	10	0	10
2015	2	0	2
2016	(D)	0	(D)
2017	10	1	11
2018	3	2	5
2019	2	(*)	2
2020	0	(*)	(*)
2021	(D)	(*)	(D)
2022	(D)	(*)	(D)
2023	(D)	(*)	(D)

Note: (D) means data are suppressed to avoid disclosure of data on individual companies. (*) means a nonzero value that rounds to zero. Data source: U.S. Bureau of Economic Analysis.

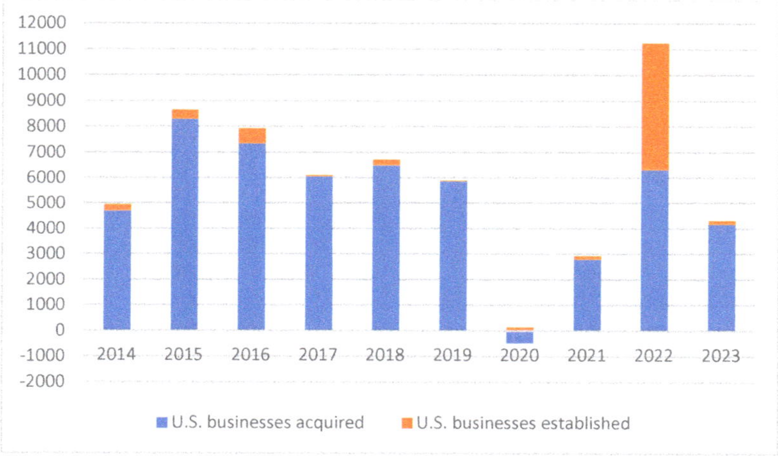

Figure 8. Net incomes from new FDI in the U.S. by type of investment (million USD). Data source: U.S. Bureau of Economic Analysis.

Based on the analysis provided above, we find support for our first and second propositions. Examination of the most recently available data on new FDI in the U.S. and specifically in the state of New Hampshire revealed notable similarities, as well as differences, in the performances of newly acquired, established, and expanded businesses during the years of mounting inflation pressures and the tail end of this inflation surge. All of the key measures, namely investment expenditures, employment, sales revenue, and net income, experienced a downward trend at both the national and the state level between 2018 and 2020, the first year of the COVID-19 pandemic. They all significantly bounced up during the economic recovery of 2021. However, during high and increasing inflation throughout the year of 2022, new FDI in New Hampshire underperformed in comparison to national-level new FDI by dropping more than proportionately in areas where both levels dropped (investment expenditures and employment) and in areas where the national level increased (sales revenue and net income). Furthermore, the cumulative negative effects of the sustained increase in prices and costs on new FDI became more salient at the national level than for their subnational counterpart in 2023. The implementation of inflation-targeting policies as an FDI driver has been extensively studied for emerging markets and developing economies (Mendonça & Tiberto, 2024). Our findings provide empirical evidence from the world's most-developed economy for this policy implication.

4.2. Existing FDI Under High Inflation: Strategic Actions Originating in New Hampshire and Beyond That Impacted New Hampshire

Analysis of existing FDI relies on qualitative interpretation of firm-level activities. Evaluation of the third proposition aims to describe FDI-related actions during the inflationary time interval of our study. Our data consist of instances of business action involving foreign-affiliated companies that took place in or that engaged businesses in our chosen subnational location. Data collection is focused on strategic actions that are consequential for a large portion of the business and its revenues or profits, and over the long term, such as significant expansions and partnerships. For context, we also evaluate overall data on business deals involving foreign-affiliated companies at our subnational location. The data are extracted from regional news and business activity information from two main reputable sources described in the section where each kinds of data are analyzed. The qualitative categorization of the data includes geographical locations where each action originated and, separately, where most of the impact was for each business action. In the creation of these categories, a description of each action is evaluated using narrative analysis. Furthermore, narrative analysis, in conjunction with classifications provided by the source of our data, is used to identify industry sectors and types of actions, as described below. Our insights are based on the qualitative exploration, interpretation, and evaluation of all the above-mentioned categories.

We see many future applications for our qualitative methods, which can be replicated for acquiring data on existing FDI at a subnational level. Our methodology provides an informational reference for how these data can be categorized, explored, and analyzed. Our data comes mainly from GlobalData, a data and analytics provider. Data sources like reputable news media and business activity reporting venues may exist to support the exploration of data at many other subnational locations for both quantitative and qualitative research in the future.

As discussed above, our data up to the year 2022 identify inflationary pressures and contractionary policies in the U.S. Thus, the year 2023 and the start of 2024 mark a period of persisting concerns about inflation, fluctuating costs of goods, and high prices for raw materials, utilities, and transportation. These circumstances likely squeezed profit margins and stretched budgets for many businesses in New Hampshire as they did for the rest of the country. We expect that, while navigating inflation, labor shortages, and decreasing demand in some industries, many businesses in the state are likely to have struggled to maintain competitiveness and profitability.

In this section, we investigate whether there was any notable firm-level response to inflation and monetary policy by foreign firms in New Hampshire and whether these conditions triggered actions that involved foreign-affiliated companies outside New Hampshire that may have affected state businesses. We were not able to find information on cost-cutting measures in our sources. However, we identified several business actions to expand overall businesses, operations, and distributions. We observed that large foreign companies in our state engaged in strategic moves that were not necessarily prompted by rising costs but rather were part of a strategy of growth. Based on our data, we find that, although inflation destabilized new FDI and caused a period of turbulence and variability, it did not significantly impact those existing companies that were already on a strategic path of growth in the past year and at the start of 2024.

During the timeframe of this study, we considered strategic actions that involved international companies that operate in New Hampshire or that engage in activities that had a lasting impact in the state. Data for small companies were not available, and therefore, our study is focused on mid-size and large companies' information and analysis. Strategic actions refer to business activities that engage a firm overall or represent a large portion of a firm, its revenues, or earnings, and that have a long-term impact. We analyzed strategic actions taken by three types of businesses: foreign subsidiaries operating in the state of New Hampshire, foreign companies outside the state that took actions that affected New Hampshire business, and companies that partnered or associated with foreign-affiliated organizations with results in terms of business in the state.

4.2.1. The Context of Business Activity in New Hampshire

Before exploring strategic actions, we aimed to understand the context in which we could interpret them. To this purpose, we investigated overall New Hampshire data on business deals that involved foreign firms. For these data, international companies were considered. Irrespective of their location, these companies entered agreements or business partnerships or alliances in the state of New Hampshire. The deals data were extracted from the "Deals" database of GlobalData's Intelligence Center (GlobalData Deals,

2025). Figures 9–11 and Table 5 are related to these data. Figure 9 below shows the 2023 proportions of total deals by type and indicates that most deals were acquisitions. A few deals addressed mergers and sales of businesses or parts of businesses. Some actions were about financing. There were few partnerships. Not represented in this figure are deal values, which are higher for financial deals. Information on strategic actions involving only foreign firms, which is presented in detail in the last part of this section, does not match this pattern, which may suggest that most of the partnerships that took place in the state involved foreign businesses, since many of our illustrative strategic actions concerned some level of partnering.

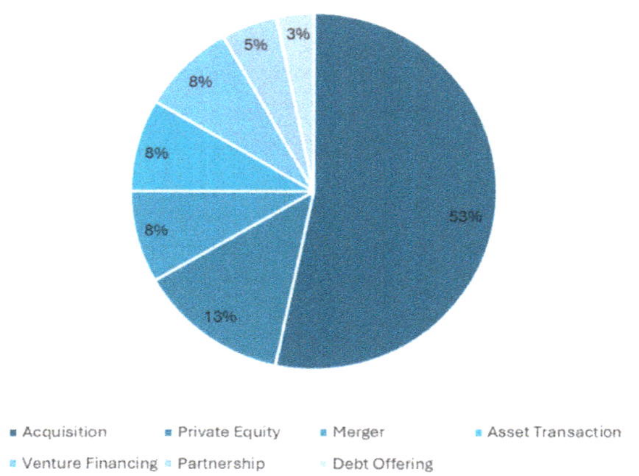

Figure 9. Proportions of strategic deals and partnerships that included or related to New Hampshire companies in 2023. Note: author's own, based on GlobalData's Intelligence Center data. Percentages were rounded down for visual simplicity, hence the overall total is less than 100 percent in the illustration. Without the rounding, each percentage has a double-digit decimal that contributes to a full total.

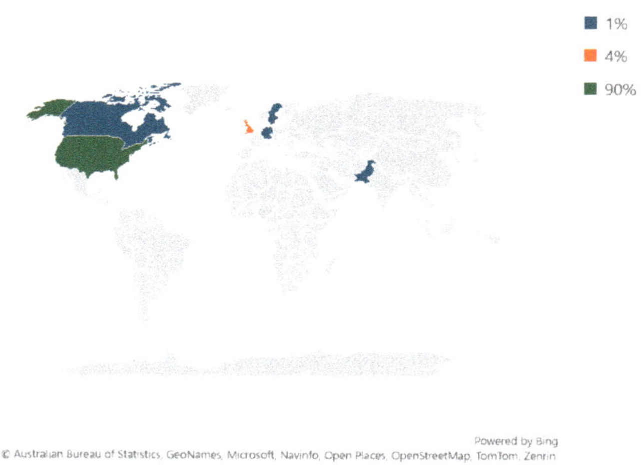

Figure 10. Business deals' geography and reach. Note: author's own, based on GlobalData's Intelligence Center data.

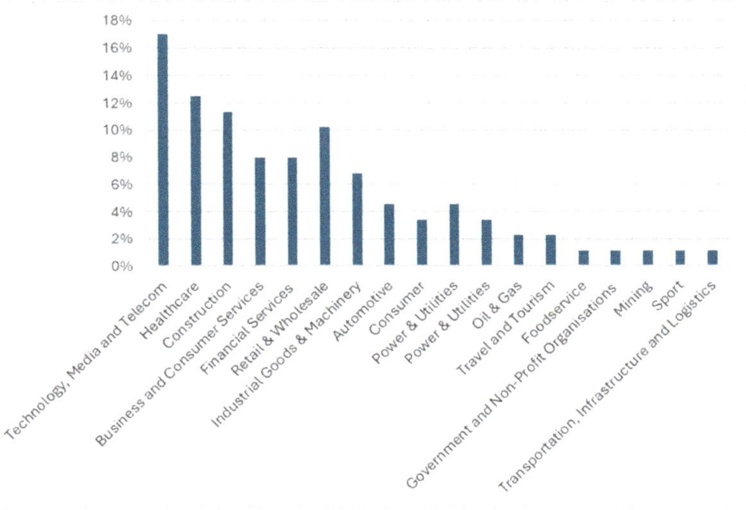

Figure 11. Deals across sectors in 2023. Note: author's own, based on GlobalData's Intelligence Center data.

Table 5. Proportions of deals across sectors in 2023.

Sector	Proportion
Technology, Media, and Telecom	17%
Healthcare	13%
Construction	11%
Business and Consumer Services	8%
Financial Services	8%
Retail and Wholesale	10%
Industrial Goods and Machinery	7%
Automotive	5%
Consumer	3%
Power and Utilities	5%
Power and Utilities	3%
Oil and Gas	2%
Travel and Tourism	2%
Foodservice	1%
Government and Non-Profit	1%
Mining	1%
Sport	1%
Transportation, Infrastructure, and Logistics	1%

Source: author's own, based on GlobalData's Intelligence Center data.

The geography of companies and reach of total activities are reflected in Figure 10, where we can identify that most companies involved were predominantly U.S. companies, and most of the strategic actions were in the U.S., in 2023. The data used for showing geography span from 1 January, 2023 to 20 February 2024. We intentionally included the start of the current year to evaluate the pattern overall, through the previous year and the start of the current year. The spatial footprint indicates that most deals with New Hampshire connections concern the U.S., rather than extensive international coverage. This may indicate a general national business orientation. The pattern of looking for in-country opportunities and activities may suggest that even foreign-affiliated companies and those associated with foreign organizations may have pursued business activities that were focused on the U.S., closer to their foreign subsidiaries' operations or aiming to gain increased distribution in the country.

As illustrated in Table 5 and Figure 11, by sector, the proportions of deals in 2023 across all sectors show a predominance of activities in technology, media, and telecom, as well as healthcare and construction, followed by retail and wholesale. Since most foreign subsidiaries in New Hampshire are in the financial and credit intermediation sector, this may explain why we did not find many activities involving foreign companies in the state. This context offers a good perspective for international business in the state versus business deals in the state overall. Many of the strategic actions involving foreign companies that we illustrate in the second part of this section are in the technology sector, as well as healthcare.

4.2.2. FDI-Related Strategic Actions in New Hampshire

For more specific investigation on strategic actions involving foreign firms in the state, we collected data on news pieces and announcements during 2023 and the start of 2024. All the data on strategic actions were extracted from the "News" database of GlobalData's Intelligence Center (GlobalData News, 2025), and they correspond to mid-size and large companies. By presence, companies affiliated with foreign parents represent 10% of a list of the biggest companies by number of employees that have locations in New Hampshire (Kolmar, 2024). These large, foreign-affiliated companies include some of the companies identified in Table 6. The companies in this table are examples of large subsidiaries included in our study, which examined a sample of strategic actions from these and other companies, both large and mid-size.

Table 6. Large companies represented in New Hampshire.

Company	Parent Affiliation and Country of Origin
Freudenberg	Freudenberg & Co. KG, Germany
Liquid Friday	Liquid Friday Ltd., UK
Lindt	Chocoladefabriken Lindt & Sprüngli AG, Switzerland
Goss International	Shanghai Electric, China
Raymarine	Raymarine Marine Electronics, UK
Highliner Food Svc	High Liner Foods, Canada
Novocure	Novocure, Switzerland
GN Netcom	GN Netcom, Denmark
Kollsman	Elbit Systems, Israel

As a notable addition, a top employer worldwide and in New Hampshire, BAE Systems (Forbes, 2024), with a parent affiliation in the UK, has significant operations in New Hampshire. FSD Pharma and INEO Tech Corp, both affiliated with Canadian-headquartered parent companies, have also engaged in significant strategic activities with impact on the state. Lonza, a Swiss multinational manufacturing company, was also active in New Hampshire during the time of the study. Konica Minolta Healthcare Americas has expanded its reach, and Amphenol Interconnect India has taken strategic actions affecting New Hampshire business. These companies represent more examples of organizations that engaged in strategic actions we considered in our investigation. We offer these examples to showcase organizations that have a notable presence in the subnational location. Our sample refers to these as well as other foreign companies with activities that had an impact on the chosen subnational location.

The sample of actions in Table 7 illustrates strategic activities involving foreign businesses in 2023 and the beginning of 2024. As noted above, data on strategic actions were extracted from the "News" database of GlobalData's Intelligence Center (GlobalData News, 2025), and we determined strategic actions to mean actions to increase the scale and value of an organization in the long term. These actions engaged a firm overall or a large portion of a firm and had a long-run impact on its revenues or earnings. For the scope of our investigation, we only considered strategic actions that involved international companies. Some activities do not originate in the state but have an impact on New Hampshire businesses, such as expanding facilities, operations, or distribution in the state. As the descriptions indicate, the data reflect a variety of business activity, with some recurrence of contract extensions and new operations' product and market expansions. The geography of each activity was classified as New Hampshire (NH) if the activity originated or had an impact on organizations in the state of New Hampshire, United States (US) if the activity originated broadly or had an impact on organizations in a number of states nationwide, or International (Int'l) if the activity originated broadly or had an impact on organizations in a number of countries outside the U.S.

Table 7. Strategic actions involving foreign companies in New Hampshire by geographic reach.

Strategic Action	Geography Where Strategic Action Is Taking Place			Geography Affected by Strategic Action		
	NH	US	Int'l	NH	US	Int'l
2024						
A foreign company with a subsidiary in the U.S. made a continuation of arrangement to provide products to an organizational buyer in the U.S. from 2020. In 2023, the company secured an extension contract for making and selling products. A portion of products will be made at facilities in NH.		✓		✓	✓	
A foreign subsidiary in NH received a modified contract with an existing organizational customer in the U.S. to develop a new product for delivery. The event signals a longer-term relationship with the customer and further development of the product in the future.	✓			✓		
An international company located overseas secured an extension of a partnership and contract to deliver one of its key products to a variety of organizational buyers in various countries. The product will be manufactured in the company's home country and across locations in the U.S., including NH.			✓	✓	✓	
A U.S. company acquired an international company and integrated the business in one of its divisions headquartered in NH.		✓	✓	✓	✓	
A joint venture involving a foreign parent with U.S. and NH subsidiaries and a U.S. company signed a contract for delivering products to an organizational buyer in the U.S.		✓	✓	✓	✓	

Table 7. *Cont.*

Strategic Action	Geography Where Strategic Action Is Taking Place			Geography Affected by Strategic Action		
	NH	US	Int'l	NH	US	Int'l
A foreign company with a subsidiary in NH agreed on a procurement contract for an organizational buyer in the U.S.		✓		✓	✓	
2023						
A foreign company with a subsidiary in NH secured funding from an outside source, planning to use the funds to modernize a facility located in NH.		✓		✓		
A foreign subsidiary in NH received an additional contract from an existing U.S. organizational buyer that addresses providing updates to a product and additional functionality for delivery.		✓		✓	✓	
A foreign company with a subsidiary in NH received a contract to develop a product for an organizational buyer in the U.S.		✓		✓		
A foreign subsidiary in NH signed a contract with an organizational customer in the U.S. to manufacture and sell a product.		✓		✓		
A foreign subsidiary in the NH secured extension of an existing contract with a U.S. organizational buyer to develop and deliver a product.		✓		✓		
A foreign subsidiary in NH extended a contract with existing organizational buyers in the U.S. to sell an additional product.		✓		✓		
A foreign company with a subsidiary in the U.S. launched a new product with a partner in the U.S. The product is the result of the development of new resources and capabilities at NH facilities.		✓		✓	✓	
A foreign subsidiary in NH signed a new contract with existing an U.S. organizational customer for the design, development, integration, testing, production, and delivery of a new product.		✓		✓	✓	
A foreign company with an NH subsidiary and US partner company completed delivery of a new product to a U.S. organizational buyer.		✓		✓		
An NH domestic company received an international license for a product, which provides the opportunity for sales in a foreign market/country.			✓			✓
A foreign company with a subsidiary in NH agreed on a new contract with an existing U.S. organizational buyer for sale of a product.	✓			✓	✓	
A foreign company with a subsidiary in NH received an extension for an existing sales contract from an organizational buyer for U.S. and international delivery.	✓			✓		✓
A U.S. foreign subsidiary expanded distribution in NH.		✓		✓	✓	
An international company entered a strategic partnership with a U.S. company to establish a facility in NH to support product development and manufacturing.		✓	✓	✓		
An international company entered a strategic partnership with a U.S. company to establish a facility in NH for product development and manufacturing.		✓	✓	✓		

Table 7. *Cont.*

Strategic Action	Geography Where Strategic Action Is Taking Place			Geography Affected by Strategic Action		
	NH	US	Int'l	NH	US	Int'l
A foreign subsidiary in NH signed contracts to sell products to organizational buyers in the U.S. and international.	✓	✓	✓	✓		
A foreign company with a subsidiary in NH proceeded with an extension contract for developing a product for a U.S. organizational buyer, including at an NH facility.		✓		✓	✓	
An international company expanded distribution of a product across the U.S., including in NH.		✓		✓	✓	
An international company signed a contract with an NH domestic company for services.			✓			✓
A foreign company with an NH subsidiary received a new contract for a product from an existing U.S. organizational buyer.		✓		✓		
A foreign subsidiary in NH secured an extension of a contract for an additional product with a U.S. organizational buyer.		✓		✓		

Note: actions are in descending chronological order; geography is noted as New Hampshire (NH), United States (US), and International (Int'l); descriptions and categorizations are created by the authors based on their own interpretations and assessments. Author's own, based on GlobalData's Intelligence Center data.

As indicated in Figure 12, most strategic actions originate from one geographic area (i.e., "geography"). The data on the geographic footprint of the sample activities show that most strategic actions impacting NH business and involving foreign businesses took place in the U.S. Internationally oriented actions also affected NH businesses. Fewest activities originated in the state. This indicates that some NH business might be at the "intersection" of national and global companies' strategies and receiving some positive impact from FDI and FDI-related activities outside the state.

The data show an almost equal split between actions that impact one of the areas and actions that impact two areas simultaneously. A total of 51% of the actions included in Table 7 impact one of the geographies, while 49% of the actions had effects on two of the three geographies. Many strategic activities involving NH businesses may be designed to have a wider reach than just the state. Since these are strategic, they are designed to have impact outside the local operations. This may reflect that FDI and FDI-related activities are not limited within statewide boundaries.

Table 8 categorizes the sample of strategic actions by business activity type. The categorization was created based on qualitative interpretation and coding of the data. The categories emerged from the descriptions of instances of actions provided by the source of data, based on the authors' subjective identifications. The categories include areas of business activity that are well known in the field and typical of strategic action. Only instances for which the description contained specific information that allowed the categorization were included. For example, actions that were categorized as partnership clearly had the word partnership or synonyms in the description, and items classified as contracts had mentions of agreement or contract. The categorization was triangulated with the classification provided in the source of data (the database provided this classification when data were extracted). Most of the items are identified as contracts. The breakdown also reveals the large extent of partnering and the fact that some actions are related to R&D. Relating these findings to the previous information on spatial footprint, data may suggest that expansion contracts and partnering often engage companies outside the borders of the state, and that innovation can push businesses to stretch activities beyond local operations.

Figure 12. Sources of origin of strategic action impacting NH. Note: author's own, based on GlobalData's Intelligence Center data.

Table 8. Strategic actions involving foreign companies in New Hampshire, categorized by business activity type.

	Strategic Action Category						
	Contracts and Tenders	Partnerships	M&A	Equity Offering	R&D	Operations	Products and Brands
2024							
A foreign company with a subsidiary in the U.S. made a continuation of an arrangement to provide products to an organizational buyer in the U.S. from 2020. In 2023, the company secured an extension contract for making and selling products. A portion of products will be made at facilities in NH.							
A foreign subsidiary in NH received a modified contract with an existing organizational customer in the U.S. to develop a new product for delivery. The event signals a longer-term relationship with the customer and further development of the product in the future.							

Table 8. *Cont.*

Strategic Action Category							
	Contracts and Tenders	Partnerships	M&A	Equity Offering	R&D	Operations	Products and Brands
An international company located overseas secured an extension of a partnership and contract to deliver one of its key products to a variety of organizational buyers in various countries. The product will be manufactured in the company's home country and across locations in the U.S., including NH.	✓	✓					
A U.S. company acquired an international company and integrated the business in one of its divisions headquartered in NH.			✓				
A joint venture involving a foreign parent with U.S. and NH subsidiaries and a U.S. company signed a contract for delivering products to an organizational buyer in the U.S.	✓	✓					
A foreign company with a subsidiary in NH agreed on a procurement contract for an organizational buyer in the U.S.	✓						
2023							
A foreign company with a subsidiary in NH secured funding from an outside source, with plans to use the funds to modernize a facility located in NH.				$			
A foreign subsidiary in NH received an additional contract from an existing U.S. organizational buyer that addresses providing updates to a product and additional functionality for delivery.	✓	✓					
A foreign company with a subsidiary in NH received a contract to develop a product for an organizational buyer in the U.S.	✓	✓			✓		
A foreign subsidiary in NH signed a contract with an organizational customer in the U.S. to manufacture and sell a product.	✓						
A foreign subsidiary in NH secured extension of an existing contract with a US organizational buyer to develop and deliver a product.	✓	✓					
A foreign subsidiary in NH extended a contract with existing organizational buyers in the U.S. to sell an additional product.	✓				✓		
A foreign company with a subsidiary in the U.S. launched a new product with a partner in the U.S. The product is the result of the development of new resources and capabilities at NH facilities.						✓	
A foreign subsidiary in NH signed a new contract with an existing U.S. organizational customer for the design, development, integration, testing, production, and delivery of a new product.	✓	✓			✓		

Table 8. *Cont.*

Strategic Action Category							
	Contracts and Tenders	Partnerships	M&A	Equity Offering	R&D	Operations	Products and Brands
A foreign company with an NH subsidiary and U.S. partner company completed delivery of a new product to a U.S. organizational buyer.							
An NH domestic company received an international license for a product, which provides the opportunity for sales in a foreign market/country.							
A foreign company with a subsidiary in NH agreed on a new contract with an existing U.S. organizational buyer for sale of a product.							
A foreign company with a subsidiary in NH received an extension for an existing sales contract from an organizational buyer for U.S. and international delivery.							
A U.S. foreign subsidiary expanded distribution in NH.							
An international company entered a strategic partnership with a U.S. company to establish a facility in NH to support product development and manufacturing.							
An international company entered a strategic partnership with a U.S. company to establish a facility in NH for product development and manufacturing.							
A foreign subsidiary in NH signed contracts to sell products to an organizational buyers in the U.S. and internationally.							
A foreign company with a subsidiary in NH proceeded with an extension contract for developing a product for a U.S. organizational buyer, including at an NH facility.							
An international company expanded distribution of a product across the U.S., including in NH.							
An international company signed a contract with an NH domestic company for services.							
A foreign company with an NH subsidiary received a new contract for a product from existing an U.S. organizational buyer.							
A foreign subsidiary in NH secured an extension of a contract for an additional product with a U.S. organizational buyer.							

Note: in descending chronological order; descriptions are created by the authors based on their own interpretations and assessments; categorizations are provided by GlobalData's Intelligence Center. Source: author's own, based on GlobalData's Intelligence Center data.

Our analysis provides insights into patterns of strategic action in the known context of inflation. Our qualitative investigation shows the types of strategic actions of companies from which FDI originates or to which FDI is related at a subnational location. We intentionally bounded our analysis to qualitative analysis so that we can answer the question "What did companies at the location do during inflation?" with actual examples of actions and begin to comprehend which strategic actions were more prevalent during this time. Our investigation did not employ a structural econometric model and drew no conclusions on any causal relationship. Our methodology conceded that many factors and developments were at play during the time of the study, and thus did not attempt to control any variables. Rather, we described the local environment and explored how it experienced inflation during an interval when inflation was a confirmed concern nationwide. Studying FDI-generating or -related actions in this environment provided us with a unique opportunity to evaluate if and how FDI reacts to and acts during inflation. Our macroeconomic data offered a relevant juxtaposition of national and subnational FDI. The firm-level data gave a view of subnational FDI and FDI-related moves.

The analysis gives evidence of subsidiary activity to increase scale and value, providing support for our third proposition expecting that existing FDI can record strategic actions despite inflationary pressures at a subnational level. Such actions are not limited to the location and often reflect a location's geography in the multinational's investment, partnering, and distribution network.

Our sample data of FDI-related business activities at the subnational level show that most actions addressed not just New Hampshire operations but had a wider reach. Most of the spatial footprint of activities was across the U.S., rather than statewide or international. We find strong support for our third proposition. The type of actions we investigated did not appear to be direct reactions to inflation, cost increases, or government policies. Activities in the sample are business actions that companies typically pursue for long-term growth. The qualitative data that forms the basis of this analysis do not identify any of these actions as reactions to inflation or policy. The business activities involving foreign firms were determined primarily by industry conditions, such as new or existing opportunities like large projects or new partnering opportunities, new markets, or expansion of demand. In interpreting the qualitative data synthesized in Table 8, we find that a relatively large proportion of the actions (37%) involve large projects. Concurrently, about a quarter of the actions (26%) concern partnering and about a quarter (26%) are about accessing new markets. The majority of actions (59%) are designed to take advantage of growing demand. A key finding of our examination is that FDI and FDI-related activities in New Hampshire are not limited to the state. Expansion contracts and partnering often engage companies outside the borders of the state, and innovation can push businesses to stretch activities beyond local operations. We discovered that at least some portion of New Hampshire business might be at the "intersection" of national and global companies' strategies and thus benefiting from the positive impact of FDI and FDI-related activities outside the state.

The current analysis and results are somewhat unique. Very few previous studies explored actual FDI and FDI-related actions during inflationary times. Foreign operations have long been seen as a place for making decisions about choosing and segmenting markets, as well as other strategic decisions in the specific context of inflation, exchange, and interest rates (Rivera & Milani, 2020). Our results align with extant findings concluding that FDI can be used by multinational companies as a hedging tool to alleviate the effects of inflation, but how companies accomplish this is more nuanced and depends on the reasons behind the investments, as well as other factors (Sayek, 2009). Previous work showed the importance of existing FDI in reducing the negative impact of inflation, which is also related to our results. The work we've pursued is similar to that of authors that recognized that the planning, distribution, and investment model of multinational companies is complex, given the varying inflation rates at the locations where they operate (Mohamed & Youssef, 2004). Our findings expand an understanding that is analogous to these studies, finding that existing FDI (a strategic approach for long-term investment commitments) influences decisions and performance of the subsidiary in the future.

5. Conclusions and Implications

Unsurprisingly, our study confirms the complicated effects of inflationary and policy pressures on FDI. Our analysis adopts both the macroeconomic approach and the international business approach to FDI and shows significant effects at all levels: global, national, and statewide. During the timeline of this research, the world's largest FDI recipient, the U.S., recorded decreasing FDI inflows from 2022 to 2023.

At the state level, for a time, New Hampshire's FDI patterns appeared to match the national trend of investment expenditures by the new FDI, which began to recover in 2021 after the pandemic but dropped notably in 2022 when the inflation pressure grew and remained low in 2023. From an employment contribution perspective, hundreds of jobs were added by new FDI in 2020; the number increased in 2021 but experienced a series of declines in 2022 and 2023. In these two measures, new FDI in New Hampshire underperformed more than proportionately when contrasted with its national counterpart. Furthermore, given elevated inflation throughout 2022, new FDI in New Hampshire experienced a decline in sales revenue and net income while the profitability of new FDI was improved at the national level. However, the negative effect of the sustained increase in prices and costs on new FDI accumulated across states and manifested itself in a significant manner at the national level approaching the tail end of the inflation surge in 2023.

Our conclusion on the economic climate highlighted both opportunities and challenges facing foreign investments in terms of acquiring and expanding existing businesses, and establishing new businesses, in the U.S. and in the state of New Hampshire, in particular. It provided relevant context for exploring strategic actions of companies that were related to foreign, international, or global business.

We found that existing foreign-affiliated companies acting in or impacting on our state continued to expand or pursue strategies to enlarge markets, collaborate with other companies, and improve operations and products. A key finding is that many of these actions that involved foreign businesses or investments flows were set in a broader footprint than just our state, with New Hampshire benefiting from the positive impact of FDI and FDI-related activities outside the state, in many cases. We also noted indications that such activities appeared to be more U.S.-focused than internationally oriented. Accordingly, we observed the distinct footprint of foreign business activities inside the U.S., with goals of increasing presence, improving distribution, or strengthening operations nationally. Many of the activities and effects we monitored in our state were the outcomes of this country-level strategic action.

Thus, despite the challenges associated with rising prices, costs, and interest rates brought about by the highest inflation since 1981 and the resulting robust tightening of monetary policy in 2022 and 2023, companies with strong positions continued their strategic path of growth. We find that many organizations in New Hampshire are partnering or cooperating with international companies, and that local foreign-affiliated organizations pursue expansion in the state and beyond.

The present study provides a valuable framework for subnational economic development. It suggests that development professionals should dedicate efforts and resources towards sustaining and incentivizing foreign direct investments that are already present at the location. Our results also point out that attracting intra-country expansion actions of FDI-related activities from outside the subnational location is also a worthwhile effort. During inflationary periods, it may be less effective to promote new FDI, and therefore, economic development agencies should place more emphasis on supporting existing FDI.

The types of FDI and FDI-related strategic actions we found taking place during an inflationary period also indicate that policymakers should dedicate incentives and even legislation designed to support partnerships, contracts, acquisitions, and expansion at the subnational location. Local economic development professionals should also showcase the value of their location in creating value for the multinational companies operating a network of activities and subsidiaries.

For corporate leaders, our results indicate that, under inflationary pressures, key investments and expansion efforts should not be abandoned. On the contrary, a period of inflation could be a good time to find new partnering opportunities, to sign new distribution or collaborative contracts, and to expand at and beyond the current subnational location. Concurrently, during inflation, there may be opportunities to benefit from the expansion strategies of companies outside the home subnational location. As other companies are investing in their regional growth, there could be many avenues to tap into new logistics, innovation, or actions to tap into new markets that these companies are planning. At the same time, when considering their own strategies, corporate and foreign subsidiary executives should expect that their competitors will invest in core business areas and will consider growth actions. To remain competitive, businesspeople should weigh their actions in the context of their rivals' priorities, whereby reducing costs or insulating the subsidiary against inflation may be less effective than taking strategic action to maintain competitiveness or grow market share.

Partnerships and contracts could be particularly important during inflation. At a time when choosing the spatial reach of the firm is essential for limiting the effects of cost increases, collaborating outside the location of the operations can lead to a better competitive position. Our results show that many companies are taking this path.

Our study provides additional insights for managerial action. Small geographical subnational locations should not be judged exclusively by the size of their markets. Rather, these locations could have advantages of proximity to growing markets, access to innovation, or potential to partner with companies aiming to grow across the region. Managers should also be warned that, although inflation is a national measure, its impact and manifestations at various subnational locations could differ. Consequently, business leaders can expect variations in inflation and plan to adapt to the characteristics of the location. In conjunction with this understanding, strategists and economic development professionals alike should recognize that focusing on the quantitative aspects of FDI may miss important developments. Qualitative assessment of existing FDI can provide a better comprehension of the FDI landscape to which they must adapt their investment decisions. At the multinational enterprise level, our findings provide insights for managers seeking to define their company's geographic reach and the scope of activities during inflationary times.

6. Limitations and Future Research

Our study is not without limitations. We wanted to delve deeply into the patterns of new and existing FDI at a subnational location, so it was expedient for us to consider a specific site and evaluate the data granularly. This approach, however, does not compare findings across various locations. A comparative study would likely add value and strength to the findings. This could be a meaningful way to expand this research strand, also emphasizing the salient patterns of FDI across subnational locations. Comparing the effects of inflation on FDI across subnational locations can also identify nuances in FDI evolution during inflationary periods and could even lead to the discovery of factors determining varying effects of inflation.

A second limitation of our study may be related to the exploration of two distinct kinds of data: a quantitative assessment of new FDI and it macroeconomic outcomes for the first two propositions, as well as a qualitative categorization of existing FDI and FDI-related activities for the last proposition. While this method may introduce inconsistencies in evidence, it provides essential detail for developing a thorough understanding of what happens to both new FDI and existing foreign businesses and the importance of variations across subnational locations owing to local characteristics during the inflationary period.

Finally, our methodology is based on an investigation of the most recent, but restricted, data and evidence that does not employ statistical modeling, which prevents us from reaching any predictive findings. Our informational study aims to shed timely light on this hotly debated topic. We expect that every inflation-shock period will be different from the next, and thus, it may be unrealistic to attempt to foresee specifically how new and existing FDI will be affected. Also, due to this methodological limitation, our findings are specific to the chosen subnational location and cannot be generalized as an inference about the underlying causal relationship. Nevertheless, statistical modeling could lead to generalizable results to add to current knowledge of FDI and inflation at the subnational level.

Our work provides timely insights into FDI when the national inflationary pressure is a key feature of the macroeconomic environment at a subnational location. Our findings give a detailed view on the phenomenon of divergence, whereby new FDI reacts to the sustained increase in prices and costs in a different way from how existing FDI does. With this understanding, corporate and economic development professionals can plan to support and incentivize foreign subsidiaries who are already operating at a location and should consider carefully the timing of new investments.

Author Contributions: Conceptualization, R.W. and C.W.; methodology, R.W. and C.W.; software, R.W. and C.W.; validation, R.W. and C.W.; formal analysis, R.W. and C.W.; investigation, R.W. and C.W.; resources, R.W. and C.W.; data curation, R.W. and C.W.; writing—original draft preparation, R.W. and C.W.; writing—review and editing, R.W. and C.W.; visualization, R.W. and C.W.; supervision, R.W. and C.W.; project administration, R.W. and C.W.; funding acquisition, R.W. and C.W. All authors have read and agreed to the published version of the manuscript.

Funding: This research received no external funding.

Institutional Review Board Statement: Not applicable.

Informed Consent Statement: Not applicable.

Data Availability Statement: The original contributions presented in this study are included in the article. Further inquiries can be directed to the corresponding author.

Conflicts of Interest: The authors declare no conflict of interest.

References

Agudze, K., & Ibhagui, O. (2021). Inflation and FDI in industrialized and developing economies. *International Review of Applied Economics*, *35*(5), 1–16. [CrossRef]

Alshamsi, K. H., Hussin, M. R., & Azam, M. (2015). The impact of inflation and GDP per capita on foreign direct investment: The case of United Arab Emirates. *Investment Management and Financial Innovations*, *12*(3–1), 132–141.

Ando, N. (2024). Multinationals' intraregional geographic expansion and foreign subsidiary performance. *International Business Review*, *33*(1), 102208. [CrossRef]

Arregle, J. L., Miller, T. L., Hitt, M. A., & Beamish, P. W. (2016). How does regional institutional complexity affect MNE internationalization? *Journal of International Business Studies*, *47*(6), 697–722. [CrossRef]

Banga, R. (2006). The export-diversifying impact of Japanese and US foreign direct investments in the Indian manufacturing sector. *Journal of International Business Studies*, *37*(4), 558–568. [CrossRef]

Beaudouin, N., Missoffe, A., & Scheidhauer, C. (2018). *Global cities investment monitor: New rankings, trends and criteria*. Available online: https://www.sciencedirect.com/science/article/pii/S1090951620301103 (accessed on 10 October 2024).

Belderbos, R., Castellani, D., & Du, H. S. (2024). Internal versus external agglomeration advantages in investment location choice: The role of global cities' international connectivity. *Journal of International Business Studies*, *55*, 745–763. [CrossRef]

Birkinshaw, J., & Hood, N. (1998). Multinational subsidiary evolution: Capability and charter change in foreign–owned subsidiary companies. *Academy of Management Review, 23*(4), 773–795. [CrossRef]

Boateng, A., Hua, X., Nisar, S., & Wu, J. (2015). Examining the determinants of inward FDI: Evidence from Norway. *Economic Modelling, 47*, 118–127. [CrossRef]

Buckley, P. J., & Ghauri, P. N. (2004). Globalization, economic geography and the strategy of multinational enterprises. *Journal of International Business Studies, 35*(2), 81–98. [CrossRef]

Caon, V. (2022, July 27). *FDI drivers in 2022: Inflation*. Available online: https://www.investmentmonitor.ai/investment-promotion/fdi-drivers-2022-inflation/?cf-view&cf-closed (accessed on 3 February 2024).

Cevik, S., Fan, A., & Naik, S. (2024). Is inflation good for business? the firm–level impact of inflation shocks in the Baltics, 1997–2020. *Economic Change and Restructuring, 57*(5), 1–19. [CrossRef]

Chidlow, A., Holmström-Lind, C., Holm, U., & Tallman, S. (2015). Do I stay or do I go? Sub-national drivers for post-entry subsidiary development. *International Business Review, 24*(2), 266–275. [CrossRef]

Coibion, O., Gorodnichenko, Y., & Ropele, T. (2020). Inflation expectations and firm decisions: New causal evidence. *The Quarterly Journal of Economics, 135*(1), 165–219. [CrossRef]

FoEh, J., Suryani, N. K., & Silpama, S. (2020). The influence of inflation level, exchange rate and Gross Domestic Product on foreign direct investment in the ASEAN countries on 2007–2018. *European Journal of Business and Management Research, 5*(3). [CrossRef]

Forbes. (2024, October 8). *World's best employers*. Available online: https://www.forbes.com/lists/worlds-best-employers/?sh=2c6721cd1e0c (accessed on 1 December 2024).

Ghemawat, P. (2003). Semiglobalization and international business strategy. *Journal of International Business Studies, 34*(2), 138–152. [CrossRef]

GlobalData Deals. (2025). *Data downloaded 11 October 2024*. Available online: https://explorer-globaldata-com.libproxy.plymouth.edu/Deals/Dashboards (accessed on 11 October 2024).

GlobalData News. (2025). *Data downloaded 11 October 2024*. Available online: https://explorer-globaldata-com.libproxy.plymouth.edu/News/Dashboard (accessed on 11 October 2024).

Granite State Times. (2024, October 16). *Inflation in New Hampshire lower than national average as of September 2024*. Available online: https://granitestatetimes.com/stories/665259915-inflation-in-new-hampshire-lower-than-national-average-as-of-september-2024 (accessed on 14 January 2025).

Gupta, E., & McGranahan, L. (2023). What is driving the differences in inflation across US regions? *Chicago Fed Letter*, 1–8.

Heinrich, J., Henderson, S., Holland, T., & Portanova, M. (2021, September 28). *6 strategies to help your company weather inflation*. Harvard Business Review. Available online: https://hbr.org/2021/09/6-strategies-to-help-your-company-weather-inflation (accessed on 2 June 2024).

Hong Nga, N., Hoang An, P., Thi Kim Loan, V., & Cuong, T. Q. K. (2024). Impact of exchange rate changes on export-import dynamics in Vietnam. *Cogent Economics & Finance, 12*(1), 2409415. [CrossRef]

Horwich, J. (2023, August 16). *Do international investment flows undermine the fight against inflation?* Federal Reserve Bank of Minneapolis. Available online: https://www.minneapolisfed.org/article/2023/do-international-investment-flows-undermine-the-fight-against-inflation (accessed on 1 October 2024).

Hutzschenreuter, T., Matt, T., & Kleindienst, I. (2020). Going subnational: A literature review and research agenda. *Journal of World Business, 55*(4), 101076. [CrossRef]

Jha, S., Awate, S., & Mudambi, R. (2024). A multilateral network perspective on inward FDI. *Journal of International Business Studies, 55*(3), 303–325. [CrossRef]

Karahan, Ö., & Bayır, M. (2022). The effects of monetary policies on foreign direct investment inflows in emerging economies: Some policy implications for post–COVID-19. *Future Business Journal, 8*(1), 39. [CrossRef] [PubMed Central]

Kastratović, R. (2020). The impact of foreign direct investment on host country exports: A meta-analysis. *The World Economy, 43*, 3142–3183. [CrossRef]

Kojima, K. (1973). A macroeconomic approach to foreign direct investment. *Hitotsubashi Journal of Economics, 14*(1), 1–21.

Kojima, K. (1982). Macroeconomic versus international business approach to direct foreign investment. *Hitotsubashi Journal of Economics, 23*(1), 1–19.

Kojima, K., & Ozawa, T. (1984). Micro–and macro-economic models of direct foreign investment: Toward a synthesis. *Hitotsubashi Journal of Economics, 25*(1), 1–20.

Kojima, K., & Ozawa, T. (1985). Toward a theory of industrial restructuring and dynamic comparative advantage. *Hitotsubashi Journal of Economics, 26*(2), 135–145.

Kolmar, C. (2024). *The 100 largest companies in New Hampshire for 2024*. Zippia. Available online: https://www.zippia.com/advice/largest-companies-in-new-hampshire/ (accessed on 1 October 2024).

Lee, K., & Jung, M. (2015). Overseas factories, domestic employment, and technological hollowing out: A case study of Samsung's mobile phone business. *Review of World Economics/Weltwirtschaftliches Archiv, 151*(3), 461–475. [CrossRef]

Mason, R. L., & Vracheva, V. (2017). The impact of inflation targeting on attracting Foreign Direct Investment. *Journal of Applied Business and Economics*, *1*(4), 79–94.

Mendonça, H., & Tiberto, B. (2024). Are prudent monetary and fiscal policy drivers of FDI inflows? *Latin American Journal of Central Banking*, *5*(1), 100120. [CrossRef]

Mensah, E., Mensah, R. O., & Danquah, D. A. (2024). Threshold effects of inflation on the FDI–growth nexus: Evidence from inflation-targeting countries in sub-Saharan Africa. *Economic Research-Ekonomska Istraživanja*, *37*(1), 2299991. [CrossRef]

Mohamed, Z. M., & Youssef, M. A. (2004). A production, distribution and investment model for a multinational company. *Journal of Manufacturing Technology Management*, *15*(6), 495–510. [CrossRef]

Mundell, R. A. (1965). Growth, stability and inflationary finance. *Journal of Political Economy*, *73*(2), 97–109. [CrossRef]

Musyoka, N., & Ocharo, K. N. (2018). Real interest rate, inflation, exchange rate, competitiveness and foreign direct investment in Kenya. *American Journal of Economics*, *3*(1), 1–18. [CrossRef]

Qian, G., Khoury, T. A., Peng, M. W., & Qian, Z. (2010). The performance implications of intra–and inter-regional geographic diversification. *Strategic Management Journal*, *31*(9), 1018–1030. [CrossRef]

ResearchFDI. (2022, August 4). *How does inflation affect FDI?* Available online: https://researchfdi.com/how-does-inflation-affect-fdi/#:~:text=Rises%20in%20inflation,%20if%20temporary,economy%20that%20influence%20FDI%20inflow (accessed on 1 October 2024).

Ridhwan, M. M. (2016). Inflation differentials, determinants, and convergence: Evidence from Indonesia subnational data. *The Journal of Developing Areas*, *50*(5), 257–276. [CrossRef]

Rivera, J., & Milani, K. (2020). Managing International Operations in Uncertain Times: Foreign exchange rates, inflation, and interest rates can weigh heavily on accountants and financial executives in charge of budgeting for overseas subsidiaries. *Strategic Finance*, *102*(5), 24.

Ronaghi, M., & Scorsone, E. (2023). The negative impact of the Ukraine war on the US economy. *Journal of Environmental Science and Public Health*, *7*, 111–122. [CrossRef]

Sabir, S., Rafique, A., & Abbas, K. (2019). Institutions and FDI: Evidence from developed and developing countries. *Financial Innovation*, *5*(1), 1–20. [CrossRef]

Sayek, S. (2009). Foreign direct investment and inflation. *Southern Economic Journal*, *76*(2), 419–443. [CrossRef]

Surowiecki, J. (2024, August 12). *How inflation shaped the companies of the Inc. 5000.* Inc.com. Available online: https://www.inc.com/james-surowiecki/how-inflation-shaped-companies-of-inc-5000.html (accessed on 13 January 2025).

Tabash, M. I., Farooq, U., Matar, A., & Al-Absy, M. S. M. (2024). Role of governance in attracting foreign direct investment inflow: Empirical evidence from South Asia region. *Cogent Economics & Finance*, *12*(1), 2358930. [CrossRef]

Tekin, R. B. (2012). Economic growth, exports and foreign direct investment in least developed countries: A panel Granger causality analysis. *Economic Modelling*, *29*(3), 868–878. [CrossRef]

Tobin, J. (1965). Money and economic growth. *Econometrica*, *33*(4), 671–684. [CrossRef]

UNCTAD. (2024, January 17). *Global investment trends monitor, No. 46.* Available online: https://unctad.org/publication/global-investment-trends-monitor-no-46 (accessed on 11 September 2024).

U.S. Bureau of Economic Analysis. (2023, September 8). *A ctivities of U.S. affiliates of foreign multinational enterprises in 2021.* Available online: https://apps.bea.gov/scb/issues/2023/09-september/0923-affiliates.htm?_gl=1*v8i7qy*_ga*NzgyMTQ3Mjc3LjE3MzMxNTk2OTM.*_ga_J4698JNNFT*MTczNjQ0NTkwMC40LjEuMTczNjQ0NjA1OC41Mi4wLjA (accessed on 14 January 2025).

U.S. Department of Commerce. (2024, January 4). *U.S. Commerce Department Announces $200 billion milestone in foreign direct investment.* Available online: https://www.commerce.gov/news/press-releases/2024/01/us-commerce-department-announces-200-billion-milestone-foreign-direct (accessed on 11 October 2024).

Wright, R., & Wu, C. (2024). Is foreign direct investment resilient post the COVID-19 pandemic? The case of a subnational economy. *Journal of Risk and Financial Management*, *17*(1), 21. [CrossRef]

Wu, C., & Rogers, C. (2018). One size does not fit all: Foreign direct investment promotion policies across US states. *Journal of Regional Analysis and Policy*, *48*(1), 23–43.

Yotzov, I., Bloom, N., Bunn, P., Mizen, P., & Thwaites, G. (2024). *The speed of firm response to inflation* (Bank of England Working Paper No. 1085). Bank of England.

economies

MDPI

Article

Financial and Economic Determinants of Banks Financial Distress in MENA Region

Abdelmoneim Bahyeldin Mohamed Metwally [1,*], Mai M. Yasser [2], Eman Adel Ahmed [3] and Mohamed Ali Shabeeb Ali [1]

1 Department of Accounting, College of Business Administration, King Faisal University, Al-Ahsa 31982, Saudi Arabia
2 Economics Department, Faculty of Management Sciences, October University for Modern Sciences and Arts, 6th of October City 12451, Egypt
3 Accounting Department, Faculty of Management Sciences, October University for Modern Sciences and Arts, 6th of October City 12451, Egypt
* Correspondence: abmetwally@kfu.edu.sa

Abstract

This study investigates the influences of financial performance and economic determinants (inflation rate and economic growth) on financial distress (FD) in the MENA region in the context of the contagion effect theory and Minsky's financial instability theory. This paper examines the determinants of financial distress in the MENA region from 2002 until 2020 using pooled OLS, fixed effect, and GMM panel estimation models; then the results are used to estimate the effect over the long run. The results show that the things that cause financial distress are changing a lot between countries in the MENA region. This shows how important it is to separate the effects of economic and financial factors. The results show the significance of economic growth, ROA, ROE, inflation, and stock market profitability using fixed effects. The results changed when we used GMM, concluding that economic growth, ROA, ROE, and stock market profitability were significant, while inflation was not significant. Therefore, there is a significant and negative relationship between financial distress and economic growth in GCC-MENA as well as other MENA countries. Our results can be of importance to investors and regulators. The introduction of a more stable political environment and engagement in international economic and financial markets will decrease the negative impacts of financial distress and boost economic growth and its sustainability in the MENA region.

Keywords: financial distress; economic growth; MENA; ROA; GCC; inflation; banking sector

JEL Classification: D53; E31; G32; O42

1. Introduction

Banks may suffer a progressive deterioration in their financial condition due to several factors, including financial crises, competition, or inadequate management approaches. In particular, the occurrence of financial difficulties within the banking sector causes significant disruption to the whole economy, given the unique role that banks have within the financial system. Due to its adverse effects on both the microeconomic and macroeconomic levels, financial distress (FD) has garnered significant attention in the research. FD and its subsequent consequences accelerate distressed banks' growth (Antoniades & Calomiris,

2020; Muñoz-Izquierdo et al., 2020). Financial distress increased a risk to businesses' profitability and decreased their value (Ibrahim et al., 2024; Kazemian et al., 2017). Banking institutions play a crucial role as the primary providers of money and financial investments in the MENA economy (Eid et al., 2023; Sghaier, 2021). The 2008 global financial crisis (GFC) and "The Arab Awakening" have resulted in economic turmoil in most countries in the MENA region, leading to a deterioration in companies' profits and increasing risk and instability (Antonia García-Benau et al., 2013; World Bank, 2016). The significant decline in the worldwide shortage of available funds has subjected a growing number of enterprises to financial instability (Galindo-Martín et al., 2021), thereby complicating their ability to attract and maintain capital and finance (Neaime, 2016). Researchers have conducted several studies to examine the impact of the crisis on the performance and stability of banks in the MENA region (Abd. Majid, 2018; Ramlan & Adnan, 2016; Zaiane & Moussa, 2021; Trad et al., 2017; Zarrouk et al., 2016) as well as the macroeconomic and bank factors that contribute to financial distress (Alam et al., 2024; Yasiru & Olajide, 2015; Ekanayake & Thaver, 2021; Supriyanto & Darmawan, 2018; Dewi et al., 2023).

The inability to pay existing debts because of liquidity problems is known as insolvency. A court-mandated disclosure of financial difficulty is necessary for company bankruptcy (Habib et al., 2020). In other words, a company experiencing financial difficulties has no choice but to file for bankruptcy (Volkov et al., 2017). Bankruptcy is a result of financial troubles; thus, in order to anticipate failure, it is preferable to categorize enterprises based on negative operating income, interest coverage ratio, and net income before special items. Due to the recent global financial crisis, bankruptcies are rising in many countries, spawning a new area of prediction literature. In terms of labor and macroeconomic conditions, a localized model fared better than a global one. Few studies predicted bankruptcy/distress worldwide or by area. Altman et al. (2017) conducted a global analysis of the original Z-score model and found that the inclusion of country-specific components increased the prediction accuracy in some countries. With 75% to 90% accuracy, the uniform model worked well in the majority of countries.

Although the factors of financial distress have been extensively examined in global banking contexts (Wasiuzzaman & Tarmizi, 2010; Muda et al., 2013; El-Chaarani et al., 2022), there is a paucity of studies addressing the particular issues encountered by banks in the MENA area. The MENA region's economy is distinctive due to its reliance on oil revenues, the presence of geopolitical concerns, and varying degrees of governmental regulation. This may influence the financial and economic variables that induce distress in manners not entirely reflected in studies from other regions (Al-Khatib & Al-Horani, 2011) (Kholisoh & Dwiarti, 2020). Much of the existing research has focused on developed economies or rising markets in Asia and Latin America. It has not examined the impact of governance structures, financial stability policies, and macroeconomic shocks on banks in the Middle East and North Africa (Trad et al., 2017). This disparity underscores the necessity to investigate whether traditional indicators of financial distress, including profitability, capital adequacy, and liquidity, function differently in the MENA region. Addressing this gap can furnish policymakers and financial institutions with customized strategies to bolster resilience and stability in the region's banking sector. Nevertheless, the majority of previous research focused on business failure models within MENA nations.

In summary, this study contributes to the existing literature by examining the determinants of banks' financial distress in the MENA region, unlike most of prior studies that focused on developed countries only. It is of significant interest to both policymakers and investors in terms of regional development policies and dedicated portfolio investment strategies in each emerging region, respectively. We used several ratios from the empirical literature on bank profitability, measured by return on assets (ROA) and return on equity

(ROE). This study aims to address the existing gap in the literature by presenting empirical information on the effects of the crisis on the banking industry. Additionally, it seeks to identify the primary factors that influence the stability of banks in the MENA region. The study analyzed the financial distress in the MENA region from 2002 to 2020. The results show the significance of economic growth, ROA, ROE, inflation, and stock market profitability using both fixed effects and the generalized method of moments (GMM). Thus, the introduction of a more stable political environment and engagement in international economic and financial markets will reduce the negative impacts of financial distress in the MENA region. By reducing political risks and enhancing participation in international economic and financial markets, the MENA region can create a more resilient economy, attract external investment, and leverage international support, all of which can help cushion the region from the adverse effects of financial distress.

This study helps MENA policymakers, investors, and banking regulators understand banks' financial distress by identifying key financial and economic factors. It improves risk assessment and early warning systems, guides regulatory reforms, supports investment decisions, promotes economic stability, tailors solutions to regional needs, and promotes sustainable banking. Policymakers can use the financial and economic determinants to create or improve early warning systems for bank financial problems. This helps fix issues quickly and reduces risks before they become systemic crises. The study also guides regulatory reforms to strengthen MENA banks' resilience, allowing central banks to tighten liquidity requirements or provide targeted liquidity support during economic downturns. The study helps investors understand regional banks' financial and economic risks, enabling them to allocate capital and identify banks with strong financial health and good risk management. The findings can help institutional investors work with bank management to improve governance and risk. The study's focus on MENA allows policymakers to tailor solutions to regional specifics, such as oil price fluctuations' effects on bank stability in oil-dependent economies. Sustainability can also encourage banks to diversify revenue streams, improve governance, and invest in digital transformation to build long-term resilience. By applying the study's findings, participants can better manage financial distress and support the MENA banking sector's long-term growth and stability.

The paper is divided into six main sections, beginning with the introduction. Then Section 2 reviews the relevant literature on the relationships between financial distress and several economic and financial banks, and develops the research hypotheses. Section 3 describes the research sample and research methodology. Section 4 discusses the results of the statistical analysis. Section 5 provides an additional robustness analysis and discussion. Finally, Section 6 concludes the paper.

2. Literature Review

Financial distress research has gained attention in recent decades (Altman, 1968; Taffler, 1983) as a means to improve measurements and models for predicting which enterprises may face bankruptcy and insolvency. The aim is to predict distress, assess loan security, assess auditors, measure portfolio risk, monitor financial institutions, and determine prices for credit-exposed instruments like bonds and derivatives (Scott, 1981). Financially disrupted firms lack the liquidity to satisfy financial commitments and debt interest payments (Gilson, 1990). Chen et al. (2020) define distress as a scenario where a firm's present worth is less than its creditors' claims. (Baldwin & Mason, 1983) define it as a firm's inability to satisfy contractual debt commitments due to lower cash flows than financial obligations. Therefore, the literature review will be divided into two main sections. The first will be theoretical in nature, explaining the main theories related to economic growth and financial distress. The second section will be divided into three main subsections: the first will deal with financial distress in the non-financial sector, the second subsection will examine financial distress in the banking sector, while the last subsection will study the relationship between economic growth and financial distress.

2.1. The Main Theories

There are many theories that study the relationships between macroeconomic factors (those that affect economic growth) and financial distress, and two of them will be presented in this section.

2.1.1. Contagion Effect Theory

A contagion effect is closely linked to a financial crisis. It occurs when there is a notable increase in cross-market connectivity between nations during or following a crisis. The contagion effect is quantified by calculating the proportion of a nation's asset prices that shift according to the same trend during a crisis as opposed to when there is no crisis. Herding behavior and the spillover effect are the two conceptually separated causes of the contagion effect (Fauzi & Wahyudi, 2016). The link between real and financial economic activity across nations often results in the spillover effect, a spreading shock effect that typically affects stock markets. An example of the herding tendency is when irrational investors panic and pull their money out due to lack of transparency or irrational economic policies (Khan & Park, 2009). The use of contagion theory is very applicable in the study of financial distress as the MENA region is an area in which a single effect is likely to become contagious across all countries, as seen in the political effects of the Arab Spring.

2.1.2. Minksy's Financial Instability Theory

According to Minsky, speculative euphoria arises during fortunate periods when corporate cash flow exceeds the amount required to pay off debt. Shortly after, debts surpass the amount that borrowers can pay off with their incoming earnings, leading to a financial crisis (Taylor & O'Connell, 1985). The connection between the time pattern of cash obligations and the time pattern of expected cash flows lies at the core of Minsky's theory of what constitutes a strong or unstable financial structure. Since the company can satisfy its obligations with its own resources, it is said to be involved in "hedge" finance if its cash flows exceed its cash commitments for each future period. In addition to anticipating the need to refinance the principal at maturity, so-called "speculative" financial arrangements also forecast cash flows that exceed interest payments on outstanding debt. This puts the company at risk if the refinancing turns out to be unanticipated, costly, or perhaps unachievable (Nasica, 2010). Financial stability is one of the main indicators that affect developing countries as they suffer from fragile financial systems and structures in addition to the inefficient use of their resources. This is the main idea that Minsky tried to apply to developing countries such as MENA.

2.2. Empirical Literature

2.2.1. Financial Distresses in the Non-Financial Sector

Numerous studies have produced conflicting findings about the primary factors influencing financial sectors in both industrialized and emerging countries. A multitude of studies have investigated FD and its underlying factors and determinants. This analysis integrates firm-specific indicators, such as current ratio, quick ratio, asset turnover, debt ratio, financial leverage, and return on assets, along with macroeconomic variables like economic growth, exchange rate, GDP, and inflation rate. In the study conducted by (Ceylan, 2021), the variable of interest, comprising the current ratio, quick ratio, asset turnover, debt ratio, financial leverage, and return on assets, was shown to have had a statistically significant positive influence on the risk of financial distress in Turkey from

2010 to 2019. This study concluded that the inflation rate was the only factor that had a negative relationship with financial distress.

Idrees and Qayyum (2018) attribute the high concentration of financial risk and the inability to identify it to insufficient management and industry performance. As a result of poor performance and low profitability, the company accumulated substantial debt, which hindered its capacity to meet its obligations and resulted in the scenario of bankruptcy. The majority of financial crises arise in either emerging or established economies characterized by the presence of high inflation rates, low growth rates, low GDP, and poor bank performance (Idrees & Qayyum, 2018; Ehigiamusoe et al., 2019).

Campbell (2011) examined the primary causes of business failure in a sample of U.S. enterprises from 1963 to 2003. The research indicates that companies with lower profitability, market capitalization, leverage, prior stock returns, cash holdings, volatility, market–book ratios, and share prices are more likely to declare bankruptcy. Leverage and firm size increase financial distress (Alfaro et al., 2019). A financial crisis hurts company profits (Du & Lai, 2018). Al-Tamimi (2010) studied 1996–2008 UAE Islamic and conventional bank performance metrics. GDP, bank size, concentration, liquidity, financial development indicators, operating expenditures, and branch count were analyzed. Concentration and liquidity damaged traditional banks' ROA and ROE.

Jahur and Quadir (2012) studied the causes of financial distress in 20 SMEs in Bangladesh during 2004–2008. The study utilized the Altman Z-score and varimax rotation factor analysis to assess and identify the FD of SMEs. Empirical data indicate that financial strain was caused by factors such as a poor accounting system, susceptibility to government policy changes, productivity and profitability, fund management and credit crunch, liquidity, macroeconomic factors, management succession, and financial control. Zaki et al. (2011) studied financial distress in UAE commercial and Islamic banks from 2000 to 2008, focusing on bank-specific factors such as cost–income ratio, equity to total assets, asset growth, and loan loss reserve to gross loans ratio. They found no evidence of macroeconomic factors' impact. In a similar vein, Maricica and Georgeta (2012) examined financial ratio forecasts for 2009 and 2010. Financial measures from Altman's model were applied to 63 listed Romanian enterprises, including size, return and margin, liquidity, financial position, cash flow, profits, indebtedness and capital structure, credit back payment, and interest payment capability. The t-test showed disparities in profitability, return, financial position, indebtedness, and capital structure across the enterprises. According to Mokhova and Zinecker (2013), the life cycle of small and medium-sized firms in the Czech Republic from 2006 to 2010, including the financial crisis years, affected their likelihood of bankruptcy. Additionally, they suggest a substantial negative correlation between liquidity and financial difficulty. Yazdanfar and Öhman (2020) examined the causes of financial distress in non-financial SMEs from 2008 to 2015. A panel data set of 3865 Swedish SMEs was analyzed with multiple binary logistic regression using macroeconomic dummy factors, firm-specific variables, and industry-specific variables. Their analysis revealed that macroeconomic factors (global financial crisis) and firm-specific characteristics (performance, financial leverage, and delayed FD) affected financial distress.

From 2003 to 2011, Charalambakis and Garrett (2019) investigated the main financial distress risk factors for 31,000 Greek private enterprises. A multiperiod logit model was used to find that firms' financial distress was based on their size, profitability, leverage, retained earnings to total assets, size, liquidity ratio, an export dummy variable, dividend payout, and real GDP growth. Additionally, other studies have examined the financial distress risk of enterprises of different sizes, particularly industrial firms, in the UK, Malaysia, Australia, Turkey, Indonesia, Nigeria, and China. According to Yazdanfar and Öhman (2020), the Global Financial Crisis and other factors such as leverage, performance, and past financial distress caused financial distress in Swedish SMEs between 2008 and 2015. Distressed enterprises have weaker liquidity, solvency, profitability, financial leverage, and repayment capacity. Researchers found a negative correlation between bank distress and failure and the liquidity holdings ratio, which is proxied by the net stable funding ratio, in financial institutions. Zhang and Xu (2021) investigated how the life cycle affects China's debt maturity structure. According to their argument, corporations have short-term loans during the launch and recession, whereas growing enterprises have higher debt ratios. Companies in recession have negative growth, resulting in reduced operational cash flow and less access to long-term loans due to increased financial distress costs.

2.2.2. Banking Sector Financial Distress

Naceur et al. (2010) utilized 1989–2005 bank-level data from 10 MENA nations. Bank efficiency was measured by three metrics: cost of intermediation, operational performance, and bank profitability. They observed that bank capitalization and credit risk increased profits significantly. In addition, regulatory and institutional factors affected bank performance. Corruption enhanced cost-efficiency and net-interest margins. The law and order variable reduced efficiency cost without compromising performance. Beyond financial issues, company traits mattered, researchers found. Size, leverage, and profitability are key determinants in business financial problems, according to research. The literature discusses firm size, leverage, and profitability. Based on data from 12 countries in MENA and Southeast Asia (70 conventional banks and 47 Islamic banks), Louati et al. (2015) analyzed the capital adequacy ratio behavior of Islamic and conventional banks in various competitive conditions. The empirical findings showed that the funding ratio affected conventional and Islamic bank behavior. Competition (measured by the Lerner Index) did not alter the weighted asset ratio or Islamic bank behavior. The authors determined that Islamic banks used their own theoretical models and behaved differently from conventional banks. Selassie et al. (2016) employed the Altman Z-score to analyze the financial healthiness of 30 Wolaita-based SMEs in manufacturing, commerce, and services in 2015. The findings showed that three services, one manufacturing, and three trade SMEs were financially distressed.

In its global economic estimates, the World Bank (2016) lists political and economic turmoil, falling oil prices, and reform obstacles in the MENA region. Its characteristics set it apart from other regions and wealthy countries. Political turmoil in Arab nations began in Tunisia in 2010 and spread rapidly. The GCC, which experienced less impact from the Arab Spring, now feels this influence. Political and military instability in the area, along with financial problems, make countries in the MENA region disposed to financial instability and a weak financial sector. The World Bank anticipates political instability will persist for years, which will harm the economies of these countries by reducing direct foreign investments and visitors. Investment in MENA nations is fragile due to ineffective bankruptcy and insolvency rules (Belkhir et al., 2016).

The civil wars in Syria, Iraq, Libya, and Yemen are destroying lives and infrastructure. However, political instability and security concerns have reduced GDP, raised unemployment rates, and damaged tourism elsewhere, notably in Egypt and Tunisia. The GCC countries, Arab oil exporters, are also suffering from low oil prices, which hurt their economies. To address these issues, MENA countries are implementing many reforms to boost economic stability, development, and growth (Celiku et al., 2018). Governmental financial issues, the COVID-19 epidemic, and inflationary pressures have plagued MENA over the last decade. These events have exacerbated the financial crisis in several countries in the region, emphasizing the importance of understanding its financial and economic causes. Therefore, the main objective of our research is to analyze several financial and macroeconomic determinants of MENA region banks and their impact on the banks' stability.

The fragility and vulnerability of financial institutions against a strengthened situation of MENA region banks (MRBs) during the global financial crisis of 2007–2008 was considered an important subject that raised a wide controversy (Parashar & Venkatesh, 2010). The subprime crisis, according to some researchers, had a significant impact on the MRBs, as evidenced by the collapse of numerous banks, including Lehman Brothers, the largest American bank. However, the partisans of Islamic finance proved that MRBs, especially Islamic banks, were not only more efficient but also more stable, with a high capacity to absorb shocks (Akmal et al., 2024; Ftiti et al., 2013; Khediri et al., 2015). In the aftermath of the 2008 financial crisis, the question of how the macroeconomic and financial characteristics of MRBs influenced the financial crisis's impact on stability has gained significant attention. To this end, various studies began in 2008, analyzing how differences in banks' internal profitability and macroeconomic factors such as inflation, GDP, exchange rate, and growth enable banks to identify potential risks.

However, most prior studies examined business failure models in MENA countries (Distinguin et al., 2010; Calice, 2014; Mateev et al., 2021), taking only economic and political factors into account, or focusing on specific countries (Al-Khatib & Al-Horani, 2011; Kholisoh & Dwiarti, 2020; Dianova & Nahumury, 2019; Moradi-Motlagh & Babacan, 2015) or a part of the region. This paper fills a research gap by examining the financial and economic factors of financial distress of listed banks in the MENA region. Other research has shown inconsistent outcomes on bank-specific and macroeconomic factors, as well as bank stability and risk. The results are all unclear and inconclusive (Bourkhis & Nabi, 2013; Louati et al., 2015; Trad et al., 2017; Fayad, 2013; Ashraf et al., 2022). In addition to bank features, the macroeconomic framework in which banks operate is a country-specific variable and a significant external element affecting bank performance. Bourkhis and Nabi (2013) and Ftiti et al. (2013) are among numerous researchers who have used external measures to study bank performance and found different outcomes. Rajhi and Hassairi (2012) examined the financial stability of 16 bank groups in the MENA region from 2000 to 2008. They employed the Z-score to measure bank stability. They found that macroeconomic factors, particularly GDP, positively and significantly affected all banks' Z-scores. Inflation is a major contributor to the instability of large South Asian banks. Muda et al. (2013) and El-Chaarani et al. (2022) indicated that real GDP affects international banks' profitability. Inflation has a significant impact on national and international bank profits. (Wasiuzzaman & Tarmizi, 2010) found that the two macroeconomic indices boost bank profitability. GDP favorably correlates with the two profitability metrics, whereas the inflation rate negatively affects only ROA.

Furthermore, multiple discriminant analyses have revealed that sales ratio, working capital, and EBIT significantly influence SMEs' financial health. Trad et al. (2017) examined how the global financial crisis affected MENA banks. The sample included 77 Islamic and 101 conventional banks in 13 countries during 2006–2013. The GMM technique revealed that bank-specific factors affected conventional and Islamic bank performance and stability. Size hurt both types of institutions. However, liquidity ratios only improved traditional bank performance, suggesting that liquidity may help to avoid bank failure. According to empirical data, inflation also hurt Islamic banks and helped conventional banks. When the dependent variable was ROA, the growth rate was positive (negative), but when it was ROE, it was negative. Research by Huy et al. (2021) identifies accounting, market, and macroeconomic factors as major predictors of financial distress in Vietnamese enterprises during 2003–2016. Financial distress was negatively correlated with liquidity, solvency, asset productivity, profitability, and stock market value, whereas inflation and short-term treasury bill interest rates were positively correlated. In the MENA region, a number of studies have examined how the Arab Spring affected bank performance and risk. By preserving a sample of 12 MENA banks from 2000 to 2012, Ghosh (2018) examined how the Arab Spring affected ROA and NIM. Bank profitability, as assessed by ROA, decreased and banking risk increased significantly after the Arab Spring. Political disputes lowered profitability and increased bank risk, according to credible empirical criteria. Bitar et al. (2016) examined regulatory capital ratios and bank performance risk. They employed the bank cost-to-income ratio, net income to total assets, net interest margin, and net income to gross loans to evaluate 168 banks in 17 MENA countries from 1999 to 2013. The empirical data revealed that capital requirements had a greater influence on big banks, particularly in crises and in well-governed nations. Previous studies revealed that most GCC countries have benefited from oil profits and rapid economic expansion, while non-GCC countries are more vulnerable to political instability and financial problems. Political instability negatively impacts the profitability of GCC banks and the efficiency of MENA banks, leading to increased risk and financial distress, particularly during the COVID-19 pandemic. Therefore, most banks work toward having greater capital ratios, which boost bank efficiency, net interest margins, and profits. Banks with high capital ratios were more cautious and managed risk better, particularly amid political upheaval.

Numerous theories can be used to outline the characteristics of a firm in financial distress: liquid asset theory, liquid and profitability theory, balance sheet decomposition measure, cash management theory, and credit risk theory all serve to describe distressed firms and their functional forms (Hotchkiss et al., 2008). In liquid asset theory, net cash flows relative to current obligations explain financial strain, with positive cash flows enabling borrowing and negative ones causing default. Technical insolvency occurs when a business lacks liquidity and expects a negative profit or net cash flow to lead to bankruptcy (Altman & Hotchkiss, 2006). A firm's health is defined by its liquidity and profitability indexes, with poor indicators putting it at risk of insolvency. Enterprises use the balance sheet decomposition measure (BSDM) to detect financial distress by assessing major balance sheet changes over time (Adnan Aziz & Dar, 2006; Monti & Garcia, 2010).

2.2.3. Financial Distress and Macroeconomic Indicators

Khoja et al. (2019) studied the causes of financial crises in the GCC, UK, and US during 2004–2012. The study found that industrial characteristics and macroeconomic trends, such as inflation, interest rates, and oil prices, significantly impact FD in dynamic situations. A recent study by ElBannan (2021) examined the main determinants of financial distress in 11 MENA countries from 2006 to 2015, controlling for the Arab Spring and using many robustness tests. She discovered that mature, profitable, liquid, small firms with high market-to-book ratios and low asset growth were less likely to experience financial distress. Well-developed financial markets in low-corruption nations reduce financial suffering. The findings include increasing earned capital and cash holdings, avoiding overinvestment, and diversifying risk. Mature enterprises also have significant cash flows to avoid capital market risk. These reasoning and research expectations strongly support the influence of the life cycle theory on company FD, as evidenced by the empirical data. This research also claims that company maturity, liquidity, profitability, market-to-book ratio, asset growth, firm size, and institutional factors, such as financial market developments and government corruption, indicate a financial crisis. Mature, profitable, liquid, small-sized enterprises with high market-to-book ratios and limited asset growth are less likely to be in financial crisis.

Unpredictable shifts in a firm's asset and liability composition increase the likelihood of losing equilibrium and facing financial difficulties. Liquidity risk theories measure the risk of a borrower defaulting on a bank loan, with the probability depending on macroeconomic factors such as unemployment, interest rates, GDP, government spending, foreign currency rates, and aggregate savings (Alifiah & Tahir, 2018).

As shown by earlier research, corporations take enormous efforts to avoid bankruptcy when they detect financial difficulties. Their options include asset and liability restructuring, asset sales, capital expenditure reduction, and/or bank debt restructuring. Companies in financial trouble may receive independent banking treatment. Financially distressed enterprises may get additional funding, defer principal and interest payments, or cancel contracts from certain banks. Some banks accelerate principal and interest payments, reduce lending limits, and increase collateral for companies. In times of crisis, corporations can liquidate assets, although industry characteristics or performance levels may limit them.

Despite comprehensive research, a consensus on the factors influencing financial distress in MENA banks remains unclear. Although bank-specific factors like size, leverage, and liquidity are essential, the influence of macroeconomic and political variables necessitates additional investigation. This study investigates the financial and economic factors influencing the stability of banks in the MENA region, offering new perspectives on the interaction between internal and external determinants as shown in the Table 1 that summarizes the most of literatures

Table 1. Summary of literature.

Literature	Application	Model	Time Framework	Variables	Results
(Rachdi & Ben Mbarek, 2011)	10 OECD countries and 6 MENA countries	Static GMM	1990–2006	CPI, private domestic credit, government consumption to GDP, liability to GDP, GDP per capita	+
(Cevik et al., 2013)	Bulgaria, the Czech Republic, Hungary, Poland, and Russia	VAR	February 2005 till January 2010	stock market index, the foreign exchange rate, international reserves, sovereign bond spreads, external debt, Z-score and real GDP	-
(Van Roye, 2014)	Germany	Threshold VAR	February 1970—December 2012	Exchange rate volatility rate, money market spread, bank return volatility relative to overall volatility, bank equity, the spread on bank securities, lending conditions expected by German banks, excess liquidity, corporate bond spread, credit default swaps on DAX30 non-financial corporations, annual stock market returns and financial distress index	-
(Alimi, 2015)	Sub-Saharan Africa	Static and dynamic GMM	1981–2013	Real GDP, private domestic credit to GDP, real interest rate, FDI	No relation
(Trad et al., 2017)	13 MENA countries 77 Islamic and 101 conventional banks	Generalized method of moments (GMM)	2006–2013	Performance, stability, GMM in system, conventional banks	+
(Guru & Yadav, 2019)	5 BRICS countries	GMM	1993–2014	Number of financial intermediaries, credit to deposit ratio, private domestic credit, stock turnover ratio, value of stock traded, inflation rate, enrollment in secondary schools, exports	+
(Arilyn, 2020)	Firms listed on the Indonesia Stock Exchange	Stepwise logit analysis	2003–2018	Financial ratios, macroeconomics variables, financial distress.	+
(Chandio & Anwar, 2020)	Nigeria	Fixed and random effects	2015–2020	Z-score, inflation, cash/debt, ROE, total debt/total assets	+
(Ekanayake & Thaver, 2021)	138 developing countries	FMOLS	1980–2018	GDP per capita, inflation rate, gross capital formation, government expenditure share of GDP, trade openness, and population growth rate	+
(Farooq et al., 2023)	214 non-financial listed on the Pakistan stock exchange l firms	Panel data analysis	2010–2018	Financial distress, short term debts, interest exchange, interest coverage	-
(Rawal & Gopalkrishnan, 2024)	31 banks operating in India	Panel data analysis	2016–2020	Financial distress, Z-score, dividend payout, debt/equity ratio	+

3. Methodology

This paper examines the main economic and financial determinants that affect financial distress in the MENA region. The financial distress was measured in different ways as some studies depend on distance to default measures, financial distress indexes, or Z-scores in the banking sectors of different nations. We used the Z-score as it is the only tool that was not previously used to measure the financial distress and macroeconomic determinants in the MENA region.

Moreover, the Z-score helps investors in predicting financial crises and bankruptcies (Elewa, 2022). Altman created the Z-score model in 1968, and its strong statistical basis and straightforward applicability across many industries have led to its extensive use as a predicted indicator of financial and economic distress. It integrates many financial statistics to evaluate a company's probability of insolvency, offering an extensive perspective on financial well-being. This model incorporates profitability, liquidity, solvency, and efficiency criteria, rendering it especially suitable for assessing organizations' overall financial stability. Its sustained prominence in academia and practice arises from its experimentally substantiated precision and versatility across various economic contexts (Altman, 1968). This study employs the Z-score owing to its proven reliability and significance in analyzing financial distress. The justification for employing the Z-score in this research is based on its empirically validated predictive efficacy, with the first studies indicating accuracy rates of up to 95% in forecasting bankruptcy one year before failure (Altman, 1968). The model's versatility across many industries and its integration of market-based metrics for public enterprises render it pertinent for evaluating financial distress in multiple scenarios (Altman et al., 2017).

In contemporary settings, the Z-score is particularly relevant for identifying financial instability arising from internal inefficiencies or external shocks, such as economic recessions or global crises (Altman & Hotchkiss, 2006). The Z-score's lasting relevance guarantees its status as one of the most employed and referenced models in financial distress literature.

The reason for choosing these countries is their variety in the following areas:

- Inflation rates in this region vary from 29% in Egypt to the lowest one in Qatar that is −2.5%.
- The banking sector in MENA is characterized by high growth rates and the use of technology, especially digital banking and artificial intelligence (AI), with wide use of the most advanced technologies in the Saudi and Emirati banking sectors.
- These countries witnessed high growth rates with high dependence of labor and capital in most countries.
- The political stability varies among them as the gulf countries such as Saudi Arabia, the United Arab Emirates, Qatar, Oman, and Bahrain are the most stable countries compared to other unstable countries such as Palestine, Libya, Yemen, and Iraq.

The model began with the main diagnostic test for correlation and heteroskedasticity. Then the stationarity test was conducted using the unit root test depending on augmented Dickey–Fuller (ADF) and Phillips–Perron (PP) statistics at level and first difference. This was examined after checking stationarity at level. If there is no stationarity at level, the first difference should be checked (Phillips & Perron, 1988). The use of the unit root test with panel data was applicable for the following reasons (Choi, 2001):

1. It was assumed that there are many kinds of stochastic and non-stochastic components in each group of panel data.
2. It was believed that each group has a distinct time series span.

Moreover, the model estimation was carried by pooled OLS, panel estimation using fixed effects, and GMM. The authors chose the fixed and random effects as they measure the heterogeneity between variables and across countries.

When dynamic endogeneity is prevalent in panel data settings, GMM is especially helpful. For example, GMM can produce reliable estimates by employing lagged values as instruments when the present values of independent variables are impacted by previous values of the dependent variable. This is essential in domains where dynamic linkages are prevalent, such as international business studies (Li et al., 2021).

In summary, while OLS is a straightforward method for regression analysis, it falls short in the presence of endogeneity. GMM, on the other hand, offers a robust alternative that can effectively address these issues through the use of instruments and moment conditions.

Furthermore, the Hausman test was used to test the significance of the fixed and random models. This helped to test the relationships between exogenous and endogenous variables, as each country or region has special characteristics (Bollen & Brand, 2010).

In order to determine the most appropriate model, the authors used the GMM that was supported by Inekwe et al. (2018), Saleem et al. (2020), and Pham et al. (2021). This can be explained by the following model (1):

$$Zscore = a_0 + a_1\ ROE + a_2ROA + a_2GDP + a_3INF + a_4STOCK + a_5ER + \varepsilon \quad (1)$$

Then the GMM model was developed into the following Equation (2):

$$\begin{gathered} Zscore = a_0 + \sum_{k=1}^{q1} a_1\ ROE + \sum_{k=2}^{q2} a_2\ ROA + \sum_{k=3}^{q3} a_1\ GDP + \\ \sum_{k=4}^{q4} a_1\ INF + \sum_{k=5}^{q5} a_1\ STOCK + \sum_{k=6}^{q6} a_1\ ER + \varepsilon \end{gathered} \quad (2)$$

The GMM model was used in order to control any endogeneity that may appear and because it is more appropriate for cross-sectional data that are greater than time (Blundell & Bond, 1998; Kruiniger, 2009). Theoretically, this model is shown in Figure 1 below, which shows the research model that was used. The validity of the model was assessed by testing the endogeneity, the serial correlation, and the independence of the variables. This was examined by using the Breusch–Godfrey LM test and the Sargan test for instrumental validity and the Breusch–Pagan–Godfrey test. Therefore, the use of diagnostic tests to examine the reliability of the model estimates was as follows:

- The use of the Breusch–Godfrey LM to test if there was no second-order serial correlation between residuals.
- The Sargan test has been an important tool used in the literature depending on the GMM model to test the independence between the variables in panel data and to examine if they are overidentified or not.
- The Breusch–Pagan–Godfrey test was used to test the heteroskedasticity.

Figure 1 explains the relationship between financial and economic variables and the Z-score, as it is suggested in the literature that financial and economic determinants should affect the Z-score.

The data were extracted from 2002 until 2020 as data were not available after 2020. Only the stock market return lagged in the data due to the huge gap between the maximum and minimum values. Thus, the variables used are shown in Table 2 and were extracted from the World Bank. All the variables used were in percentages except exchange rates. These data were applicable to some countries only due to the lack of data. The applicable countries were Egypt, Saudi Arabia, United Arab Emirates, Israel, Oman, Morocco, Tunisia, Qatar, Turkey, and Jordan.

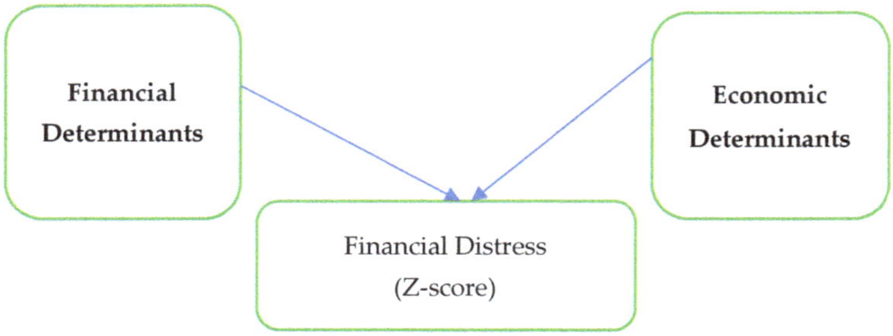

Source: created by the authors

Figure 1. Research model.

Table 2. List of variables.

Variable	Symbol	Definition	Unit	Source
Dependent variable				
Z-score (dependent)	Z-score	It is one of the indicators of bank stability and risk, estimated by the following equation: Z-score $= \frac{ROE+\left(\frac{equity}{assets}\right)}{standard\ deviation\ of\ ROE\ to\ ROA}$	percentage	World Bank
Economic variables (independent variables)				
Exchange rate	ER	Average of the official exchange rate to US dollars on an annual basis	US $	World Bank
Inflation rate	INF	It is calculated by using the consumer price indices as follows: Inflation rate $= \frac{CPI\ new - CPI\ old}{CPIold} \times 100$	percentage	World Bank
GDP growth rate	GDP	GDP growth rate $= \frac{GDPnew - GDPold}{GDPold} \times 100$	percentage	World Bank
Profitability variables (independent variables)				
Return on assets	ROA	$\text{ROA} = \frac{Net\ income\ after\ taxes}{total\ assets}$	percentage	World Bank financial data
Return on equity	ROE	$\text{ROE} = \frac{Net\ income\ after\ taxes}{total\ equity}$	percentage	World Bank financial data
Stock market return	Log_STOCK	The growth rate of the annual average stock market index	percentage	World Bank

Thus the study examines the following hypotheses:

Studies have demonstrated a substantial negative relationship between economic growth and financial distress. Robust economic growth enhances credit conditions, bolsters consumer confidence, and increases borrower repayment abilities, thereby alleviating financial distress (Wasiuzzaman & Tarmizi, 2010). Bourkhis and Nabi (2013) assert that economic downturns, which decrease GDP growth, increase financial distress by decreasing asset values and elevating bank default rates. El-Chaarani et al. (2022) find that banks' financial stability enhances during economic expansion due to increased lending revenues and decreased non-performing loans. Nevertheless, certain researchers, including Fayad (2013), Louati et al. (2015), and Ashraf et al. (2022), contend that quick and unsustainable economic expansion may precipitate credit bubbles and financial crises over time. When looking at how economic growth affects financial distress, it is important to take into account things that are unique to each country, the rules that govern them, and how strong the banks are. This conflict makes this point clear. Thus the first hypothesis was developed as follows:

H1. *There is a negative and significant relationship between economic growth and financial distress.*

Previous studies have analyzed inflation and financial distress from various perspectives. Boyd et al. (2001) assert that elevated inflation diminishes the real value of financial assets and heightens uncertainty, leading to inefficient resource allocation and financial instability. According to Ehigiamusoe et al. (2019), inflation increases transaction costs and diminishes borrower credit quality, thereby heightening financial instability. Numerous studies indicate that moderate and stable inflation may exert a neutral or even beneficial impact on the economy by fostering predictable financial conditions and consistent economic growth. Ekanayake and Thaver (2021) argue that hyperinflation or high price volatility has historically caused banking crises and financial instability. Trad et al. (2017) assert that inflation indirectly influences financial distress by increasing interest rates, thereby increasing borrowing costs for both firms and individuals. The different points of view show how complicated the link is between inflation and financial distress. More research is needed to find out how inflation's effects may be different in countries with different economic conditions and institutional structures. Thus the second hypothesis was developed as follows:

H2. *The inflation rate has a significant relationship with financial distress.*

Institutions' financial health depends on profitability, and many researchers have studied its relationship with financial distress. In his fundamental Z-score model, Altman (1968) identified profitability as a key predictor of financial distress, arguing that firms with higher profitability can better meet their financial obligations and avoid distress. Beaver et al. (2006) noted that profitability indicates a firm's ability to cover expenses and avoid default. According to Antonia García-Benau et al. (2013), low profitability indicates financial distress due to operational inefficiencies and low earnings potential. However, Bitar et al. (2016), Calice (2014), and El-Chaarani et al. (2022) argue that profitability is important, but leverage and liquidity may mitigate its effect. Profitability may also delay financial distress because firms may use short-term financing in order to conceal problems, according to Das et al. (2024). These different points of view show how important profitability is in times of financial trouble, especially when looked at with other financial and operational indicators. Thus, the third hypothesis was developed.

H3. *Profitability has a significant relationship with financial distress.*

4. Results

The main determinants of financial distress were investigated using the GMM model. This was carried out depending on several tests, the first being the analysis of the descriptive data and validity of the data using the diagnostics tests. The second was the integration and multicollinearity of data, while the third examined the GMM model. Finally, a robustness test was conducted.

4.1. Descriptive and Diagnostics Results

In order to estimate the results, descriptive data were collated in Table 3 for 200 observations over 20 years in 10 countries. The Z-scores averaged 27.265667 with standard deviation of 12.62972; the lowest Z-score was 0.2 in Turkey and the highest was 66.27002 in Jordan. This shows the huge variation between banks in the MENA region. Regarding ROE, the mean was 12.47828 with a maximum of 31.62065 and a minimum of −7.204117. Furthermore, the difference between the mean and standard deviation was very narrow for the stock market return, exchange rate, GDP growth rate, inflation rate, and return on assets. The significant standard deviations in both Z-score and ROE when interpreting these data set the tone for the regression study, in which we examined how these factors contribute to short-term growth and their diminishing long-term returns.

Table 3. Descriptive data.

	Z-Score	Log_STOCK	ER	GDP	INF	ROE	ROA
Mean	27.26567	2.335148	3.852769	4.211648	4.267115	12.47828	1.388016
Std. dev	12.62972	1.302789	3.272135	4.207495	5.567157	5.600596	0.8043568
Max	66.27002	5.134698	17.78253	26.17025	44.96412	31.62065	3.983963
Min	0.2	−2.599947	0.3845	−8.591826	−4.863278	−7.204117	−0.922874
No	200	200	200	200	200	200	200

Source: authors' calculations.

Moreover, Table 4 shows the functionality of the model in terms of the heteroskedasticity and serial correlation. There was no serial correlation between the data, as shown in the results. Also, the results of Sargan test on the instrumental variables were insignificant, which indicates that there was no endogeneity between variables.

Table 4. Diagnostics results.

Test	t-Statistic	Result
Breusch–Godfrey serial correlation LM	126.4136 ***	No serial correlation
Sargan test for instrumental validity	85.687	no overidentified
Breusch–Pagan–Godfrey test	282.4447 ***	No heteroskedasticity

*** significant at 1%, Source: authors' calculations.

4.2. Correlation Results

The correlation test results are depicted in Table 5, showing that the highest correlation was between the Z-score and ROE and the Z-score and the inflation rate, which indicates the lack of multicollinearity between variables. The Z-score was negatively and significantly correlated with ROA, ROE, STOCK, and INFL. But there was a positively insignificant relation between the Z-score and GDP, which implies a need to conduct unit root tests and panel regression methods (see Sections 4.3 and 4.4).

Table 5. Correlation results.

Correlation	Z-Score	ER	ROA	ROE	STOCK	INFL	GDP
Z-score	1						
ER	−0.047307	1					
ROA	−0.158779 **	−0.058077	1				
ROE	−0.242651 ***	0.182463 ***	0.866999 ***	1			
Log_STOCK	−0.171006 **	0.033659	0.004956	0.105665	1		
INFL	−0.295809 ***	0.173432 ***	0.012777	0.130868 *	0.130125 *	1	
GDP	−0.034195	0.023820	0.349154 ***	0.298798 ***	0.162814 **	0.240997 ***	1

*** significant at 1%, ** significant at 5% * significant at 10% Source: authors' calculations.

After conducting Pedroni panel cointegration and Kao integration tests, the variables were found to be significant in most tests at 10% or 5%—except rho and v statistics (see panel A of Table 6). Therefore, the null hypothesis, which assumed that there is no cointegration, was rejected—there is integration in the long run. Then, Kao integration was found to be significant (see Panel B) at 1% with long-run integration relationships.

Table 6. Pearson cointegration tests.

Panel A: Pedroni Panel Cointegration Test			
	Statistic (All Countries)		Statistic (All Countries)
Panel v statistic	−2.008787	Panel v statistic (weighted)	−2.081182
Panel rho statistics	2.284053	Panel rho statistics (weighted)	1.554250
Panel PP statistic	−2.854576 ***	Panel PP statistic (weighted)	−4.895711 ***
Panel ADF statistic	−2.647123 ***	Panel ADF statistic (weighted)	−1.697424 **
Group rho statistic	2.827199	Group ADF statistic	−0.600409
Group PP statistic	−4.564815 ***		
Panel B: KAO Integration Statistic			
statistic	−5.726189 ***		

*** significant at 1%, ** significant at 5%, Source: authors' calculations.

4.3. Unit Root Results

The stationarity of the data was examined using the unit root test. This was performed at the level and at the first difference using Dickey–Fuller and Phillips–Perron (PP) tests. The results collated in Table 7 show that the variables were significant in the long run more than the short run.

Table 7. Unit root tests.

Panel A: ADF Results				
	Level		First Difference	
	Constant	Constant with Trend	Constant	Constant with Trend
Z-score	36.5078 **	42.1329 ***	97.5002 ***	72.1759 **
ER	5.58331	6.7690	33.7025 ***	21.74497 **
ROA	47.2644 ***	67.6363 ***	106.504 ***	71.1917 ***
ROE	37.1886 **	60.7045 ***	95.7407 ***	65.6223 ***
Log_STOCK	49.5592 ***	44.0349 ***	131.161 ***	97.0456 ***
INF	31.0194 *	32.4364 **	96.0029 ***	68.8142 ***
GDP	42.3991 ***	50.0083 ***	113.052 ***	80.8820 ***
Panel B: PP Results				
	Level		First Difference	
	Constant	Constant with Trend	Constant	Constant with Trend
z-score	42.4052 ***	58.3316 ***	289.103 ***	116.604 ***
ER	8.86482	11.3986	53.4479 ***	37.4290 ***
ROA	54.6445 ***	68.7249 ***	193.535 ***	133.648 ***
ROE	44.7739 ***	54.9498 ***	197.667 ***	138.385 ***
Log_STOCK	78.1886 ***	71.2588 ***	765.211 ***	207.121 ***
INF	78.3756 ***	69.9276 ***	355.086 ***	168.068 ***
GDP	71.0250 ***	88.0908 ***	577.535 ***	162.723 ***

*** significant at 1%, ** significant at 5% * significant at 10% Source: authors' calculations.

4.4. Panel Data Estimations

Then, different regression methods were used (pooled OLS, fixed effect OLS, and random effects, see Appendix A), and the robustness of the data was tested to estimate the relationship between variables in the long run. The results in panel A of Appendix A show the significance of all variables with Z-scores, except stock market return and the inflation rate. This was not the same situation when comparing MENA-GCC oil-producing countries with other countries in the region, as the former showed significant relationships between the Z-score and ROA and between ROE and the exchange rate compared to the latter category, which showed significant relationships between Z-score and all variables except stock market return. The situation was different in panel B, which shows the significance of the Z-score with all variables in the MENA region as a whole, with no significance for GDP per capita and exchange rate in MENA other countries and MENA-GCC oil ones. Finally, panel C shows the significance of financial distress and economic growth using the RE-OLS model. The results in Panel C show the significance of the relationship between GDP per capita and the Z-score in GCC oil-producing countries and in the other countries in the region.

5. Discussion

The results of the study are consistent with some previous studies (Cevik et al., 2013; Van Roye, 2014), which demonstrates the relationship between economic growth and financial distress in the MENA region. The results were divided into three main scenarios: the first devoted to all countries of MENA region, the second to the GCC oil-producing countries in the region, and the last one to the remaining countries in the region. The reason behind that division is the differences in income levels and political conditions that each country faces. Regarding the first scenario (the whole MENA region), the insignificant relationship between economic growth and financial distress depends on the Z-score as a dependent variable. Compared to the results of the FE-OLS and GMM methods, there is a significant and negative relationship between financial distress and economic growth in most scenarios. This can be explained by the different political and economic circumstances that the MENA region faces, such as political instability, the Arab Spring effect, and the high inflation rates in some countries that affect the region as a whole.

Regarding the GCC countries, the situation is totally different as those countries (the oil-producing ones) are characterized by political stability and high growth rates. The results of the panel regressions collated in Appendix A show the negative relationship between economic growth and financial distress in all countries besides the oil producing countries. This can be explained by low income levels, GDP per capita, and high population growth rates. Also, this relationship is characterized by levels of significance that range from no significance to 5%, and this is consistent with studies that relate financial distress in MENA to external or internal shocks (Elsayed & Yarovaya, 2019) or to the very loose integration between MENA countries that decreases the contingency effect (Neaime, 2016). Therefore, we conducted an impulse effect (see Figure 2) to test the results in the MENA region.

Figure 2 is consistent with the results computed from Appendix A as the exchange rate has a positive relationship with the Z-score in the fixed effects and GMM models. ROA and STOCK have negative relationships with the Z-score. Also, inflation has a positive relationship with the Z-score in the fixed effects and GMM models that reaches a steady state in the long run. Only GDP per capita has a positive relationship with the Z-score, which contradicts the results of the panel regression because of other factors that were ignored due to lack of data such as corruption rate (Song et al., 2021), political instability, and economic uncertainty (Das et al., 2024). These variables can be used in further studies whenever such data become available. Therefore the results support some hypotheses and reject others, as shown in Table 8.

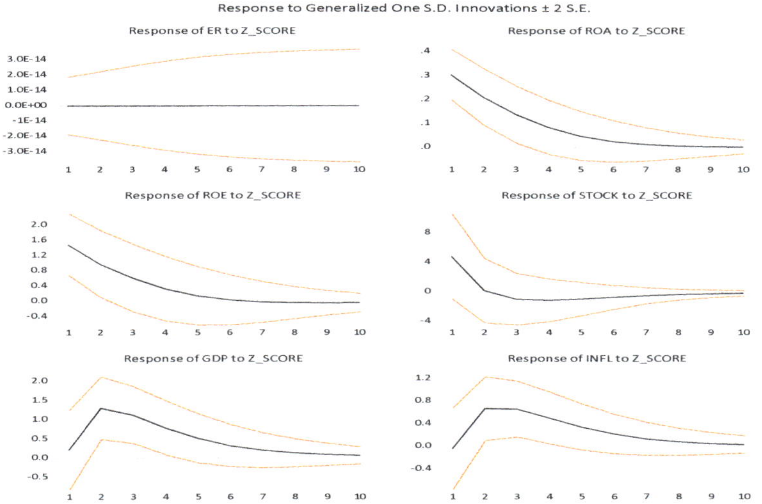

Source: authors' calculations.

Figure 2. Impulse effect.

Table 8. Results of hypotheses.

Hypothesis	Result in MENA	Result in GCC OIL-MENA	Result in the Rest of MENA
H1. There is a negative and significant relationship between economic growth and financial distress	Accept	reject	accept
H2. The inflation rate has a significant relationship with financial distress	Reject	accept	accept
H3. Profitability has a significant impact on financial distress	Accept	accept	reject

6. Conclusions and Policy Implications

This study aimed to examine the relationship between financial distress, profitability, and macroeconomic indicators not only in the MENA region as a whole but also by comparing MENA-GCC oil-producing countries with other countries in the region. This was carried out using 10 countries only because of the political tensions that the region suffers from in many countries such as Sudan, Palestine, Syria, Lebanon, Yemen, Libya, and Iraq. One more reason to minimize the number of the countries to 10 was the unavailability of data from the banking sectors in Kuwait, Algeria, and Iran. The relationship between financial distress and economic growth was examined using a number of regression methods—OLS, FE, and static GMM—using data published by the World Bank from 2002 to 2020. The results are consistent with the previous literature (Cevik et al., 2013; Van Roye, 2014). This model is considered the first to use Z-scores as an indicator to measure financial distress, as most of the previous literature relied on a financial distress index (Cevik et al., 2013) or private domestic credit to GDP (Alimi, 2015; Rachdi & Ben Mbarek, 2011; Guru & Yadav, 2019).

Furthermore, measuring financial distress in the MENA region was not discussed in the previous literature, except by Rachdi and Ben Mbarek (2011), who compared MENA to the OECD without mentioning the main determinants that affect the relationship between financial distress and economic conditions in the MENA region. Our results have many implications in practical life as financial data should be available to all, especially in times of crises such as COVID-19 or financial crises. This is obvious in the MENA region as the region suffers from many political, economic, and social tensions. Moreover, capital management should be conducted efficiently in order to cover expected and unexpected loan losses. Therefore, we propose some policy recommendations:

- There is a need for more improvement in the financial sector as there should be more awareness regarding the policies that promote a strong financial sector and enhance financial inclusion.
- The public sector needs to be restructured to decrease corruption and to increase the transparency of data and policies.
- There is a need to promote more credit resource allocation in all sectors of the economy.
- There is a need to align monetary and fiscal policy with policies that target inflation.

For further studies, it will be very beneficial to include all MENA countries and study them in terms of income, ranging from low-income countries to middle- and high-income ones. Also, incorporating the quality of corporate governance and corruption into future studies may reveal links to economic growth and economic development. The effect of elections and political factors can be incorporated into further studies.

Author Contributions: Conceptualization, A.B.M.M., M.M.Y., E.A.A. and M.A.S.A.; methodology, A.B.M.M., M.M.Y., E.A.A. and M.A.S.A.; software, A.B.M.M., M.M.Y., E.A.A. and M.A.S.A.; validation A.B.M.M., M.M.Y., E.A.A. and M.A.S.A.; analysis and interpretation of the data A.B.M.M., M.M.Y., E.A.A. and M.A.S.A.; the drafting of the paper A.B.M.M., M.M.Y., E.A.A. and M.A.S.A.; revising it critically for intellectual content A.B.M.M., M.M.Y., E.A.A. and M.A.S.A.; funding acquisition, A.B.M.M. and M.A.S.A. All authors have read and agreed to the published version of the manuscript.

Funding: This work was funded by the Deanship of Scientific Research, Vice Presidency for Graduate Studies and Scientific Research, King Faisal University, Saudi Arabia. [Project No. KFU241858].

Informed Consent Statement: No consent statement was required as there was no study on humans.

Data Availability Statement: Data are available upon request from researchers who meet the eligibility criteria. Kindly contact the corresponding author privately through e-mail.

Conflicts of Interest: The authors declare no conflicts of interest.

Abbreviations

FD	financial distress
FE	fixed effect
FMOLS	fully modified ordinary least squares model
GFC	global financial crisis
GMM	generalized method of moments
MENA	Middle East and North Africa
MRB	MENA region banks
OECD	organization of economic cooperation and development
OLS	ordinary least squares model
ROA	return on assets
ROE	return on liability
ROI	return on investment
SMEs	small and medium enterprises
VAR	vector auto regression model

Appendix A

Table A1. Regression results.

		Panel A: Static Panel Regression (pooled OLS)	
Variables	**Statistic (All Countries)**	**Statistic (GCC-Oil Producing Countries)**	**Statistic (Other MENA Countries)**
ER	0.265001	1.687698 ***	0.2651554
ROA	−2.727512	10.59423 ***	11.2762 **
ROE	−0.0598682	−1.313006 ***	−1.403209 **
Log_STOCK	−1.598308 *	−0.0114681	−0.8805222
INF	−0.686425 ***	−0.032477	−0.8333628 ***
GDP	0.3199478	0.0519168	−1.332586 **
C	35.2253 ***	15.53617 ***	43.67618 ***
		Panel B: Static Panel Regression (FE OLS)	
	Statistic (All Countries)	**Statistic (GCC-Oil Producing Countries)**	**Statistic (Other MENA Countries)**
ER	0.2948784 *	0.568921	0.2082327
ROA	11.97984 ***	10.04718 ***	14.55605 ***
ROE	−1.176469 ***	−1.137099 ***	−1.286094 ***
Log_STOCK	−0.377678 *	0.2215798 *	−0.8259574 **
INF	0.1020422 *	−0.0536356	0.1876155 **
GDP	−0.1793483 *	−0.0053157	−0.1152506
C	24.62937 ***	18.78091 ***	28.27984 ***
		Panel C: Static Panel Regression (GMM)	
	Statistic (All Countries)	**Statistic (GCC-Oil Producing Countries)**	**Statistic (Other MENA Countries)**
ER	0.30691995 *	1.687698 ***	0.2651554
ROA	11.66203 ***	10.59423 ***	11.2762 **
ROE	−1.148273 ***	−1.313006 ***	−1.403209 **
Log_STOCK	−0.3946719 *	−0.0114681	−0.8805222
INF	0.916024	−0.0324777	−0.8333628 ***
GDP	−0.1714445 *	0.519168	−1.332586 **
C	25.23527 ***	15.53617 ***	45.65824 ***
Hausmen test	12.02 **	32.28 ***	63.43 ***

*** significant at 1%, ** significant at 5% * significant at 10% Source: authors' calculations.

References

Abd. Majid, M. S. (2018). Stability and resilience of equity markets amidst the 2008 global financial crisis: Islamic versus conventional markets. *DLSU Business & Economics Review*, *28*(1), 34–48. Available online: https://www.dlsu.edu.ph/wp-content/uploads/2019/03/2majid-100218.pdf (accessed on 1 July 2024).

Adnan Aziz, M., & Dar, H. A. (2006). Predicting corporate bankruptcy: Where we stand? *Corporate Governance: The International Journal of Business in Society*, *6*(1), 18–33. [CrossRef]

Akmal, M., ur Rehman, J., & Rashid, A. (2024). Impact of internal and macroeconomic risks on financial performance, growth, and stability of domestic and foreign banks in Pakistan. *Journal of Finance and Accounting Research*, *6*(1), 28–49. [CrossRef]

Alam, S., Das, S. K., Dipa, U. R., & Hossain, S. Z. (2024). Predicting financial distress through ownership pattern: Dynamics of financial resilience of Bangladesh. *Future Business Journal*, *10*(1), 91. [CrossRef]

Alfaro, L., Asis, G., Chari, A., & Panizza, U. (2019). Corporate debt, firm size and financial fragility in emerging markets. *Journal of International Economics*, *118*, 1–19. [CrossRef]

Alifiah, M. N., & Tahir, M. S. (2018). Predicting financial distress companies in the manufacturing and non-manufacturing sectors in Malaysia using macroeconomic variables. *Management Science Letters*, *8*(6), 593–604. [CrossRef]

Alimi, S. (2015). *Financial deepening and economic growth: A System GMM Panel Analysis with application to 7 SSA countries. MPRA Paper No. 65789*. University Library of Munich. Available online: https://mpra.ub.uni-muenchen.de/65789 (accessed on 5 September 2024).

Al-Khatib, H., & Al-Horani, A. (2011). Predicting financial distress of public companies listed in Amman Stock Exchange. *European Scientific Journal, 8*(15), 1–17. Available online: https://www.researchgate.net/publication/266162851_Predicting_financial_distress_of_public_companies_listed_in_Amman_stock_exchange (accessed on 4 August 2024).

Al-Tamimi, H. A. H. (2010). Factors influencing performance of the UAE Islamic and conventional national banks. *Global Journal of Business Research, 4*(2), 1–9.

Altman, E. I. (1968). Financial ratios, discriminant analysis and the prediction of corporate bankruptcy. *The Journal of Finance, 23*(4), 589–609. [CrossRef]

Altman, E. I., & Hotchkiss, E. (2006). *Corporate financial distress and bankruptcy: Predict and avoid bankruptcy*. Wiley & Sons. Available online: https://books.google.com.eg/books?hl=en&lr=&id=_5n0-J37Zz4C&oi=fnd&pg=PA10&dq=Altman+and+Hotchkiss,+2006&ots=E6vjb5GzfR&sig=IedH7LC3orCuh1BMnHJusLwLVXk&redir_esc=y#v=onepage&q=Altman%20and%20Hotchkiss,%202006&f=false (accessed on 10 July 2024).

Altman, E. I., Iwanicz-Drozdowska, M., Laitinen, E. K., & Suvas, A. (2017). Financial distress prediction in an international context: A review and empirical analysis of altman's Z-score model. *Journal of International Financial Management & Accounting, 28*(2), 131–171. [CrossRef]

Antoniades, A., & Calomiris, C. W. (2020). Mortgage market credit conditions and U.S. Presidential elections. *European Journal of Political Economy, 64*, 101909. [CrossRef]

Antonia García-Benau, M., Sierra-Garcia, L., & Zorio, A. (2013). Financial crisis impact on sustainability reporting. *Management Decision, 51*(7), 1528–1542. [CrossRef]

Arilyn, E. J. (2020, February 19–21). *The effect of financial ratios and macroeconomic variables to financial distress of agriculture industry listed in the indonesia stock exchange from 2013 to 2018*. 17th International Symposium on Management (INSYMA 2020), Vung Tau City, Vietnam. [CrossRef]

Ashraf, B. N., Tabash, M. I., & Hassan, M. K. (2022). Are Islamic banks more resilient to the crises vis-à-vis conventional banks? Evidence from the COVID-19 shock using stock market data. *Pacific-Basin Finance Journal, 73*, 101774. [CrossRef]

Baldwin, C. Y., & Mason, S. P. (1983). The resolution of claims in financial distress the case of massey ferguson. *The Journal of Finance, 38*(2), 505–516. [CrossRef]

Beaver, W. H., Shakespeare, C., & Soliman, M. T. (2006). Differential properties in the ratings of certified versus non-certified bond-rating agencies. *Journal of Accounting and Economics, 42*(3), 303–334. [CrossRef]

Belkhir, M., Ben-Nasr, H., & Boubaker, S. (2016). Labor protection and corporate Debt maturity: International evidence. *International Review of Financial Analysis, 45*, 134–149. [CrossRef]

Bitar, M., Saad, W., & Benlemlih, M. (2016). Bank risk and performance in the MENA region: The importance of capital requirements. *Economic Systems, 40*(3), 398–421. [CrossRef]

Blundell, R., & Bond, S. (1998). Initial conditions and moment restrictions in dynamic panel data models. *Journal of Econometrics, 87*(1), 115–143. [CrossRef]

Bollen, K. A., & Brand, J. E. (2010). A general panel model with random and fixed effects: A structural equations approach. *Social Forces, 89*(1), 1–34. [CrossRef]

Bourkhis, K., & Nabi, M. S. (2013). Islamic and conventional banks' soundness during the 2007–2008 financial crisis. *Review of Financial Economics, 22*(2), 68–77. [CrossRef]

Boyd, J. H., Levine, R., & Smith, B. D. (2001). The impact of inflation on financial sector performance. *Journal of monetary Economics, 47*(2), 221–248. [CrossRef]

Calice, P. (2014). *Predicting bank insolvency in the middle east and North Africa. Policy research paper 6969 world bank group*. World Bank Group. [CrossRef]

Campbell, J. L. (2011). The US financial crisis: Lessons for theories of institutional complementarity. *Socio-Economic Review, 9*(2), 211–234. [CrossRef]

Celiku, B., Maseeh, A. N., & Sharma, D. (2018). *Iraq economic monitor, fall 2018: Toward reconstruction, economic recovery and fostering social cohesion*. World Bank Group. Available online: https://www.researchgate.net/publication/328432107_Iraq_Economic_Monitor_Toward_Reconstruction_Economic_Recovery_and_Fostering_Social_Cohesion (accessed on 20 July 2024).

Cevik, E. I., Dibooglu, S., & Kutan, A. M. (2013). Measuring financial stress in transition economies. *Journal of Financial Stability, 9*(4), 597–611. [CrossRef]

Ceylan, I. E. (2021). The impact of firm-specific and macroeconomic factors on financial distress risk: A case study from Turkey. *Universal Journal of Accounting and Finance, 9*(3), 506–517. [CrossRef]

Chandio, J. A., & Anwar, S. (2020). What causes financial distress? A study of inflation, solvency, profitability and liquidity: A random effect analysis. *International Journal of Disaster Recovery and Business Continuity, 11*(3), 3605–3618. Available online: https://www.researchgate.net/profile/Sadia-Anwar-8/publication/364315087_What_Causes_Financial_Distress_A_Study_of_Inflation_Solvency_Profitability_and_Liquidity_A_Random_Effect_Analysis/links/634693a0ff870c55ce1da014/What-Causes-Financial-Distress?-A-Study-of-Inflation,-Solvency,-Profitability-and-Liquidity:%20A-Random-Effect-Analysis (accessed on 29 August 2024).

Charalambakis, E. C., & Garrett, I. (2019). On corporate financial distress prediction: What can we learn from private firms in a developing economy? Evidence from Greece. *Review of Quantitative Finance and Accounting, 52*(2), 467–491. [CrossRef]

Chen, C., Chen, C., & Lien, D. (2020). Financial distress prediction model: The effects of corporate governance indicators. *Journal of Forecasting, 39*(8), 1238–1252. [CrossRef]

Choi, I. (2001). Unit root tests for panel data. *Journal of International Money and Finance, 20*, 249–272. [CrossRef]

Das, B. C., Hasan, F., & Sutradhar, S. R. (2024). The impact of economic policy uncertainty and inflation risk on corporate cash holdings. *Review of Quantitative Finance and Accounting, 62*(3), 865–887. [CrossRef]

Dewi, D. N., Murhadi, W. R., & Sutejo, B. S. (2023). Financial ratios, corporate governance, and macroeconomic indicators in predicting financial distress. *Journal of Law and Sustainable Development, 11*(4), e893. [CrossRef]

Dianova, A., & Nahumury, J. (2019). Investigating the effect of liquidity, leverage, sales growth, and good corporate governance on financial distress. *Journal of Accounting and Strategic Finance, 2*(2), 143–156. [CrossRef]

Distinguin, I., Hasan, I., & Tarazi, A. (2010). The use of accounting data to predict bank financial distress in MENA countries. *International Journal of Banking, Accounting and Finance, 2*(4), 332. [CrossRef]

Du, X., & Lai, S. (2018). Financial distress, investment opportunity, and the contagion effect of low audit quality: Evidence from China. *Journal of Business Ethics, 147*(3), 565–593. [CrossRef]

Ehigiamusoe, K. U., Lean, H. H., & Lee, C.-C. (2019). Moderating effect of inflation on the finance–growth nexus: Insights from West African countries. *Empirical Economics, 57*(2), 399–422. [CrossRef]

Eid, Q. M. A., Al Houl, M. A. A., Alqudah, M. T. S., & Almomani, M. A.-A. (2023). The role of financial inclusion in the stability of Islamic banks. *International Journal of Professional Business Review, 8*(4), e01214. [CrossRef]

Ekanayake, E. M., & Thaver, R. (2021). The nexus between financial development and economic growth: Panel data evidence from developing countries. *Journal of Risk and Financial Management, 14*(10), 489. [CrossRef]

ElBannan, M. A. (2021). On the prediction of financial distress in emerging markets: What matters more? Empirical evidence from Arab spring countries. *Emerging Markets Review, 47*, 100806. [CrossRef]

El-Chaarani, H., Ismail, T. H., El-Abiad, Z., & El-Deeb, M. S. (2022). The impact of COVID-19 on financial structure and performance of Islamic banks: A comparative study with conventional banks in the GCC countries. *Journal of Economic and Administrative Sciences, 40*, 769–797. [CrossRef]

Elewa, M. (2022). Using altman Z-score models for predicting financial distress for companies—The case of egypt panel data analysis. *Alexandria Journal of Accounting Research, 6*(1), 1–28. [CrossRef]

Elsayed, A. H., & Yarovaya, L. (2019). Financial stress dynamics in the MENA region: Evidence from the Arab Spring. *Journal of International Financial Markets, Institutions and Money, 62*, 20–34. [CrossRef]

Farooq, M., Hunjra, A. I., Ullah, S., & Al-Faryan, M. A. S. (2023). The determinants of financial distress cost: A case of emerging market. *Cogent Economics & Finance, 11*(1), 2186038. [CrossRef]

Fauzi, R., & Wahyudi, I. (2016). The effect of firm and stock characteristics on stock returns: Stock market crash analysis. *The Journal of Finance and Data Science, 2*(2), 112–124. [CrossRef]

Fayad, M. (2013). Comparative performance study of conventional and Islamic banking in Egypt. *Journal of Applied Finance & Banking, 3*(2), 1–14. Available online: https://www.scienpress.com/Upload/JAFB/Vol%203_2_1.pdf (accessed on 24 August 2024).

Ftiti, Z., Nafti, O., & Sreiri, S. (2013). Efficiency of Islamic banks during subprime crisis: Evidence of GCC countries. *Journal of Applied Business Research (JABR), 29*(1), 285. [CrossRef]

Galindo-Martín, M.-Á., Castaño-Martínez, M.-S., & Méndez-Picazo, M.-T. (2021). Effects of the pandemic crisis on entrepreneurship and sustainable development. *Journal of Business Research, 137*, 345–353. [CrossRef]

Ghosh, S. (2018). Governance reforms and performance of MENA banks: Are disclosures effective? *Global Finance Journal, 36*, 78–95. [CrossRef]

Gilson, S. C. (1990). Bankruptcy, boards, banks, and blockholders. *Journal of Financial Economics, 27*(2), 355–387. [CrossRef]

Guru, B. K., & Yadav, I. S. (2019). Financial development and economic growth: Panel evidence from BRICS. *Journal of Economics, Finance and Administrative Science, 24*(47), 113–126. [CrossRef]

Habib, A., Costa, M. D., Huang, H. J., Bhuiyan, M. B. U., & Sun, L. (2020). Determinants and consequences of financial distress: Review of the empirical literature. *Accounting & Finance, 60*(S1), 1023–1075. [CrossRef]

Hotchkiss, E. S., John, K., Mooradian, R. M., & Thorburn, K. S. (2008). Bankruptcy and the Resolution of Financial Distress**We thank the editor, B. Espen Eckbo, for helpful comments and suggestions. In *Handbook of empirical corporate finance* (pp. 235–287). Elsevier. [CrossRef]

Huy, D. T. N., Nhan, V. K., Bich, N. T. N., Hong, N. T. P., Chung, N. T., & Huy, P. Q. (2021). Impacts of internal and external macroeconomic factors on firm stock price in an expansion econometric model—A case in vietnam real estate industry. In N. Ngoc Thach, V. Kreinovich, & N. D. Trung (Eds.), *Data science for financial econometrics* (vol. 898, pp. 189–205). Springer International Publishing. [CrossRef]

Ibrahim, S. N., Ismail, S., Abd Rahman, N. H., Malan, I. N. B., & Ismail, W. M. W. (2024). Financial distress prediction of islamic banks in top sukuk-issuing countries: An application of Altman's z-score model. *Information Management and Business Review*, *16*(2(I)), 28–36. [CrossRef]

Idrees, S., & Qayyum, A. (2018). The impact of financial distress risk on equity returns: A case study of non-financial firms of Pakistan Stock Exchange. *Journal of Economics Bibliography*, *5*(2), 49–59. Available online: https://ideas.repec.org/p/pra/mprapa/85346.html (accessed on 24 August 2024).

Inekwe, J. N., Jin, Y., & Valenzuela, M. R. (2018). The effects of financial distress: Evidence from US GDP growth. *Economic Modelling*, *72*, 8–21. [CrossRef]

Jahur, M. S., & Quadir, S. M. N. (2012). Financial distress in small and medium enterprises (SMES) of Bangladesh: Determinants and remedial measures. *Economia. Seria Management, Faculty of Management, Academy of Economic Studies, Bucharest, Romania*, *15*(1), 46–61. Available online: https://ideas.repec.org/a/rom/econmn/v15y2012i1p46-61.html (accessed on 1 September 2024).

Kazemian, S., Shauri, N. A. A., Sanusi, Z. M., Kamaluddin, A., & Shuhidan, S. M. (2017). Monitoring mechanisms and financial distress of public listed companies in Malaysia. *Journal of International Studies*, *10*(1), 92–109. [CrossRef]

Khan, S., & Park, K. W. K. (2009). Contagion in the stock markets: The Asian financial crisis revisited. *Journal of Asian Economics*, *20*(5), 561–569. [CrossRef]

Khediri, K. B., Charfeddine, L., & Youssef, S. B. (2015). Islamic versus conventional banks in the GCC countries: A comparative study using classification techniques. *Research in International Business and Finance*, *33*, 75–98. [CrossRef]

Khoja, L., Chipulu, M., & Jayasekera, R. (2019). Analysis of financial distress cross countries: Using macroeconomic, industrial indicators and accounting data. *International Review of Financial Analysis*, *66*, 101379. [CrossRef]

Kholisoh, S. N., & Dwiarti, R. (2020). The analysis of fundamental variables and macro economic variables in predicting financial distress. *Management Analysis Journal*, *9*(1), 81–90. [CrossRef]

Kruiniger, H. (2009). GMM estimation and inference in dynamic panel data models with persistent data. *Econometric Theory*, *25*(5), 1348–1391. [CrossRef]

Li, J., Ding, H., Hu, Y., & Wan, G. (2021). Dealing with dynamic endogeneity in international business research. *Journal of International Business Studies*, *52*, 339–362. [CrossRef]

Louati, S., Gargouri Abida, I., & Boujelbene, Y. (2015). Capital adequacy implications on Islamic and non-Islamic bank's behavior: Does market power matter? *Borsa Istanbul Review*, *15*(3), 192–204. [CrossRef]

Maricica, M., & Georgeta, V. (2012). Business failure risk analysis using financial ratios. *Procedia—Social and Behavioral Sciences*, *62*, 728–732. [CrossRef]

Mateev, M., Moudud-Ul-Huq, S., & Nasr, T. (2021). Capital regulation and market competition in the MENA region: Policy implications for banking sector stability during COVID-19 pandemic. *Global Business Review*, 097215092110644. [CrossRef]

Mokhova, N., & Zinecker, M. (2013). Liquidity, probability of bankruptcy and the corporate life cycle: The evidence from Czech Republic. *International Journal of Globalisation and Small Business*, *5*(3), 189. [CrossRef]

Monti, N. E., & Garcia, R. M. (2010). A statistical analysis to predict financial distress. *Journal of Service Science and Management*, *3*(03), 309–335. [CrossRef]

Moradi-Motlagh, A., & Babacan, A. (2015). The impact of the global financial crisis on the efficiency of Australian banks. *Economic Modelling*, *46*, 397–406. [CrossRef]

Muda, M., Shaharuddin, A., & Embaya, A. (2013). Comparative analysis of profitability determinants of domestic and foreign Islamic banks in Malaysia. *International Journal of Economics and Financial Issues*, *3*(3), 559–569. Available online: https://www.econjournals.com/index.php/ijefi/article/view/462/pdf (accessed on 5 September 2024).

Muñoz-Izquierdo, N., Laitinen, E. K., Camacho-Miñano, M., & Pascual-Ezama, D. (2020). Does audit report information improve financial distress prediction over Altman's traditional Z-Score model? *Journal of International Financial Management & Accounting*, *31*(1), 65–97. [CrossRef]

Naceur, S. B., Cherif, M., & Kandil, M. (2010). What drives financial sector development in the MENA region? *SSRN Electronic Journal*. [CrossRef]

Nasica, E. (2010). Rational and innovative behaviors at the core of financial crises: Banking in Minsky's theory. In D. B. Papadimitriou, & L. R. Wray (Eds.), *The elgar companion to hyman minsky*. Edward Elgar Publishing. [CrossRef]

Neaime, S. (2016). Financial crises and contagion vulnerability of MENA stock markets. *Emerging Markets Review*, *27*, 14–35. [CrossRef]

Parashar, S. P., & Venkatesh, J. (2010). How did Islamic banks do during global financial crisis? *Banks and Bank Systems*, *5*(4), 54–62. Available online: https://www.businessperspectives.org/index.php/journals/banks-and-bank-systems/issue-167/how-did-islamic-banks-do-during-global-financial-crisis (accessed on 1 September 2024).

Pham, T. T., Dao, L. K. O., & Nguyen, V. C. (2021). The determinants of bank's stability: A system GMM panel analysis. *Cogent Business & Management*, *8*(1), 1963390. [CrossRef]

Phillips, P. C. B., & Perron, P. (1988). Testing for a unit root in time series regression. *Biometrika*, *75*(2), 335–346. [CrossRef]

Rachdi, H., & Ben Mbarek, H. (2011). The causality between financial development and economic growth: Panel data cointegration and gmm system approaches. *International Journal of Economics and Finance*, *3*(1), 143–151. Available online: https://epe.lac-bac.gc.ca/100/201/300/intl_journal_economics_finance/2011/IJEF-V3N1-All.pdf#page=145 (accessed on 5 September 2024). [CrossRef]

Rajhi, W., & Hassairi, S. A. (2012). Islamic banks and financial stability: A comparative empirical analysis between MENA and southeast Asian countries. *SSRN Electronic Journal*. [CrossRef]

Ramlan, H., & Adnan, M. S. (2016). The profitability of Islamic and conventional bank: Case study in Malaysia. *Procedia Economics and Finance*, *35*, 359–367. [CrossRef]

Rawal, A., & Gopalkrishnan, S. (2024). Impact of financial distress on the dividend policy of banks in India: Evidence using panel data. *Future Business Journal*, *10*(1), 27. [CrossRef]

Saleem, R., Hussain, A., & Ibraheem, R. (2020). Banking industry specific determinants of financial distress: Empirical evidence from ASEAN countries. *iRASD Journal of Economics*, *2*(2), 113–123. [CrossRef]

Scott, J. (1981). The probability of bankruptcy. *Journal of Banking & Finance*, *5*(3), 317–344. [CrossRef]

Selassie, E., Tarekegn, G., & Ufo, A. (2016). Analysis of financial distress and its determinants in selected SMEs in Wolaita Zone. *Global Journal of Management and Business Research: C Finance*, *16*(8), 35–41. Available online: https://globaljournals.org/GJMBR_Volume16/5-Analysis-of-Financial-Distress.pdf (accessed on 11 August 2024).

Sghaier, I. (2021). Remittances and economic growth in MENA countries: The role of financial development. *Economic Alternatives*, *27*(1), 43–59. [CrossRef]

Song, C.-Q., Chang, C.-P., & Gong, Q. (2021). Economic growth, corruption, and financial development: Global evidence. *Economic Modelling*, *94*, 822–830. [CrossRef]

Supriyanto, J., & Darmawan, A. (2018). The effect of financial ratio on financial distress in predicting bankruptcy. *Journal of Applied Managerial Accounting*, *2*(1), 110–120. [CrossRef]

Taffler, R. J. (1983). The assessment of company solvency and performance using a statistical model. *Accounting and Business Research*, *13*(52), 295–308. [CrossRef]

Taylor, L., & O'Connell, S. A. (1985). A Minsky crisis. *The Quarterly Journal of Economics*, *100*, 871–885. [CrossRef]

Trad, N., Rachdi, H., Hakimi, A., & Guesmi, K. (2017). Banking stability in the MENA region during the global financial crisis and the European sovereign debt debacle. *The Journal of Risk Finance*, *18*(4), 381–397. [CrossRef]

Van Roye, B. (2014). Financial stress and economic activity in Germany. *Empirica*, *41*(1), 101–126. [CrossRef]

Volkov, A., Benoit, D. F., & Van Den Poel, D. (2017). Incorporating sequential information in bankruptcy prediction with predictors based on Markov for discrimination. *Decision Support Systems*, *98*, 59–68. [CrossRef]

Wasiuzzaman, S., & Tarmizi, H. A. A. (2010). Profitability of Islamic banks in Malaysia: An empirical analysis. *Mic Bank Training and Research Academy Journal*, *6*(4), 53–68. Available online: https://www.semanticscholar.org/paper/Profitability-of-Islamic-Banks-in-Malaysia-:-An-Wasiuzzaman-Tarmizi/e05cd0ffbd0c4ae89caf7ac8fe9509e3f219ff7e (accessed on 24 August 2024).

World Bank. (2016). *Global economic prospects, January 2015: Having fiscal space and using it*. World Bank. Available online: https://documents.worldbank.org/en/publication/documents-reports/documentdetail/444361468127152333/global-economic-prospects-january-2015-having-fiscal-space-and-using-it (accessed on 24 August 2024).

Yasiru, A. O., & Olajide, A. J. (2015). Assessment of global economic and financial reforms in developing countries: Evidences from Sub-Saharan Africa (SSA). *International Journal of Physical and Social Sciences*, *5*(4), 325–343.

Yazdanfar, D., & Öhman, P. (2020). Financial distress determinants among SMEs: Empirical evidence from Sweden. *Journal of Economic Studies*, *47*(3), 547–560. [CrossRef]

Zaiane, S., & Moussa, F. B. (2021). What drives banking profitability during financial crisis and political turmoil? Evidence from the MENA region. *Global Journal of Emerging Market Economies*, *13*(3), 380–407. [CrossRef]

Zaki, E., Bah, R., & Rao, A. (2011). Assessing probabilities of financial distress of banks in UAE. *International Journal of Managerial Finance*, *7*(3), 304–320. [CrossRef]

Zarrouk, H., Ben Jedidia, K., & Moualhi, M. (2016). Is Islamic bank profitability driven by same forces as conventional banks? *International Journal of Islamic and Middle Eastern Finance and Management*, *9*(1), 46–66. [CrossRef]

Zhang, X., & Xu, L. (2021). Firm life cycle and debt maturity structure: Evidence from China. *Accounting & Finance*, *61*(1), 937–976. [CrossRef]

economies

MDPI

Article

Unveiling Inter-Market Reactions to Different Asset Classes/Commodities Pre- and Post-COVID-19: An Exploratory Qualitative Study

Siddhartha S. Bannerjee [1], Rekha Pillai [2], Mosab I. Tabash [3,*] and Mujeeb Saif Mohsen Al-Absy [4]

[1] Department of International Finance, Poznan University of Economics and Business, 61-875 Poznan, Poland; 87486@student.ue.poznan.pl
[2] Faculty of Business and Law, British University in Dubai, Dubai P.O. Box 345015, United Arab Emirates; rekha.pillai@buid.ac.ae
[3] Department of Business Administration, College of Business, Al Ain University, Al Ain P.O. Box 64141, United Arab Emirates
[4] Accounting and Financial Science Department, College of Administrative and Financial Science, Gulf University, Sanad 26489, Bahrain; dr.mujeeb.saif@gulfuniversity.edu.bh
* Correspondence: mosab.tabash@aau.ac.ae

Abstract

Comprehending intermarket relationships among asset classes/commodities and the changing dynamics among the gold, bitcoin, and oil markets under high or low-volatility indexes is now imperative for investors. This paper presents a qualitative study to elicit expert views on the relationships between two major commodities (gold and oil) and bitcoin, specifically emphasizing the pre- and post-COVID-19 era. The thematic analysis of 30 finance experts revealed gold as a safe haven and portfolio diversifier; however, it has lost importance as an inflation hedge post-COVID-19 (2020–2022). Moreover, findings indicated that bitcoin was not a substitute for gold and that there was a positive correlation between gold and oil and the gold volatility index (VIX). Furthermore, there was a negative correlation between the oil VIX and the bitcoin VIX, with no correlation between the gold–bitcoin or oil–bitcoin nexus. These findings are pertinent for investors and scholars in the context of portfolio allocation/portfolio design that comprise these vital asset classes/commodities.

Keywords: intermarket relationships; asset classes; portfolio; pre- and post-COVID-19 era

1. Introduction

The intermarket relationships among asset classes/commodities are changing and becoming more complex (Y. Zhou et al., 2023). Hence, it is vital to appreciate the asset class/commodity dynamics that play a significant role in portfolio design, which include gold, oil, and bitcoin. The proper determination and forecast of asset volatility is extremely important for investors (Souto & Moradi, 2023). Gold was one of the first metals used by humans, and the history of gold use goes back 5000 years or more to Egypt and Nubia. The gold-centric monetary standard or the "Gold Standard", which links the economic unit of account to a fixed quantity of gold, was followed from the 1870s to 1971. Gold is important not just to central banks but also to governments, households, and institutional investors. Gold also provides diversification benefits owing to its negative correlation with equity markets (Artigas, 2010). Thus, it provides downside protection during economic downturns and works as an inflation hedge in a bull market (McCown & Zimmerman, 2006). The COVID-19 pandemic in 2020 caused gold prices to soar, peaking at USD 2075 an ounce in August 2020 and USD 2135 an ounce in 2023 as per the figures by Bloomberg. Currently, because of global inflation and the consequence of several rate hikes by various central banks (Federal Reserve, European Central Bank, Bank of England, etc.), gold has again started to play an important role.

With respect to oil, in the post-World War II era, countries like Iran and Saudi Arabia attempted to nationalize oil production. Although this was partly achieved, the main power over the market initially remained with the USA and the Soviet Union. Later, in 1960, the Organization of Petroleum Exporting Countries (OPEC) was formed by Iran, Iraq, Kuwait, Saudi Arabia, and Venezuela. This was later expanded to 13 members and aimed to have more control over prices and to strengthen collaboration among the oil-producing countries[1]. Today, the oil price is one of the indicators of economic expansion (Mlaabdal et al., 2020). The peak oil price was recorded for West Texas Intermediate (WTI) crude on 11 July 2008 at USD 147.27 per barrel. In April 2020, during the COVID-19 pandemic, WTI was negative for the first time in history (USD −37/per barrel) owing to a severe shortage of storage capacity that outweighed the benefits of price (Chiaramonti & Maniatis, 2020). Considering oil scarcity, early studies (e.g., Kober et al., 2020) opined that by 2060, the reserves would be depleted, and the world would move into more sustainable alternative energy sources.

Bitcoin, a recent and unconventional asset, is a part of the crypto-asset family and arguably the most important one. Bitcoin is a digital token created by a code (protocol) running on multiple computer hubs to form a decentralized network. The bitcoin network creates and moves around bitcoin digital tokens. Increasingly, bitcoin is being accepted by investors like any other government- or central bank-controlled fiat currency (e.g., USD, EURO, GBP, etc., which are issued by the government and not backed by a commodity). The fundamental difference is that a single person, institution, central bank, or government does not own bitcoin. There is a bitcoin cap of a maximum of 21 million (Chohan, 2022). Countries like China, Russia, India, Vietnam, Bolivia, Columbia, and Ecuador have strong regulations against bitcoin. However, the USA, Canada, Australia, and the European Union have shown a positive tilt towards bitcoin.

Looking at the interrelationships between these three major assets which belong to the asset classes of commodities and cryptocurrencies, the pre-COVID-19 era was a period of low correlation between gold and bitcoin, and there was also a relatively weak correlation between oil and gold and oil and bitcoin (Maghyereh & Abdoh, 2022). Post-COVID-19, the relationship has become more dynamic. The oil price has increased owing to more demand after the opening of the global economy and to the geopolitical crisis caused by the Russia–Ukraine conflict. If we analyze recent studies, Tanin et al. (2022) concluded that the gold–oil relationship holds true in the short term and oil can be used to predict gold. However, this finding was contradicted by Benlagha and El Omari (2022), who found a significant relationship between gold and oil during COVID-19. Ji et al. (2020), Mensi et al. (2020), and Syuhada et al. (2022) compared gold and bitcoin, and concluded that gold was more consistent and was a superior hedge in terms of reducing portfolio risk. Moreover, Jareno et al. (2021) concluded that the relationship between oil price shocks and crypto currency returns was higher during the COVID-19 crisis period compared with the pre-COVID-19 period.

Equity is another important asset class that may be incorporated to analyze against the above-mentioned asset classes. However, selecting one index may not represent the whole equity market. Instead, the movements of the above asset classes may be analyzed using equity volatility. Whaley (2009) remarks that the Chicago Board Options Exchange's 'CBOE Volatility Index' (VIX), which gauges the anticipated volatility of S&P 500 index options, is the most accurate indicator of equity volatility.

The concept of the VIX[2] (Sigma Index) was coined by Menachem Brenner and Dan Galai in Financial Analyst Journals in 1989. The VIX is frequently referred to as the fear index or fear gauge because many investors use it to quantify risk, anxiety, or tension in the equities market (Carr, 2017). Using options-based theory (Fernandes et al., 2014) and up-to-date options market data, the current VIX index value is the anticipated annualized change in the S&P 500 index over the next 30 days. On 16 March 2020, the VIX closed at 82.69, the highest since its inception. Looking at the relationships between these asset classes pre- and post-COVID-19, oil was relatively stable and was influenced by supply and demand and geopolitical events. During COVID-19, there was a low correlation between gold and bitcoin and a relatively weak correlation between oil and gold and oil and bitcoin (P. Wang et al., 2021). Post-COVID-19, the relationship has become more dynamic. Gold retreated initially, then showed a steady growth trajectory as an inflation hedge and counter to potential dollar (USD) weakness. In contrast, bitcoin initially surged because of risk-on sentiments, signaling a declining trend due to risk-off sentiment and regulatory tightening. Prior research has attested to the return unpredictability in cryptocurrency markets, and this is still drawing attention in the research arena (Karasiński, 2023).

Extending the recent and previous work of these scholars, the current paper aims to answer the research question '*What are the intermarket relationships between the gold, bitcoin, and oil markets under different economic scenarios using the health of the economic situation or the volatility?*' The VIX tracks economic uncertainty or volatility. The non-standard features of VIX are fruitful for long-term investors searching for profitable portfolio diversification (Latoszek & Ślepaczuk, 2020). The key contributions of the paper are multi-fold. First, it explores the changes in intermarket relationships in asset classes before and after COVID-19. Second, to the best of our knowledge, this is the first comprehensive study to analyze three assets—gold, oil, and bitcoin—together. This is important because few papers highlight the relationships among these asset classes and link them to the VIX, especially over varied time horizons like pre- and post-COVID-19. Volatility as an asset class is a relatively new concept in financial theory, but due to its rapid development and new investment possibilities, the interest of academia and professionals has increased remarkably. Third, the paper addresses the gap in knowledge regarding the behavioral aspects of finance. Fourth, this is the first paper of its kind to highlight the role of information theory in the domain of applied finance. Fifth, this is the first paper, to the best of our knowledge, to conduct a qualitative study, a design that has garnered limited attention in research (Y. Kim, 2011, p. 191), to unveil the views of mixed expert groups practically and frequently contributing to the domain. Finally, the paper accommodates a multi-theoretical approach by integrating behavioral theory, information theory, and entropy theory when addressing the interrelationships of the asset classes like gold, oil, bitcoin, and VIX.

The remainder of the paper is organized as follows: Section 2 covers the theoretical foundations while Section 3 contains the literature review. The data and methodology used for the study are shown in Section 4. Section 5 reports the findings, while Sections 6 and 7 contain the discussion and the limitations, implications, and recommendations, respectively.

2. Theoretical Foundation

The behavior and the performance of asset classes need to move beyond fundamental or technical analysis (Chandra & Thenmozhi, 2017). For example, the bias of investors and experts plays a major role in defining the performance of the assets. However, behavioral aspects are a missing link in the arbitrage of financial assets, and these are not captured by mathematical models (Leković, 2019). In addition, the growing abundance of information in recent years poses a challenge for rational investment decision-making. This paper employed a novel entropy and information theory approach as well as the more commonly used behavioral finance theory to investigate the behavioral aspects of investment.

2.1. Entropy and Information Theory

Information theory (Shannon, 1948) is a mathematical theory of communication, and it has only recently begun to be applied in economies and finance. The theory is based on developing a "usable measure" from the information communicated. Here, the net received information can be defined as total information generated minus information asymmetry (Chen, 2004). However, the amount of information received may vary across investors. Shannon's entropy theory (Shannon, 1948), which was originally considered in relation to technical problems of information transmission across channels, has been used by economists to connect the information theories for economics and finance. Entropy is used in a mean-variance model to replace variance for options pricing and asset probability distributions (R. Zhou et al., 2013). Another critical theory is the Rényi entropy (Rényi, 1960) which is considered the generalized version of Shannon's entropy (Lahmiri & Bekiros, 2020). A study that used Rényi entropy to assess the return time series of bitcoin, S&P 500, WTI, Brent, gas, gold, silver, and VIX revealed some important observations. For example, any portfolio composed of two assets which included bitcoin reflected more disorder or randomness during low probability extreme events. However, an exception was found in assets comprising bitcoin and gas. In contrast, the lowest levels of disorder or more diversification during the COVID-19 pandemic were experienced by two asset-balanced portfolios like "gas and silver", "gold and silver", "gold and gas", "Brent and silver", "Brent and gold", or "gas and VIX" (Lahmiri & Bekiros, 2020).

Another multiscale entropy study was conducted regarding the market efficiency of the S&P 500, gold, bitcoin, and the USD index during COVID-19 by J. Wang and Wang (2021). A contagion effect and reduced market efficiency were observed in all assets during the COVID-19 pandemic; however, the S&P 500 was the worst impacted asset class and bitcoin showed more resilience compared with the other assets.

2.2. Behavioral Finance Theory

As the name suggests, behavioral finance theory is based on the rationality of conventional finance but goes beyond the modern portfolio theory by Markowitz (1952) or the efficient market hypothesis (Fama, 1965). Kahneman and Tversky (1979) are considered to be the founders of behavioral finance with their prospect theory which is based on human bias. According to the prospect theory (also known as the loss aversion theory), investors have different values for an equivalent amount of gain and loss. Since losses have a greater emotional impact on investors, the amount of gain must be greater than the amount of loss.

Subsequently, Peter and Tversky (1993) revised the prospect theory to the cumulative prospect theory where investment assessments were linked with biases. Likewise, Statman (1995) opined that the financial decisions for investors and portfolio managers were based on risk management and the way of presenting the information. Simon (1997) developed a concept of bounded rationality where the investor decision is based on satiety, though the results may not be optimal. Then, Barber and Odean (1999) explained the "gender bias" whereby male traders are more confident than females while trading. However, at times male traders make erroneous judgements due to overconfidence. Also, Shefrin (2000) suggested that investors should be aware of their mistakes and counterparty errors and that the loss of one party may be the gain of the other party. Hence, the evolution of behavioral finance cannot be ignored when analyzing the intermarket relationships of various assets.

3. Empirical Review

3.1. Gold and Oil

First, this investigation investigated the connection between oil and gold. When compared with equities across all markets, gold was a safe haven, but not when compared with bonds (Baur & Lucey, 2010). Due to their inverse relationship with stock markets, Sujit and Kumar (2011) determined that investments tied to oil were the best risk hedge during periods of uncertainty in oil prices. However, these studies are relatively outdated, and the market volatility and previously unheard-of external factors that influence the link have changed. Moreover, the appreciation of gold has recently served as a hedge against geopolitical crises in relation to the yield augmentation (price depreciation) of 10-year US Treasury notes following Russia's invasion of Ukraine (Neely, 2022).

Thus, it may be concluded that gold has served as a safe haven throughout times of crisis, even when bonds were on the decline. M. H. Kim and Dilts (2011) found that the USD–oil and USD–gold relationships had an inverse connection. Later, Ciner et al. (2013) looked at five main assets: the USD, equities, bonds, oil, and gold. They discovered that gold was a safe haven for investors compared with oil. Again, because both gold and the USD have appreciated, M. H. Kim and Dilts' (2011) conclusions are less applicable in the present geopolitical environment. Similarly, Reboredo (2013) stated that gold served as a hedge against sharp fluctuations in the price of oil. Nevertheless, in order to understand the intermarket relationship between these two asset classes before and after COVID-19, as well as up to Q1 2022 to account for the recent Russia–Ukraine war and related geopolitical crisis, we contend that more research is necessary to test the findings of both Ciner et al. (2013) and Reboredo (2013).

The study on crude oil's capacity to forecast stock market conditions using implied volatility data was extended by Al-Khazali et al. (2018). The study used a bi-variate cross-quantilogram approach and focused on the efficient frontier hypothesis (Han et al., 2016). Their methodology, which worked best in a non-crisis financial time, showed that directional prediction was weak when crude oil implied volatility was at a medium or high level. In contrast, sustained predictability was high when it was low. Gharib et al. (2021) employed Granger causality tests to deduce the bilateral contagion bubble effects in oil and gold markets during the initial phase of the pandemic.

Similarly, Salisu et al. (2020) used a VARMA-GARCH model to determine the function of gold as an appropriate hedging mechanism against crude oil price anomalies during the early pandemic; however, Mensi et al. (2020) observed an asymmetrical multifractality behavior in gold and oil prices. The VAR-BEKK-AGARCH model was also used by Huang and Wu (2021) to demonstrate strong asymmetric spillover effects from the oil to the gold market during the pandemic. They specifically concluded that negative information shocks in the oil market significantly impacted the volatility of gold returns during the pandemic.

More recently, Tanin et al. (2022) conducted a thorough analysis of the link between oil and gold before and after COVID-19 in five major stock markets. The findings indicated that there was only a short-term association (to differing degrees depending on the market); oil prices could not forecast gold prices. However, in five major stock markets, Benlagha and El Omari (2022) concluded that gold and oil were related, with gold as a favorable receiver and oil as the shock transmitter during COVID-19.

3.2. Gold, Oil and Bitcoin

Second, a particular school of thinking examining the connections between bitcoin, oil, and gold has just surfaced. While Gajardo et al. (2018) found that bitcoin had a higher cross-correlation with the WTI, Selmi et al. (2018) found that both gold and bitcoin demonstrated hedging qualities against oil fluctuation. According to Das et al. (2020), gold proved to be a better safe haven in dire circumstances, even though bitcoin was more effective at hedging the oil volatility index (OVX). In addition, Yin et al. (2021) reported on the relationship between the oil market and cryptocurrency. They highlighted the significance of fluctuations in the oil price as indicators of uncertainty in the cryptocurrency market because of the latter's relationship to macroeconomic variables, including monetary policy, global interest rates, and inflation.

More recently, Wen et al. (2022) concluded that gold was a superior option to protect against the volatility of the stock market and oil during the pre-COVID-19 era. However, bitcoin had a decent hedging effect against oil. Jiang et al. (2022) used the Markov Chain Monte Carlo technique and the TVP-VAR model to measure volatility spillovers. They found that gold showed consistently positive spillovers, confirming its status as a safe haven. Conversely, they proposed that bitcoin might be considered an investment hedge, with oil being marginalized as a hazardous asset. However, over time, it might be wiser to back up Das et al.'s (2020) claims about gold's superior safe haven qualities over bitcoin. Similarly, Syuhada et al. (2022) stated that adding gold to their energy portfolio clearly reduced risk because bitcoin's safe haven qualities in the portfolio were inconsistent in their capacity to reduce risk (see also Ji et al., 2020; Mensi et al., 2020).

3.3. Gold and Bitcoin

Third, the existing body of research has examined the connection between bitcoin and gold, with conflicting findings to date. Earlier, Glaser et al. (2014) identified bitcoin as a speculative asset rather than a currency or a means of payment, while Yermack (2015) found that bitcoin was a poor diversifier and had little association with gold and other currencies. According to Dyhrberg (2016), who positioned bitcoin between gold and the USD (commodities and currencies), it had many characteristics of both the USD and gold's hedging capabilities. At the same time, Urquhart (2016) concluded that bitcoin was inefficient from 2010 to the middle of 2016 (Caporale et al., 2018; Kristoufek, 2018), after which it progressively became more efficient. Wei (2018) and Nadarajah and Chu (2017) also concluded that bitcoin was now nearly efficient.

Nonetheless, according to Klein et al. (2018), gold was a better hedge than bitcoin during market stress, while Al-Yahyaee et al. (2018) proposed that gold, stocks, and cash had higher efficiency than bitcoin. Similar findings were made by Al-Khazali et al. (2018), who discovered that bitcoin was less impacted by surprises than gold, which consistently responded to macroeconomic news surprises in line with its historical function as a safe haven. Taking a broader view, Aggarwal et al. (2018) looked at six asset classes: commodities, real estate, gold, fixed income, equity, and alternative investments. They concluded that bitcoin had significant potential to improve risk-adjusted returns.

Market characteristics became a determining role in the risk-safety aspects of bitcoin. Dorfleitner and Lung (2018) concluded that cryptocurrency was only a safe haven when the market was mature, with positive markets being the only relevant times. According to Bouoiyour et al. (2019), bitcoin was more effective at transferring values, while gold was a superior diversifier. They also claimed that there were clear distinctions between gold and bitcoin in dire circumstances. Wu et al. (2019) developed this idea and further concluded that uncertainty at lower and higher quantiles made bitcoin more unstable. Similarly, Symitsi and Chalvatzis (2019) found that bitcoin showed little return when combined with other assets, and that economic factors like uncertainty surrounding trade policy had a negative effect on bitcoin acceptance. Times of crisis also caused significant co-movements and undulations in bitcoin (Kang et al., 2019). However, the former authors' pre-COVID-19 study period begs the question of whether the risk-adjusted higher return is still relevant.

In order to hedge the bitcoin spot price in the post-COVID-19 period, Zhang et al. (2021) compared gold and bitcoin futures during the COVID-19 phase. They concluded that bitcoin futures were a stronger hedge than conventional gold futures and that there was a strong correlation between bitcoin spot and futures using the VAR-DCC-GARCH and VAR-BEKK-GARCH models. Additionally, they proposed that there was bidirectional volatility spillover between bitcoin futures and spot. In the same spirit, Shehzad et al. (2021) assessed the safe haven qualities of gold over bitcoin. They asserted that throughout the epidemic, gold became the most favored asset in the Asian, US, and European stock markets.

Gold was also mentioned by Parvini et al. (2022) as a more accurate indicator of bitcoin movements from 28 June 2018 to 4 April 2020. In contrast, Chemkha et al. (2021) used the A-DCC model to study the US, UK, Japanese, and European markets. They concluded that gold and bitcoin could be effective hedges during periods of stability and external shocks. Gold had a weak advantage in maintaining safe haven properties, except for the Nikkei 225, while bitcoin could not withstand contingencies. It is interesting to note that Wen et al. (2022) examined the various dimensions of these asset classes and used the TVP-VAR model to suggest that these two assets were better hedging tools before COVID-19, with gold continuing to be a significant hedging tool against stock and oil markets during the early and peak COVID-19 periods while bitcoin lost its prominence. Conversely, Barbu et al. (2022) show a positive association between bitcoin and gold, suggesting that cryptocurrencies were a safe haven during the COVID-19 pandemic, demonstrating the maturity of the cryptocurrency market.

3.4. Bitcoin–Oil and Bitcoin–S&P 500

Fourth, Jareno et al. (2021) established the relationship between oil and cryptocurrency using the NARDL model to explore more unusual commodities. They discovered that, in comparison with the pre-COVID-19 period (20 November 2018 to 28 February 2020), the degree of interconnection between oil price shocks and cryptocurrency returns peaked during the COVID-19 crisis period (2 March to 30 June 2020). With the exception of Tether, every cryptocurrency exhibited a strong positive correlation with oil price demand shocks, a strong negative correlation with oil price risk shocks, and no association with supply side shocks at any point in time.

Results also evinced that throughout the pandemic, cryptocurrency returns were correlated with oil price variations. A related study was conducted by Vukovic et al. (2021) to investigate bitcoin as a hedge against risky investments. With the exception of Tether, which was more stable than other cryptocurrencies, the analysis found that risky assets like the S&P 500 had a direct impact on all cryptocurrencies using OLS and quantile regression estimations. The wavelet coherence analysis verified no contagion effect and poor coherence in crypto pairings, including Tether. As a result, Tether—but not bitcoin—may take the role of gold as a hedging instrument.

These investigations conclude that bitcoin might not be a good hedge against the S&P 500 and oil shocks. The Tether investigation highlights future research prospects, even though it is outside the purview of this publication. Furthermore, research could also be expanded to determine whether the correlations between bitcoin, oil, and the S&P 500 still exist in the present context.

3.5. Gold, Bitcoin, and the Volatility Index (VIX)

The last body of literature involves studies highlighting the different aspects of the gold, bitcoin, and volatility index nexus to demonstrate their multipath interactions. To determine the safe haven qualities of gold and VIX for the US stock market, Matthew and Farooq (2013) used data from November 1995 to November 2010; both gold and

VIX displayed a negative association with the stock market. Compared with gold, VIX displayed a weaker correlation and, thus, better safe haven qualities. Using a GARCH and Exponential GARCH model to assess the pattern of bitcoin volatility, López-Cabarcos et al. (2021) more recently investigated investor sentiments in their study to determine the impact of social network sentiment, the S&P 500, and VIX on bitcoin volatility. The findings showed that investors were knowledgeable about the volatility of bitcoin and that when stock markets were stable, they became more speculative.

Despite being pertinent to the pre-COVID-19 era, Matthew and Farooq's (2013) findings are outdated. To create novel asset-commodity connections, hitherto unheard-of socioeconomic and political shocks must be taken into account. Furthermore, in light of the elevated uncertainties and high VIX, the characteristics of gold and bitcoin must be contrasted.

The empirical review justifies our examination of safe haven assets amidst the pandemic fears, investigating investors' preference for gold in comparison with oil and bitcoin during high and low stock market volatility in the pre- and post-COVID-19 eras. This approach is backed by Markowitz's modern portfolio theory of optimal selection and behavioral theories, where the former focuses on the expected risk–return relationship and the latter attributes herd behavior among investors who make heuristics-based decisions rather than fact-based or rationale-based decisions.

4. Methodology

The paper utilized a qualitative research design to expand the theoretical studies. Few papers have explored the influence of the behavioral aspect on the relationship between the different asset classes/commodities (Peter & Tversky, 1993). There is little guidance about the sample size required for a qualitative study (Hertzog, 2008). Browne (1995) suggested a sample size of 30, while Julious (2005) suggested 12 samples per group as a rule of thumb, and Teare et al. (2014) considered 70 as the acceptable size. The current study conformed with Browne (1995) and adopted 30 as the sample size. The respondents in this study were chosen using convenience sampling techniques. We targeted candidates with CFA or CA qualifications, an MBA in Finance, and/or relevant experience and expertise in economics and finance. The group comprised wealth management experts, bankers, relationship managers, investment advisors, and product specialists in economics and finance.

Semi-structured interviews were conducted in-person and online between Q4 2022 and Q1 2023, each lasting roughly 45 min. Potential subjects received an email inviting them to participate in the study. A consent form with details on the subjects' voluntary involvement, confidentiality, anonymity, and ability to withdraw at any time, as well as information relevant to the goals and objectives of the current research study, were distributed. The corresponding participants received the transcripts to review and comment on the details they had supplied during the interview. This increases the reliability and validity of participatory and collaborative research strategies (Thomas, 2017). We approached 100+ experts and received responses from 30 experts. Building on the work of Jones et al. (2011), we adopted an inductive, evaluation-centered approach to identify inherent themes and subthemes within the dataset. Thematic analysis, a technique grounded in psychology, is acknowledged as a valuable method for "analysing and reporting patterns in data" (Braun & Clarke, 2006), where a theme captures the essential ideas generated from the information analyzed.

The thematic analysis used in this study was based on the analysis of qualitative data described by Braun and Clarke (2006). Qualitative thematic analysis was selected to identify, analyze, and report patterns and themes in the interview data from 30 finance experts about intermarket correlations of gold, oil, and bitcoin. The six steps of the analysis process included familiarization with data, initial coding, searching for themes, reviewing themes, defining and naming themes, and producing the final report. Respondent validation was employed, in which participants were asked to review the accuracy of their individual interview transcripts to enhance the credibility of the thematic analysis. The themes were further corroborated using triangulation with the extant literature on intermarket relationships. Researcher reflexivity was an integral component of the team process, with the research team recording potential biases and assumptions to facilitate a balanced interpretation of the data.

5. Results

5.1. Demographic Profile

Of the respondents, 70% were male, while 30% were female (Table 1). The age groups of the experts were between 25–50, with 66% of the respondents being between 36–45 years. Indian nationals dominated the expert group (67%). Sixty percent of the respondents were either CFA or studying CFA or held dual professional qualifications like CA and CFA. Thirty percent of the respondents belonged to wealth management. The respondent profile showed that the group was dominated by males, mid-career professionals, with most of them in their late 30s to early 40s and with significant experience in the financial and investment sectors. The high proportion of Indian and Arabic nationals suggests a regional dominance, possibly of the demographic of the financial industry in such markets. The high percentage of CFA certification holders, complemented by a high proportion of CA and higher academic degree holders, indicated that the respondents were well-qualified professionals with sound technical background in finance, investment, and wealth management. The fact that they were diversified across industries with a focus in advisory, treasury, and product management roles indicated their role as decision-makers and strategists in financial planning and investment management areas. The availability of CFOs, CIOs, and finance educators also showed a combination of leadership, technical knowledge, and knowledge transfer in the sector.

Table 1. Characteristics of respondents.

Characteristics			
Gender		Value	Percentage
	Male	21	70%
	Female	9	30%
Age Group			
	25–30	5	17%
	30–35	4	13%
	36–40	10	33%
	41–45	9	30%
	45–50	2	7%
Nationality			
	Indian	20	67%
	Arabic	6	20%
	British	2	7%
	Canadian	1	3%
	Chinese	1	3%

Table 1. *Cont.*

Characteristics			
Education *			
	CFA	11	37%
	CA	3	10%
	CA and CFA	3	10%
	CFA L2	4	13%
	Masters	6	20%
	Graduate	2	7%
	PhD	1	3%
Sector			
	Wealth Management Investment Advisory	9	30%
	Treasury and Forex Analyst	5	17%
	Wealth Management Product Managers	4	13%
	Wealth Management Sales	3	10%
	Business Manager	3	10%
	Educationalist related to Finance	3	10%
	Group Reporting Analyst	1	3%
	Wealth Management Chief Investment Officer	1	3%
	Chief Financial Officer	1	3%

* Many of the respondents held multiple qualifications, and the highest education or related professional education was selected. Source: Authors' own work.

5.2. Interview Findings

The audio recordings of the interviews were transcribed, and the transcripts were reviewed several times to familiarize with the data. This was followed by separate coding processes. Key extracts were highlighted using NVivo software (version 12) for qualitative analysis and then coded descriptively. The codes included "safe haven", "portfolio diversification", "high volatility impact", and "post-COVID shifts". The coding was iterative, with new codes developed as patterns were identified in the data. Figure 1 below shows the word cloud generated from the analysis.

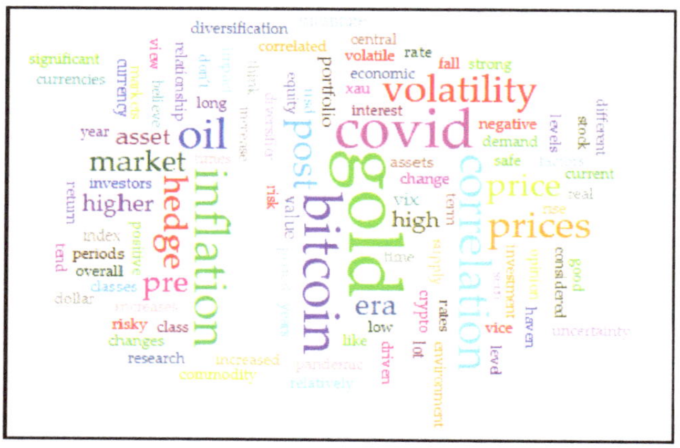

Figure 1. Thematic analysis word cloud.

Following the analysis, key themes that corresponded closely with the study's focus were identified and described in the findings section. The following were identified as the key themes and subthemes:

a. Gold as a safe haven and hedge;
b. Bitcoin's role in portfolios;
c. Intermarket relationships;
d. Volatility dynamics.

The correlations between these core themes and subthemes emerging from the analysis are illustrated in a mind map (Figure 2).

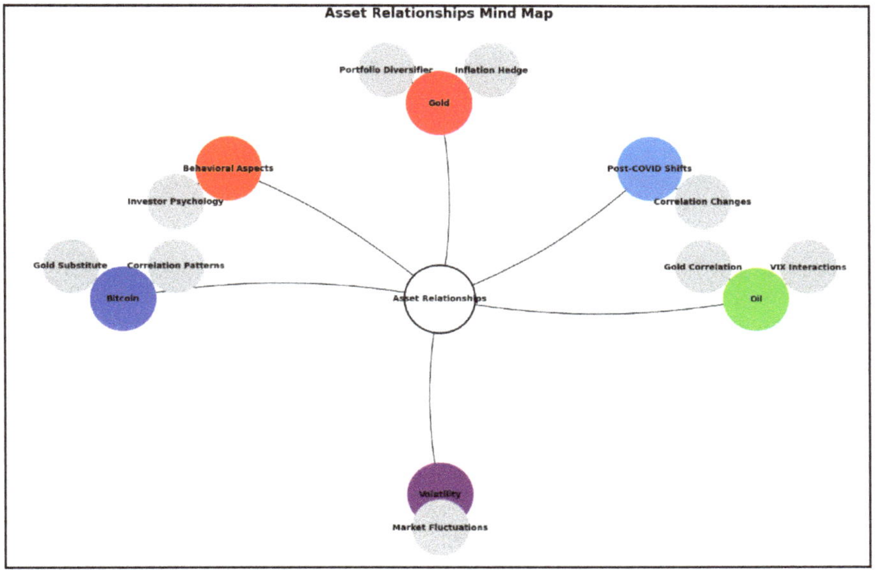

Figure 2. Mind map of asset relationships.

5.3. Analysis of Themes

5.3.1. Gold as a Safe Haven and Hedge

Out of 30 interviewees, 19 experts claimed that gold was a portfolio diversifier, with one expert disagreeing with the majority by stating that the asset had no intrinsic value or cash flow. Hence, it could not be considered a diversifier. Most experts opined gold as a safe haven investment that hedged geopolitical risks and weathered extreme market fluctuations but exhibited high volatility. Moreover, its negative correlation with the USD was an important diversification against the USD as a currency not only to investors but also to central banks.

For example, Expert 1 mentioned that historically, gold had been a hedge when the VIX increased due to volatility. However, this commodity was driven by sentiment and had no industrial use. In the medium-term, gold was a strong diversifying asset class but its correlation with traditional assets increased with time, especially with the emergence of other alternative options. Expert 7 identified that participation in gold diversification could be broadly in two forms: through gold shares and bullion. However, depending on the choice of diversification, gold could be an erratic diversifier. The volatility levels of gold shares were far higher than other assets, while gold bullion risked being stagnant with no gains to be made for long periods of time. For example, gold shares were stable for

15 years from 1986 until approximately 2000–2001, then grew eight-fold in the following 10 years. They grew by a further 40% in a month during the COVID-19 pandemic in 2020.

Therefore, depending on the market crisis and the extent of the downturn (with other possible safe havens also not yielding much), gold could be a relevant store of wealth. For instance, during COVID-19, the S&P 500 dropped by 34% in a month. Market players switched from riskier options, like stocks and emerging currencies, to assets typically considered safe havens, like precious metals, in this atmosphere of widespread fear and uncertainty. The reliance structure between the many assets that make up a portfolio was the most important component of a diversification strategy. Because gold and stock markets have an inverse relationship, investors could lower their overall risk exposure because possible losses in stocks could be offset by gains in gold, or at the very least, the effect of the losses could be lessened.

Gold was an excellent diversifier during the 2008 global financial crisis (GFC) because there was a severe market downturn, with most assets in the negative, and even alternate sources that might typically be considered safe havens also yielding low or zero returns due to the drastic cut in interest rates by the US Federal Bank. However, during times when other safe haven assets (e.g., US Treasuries) start to offer yield or income, gold could lose its diversifier impact because gold is an asset that does not yield any income, unlike Bonds or Treasuries. If, within a portfolio of equities and bonds, equity shares of gold companies rather than gold bullion were used (approximately 10% of the portfolio), then the portfolio showed better outcomes in terms of returns. However, higher returns came with a higher risk as well.

With respect to gold as an inflation hedge, 16 out of the 30 experts pointed out that gold had lost its value as an inflation hedge, with a few experts stating that gold might remain an inflation hedge against low and stable inflation under "normal" market conditions. For example, Expert 10 mentioned that "inflation over 2012–2019 averaged at under the 2% target whereas XAU (gold) saw a 45% swing from high to low and ended that period 15% down from its 2012 high. With inflation albeit low but positive during the period and XAU depreciating in USD value, it cannot be argued that XAU was an inflationary hedge over the whole period between 2012 to 2019. Looking more minutely, from 2015 to July 2016, however, inflation went from 0% to around 1.5% while XAU sharply appreciated 31.11%, giving a net appreciation in USD value ~28.6%".

To elaborate further, if we looked at the correlation between the XAU and inflation, they clearly tracked each other. As inflation rose, the XAU rose in value with the XAU percentage increases being greater than that of inflation. Thus, it can be argued that the XAU is a valid hedge against inflation although this depended on inflation stability and the market condition. However, if there was an exogenous shock in the economy in the form of extremely loose monetary policies or a large fiscal response, gold would lose its value to the USD or USD-denominated assets like the US Treasury. Also, during different time periods, the price change of gold did not necessarily match the change in inflation; hence, it is difficult to call gold a complete inflation hedge. Some of the experts pointed out that during lockdown and post-COVID-19, especially during geopolitical tensions such as the Russia–Ukraine war, governments had settled expensive energy prices in USD. Thus, the USD acted as a better inflation hedge than gold or any other commodities. Expert 23 opined that two factors held back a rise in the gold price. First, because gold did not pay interest, during inflation, consumer product price increases affected the disposable income of the household. Thus, consumers wanted their investments to provide returns periodically to meet the price increase. During inflation, the bond yield increased; for example, the current 10-year yield rate is 3.50%, which increased from 1.5% between 2021 and 2022. Thus, investors would incur an opportunity cost if they held onto gold compared with 10-year bonds. Second, the USD had appreciated rapidly and had reached its highest point in two decades. Because the gold price was also quoted in USD, it was more expensive for foreign investors who used currencies other than USD to invest in gold. During inflation, the adverse impact of the USD strengthening was further magnified. Therefore, gold tended to perform poorly when the USD strengthened.

5.3.2. Bitcoin's Role in Portfolios

Out of 30 interviewees, 24 categorically rejected bitcoin as a substitute for gold in terms of an inflation hedge or portfolio diversifier. Expert 3 elaborated that, pre-COVID-19, bitcoin had the potential to be a substitute for gold in the portfolios due to the simplicity of holding and buying it. It was mainly adopted by the millennial generation rather than by other investors and traders due to a lack of regulations and high uncertainty. However, post-COVID-19, the significant drop in bitcoin value showed the poor hedging and diversification properties of bitcoin. Expert 3 also highlighted that bitcoin had other limiting factors, such as no intrinsic value, a high correlation with the technology sector, higher volatility, relatively less historical track record, and regulatory nonacceptance. The rise of bitcoin is probably noteworthy for the three years from 2017 when the Chicago Mercantile Exchange (CME) announced that it would launch bitcoin futures, and there were many more advocates of cryptocurrencies. With prolonged shutdowns and several rounds of government economic stimulus payouts, the COVID-19 epidemic in 2020 left many people with extra cash and free time, which contributed to a late 2020 spike in bitcoin values.

There was one strong voice in support of cryptocurrency. Expert 11 elaborated that they thought bitcoin would emerge as a substitute for gold due to factors such as: (a) gold storage versus bitcoin network security. The bitcoin network, by design, is very secure and cannot be easily hacked. It requires substantial computing power to perform a 51% network attack, which may indeed be impossible. The cost to store bitcoin is very cheap. In contrast, gold is a safe haven asset that has to be stored in a secure location, and this incurs a cost; (b) transferability: bitcoin can be transferred more easily than gold; (c) scarcity: the total production of bitcoin is fixed, and it is not abundant like gold. While bitcoin may be driven by speculation today, as adoption and regulation increase, it will continue to gain an allocation within investment portfolios as an asset class. Bitcoin may become a valuable addition as a diversifier and inflation hedge once regulatory acceptance increases.

Expert 23 mentioned that bitcoin was meant to work well as an inflation hedge only when the inflation was caused by monetary policy inflation, i.e., when a central bank reduced the interest rates to increase the liquidity in the market, which in turn increased people's spending power. When inflation was caused by other reasons, such as the current economic environment due to war, energy crises, and food supply shortages like wheat because of sanctions imposed on Russia, and the Federal Reserve rapidly increased interest rates to tighten monetary policy, there was a sense of fear within the public that the economy may be heading towards recession. During these times, people reflected a flight to safety behavior and invested in safe assets such as government bonds rather than volatile assets such as bitcoin.

5.3.3. Intermarket Relationships

Correlation of Gold and Bitcoin, Pre- and Post-COVID-19

Out of 30 interviewees, 19 experts found no or a weak correlation between gold and bitcoin. They based their opinions on Horstmeyer and Kowalski (2022), which observations on bitcoin–gold associations (see Table 2 below). In contrast, five experts found a positive correlation between the assets, and two experts reported negative correlations. Expert

4 elaborated that bitcoin was not a diversifier against equities because both were highly correlated. Gold offered diversification over the long term. Bitcoin and gold had less correlation with each other. Therefore, in the case of equity being sold off, bitcoin might also be sold off, and gold might help diversify, both only in normal times. In situations like COVID-19 or a financial crisis, diversification might not work. Expert 7 reported a slight positive connection of 0.057 between bitcoin and gold amid an upswing in the stock market. The correlation only marginally increased to 0.064 during a stock market meltdown. As a result, the correlation between gold and bitcoin was nearly zero regardless of the status of the equities markets.

Table 2. Crash correlations: bitcoin and gold. Source: (Horstmeyer & Kowalski, 2022).

	Correlations
First Crash: 26 January–7 February 2018	−0.194
Second Crash: 21 September–28 December 2018	0.107
Third Crash: 6 May–6 June 2019	0.277
Fourth Crash: 20 February–28 March 2020	0.275
Fifth Crash: 1 January–11 March 2022	−0.179
Average Correlation during Crashes	0.057
Average Correlation Outside of Crashes	0.064

According to Expert 20, the correlation was purely based on press coverage on gold, the USD, bitcoin, and government adaptation of cryptocurrencies. At times, gold and bitcoin have shown correlation and similar price movements. During highly volatile market movements different speculation can arise around the safety of the major developed market currencies in terms of their real value vs. a basket of goods.

Correlation of Gold and Oil, Pre- and Post-COVID-19

Of 30 interviewees, 18 experts commented on the positive correlation between gold and oil. The experts pointed out some crucial commonalities like both assets being priced in USD and correlated with geopolitical concerns. However, many of them observed that the strong positive correlation of the assets pre-COVID-19 changed to a negative correlation during COVID-19 and a weak positive correlation post-COVID-19. Expert 12 commented that there was a positive correlation between gold and oil in the long run, which broadly stayed true in the pre-COVID-19 era. The post-COVID-19 era has been more driven by oil from a demand and supply disruption perspective, with oil coming back very sharply due to the demand bump and supply constraints while gold had experienced a bounded range. The correlation has declined in the post-COVID-19 world. According to Expert 16, the moderately positive pre-COVID-19 correlation (range 0.40–0.48) between gold and oil changed to a weak positive correlation (range 0.19–0.22). Because gold is normally considered a safe haven in volatile times, in the COVID-19 times the gold price rose above 2000 levels while the oil price dropped due to an increase in oil supply and lower demand in the contracted COVID-19 economy. This reduced the overall correlation between gold and oil, which historically was moderately strong.

In contrast, two experts reported a negative correlation between gold and oil, and eight experts found no correlation or no consistent correlation because of the different nature of the two assets. Expert 15 stated that the oil price was more a function of geopolitics and speculation (price driven by traders) than pure demand and supply. OPEC+ largely controls the oil price by adjusting the production levels; this adjustment is not entirely based on demand and supply but also on geopolitics. Gold, in contrast, is a demand and supply-driven price. For example, the XAUUSD rises when central bankers accumulate gold or when the festive season occurs in countries like India. The XAUUSD is also sensitive to US Treasury yields and the USD strength. Higher US Treasury yields lead to a fall in the XAUUSD price because the XAUUSD is a non-income-yielding asset. Therefore, Expert 15 did not think there was a meaningful correlation between the XAUUSD and oil. Similarly, Expert 28 stated that the correlation between gold and oil historically was complex, with fluctuations in the price of one asset sometimes affecting the price of the other. During the pre-COVID-19 era, from 2012 to 2019, the correlation between gold and oil was relatively low, suggesting that they were not strongly linked. However, in the post-COVID-19 era, from 2020 to the present, the correlation between gold and oil increased somewhat, likely due to the economic uncertainty brought on by the pandemic. It is important to note that the correlation may change depending on market conditions and geopolitical events.

Correlation of Bitcoin and Oil, Pre- and Post-COVID-19

Out of 30 interviewees, 15 experts found no correlation between bitcoin and oil. Although both prices are driven by demand and supply, bitcoin is more speculative. Oil, however, reflects the economic outlook, and there was no difference between pre-COVID-19 and post-COVID-19. Bitcoin is a software code, while oil requires physical production. These asset classes are attractive to different investors and traders, and it is unlikely that any correlation will be seen unless there is a major move on the USD because both assets are priced against the dollar. Bitcoin was a hedge that could help reduce crude oil's portfolio risk. However, post-pandemic, the correlation has come under question. Moreover, Expert 7 opined if individuals had more money, they would invest more in bitcoin. As a result, while oil and gas costs may not directly affect bitcoin prices, the cryptocurrency would likely increase or fall less if consumers did not have to spend more on necessities.

In contrast, 10 experts found a positive correlation between bitcoin and oil. It may be possible in the post-COVID-19 era to see oil being priced and paid for in bitcoin, which will have a direct impact on the oil–bitcoin correlation. As explained by Expert 12, a positive correlation between oil and bitcoin is visible in the long run, thus revealing their volatility. Post-COVID-19, the correlation has been reduced because bitcoin has shown a higher correlation with risky equity-like tech/semiconductors/commercial services, while oil has been data and demand-driven. Some of the correlation metrics may revert once the supply issues are normalized. According to Expert 16, there was a negative correlation between bitcoin and oil in pre-COVID-19 times in the range of −0.19 to 0.18. However, the correlation increased to +0.47–0.50 levels during the COVID-19 and post-COVID-19 era.

Nevertheless, Expert 26 mentioned that the correlation between bitcoin and oil in the pre-COVID-19 era was lower, at approximately 0.20, and it would have gone higher to approximately 0.40 in the post-COVID-19 era. Similar views were echoed by Expert 28, who said that, during the pre-COVID-19 era, from 2012 to 2019, the correlation between bitcoin and oil was relatively low, suggesting that they were not strongly linked. However, in the post-COVID-19 era, from 2020 to the present, the correlation increased somewhat, likely due to the economic uncertainty brought on by the pandemic. It is important to note that the correlation may change depending on market conditions and investor preferences.

5.3.4. Volatility Dynamics

Correlation of Gold and the Volatility Index (VIX), Pre- and Post-COVID

Eighteen interviewees out of thirty agreed on the positive correlation between gold and the VIX. During COVID-19, between February to June 2020, the VIX was very high. Similarly, the price movement of gold was also high because the gold price followed an upward trend during periods of uncertainty for equity. When the VIX is relatively low, the fluctuation of the gold price tends to be relatively lower or stable. The fluctuation of the gold price also depends on many other factors like inflation, the interest rate level and the USD. During pre-COVID-19, gold was considered a safe haven, and prices were assumed to spike during high volatility. During and after the pandemic, many central banks reassessed their economic prospects and increased their allocation towards gold as a safe haven asset, including gold as a reserve holding. This reiterates the reported correlation between gold and volatility. However, the VIX was much higher post-COVID-19 due to various events and geopolitical crises. Expert 7 clarified that during periods of significant market volatility, there could be strong correlations between gold and the VIX. Gold typically appreciates after a major market downturn, such as the 2008 GFC, because it is a safe asset. Because it offers a safety net against risk, investors frequently seek refuge in non-yield-bearing gold during market downturns. Although the relationship between gold and the VIX may not always be stable in times of severe uncertainty, historically, the two have been in sync. When price volatility increases, gold often performs better than US stocks. The gold:S&P 500 ratio tends to rise in tandem with each market shock. Conversely, a low volatility regime is typically linked to gold's poor performance (relative to stocks). During the COVID-19 crisis, there was a significant co-movement between the two-time series. In Q1 2020, gold prices increased by 3.6% while US stocks fell by 20% (the S&P 500 fell 35% from peak to trough during that time).

Interestingly, the relationship does not seem to have changed between VIX and gold, post-COVID-19 compared with the COVID-19 era. As identified by Expert 28, gold has historically been seen as a safe haven asset, with its price tending to rise during economic volatility and uncertainty. During the pre-COVID-19 era, from 2012 to 2019, the gold price tended to rise during periods of high market volatility, suggesting that it was seen as a safe haven asset during such times. However, in the post-COVID-19 era, from 2020 to the present, gold's price movements have been more complex, with both increases and decreases in price occurring during periods of high volatility. It is important to note that the relationship between the gold price and volatility may change depending on market conditions and individual investor preferences.

Ten interviewees out of thirty expressed a different opinion to the majority. Most of these experts reported a negative correlation, and a few found no correlation in the long run. According to the experts, all assets have a separate volatility. In fact, other risk assets showed more volatility compared with gold when the VIX was high. The gold price was inversely correlated with the VIX. If volatility was high, then liquidity flowed out from risky assets and moved to safer haven assets like gold. However, it was vital to watch the movement of the USD against its peers because gold exhibited the strongest positive correlation with the USD. If risk-off sentiments triggered asset flows into USD, then gold would most likely see a fall and vice versa. According to Expert 16, the gold price showed some volatility during higher VIX periods. For example, during the COVID-19 period, when the VIX was highest from February to June 2020, the gold price went down to 1470 and up to 2000 in August 2022. Pre-COVID-19, when the VIX was high in 2017, the gold price did not show much volatility. Bitcoin is being traded as a risky asset and has a high positive correlation with other risky assets. Risky assets tend to have a high negative correlation with the VIX, and that correlation tends to be higher under a higher volatility regime. However, as bitcoin emerges as a substitute for gold, we would expect to see a positive correlation with volatility rather than a negative correlation.

Correlation of Bitcoin and the Volatility Index (VIX), Pre- and Post-COVID

Fifteen experts out of thirty interviewees agreed that the bitcoin price went down when the VIX was higher, which meant that the assets showed a negative correlation.

Bitcoin does not have an intrinsic value, and when the equity uncertain level or VIX is higher, investors tend to sell off risky assets, including bitcoin. There was no change in this relationship for pre- or post-COVID-19. Post-COVID-19, bitcoin, a risky asset, has been highly correlated with riskier assets. Also, as a substitute for gold, investors would expect to see a positive correlation with volatility than a negative correlation. Also, post-COVID-19, the volatility is higher. Therefore, the change in prices across different asset classes is stronger. It should be noted that this relationship is not only due to COVID-19 but also to events like current geopolitical crises, which increase volatility. The event type determines the price change. As stated by Expert 23, bitcoin reached a new high during 2021 and 2022, while the VIX reached a new low during those years. In 2018, when the VIX started to rise, bitcoin fell. The VIX generally performs well when the markets start to fall, and when markets fall, bitcoin also falls because bitcoin is an expensive investment. During a market fall, people have money constraints, and thus do not invest in bitcoin, which drives prices down. Therefore, bitcoin falls when the VIX rises and vice versa.

Three experts found no or low correlation between these assets. Bitcoin has a volatility of its own, which is exacerbated by overall equity market volatility. However, it did not follow a pattern similar to that of the VIX over the coverage period. A number of factors determine bitcoin volatility, such as demand and supply, the financial market, market sentiment, macroeconomic conditions, and the bitcoin environment. The speculation about price changes has played a major role in bitcoin's value at any given moment, causing a rise in commodity market value.

Correlation of Oil and the Volatility Index (VIX), Pre- and Post-COVID-19

Fifteen experts out of thirty interviewees concluded there was a negative correlation between oil and the VIX. Many factors impact the oil price, for example, oil supply and demand, and political stability or instability (because oil producers are highly concentrated in a few countries in the world). When the volatility level is higher, the economic outlook is expected to be uncertain. The volatility in the post-COVID-19 era is even higher than in the pre-COVID-19 period due to the unpredictable demand patterns of the oil. Lockdowns and COVID-19 spikes across the bigger economies had a direct bearing on demand. Geopolitical concerns and war have added to the volatility in the demand and price. Experts have also indicated a negative oil price under high VIX during the COVID-19 period due to higher supply, lack of demand and storage capabilities. Post-COVID-19, with the emergence of close substitutes such as nuclear power, solar power, ethanol, and wind power, demand for oil in the commodity market has dropped. This was highlighted by Expert 27 who stated that oil prices were notoriously volatile, and there was a well-established relationship between oil prices and market volatility. Oil prices tend to be more volatile during high volatility and vice versa. During the pre-COVID-19 era, oil prices were positively correlated with market volatility. This was largely due to the significant supply disruptions and geopolitical tensions that drove oil prices higher. However, the COVID-19 pandemic caused a sharp drop in oil prices as demand for oil plummeted due to the economic slowdown. Since then, oil prices have rebounded somewhat, but the future relationship between oil prices and volatility remains unclear. There are concerns that the ongoing pandemic and the increasing shift towards renewable energy sources could further dampen demand for oil and make it a less reliable hedge against market volatility.

Five experts reported positive correlations. One important fact, suggested by Expert 14, was an inverse correlation in the VIX and oil price in general but with idiosyncratic factors (like the present Ukraine–Russia conflict) temporarily resulting in a positive correlation between the two. As stated by Expert 7, the relationship between the two is multifaceted. Regardless of the price connection, one cannot ignore the positive relationship between oil and stock market volatility. The OVX is the equivalent of the VIX for oil markets, and the two have tended to move in lockstep. The relationship between oil and stock price volatility was relatively stable during the 2008 GFC period, possibly because it was restricted to the financial markets. Prior to 2020, the most extreme levels for this measure were during the OPEC price war that started in November 2014. Looking at market volatility during that time, we know this was more of an oil crisis. In and post-2020, it seemed that oil might be responsible for the volatility that investors saw throughout asset markets after the initial COVID-19 period. As long as oil volatility remains high, there will be a flow to the many asset classes tied to oil prices. Many high-yield bonds are energy-related, issued by US companies that could struggle at these low-price levels. Stock portfolios following a classic value sector approach will usually be tilted toward energy stocks. In many cases, a multi-asset portfolio with asset classes or even direct commodity investments must calibrate volatility exposures in an extremely difficult environment.

Three experts found no correlation between oil and the VIX. Oil is an inelastic essential whose price is mostly supply-side driven. As a tool for hedging purposes, the returns skew to the left-over time. Given the substantial influence of OPEC on oil prices, it is not an asset whose price is determined by the market.

In summary, Figure 3 below visualizes the relative frequency of key terms—oil, inflation, gold, COVID, and bitcoin—across ten document segments from an expert interview schedule analysis. The segments are divisions within the text used to track topic frequency variations over sections of the documents. The trends show varying focus on these topics over the segments. For instance, oil (blue line) sees a peak in the later segments (around segments 8–9), while inflation (green) demonstrates more activity early on and again in the middle. Gold (light green) shows peaks at segments 4 and 8, while COVID-19 (pink) has consistent moderate relevance across segments. Bitcoin (purple) fluctuates, with notable spikes in segments 5 and 9. These variations indicate shifting topical emphasis within the analyzed interviews.

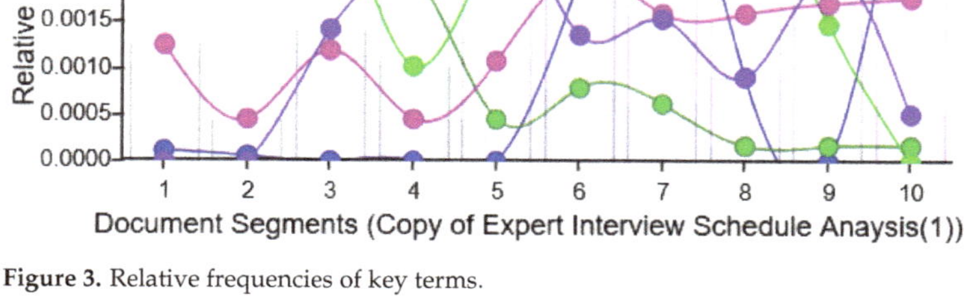

Figure 3. Relative frequencies of key terms.

6. Discussion

Using the VIX, the current study aimed to identify the intermarket relationships among the gold, bitcoin, and oil markets under different scenarios (e.g., before, during, and after recent economic shocks such as COVID-19 and the war between Ukraine and Russia). Gold, oil, and bitcoin are major portfolio assets but their roles as hedgers and diversifiers have changed in recent times because of global events. Therefore, the research contributes to a clearer understanding of the characteristics of different asset classes in different market conditions or entropy levels (Lahmiri & Bekiros, 2020). Importantly, it compares and contrasts the findings of empirical studies with expert opinion. The behavioral aspects of investment and portfolio management may have a significant role in defining the performance of different asset classes, as identified by behavioral finance theory (Peter & Tversky, 1993) and deciphering the relevant information (Information theory, Shannon, 1948) for the informed decision-making process.

Previous quantitative studies and the experts in the qualitative study both generally concurred that gold was a portfolio diversifier and safe haven asset of the class commodities before and after the COVID-19 pandemic (e.g., Ciner et al., 2013; Jiang et al., 2022; Salisu et al., 2020; Wen et al., 2022). Gold was strongly favored in times of high uncertainty (Das et al., 2020) and was an effective hedge against volatility in bitcoin (Bouoiyour et al., 2019; Klein et al., 2018) and in oil prices during and after the pandemic. A few experts stated that gold was not as effective a hedge as the USD or Federal bonds in times of high inflation because it did not pay interest. Both types of study generally agreed on the positive correlation between gold and oil before the pandemic but found a reversal in this relationship during the pandemic. For example, Huang and Wu (2021) and Benlagha and El Omari (2022) found an inverse relationship with negative shocks in the oil market leading to positive effects on the gold price during the COVID-19 pandemic, where the gold price reached a high of USD 2075 per ounce while oil prices were low and even negative (Chiaramonti & Maniatis, 2020). However, Tanin et al. (2022) studied the oil–gold nexus pre- and post-COVID-19 in five leading stock markets and found that oil prices could not predict gold prices.

As an example of cryptocurrency assets, the role of bitcoin showed some strong variations when comparing its pre- and post-COVID-19 status. Most experts in the qualitative study and recent empirical studies rejected bitcoin as a better substitute for gold as a diversifier. It was viewed as a risky asset, which meant that it tended to have a negative correlation with the VIX and, hence, a negative or no correlation with the gold price. In a bull market, bitcoin tended to do well, as identified by López-Cabarcos et al. (2021). Their study reported that investors were aware of bitcoin volatility, which became more speculative in stable stock markets. Expert opinion was somewhat divided on this asset. A substantial minority saw bitcoin as a niche asset less attractive to mainstream investors and traders because of its high uncertainty and lack of intrinsic value. The significant drop in bitcoin value post-COVID-19 showed its poor hedging and diversification properties. Generally, most experts reported little or no correlation between bitcoin and oil. However, the relationship between bitcoin and oil changed between pre- and post-COVID-19 times, and a higher correlation was found post-COVID-19 (Jareno et al., 2021). Yin et al. (2021) examined the oil market–crypto nexus and reported that oil price undulations were precursors of uncertainties in the crypto market.

In summary, both the empirical studies and experts in the qualitative study supported Markowitz's portfolio theory of optimal selection and behavioral theories. The change in portfolio share from bitcoin to gold during times of high risk reflected the expected risk–return relationship shown by portfolio theory as well as herd behavior among investors who made heuristic rather than fact-based or rationale-based decisions, according to the volatility of the stock market in the pre- and post-COVID-19 era.

7. Conclusions, Limitations, Implications, and Recommendations

This study used a qualitative study of 30 experts in the finance and economics fields, but this approach has certain strengths and limitations. A qualitative study is an initial step for exploring a concept. It is useful to identify the feasibility and clarify potential amendments in the design; however, it cannot be used for hypothesis testing (Leon et al., 2011).

The strength of our study also led to limitations because the work was based on expert opinion, and hence was not free from expert bias. Moreover, the generalizability of convenience sampling is limited because it tends to produce a non-representative sample, hence leading to selection bias and reduced diversity. This limits the generalizability of findings to a larger population and can threaten external validity. Researchers can diversify participant recruitment strategies, increase sample size, use stratified sampling, and include multiple data sources to enhance the generalizability of findings and capture various subgroups within the population for more balanced insights. Future studies can highlight the significance of other asset classes to provide a more comprehensive picture. Although there are many other asset classes like Central Bank Interest Rate, Developed Markets Investment Grade Bonds Indices, and Credit Default Swap (CDS) that may be incorporated in future studies, those asset/classes are beyond the scope of the current paper. Assets like US Treasury bonds, the USD Index, and Developed Market Property Indices may also be explored in the future studies. Future studies can employ quantitative analysis and compare the actual results with the current qualitative study to arrive at more holistic conclusions.

It is also recommended to incorporate longitudinal studies that can determine the stability of the correlations that have been observed between gold, oil, and bitcoin over different time horizons and investigate how macroeconomic shocks, such as geopolitical crises or monetary policy shifts, affect these correlations. Researching market sentiment and behavioral finance can also provide useful insights into how investor speculations, social media influences, and cognitive biases affect the intermarket relationships under both high- and low-volatility regimes. The application of artificial intelligence and machine learning-based models can enhance the accuracy of volatility spillover prediction and dynamic correlations and make it easier to compare conventional econometric models with deep learning models. In addition, analysis of regional and sectoral differences can detect heterogeneity across emerging and developed markets in these intermarket relationships as well as industry-specific effects, especially in energy-intensive industries. Lastly, the effects of regulatory policies, including central bank interventions and cryptocurrency regulations, must be considered to determine their contribution to the safe-haven quality of bitcoin and gold and broader implications for portfolio management and risk management strategies. The methodology could also be strengthened by involving respondents with asset management experience and varied positions within finance. Investment managers, traders, and other finance practitioners often have special vantage views of the world due to their roles. They could offer a more holistic vision of the assets being researched.

The results have widespread implications for portfolio managers who adopt dynamic adaptive investment strategies by maintaining a robust allocation of gold, particularly during periods of geopolitical tension/economic instability. This is because gold has retained its position as a safe-haven asset that can mitigate portfolio risk and preserve value during market downturns. Moreover, given bitcoin's diminishing role as an inflation hedge due to its volatile risk–return profile, investors should be cautious about its proportion held in their portfolios as this approach can optimize portfolio resilience while potentially improving risk-adjusted returns. In contrast, investors should be cognizant that while gold exhibits relatively lower volatility and ensures stable long-term returns during periods of economic uncertainty, bitcoin, with its high volatility, may serve as a high-risk, high-return component. However, the degree of its inclusion should be balanced with the investor's risk tolerance and investment horizon to avoid unwanted exposure to market turbulence.

Author Contributions: Conceptualization, S.S.B.; methodology, R.P. and S.S.B.; software, S.S.B.; validation, S.S.B., R.P. and M.I.T.; formal analysis, S.S.B. and R.P.; investigation, S.S.B., R.P., M.I.T. and M.S.M.A.-A.; resources, S.S.B., R.P., M.I.T. and M.S.M.A.-A.; data curation, S.S.B. and R.P.; writing-original draft preparation, S.S.B. and R.P.; writing—review and editing, S.S.B., R.P., M.I.T. and M.S.M.A.-A.; visualization, S.S.B. and R.P.; supervision, M.I.T. and M.S.M.A.-A.; project administration, S.S.B., M.I.T. and M.S.M.A.-A. All authors have read and agreed to the published version of the manuscript.

Funding: This research received no external funding.

Informed Consent Statement: Informed consent was obtained from all subjects involved in the study.

Data Availability Statement: The data presented in this study are available on request from the corresponding author.

Conflicts of Interest: The authors declare no conflict of interest.

Notes

1 There are many oil classifications used globally; however, West Texas Intermediate (WTI) crude and Bent crude are the largest global indicators. Brent is drilled in the North Sea and controlled by the UK and Norway, while WTI is extracted in the US.

2 The CBOE VIX for the CBOE S&P 100 Index (OEX) option pricing was accommodated and customized by the Chicago Board Options Exchange on 19 January 1993 (Osterrieder et al., 2019). In 2003, Goldman Sachs worked with the CBOE VIX to modify it. The CBOE S&P 500 Index (SPX) replaced the underlying CBOE S&P 100 Index (OEX).

References

Aggarwal, S., Santosh, M., & Bedi, P. (2018). Bitcoin and portfolio diversification: Evidence from India. In A. Kar, S. Sinha, & M. Gupta (Eds.), *Digital India. Advances in theory and practice of emerging markets* (pp. 99–115). Springer. [CrossRef]

Al-Khazali, O., Bouri, E., & Roubaud, D. (2018). The impact of positive and negative macroeconomic news surprises: Gold versus Bitcoin. *Economic Bulletin*, *38*(1), 373–382.

Al-Yahyaee, K. H., Mensi, W., & Yoon, S. M. (2018). Efficiency, multifractality, and the long-memory property of the Bitcoin market: A comparative analysis with stock, currency, and gold markets. *Finance Research Letters*, *27*, 228–234. [CrossRef]

Artigas, J. C. (2010). Rediscovering gold as an asset class. *Journal of Indexes*, *13*(6), 26–33. Available online: https://www.etf.com/docs/magazine/2/2010_176.png?iu=1#page=27 (accessed on 22 October 2022).

Barber, B., & Odean, T. (1999). Do investors trade too much. *American Economic Review*, *89*(5), 262. Available online: https://www.safalniveshak.com/wp-content/uploads/2012/07/Why-Do-Investors-Trade-Too-Much.png (accessed on 12 March 2023).

Barbu, T. C., Boitan, I. A., & Cepoi, C. O. (2022). Are cryptocurrencies safe havens during the COVID-19 pandemic? A threshold regression perspective with pandemic-related benchmarks. *Economics and Business Review*, *8*(2), 29–49. [CrossRef]

Baur, D. G., & Lucey, B. M. (2010). Is gold a hedge or a safe haven? An analysis of stocks, bonds and gold. *Financial Review*, *45*, 217–229. [CrossRef]

Benlagha, N., & El Omari, S. (2022). Connectedness of stock markets with gold and oil: New evidence from COVID-19 pandemic. *Finance Research Letters*, *46*(B), 102373. [CrossRef]

Bouoiyour, J., Selmi, R., & Wohar, M. (2019). Bitcoin: Competitor or complement to gold? *Economics Bulletin*, *39*(1), 186–191. Available online: https://hal.science/hal-01994187v1/document (accessed on 11 November 2023).

Braun, V., & Clarke, V. (2006). Using thematic analysis in psychology. *Qualitative Research in Psychology*, *3*(2), 77–101. [CrossRef]

Browne, R. H. (1995). On the use of a pilot sample for sample size determination. *Statistics in Medicine*, *14*(17), 1933–1940. [CrossRef]

Caporale, G. M., Gil-Alana, L., & Plastun, A. (2018). Persistence in the cryptocurrency market. *Research in International Business and Finance*, *46*, 141–48. [CrossRef]

Carr, P. (2017). Why is VIX a fear gauge? *Risk and Decision Analysis*, *6*(2), 179–185. [CrossRef]

Chandra, A., & Thenmozhi, M. (2017). Behavioural asset pricing: Review and synthesis. *Journal of Interdisciplinary Economics*, *29*(1), 1–31. [CrossRef]

Chemkha, R., BenSaïda, A., Ghorbel, A., & Tayachi, T. (2021). Hedge and safe haven properties during COVID-19: Evidence from bitcoin and gold. *The Quarterly Review of Economics and Finance*, *82*, 71–85. [CrossRef] [PubMed]

Chen, J. (2004). Generalized entropy theory of information and market patterns. *Corporate Finance Review*, *9*(3), 21–32. Available online: https://web.unbc.ca/~chenj/papers/GETI.png (accessed on 15 April 2022).

Chiaramonti, D., & Maniatis, K. (2020). Security of supply, strategic storage and COVID-19: Which lessons learnt for renewable and recycled carbon fuels, and their future role in decarbonizing transport. *Applied Energy*, *271*, 115216. [CrossRef]

Chohan, U. W. (2022, February 5). *A history of bitcoin*. Available online: https://ssrn.com/abstract=3047875 (accessed on 29 December 2022).

Ciner, C., Gurdgiev, C., & Lucey, B. M. (2013). Hedges and safe havens: An examination of stocks, bonds, gold, oil, and exchange rates. *International Review of Financial Analysis, 29*, 202–211. [CrossRef]

Das, D., Le Roux, C. L., Jana, R. K., & Dutta, A. (2020). Does bitcoin hedge crude oil implied volatility and structural shocks? A comparison with gold, commodity and the US dollar. *Finance Research Letters, 36*, 101335. [CrossRef]

Dorfleitner, G., & Lung, C. (2018). Cryptocurrencies from the perspective of euro investors: A re-examination of diversification benefits and a new day-of-the-week effect. *Journal of Asset Management, 19*, 472–494. [CrossRef]

Dyhrberg, A. H. (2016). Bitcoin, gold and the dollar—A GARCH volatility analysis. *Finance Research Letters, 16*, 85–92. [CrossRef]

Fama, E. (1965). The Behavior of Stock Market Prices. *Journal of Business, 38*, 34–105. [CrossRef]

Fernandes, M., Medeiros, M. C., & Scharth, M. (2014). Modeling and predicting the CBOE market volatility index. *Journal of Banking & Finance, 40*, 1–10. [CrossRef]

Gajardo, G., Kristjanpoller, W. D., & Minutolo, M. (2018). Does bitcoin exhibit the same asymmetric multifractal cross-correlations with crude oil, gold and DJIA as the Euro, Great British Pound and Yen? *Chaos, Solitons & Fractals, 109*, 195–205. [CrossRef]

Gharib, C., Mefteh-Wali, S., & Jabeur, S. B. (2021). The bubble contagion effect of COVID-19 outbreak: Evidence from crude oil and gold markets. *Finance Research Letters, 38*, 101703. [CrossRef] [PubMed]

Glaser, F., Zimmermann, K., Haferkorn, M., Weber, M. C., & Siering, M. (2014, June 9–11). *Bitcoin-asset or currency? Revealing users' hidden intentions*. Twenty Second European Conference on Information Systems, Tel Aviv, Israel.

Han, H., Linton, O., Oka, T., & Whang, Y. J. (2016). The cross-quantilogram: Measuring quantile dependence and testing directional predictability between time series. *Journal of Econometrics, 193*(1), 251–270. [CrossRef]

Hertzog, M. A. (2008). Considerations in determining sample size for pilot studies. *Research in Nursing & Health, 31*(2), 180–191. [CrossRef]

Horstmeyer, X. J., & Kowalski, M. (2022). *Digital gold or fool's gold: Is crypto really a hedge against equity risk?* Available online: https://blogs.cfainstitute.org/investor/2022/07/12/digital-gold-or-fools-gold-is-crypto-really-a-hedge-against-equity-risk/ (accessed on 28 December 2022).

Huang, W., & Wu, M. (2021). Are spillover effects between oil and gold prices asymmetric? Evidence from the COVID-19 pandemic. *Energy Research Letters, 2*(4), 28127. [CrossRef]

Jareno, F., Gonzalez, M. D. L. O., Lopez, R., & Ramos, A. R. (2021). Cryptocurrencies and oil price shocks: A NARDL analysis in the COVID-19 pandemic. *Resources Policy, 74*, 102281. [CrossRef]

Ji, Q., Zhang, D., & Zhao, Y. (2020). Searching for safe-haven assets during the COVID-19 pandemic. *International Review of Financial Analysis, 71*, 101526. [CrossRef]

Jiang, S., Li, Y., Lu, Q., Wang, S., & Wei, Y. (2022). Volatility communicator or receiver? Investigating volatility spill over mechanisms among bitcoin and other financial markets. *Research in International Business and Finance, 59*, 101543. [CrossRef]

Jones, M. V., Coviello, N., & Tang, Y. K. (2011). International entrepreneurship research (1989–2009): A domain ontology and thematic analysis. *Journal of Business Venturing, 26*(6), 632–659. [CrossRef]

Julious, S. A. (2005). Sample size of 12 per group rule of thumb for a pilot study. *Pharmaceutical Statistics, 4*(4), 287–291. [CrossRef]

Kahneman, D., & Tversky, A. (1979). Prospect theory: An analysis of decision under risk. *Econometrica, 47*, 263–291. [CrossRef]

Kang, S. H., McIver, R. P., & Hernandez, J. A. (2019). Co-movements between bitcoin and gold: A wavelet coherence analysis. *Physica A: Statistical Mechanics and Its Applications, 536*, 120888. [CrossRef]

Karasiński, J. (2023). The adaptive market hypothesis and the return predictability in the cryptocurrency markets. *Economics and Business Review, 9*(1), 94–118. [CrossRef]

Kim, M. H., & Dilts, D. A. (2011). The relationship of the value of the dollar, and the prices of gold and oil: A tale of asset risk. *Economics Bulletin, 31*(2), 1151–1162.

Kim, Y. (2011). The pilot study in qualitative inquiry: Identifying issues and learning lessons for culturally competent research. *Qualitative Social Work, 10*, 190–206. [CrossRef]

Klein, T., Thu, H. P., & Walther, T. (2018). Bitcoin is not the new gold—A comparison of volatility, correlation, and portfolio performance. *International Review of Financial Analysis, 59*, 105–116. [CrossRef]

Kober, T., Schiffer, H. W., Densing, M., & Panos, E. (2020). Global energy perspectives to 2060—WEC's world energy scenarios 2019. *Energy Strategy Reviews, 31*, 100523. [CrossRef]

Kristoufek, L. (2018). On bitcoin markets (in) efficiency and its evolution. *Physica A: Statistical Mechanics and Its Applications, 503*, 257–262. [CrossRef]

Lahmiri, S., & Bekiros, S. (2020). Renyi entropy and mutual information measurement of market expectations and investor fear during the COVID-19 pandemic. *Chaos, Solitons and Fractals, 139*, 110084. [CrossRef]

Latoszek, M., & Ślepaczuk, R. (2020). Does the inclusion of exposure to volatility into diversified portfolio improve the investment results? Portfolio construction from the perspective of a Polish investor. *Economics and Business Review, 6*(1), 46–81. [CrossRef]

Leković, M. (2019). Behavioral portfolio theory and behavioral asset pricing model as an alternative to standard finance concepts. *Economic Horizons*, *21*(3), 255–279. [CrossRef]

Leon, A. C., Davis, L. L., & Kraemer, H. C. (2011). The role and interpretation of pilot studies in clinical research. *Journal of Psychiatric Research*, *45*(5), 626–629. [CrossRef] [PubMed]

López-Cabarcos, M. Á., Pérez-Pico, A. M., Piñeiro-Chousa, J., & Šević, A. (2021). Bitcoin volatility, stock market and investor sentiment. Are they connected? *Finance Research Letters*, *38*, 101399. [CrossRef]

Maghyereh, A., & Abdoh, H. (2022). COVID-19 and the volatility interlinkage between bitcoin and financial assets. *Empirical Economics*, *63*, 2875–2901. [CrossRef] [PubMed]

Markowitz, H. (1952). The utility of wealth. *Journal of Political Economy*, *60*(2), 151–158. [CrossRef]

Matthew, H., & Farooq, M. (2013). Is gold the best hedge and a safe haven under changing stock market volatility. *Review of Financial Economics*, *22*(2), 47. [CrossRef]

McCown, J. R., & Zimmerman, J. R. (2006, July 24). *Is gold a zero-beta asset? Analysis of the investment potential of precious metal*. Available online: https://ssrn.com/abstract=920496 (accessed on 28 December 2022).

Mensi, W., Sensoy, A., Vo, X. V., & Kang, S. H. (2020). Impact of COVID-19 outbreak on asymmetric multifractality of gold and oil prices. *Resource Policy*, *69*, 101829. [CrossRef]

Mlaabdal, S., Chygryn, O., Kwilinski, A., Muzychuk, O., & Akimov, O. (2020, November 4–5). *Economic growth and oil industry development: Assessment of the interaction of national economy indicators*. Proceedings of the 36th International Business Information Management Association (IBIMA), Granada, Spain.

Nadarajah, S., & Chu, S. (2017). On the inefficiency of bitcoin. *Economics Letters*, *150*, 6–9. [CrossRef]

Neely, C. J. (2022). Financial market reactions to the Russian invasion of Ukraine. *Federal Reserve Bank of St. Louis Review*, *104*(4), 266–296. [CrossRef]

Osterrieder, J., Vetter, L., & Röschli, K. (2019, January 7). *The VIX volatility index—A very thorough look at it*. Available online: https://ssrn.com/abstract=3311727 (accessed on 28 December 2022).

Parvini, N., Abdollahi, M., Seifollahi, S., & Ahmadian, D. (2022). Forecasting bitcoin returns with long short-term memory networks and wavelet decomposition: A comparison of several market determinants. *Applied Software Computing*, *121*, 108707. [CrossRef]

Peter, W., & Tversky, A. (1993). An axiomatization of cumulative prospect theory. *Journal of Risk and Uncertainty*, *7*(2), 147–175. [CrossRef]

Reboredo, J. C. (2013). Is gold a hedge or safe haven against oil price movements? *Resources Policy*, *38*(2), 130–137. [CrossRef]

Rényi, A. (1960). On measures of information and entropy. In *Proceedings of the 4th Berkeley symposium on mathematics, statistics and probability* (pp. 547–561). University of California.

Salisu, A. A., Vo, X. V., & Lawal, A. (2020). Hedging oil price risk with gold during COVID-19 pandemic. *Resource Policy*, *70*, 101897. [CrossRef]

Selmi, R., Mensi, W., Hammoudeh, S., & Bouoiyour, J. (2018). Is bitcoin a hedge, a safe haven or a diversifier for oil price movements? A comparison with gold. *Energy Economics*, *74*, 787–801. [CrossRef]

Shannon, C. E. (1948). A mathematical theory of communication. *The Bell System Technical Journal*, *27*(3), 379–423. [CrossRef]

Shefrin, H. (2000). Recent developments in behavioral finance. *The Journal of Wealth Management*, *3*(1), 25–37. [CrossRef]

Shehzad, K., Bilgili, F., Zaman, U., Kocak, E., & Kuskaya, S. (2021). Is gold favourable than bitcoin during the COVID-19 outbreak? Comparative analysis through wavelet approach. *Resources Policy*, *73*, 102163. [CrossRef] [PubMed]

Simon, H. A. (1997). *Models of bounded rationality: Empirically grounded economic reason* (Vol. 3). MIT Press.

Souto, H. G., & Moradi, A. (2023). Forecasting realized volatility through financial turbulence and neural networks. *Economics and Business Review*, *9*(2), 133–159. [CrossRef]

Statman, M. (1995). Behavioral finance versus standard finance. In *AIMR conference proceedings*. CFA Institute.

Sujit, K. S., & Kumar, R. (2011). Study on dynamic relationship among gold price, oil price, exchange rate and stock market returns. *International Journal of Applied Business and Economic Research*, *9*(2), 145–165.

Symitsi, E., & Chalvatzis, K. J. (2019). The economic value of bitcoin: A portfolio analysis of currencies, gold, oil and stocks. *Research in International Business and Finance*, *48*, 97–110. [CrossRef]

Syuhada, K., Suprijanto, D., & Hakim, A. (2022). Comparing gold's and bitcoin's safe-haven roles against energy commodities during the COVID-19 outbreak: A vine copula approach. *Finance Research Letters*, *46*(B), 102471. [CrossRef]

Tanin, T. I., Sarker, A., Brooks, R., & Do, H. X. (2022). Does oil impact gold during COVID-19 and three other recent crises? *Energy Economics*, *108*, 105938. [CrossRef] [PubMed]

Teare, M. D., Dimairo, M., Shephard, N., Hayman, A., Whitehead, A., & Walters, S. J. (2014). Sample size requirements to estimate key design parameters from external pilot randomised controlled trials: A simulation study. *Trials*, *15*, 264. [CrossRef] [PubMed]

Thomas, D. R. (2017). Feedback from research participants: Are member checks useful in qualitative research? *Qualitative Research in Psychology*, *14*(1), 23–41. [CrossRef]

Urquhart, A. (2016). The inefficiency of bitcoin. *Economic Letters*, *148*, 80–82. [CrossRef]

Vukovic, D., Maiti, M., Grubisic, Z., Grigorieva, E. M., & Frömmel, M. (2021). COVID-19 pandemic: Is the crypto market a safe haven? The impact of the first wave. *Sustainability*, *13*(15), 8578. [CrossRef]

Wang, J., & Wang, X. (2021). COVID-19 and financial market efficiency: Evidence from an entropy-based analysis. *Finance Research Letters*, *42*, 101888. [CrossRef]

Wang, P., Zhang, H., Yang, C., & Guo, Y. (2021). Time and frequency dynamics of connectedness and hedging performance in global stock markets: Bitcoin versus conventional hedges. *Research in International Business and Finance*, *58*, 101479. [CrossRef]

Wei, W. (2018). The impact of tether grants on bitcoin. *Economics Letters*, *171*, 19–22. [CrossRef]

Wen, F., Tong, X., & Ren, X. (2022). Gold or bitcoin, which is the safe haven during the COVID-19 pandemic? *International Review of Financial Analysis*, *81*, 102121. [CrossRef] [PubMed]

Whaley, R. E. (2009). Understanding the VIX. *The Journal of Portfolio Management*, *35*(3), 98–105. [CrossRef]

Wu, S., Tong, M., Yang, Z., & Derbali, A. (2019). Does gold or bitcoin hedge economic policy uncertainty? *Finance Research Letters*, *31*, 171–178. [CrossRef]

Yermack, D. (2015). Is Bitcoin a real currency? An economic appraisal. In *Handbook of digital currency* (pp. 31–43). Academic Press. [CrossRef]

Yin, L., Nie, J., & Han, L. (2021). Understanding cryptocurrency volatility: The role of oil market shocks. *International Review of Economic Finance*, *72*, 233–253. [CrossRef]

Zhang, Y., Zhu, P., & Xu, Y. (2021). Has COVID-19 changed the hedge effectiveness of bitcoin? *Frontiers in Public Health*, *9*, 704900. [CrossRef] [PubMed]

Zhou, R., Cai, R., & Tong, G. (2013). Applications of entropy in finance: A review. *Entropy*, *15*(11), 4909–4931. [CrossRef]

Zhou, Y., Xie, C., Wang, G.-J., Zhu, Y., & Uddin, G. S. (2023). Analysing and forecasting co-movement between innovative and traditional financial assets based on complex network and machine learning. *Research in International Business and Finance*, *64*, 101846. [CrossRef] *economies*

MDPI

Article

An Asymmetric Analysis of the Impact of Foreign and Domestic Debt on South Africa's Economic Growth

Gisele Mah

Department of Economics, North-West University, Mafikeng 2735, South Africa; gisele.mah@nwu.ac.za

Abstract

South Africa has been struggling with high levels of gross debt. The COVID-19 pandemic has worsened as the government has had to adjust its budget continuously, resulting in fiscal stance and debt sustainability becoming a matter of concern. This research aims to assess the possible asymmetric effect of foreign and domestic debt on economic growth in South Africa. Annual data from 1960 to 2023 was obtained from the South African Reserve Bank for the following variables: total domestic debt as a percentage, total foreign debt as a percentage, and gross domestic product. The nonlinear autoregressive distributed lag was used, and the results reveal that a positive change in total domestic debt has a negative and significant effect on GDP. A negative change in total domestic debt as a percentage has a positive and significant effect on GDP. These results suggest that South Africa's GDP responds significantly to a decrease in total domestic debt when compared to an increase in total domestic debt. A positive change in total foreign debt as a percentage has a positive and statistically significant effect on GDP. A negative change in total foreign debt as a percentage has a negative and statistically insignificant relationship with GDP. In South Africa, foreign debt has a positive relationship, while domestic debt has a negative relationship with gross domestic product in South Africa. This means that for the gross domestic product to increase, there is a need for an increase in foreign debt and a decrease in total domestic debt in South Africa. The foreign debt should be at a certain level to avoid high debt services.

Keywords: foreign debt; domestic debt; NARDL; GDP gap; South Africa

JEL Classification: H63; H68; O43; C14

1. Introduction

The government debt of most countries around the world has been increasing over the years. Most developed countries had the highest debt-to-GDP ratio during and after COVID-19. The countries with the highest amount of debt are countries found in Europe. It is evident that, in 2020, all countries had the highest debt-to-GDP ratio. Croatia had 687.99% in 2018, increasing to 633.16% in 2021 (World Bank, 2023). This is followed by Greece with 237.12% in 2018, increasing to 208.81% in 2021, and Japan with 198.02% in 2018, increasing to 217.61% in 2021 (World Bank, 2023). The second set of countries with the highest debt is North America, followed by Asia. Most African countries have the lowest debt compared to other countries worldwide (World Bank, 2023).

Over the years, South Africa has been continually accumulating government/public debt. According to the Reserve Bank of South Africa, total public debt has sharply risen to 68.9% of the GDP in 2020, 68.7% in 2021, 70.2% in 2022, and 73.4% in 2023 (South African

Reserve Bank, 2024). This has raised some concern among different economic role-players about the future of South Africa's debt path. High levels of public debt, if allowed to grow beyond the country's productive capacity, would likely work against the growth and development of the economy (Dabrowski, 2014). The COVID-19 pandemic appeared to have made it worse as the government had to continuously adjust its budget upwards, resulting in fiscal imbalances and debt sustainability becoming a matter of concern. Saungweme and Odhiambo (2020) mentioned that aggregate public debt negatively impacts growth.

Sovereign debt in South Africa arises primarily from the government's budget deficit. In the past decades, debt levels have been continuously increasing worldwide, worsening due to the COVID-19 pandemic, which has caused many governments to have a deficit in their finances. South African debt is associated mainly with the budget deficit; the government cannot cover its planned expenditure, and therefore, the deficit arises. Increased budget commitment to different sectors requires the government to have enough revenue to ensure that there is no deficit in its budget (Galodikwe & Mah, 2023).

South Africa has been struggling with high levels of gross debt. Even though this concern is reasonable and acceptable, it might be useful to decompose the total debt into its domestic and foreign components and discover some interesting patterns that may assist in macroeconomic policymaking. Total debt in South Africa consists of both domestic debt and foreign debt. Domestic debt is the money borrowed by the government from local banks, individuals, and companies through government securities sales such as treasury bonds and bills. Foreign debt is the money the government borrows from another country's government or foreign private lenders.

As shown in Figure 1, according to the Reserve Bank of South Africa, the portion of domestic debt rose from 50.3% in 2019 to 65% in 2023, while foreign debt rose from 5.8% in 2019 to 8.3% in 2023 (South African Reserve Bank, 2024). With an increase of 12.8% in total public debt from 2019 to 2020, it is interesting to note that while 11.5% was domestic, only 1.2% was foreign. However, when total debt decreased by 1% from 2020 to 2021, it was discovered that although domestic debt also decreased by the same 1%, the portion of foreign debt increased by 1%. Similarly, from 2021 to 2022, there was a 2.3% increase in total debt: 1.5% was domestic debt, while 0.8% was foreign debt. Most of the time, domestic debt is acquired mainly to finance the country's primary deficits and ensure that appropriate monetary policies are implemented.

Figure 1. GDP, domestic debt, and foreign debt in South Africa.

The relationship between foreign debt and economic growth has both positive and negative effects. Zakaria (2012) highlights that the productive use of borrowed funds is crucial for realising any potential economic benefits from debt, while Ajuh and Oyeanu (2021) mentioned that, in Nigeria, external debt often correlates negatively with growth outcomes. Koyuncu and Demirhan (2020) found that while external debt may positively impact growth under certain circumstances, its effects can quickly turn negative when thresholds of sustainability are breached. Tchereni et al. (2013) mentioned the detrimental effects of foreign debt, which are crowding out domestic investment, leading to increased vulnerability to external shocks. This can outweigh the potential benefits if the debt management is not robust.

Several studies support the assertion that domestic debt has a significant positive relationship with economic growth in Nigeria (Didia & Ayokunle, 2020). Akram (2015) suggested that well-managed domestic debt can act as a catalyst for growth, provided it does not crowd out private investment. In Jordan, it has been shown that domestic borrowing effectively fosters economic expansion, albeit with consideration for its macroeconomic implications (Fseifes & Warrad, 2020). Saungweme and Odhiambo (2020) argue that aggregate public debt negatively impacts growth, and the influence of domestic debt is significantly positive in the short run. Domestic debt may exert undue pressure on government revenues due to high interest burdens, potentially diminishing funding available for pro-growth sectors. Moreover, the relationship between domestic debt levels and economic growth often exhibits nonlinear characteristics, suggesting that there is an optimal level of domestic debt that supports growth, while exceeding this threshold could be detrimental (Mbate, 2013).

Results from diverse geographical contexts reveal that while domestic debt can strengthen growth if managed prudently, foreign debt frequently carries risks that require careful handling. The overall consensus is that the potential benefits of both domestic and foreign debt significantly depend on how the funds are utilised and the strength of institutional frameworks that can mitigate risks associated with high debt levels while enhancing growth prospects (Saungweme & Odhiambo, 2021b). Most studies focus on public debt as a whole, but few focus on the asymmetric effect of foreign and domestic debt in South Africa. This study will assess the positive and negative effects of foreign and domestic debt on growth in South Africa. The rest of this study is structured as follows: Section 2 reviews the theoretical and empirical literature; Section 3 presents the econometric methods; Section 4 provides the empirical results; lastly, Section 5 outlines the conclusion of this study.

2. Literature Review

One theoretical approach that has received widespread attention within this context is the Keynesian perspective. Keynes (1937) emphasises the role of government intervention in stimulating economic growth and stability. In the Keynesian theory of public debt, governmental borrowing is perceived as a necessary tool for addressing the economic impulses of recession and reducing unemployment levels. As such, public debt is seen as a means by which the government can support economic recovery and mitigate potential negative impacts of economic contraction.

The main idea of the public debt overhang theory is that having too much debt can harm future economic growth. This theoretical concept posits that when a country's debt goes up, it can cause less economic growth because the government has to use more of its money to pay off the debt. The theory suggests that this can create a self-reinforcing cycle, as lower economic growth means reduced resources to manage debt, further exacerbating the problem. In simple words, Krugman (1988) suggests that people who want to invest money would be more worried about banks having to pay a lot of taxes to cover the government's debt than they would be about the costs of investing in something that will make money in the future. Debt overhang means having too much debt that it becomes burdensome and difficult to repay.

The relationship between foreign debt and economic growth has both positive and negative effects. Saungweme and Odhiambo (2021b) emphasise the importance of examining both domestic and foreign public debt separately, as their impacts on economic growth can differ significantly. Their findings suggest that while foreign debt can potentially stimulate growth under certain conditions, excessive reliance on it can lead to adverse outcomes, such as increased vulnerability to external shocks and higher debt servicing costs. Research conducted in Nigeria indicates that while foreign debt positively influences private investment, domestic debt has a negative impact in both the short- and long run (Simon et al., 2023). This suggests that the effects of debt are not uniform and can vary significantly based on whether the debt is domestic or foreign. Similarly, studies in Egypt and Sri Lanka have shown that external debt can have both positive and negative effects on economic growth, depending on the economic context and the nature of the debt (Sharaf, 2021; Sumanaratne, 2022).

Olaoye et al. (2022) indicate that excessive reliance on foreign borrowing can lead to vulnerabilities in the economy, including currency mismatches and increased susceptibility to external shocks. This phenomenon is mentioned within other contexts, where the presence of high levels of public debt can lead to reduced private sector investment due to increased competition for financial resources (Matthew & Adetayo, 2022; Lashari et al., 2017). The NARDL model provides a robust framework for understanding the complex interplay between domestic and foreign debt and their respective impacts on economic growth, inflation, and investment. The findings from various studies underscore the necessity for policymakers to carefully consider the composition of public debt and its implications for economic stability and growth. In Sri Lanka, the NARDL analysis demonstrated that both the stock of external debt and debt service payments significantly affect economic growth, underscoring the importance of managing foreign debt levels to ensure economic stability (Sumanaratne, 2022). Furthermore, the crowding-out effect of public debt on domestic investment has been documented in various studies. In Sri Lanka, for instance, both domestic and foreign debt were found to crowd out domestic investment, which can hinder long-term economic growth (Shiyalini & Suresh, 2022).

Baaziz et al. (2015) found that public debt becomes detrimental to growth when it surpasses 31.37% of the GDP, highlighting the critical threshold that policymakers must consider. This is further supported by Zhang et al. (2022), who note that excessive public debt can lead to crowding out of private investment, thereby stifling growth prospects. The implications of these findings suggest that while some level of debt may be necessary for development, a delicate balance must be maintained to avoid negative repercussions. Additionally, the interaction between debt service obligations and economic growth has been a focal point of research. Saungweme and Odhiambo (2021a) argue that high debt service payments can constrain public investment, which is essential for economic growth. Mhlaba and Phiri (2019) assert that the long-run effects of public debt on growth are often negative due to the crowding out of productive investments. These studies collectively highlight the critical need for effective debt management strategies that prioritise growth-enhancing investments. Furthermore, the role of external factors, such as country risk and macroeconomic stability, cannot be overlooked. Zakaria (2012) highlights that the productive use of borrowed funds is crucial for realising any potential economic benefits from debt. Musa et al. (2023) found that in the presence of good governance, public debt promotes economic growth in the medium to higher quantiles.

Ajuh and Oyeanu (2021) found that, in Nigeria, external debt often correlates negatively with growth outcomes. Fseifes and Warrad (2020) reported that external debt negatively impacts Jordan's growth, which aligns with findings from Pakistan by Shah et al. (2016), where high debt servicing burdens curtailed investment and productivity. Akram (2015) mentioned that domestic debt can lead to the crowding out of private sector investment, thereby stunting economic growth. Wulandari et al. (2022) argue that foreign debt can enhance liquidity and provide much-needed capital for infrastructure projects, which is crucial for economic expansion in developing countries. Junaedi et al. (2022) found a correlation between foreign debt and Indonesia's GDP and poverty levels, suggesting that well-managed foreign debt can stimulate economic activity and lead to poverty alleviation. Changyong et al. (2012) assert that foreign capital inflows can facilitate domestic investment and accelerate a country's transition towards self-sustaining growth. Koyuncu and Demirhan (2020) found that while external debt may positively impact growth under certain circumstances, its effects can quickly turn negative when thresholds of sustainability are breached. The relationship between foreign debt and economic growth often follows a nonlinear pattern, with a threshold identified beyond which additional debt can restrict growth (Changyong et al., 2012). Pattillo et al. noted a critical point around 35 to 40% of GDP at which foreign debt begins to inversely correlate with growth potential (Changyong et al., 2012).

Omimakinde and Onifade (2022) found that while domestic debt may yield positive short-term effects, its long-term implications can be negative unless directed towards growth-enhancing projects. Didia and Ayokunle (2020) suggest that domestic debt significantly contributes to economic growth in Nigeria over the long term, contrasting with the persistent negative effects associated with external debt. Several studies support the assertion that domestic debt has a significant positive relationship with economic growth in Nigeria (Didia & Ayokunle, 2020). Well-managed domestic debt can act as a catalyst for growth, provided it does not crowd out private investment (Akram, 2015).

Saungweme et al. (2023) examined the symmetric and asymmetric impact of public debt on economic growth in Côte d'Ivoire using both linear and nonlinear autoregressive distributed lag (ARDL) models. The nonlinear autoregressive distributed lag (NARDL) findings indicate that, on average, positive changes to public debt led to economic decline in the long run, while negative changes caused an economic upturn in the short run. The findings also show that GDP growth responds rapidly and strongly to negative changes in public debt. Eric (2024), on Nigeria's government debt and its impact on GDP growth from the period 1991 to 2022, shows that the responsiveness of GDP growth is stronger for the negative than positive values of debt. Aloulou et al. (2023) examined the symmetric and asymmetric impact of external debt on economic growth in Tunisia between 1965 and 2019. The linear autoregressive distributed lag ARDL model was used, and the results show that economic growth is more sensitive and favourable to decreases than to increases in external debt, which, in turn, means that maintaining debt at relatively high levels is detrimental to Tunisian economic growth. Sharaf (2021) determined the asymmetric and dynamic effects of public debt on private investment in Nigeria from 1990 to 2019. According to the NARDL modelling technique, there was a significant instant positive impact on domestic and foreign debt shocks in the short run. Sharaf (2021) examined the asymmetric and threshold impact of external debt on economic growth in Egypt during the period 1980 to 2019. The paper uses an NARDL bounds testing approach. The results of the NARDL model show a robust, statistically significant negative long-run impact on economic growth stemming from both positive and negative external-debt-induced shocks. In terms of magnitude, on the one hand, the impact of external-debt-induced negative shocks exceeds that of the positive. In the short and long run, on the other hand, the growth impact of external debt in Egypt is symmetric. Sharaf et al. (2024), in the estimation of the NARDL model for Brazil, revealed that foreign debt does not have a statistically significant long-term impact on inflation, contrasting with findings from other countries where such relationships were more pronounced. This discrepancy highlights the importance of context when analysing the effects of debt, as different countries may exhibit unique responses to similar debt levels. Mosikari and Eita (2021) investigated the asymmetric relationship between government debt and GDP growth in Namibia. This study applied the NARDL methods to determine the asymmetrical effect of government debt on GDP growth. This shows that the responsiveness of GDP growth to positive values of debt is different to that of negative values of debt. The responsiveness of GDP growth to negative values of debt is greater than to positive values of debt. This implies that it is important for Namibia to have manageable debt and fiscal sustainability in order to increase its GDP growth.

The impact of foreign and domestic debt on South Africa's economic growth is a complex and multifaceted issue that has garnered significant attention in recent academic studies. A notable research gap exists in understanding the nuanced effects of these two types of debt, particularly within the context of South Africa's unique economic landscape.

3. Econometric Methods

The model below is used to determine the linear and nonlinear effects of debt on economic growth in South Africa. The model of Redda (2020) was modified to obtain the following equation:

$$GDP_t = \beta_0 + \beta_1 DDEBT_t + \beta_2 FDEBT_t + e_t \tag{1}$$

where GDP_t is the gross domestic product, $DDEBT_t$ is domestic debt as a percentage and $FDEBT_t$ is total foreign debt as a percentage, β_0, β_1, β_2, are the coefficients, and e_t is the error term. Annual data from 1960 to 2023 was obtained from the South African Reserve Bank (South African Reserve Bank, 2024) for the following variables: total domestic debt as a percentage, total foreign debt as a percentage, and gross domestic product.

The nonlinear autoregressive distributed lag (NARDL) technique is used. Shin et al. (2014) developed the NARDL model, where the independent variables are decomposed into positive and negative results. The NARDL method of analysis is used to avoid model misspecification errors, as the NARDL method considers the asymmetric relationship between the dependent and the independent variables (Shin et al., 2014). The NARDL method accommodates variables of mixed integration orders I(0) and I(1) while Johansen cointegration approaches require that the variables be all I(1). The advantage of the NARDL method is its ability to detect asymmetric effects, which is crucial for understanding complex economic dynamics. It captures both short- and long-run asymmetries, differentiating the effects of positive and negative changes in independent variables, which other techniques, such as the Vector Error Correction Model and Engle–Granger, cannot (Shrestha & Bhatta, 2018).

The estimation starts with descriptive statistics, correlation, and then the unit root test. The order of integration is determined, and the next step is the lag length selection criteria. After the appropriate lag is chosen, the NARDL bounds cointegration follows. The next step is the estimation of the long- and short-run nonlinearity of the debt variables. The diagnostic and stability tests then follow it.

To analyse multicollinearity, this study uses the correlation matrix method. While this approach is traditionally applied to detect multicollinearity among independent variables, it is also effective in evaluating the relationship between the dependent variable and the independent variables. Therefore, the correlation matrix not only identifies multicollinearity among predictors but also examines the complex interactions between the dependent variable and independent variables. Correlation is a method used to detect multicollinearity (Gujarati & Porter, 2008). Multicollinearity occurs when a regression model includes multiple explanatory variables that show significant correlations with each other and with the dependent variable (Young, 2018). A common guideline suggests that if the pairwise or zero-order correlation coefficient between two predictors exceeds 0.8, it indicates a potential multicollinearity problem (Gujarati & Porter, 2008).

The augmented Dickey–Fuller (ADF) and Phillips and Perron (PP) unit root tests were used to test for stationarity. The ADF has heterogeneity in the distribution of the disturbance term, and the PP test was carried out to determine the confirmatory unit root results (Asteriou & Hall, 2011). The Phillips–Perron tests (PP) correct the t-statistics of the coefficient in the autoregressive regression model (Asteriou & Hall, 2011; Phillips & Perron, 1988). It is performed at the intercept, intercept and trend, and none.

When the variables are stationary at level, it is integrated at I(0); if they are at the first difference, then they are integrated at I(1), and if they are at the second difference, then they are integrated at I(2) (Asteriou & Hall, 2011). If the variables are stationary at I(0) and I(1), then the ARDL is best. The next step is the bounds cointegration.

The bounds test, developed by Pesaran and Shin (1995) and Pesaran et al. (1996), is ideal when dealing with one co-integrating vector. When employing the bounds test of cointegration and considering the null-hypothesis to come to a decision, the F-statistic of the test should be statistically significant to reject the null hypothesis of no long-run relationship or no cointegrating relationship, and therefore, the alternative hypothesis of a cointegrating relationship will be concluded. This study finds it very crucial to determine the presence of asymmetry in the relationship between domestic debt, foreign debt, and GDP. After the confirmation of the cointegration, this study estimated the long-run asymmetries.

$$GDP_t = \beta_0 + \beta_1 DDEBT^{+}{}_{t-1} + \beta_2 DDEBT^{-}{}_{t-1} + \beta_3 FDEBT^{+}{}_{t-1} + \beta_4 FDEBT^{-}{}_{t-1} + \varepsilon_t \quad (2)$$

The short-run dynamics are presented as shown below.

$$\begin{aligned} \Delta GDP_t = \textstyle\sum_{i=0}^{q} \alpha_1^{+} \Delta DDEBT_{t-i}^{+} + \sum_{i=0}^{q} \alpha_1^{-} \Delta DDEBT_{t-i}^{-} + \sum_{i=0}^{q} \alpha_2^{+} \Delta FDEBT_{t-i}^{+} \\ + \textstyle\sum_{i=0}^{q} \alpha_3^{-} \Delta FDEBT_{t-i}^{-} + \varepsilon_t \end{aligned} \quad (3)$$

Diagnostic tests are used to confirm that the model is appropriately stated. For the normality test, the Jarque–Bera test is used since it is the most commonly used for large samples (Brooks, 2014). For heteroscedasticity, the white heteroscedasticity test is performed to see whether the residuals and explanatory variables are related. Serial correlation is the relationship between several series of observations over time or place (Gujarati & Porter, 2008). This is predicated on the idea that the disturbance term associated with any given observation is independent of the disturbance term associated with any other observation (Gujarati & Porter, 2008).

For the stability test, the Ramsey reset test is used to determine whether the response variable can be described by the fitted values of nonlinear combinations of the study that was utilised in the model. The test is carried out to ensure that no misspecifications of any kind, i.e., ensuring stability, occur (Brooks, 2014).

4. Empirical Results

The asymmetric results of foreign and domestic debt on South Africa's economic growth are discussed below. It starts with a summary of statistics.

4.1. Summary Statistics of Variables

The average value of domestic debt is 33.3%, foreign debt is 2.7%, and the GDP is 0.71% in South Africa, as shown in Table 1 below.

Table 1. Summary statistics of variables.

	GDP	FDEBT	DDEBT
Mean	0.714063	2.739063	33.73438
Median	0.900000	2.400000	33.30000
Maximum	5.000000	8.200000	63.10000
Minimum	−7.400000	0.500000	19.70000
Std. dev.	2.462859	1.781440	9.091636
Skewness	−0.640819	1.061837	1.343885
Kurtosis	3.625517	3.679952	5.341210
Jarque–Bera	5.423647	13.25954	33.88099
Probability	0.066416	0.001320	0.000000
Sum	45.70000	175.3000	2159.000
Sum sq. dev.	382.1373	199.9323	5207.444
Observations	64	64	64

4.2. Correlation Matrix of Variables

According to Shieh (2010), multicollinearity is not a problem when dealing with dynamic models such as NARDL. However, we have to check the correlation among the variables of this. According to Gujarati and Porter (2008), a correlation coefficient that is greater than 0.8 indicates severe multicollinearity. Table 2 shows low correlations among the variables in this study. Table 2: Correlation matrix of variables.

Table 2. Matrix of variables.

	GDP	FDEBT	DDEBT
GDP	1.000000 -----		
FDEBT	−0.056277 0.6587	1.000000 -----	
DDEBT	−0.003495 0.9781	0.483157 0.0001	1.000000 -----

4.3. Structural Break

Table 3 presents the analysis of structural breaks utilising dummy variables. This approach uncovers relationship alterations within the data over time by integrating dummy variables into the regression equation. These variables assist in identifying changes in intercepts or slopes, signalling structural modifications in the fundamental data-generating mechanism across various time frames.

Table 3. Structural break.

Break Year	Name of the Dummy	Coding Dummies
2009	DUM09	➢ DUM09 =1; in 2000 ➢ DUM09 = 0; Period before and after the break.
2020	DUM20	➢ DUM20 = 1; in 2020 ➢ DUM20 = 0; Period before and after the break

4.4. Unit Roots

The unit root results reveal that GDP is stationary at level I(0), while FDEBT and DDEBT are stationary at the first difference, I(1), as shown in Table 4 below.

Table 4. ADF and PP unit root tests at difference levels.

Variables	Formula	Levels				Conclusion
		ADF		PP		
		T-Values (Lags)	5% Critical Value	T-Values (Band Width)	5% Critical Value	
GDP	Intercept	−5.416 ***	−2.908	−5.423 ***	−2.908	Stationary
	Trend and intercept	−5.640 ***	−3.483	−5.640 ***	−3.483	Stationary
	None	−5.152 ***	−1.946	−5.143 ***	−1.944	Stationary
FDEBT	Intercept	−0.340	−2.908	−0.130	−2.908	Non-stationary
	Trend and intercept	−1.725	−3.483	−1.628	−3.483	Non-stationary
	None	0.607	−1.946	0.944	−1.946	Non-stationary
D(FDEBT)	Intercept	−7.449 ***	−2.909	−7.423 ***	−2.909	Stationary
	Trend and intercept	−7.762 ***	−3.484	−7.836 ***	−3.484	Stationary
	None	−7.435 ***	−1.946	−7.413 ***	−1.946	Stationary
DDEBT	Intercept	−0.644	−2.909	−0.125	−2.909	Non-stationary
	Trend and intercept	−1008	−3.484	−0.399	−3.484	Non-stationary
	None	0.474	−1.946	0.903	−1.946	Non-stationary
D(DDEBT)	Intercept	−5.088 ***	−2.909	−5.109 ***	−2.909	Stationary
	Trend and intercept	−5.520 ***	−3.484	−5.540 ***	−3.484	Stationary
	None	−5.078 ***	−1.946	−5.093 ***	−1.946	Stationary

Note: *** indicate significance levels at 1%, respectively.

4.5. NADRL Bounds Cointegration Results

Table 5 reveals the NARDL bounds cointegration results. The results reveal that there is cointegration among our variables since the F-statistic value is greater than the upper-bound values.

Table 5. NADRL bounds cointegration results.

F-Bound Test	Null Hypothesis: No Levels of Relationship			
Test Statistic	Value	Signif.	I(0)	I(1)
		10%	2.2	3.09
F-statistic	11.23062	5%	2.56	3.49
K	4	2.5%	2.88	3.87
		1%	3.29	4.37

After determining cointegration, we proceed to estimate the long-run relationship.

4.6. Long-Run Relationship Results

The asymmetric cointegration long-run results are presented in Table 6. It shows the statistical significance and the relationship of domestic debt and foreign debt with gross domestic product in symmetry for South Africa.

Table 6. The long-run relationship results.

Variable	Coefficient	Std. Error	t-Statistic	Prob.
FDEBT_POS ***	2.675264	0.511243	5.232864	0.0000
FDEBT_NEG	−0.310690	0.550256	−0.564629	0.5749
DDEBT_POS ***	−0.233567	0.063758	−3.663305	0.0006
DDEBT_NEG ***	0.686992	0.183684	3.740071	0.0005
C	1.778726	0.995780	1.786263	0.0802

Note: *** indicate significance level at 1%, respectively. EC = GDP − (2.6753 × FDEBT_POS − 0.3107 × FDEBT_NEG − 0.2336 × DDEBT_POS + 0.6870 × DDEBT_NEG + 1.7787).

A positive change in foreign debt in the long run in South Africa has a positive and statistically significant effect on economic growth. Every 1-unit increase in foreign debt will lead to a 2.214443-unit increase in gross domestic product. This means that, in the long run, the increase in foreign debt leads to an increase in gross domestic product. Sharaf (2021) obtained the same results, which confirm our results. On the other hand, there is a negative change in foreign debt in South Africa, which causes gross domestic product to decrease, but the relationship is statistically insignificant. From these results, an increase in foreign debt will lead to an increase in gross domestic product in South Africa, which is contrary to the results of Ajuh and Oyeanu (2021) but in line with that of Koyuncu and Demirhan (2020), who found out that external debt may positively impact growth under certain circumstances.

The positive effect of foreign debt on economic growth in South Africa stems from its relatively lower cost, discipline-imposing nature, and its external financing benefits. Foreign borrowing usually comes with greater scrutiny from international lenders or capital markets. The need to adhere to repayment obligations and maintain credibility in global markets often imposes fiscal discipline and incentivises sound macroeconomic policy, thereby encouraging better debt management.

A positive change in domestic debt in South Africa has a negative and significant effect on gross domestic product in South Africa. Every 1-unit increase in domestic debt will lead to a 0.233567-unit decrease in the gross domestic product in South Africa. In other words, in the long run, an increase in domestic output leads to a decrease in gross domestic product in South Africa. On the other hand, a negative change in domestic debt has a positive and significant effect on gross domestic product. A 1-unit decrease in domestic debt will lead to a 0.686992-unit decrease in gross domestic product in South Africa. In other words, in the long run, the decrease in domestic debt leads to an decrease in gross domestic product in South Africa. Omimakinde and Onifade (2022) state that, in the long term, domestic debt has a negative relationship with growth, which is in line with our results.

Domestic debt is more likely to be expensive, inefficiently used, and fiscally destabilising, largely due to institutional weaknesses, poor fiscal discipline, and limited financial market depth. The negative effect of domestic debt on economic growth in South Africa's gross domestic product could be due to the mismanagement of State-Owned Enterprises. Much of the domestic debt is absorbed by funding bailouts for inefficient public entities, such as Eskom and the South African Airlines. Domestic debt is often more prone to fiscal indiscipline, with low accountability and politicised allocation of resources. Also, South Africa's domestic debt carries relatively higher interest rates, as the government borrows at premium rates due to risk perceptions, inflation expectations, and a narrow savings base. This raises the cost of servicing the debt and crowds out private investment. Lastly, rising domestic debt signals fiscal stress and a shrinking tax base, raising concerns about sustainability and deterring both foreign and domestic investment.

In the long run, in South Africa, an increase in foreign debt will cause the gross domestic product to increase. An increase in domestic debt in South Africa will cause gross domestic product to decrease, while a decrease in domestic debt will cause gross domestic product to increase in South Africa. This means that for the gross domestic product to increase, there is a need for an increase in foreign debt and total domestic debt in South Africa.

4.7. Short-Run Relationship Results

A negative and statistically insignificant relationship was found between foreign debt and GDP in South Africa. The asymmetric short-run results are presented in Table 7 below.

Table 7. The short-run results.

C	**1.922948**	**1.038308**	**1.852002**	**0.0698**
D(FDEBT_POS)	0.007368	0.356293	0.020681	0.9836
D(FDEBT_POS(−1)) ***	−1.266977	0.415081	−3.052362	0.0037
D(DDEBT_POS) ***	0.292764	0.100596	2.910302	0.0054
D(DDEBT_NEG) *	−0.311886	0.166370	−1.874652	0.0668
DUMMY09 **	−3.699954	1.525702	−2.425083	0.0190
DUMMY20 ***	−8.171028	1.651734	−4.946940	0.0000
CointEq(−1) ***	−0.831359	0.096474	−8.617400	0.0000
R-squared	0.612473	Mean dependent var		−0.060656
Adjusted R-squared	0.746139	S.D. dependent var		2.860844
F-statistic	17.38509	Durbin-Watson stat		1.836217
Prob (F-statistic)	0.000000			

Note: ***, ** and * indicate significance levels at 1%, 5%, and 10%, respectively.

In the short run, a positive change in foreign debt and lag-one of foreign debt are negative, but the positive change in foreign debt is significant, while lag-one of the positive changes in foreign debt is insignificant. Furthermore, in the short run, an increase in domestic debt has a positive and significant relationship with GDP. A decrease in domestic debt has a negative and statistically significant relationship with GDP. Saungweme and Odhiambo (2020) argue that aggregate public debt negatively impacts growth, and the influence of domestic debt is significantly positive in the short run. The positive changes to public debt led to economic decline in the long run, while negative changes caused an economic upturn in the short run and long run; on the other hand, the growth impact of external debt in Egypt is symmetric.

The error term is negative and statistically significant, with a speed value of −0.831359 for equilibrium to be established in this model. The probability value of the F-statistic is significant. Since his model is good, we proceed to check the evidence of asymmetric among our variables.

4.8. Parsimonious Asymmetric Test Results

The parsimonious asymmetric model on which the Wald test is performed to confirm the presence of asymmetric results is presented in Table 8. This is the model that was discussed above; it has been rearranged to obtain the right identification to test for asymmetry.

Table 8. Parsimonious asymmetric test results.

Variable	Coefficient	Std. Error	t-Statistic	Prob.
C *	1.483130	0.813467	1.823221	0.0743
GDP(−1) ***	−0.831494	0.117269	−7.090459	0.0000
FDEBT_POS(−1) ***	2.221548	0.380206	5.843008	0.0000
FDEBT_NEG	−0.254842	0.392390	−0.649461	0.5190
DDEBT_POS(−1) ***	−0.193776	0.042307	−4.580206	0.0000
DDEBT_NEG(−1) ***	0.569907	0.123668	4.608350	0.0000
DUMMY09 **	−3.700479	1.693016	−2.185731	0.0335
DUMMY20 ***	−8.162760	1.686932	−4.838821	0.0000
D(FDEBT_POS(−1)) **	−1.267935	0.473352	−2.678628	0.0100
D(DDEBT_POS) **	0.292949	0.140022	2.092165	0.0415
D(DDEBT_NEG)	−0.313438	0.187917	−1.667965	0.1016
R-squared	0.746138	Mean dependent var		−0.060656
Adjusted R-squared	0.695365	S.D. dependent var		2.860844
F-statistic	14.69573	Durbin-Watson stat		1.836527
Prob(F-statistic)	0.000000			

Note: ***, ** and * indicate significance levels at 1%, 5%, and 10%, respectively.

4.9. Wald Test Results

The Wald test results were performed on the model in Table 9 above, and the results presented in Table 9 represent the asymmetric results for both the long and short run.

Table 9. Long-run and short-run asymmetries results.

Long-Run Asymmetry of DDEBT, C(3) = C(4)				Conclusion
t-statistic	4.4711322	50	0.0000	There is evidence of long-run asymmetry between DDEBT and GDP in South Africa.
F-statistic	19.99102	(1, 50)	0.0000	
Chi-square	19.99102	1	0.0000	
Long-run asymmetry of FDEBT C(5) = C(6)				
t-statistic	−5.059659	50	0.0000	There is evidence of long-run asymmetry between FDEBT and GDP in South Africa.
F-statistic	25.60015	(1, 50)	0.0000	
Chi-square	25.60015	1	0.0000	
Short-run asymmetry of DDEBT C(10) = C(11)				
t-statistic	2.365232	50	0.0219	There is evidence of short-run asymmetry between DDEBT and GDP in South Africa
F-statistic	5.594320	(1, 50)	0.0219	
Chi-square	5.594320	1	0.0180	

Table 9 shows that there is evidence of long-run asymmetry between domestic debt and GDP in both the long and short run in South Africa. In the short and long run, there exists an asymmetric relationship between growth and external debt, as mentioned by Sharaf (2021), which confirms our results of asymmetry.

4.10. Stability Test Results

As shown in Figures 2 and 3, the estimated model is stable since the residuals are within the 5% significance interval.

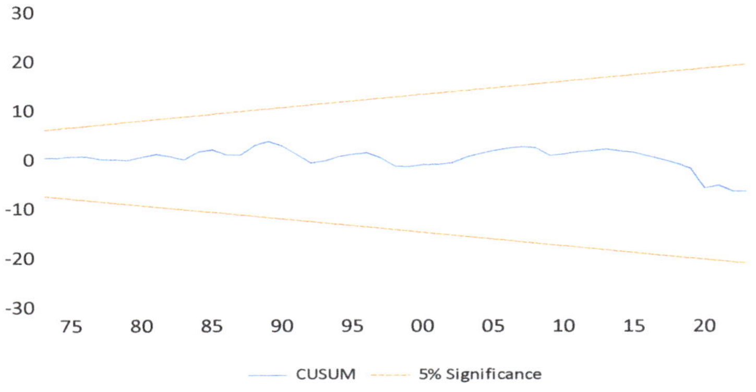

Figure 2. Stability results for CUSUM.

Figure 3. Stability results for CUSUM of squares with dummies.

4.11. Diagnostic Test Results

The stability test results are all good. They meet all classical linear assumptions as shown in Table 10 below.

Table 10. Diagnostic test results.

Breusch-Godfrey Serial Correlation LM Test Results				
F-Statistics	**Obs R-square**	**Prob. F(2,47)**	**Prob. Chi-Square**	**Conclusion**
0.031	1.280803	0.6073	0.5271	There is no serial correlation
Heteroskedasticity Test: Breusch–Pagan–Godfrey results				
F-statistics	**Obs R square**	**Prob. F(11,49)**	**Prob. Chi-Square**	**Conclusion of heteroskedasticity**
3.613	17.25480	0.063	0.1006	No heteroskedasticity
Results of Jarque–Bera normality test				
Jarque–Bera		**Prob.**	**Conclusion**	
0.838287		0.657610	The model is normally distributed	

5. Conclusions

This research aims to assess the possible asymmetric effect of foreign and domestic debt on economic growth in South Africa using the NARDL method. The results reveal that a positive change in total domestic debt will cause an increase in gross domestic product in South Africa. A positive change in domestic debt will cause the gross domestic product to decline, while a negative change in domestic debt will cause the gross domestic product in South Africa.

In South Africa, a positive change in foreign debt will cause the gross domestic product to increase. South Africa's post-COVID debt management strategy for foreign debt must reduce exchange rate vulnerability, limit reliance on costly commercial debt, strengthen institutional frameworks, and improve transparency and investor confidence. By integrating foreign debt policy into a coherent macroeconomic framework and leveraging concessional funding for strategic development objectives, South Africa can manage its foreign debt prudently while supporting inclusive and resilient economic recovery.

A positive change in domestic debt will cause the gross domestic product to decrease. The results exhibit that a positive change in domestic debt will lead to a decline in economic growth, whereas a negative change in domestic debt leads to an increase in gross domestic product in the long run.

Post-COVID-19, South Africa's domestic debt management must be rooted in lengthening the maturity profile of debt, deepening domestic capital markets, containing debt-service costs, boosting growth through structural reforms, and ensuring debt remains aligned with broader fiscal and monetary policy goals. Maintaining a credible medium-term fiscal consolidation plan anchored by effective debt management will be essential for preserving South Africa's macroeconomic stability and regaining policy flexibility.

Future research could benefit by considering other macroeconomic variables (e.g., exchange rate volatility and political risk) in the debt–growth relationship. This study further recommends that future studies in this area should use panel estimation techniques to examine the relationship between debt variables and economic growth at the provincial level. A key limitation of this study was the lack of quarterly data for all the variables of the study.

Funding: This research received no external funding, the APC was funded by the research office, Faculty of Economics and Management Sciences, North-West University.

Institutional Review Board Statement: Not applicable.

Informed Consent Statement: Not applicable.

Data Availability Statement: Suggested Data Availability Statements are available in section "The South African Reserve Bank" at https://www.resbank.co.za/en/home/what-we-do/statistics/releases/online-statistical-query (accessed on 12 February 2025).

Conflicts of Interest: The author declare no conflict of interest.

References

Ajuh, A. I., & Oyeanu, E. (2021). Impact of external debt on economic growth in Nigeria. *International Journal of Mechanical Engineering and Technology (IJMET)*, *12*(7), 49–57.

Akram, N. (2015). Is public debt hindering economic growth of the Philippines? *International Journal of Social Economics*, *42*(3), 202–221. [CrossRef]

Aloulou, R., Kalai, M., & Helali, K. (2023). The symmetric and asymmetric impacts of external debt on economic growth in Tunisia: Evidence from linear and nonlinear ARDL models. *SN Business & Economics*, *3*(7), 112.

Asteriou, D., & Hall, S. G. (2011). *Applied econometrics* (2nd ed., p. 512). Palgrave Macmillan.

Baaziz, Y., Guesmi, K., Heller, D., & Lahiani, A. (2015). Does public debt matter for economic growth?: Evidence from South Africa. *Journal of Applied Business Research*, *31*(6), 2187. [CrossRef]

Brooks, C. (2014). *Introductory econometrics for finance*. Cambridge University Press.
Changyong, X., Jun, S., & Chen, Y. (2012). Foreign debt, economic growth and economic crisis. *Journal of Chinese Economic and Foreign Trade Studies*, *5*(2), 157–167. [CrossRef]
Dabrowski, M. (2014). *Factors determining a 'safe' level of public debt*. Warsaw—Moscow, February–March. Higher School of Economics Publishing House.
Didia, D., & Ayokunle, P. (2020). External debt, domestic debt and economic growth: The case of Nigeria. *Advances in Economics and Business*, *8*(2), 85–94. [CrossRef]
Eric, C. R. (2024). *Asymmetric impact of government public debt and GDP growth: Case study from Nigeria*. Available online: https://ssrn.com/abstract=4693281 (accessed on 11 January 2024).
Fseifes, E. A., & Warrad, T. M. (2020). The impact of domestic and external public debt on the economic growth of Jordan. *International Journal of Business and Economics Research*, *9*(4), 254. [CrossRef]
Galodikwe, I. K., & Mah, G. (2023). Budget deficit and economic growth in BRICS countries: Panel approach. *African Journal of Business & Economic Research*, *18*(2), 295–317.
Gujarati, D. N., & Porter, D. C. (2008). *Basic econometrics* (5th ed.). McGraw Hill.
Junaedi, D., Norman, E., Salistia, F., Arsyad, M. R., & Paramansyah, A. (2022). The analysis of the impact of debt on the Indonesian economy for the period 1976–2021. *ManBiz: Journal of Management and Business*, *1*(1), 1–18.
Keynes, J. M. (1937). The general theory of employment. *The Quarterly Journal of Economics*, *51*(2), 209–223. [CrossRef]
Koyuncu, T., & Demirhan, H. (2020). Impact of external debt on economic growth in Brazil: An ARDL bound testing approach. *The Journal of International Scientific Researches*, *5*(3), 191–202. [CrossRef]
Krugman, P. (1988). Financing vs. forgiving a debt overhang. *Journal of Development Economics*, *29*(3), 253–268. [CrossRef]
Lashari, G. Z., Akbar, M., & Khan, R. (2017). Choice between domestic and foreign debt: A case study of Pakistan. *International* Journal of Economics, Finance and Management Sciences, *5*(6), 284–293. [CrossRef]
Matthew, A. O., & Adetayo, A. O. (2022). *Debt sustainability and economic growth in Nigeria* (Vol. 1054, No. 1, p. 012053). IOP conference series: Earth and environmental science. IOP Publishing.
Mbate, M. (2013). Domestic debt, private sector credit and economic growth in Sub-Saharan Africa. *African Development Review*, *25*(4), 434–446. [CrossRef]
Mhlaba, N., & Phiri, A. (2019). Is public debt harmful towards economic growth? New evidence from South Africa. *Cogent Economics & Finance*, *7*, 1603653.
Mosikari, T. J., & Eita, J. H. (2021). Asymmetric effect of government debt on GDP growth: Evidence from Namibia. *Public Sector Economics*, *45*(4), 543–558. [CrossRef]
Musa, K., Sohag, K., Said, J., Ghapar, F., & Ali, N. (2023). Public debt, governance, and growth in developing countries: An application of Quantile via Moments. *Mathematics*, *11*(3), 650. [CrossRef]
Olaoye, O. O., Tabash, M. I., Omokanmi, O. J., Ogunjumo, R. A., Ojelade, M. O., & Ishola, J. A. (2022). Macroeconomic implications of escalating stock of public debt: Evidence from sub-Saharan African economies. *African Development Review*, *34*(4), 527–540. [CrossRef]
Omimakinde, J. A., & Onifade, S. Z. (2022). Relationship between domestic debt and economic growth of Nigeria. *International Journal of Social Science of Human Research*, *5*(6), 2153–2159. [CrossRef]
Pesaran, M. H., & Shin, Y. (1995). *An autoregressive distributed lag modelling approach to cointegration analysis* (Vol. 9514, pp. 371–413). Department of Applied Economics, University of Cambridge.
Pesaran, M. H., Shin, Y., & Smith, R. J. (1996). *Testing for the 'existence of a long-run relationship'* (No. 9622). Faculty of Economics, University of Cambridge.
Phillips, P. C., & Perron, P. (1988). Testing for a unit root in time series regression. *Biometrika*, *75*(2), 335–346. [CrossRef]
Redda, E. H. (2020). Sustainability of public debt and budget deficit in South Africa. *Journal of Management Information and Decision Sciences*, *23*(3), 164–174.
Saungweme, T., Maluleke, G., & Odhiambo, N. M. (2023). The impact of public debt on economic growth in Côte d'Ivoire: New evidence from linear and non-linear ARDL approaches. *Croatian Review of Economic, Business and Social Statistics*, *9*(1), 61–77. [CrossRef]
Saungweme, T., & Odhiambo, N. M. (2020). The impact of public debt service on economic growth: Empirical evidence from Zambia. *International Journal of Revenue Management*, *11*(3), 172–189. [CrossRef]
Saungweme, T., & Odhiambo, N. M. (2021a). Public debt service in South Africa and its impact on economic growth: An empirical test. *The Review of Black Political Economy*, *48*(3), 313–327. [CrossRef]
Saungweme, T., & Odhiambo, N. M. (2021b). Relative impact of domestic and foreign public debt on economic growth in South Africa. *Journal of Applied Social Science*, *15*(1), 132–150. [CrossRef]
Shah, M. I., Ullah, I., Rahman, Z. U., & Nadeem, J. A. N. (2016). The debt overhang hypothesis: Evidence from Pakistan. *Studies in Business and Economics*, *11*(1), 140–151. [CrossRef]

Sharaf, M. F. (2021). The asymmetric and threshold impact of external debt on economic growth: New evidence from Egypt. *Journal of Business and Socio-Economic Development*, *2*(1), 1–18. [CrossRef]

Sharaf, M. F., Shahen, A. M., & Binzaid, B. A. (2024). Asymmetric and nonlinear foreign debt–inflation nexus in Brazil: Evidence from NARDL and Markov regime switching approaches. *Economies*, *12*(1), 18. [CrossRef]

Shieh, G. (2010). On the misconception of multicollinearity in detection of moderating effects: Multicollinearity is not always detrimental. *Multivariate Behavioral Research*, *45*(3), 483–507. [CrossRef]

Shin, Y., Yu, B. C., & Greenwood-Nimmo, M. (2014). Modelling asymmetric cointegration and dynamic multipliers in a nonlinear ARDL framework. In R. Sickels, & W. Horrace (Eds.), *Festschrift in honor of Peter Schmidt: Econometric methods and applications* (pp. 281–314). Springer. [CrossRef]

Shiyalini, S., & Suresh, K. (2022). The impact of public debt on domestic and foreign direct investments in developing market: An ARDL bounds testing approach. *Corporate Law & Governance Review*, *4*(1), 8–18.

Shrestha, M. B., & Bhatta, G. R. (2018). Selecting appropriate methodological framework for time series data analysis. *The Journal of Finance and Data Science*, *4*(2), 71–89. [CrossRef]

Simon, E. O., Ibenta, S., Yua, H., & Clement, N. (2023). Domestic and foreign debt dynamics and nonlinear effects on private investments in Nigeria: Evidence with asymmetric ARDL and causality. *African Journal of Accounting and Financial Research*, *6*(1), 1–21.

South African Reserve Bank. (2024). *Online statistical query*. Available online: https://www.resbank.co.za/en/home/what-we-do/statistics/releases/online-statistical-query (accessed on 20 March 2024).

Sumanaratne, B. M. (2022). External debt sustainability and economic growth in Sri Lanka. *Journal of Social Sciences and Humanities Review*, *7*(4), 271–293. [CrossRef]

Tchereni, B. H. M., Sekhampu, T. J., & Ndovi, R. F. (2013). The impact of foreign debt on economic growth in Malawi. *African Development Review*, *25*(1), 85–90. [CrossRef]

World Bank. (2023). *Data*. Available online: https://data.worldbank.org/ (accessed on 28 September 2023).

Wulandari, A., Giri, N. P. R., & Jayawarsa, A. K. (2022). Analysis of foreign debt and foreign investment on economic growth. *Journal of Tourism Economics and Policy*, *1*(3), 87–94. [CrossRef]

Young, D. S. (2018). *Handbook of regression methods*. Chapman and Hall/CRC.

Zakarıa, M. (2012). Interlinkages between openness and foreign debt in Pakistan. *Doğuş Üniversitesi Dergisi*, *13*(1), 161–170. [CrossRef]

Zhang, M., Brookins, O. T., & Huang, X. (2022). The crowding out effect of central versus local government debt: Evidence from China. *Pacific-Basin Finance Journal*, *72*, 101707. [CrossRef]

MDPI AG
Grosspeteranlage 5
4052 Basel
Switzerland
Tel.: +41 61 683 77 34

Economies Editorial Office
E-mail: economies@mdpi.com
www.mdpi.com/journal/economies

www.ingramcontent.com/pod-product-compliance
Lightning Source LLC
Chambersburg PA
CBHW061619220926
51850CB00005B/544
9783725874989